ONE WEEK LOAN

- 6 JAN 2006

1 0 OCT 2006

1 1 JAN 2007

- 9 MAY 2007

2 3 MAY 2008

2 8 NOV 2005

1 6 DEC 2005

Also by Jill Forbes:

The Cinema in France: After the New Wave

Les Enfants du paradis

Contemporary France: Essays and Texts on Politics, Economics and Society
  (with Nick Hewlett)

French Cultural Studies (with Michael Kelly)

Also by Sarah Street:

British National Cinema

British Cinema in Documents

Cinema and State: The Film Industry and the British Government, 1927–84
  (with Margaret Dickinson)

Moving Performance: British Stage and Screen, 1890s–1920s (with Linda Fitzsimmons)

European Cinema

An Introduction

Jill Forbes and Sarah Street

palgrave

First published 2000 by
PALGRAVE
Houndmills, Basingstoke, Hampshire RG21 6X5 and
175 Fifth Avenue, New York, N. Y. 10010
Companies and representatives throughout the world

PALGRAVE is the new global academic imprint of St. Martin's Press LLC
Scholarly and Reference Division and Palgrave Publishers Ltd
(formerly Macmillan Press Ltd).

ISBN 0–333–75209–0 hardback
ISBN 0–333–75210–4 paperback

This book is printed on paper suitable for recycling and
made from fully managed and sustained forest sources.

A catalogue record for this book is available
from the British Library.

Library of Congress Cataloging-in-Publication Data

European cinema: an introduction/edited by Jill Forbes and Sarah Street.
    p. cm.
  Includes bibliographical references and index.
  ISBN 0–333–75209–0—ISBN 0–333–75210–4 (pbk.)
  1. Motion pictures—Europe. I. Forbes, Jill. II. Street, Sarah.
  PN1993.5.E8 E96 2000
  791.43'094—dc21

                                                          00–031111

10 9 8 7 6 5 4 3 2 1
09 08 07 06 05 04 03 02 01 00

Printed and bound in Great Britain by
Creative Print & Design (Wales), Ebbw Vale

Contents

List of Illustrations

Acknowledgements

The authors gratefully acknowledge the support of the University of Bristol and of the Arts and Humanities Research Board in the preparation of this book. They have also benefited from the advice and help of many individuals and, in particular, Ross Chambers, Peter Evans, David Forgács, Jeremy Hicks, Jo Labanyi, Geoffrey Nowell-Smith, Keith Reader, Richard Taylor, and Ingrid Wassenaar. Special thanks are due to Michael Liversidge who, as Dean of the Faculty of Arts at Bristol, first encouraged the development of a course in European cinema and to the students whose comments and reactions did much to determine its final shape. We would also like to thank the following for permission to reproduce illustrations: Artificial Eye Ltd; the Bibliothèque du film (BIFI), Paris; the British Film Institute Stills, Posters and Designs Department; Igor Gnevashev; the Kobal Collection; Professor Richard Taylor.

Every effort has been made to trace all copyright holders, but if any have been inadvertently overlooked, the publishers will be pleased to make the necessary arrangements at the first opportunity.

Bristol and London

Introduction

This book was inspired by the attempts of its authors to design and teach an undergraduate course on European cinema. In so doing we were led to consider not just how European cinema might be defined but also how it might be studied, and we encountered the immediate difficulty that while there is a large, and growing, body of academic work in English devoted to national cinemas in Europe, there was until recently very little academic interest in questions of European cinema.

One of the reasons for this can be found in the way film studies have developed in the last twenty or even thirty years. Although the study of film as a cultural phenomenon – that is, outside the practice-related approach of art schools and film schools – is now well-established in Britain and the United States, it has been much slower to develop in continental Europe. Thus although there are several excellent textbooks which can be recommended to students wishing to be initiated into the academic study of films, such as those by Bordwell and Thompson, Cook, or Monaco, the case studies they use and the paradigms they establish almost always refer to Hollywood cinema which is considered the 'norm' or the 'classic'. In a different way this is also true of film theory, since it has almost always been tested in relation to Hollywood cinema whose characteristics it is, more often than not, designed to elucidate. A case in point might be Mulvey's celebrated and frequently reprinted essay 'Visual Pleasure and Narrative Cinema' which was explicitly conceived to account for the pleasurable experience of viewing 'classic' or 'mainstream' Hollywood cinema (Mulvey, 1975). The global reach of English-language publishing houses, together with the earlier institutionalisation of film studies in English-language territories, have compounded this emphasis. While 'film theory' has often relied on a range of sources, many not written in the English language, it is invariably when theoretical works are published in English translation that they begin to achieve an international impact and to inform film studies generally. For example, the success of Kracauer's *From Caligari to Hitler*, which in 1947 persuasively offered an analysis of German cinema that Anglo-Americans wished to read, overshadowed the same author's equally interesting – but less apparently politically relevant – work on French culture, not translated until 1995. Comparable observations might be made about the reputations of Christian Metz or more recently of Gilles Deleuze and, pre-eminently, of Russian-language writers, whose contribution to film theory has had a chequered history in the west and one which only recently began to be explored, in the path-breaking work of Taylor and Christie.

However, another tradition began to emerge in the 1990s. In the work of Sorlin in Paris, in that of Dyer and Vincendeau at Warwick and, above all, in the continuing investigations of Nowell-Smith and his collaborators, we can detect an urgent interest in questions of European cinema and an increasing dissatisfaction with the way film histories have been written in the past. Political developments such as the fall of the Berlin Wall, *glasnost* and *perestroika*, as well as the completion of the Single European Market and the creation of the European Union, have naturally had their part to play in this upsurge of interest. It was Mikhail Gorbachev who tellingly referred to the 'single European home', since when commentators have continued to explore the cultural implications of his remark. In their introduction to a selection of papers from a conference on popular European cinema, presciently held in 1989, two months before the breach of the Berlin Wall, Dyer and Vincendeau wrote: 'Europe has never appeared a more contested notion, as the European Community seeks to engineer a new economic and political (and cultural?) unity into place, and as the nature and allegiances of eastern Europe change daily as we write (summer 1991)' (Dyer and Vincendeau, 2).

From 1992 the effects of a European Union policy for the media began to be seen, on European film production and, although less clearly, on film distribution. At the same time the increasingly global nature of the media industries, of which cinema is now a small part, gave rise to a counter-interest in the heritage of the past, a heritage whose specificities, it is sometimes feared, are rapidly being submerged or effaced. The funds the European Union allocates to research and conservation, spectacularly evident at the time of the celebration of the centenary of cinema in 1995/6, have already enhanced our knowledge of European cinema and will certainly continue to do so in the future. As archives are opened and films are restored, and as new technologies make previously little-known films more readily and widely available, our critical assumptions and our canons will require revision. For the present, however, there remain immense historiographical lacunae in the study of the first century of European cinema.

The contents and organisation of this book require some explanation. Part I is an introductory survey which attempts to place European cinema in its economic and political context and to raise questions relating to its ideology, aesthetics and style. The intention is to introduce students to areas of debate and to suggest ways in which they can explore such topics further. There are major difficulties in attempting to survey the economy of European cinema which were raised by Thomas Guback, as long ago as 1969, in his fascinating account of the international film industry. He wrote:

On the elementary question of foreign films coming into a country several standards exist. One nation may state this in terms of total meters of exposed film imported. Another nation may decide to tabulate the number of pictures that have actually gone through the customs office. A third may base its measure on the number submitted to censorship. And a fourth may count the business licenses issued which permit films to be exhibited.   (Guback, 37)

Not only are statistics collected differently according to the territory, they are also, frequently, massaged for political and economic purposes. From 1992, uniform statistics on the economics of film-making and film distribution within the European Union have, in theory, been collected and are published, but for earlier periods comparative work, except of a very broad-brush kind, is virtually non-existent. Kristin Thompson's meticulous and groundbreaking study of American cinema in the pre-Second World War world film market attempted to 'lay the groundwork for further, more detailed studies' (Thompson, x) but to date these have not been forthcoming. As we have found in attempting to describe the economics of European cinema, the available information depends on the questions which have been asked, most of which relate to Hollywood in Europe. The account we present here is therefore distilled from existing sources. Its broad outlines are, we hope, accurate, but there is an urgent need for the detail to be filled out with further research of a comparative kind.

If the economics of European cinema are difficult to study, what of its politics? Here film scholars are at the mercy of events which have had a direct impact on their approach to their subject. The Russian Revolution and the rise of totalitarian dictatorships precipitated movements of film personnel across Europe, and ultimately, in many cases, to Hollywood, to the greater benefit of the American film industry. The censorship of Russian films in the west, and in the Soviet Union; the banning of American films from many European territories before and during the Second World War; the Cold War and the Iron Curtain, which for many years closed eastern archives to scholars and filtered the export of eastern-bloc films to the west; and the ruthlessness of the American film industry in dressing up its commercial policies as the triumph of democracy, all these factors have affected not only the interpretation of films that are released, but perhaps more important, whether films are released in the first place. As Taylor and Christie suggest, and as is discussed in this book, the marketing success of *The Battleship Potemkin* is an excellent illustration of the way in which the international availability of the output of an entire film industry can be determined by political considerations whose pertinence may have long since disappeared.

This is not merely a question of overt censorship, whose study has tended to fetishise the lost fragment, to the exclusion, as is suggested here, of much else that is interesting. The censorship and certification regimes, which exist in all countries, contribute to the creation of images which will be acceptable in national and international markets and which will conform to the picture each country desires to present to the outside world. An earlier and perhaps simplistic view of censorship under communism and fascism has given way, in more recent scholarship, to detailed national studies by Lindeperg, Taylor, Petley, and others, which have suggested that censorship was almost invariably more subtle, and more interesting, than had been supposed. Vasey has carried out groundbreaking work on this topic but although her book contains much that is of interest and relevance to European cinema it does not focus centrally on it, and primarily discusses Hollywood cinema and especially the 'Hays' Code'.

Censorship relates to questions of ideology, aesthetics and style, which are the subject of the last part of the Introduction. For example, the close involvement of the French and Italian governments, followed later by the German and Spanish, in subsidising and, as important, promoting a particular kind of art cinema has encouraged the development of critical narratives which seek to place the film production of a particular country or set of countries within recognised frameworks which can then be used to influence production. Thus French cinema is frequently placed within the framework 'new wave', Spanish cinema within 'surrealism', Italian cinema within 'neo-realism', and so on, all of which reinforce the notion that European cinema is art cinema. Alongside this kind of cinema, however, there exists, or existed, European popular cinema which was targeted at a small regional or national audience and did not fit into the preferred, and internationally recognised, critical canons. This cinema is not well known because it is defined, to use Jeancolas's term, by being 'unexportable' (in Dyer and Vincendeau, 141). Although, today, it has largely been replaced by television, this does not mean that European popular cinema or the structures which produced it do not merit study.

Studios, genres, and stars are generally considered to have been the constitutive elements of the 'Hollywood system', the source of its industrial efficiency, economies of scale, and capacity to produce for the mass market. However, before the Second World War, and to some extent after it as well, studios also made a major contribution to the cinema in Europe. Scholars have certainly examined individual studios such as Albatros, Éclair, Gainsborough or Ealing, or indeed, the Soviet Film Factory, but the work of synthesising this knowledge and identifying the specific contribution of film studios in Europe has only just begun. Similarly, little has been published on the role of film stars in Europe, or on the development of specific genres and their function in European cinema.

The existence of European studios, genres and stars brings into focus the central question which this book raises but naturally does not answer: What, if any, are the common features of European cinema? Whatever the policy developments within the European Union, a European cinema cannot be brought into being by fiat, and in any case the Union is not co-terminous with Europe. Is European cinema a collection of national cinemas, some more vibrant and successful than others? Is it increasingly characterised by featureless co-productions, 'europuddings', in which the composition of an international cast list and a choice of international locations is determined by the relative significance of each country's financial input? Is it now influenced, primarily, by Hollywood's vision – or fantasy – of Europe, just as in the past it offered the occasion for the *mise-en-scène* of European fantasies of the American myth, and by the narrative structures preferred in Hollywood which are often inimical to other, national traditions? How has gender been represented and does the more open narrative often favoured in European cinema allow for more mobile conceptions than elsewhere? Is it, as Nowell-Smith suggests, wedded to realism, 'a commodity deeply rooted in European culture' but, in his view, inimical to a successful cinema which must '[reconnect] with the everyday mythologies of fear and desire' (Nowell-Smith and Ricci, 13)? And what of European audiences, about whom there are many statistics but remarkably few studies? The essays which follow are intended to engage with these questions, and to raise others, rather than to provide answers.

Part II consists of a series of 'case studies', free-standing analyses of individual films (two from each of six major European film-producing countries) together with a filmography and suggestions for further reading. The studies are intended to exemplify some of the salient features of particular national cinemas and European film styles as well as to offer points of cross-national comparison relating to the questions outlined above. Thus they can be read separately by students interested in a particular director's work or a particular national cinema, but they also provide the material for aesthetic and thematic comparisons across European national boundaries.

We have adopted a definition of 'Europe' which encompasses both Britain and Russia since the film production of these two countries is important for our purposes – Britain because it shares a language with the United States and because its film industry has, perhaps, been more intimately connected with Hollywood than that of any other European country; Russia because the post-*glasnost* rediscovery of Russian cinema has altered, and will continue to alter, our perception of cinema and of film history. It may well be objected that by not including films from Scandinavian countries, from the Czech Republic, from Hungary, from Poland, from Portugal or, indeed, from Ireland, we have distorted the picture of European cinema. It might also be objected that the present volume does little to disturb what Dyer and Vincendeau described as the 'high white tradition' (2), even though some of the most fascinating modern cinema is made in territories which are former European colonies and/or by ethnic or immigrant groupings within Europe. We can only plead lack of space in extenuation.

Our choice is not canonical; it is not intended to celebrate 'great' films or 'masterpieces of European cinema'. Instead, it has been guided by a number of practical considerations and critical needs. On the practical side we have attempted to choose films that will appeal to student audiences, that will be stimulating to viewers who do not necessarily have a highly developed knowledge of the cinema, and that will offer a range of critical points of entry. We also wished to achieve a reasonable chronological spread so as to include films from the silent era (_The Battleship Potemkin_, _The Lodger_) as well as films made within the last decade (_La haine_, _Trainspotting_). And we considered it essential that the films chosen should be readily available in sub-titled versions – a criterion which, of course, massively restricts the possibilities as far as concerns the film output of many countries, particularly Russia.

Beyond these practical considerations, it is intended that the case studies will illustrate ways in which themes such as modernism and the avant-garde, gender, reception, heritage, performance, narrative or language, are differently inflected in different national cinemas but can be illuminated by cross-national comparison. To take the most recent works first, _La haine_ and _Trainspotting_ share characteristics which we recognise as postmodern: both are firmly rooted in their local contexts but both are also designed to appeal to international audiences through their playful use of visual styles derived from television, their use of popular, internationally recognised music, and in their manipulation of elements of western youth culture. However, the treatment of race relations, of the aspirations of young people, and of space, also permits fascinating comparisons between _La haine_ and _Das Versprechen_, even though each film apparently engages with very local cultural concerns. Again, despite their differences of style and subject-matter, _La règle du jeu_, _Ossessione_, _Viridiana_ and _Das Versprechen_ all deal with the Second World War and its legacy: none of them is a 'war film' in the traditional sense since none involves a _mise-en-scène_ of the events of the war, but all attempt to confront the ideological issues arising from it. It is perhaps hardly surprising that such a major conflict should have been frequently represented in European cinema but it is interesting that the theme should persist in Europe throughout the twentieth century and should give rise to such a variety of treatments. By the same token, these films stage the confrontation between traditional ideologies and modernisation, which is a constant theme of European cinema. This is already evident in _The Battleship Potemkin_, frequently cited as an example of modernism, but can also be seen in _The Lodger_, whose less well known modernism is made explicit by a juxtaposition with _Potemkin_. Similarly, _Alice in den Städten_ and _Good Morning Babilonia_ explicitly examine the often fraught but always productive relationship between European cinema and Hollywood, which is less overt but none the less present in _La haine_, _Das Versprechen_ and _Ossessione_. Though this relationship is seen through different national prisms, it also becomes a metaphor for the processes of modernisation and for the acute sense of cultural loss that such processes often generated, suggesting that ambivalence in the face of modernisation is a defining European experience and one which the cinema was particularly capable of documenting. By contrast, _Carmen_ and _The Barber of Siberia_ illustrate the opposite trend, namely a desire and even an obligation to celebrate the national heritage, even to the point where it becomes stereotypical, and to treat cinema as a privileged medium in which to debate questions of national culture.

Such categorisations can never be definitive and readers of more than one case study will detect other points of comparison which are constants in film studies and especially in the study of European cinema. Thus Birgit Beumers explores the relationship between the use of montage and the narration of history in *The Battleship Potemkin*, while Sarah Street considers the way reference to expressionism inflects the depiction of gender in *The Lodger*. Jill Forbes shows how a literary and cultural tradition is worked into a political critique in *La règle du jeu* and how its impact has increased over the years, while Derek Duncan considers the way an American source was controversially adapted in *Ossessione* to provide a critique of fascism through the subversion of gender relations. Annella McDermott suggests how *Viridiana* uses the iconography and thematics of Catholicism and surrealism to expose the oppressive nature of Franco's Spain and to plead for the country's reintegration into the European mainstream, while in *Das Versprechen* Stuart Taberner discovers similar artistic and intellectual ambiguities in the reintegration of the two Germanies in the 1990s. In examining the extraordinary intertextuality of *Alice in den Städten* and of *Good Morning Babilonia* Stuart Taberner and Derek Duncan raise questions about European film culture in a context made ever more pertinent by globalisation. One response, explored by Annella McDermott in *Carmen* and Birgit Beumers in *The Barber of Siberia*, is the deliberate and flamboyant juxtaposition of the new with the old aesthetics, gender politics and nationalism. However, a different answer is provided by two recent European successes, *La haine* and *Trainspotting*, examined by Jill Forbes and Sarah Street. It is one which challenges the notion that 'realism' is a defining impetus of European cinema and which suggests that a more fluid and more hybrid aesthetic will be characteristic of Europe at the dawn of the twenty-first century.

References

Bordwell, David and Thompson, Kristin 1993: *Film Art*. New York: McGraw Hill.

Cook, Pam 1985: *The Cinema Book*. London: British Film Institute.

Dyer, Richard and Vincendeau, Ginette (eds) 1992: *Popular European Cinema*. London: Routledge.

Guback, Thomas 1969: *The International Film Industry*. Bloomington: Indiana University Press.

Kracauer, Siegfried 1947: *From Caligari to Hitler*. Princeton: Princeton University Press.

Kracauer, Siegfried 1995: *The Mass Ornament*. Translated by Thomas Levin. Cambridge, MA: Harvard University Press.

Lindeperg, Sylvie 1997: *Les Écrans de l'ombre*. Paris: CNRS Éditions.

Monaco, James 1981: *How to Read a Film*. New York: Oxford University Press.

Mulvey, Laura 1975: 'Visual Pleasure and Narrative Cinema'. In *Screen*, 16, 3, 6–18.

Nowell-Smith, Geoffrey (ed.) 1996: *The Oxford History of World Cinema*. Oxford: Oxford University Press.

Nowell-Smith, Geoffrey and Ricci, Steven (eds) 1998: *Hollywood & Europe*. London: British Film Institute.
Petley, Julian 1979: *Capital and Culture: German Cinema, 1933–45*. London: British Film Institute.
Sorlin, Pierre 1991: *European Cinemas, European Societies*. London: Routledge.
Taylor, Richard 1998: *Film Propaganda: Soviet Russia and Nazi Germany*. London: I. B. Tauris.
Taylor, Richard and Christie, Ian 1988: *The Film Factory*. London: Routledge & Kegan Paul.
Thompson, Kristin 1985: *Exporting Entertainment: America in the World Film Market, 1907–34*. London: British Film Institute.
Vasey, Ruth 1997: *The World According to Hollywood*. Exeter: Exeter University Press.

Part I

European Cinema: An Overview

1
Economics and Politics

In the space of a century, the cinema has grown from a curiosity exhibited in the fairgrounds of western Europe and America to be part of a multi-billion-dollar business. In the early years, cinema was dominated by buccaneering capitalists like Charles Pathé; today it is an integral part of a global electronics industry which is likely to expand massively in the twenty-first century, with feature films making up a 'significant element' alongside sports programming and news gathering, and playing 'a leading role in the growth of fresh ancillary and new technology-driven markets' (Finney, 1). In this introduction we seek to trace the means by which cinema in Europe gradually became a vital component of the culture industries and, in the process, acquired a symbolic function in Europe's fight to protect itself against economic and cultural domination by the United States.

The First World War and After

Until 1914 the French film industry was the most important in the world, and its closest competitors were the industries of Italy and Denmark. It was founded on the success of the Lumière Brothers' *cinématographe*, which was publicly demonstrated for the first time in Paris in December 1895, and on the brilliant inventiveness of the theatre impresario Georges Méliès, whose Star Film Company built a world-wide empire with offices in London, Barcelona, Berlin and New York. However, it was the business genius of the gramophone manufacturer Charles Pathé which transformed the cinema in France from a series of small-scale, craft-based operations into a large, vertically and horizontally integrated company. Pathé's company manufactured film, built studios, set up processing laboratories and created subsidiaries abroad, and it owned the means of production, distribution and exhibition (Sadoul, 2: 221). Pathé expanded rapidly outside France, opening offices across Europe, including Russia, as well as in the United States and the Far East. One reason for its success was that the film business was extraordinarily profitable in the early years. According to the historian Georges Sadoul, the entire production of the Vincennes Studio for the year 1905 was amortised in 12 days, and in a situation where most films were less than 300 metres long it was enough to sell 20 copies for the initial outlay to be recouped (Sadoul, 2: 225, 235). However, although the French and Italian film businesses were the most dynamic in Europe before the First World War, they operated in societies that were still very rural, with the result that continuous film exhibition was limited to a few large towns and cities. Thus both these film industries relied on exports for their profits and their largest market was the United States, where, in the decade preceding the First World War, only about one-third of the films screened were American (Nowell-Smith, 1996, 24).

The First World War dramatically altered this state of affairs. The war mobilised personnel, diverted natural resources and industrial capacity, and disrupted patterns of trade. It consolidated the position of the United States as an exporting nation since, even before the US entered the war in 1917, the Allies turned to the US to import munitions and foodstuffs. It also helped the US and Japan to supplant Britain as a major shipping power since the British merchant fleet was mobilised for the war effort. Even European countries like Sweden, which remained neutral, or which were engaged in a civil war, like Russia, did not escape the impact of the hostilities.

By 1914, films had become an important element of world trade and were naturally affected too. During the first two years of hostilities the Americans exported fewer films to Europe, but by 1916 American sales were increasing in Italy, France, Spain and, above all, in Britain where, by this time, only 9 per cent of films screened were domestically produced and American films represented between 75 per cent and 90 per cent of those exhibited (Thompson, 67). Likewise in France, domestic productions had accounted for about 80 per cent of films screened before the war, but this figure had dropped to about 37 per cent by 1917, with approximately 30 per cent of the remainder being taken by American films. In Italy, the domestic industry had competed successfully against the Americans both at home and abroad but this was less and less the case by the end of the war, while in non-combatant Spain the Americans had captured almost 50 per cent of the domestic market by 1918 (Thompson, 91). Not surprisingly, the export manager of one American film company wrote of 'cashing in on Europe's war' and of 'invading' European and world markets (Thompson, 50).

However, the war was not the only factor which dented the economic strength of the film industries in Britain, France and Italy. In Britain the production of films had only really been buoyant in the early years of the century and the quality of British films was often poor or imitative of American products. Because London was still the financial and trading centre for a large Empire and because the British merchant navy still dominated the seas, London very quickly became the centre for processing American films and for re-exporting them across the world, not just to the British Empire but to other countries too. Film negatives would be shipped to London, positive prints would be struck in British laboratories, and agents would take advantage of British trading expertise and facilities to ship American films to the Far East, Australasia and, indeed, to Latin America. By 1910, hiring out films was proving much more lucrative than making them as far as the British were concerned, and it is from these pre-war imperial arrangements that the British tradition of providing technical facilities for American productions can be dated.

In France, where pre-war American films had been seen primarily in large towns, it was not just a decline in film production which allowed the Americans to export more, but also a change in the content and quality of the films themselves. The serial, which was Pathé's showcase product, became far less popular while the new feature films which came from America during 1915 and 1916 proved extremely successful (Thompson, 89). At the same time as the Americans were making significant inroads into the French market for the first time, French producers were losing their share of foreign markets. Pathé, Gaumont and Éclair had all set up production facilities in the US. The latter two were not part of the American motion picture producers' cartel and found operating in the American market difficult as a result. Pathé, however, was initially very successful but, from 1913 onwards, transformed itself into a distribution rather than a production company in America, a miscalculation which meant it lost its early advantage (Thompson, 59). French producers also lost considerable ground world-wide, especially in Latin America and the Far East from where much of their profit derived. The same is true of Italy whose small domestic market had been boosted by profits from Spain and especially Latin America, which had allowed the Italian industry to invest in expensive, longer than average spectaculars, with elaborate sets and large numbers of extras, the best known of which are Enrico Guazzoni's *Quo vadis?* (1913) and Giovanni Pastrone's *Cabiria* (1914). Until 1915 or 1916 such productions successfully rivalled American films, in Italy and America as well as farther afield, and stimulated many imitations.

Perhaps the war would not have enabled the Americans to compete successfully in Europe if the change in the style and content of American films had not been matched by significant changes in the structure and organisation of the American industry. The creation of the cartel known as the Motion Picture Patents Company (MPPC) in 1908 had ended undercutting and patents wars and had created a relatively stable oligopoly, reinforced by the end of the initial period of frenetic technological experimentation. It also tended to favour domestic production, and although it included the largest foreign companies, it tended to freeze out foreign competition (Nowell-Smith, 1996, 25). After the MPPC was declared illegal in 1915, the American industry, which had relocated to Hollywood, began to organise itself into vertically integrated conglomerates which controlled all stages of the production and sales process and which competed not through price and patent wars, as before, but through product differentiation based on named stars, who were used as marketing devices. The teens were thus the period when the 'Hollywood system' was established, a system based on 'a division of labour, maximum exploitation of resources, and the canons of beautiful cinematography' (Thompson, 89). The Americans were thus organised like a big business whereas the European industries, with the exception of Pathé, remained small and craft-based.

In this way, the First World War enabled the US to establish a world-wide hegemony in exporting films, which was helped by standards of quality and reliability that created international benchmarks for production. This reduced the European (and especially French) presence in America and increased the American penetration of Europe, especially in Britain, France and Italy. However, it should not be forgotten that this process did not take place throughout Europe, as is sometimes assumed. In Russia, where in any case relatively few American films were seen by the very scattered population, currency devaluation and transport difficulties meant that American films lost ground during the war. Then came the Revolution of 1917 and the Civil War, followed by a trade blockade of the Soviet Union by the western powers which was not lifted until 1921. This not only cut off imports of foreign films but also led to an acute shortage of film stock which stifled national film production. At the same time, Lenin declared film to be 'the most important art' and attempted to encourage domestic production and exhibition. Meanwhile in Germany, an Allied blockade and a ban on supplying films to Germany (lest the nitrate used in film production could be diverted for military purposes) meant that the German film industry had to supply its domestic market. It was consolidated by the creation of the partly nationalised Universumfilm Aktiengesellschaft (UFA) holding company in 1917, a move which was to have an immense impact on the European film industries and which was to enable the German film industry, alone, to present a significant challenge to Hollywood in the aftermath of the First World War.

The 'Silent Salesman'

The War demonstrated the potential for the use of cinema in information and propaganda and it also consolidated the belief in the broader, indirect, economic significance of the cinema. The magazine *Collier's Weekly* wrote in 1918: '[T]he American moving picture is...familiarising South America and Africa, Asia and Europe with American habits and customs. It is showing American clothes and furniture, automobiles and homes. And it is subtly but surely creating a desire for these American-made articles' (quoted in Thompson, 121–2). Indeed, the idea that 'trade follows the film' came to replace the earlier imperialist notion that 'trade follows the flag'. This was reinforced by social changes which occurred partly as a result of the war, especially in the position of women who, symbolically, gained the vote in Britain and America and who, throughout the west, were the prime targets of the consumer boom that took place in the 1920s. This was not lost on most European film-producing countries, which attempted to protect their film and other industries by using import quotas to fight Hollywood domination. The Soviet Union, however, adopted a different and, as we shall see, arguably more effective approach to the American domination of the world film industry.

Protecting the domestic market was led by Germany. In 1916 an embargo was imposed on inessential imports, which continued beyond the armistice until 1920. Then, in 1921, Germany introduced the first of a series of quota measures designed to limit film imports, based initially on a fixed percentage of footage and from 1925 on a proportional basis which stipulated that one foreign feature film could be imported for every German feature film distributed. In theory, this should have limited the number of foreign films in distribution in Germany to 50 per cent. In practice the figure seems to have been slightly lower, perhaps because, until 1923, hyper-inflation meant that German distributors could not afford to buy foreign films. Throughout the silent period, Germany managed to supply much more of its domestic market than did other European countries. In 1927, the quota was again altered to the so-called 'Kontingent' system under which imports were based on an estimate of the 'needs' of the market, and this remained in force throughout the Nazi period (Thompson, 211–12).

The German example was imitated more or less effectively in other European film-producing countries. Britain introduced a quota in 1927 which stipulated that 7.5 per cent of films handled by British renters (distributors) and 5 per cent shown by British exhibitors must be British films; both quotas to rise gradually to 20 per cent by 1936. The measure was only partially successful since although it led to an increase in the number of British films screened, it also stimulated the production of what were known as 'quota quickies', that is poor quality films made in Britain, by foreign and often American companies, in order to fulfil the requirements of the quota. But it nevertheless protected the industry to some extent and the British film industry recovered from its weak position in the 1920s as British films – even some 'quickies' – became more popular. In 1927, Italy attempted to impose a rule that 10 per cent of screen time should be devoted to Italian films, although the measure could not be enforced for lack of domestic product, while France imposed a highly ambitious quota of seven French films for one foreign film, with import licences granted only on the basis of French film exports, and which resulted in a temporary American boycott of the French market (Thompson, 121).

The economic impact of these measures is difficult to assess. It appears incontestable that import restrictions limited – more or less, depending on the territory – the number of American films imported into Europe (Thompson, 127). This in turn confirmed the treatment of films as a commodity to be exported like any other and underlined the extent to which Hollywood movie production had become big business. Indeed, in 1926, the American Congress voted funds to support a 'Motion Picture Section' within the Department of Commerce's Bureau of Foreign and Domestic Commerce. At the same time the American government supported the film boycott of France for fear that strict quotas for film imports might set a precedent for the imposition of quotas on other American products. On the other hand, the number of films exported to a given country does not necessarily equate with box office receipts within that country, and those are much more difficult to assess. Furthermore, by reducing the number of American imports, it has been suggested that European governments rendered a service to the Hollywood exporters, who, as a result, enhanced the quality of their product and increased profitability: '[f]ewer movies not only meant a better return per picture but also assisted the American industry by boosting the prestige of the Hollywood product' (Vasey, 89).

The Soviet approach was, interestingly, to use imported films to help the USSR's own industry recover from the effects of war and revolution, a system that was not generally adopted in western Europe until after the Second World War. The film industry was partially nationalised in 1919 and in 1922 was concentrated and centralised into the organisation Goskino. Part of the impetus for this was to control scarce resources. Most cameras were imported but spare parts were unavailable because of the trade blockade. Film production slumped and many cinemas closed for lack of anything to exhibit. From 1922 onwards Lenin therefore ordered the importing of foreign films into the USSR but under an arrangement which provided, first, that imported films should be exhibited alongside Soviet educational and propaganda shorts – this was the so-called 'Leninist film proportion' – and secondly, that revenues from exhibiting foreign films should be ploughed back into Soviet film production. This meant that by the mid-1920s, 85 per cent of films in the Soviet market came from abroad, and many of these were American. At the same time, Soviet production rose from a meagre 13 feature films in 1923 to 109 by 1928, suggesting that the policy had been rather successful (Kepley, 65, 77).

Pan European Cooperation

The other line of European defence, especially in the 1920s, was to develop cooperation through the 'Film Europe' movement, which some commentators have considered a precursor of today's European Union policies. The impetus came initially from Germany, and the reasons are understandable. In the period after the First World War, Germany probably had the most dynamic film industry in Europe. As we have seen, its domestic market was protected. Hyper-inflation meant that until the currency was stabilised in 1923, imported films were prohibitively expensive, and in 1917, with state backing, much of the film industry had been concentrated into the UFA holding company which brought together the government film propaganda unit and a variety of small production companies. UFA also owned offices, laboratories, film equipment and processing plant, cinemas, and new, purpose-built studios at Babelsberg. UFA was further strengthened by taking over another large production company, DECLA, in 1921, and the conglomerate was backed both by the Deutsche Bank and by the electrical and chemical industries. The involvement of finance and industry in film production illustrates a new attitude towards the significance of the cinema, and more broadly the culture industries, in the 1920s, and in this the Germans led the way.

However, a further important reason for the Germans to preach cooperation was that the war had made European audiences xenophobic. In France, for example, it was considered highly unpatriotic to appreciate German culture or to buy German goods. Thus if UFA was to export, it had to win over foreign viewers and it was helped by the international success of Lubitsch's *Madame du Barry* (1919), the subject-matter of which was 'French', and of Wiene's *Das Kabinett des Dr Caligari* (*The Cabinet of Dr Caligari*, 1919), produced by DECLA, which inaugurated the expressionist style that came to be considered distinctive of German cinema in the 1920s. Indeed, Elsaesser has suggested that the expressionist masterpieces, which include celebrated films such as Fritz Lang's *Der müde Tod* (*Destiny*, 1921) and *Metropolis* (1926), or F. W. Murnau's *Der letzte Mann* (*The Last Laugh*, 1924), were deliberately encouraged as a means of distinguishing German film production from that of Hollywood and of recruiting the middle-class and intellectual audience abroad to support German films (Elsaesser, in Nowell-Smith, 1996, 144).

Shortly after becoming overall head of UFA, Erich Pommer declared in an interview in a French film magazine: 'It is necessary to create "European Films" which will no longer be French, English, Italian or German films; entirely "continental" films, expanding out into all Europe and amortising their enormous costs, can be produced easily' (quoted in Thompson, 113), and he did so in order to promote his new distribution agreement with one of the major French film distributors, the Établissements Aubert (Thompson, 112). Similar agreements followed: in 1926 the Alliance cinématographique européenne provided further outlets for UFA films in France; in October 1926 a joint Russian–German production and distribution company, DERUFA, was created which, before it went bankrupt in 1929, had imported into Germany Barnet's *Devushka s korobkoi* (*The Girl with a Hat Box*, 1927), Pudovkin's *Konets Sankt Peterburga* (*The End of St Petersburg*, 1927), and Eisenstein's *Staroe i novoe* (*Old and New/The General Line*, 1929) (Thompson, 116); in 1927 UFA signed an agreement with Gaumont-British, and in June 1928 UFA and the Italian state company LUCE agreed to distribute each other's films.

One of the weaknesses of Pommer's proposals was that they were confined to distribution and exhibition. They were not sufficient to prevent the financial difficulties which struck UFA in 1925 and which enabled the Americans to buy a share of the company, effectively circumventing distribution restrictions. However, another German company, Westi Films, concluded an agreement with Pathé in December 1924 and its owner suggested collaboration on the production of expensive and artistically meritorious European films via a European 'syndicate' of the major European film-producing companies (Danilowicz, 54–6), and indeed the company invested in arguably the most spectacular European film of the 1920s, Abel Gance's *Napoléon* (1927).

At the same time, proposals for European cooperation were not entirely self-interested. The League of Nations, founded in 1919 to promote international peace and understanding, agreed to make cinema one of its areas of concern and convened a congress which took place in Paris in September–October 1926 (Thompson, 111). It was attended by many of the leading film-makers of the day, it served to publicise the possibility of cooperation, and it passed resolutions that films should avoid inflammatory, racist or nationalistic material and should promote understanding between peoples. One example of such a cooperative approach was G. W. Pabst's film *Kameradschaft* (*Comradeship*, 1931), a Franco-German co-production, set in a mining town on the Franco-German border, which depicts French and German miners working together to rescue people after an accident in the mine. Yet, ironically, it appears that Pabst shot two endings, one of which shows this ideal cooperation continuing, the other which shows the border re-established under ground after the mine is reopened – alternatives which were, perhaps, symbolic of the uncertainty many felt about putting pan European cooperation into practice.

Technology and the Birth of the 'Culture Industries'

The advent of sound cinema further underlined cinema's role as a showcase for and locomotive of new technologies and the participation of big business in film production. It also, initially, provided the means for further economic protectionism in Europe. The first successful American sound film, Alan Crosland's *The Jazz Singer* (1927), reached Europe in 1928–9 and immediately revitalised interest in sound technology, precipitating a turf war in Europe. Huge sums of money were at stake for film producers, for those who owned the patents of the sound processes and for those who supplied the equipment to wire the cinemas. Once again, Germany led the way with the creation, in 1929, of a cartel called Tobis-Klangfilm, which had been formed by the merger of two powerful companies, the former including Swiss and Dutch venture capital, the latter significantly bringing together two large German electrical companies, AEG and Siemens. Tobis-Klangfilm, in a series of successful lawsuits, prevented Western Electric, the holder of the main series of American sound patents, from operating in Europe until July 1930 when an agreement was reached on an international cartel which essentially divided the European market between the two systems, one German-controlled, the other American-controlled.

The advent of sound in Europe temporarily arrested American domination of the European film industries – a moratorium which lasted until dubbing techniques had been perfected, or, more important, accepted by non-English-speaking audiences, around 1932. It also helped to consolidate German investment in other European markets, especially in France where Tobis built its own studio. On the American side, sound accelerated the standardisation of the product, which was no longer exported 'semi-finished', as well as its cultural specificity. And it also marked the moment, as the Germans realised, when the audio and visual industries came together for their mutual benefit and cinema became a significant element in the expansion of electrical conglomerates. Finally, sound posed questions, as perhaps the silent cinema had never done, about 'national cinema' and put an end to embryonic European cooperation.

Censorship and Propaganda

All European countries had various systems of censorship, either directly controlled by the state, or via systems of self-regulation which were instituted by the film industries with tacit approval from their governments. These were frequently instituted under the guise of safety regulations, but then extended to content control. In any examination of European cinema it is important to consider the extent to which censorship influenced film content in the direction of promoting specific, officially sanctioned 'national' images. As Richard Maltby explains, censorship is 'a practice of power, a form of surveillance over the ideas, images, and representations circulating in a particular culture' (quoted in Nowell-Smith, 1996, 235). The existence of censorship had different effects in different periods: in wartime or dictatorship, for example, it was more acute and focused than in peacetime. It is without question, however, that whatever the period, it exercised a significant constraint on what could be shown. Once these strictures became accepted by film-makers as facts of life they inhibited them from broaching delicate or forbidden subjects in their films. While there are many cases of film-makers managing to get around the letter of censorship laws by including subtle yet risqué material, for example, the celebrated sexual scene (which would not have been apparent in the script) in Alfred Hitchcock's *The Thirty-Nine Steps* (1935) when Madeleine Carroll and Robert Donat are handcuffed together, the overall impact of regulatory systems acted as a force which contributed to the shape of a particular country's film production. And, by exercising control over film imports, European countries could, via censorship, regulate images from abroad which were deemed to be 'unsuitable', or which were set up as objectionable in comparison with indigenous films. They could also, and frequently did, use dubbing to excise politically or morally unacceptable references from films.

The British system of censorship was founded in 1912 when the film industry established the British Board of Film Censors (BBFC), a body which received government approval. The Board had no statutory power but its rulings tended to be accepted by local authorities, who could ban films as an extension of their control over saftey regulations in cinemas. The Board proceeded to classify films under categories including sex and politics, and in the 1930s required film producers to send them scripts so that time and money would not be wasted on films which were unlikely to satisfy the censors. This system was fairly strict and served to exclude films which were considered to be 'dangerous' in political terms, including imports from the USSR so that Eisenstein's *Bronenosets Potemkin* (*The Battleship Potemkin*, 1926) was banned from 1926 to

1954. Films such as *Potemkin* were seen in Britain, but only by members of film societies, which were allowed to show banned films because of their status as private (and expensive) clubs, and this meant that they were viewed only by a minority of the intelligentsia. The films which broached contentious subjects like unemployment in the 1930s were not allowed to be produced, a famous case being the filming of Walter Greenwood's novel *Love on the Dole*, which could only be made after the outbreak of the Second World War when unemployment was no longer a politically sensitive issue. In the 1930s, as Jeffrey Richards has shown, censorship in Britain bolstered the National Government, reinforced its political ideology of 'consensus' and helped to defend the status quo (Richards, 89–107). Direct state involvement was not necessary since the film industry colluded with a system which purported to be independent yet at the same time could be subject to official influence since the President of the BBFC had to be approved by the Home Secretary.

In France the Ministry of the Interior established a Commission in 1916 which issued visas to films that were deemed to be acceptable for exhibition. As in Britain, the localities also had power to ban films, and films made in the USSR received particulary harsh treatment. By contrast, censorship in Germany, during the Weimar period, became more liberal and encouraged the importing of films from the USSR as a political move to forge closer relations between the two countries. Consequently, *The Battleship Potemkin* was a huge success with working-class audiences in Berlin, more so than with audiences in the Soviet Union. Much of its status as a classic of silent cinema rests on its reputation as a 'banned' film which was nevertheless seen by key groups of critics and admirers, and on the enthusiasm with which it was received by the European intelligentsia. Its success in Germany, however, is interesting because it provides evidence for the film as an accessible and *popular* film amongst the audiences for whom it was intended. In this instance, therefore, censorship had a direct impact on the critical reception and popular memory of what became probably the USSR's most famous film in the west.

The rise of the totalitarian regimes had the most dramatic impact on the established norms of censorship regulation in Germany, Italy, Spain and the USSR. The Nazi regime was intent on controlling cinema and it excluded films made in other countries, primarily Hollywood, which competed with German films in the ideological sphere. In Italy the cinema was subject to similar strictures, although Mussolini was less successful than Hitler in completely banning foreign films. The Catholic Church also exerted a conservative influence over film content, as it did in Spain where censorship was draconian, particularly after the Supreme Film Censorship Board was established in 1937 and proceeded to ban films made in the Catalan language and to require, from 1941, that foreign film imports were dubbed. The Church had its own body, the National Board of Classification of Spectacles, which pronounced on the suitability of film projects and raised objections according to its strict moral codes. In this sense both Spain's and Italy's censorship regulations sought to ensure that their respective film cultures were perceived both nationally and internationally as conservative and Catholic.

In Soviet Russia the Stalinist period was more draconian than the 1920s, when during the first part of the decade American films were exhibited and greeted with enthusiasm, particularly films by Buster Keaton, Charlie Chaplin, Douglas Fairbanks and Mary Pickford. Stalin's attempts to create an insular culture, based on the ideology of Socialist Realism, led to the USSR banning the entry of foreign films while at the same time protecting and encouraging the development of the Soviet film industry. Eisenstein's former assistant Grigori Alexandrov developed popular genres such as the musical, and the title sequence of one of his films even contained the lines 'Buster Keaton and Charlie Chaplin do not star in this film,' followed by a list of the Soviet actors who did. As in Germany, 'entertainment' and 'propaganda' went hand-in-hand and directors, including Eisenstein, who did not find favour with Boris Shumyatsky, the official in charge of Stalin's political cinema, were not allowed to make their projects. After *The Battleship Potemkin*, Eisenstein's films became more involved with 'intellectual montage' and even his celebrated classic *Oktiabr'* (*October*, 1928) was accused of being unintelligible to the masses. However, he was reinstated as a Soviet film-maker after Shumyatsky became a victim of Stalin's purges in 1938, and his contribution to the anti-fascist cause was *Aleksandr Nevskii* (*Alexander Nevsky*, 1938). In this case it was expedient for the state to use a film-maker who had proved that he could make films with overt propagandist intent in the 1920s.

During the Second World War these major methods of film censorship continued, and were reinforced by official concerns not just for morality but for national security and morale as well, and in the Axis powers imports of films from the United States and Britain were banned. In Italy, Visconti's *Ossessione* (1942), an adaptation of James M. Cain's novel *The Postman Always Rings Twice*, on its release, was severely criticised by the Fascist hierarchy and the Church who were concerned by its depiction of lust, murder and infidelity. Mussolini's censorship laws decreed that crime and immorality were not suitable screen subjects because they were supposed to have been eradicated by the Fascist regime. As a result, *Ossessione* was cut to under half its original length, given only a limited release in Italy, and all the original copies were destroyed. In Spain, censorship under Franco prevented the introduction of a Spanish branch of neo-realism despite attempts by film-makers such as Luis García Berlanga and Juan Antonio Bardem.

However, in the 1950s most European countries relaxed their censorship laws partly in response to a general trend of liberalisation and the need to support cinema in the face of competition from television. France, in particular, became much more liberal in its attitude towards the depiction of sexuality while in Britain the introduction of the 'X' certificate in 1951 permitted more sexually explicit films to be exhibited. On the other hand, France maintained political censorship until the 1970s, banning films such as Godard's *Le petit soldat*

(*Little Soldier*, 1963), Pontecorvo's *La Bataille d'Alger* (*The Battle of Algiers*, 1966), and even Yorkin's comedy *Start the Revolution Without Me* (1970). Censorship was not abolished in Spain until 1977 after decades during which directors had to make films which satisfied the censors but on occasion, as with the work of Carlos Saura, contained covert elements of critique. By utilising techniques such as allegory, ellipsis and subtle characterisation, Saura achieved a veiled critique of Francoism in films such as *Peppermint Frappé* (1967).

In 1986 *glasnost* liberated Soviet cinema from the straitjacket of totalitarian censorship, the most extreme case of which was, perhaps, Sergei Paradjanov's five years' hard labour for 'speculating in art' and for homosexuality. Paradjanov's *Nran Gouyne* (*The Colour of Pomegranates*, 1969) had been banned for its 'incorrect', surrealistic account of the life of the eighteenth-century poet Sayat Nova. A host of shelved and banned films were released including Alexander Askoldov's *Komissar* (*The Commissar*, 1967), finally completed in 1987, and Alexei Gherman's *Moi drug Ivan Lapshin* (*My Friend Ivan Lapshin*, 1984), and directors like Sergei Paradjanov and Andrei Tarkovsky, who had had their careers blocked in the 1970s, received international acclaim. As the western market economy has been reintroduced, however, American films have been greeted with enthusiasm while the Russian cinema continues to be vulnerable and unstable, dogged by different, but equally acute problems. As in Germany after the Second World War, it has been found that the legacy of dictatorship and censorship cannot be discarded overnight. A survey published in 1995 concluded that most European countries currently adopt a more lenient attitude towards censorship than twenty-five years ago, with the exception of Germany, which seeks to control neo-Nazism and to protect youth, and Britain, which seeks to censor domestic video.

The use of film as propaganda was an adjunct to censorship and can be seen as part of a dual system of forbidden and promoted images. Censorship was used to shape the perception of a country's national output in ways which were perceived by European governments as acceptable, or in accord with other elements of dominant conceptions of nationalist culture. It was generally accepted that film was an important means of national persuasion in times of national emergency; and while film propaganda had been a significant development in the 'total war' of 1914–18 it was the Second World War which accelerated its conscious use by European governments. In Germany, where the major film-production conglomerate was already nationalised, film was seen as a superb medium for the dissemination of Nazi ideas through newsreels and the spectacular documentaries devoted to the celebratory rallies the Nazis held in Nuremberg in 1933 and 1934, filmed by Leni Riefenstahl as *Sieg des Glaubens* (*Victory of Faith*, 1933) and *Triumph des Willens* (*Triumph of the Will*, 1935) and the profoundly anti-semitic *Der ewige Jude* (*The Eternal Jew*, 1940). A few films rewrote history from a Nazi perspective. *Titanic* (1943), for example, claimed that the famous liner sank because of British and Jewish aristocratic and capitalist agency despite the efforts of a heroic German officer to prevent collision with an iceberg, while *Aufruhr in Damaskus (Uproar in Damascus,* 1939) portrayed Lawrence of Arabia as an insurrectionist who incited Syrian rebellion against Germany in the First World War. But since Hollywood films were banned in Germany, Josef Goebbels, the Minister of Propaganda, considered that German feature films should mirror Hollywood entertainment values, and genres such as comedies, melodramas and musicals, and while they could in no way criticise the Nazi regime, most of them did not contain heavy-handed insertions of Nazi doctrines. For this reason, only one-sixth of the 1097 feature films made in Germany from 1933 to 1945 were subsequently banned in the post-war period by Allied censors because they could be construed as Nazi propaganda (Bordwell and Thompson, 308).

In Italy, the Fascists took a keen interest in the cinema. The LUCE (L'Unione cinematografica educativa) company was granted a monopoly of newsreel and documentary production and in 1926 it was decreed that every cinema programme had to include one of the four Mussolini-approved LUCE newsreels that were produced every week. Other measures to protect and promote the film industry included requiring films to be dubbed into Italian in Italy, a tax on dubbed films (levied from 1934 onwards), the creation of the Venice Film Festival (1934), a system of subsidies and prizes for 'high quality' films, and state funding for the new Cinecittà studios, which were opened by Mussolini in 1937. Thus by the end of the 1930s the state 'had a powerful distribution chain, a chain of first rate cinemas and a major production facility' (Wagstaff, 165–7). In 1938, the major American companies withdrew from the Italian market in protest against the monopoly on importing and distributing foreign films which was assigned to a state-run organisation, with the result that the Italian market was virtually closed to foreign imports and there was a concomitant increase in Italian film production. Popular cinema flourished, especially comedies and melodramas, but the facilities of Cinecittà also provided an important training ground for individuals who went on to become crucial figures in neo-realist cinema, including the directors Visconti and Rossellini, and de Sica who was originally a star actor. Similarly, in Spain popular genres like the *folklóricas* were used to glorify Spanish masculinity, and history was used as a blatant excuse to promote Francoism.

In the Soviet Union, the cinema operated within a command rather than a market economy and in the 1930s became a large, studio-based industry to which the state devoted considerable sums of money not just in Moscow and Leningrad but in the regions and outside Russia as well. Stalin's approach was to combine censorship with entertainment, while directors like Mikhail E. Chiaureli were used to inculcate the Stalinist 'cult of personality' in films such as *Velikoe zarevo (The Great Dawn,* 1938), *Kliatva (The Vow,* 1946) and *Padenie Berlina (The Fall of Berlin,* 1949). Despite censorship and Stalin's intimate involvement in film production, the 1930s and 1940s produced many film classics (whose value was ignored until very recently by film scholars) and Soviet citizens became enthusiastic movie-goers (Taylor and Christie, xix–xxi; Nowell-Smith, 1996, 640–1).

In occupied France a German company, Continental, absorbed the major Parisian film studios, took over many expropriated Jewish businesses, and produced French-language films, such as Henri Decoin's *Les inconnus dans la maison* (*Strangers in the House*, 1941). Censorship was circumvented by avoiding contemporary settings and subject-matter and by using the past, as with Marcel Carné's two wartime masterpieces *Les visiteurs du soir* (*The Devil's Own Envoy*, 1942) and *Les enfants du paradis* (*Children of Paradise*, 1945), to compose potentially allegorical narratives of tyranny and freedom. If anything, censorship was more severe in the immediate post-war period when supposedly collaborationist directors like Henri Clouzot were blacklisted, and when the scenarios of films were subject to pre-production vetting by a powerful committee of trade union representatives who had been active in the Resistance (Lindeperg, 145–67).

In Britain the Ministry of Information's propaganda directives urged documentaries and feature films to highlight what Britain was fighting for, how it was fighting the war, and the need for sacrifice at all levels if the war was to be won. A common strategy was to collapse class conflict into narratives which featured everybody 'pulling together': a united nation in the face of national emergency. Both *In Which We Serve* (1942) and *San Demetrio, London* (1943) used the device of a ship as a microcosm of society, loyalty to which united people from different class backgrounds. The home front was also considered to be an important arena for propaganda. *Millions Like Us* (1943) focused on a group of women who had been conscripted to work in a munitions factory, and *The Gentle Sex* (1943) on the training of women in the Auxiliary Territorial Service (ATS). Popular music-hall stars also contributed to maintaining home-front morale by making films which used comedy to communicate the same broad message that everyone must 'do their bit' in the fight against fascism. George Formby had been a popular star in the 1930s and his wartime films included *Let George Do It* (1940), in which a concert performer is mistaken for a British intelligence agent and becomes a hero when he passes a vital message which facilitates the destruction of a Geman U-boat.

The Second World War was therefore a key period when most European governments exerted a considerable degree of control over film production, and even when the war had ended all the Allies continued to see cinema as a key ideological weapon. The Psychological Warfare Branch (PWB) of the American army arrived in Italy and Germany bearing American documentary and feature films. In Berlin, the occupying forces vied with each other to re-open or rebuild cinemas in their respective zones (Bance, 153–68) and Allied funds went to assist the making of suitably anti-fascist films such as Rossellini's *Paisà* (1946), funded by American money, and Wolfgang Staudte's *Die Mörder sind unter uns* (*The Murderers are Among Us*, 1946), which was supported by the Russians. But as Vincendeau has pointed out, the war did not become 'the epic of modern Europe', largely because it affected the various European countries differently and they had to come to terms with their experience in different periods and in their own particular ways (Vincendeau, 1995, xv). France, for example, was unable to deal with the issue of collaboration until many years after the war, and post-war German cinema largely avoided its own recent history, while British films of the 1950s, like *The Dam Busters* (1954), tended to displace problems of masculine identity onto war subjects and generally adopted a less positive attitude towards heroism than in propaganda films made during the war.

To sum up, it would appear that while European governments tried to exercise control over film content via censorship and propaganda, this was not always successful in producing a monolithic and one-dimensional impression of a particular country's film culture. Censorship systems tended to be reactive – attempting to excise 'objectionable' images but operating in such a way that film-makers became unconsciously aware of their concerns, which could act as constraints on, or in some cases, as challenges to, their art. Propaganda, on the other hand, was more pro-active in seeking to perpetuate images which articulated particular expressions of dominant ideology, whether they were fascist, socialist or consensual. The aim of both systems – formal and informal – was to create preferred expressions of national culture, expressions which invariably neglected other competing representations and ideologies.

Protectionism and Subsidy

After 1945, thanks to the experience of the war, state intervention in the European film industries was motivated by cultural as well as economic considerations. There is ample evidence that the Americans wished to dump films in the European markets, but they presented this as the promotion of democracy and freedom. American lobbyists shamelessly associated the triumph of democracy with the export of American movies: 'Whether one calls it propaganda or information, it is evident that as a result of World War II, the motion picture from this day must be regarded as an instrument of public policy as well as a great popular medium of entertainment', wrote the editor of *Film Daily* (quoted in Dickinson and Street, 176).

In Germany, after the collapse of the Nazi regime, the Hollywood film industry was able to 'hold the military government to ransom over the use of American films for education and propaganda purposes' (Elsaesser, 1989, 9) and ensure that the trading arrangements were extraordinarily advantageous to the US. In Italy, similarly, the American chairman of the film section of the Allied Commission declared that 'Italy, as a rural and former fascist country, did not need a film industry and should not be allowed to have one' (Nowell-Smith and Ricci, 6). But in other countries the Americans had a much less easy ride, largely because economic priorities lay elsewhere. Thus in Britain, film imports were associated with food shortages, leading one Member of Parliament, Robert Boothby, to use the graphic comparison of a choice between 'bacon' and 'Bogart' (Dickinson and Street, 180), while in France it was similarly acknowledged that it might be necessary to sacrifice the film industry 'in the higher interests of France' (Jeancolas, 17).

The Americans saw the end of the war as an opportunity to promote free trade which they wished to enshrine in the first General Agreement on Tariffs and Trade (GATT) concluded in 1947. The Europeans were much more ambivalent, as can be seen from the indirect treatment of the topic in films such as Rossellini's *Roma, città aperta* (*Rome, Open City*, 1945) or Cornelius's *Passport to Pimlico* (1949). Films were one of the Americans' major export commodities, the more so since a backlog of unexported movies had built up during the years of the war. The Motion Picture Association of America (MPPA) formed a subsidiary association devoted to questions of trade (the Motion Picture Export Association of America, MPEA) to lobby on behalf of American interests, primarily in Europe. But the cinema was of much greater significance in the American economy than it was in any of the European economies. For example, in 1947, dollar remittances from Britain to the US for films accounted for only 4 per cent of all dollar remittances, the major part being spent on foodstuffs and fuel (Dickinson and Street, 179).

European governments were aware of the popular desire to see American movies, of the need to provide leisure activities, and of the need to offer their people something to buy at a time of great austerity. They were concerned lest disputes over film imports would impede progress on discussion of aid for reconstruction. They were also urged on by powerful lobbies of exhibitors who were anxious for films to screen, since domestic film production had either collapsed, as in Germany, or was severely hampered by the shortage of raw materials. But they could not afford the outflow of dollars needed to import American films. Food rationing in Britain was stricter in the years following the war than it had been during the war. In Germany and Russia people were starving, and in the harsh winter of 1946–7 there was an acute shortage of fuel throughout Europe.

Gradually the arguments about the relative advantages and disadvantages of open and closed markets turned into a recognition of the need to subsidise film production in Europe. The measures put in place during the war to provide state support for the domestic film industries in countries such as France, Italy and Britain, survived in modified form and immediately after the war several European governments took steps to protect their industries against American competition. In August 1947 the British imposed a 75 per cent tax on the value of every foreign film. This led to a boycott of the British market by the MPEA, which was resolved by the Anglo-American Film Agreement of 1948 limiting the dollar remittances allowed to American companies but not the number of films which could be imported. It also encouraged American companies to spend their dollar earnings in Britain.

In France, where the market had been regulated until the war by the 1936 Marchandeau Agreement limiting the number of dubbed films imported (about 150 of which in any one year were American), a screen quota was instituted in

1946. This placed no restriction on the number of films that could be imported, but it obliged exhibitors to devote 4 weeks per trimester (or 16 weeks a year) to screening French films, increased to 5 weeks per trimester in 1948 (Jeancolas, 19).

In Italy the Andreotti Act of July 1949 instituted a system of taxing imports to support local production by means of the so-called 'dubbing certificate'. For each dubbed film imported, the distributor had to deposit a sum of money with the national Banca Nazionale di Lavoro, which was used to create a fund from which Italian producers could borrow at low interest. There was no restriction on the number of films imported, and exemption from the dubbing certificate could be acquired in return for export licences for Italian films (ironically, the Americans could not benefit from this since they had no restrictions on imports). In addition, a screen quota similar to that of France was imposed which was advantageous for film production in Italy.

In Germany and Spain circumstances were somewhat different. The Allies deliberately held back the growth of the German film industry while Americans secured a stranglehold on distribution so that there was little attempt to limit American imports (Elsaesser, 1989, 15). In Spain, imports of American films rose dramatically after the war and it was not until the mid-1950s that the government introduced the so-called 'Baremo', a term which refers to a complex points system by which distributors were allowed to distribute foreign films. Spain proposed to reduce American imports to a total of about 80 films and demanded in return that Spanish films should be distributed in the US, and this led to an American boycott of the Spanish market which lasted for nearly three years. The Baremo was extremely effective in limiting American imports into Spain and encouraging Spanish film production (Guback, 27–30).

After the financial crises of the late 1940s were resolved, western Europe embarked on a period of reconstruction, modernisation and economic growth which in most cases lasted until the first oil crisis of 1973. In societies like those of France, Italy and Spain, which were still very rural in 1945, large numbers of people left the countryside to work in towns. Mass secondary education was introduced in most countries, women were enfranchised and, in the 1960s, the 'baby boomers' of the post-war years came to maturity as a distinctive socioeconomic generation. The profound social, economic and technological changes which resulted from the modernisation of the 1950s and 1960s had a significant impact on forms of culture, leisure and entertainment and on the tastes of European populations. Perhaps the most significant were those produced by the spread of car ownership and the rise of television. However, these changes were often opposed as passionately as they were welcomed and were frequently believed to represent an undesirable 'Americanisation' of Europe. In France and Italy, which both had electorally powerful Communist parties, the Cold War increased pressure on governments to resist 'Coca-Cola culture' and 'American imperialism' as embodied in Hollywood cinema.

Modernisation changed the relationship between European governments and European film industries. In the 1950s cinema attendances began to decline, more rapidly in some countries than in others, while television gradually replaced cinema as the mass medium of entertainment, again more rapidly in some countries than in others. Films continued to be produced for the mass domestic audience in all European countries, but they were not necessarily exported. At the same time, the audience that continued to go to the cinema became socially and generationally fragmented and this, in turn, altered the economic significance of the film industries in Europe.

Throughout the 1950s these changes translated into a spectrum of interventionist measures, some designed to encourage the production of more films, others to foster particular kinds of production. At one extreme, the British 'Eady Levy' on ticket sales returned the greatest amount of money to the producers of the biggest box-office successes, regardless of quality. At the other end of the spectrum was the series of measures developed in France which, in addition to 'automatic aid', of the Eady kind, gradually placed more and more emphasis on qualititative criteria for financial support. Thus in 1948 French producers were offered 'automatic aid' in return for accepting the newly agreed screen quota, which gave them a proportion of the box-office receipts from their films provided a new French film was produced, generating about 17 per cent of total investment in film production in the 1950s. However, in 1953 a proportion of the available subsidy was set aside specifically for projects which were 'French and of a kind to serve the cause of cinema or open new perspectives in the art of cinematography', and in 1959 a fund was created which provided interest-free loans to film-makers (*avances sur recettes*) granted on the basis of an outline or an idea, which was only repayable if the film earned a profit (Forbes, 5–6).

Alongside these various forms of subsidy were other measures designed to boost the supply side. Following the 'Film Europe' initiative of the 1920s, co-production agreements were seen as a means to secure large enough budgets and sufficient distribution guarantees to ensure international box-office success. The very fertile Franco-Italian agreement of 1949 took up an initiative which had begun in 1939 when Jean Renoir went to work in Italy, and had continued in the early years of the war when Italian money was invested in the Victorine Studios in Nice and Antonioni went to work in France. Both the Venice and Cannes film festivals (the former created in 1934, the latter in 1939 but relaunched after the war) became immensely significant as showcases for European films, as did the Forum of Young Cinema introduced at the Berlin Film Festival in 1970. Cannes, especially, became an extremely important meeting place for critical and commercial interests and for European attempts to sell films on the basis of their artistic quality. The films individual countries selected to represent their industries at such festivals were extremely influential in determining the image of a particular country's cinema and especially significant in fostering the notion that European cinema is 'art' cinema.

Modernisation and 'New Cinema'

The 1960s saw 'new cinema' flourishing almost everywhere in Europe. In the Soviet Union, Khrushchev's denunciation of Stalin's 'personality cult' at the 20th Communist Party Congress in 1956 led to a general cultural thaw, and, as far as cinema was concerned, to the release of many banned films, to a period of aesthetic experimentation and to massive investment in the cinema with production rising from ten films a year in the early 1950s to about a hundred in 1960. The west responded by awarding the Golden Palm at Cannes to Mikhail Kalatozov's *Letiat zhuravli* (*The Cranes are Flying*) in 1957 and the Golden Lion at Venice to Andrei Tarkovsky's *Ivanovo detstvo* (*Ivan's Childhood*) in 1962. In France, François Truffaut's *Les quatre cents coups* (*The 400 Blows)* won the Best Director prize at Cannes in 1959, inaugurating the 'nouvelle vague' (new wave) of young directors which included Godard, Chabrol, Rohmer and Rivette, who all made their first films at this time. Similarly, in Italy with Antonioni and Fellini, in Britain with Anderson, Richardson and Reisz, and in Spain with Carlos Saura there was an upsurge of 'new cinema' stimulated by young directors, technological innovation and aesthetic experimentation, in which state intervention sometimes, but not always, played a small but significant role.

However, critical success was not matched by success at the box office. Cinema attendances declined dramatically, especially in Britain and in Germany – in the latter they dropped from 800 million to 180 million at the beginning of the 1960s. In France, Italy, Spain and the Soviet Union, the decline was delayed until the 1970s, no doubt because television spread more slowly in those countries. Ticket sales halved in Italy in the latter part of the 1970s, falling from 514 million to 270 million, and continued to drop to a point below 100 million in the 1990s. In Spain, likewise, cinema audiences declined by two-thirds between 1971 (331 milllion tickets) and 1985 (101 million tickets), and in the Soviet Union they fell from 5 billion in the 1960s to 4 billion by the end of the 1970s. Even in France, where cinema audiences held up better than in any other country, the 1970s was a period of significant decline. This was accompanied in many countries by a production crisis. The British industry became so dependent on American investment that by 1969, 90 per cent of investment in British cinema came from the United States. In Italy in the 1960s, the industry was propped up by the production of comedies but entered a crisis when their popularity declined. In Germany, the loss of 75 per cent of the audience to television gave rise to the Oberhausen Manifesto of young German film-makers in 1962, which called for government intervention and was sympathetically received. From that point on it was recognised that cinema required state support in West Germany, even though debates raged about the amount and the kind of films supported. By the 1980s state intervention in the cinema had become overtly cultural rather than implicitly industrial and films were subsidised in the same way, although less generously, as other art forms such as theatre or opera. A similar process is evident in the policies advocated by Pilar Miro as Director-General of Cinema in Spain in the 1980s, where it was recognised that advance credits of up to 50 per cent of production costs would be needed to produce fewer, but higher-quality films (Jordan and Morgan-Tamosunas, 3).

Cinema and Television

From the 1960s onwards the scale of American investment in European cinema and the general decline in cinema attendances were rendering screen and import quotas irrelevant. The major preoccupation of film industries throughout the developed world was the loss of audience to television, and the relationship between these two media became the focus of state intervention.

In the 1950s and 1960s most European television was publicly funded and operated as a public service (Britain was exceptional in having a mixed public/ private economy). Governments imposed strict quotas on the amount of foreign and foreign-language material which national television stations were allowed to screen, as well as regulating the proportions of each genre of programme. As audiences increasingly saw their films on television, so television and cinema operated in a climate of intense competition in the 1960s and 1970s. This evolved into one of necessary co-existence and cooperation in the 1980s and 1990s when television became the most important source of funding for European films.

Initially television's investment in cinema concentrated on radical or experimental films. In Germany, legislation enacted in the early 1970s permitted television to invest in cinema films, which led to the production of 74 films between 1974 and 1979. In France, similarly, the ban on television investing in cinema was lifted in 1979 and both the first and second channels became major players in cinema. Britain followed suit with the launch of Channel Four in 1982. Initially, investment favoured radical or experimental productions. Germany's second television channel, ZDF, adopted a 'philosophy of artistic patronage' with their series *Das kleine Fernsehspiel*, which financed such works as Hans-Jürgen Syberberg's *Ludwig – Requiem für einen jungfräulichen König* (*Ludwig – Requiem for a Virgin King*, 1972) and Theo Angelopoulos's *Alexander the Great* (1980) (Hartnoll and Porter, 12). In France, the Institut National de l'Audiovisuel, created in 1975, adopted a policy of funding experimental films by many of the most radical European film-makers between 1975 and 1979. By the 1980s, however, this period of experimental film production financed by television appeared to be over. Television finance for cinema films was increasingly devoted to mainstream film production, often of a kind which had to be able to be 'sold on the international market' (Hartnoll and Porter, 17), while in some cases television channels became instruments for the direct or indirect promotion of the interests of politicians. Thus in Italy in the late 1980s Silvio Berlusconi owned three large private televison networks through his company Fininvest, and a substantial share of the distribution company Penta Film, and this allowed him to use his media influence to promote his political campaigns and those of his party Forza Italia.

At the outset, television's contribution to the production of films for the cinema was an indirect form of public subsidy since European television stations were almost all operated as state-funded public services. However, the 1980s saw rapid changes in the way films were delivered to audiences, with many films becoming available on video cassettes for sale or for rental and with satellite and cable channels becoming widespread. Television was deregulated in Italy in the mid-1970s, in France and Spain in the 1980s, and in Russia after the fall of the Berlin Wall, so that commercial television channels became increasingly involved in both producing and screening cinema films. In Italy, for example, 80 per cent of feature films were financed by television by the end of the 1980s, while Canal Plus, one of the most dynamic of the new channels, which originated in France in 1984, had built up a production and distribution empire that covered much of Europe by the end of the 1990s. In anticipation of the completion of the Single Market in 1986, the European Commission addressed the question of cross-frontier broadcasting, or so-called 'television without frontiers', making it clear that the aim was to use television to create 'an increasingly integrated economic, social and political entity' in which questions of competition, particularly in relation to advertising and intellectual property, would require resolution. Thus a curiously contradictory situation arose. As competition between TV stations became more acute and revenues more and more dependent on the size of the audience, so television became another means by which American films, which were cheap to buy and popular, were distributed in Europe.

On the other hand, many European governments took a renewed interest in financing the cinema. In Britain, a government that was committed to privatisation and to shrinking the state, phased out tax breaks for investors in the film industry, abolished the Eady Levy and dismantled the National Film Finance Corporation in 1985, a year later establishing British Screen, a private company whose role was to lend money to finance film production. In France, the socialist government of the 1980s created three new television channels (two of them private), generating cut-throat competition for audiences and profit, which led to large increases in American imports, but at the same time increased the amount available for *avances sur recettes*, involved the Ministry of Culture directly in financing film production, and created a tax shelter system to encourage investment in films. In Russia in the early 1990s, immediately after the collapse of the Soviet Union, investment in film production became a preferred method of money-laundering while video-piracy made significant inroads into the distribution sector. More recently, the major television channels have operated a cartel for purchasing screening rights, which keeps the price of features artifically low and starves the film industry of funds for production. They devote one-third of their schedules to feature films but achieve high ratings by screening old Soviet films.

Cinema and the European Union

In Europe, state intervention in the film industries was invariably designed to prop up domestic industries or to encourage co-productions and it was often designed to support film-making in 'minority' languages. Until the completion of the Single Market in 1986 there was little thought of a European film policy, although, as we have seen, a unified television policy was adumbrated in 1984. However, in the 1980s and 1990s such a policy became both feasible and desirable. The fall of the Berlin Wall in 1989 and the re-unification of Germany in 1990 altered the perception of 'Europe' and gave western Europe economic and cultural responsibilities towards the former eastern bloc. The Treaty of Maastricht and the creation of the European Union made harmonisation and concerted action necessary both to manage competition, to ensure a strong European presence in the increasingly convergent telecommunications, computing and information markets, and in order to foster the cultural idea of Europe. The privatisation of television and telecommunications which began in the 1980s and gathered pace throughout the decade, the successive waves of mergers and takeovers in international media corporations, rapid technological change, and the birth of the information highway, all served to anchor cinema within the global media industries, which are, of course, dominated by the United States. Films made for cinema are used to attract customers to purchase other goods and services sold via the new media, and to underpin infrastructural investment, so that although film production forms a very small part of total media activity, it is an immensely significant element of the global media economy, as is the ownership of catalogues of films.

The global economic significance of the audio-visual sector was confirmed by the Uruguay round of negotiations which led to the 1993 GATT. The Americans sought a deregulation of the European market – an abolition of quotas and subsidies – in the cause of free trade, while the European Union, inspired by the French, argued that audio-visual products were cultural products and thus should be exempted from free trade provisions. The EU's refusal to shift its position almost caused a failure of the Agreement, which was finally concluded by omitting audio-visual products and by an 'agreement to disagree'.

The timing of this confrontation is interesting. In France it coincided with the release of Claude Berri's film of Emile Zola's novel *Germinal*, leading to an opposition between 'Cola' and 'Zola' which recalled an argument between the Europeans and the Americans that can be traced back, as we have seen, to 1945 if not to the 1930s. For Michael Chanan the argument is to be explained by the value of what was at issue (Chanan, 57). The 1980s saw transnational media corporations like Microsoft, News International and Time Warner massively increase their power. Thus the traditional argument between European and American film industries had been transformed in the 1990s into an argument about who would secure the multi-billion dollar profits from world media domination, in which cinema plays a small but significant part.

The GATT discussions gave further impetus to a series of Europe-wide initiatives tentatively begun in the 1980s when it was agreed that Europe's television channels would screen a fixed quota of EU-originated programmes. In 1989 the Council of Europe (whose members included eastern-bloc countries as well as those in the European Community) initiated the Eurimages programme, a fund for multi-lateral European co-productions between countries who are contributing members, which supports co-production through a loan mechanism and also supports documentaries, exhibition and marketing. Some of the most critically successful European films of the 1990s were supported by this fund. In addition, the European Community/Union has had two cinema initiatives, MEDIA I (1991–5) and MEDIA II (from 1995). While the former has been criticised for its 'scattergun' approach (Finney, 3), the second project, with a budget of 310 million ECU, concentrates on development, distribution and training as well as on the key industrial sectors of animation, new technology and heritage (Finney, 133). Its inspiration is clearly the Hollywood film industry, whose size is considered to offer significant economies of scale but, as important, a means to spread risk in what is an inherently uncertain business. Based on the knowledge that only 10 per cent of European films are screened in another European country, MEDIA II considered distribution to be a major weakness of the European film industries. A report by the consultants Coopers and Lybrand (cited in Finney, 141) identified the advantages of the American majors in respect of distribution, an illustration of which might be the extremely favourable deals imposed by George Lucas on theatres wishing to screen his prequel *Star Wars Episode 1: The Phantom Menace* (1999). Thus the European Union has made efforts to create industrial structures in the cinema to compare with and rival those of Hollywood, reinserting cinema into a commercial discourse from which it emerged in the aftermath of the Second World War, and reinforcing it by its policy of promoting fair competition.

Paradoxically, perhaps, new technologies have encouraged the production of new feature films and enhanced the value of back catalogues by increasing the outlets and demand for audiovisual products, so that the EU has been well placed to take advantage of the market expansion offered by globalisation. However, because the European Union also promotes cultural diversity, this creates uncertainty as to what should be the focus of public policy towards the cinema and whether, indeed, a common policy is feasible or desirable. What, if anything, defines 'European cinema' remains an open question, and it is this which forms the subject of the following chapter.

2

Ideology, Aesthetics and Style

The preceding pages have discussed the history of cinema in Europe from an economic and political point of view, stressing the importance national governments of all political persuasions came to attach to controlling and supporting what was, for much of the twentieth century, the most important audio-visual medium and the most significant form of mass entertainment. The Russian Revolution, the rise of fascism in Italy, Germany and Spain, the two world wars, the collapse of the Soviet Union, together with the creation and extension of the European Union, have all been seen to have had a profound impact on the cinema and to have affected the film industries in Europe.

The pages which follow will focus on questions of aesthetics and style and how these have been used to define the nationality of films. They will ask whether European cinema is merely the sum of different national cinemas or whether there are identifiable genres, styles, production norms and practices which differentiate European cinema from other regional cinemas and, especially, from Hollywood cinema. They will also consider whether the relationship between European cinema and Hollywood cinema can most productively be described as one of mutual creative tension, and what the cultural role of cinema in Europe will be in the context of twenty-first-century globalisation.

The Rise of National Cinema

In the 1920s the economic, political and ideological role of cinema was hotly debated and the idea of national cinema took root in Europe. In Italy, the Soviet Union, Germany and Spain, the context was the rise of nationalism and the increasingly totalitarian regimes in these countries. In other major European film-producing countries such as Britain and France, the nationalist emphasis was more obviously cultural than political. Elites were worried about the influence of the cinema in general and of the American cinema in particular. It has been argued that the standardisation and homogenisation of mass culture evident in American films purveyed a democratic egalitarianism which ran counter to the more hierarchical structures of European societies and posed a threat to bourgeois elites. Thus one commentator in Britain complained of 'youths belonging to all classes whose experience of life is based largely on the narrow and frequently sordid plots of American films' (Thompson, 70); another criticised the fact that in the America depicted in the movies, 'no sentiment is too sacred to be compared with the pleasures of the commodities displayed' (quoted in Ďurovičová, 140). A particular concern was that the emphasis on material objects not only damaged European industries but was also particularly attractive to women, who were the 'ideal consumers' targeted by Hollywood (Eckert, 16), and that this was subversive of their traditional place in society. Hence another British writer's reference to 'women who, to all intents and purposes, are temporary American citizens' as a result of watching movies (Maltby and Vasey, 71). In response to the combination of moral and ideological panic induced by the popularity of American films in Britain a Commission on Educational and Cultural Films was set up in 1929 (Dickinson and Street, 48), and in a report on *The Film in National Life*, called for the production of films which were 'an unequivocal expression of British life and thought, deriving character and inspiration from our national inheritance' (Maltby and Vasey, 72–3).

The 'America' of the movies was a utopia which 'presented itself less as a geographical territory than as an imaginative one. It was a territory that deliberately made itself available for assimilation in a variety of cultural contexts,' and it 'was not a foreign country to its aficionados whatever their nationality' (Maltby and Vasey, 69, 79). American studio bosses made much of this utopianism and used the idea of a Hollywood 'melting pot' to promote Hollywood's universal appeal and to suggest that the American film industry was 'a cultural microcosm gathering the best and the brightest from all continents' (Ďurovičová, p. 141).

In seeking to offer economic protection to their domestic film industries, European governments were led to attempt to define a national film since this was both a form of distinctiveness and a useful counterweight to the supposed 'universalism' of Hollywood. The difficulties they experienced and the solutions they devised offer an interesting approach to the question of national cinema and its relation to European cinema.

The nationality of a film could be defined by where it is made and who invests in its production and distribution (Higson, 36). But the various quota systems introduced in Europe illustrate how ineffective this definition could be. In Germany, for example, the American studios Paramount and Metro-Goldwyn Corporation bought a large share of UFA in 1925, while in Britain and Italy 'quota quickies' were filmed locally but using American money. The fact that a film is shot in a particular country is no indication of who has invested in it, who owns the finished product, or even who benefits from distributing it.

A second definition might concern the national origins of those who work on a film. Thus the British 'Quota Act' of 1927 defined whether or not a film was British by the 'proportion of labour costs paid to British nationals' (Maltby and

Vasey, 69). However, the film industry throughout Europe and the United States was extremely cosmopolitan. Hollywood employed individuals from all sorts of different national backgrounds – indeed, it was an industry in which immigrants were able to succeed with relative ease, whether as actors, directors, producers or technicians. Hollywood also proved a magnet to Europeans: some, like Chaplin, Hitchcock or Lubitsch, went to seek their fortunes; others emigrated for political reasons. The European film industries also employed waves of immigrants: Russians emigrated after the Bolshevik Revolution of 1917 to Berlin or to Paris where the Russian-owned and run Albatros Studios flourished in the 1920s; Alexander Korda, the most powerful film producer in England in the 1930s, was Hungarian by birth. When Hitler came to power in 1933 many Jews in the film business fled to France, England or America – Fritz Lang being perhaps the best known – and the German-trained cameramen who found work in France had an influence on the visual style of French films right up to the 1950s. When the Germans invaded France many French actors and directors, among them Renoir, Clair, Duvivier, Gabin and Jouvet, left for North or South America and did not return until after the war. Luis Buñuel went into political exile from Spain as a result of the Civil War and did not make a film there again until *Viridiana* in 1961; many Eastern European film-makers, like Roman Polanski or Milos Forman, emigrated to America during the Communist period; and since the fall of the Berlin Wall, many film-makers from Eastern Europe and Russia, such as Krzysztof Kieslowski, have worked in the west, especially in France, while large numbers of European film-makers, like Luc Besson, Ridley Scott and Wim Wenders, continue to work in Hollywood.

A more promising definition of national cinema might concern what it represents. Hollywood cinema is deliberately escapist and film studios became adept at creating sets to look like anywhere in the world, from Ancient Rome and Biblical Babylon, as in D. W. Griffith's *Intolerance* (1916), to modern Paris, London or Moscow. During the 1920s and 1930s, especially, set decorators worked from photographic records, embellished by their own invention, to re-create landscapes or cities thought to be typical of well-known locations like the cities of London, Paris, Berlin or New York. Indeed, the Paris photographic agency Seeberger Frères specialised in supplying Hollywood studios with images of 'typical' Paris street scenes and were thus influential in determining for decades how Paris would be represented by Hollywood. The need for a location to be recognisable often led to the flouting of verisimilitude. For example, Pabst's *Die Dreigroschenoper* (*The Threepenny Opera*) (1931), based on the eighteenth-century English play *The Beggars' Opera* by John Gay, was made in Berlin but set in a London in which, contrary to reality, the docks and Soho are contiguous. But these features are used as indices of London in much the same way as a meteorological commonplace such as the London fog in Hitchcock's *The Lodger*, or a monument such as the Eiffel Tower, which signifies Paris in *La haine*. Such features are incorporated into a shot to let the viewer know where the film is supposed to be set, which may be many thousands of miles away from where it is shot.

During the 1930s, European cinema often self-consciously shared Hollywood's utopianism, as can be seen in the extravagant sets of Italian spectaculars or the fantastic design of German expressionist films such as *Metropolis* or *The Cabinet of Dr Caligari*, as well as in the studio-produced historicism of internationally successful films such as Korda's *The Private Life of Henry VIII* (1933) or Feyder's *La kermesse héroïque* (*Carnival in Flanders*, 1935). Gradually, however, we can see the beginning of a movement towards realism, exemplified in Renoir's *La règle du jeu*, released just before the Second World War in 1939. This was taken up after the war in the Italian neo-realist cinema and gradually became a commonplace in European cinema in the 1960s. But even films shot 'on location' are not necessarily shot in the real location. Hollywood spectaculars such as Anthony Mann's *El Cid* (1961) or *The Fall of the Roman Empire* (1964) were shot in Spain, as were the so-called 'spaghetti westerns'. Today, modern technology makes it possible to create an authentic-looking location entirely within a film studio or on a computer screen, as was amusingly illustrated in Barry Levinson's *Wag the Dog* (1997). The result is that although the nationality of a film may be legally defined by where it is made, this definition may well be at odds with what the film represents and, therefore, what the audience believes, or is intended to believe, about its national origins. Hollywood 'represented' Europe and Europe fantasised about America.

Sound and Style

The arrival of the talkies at the end of the 1920s, however, seemed to offer an obvious way of defining a film's nationality. In the silent period language was certainly no guide to the nationality of a film. Many of the early film theorists considered that the silent cinema constituted an 'international language', either because it dealt with simple melodramatic or comic themes, which easily crossed national boundaries, or because its iconography and performance styles were based on a set of simplified, exaggerated and easily 'legible' codes. It was also suggested that cinema not only mobilised universal themes and genres but could also be used to promote humanist ideals. But films were primarily 'an international language' because they were exported as 'semi-finished products' (Maltby and Vasey, 77). For technical reasons European release prints were often made from negatives different from the ones used for American release prints and when they were exhibited it was in conditions which varied widely from place to place. There could be different musical accompaniments, and intertitles in the local language whose content was often radically modified to take account of local sensibilities; they could be projected at different speeds, with different colour tints; and they were often re-edited so that the versions screened could be of widely varying lengths. In the Soviet Union, when there was a dearth of imported films during the post-revolutionary blockade, a deliberate policy of re-editing imported films was developed both for aesthetic and for political reasons. The shortage of new imported films stimulated the 're-use' of those already in the country, which were often recut to make something new, while at the same time aesthetic experimentation in all the arts was predicated on the deliberate destruction of the old. The theories of montage, by which new aesthetic experiences are generated through the juxtaposition of different images, is said to have derived from this practice. But as well as existing in a range of sometimes quite different versions, adapted to local circumstances, silent films were 'naturalised' because audiences read into them whatever local interpretations they chose. Anthropologists have noted that groups unfamiliar with western narrative genres will appropriate western audio-visual material according to their individual world views (Michaels, 81–95), and a similar process probably took place with silent films. Sound cinema, on the other hand, made comprehension difficult, emphasised cultural specificity, and also offered greater opportunities for defining the nationality of a film.

Sound cinema had been technically feasible for some considerable time but it became commercially viable with the success of Crosland's *The Jazz Singer* (1927), starring the popular vaudeville singer Al Jolson. Designed to revive the flagging fortunes of the Warner Brothers Studio, which it did beyond all expectation, sound cinema also precipitated cut-throat technological and artistic competition. On the technological side, sound completed the industrialisation of cinema by introducing greater uniformity and standardisation. According to Williams, 'everywhere the coming of sound appears to have reduced diversity and acted against those who would oppose the classical Hollywood cinema with an alternative of their own' (Williams, 136). It also integrated the various elements of popular entertainment, such as song, music and dance, into the 'culture industries', and marked the beginning of the link, which is of immense significance today, between the film industry, the electrical and electronic industries, and big business. In Europe, sound reinforced national rivalries, stifled the cooperation that had been adumbrated in 'Film Europe', but also offered temporary protection from Hollywood. However, in Europe it was only in Germany that the link was made between big business and the cinema, through the investment of companies such as AEG and Siemens in the conversion to sound.

Artistically, many in Europe feared the standardisation that sound would bring not just to American films but to European cinema too, and believed that the constraints of filming on sound stages and the novelty of hearing people talk would put an end to visual experimentation. This was perhaps most acutely felt in the Soviet Union. Soviet films had often been conceived with musical accompaniments in mind – Eisenstein, for example, worked with the German composer Edmund Meisel on a specially composed score to accompany *The Battleship Potemkin* (Eisenstein, 177–8), and he maintained the habit of working closely with composers, as can be seen from his collaboration with

Prokofiev on *Alexander Nevsky*. But the organic development of musical accompaniments was a very different matter from the integration of dialogue. In 1928, Eisenstein, Pudovkin and Alexandrov published a 'Statement' on sound cinema in which they expressed concern that 'this new technical discovery may not only hinder the development and perfection of the cinema as an art, but also threaten to destroy all its present formal achievement' (Eisenstein, 257–9). They particularly feared that sound would destroy the aesthetic principles of montage, which was the national specificity of Soviet cinema and the foundation of 'the success of Soviet films on the world's screens', and they predicted, rightly, that sound would usher in 'an epoch of its automatic utilisation for "highly coloured dramas" and other photographical performances of a theatrical sort' and called for 'experimental work with sound...along the line of its distinct non-synchronisation with the visual images', for the 'contrapuntal use' of sound.

This 'Statement' is significant for a number of reasons. The first is that it embraces sound but not dialogue, whereas elsewhere the question of national cinema crystallised around dialogue in particular rather than sound in general. Secondly, it confirms a divorce, at this point, between the development of cinema in the west and in the Soviet Union. As Eisenstein and his co-authors acknowledged, it was to be several years before the Soviet Union was equipped for sound, and silent films continued to be made and distributed in that country until the Second World War (Nowell-Smith, 1996, 390), whereas in western Europe sound was initially viewed as an opportunity for national differentiation. But thirdly, as envisaged, when sound did eventually become general in Soviet films its advent took on political force as Socialist Realism was adopted as the party line and as Stalin's censorship bit hard: 'According to official doctrine, it was the scriptwriter rather than the director who was the crucial figure.... Publicists of the time insisted on the "iron scenario" strictly limiting the independence of the director and denounced the idea of directorial freedom as a remnant of formalism' (Nowell-Smith, 1996, 390). Indeed, it has been suggested that like Goebbels in Germany, Stalin 'micro-managed' the cinema and instituted himself as the supreme censor.

But in western Europe too, even where political totalitarianism was absent, artistic experimentation was killed off by sound. This is interestingly dramatised in one of René Clair's early sound films, *A nous la liberté* (1932), in which a gramophone-record factory is visually likened to a prison because both use the principles of mass production, in which tasks are measured, timed and infinitely repeated in order to achieve maximum efficiency. The film, which is said to have influenced Chaplin's *Modern Times* (1936), satirises the totalitarian slogan 'work is freedom' (later to be found over the entrance to concentration camps) and ends with its two heroes abandoning a life of industry-generated wealth for a life as tramps on the open road.

In the very early years of film with dialogue it appeared that the film industry might fragment into a series of national markets and audiences. Early sound films such as *The Jazz Singer*, in which music is much more important than spoken dialogue, solved the problem of language differences by projecting intertitles onto an adjacent screen, much as is frequently done for opera today (Thompson, 158). But subtitling or handing out a translation of the scenario somewhat undermined the novelty of films in which people spoke and could be understood. On the other hand, dubbing techniques remained unsatisfactory until the invention of the Moviola in 1930, when the mixing and accurate synchronisation of sound tracks became feasible. The result was that, for a brief period, films were often made in several different language versions. This was done either by setting up production facilities abroad or by hiring foreign actors to work in the domestic industry. The American studios were most active because they had most to lose. Paramount established a branch studio at Joinville just outside Paris, which came to be known as 'Babel on Seine'; MGM and Universal hired European actors to make foreign-language versions in Hollywood (Vincendeau, 1988, 29); but the Germans also operated abroad, with the Tobis studios at Epinay in the Paris suburbs, while many British and French actors travelled to Berlin to make films in their native languages.

The experiments with foreign-language versions are useful in considering whether language is axiomatic to defining national cinemas. The failure to respect language sensibilities led to riots in Prague in 1930, possibly discreetly fostered by American firms, when German-speaking films were screened, leading distributors to prefer French versions with Czech subtitles (Ďurovičová, 23, n. 25). Similarly, films made in Spanish in Hollywood, using Latin American actors, were ill-received in Spain because of its variety of linguistic communities. Sometimes there could simply be a failure of comprehension, as in Portugal where Brazilian speakers were not understood. Beyond this, dialogue increased social and cultural specificity both within films and between films and foregrounded the social and national origins of actors and characters. Films which Hollywood had passed off as 'universal', or in which nationality had not been an issue, now became identifiably American and therefore less amenable to local assimilation. In Britain where audiences ostensibly understood Hollywood's language, American idioms initially proved incomprehensible (they would not be today, thanks to the mass media), but on the other hand, audiences in the north of England and in Scotland preferred the apparently 'classless' accents of American actors to the relentlessly upper middle-class southern English accents of most British screen actors. Nationality differences were sometimes incorporated diegetically in order to allow different languages to be spoken. Thus Duvivier's *Allô Berlin? Ici Paris* (1932) is a comedy about male German telephonists falling in love with female French telephonists, based around language differences and stereotypical national behaviour. It is often said that the advent of sound destroyed many acting careers, but it was the making of others. Greta Garbo or Emil Jannings, who were bi- or multi-lingual, found their careers boosted by their transnational appeal, while Maurice Chevalier was apparently instructed not to lose his French accent, so that he could continue to incarnate a 'typical' French man in Hollywood.

Scholars have suggested that foreign-language versions were unpopular because audiences perceived them as somehow 'inauthentic', based as they were on a minimalist definition of the national as 'simply the difference between the least possible and the least necessary inflection of the basic text' (Ďurovičová, 144). In a film industry built around stars it was pointless to replace a well-known figure simply in order that the film's dialogue could be understood. More significantly, foreign-language versions underscored the fact that cultural discourse was just as important as dialogue in the reception of a film. Nataša Ďurovičová cites the fascinating example of the Swedish version of a Hollywood film in which 'the sense of comfort with which the Swedish actors speak their lines is essentially incompatible with the non-Swedish social mannerisms, surroundings and psychological types of the characters' (146). With the coming of sound, the corporeal expressiveness of silent cinema gave way to a certain 'casualness' which became the mark of authenticity and realism, but this was a way of 'being in the world' which was culturally specific. In this way sound cinema required films to adopt a recognisable cultural idiom so as to appear authentic.

Sound was also instrumental in shifting the origin of language from a geographical to a technological space (Ďurovičová, 142). The two methods quickly perfected for distributing foreign-language films were dubbing and subtitling (preferences for one or the other varied from country to country) and both could be used to promote national requirements. Italy, France and Germany all required dubbing to be carried out in those countries and not, for example, in America or Britain. The requirement that all foreign films screened in Italy should be dubbed into Italian was both a protectionist measure and a nationalist one since it imposed on Italian cinema a linguistic uniformity which the Italian state, with its many and varied regional dialects and languages, did not have (Nowell-Smith, 1968, 146). It also began the tradition of post-synchronisation which persists in Italian cinema today. The Italian used in dubbing was, in the main, a 'standard Italian' designed to eradicate dialect and foreign words, but more recently, for the dubbing of a film such as *Trainspotting*, a kind of colloquial Italian is used which is largely self-referential (that is, rather than mirroring how people actually speak, it signifies 'the colloquial register in cinema'). From 1941 onwards, Spain likewise imposed dubbing into Spanish (Bosch and del Rincón, 119), and on occasion this proved an extremely useful tool of censorship. In Franquist Spain, for example, all references to Rick's (Humphrey Bogart's) participation in the Spanish Civil War in Curtiz's *Casablanca* (1942), were simply excised (Bosch and del Rincón, 122–3). But even where political censorship was non-existent, references which were considered obsure were frequently 'naturalised' and the film's meaning was often altered in the process (Nowell-Smith, 1968, 147). In such cases it would be difficult to argue that audiences in different countries were seeing the 'same' version of a film.

To sum up, therefore, sound cinema required the 'proper bodies' to make the 'proper noises'. Usually the proper noises were the national language, which could be a dialect invented for the purpose, as in Italy, or, as in Britain, a foreign dialect such as 'American English', which had the advantage of not being regionally specific. The 'proper bodies' were often more problematical because the norms to which they were required to conform were, and are, less well codified: the 'grammar' of physical comportment is less highly developed than the grammar of spoken dialogue.

Film-makers sometimes used national stereotypes to comic effect. Knowing that the west was both suspicious and curious about the post-revolutionary Soviet Union, the Russian film-maker Lev Kuleshov made a spoof entitled *The Extraordinary Adventures of Mr West in the Land of the Bolsheviks* (1924), in which Bolsheviks dress up like the tribal bandits the Americans imagine them to be in order to fleece the American visitors. Similarly, the Spanish film-maker Luis Buñuel, making *Cet obscur objet du désir* (*That Obscure Object of Desire*, 1977) in France, investigated the themes of Frenchness and Spanishness through body language and speech in 'a film by a Spaniard who has lived in France adapting a French novel (Pierre Louÿs's *La femme et le pantin*) whose Spanish protagonist is transformed by Buñuel into a Frenchman played by a Spaniard and dubbed by a Frenchman' (Shohat and Stam, 50). Conversely, in Claude Chabrol's film of Simone de Beauvoir's novel *Le sang des autres* (*The Blood of Others*, 1984), made in English for the American cable network HBO and starring American and Australian actors, the question of nationality is not foregrounded, so that both the body-language of the actors and the confrontational dialogue, as well as the fast-paced editing, combine to produce a representation which more closely resembles *Dallas* than Paris in the 1950s.

The European Film Studios

Most film historians attribute the world-wide success of American cinema to the studio system. 'By concentrating production within vast, factory-like studios and by vertically integrating all aspects of the business, from production to publicity to distribution to exhibition, they created a model system – the "studio system" – which other countries had to imitate in order to compete' (Gomery, in Nowell-Smith, 1996, 43). Indeed, the use of the word 'studio', which simultaneously connotes an artist's workshop and the place where the pupils and followers of a great artist produce imitations of his work, neatly encapsulated the cinema's role as industry masquerading as art.

As we have seen, the studio system was a key factor in helping the Americans to consolidate their European domination at the time of the First World War, when American products proved technically and artistically superior to those in Europe. It was also crucial after the advent of sound cinema when technological superiority was achieved through the involvement of big corporations, especially those from the electrical industries, in the modernisation and expansion of the studios. Is it the case, however, that the Europeans had to 'imitate the Americans' in order to compete?

It is certainly true that they thought they did. In France during the 1930s, when film-production companies came and went bankrupt with alarming rapidity and when it appeared impossible to achieve continuity in film production, Jean Renoir, Marcel L'Herbier, and several other film-makers tried to persuade the government to create a 'Hollywood on the Côte d'azur'. Ironically, this was only achieved during the Occupation when the mass exodus from Paris of people involved in the film business led to the creation of a prototype film school and production centre near Nice (Bertin-Maghit, 42–8). In Italy, Luigi Freddi, the Fascist Party's head of propaganda, went to Hollywood to study the organisation of the film industry and, after he became head of cinema, promoted vertical integration in the Italian industry and secured state funding to build the new Cinecittà studios, opened in 1937.

In the Soviet Union the Hollywood model proved equally seductive although it operated within the overall context of state control. Boris Shumyatsky, appointed head of Soyuzkino by Stalin in 1930, visited Hollywood. He applied its lessons by successfully managing the transition to sound, by re-organising Soviet film production on Hollywood lines. Similarly in Germany, after the Nazis came to power, Goebbels worked closely with the film industry to concentrate film production into a small number of highly capitalised, efficiently organised studios which successfully produced high-quality entertainment, often inspired by Hollywood genres, for Germany's expanding market. These examples, and that of Tobis-Klangfilm or Paramount, who built studios in Paris in order to exploit their respective sound systems, suggest that some European studios were, indeed, vehicles for factory-style mass production.

However, this was not always the case, nor is it necessarily what they are best remembered for. Babelsberg, owned by UFA, became celebrated for a distinctive style of film-making based initially on complex and intriguing sets and lighting, and later, on a style of 'cold' cinematography which was exported to France and to America through the emigration of cinematographers after the Nazis came to power. The Albatros film studio at Montreuil near Paris was taken over in 1920 by the Russian émigré Ermolieff. It became the vector through which much contemporary Russian art and design and a certain orientalism reached a wide public in western Europe, while its leading actor, Ivan Mosjoukine, became one of the first film stars to emerge in Europe (Albera, 19–31). The Tobis-owned Epinay film studio in the Paris region became known, under the designer Lazare Meerson, for its elaborate sets, seen in many of René Clair's films, as did the Victorine studios in Nice where *Les enfants du paradis* was shot. The UFA and Albatros models are arguably more typical of European film studios, which were primarily artistic or stylistic communities rather than factories of films. With the exception of the Soviet studios, which were devoted to catering for the masses, their major function was not to serve as the centre of vertically integrated businesses but to provide an artistic home and a means of artistic expression for communities of like-minded individuals.

The 1920s and 1930s were probably the period when studio styles had the greatest influence on cinema in Europe. After the Second World War, under the influence of the Italian neo-realists who shot their films on location rather than on elaborate sets, their influence declined, but it did not disappear. In Britain, Michael Balcon used the Ealing Studios, which he took over in 1938 but whose period of greatest celebrity was the late 1940s and early 1950s, to promote an ideology more than an aesthetic through the genre of comedy, consciously putting 'film to work in the national interest' (Barr, 7) and aiming to make films 'projecting Britain and the British character'. But perhaps the most celebrated of all post-war European studios was Rome's Cinecittà, the 'Hollywood on the Tiber' that Pasolini called 'the belching stomach of Italy'. It created its own star system of 'sex-pot divas' such as Gina Lollobrigida and Sophia Loren, who subsequently became world famous thanks to Hollywood, and it specialised in mass producing a rapidly changing range of 'B' features and genre films – popular melodramas, comedies, horror films, sword and sandal epics and, most famous of all, 'spaghetti westerns'. The increasingly parodic self-reflexiveness of the spaghetti westerns underlined the ambiguous function of a film studio attempting to copy pre-war Hollywood in the post-Second World War era. The conflicts between a 'European' artistic community and 'American' big business inherent in Cinecittà's approach to film-making is also dramatised in Jean-Luc Godard's film *Le mépris* (*Contempt*, 1962), itself a Franco-Italian co-production shot at Cinecittà and on location in Italy. However, François Truffaut's *La nuit américaine* (*Day for Night*, 1983), whose ambiguous title 'the American night' does not come across in English, is a nostalgic evocation of studio-based film-making which suggests both the positive and negative aspects of the studios, as does Federico Fellini's equally nostalgic *Ginger e Fred* (*Ginger and Fred*, 1985). Such exercises in nostalgia underline the important but frequently neglected contribution of studios to European film-making.

Hollywood, For and Against: Art Cinema and Popular Cinema

As we have seen, for much of the twentieth century European countries were concerned about the threat of 'Americanisation', or to be more specific, 'Hollywoodisation'. 'Americanisation' was synonymous with 'Hollywoodisation' because of the US motion picture industry's success at exporting its films all over the world and the assumption that films carried cultural meanings: Uncle Sam invades Europe. The dilemma hinged on the extent to which separation from Hollywood was possible or, indeed, desirable. For many in Europe, particularly cultural and political elites who feared the impact of mass exposure to Hollywood's messages of democracy, this was something to be taken seriously (Maltby, in Nowell-Smith and Ricci, 104–15). Throughout the twentieth century the existence of Hollywood as a major international competitor has exerted a profound influence over the direction of European film industries as European states have sought to protect their national cinemas against Hollywood competition. In the totalitarian states the film industries were carefully developed and nurtured for nationalist economic and cultural reasons, either by massive state investment, as in the USSR, or, as in Germany, through the close involvement of the banks in financing the film industry. Indeed, with Goebbels's encouragement, the cinema developed into the fourth largest industry of the Third Reich (Petley, 86). In France and Britain, pre-war state involvement was patchy and in the main confined to forms of import regulation.

At the end of the Second World War, European governments became more actively involved in the promotion of cinema through various forms of state subsidy, and later, through the regulation of television and the mechanisms of the European Community/Union. France took the lead in the 1950s, followed by Germany and, after Franco's death, Spain, in promoting the art film or *auteur* film, which some scholars would consider a characteristic form of European cinema. The art film existed alongside the popular film genres which continued to be produced in Europe, but for a period of about twenty years from the late 1950s art cinema came to be seen as distinctively European because it was the form of cinema in which states invested the greatest financial support and which they promoted abroad.

In an interesting article published in 1979, Bordwell suggested that art cinema was a post-war 'mode of film production' which grew up 'as the dominance of Hollywood cinema was beginning to wane' (Bordwell, 57). He attempted to define art cinema by stating what it is not – in other words by positing Hollywood as the classic or the 'norm' and describing how art cinema deviates from it. According to Bordwell, in Hollywood cinema the *mise en scène*, editing, sound, and cinematography all function to advance the narrative and to create compositional unity so that the narrative represents a 'cause-effect chain'. Classic Hollywood cinema is thus transparent, easy to read, goal-oriented, and structured around narrative closure. Art cinema, on the other hand, rejects cause and effect and favours narratives motivated by realism and authorial expressivity. Its protagonists are psychologically complicated, reality is ambiguous and subjective, while the author is foregrounded as a structure in the film's system.

The aesthetic origins of art cinema are undoubtedly to be found in European modernism. The narrative structures and the focus on subjectivity, as well as the self-reflexiveness, which are typical of art cinema, all have their counterpart in the experimental European novel of the 1920s to the 1960s, while the playfulness, intertextuality and fragmentary nature of much art film is equally central to modernist writing whether prose or poetry. Thus a typical art film might be Antonioni's *L'Avventura* (1960), with its apparently inconsequential narrative, unexplained shifts of focus, and characters who are engaged in a compelling but unresolved quest. Similarly, Truffaut's first two feature films, *Les quatre cents coups* (*The 400 Blows*, 1959) and *Tirez sur le pianiste* (*Shoot the*

Pianist, 1960), the former the subjective narrative of the adolescent Antoine Doinel, the latter with its playful references to Hollywood gangster films, its narrative flashbacks, its abrupt shifts of tone and strange mixture of genres, fall centrally within the modernist narrative and aesthetic tradition. The art film addressed its audience in a different way from the Hollywood film and the audience it addressed was different. Hollywood sought to federate its spectators and, in Steve Neale's words, 'succeeded in... producing a unified and unifying mode of textual address, a genuinely popular form of entertainment with a mass rather than a class-based audience' (Neale, 29). Art films, on the other hand, reflecting the fact that the cinema audience in the post-war world was no longer a mass audience, deliberately sought out the fraction that was more middle-class, better educated and more receptive to narrative experimentation.

The existential quest, the interrogation of subjectivity, and experiment with narrative form which appear to lie at the heart of art cinema mirror a structure of production in which the director is the linchpin of the film. The film is a personal statement by the director, who has himself invented the project, probably written the script, raised the finance, used his house as a location and cast his friends and family in the leading roles. Making a film thus becomes more like writing a private diary than manufacturing a car, and the camera becomes the instrument for writing rather than a machine for producing. The film is sold on the director's name rather than that of the star and it remains the intellectual property of the director rather than that of the studio, as in the Hollywood tradition.

Is Bordwell right to suggest that 'realism' is also characteristic of art cinema? In the 1950s, the British and Italian film studios continued to construct fantasy worlds and utopian environments while the French cinema frequently invested in costume dramas and adaptations of nineteenth-century novels. But at the same time the neo-realist movement in Italy adumbrated a new approach to subject-matter, to performance and to setting. This is exemplified in Visconti's *Ossessione*, which takes a theme that is treated in a heightened, melodramatic manner in the American cinema and adapts it to the circumstances of Italian village life. By the 1960s, territories such as Spain, which remained politically and culturally isolated, continued, as Buñuel's *Viridiana* (1961) suggests, to give a national inflection to artistic traditions. But elsewhere the realist approach had become general in European cinema and it can be found in films as diverse as the French New Wave and the 'kitchen sink' dramas of British 1960s cinema. The realism in question often consisted in choosing subjects from everyday life, enacted by ordinary people in settings which were not obviously glamorised, so that one of its extremely significant features was a naturalistic approach to performance that often relied on young, relatively unknown actors, anti-heroes and anti-stars whose consciousness rather than their public role was the mainspring of the film's action and who lent the films a degree of authenticity.

An important aspect of this new authenticity was a willingness to depict sexual relations more openly and realistically, and this was to prove a major selling point for European cinema at a time when Hollywood films were still too frightened of public reaction to do so. The typical plot of a New Wave film concerns the relationship of a young man and a young woman, while much of the foreign reputation of the French cinema in the late 1950s was based on the corporeal freedom symbolised by Brigitte Bardot who, of course, quickly became a star in the Hollywood sense of the word, able to sell films on the basis of her appearance in them. In Godard's film *Le mépris*, Bardot becomes the pretext for a confrontation between the European art film and the American popular cinema, since *Le mépris* depicts the American producer of an Italian film who wishes to seduce the wife (Bardot) of the French scriptwriter and to people the film adaptation of a world literary classic, *The Odyssey*, with naked mermaids as in a sex film.

Neale suggests that the representation of the body was a site of crucial difference between art cinema and Hollywood cinema. Whereas 'the body in Hollywood became simultaneously the incarnation of fictional characterisation and the nodal site of a fetishistic regime of eroticisation and sexual representation... [t]ogether with a reticence of gesture and (later) vocal delivery', European cinema exploited a freedom which was the result of a tradition stretching back to the 1920s, and which can be seen in Eisenstein's use of 'types', Renoir's stress on the artifice of acting in *La règle du jeu*, Visconti's use of non-professional actors in *La terra trema* (1948), and so on (Neale, 31). From the mid-1950s onwards, this freedom enabled European films 'to trade more stably and commercially both upon their status as "adult" art and upon their reputation for "explicit" representations of sexuality' (33), so constituting a recognisable export genre within world cinema trade.

Bordwell's thesis that art cinema is a 'mode of production' must therefore be placed alongside Neale's view of art cinema as a 'mode of consumption'. Neale points out that the exhibition basis for art cinema was provided by the film clubs developed in the 1920s to view censored Soviet films. Film education was an important element of fascist film policy in Italy in the 1930s and was instrumental in the careers of the neo-realist directors. Similarly, in France in the 1950s, film clubs sprang up whose initial purpose was to educate the public in the critical interpretation of films through the organisation of screenings and discussions, and through film magazines, such as *Cahiers du cinéma* and *Positif*. Eventually, as in Italy, it was from these groupings that the new generation of film-makers emerged as the New Wave. In Germany, a little later, the conscious attempt to create a 'film culture', that is a domestic audience capable of appreciating and understanding the films that were produced as art, was, as Elsaesser has pointed out, an absolutely central element in the success of the New German Cinema both domestically and internationally: 'Almost as important as the films, the film schools and cinémathèques and the contacts with an avant-garde cinema were the new writing about the cinema, the publishing ventures and other local and regional media initiatives – all of which revalued the experience of going to the cinema' (Elsaesser, 1989, 27).

Whilst Nowell-Smith may be right to dismiss attempts to treat art cinema as a 'distinct genre analogous to those that flourished in Hollywood and other mainstream commercial cinemas' as a 'mockery', on the grounds that art cinema is too heterogeneous, it certainly is the case that 'art cinema' became a useful marketing device capacious enough and flexible enough to accommodate the differential promotion of films according to the audience targeted (Nowell-Smith, 1996, 569). Thus it is perfectly possible, indeed quite common, for a film which is sold as 'popular' in its home territory to be designated 'art' when exported. This is particularly true of the so-called 'heritage' or 'nostalgia' film which became fashionable in the 1980s and 1990s in Britain, France, Italy and, slightly later, in Russia. Such films play on the anxieties of modernisation, particularly acutely felt at a time of rapid industrial change, and set out to re-create a lost era which, they imply, was better, more agreeable and more exemplary of the national experience than the present. A film such as Claude Berri's *Jean de Florette* (1986) was an immense popular success in France and overseas, but in France this was based on the re-creation of a regionalism which had disappeared with the post-war rural exodus, whereas abroad the film addressed an audience who liked to consume French products, including holidays in the French countryside. Not surprisingly, an imitation of the film, using the same music, was used in a commercial for Stella Artois beer.

Cinema and the National Question

The heritage film points to another distinguishing feature of European art cinema, namely its engagement with the national question, which in cinema terms takes the form of a dialectical relationship with Hollywood cinema. In French film writing of the 1950s, Hollywood cinema is seen as embodying a classicism which is the guarantor of its cultural centrality, rather as French eighteenth-century literature had embodied a classicism which claimed to represent universal truths and values – hence its use as an intertext by Renoir in *La règle du jeu*. If Hollywood represents the classical, then the French or any other European cinema necessarily has a marginal existence which is defined only in relation to the centre. Another version of this belief is found in the 'colonial paradigm' identified by Elsaesser as typical of the relationship of German cinema to Hollywood, and embodied in the famous statement in Wim Wenders's film *Im Lauf der Zeit* (*Kings of the Road*, 1976) that 'the Yanks have colonised our subconscious'. Like 'minority' literatures, or writers who come from 'minorities', European cinema inevitably places the national question at its centre since this is what defines both its structure and its content.

The national question is, of course, more acutely felt by some film-makers than by others, but it is nevertheless a constant of European cinema and it finds a range of expressions. One is the reworking or re-appropriation of genres felt to be typically American, as seen in the Italian spaghetti western, the French crime film or *polar*, or the German road movie. Another is the attempt to repossess the national history, a particularly acute problem in relation to Germany and Russia. Thus Edgar Reitz wrote: 'the most serious act of expropriation occurs when people are deprived of their history', and explicitly conceived *Heimat* (*Home*, 1984) 'as a riposte to [the American TV series] *Holocaust*' (Elsaesser, in Nowell-Smith, 1996, 143), while Mikhalkov turns to the history of Tsarist Russia as a source of values for the contemporary spectator. Indeed, revisionist history, the desire to use film to tell a different version of past events, is an important strand of film-making not just in Germany and Russia but in Italy and France too. The national question may be a pretext for experimental uses of colour and iconography, as in Godard's recourse to a tricolour palette (blue, white, red) or his oblique references to Joan of Arc and Marianne as symbols of France and the Republic, while the dialectical relationship with Hollywood may account for the split or fragmented narratives which are a common feature of many art films, the double narrative of Godard's *A bout de souffle* (*Breathless*, 1959) being a case in point.

Perhaps the most interesting representation of the national question is through the sensibilities, and above all, over the bodies, of women. We have already noted how, in *Le mépris*, the body of Brigitte Bardot became the site of a cultural contest between Europe and America, the locus of both pleasure and conflict. In the New German Cinema, and especially perhaps in films such as Rainer Werner Fassbinder's *Die Ehe der Maria Braun* (*The Marriage of Maria Braun*, 1978) or Helma Sanders-Brahms's *Deutschland bleiche Mutter* (*Germany, Pale Mother*, 1980), the suffering, sometimes prostituted, woman becomes the symbol of the state of Germany, while in Spanish cinema of the 1980s and 1990s, in the work of the director Almodóvar, sexually mobile bodies establish 'a new cultural stereotype for a hyperliberated Spain' (Kinder, 3) in films like *Matador* (1986) and *La ley del deseo* (*The Law of Desire*, 1987).

The inscription of the relationship with Hollywood underlines the double address of national cinemas, simultaneously speaking to a domestic audience and embodying the national stereotype for foreigners. This frequently gives rise to complex texts. For example, in *Kings of the Road* mentioned above, the reference to colonisation is, as Elsaesser reminds us, both approving and critical. In Luis García Berlanga's *Bienvenido Mister Marshall* (*Welcome Mr Marshall*, 1952), an *españolada*, or folkloric comedy, is rendered satirical by having the inhabitants of a village dress up as Andalusian peasants in order to look like the Spaniards the American visitors expect to see, while the Hollywood intertext is used for subversive purposes to circumvent censorship and criticise the Franco regime.

While it would be tempting to view Europe as simply being imposed upon by Hollywood, it is important however to appreciate that American films were popular, and, as Martin Scorsese acknowledges, that directors of the 'new'

Hollywood were inspired by European cinema (Scorsese, in Thompson and Christie, 14). Scorsese was a film student from 1960 to 1965, during the height of the French New Wave, and his films, as well as others produced by his generation of film-makers, pay homage to European cinema as well as to the traditions of Hollywood genre cinema. Those who used political rhetoric in their arguments against 'cultural imperialism' and 'the Hollywood invasion' often neglected to appreciate the complexities of Hollywood's relations with Europe or to recognise that most of Hollywood's personnel were descendants of European immigrants. European cinema is often explained in terms of its resistance to Hollywood styles, its determination to offer an artistic alternative to crass commercialism, but it is also productive to consider European cinema in terms of the overlaps, distinctive qualities, genres and stars which resulted from operating in a position of market inferiority that nevertheless was also characterised by cultural symbiosis. Foregrounding this dynamic broadens analysis to encompass questions about the relationship between art and popular cinema and the existence of popular European genres and stars. In part, these are a facet of Europe's response to Hollywood, but they also relate to national cultural traditions.

Popular European Cinema: Genres and Stars

Hollywood developed film studios and genres into a highly sophisticated and resilient system which was designed to ensure continuity of production on a 'factory' basis, streamlined into an operation which worked to reduce the high element of financial risk involved in film production. Film genres were integral to the functioning of this system since they provided a key dynamic to the challenge of judging which films would be popular. European cinemas also thrived on film genres that were popular with domestic audiences, many of which share affinities with American genres in their ability to change and develop over several decades, yet at the same time display a set of consistent themes and preoccupations, for example musicals, comedies, melodramas and crime thrillers. Thrillers are an interesting case in point in terms of their overlap with American styles and themes and, in exchange, the incorporation of European sensibilities into Hollywood cinema. The crime/thriller genre was popular throughout Europe: in Britain crime was a staple genre, particularly the 'spiv' films of the 1940s featuring characters who were swindlers and blackmarketeers; in Spain the *Cine Negro* genre, which dramatised social discontent in the 1950s and 1960s, was akin to both American *films noirs* and French *polars*, while the post-war German *Trümmerfilme* (ruin films) also demonstrated close affinities with *film noir*. Similarly, contemporary Russian *chernukha* ('made black') films depict a bleak reality with the killer as hero. From this perspective, variations of *noir* thrillers can be examined as a pan European genre which shares similarities but is also integral to each particular country's national output.

The French *polar* or crime film, bearing close resemblance to the American *film noir*, is interesting because it often contained explicit reference and even homage to its Hollywood counterparts. This was particularly evident in the 1950s films of Jacques Becker, or of Jean-Pierre Melville who in turn is much admired by Quentin Tarantino. Similarly, many of the early films of Godard and Truffaut, like *A bout de souffle* and *Tirez sur le pianiste*, contain references to, or pastiches of, *film noir*. In more recent years the so-called *cinéma du look* exemplified in films such as Beineix's *Diva* (1980) or Besson's *Nikita* (1990) has been highly influenced by Hollywood images, evincing a fascination with youth, fashion, 'trash' culture and the aesthetic of music videos and commercials. These films contain slick images, bright colours, and crisp editing which are influenced by television commercials. Similarly, much of Kassovitz's *La haine* is filmed in the so-called MTV style.

By contrast, pre-1945 German cinema was on the whole more resilient to the absorption of external styles and influences, in part owing to the strength of its system of economic protectionism and the exclusion of American films during the Nazi period, and in the 1920s German films were successfully exported, particularly the spectacular costume films directed by Ernst Lubitsch. Although box-office earnings and the number of films produced by the German expressionist movement were not especially high, their international reputation ensured that they were thereafter considered to be the most significant development in German cinema of the 1920s. German expressionist cinema had a profound impact on Hollywood, particularly the *film noir* genre, and directors including Fritz Lang, who fled from fascism in the 1930s, carried this style with them and provide a key example of how the influence of European cinema is present in many of Hollywood's films. German expressionism's distinctive, 'unrealistic' *mise en scène* functioned as a focus for a film's overall artificial, constructed look and gestural acting styles. In Germany, Lang directed the expressionist classic *Dr Mabuse, der Spieler* (*Dr Mabuse, the Gambler*, 1922), a film which is very similar, in its obsession with guilt, innocence and fear of mental illness, to *Ministry of Fear*, which he made in 1943 in Hollywood.

American stylistic influence can also be traced in the work of European *auteurs*; for example, the films of Pedro Almodóvar deploy comedic and melodramatic traditions that combine an acute sense of national specificity with cultural fascinations which cross national boundaries. Martin Scorsese, whose films are a point of reference for the French characters in *La haine*, has acknowledged his debt to European art cinema of the 1960s as has Tarantino, whose obtrusive displays of cinematic allusion in his films frequently reference classics of European cinema. Similarly, Wim Wenders's *Alice in den Städten* (*Alice in the Cities*, 1974) is an exploration of European identity *vis à vis* America. The relationship, therefore, between Hollywood and Europe is clearly at best a productive example of cultural cross-fertilisation and at worst an attempt to simply ape an economically successful formula at the expense of indigenous experiment.

As argued above, European cinema is frequently taken to be synonymous with art cinema. The concept of art cinema has provided Europe with a set of distinctive directors and genres and is broadly associated with experimentation with the film medium. The impact of German expressionism, Soviet montage, French impressionism, Italian neo-realism, Spanish surrealism, and the avant-gardes of Europe has been profound and sustained, so much so that in international terms art cinema *is* popular cinema. As a result, however, for many years the dominant critical position held by *auteur* theories privileged art cinema above 'entertainment' genre cinema, resulting in an often distorted notion of a nation's cinematic output. Indeed, the films which influenced Scorsese were made by celebrated *auteurs* including Godard, Truffaut, Antonioni, and Powell and Pressburger. No mention is made of American film schools showing their students films by other, less-renowned directors.

Films that were more popular at the box office but not much admired by critics tended to be forgotten in histories which attempted to emphasise European cinema as a superior alternative to Hollywood. It is possible, however, to view art cinema as part of a nation's generic heritage ('expressionism', for example, can be referred to as a German cinematic genre, as can Italian neo-realist films), so that it can be examined alongside popular films which were not so easily exportable and are therefore less well known. Arguably, it is these films which made fullest use of national traditions and, by dint of their box-office success, say much about a particular country's collective psyche. In France, while most film histories quite properly chronicle the work of Jean Renoir and Marcel Carné, the box office in the 1930s was dominated by musicals (filmed operettas) and screen adaptations of boulevard theatre. As this book demonstrates, while *La règle du jeu* is undoubtedly a key film of 1939, we nevertheless need to be aware of the commercial and political context of its release – it was a box-office failure and was banned for most of the Second World War – and its relation to the overall corpus of French national film production. In Britain most critics praised David Lean's *Brief Encounter* (1945), but it is only in recent years that film historians have recognised the social importance of a more risqué film, Leslie Arliss's *The Wicked Lady* (1945), a Gainsborough melodrama which outstripped *Brief Encounter* at the box office. That edge of popularity prompts the conclusion that contemporary audiences preferred the image of unrepentant female transgression which pervades most of *The Wicked Lady*, as opposed to the guilt-ridden depiction of marital infidelity presented in *Brief Encounter*. Considering art cinema alongside popular cinema and appreciating the links between the two is not to detract from a country's accepted cinematic heritage; it is rather to dismantle the artificial division between 'high' and 'low' art.

In the 1920s, while the classics of German expressionist cinema, *The Cabinet of Dr Caligari* and *Nosferatu* (1922), were receiving international acclaim, the *Strassenfilme* ('street' films) was another significant genre. The *Strassenfilme* were associated with particular directors, including G. W. Pabst (particularly *Die freudlose Gasse* (*The Joyless Street*, 1925)) and Bruno Rahn (*Dirnentragödie*

(*Tragedy of the Street*, 1928)), and the films depicted life in the urban milieu, providing a location for narratives which associated the city with vice and temptation. As the chapter on Hitchcock's *The Lodger* demonstrates, this representation of the city was highly influential in Britain in the mid-late 1920s. While Germany's most popular genres were light entertainment comedies or *Lustspielfilme*, and musicals, *Heimat* films came to prominence in the 1950s and were distinctive for their engagement with issues of national identity. Also operating as a critique of city life, the *Heimatfilm* genre drew on Germanic folklore, celebrating traditional values and a conservative rural utopia with the effect of 'sustaining cultural boundaries and boundedness' (Morley and Robbins, 2–3). Again, we see an interesting example of how genres relate to each other, and can conclude that a dominant theme in the European cinematic imagination has been the often fraught tension between the city and the countryside.

In Spain an indigenous genre of musicals known as the *folklóricas*, rooted in traditional values, again depicted the city as vice-ridden, and promoted flamenco performances. Saura's *Carmen* exploits this strongly national tradition. In Italy, the figure of the athletic slave, Maciste, first seen in *Cabiria*, proved so popular that it gave rise to an entire series (Nowell-Smith, 1996, 129), while elevation of the past to a mythic level was also a staple of one of Italy's most popular film genres, the 'peplum' adventure spectacles of the late 1950s and early 1960s. These films glorified the ancient world and the films featured heroes including Spartacus and Hercules. Italian westerns, known as 'spaghetti westerns', were also extremely popular and received international acclaim in the 1960s. They retained some qualities of the 'peplum' films but also resembled American westerns before developing into the most dominant strain of cinema in Italy, with its greatest *auteur* being Sergio Leone, director of *Per un pugno di dollari* (*For a Fistful of Dollars*, 1964), *Per qualche dollari in più* (*For a Few Dollars More*, 1965) and *Il buono, il brutto e il cattivo* (*The Good, the Bad and the Ugly*, 1966). In these films the negotiation of geographical 'spaces' (they were filmed in Spain) came to be invested with national overtones as the films became less 'Hollywoodised' and more rooted in Italian or European culture and concerns.

In the 1920s and 1930s the Soviet Union also had its fair share of *auteurs* and popular genres. Eisenstein's contribution to world cinema is well known, and *The Battleship Potemkin* (1926) was a popular (particularly in international markets) and artistic success. Although it has a clear narrative structure the film indirectly critiques Hollywood's methods by employing symbolism as ironic counterpoint and utilising the technique of ideological montage. While the Soviet state was anti-capitalist and critical of America, there was, as we have seen, considerable admiration for the efficiency of Hollywood's studio system, and Alexandrov's popular musicals such as *The Circus* (1936) and *Volga-Volga* (1938) were intended to combine progaganda with entertainment and were part of an attempt to 'Hollywoodise' Soviet cinema in the 1930s. Again, it is important to view this connection with Hollywood as a key dynamic in art and genre cinema, something which could be drawn upon, adapted and critiqued.

Another way to examine the specificity of European cinema is to look at its film stars. In the early twentieth century several stars were associated with a particular national genre; for example, in Italy female stars Lyda Borelli and Francesca Bertini were known as 'divas', while in France the Russian émigré Ivan Mosjoukine embodied a certain orientalism. These stars were the focus of their films, which encouraged fans to worship them and admire their lavish costumes and lifestyles, both on and off screen. Frequently associated with genre and popular cinema, stars acquire iconic status and come to represent the essence of a national cinema for the export market. Thus in the 1930s, for instance, Arletty and Jean Gabin conjure up French cinema; in the 1940s Margaret Lockwood and James Mason suggest a conception of British cinema; and after the Second World War Marcello Mastroianni *is* Italian cinema, at least for foreign audiences. While considerable academic enterprise has been expended on examining Hollywood's stars, their personas and their social function, less attention has been paid to stardom in a European context.

European cinema had, and continues to have, many important film stars. Like Hollywood's stars, they were followed by loyal fans and were part of an industrial infrastructure which produced fan magazines, photographs and merchandise. Stars give particular films a sense of 'national essence' and it is clear that more than one star can occupy the role of communicating this 'essence' even though they might be completely different performers and represent very different aspects of that 'national essence'. In Britain, Gracie Fields and Anna Neagle could not be more opposed in their acting styles, personas and class appeal, yet in their distinct ways they embody particular aspects of 'Britishness': Gracie Fields as the down-to-earth working-class singer with a good heart and Anna Neagle as the upper middle-class 'lady' who was plucky, refined and moral. Both national and international popularity has been attained by Gérard Depardieu, who represents what Ginette Vincendeau describes as 'an idealised masculinity, merging working-class virility with romanticism' (Vincendeau, 1995, 111). On the other hand, actresses like Catherine Deneuve and Isabelle Adjani can be said to represent different facets of French femininity, respectively elegance and glamour, underlined by their employment as models to advertise the perfume and cosmetics manufactured by the French couture houses.

Interesting divergences emerge when international reputation is compared with internal box-office success. While, at an international level, French cinema of the 1960s is associated with stars such as Jean-Paul Belmondo and Simone Signoret, in terms of box-office success the biggest star of the period was Louis de Funès, who appeared in popular comedies rather than the showcase New Wave films. There was a similar tendency in Italian cinema. It is ironic, considering the anti-American aims of the neo-realist project, that Anna Magnani and the 'stars' of neo-realism were well known world-wide and came to represent

Italian cinema, even though at the domestic box office they were eclipsed by other less critically applauded stars, including the popular comic actors Erminio Macario and Walter Chiari. Similarly, the British actors Alec Guinness and Laurence Olivier are far better known internationally than stars such as Will Hay and George Formby, who consistently topped the domestic box office in the 1930s and 1940s. The star, of course, conveys his or her identity through a particular acting style which can be associated with their country. In Spain, the *folklóricas* films were characterised by musical performance interludes which would have been most familiar to, and easily understood by, domestic audiences. A key star in relation to this type of performance is Lola Flores, who was an extremely well known Spanish dancer, singer and actress in the 1950s. It is important, therefore, to appreciate the extent to which stardom can operate in different ways and on several levels according to national and international circulation.

In spite of the Soviet cinema's apparent rejection of Hollywood's norms and the capitalist associations of star systems, there were popular stars in the 1920s, like Igor V. Ilyinsky, who managed to develop an individual comic persona and at the same time to fulfil the propagandist function of playing a classic 'type', the bureaucrat. Britain shared this ambivalence towards copying Hollywood's formulas. This arose partly because of the assumption that Hollywood's stars were manufactured and that 'good acting' could never result from such a system, for it was believed that 'good acting' had its origins on the stage. Many of Britain's most famous screen actors had established stage careers, including Ivor Novello, Laurence Olivier and John Gielgud. In France, as in Britain, there were strong links between stage and film careers, for example Jean-Louis Barrault (perhaps his most famous role was as Baptiste in *Les enfants du paradis*), Jules Berry, Harry Baur and Pierre Brasseur are just a few of the many stars who were known as theatre and film actors. Reservations apart, these actors were involved in the pursuit of screen stardom, but at the same time film producers were keen to differentiate them from popular Hollywood stars. One way to achieve this was to incorporate aspects of Hollywood's publicity methods but colour them with specific national associations. The Rank Organisation did this in Britain in the 1940s and 1950s when it developed 'The Charm School', which involved figures such as Diana Dors, Phyllis Calvert, Stewart Granger, Margaret Lockwood, James Mason and Patricia Roc. Actors and actresses under contract were required to attend film premières and publicity events. The aim was to inject glamour into British cinema but at the same time identify this as unmistakably British. British stars were to be associated with class and decorum whereas American stars were represented in fan magazines as much more ambitious and mercenary. In this way we can see another instance of Europe's ambivalent attitude towards Hollywood, simultaneously trying to incorporate and to reject many of its norms.

The diversity which characterised European cinema increased as the century progressed towards the Millennium and as globalisation erased national boundaries in economic and ideological terms. Cinema is now part of a huge, multinational system which consists of television networks, the pursuit of new technologies in media production, and co-productions between countries. Inevitably, the existence of this system militates against the perpetuation of rigid national boundaries and the ossification of nationalist conceptions of identity. This state of flux is reflected in much contemporary cinema. As Everett has put it: 'European cinema is not a monolith, but a series of expressions of different ways of questioning and portraying itself and the world' (Everett, 5). While many elements of identity are historical and draw upon references of collective cultural memory, globalisation has the dual and frequently contradictory effect of erasing national barriers but at the same time prompting a defence against, or negotiation with, its perceived reality as yet another development in American economic and cultural hegemony: 'Coca-Cola' culture has an economic, cultural and ideological face.

The pursuit of overseas markets encourages European films to present narratives that will 'travel' well, such as the films of Luc Besson, or Wim Wenders's internationally acclaimed works, particularly *Paris, Texas* (1984). Yet it is paradoxical that despite the push towards globalisation and hybridity, films that do best in overseas markets are often quite specific in their engagement with issues of national identity. Both *La haine* (1995) and *Trainspotting* (1996) are examples of films which contain particular conceptions of 'Frenchness', 'Britishness' and 'Scottishness' but these may well be essential components of their international appeal. This is not to say that globalisation has intensified the defence of traditional nationalism; rather it is to observe that contemporary cinema articulates the crisis experienced by European identities when challenged by the economic and cultural forces of globalisation. This crisis has been aptly described by Antoine Compagnon (in Petrie, 113): 'Europe is everywhere and yet invisible; the circumference is everywhere and the centre nowhere.' Indeed, negotiating a cultural space for the fluid, unstable and ever-changing facets of European identity is the challenge which faces cinema in the twenty-first century.

References and Suggestions for Further Reading

Albera, François 1995: *Albatros: des Russes à Paris, 1919–1929*. Milan: Edizioni Gabriele Mazzotta.

Bance, Alan (ed.) 1997: *The Cultural Hegemony of the British Occupation in Germany*. Stuttgart: Verlag Hans-Dieter Heinz.

Barr, Charles 1993: *Ealing Studios*. London: Studio Vista.

Bertin-Maghit, Jean-Pierre 1989: *Le Cinéma sous l'Occupation*. Paris: Olivier Orban.

Bordwell, David 1979: 'The Art Film as Mode of Film Practice'. In *Film Criticism*, 4, 1, 56–64.

Bosch, Aurora and del Rincón, Maria Fernanda 1998: 'Franco and Hollywood'. In *New Left Review*, 232, 112–127.

Chanan, Michael 1994: 'What was GATT About?' In *Vertigo*, Spring, 57–58.

Danilowicz, C. de 1924: 'Les projets de Monsieur Wengeroff'. In *Cinémagazine*, 10, October, 54–56.

De Grazia, Victoria 1989: 'Mass Culture and Sovereignty: The American Challenge to European Cinemas, 1920–1960'. In *Journal of Modern History*, 61, 1, 53–87.

Dickinson, Margaret and Street, Sarah 1985: *Cinema and State: The Film Industry and the British Government, 1927–84*. London: British Film Institute.

Ďurovičová, Nataša 1992: 'Translating America: The Hollywood Multilinguals'. In Rick Altman (ed.), *Sound Theory, Sound Practice*. London: Routledge, 138–153.

Eckert, Charles 1978: 'The Carole Lombard in Macy's Window'. In *Quarterly Review of Film Studies*, 3, Winter, 1–21.

Eisenstein, Sergei 1957: *Film Form, Film Sense*. Edited and Translated by Jay Leyda. New York: Meridian Books.

Elsaesser, Thomas 1989: *New German Cinema: A History*. London: Macmillan.

Elsaesser, Thomas 1996: 'Germany: The Weimar Years'. In Geoffrey Nowell-Smith (ed.), *The Oxford History of World Cinema*. Oxford: Oxford University Press, 136–51.

Everett, Wendy (ed.) 1996: *European Identity and Cinema*. Exeter: Intellect Books.

Finney, Angus 1996: *The State of European Cinema*. London: Cassell.

Forbes, Jill 1992: *The Cinema in France: After the New Wave*. London: Macmillan.

Gomery, Douglas 1996: 'The Hollywood Studio System'. In Geoffrey Nowell-Smith (ed.), *The Oxford History of World Cinema*. Oxford: Oxford University Press, 1996, 43–52.

Guback, Thomas 1969: *The International Film Industry*. Bloomington: Indiana University Press.

Guback, Thomas 1974: 'Cultural Identity and Film in the European Economic Community'. In *Cinema Journal*, 14, 1, 2–17.

Hartnoll, Gillian and Porter, Vincent 1982: *Alternative Film-Making in Television: ZDF A Helping Hand*. London: British Film Institute.

Higson, Andrew 1989: 'The Concept of National Cinema'. In *Screen*, 30, 4, 36–46.

Jeancolas, Jean-Pierre 1993: 'Blum-Byrnes: L'Arrangement, 1945–48'. In *1895*, 13, 7–21.

Jordan, Barry and Morgan-Tamosunas, Rikki 1998: *Contemporary Spanish Cinema*. Manchester: Manchester University Press.

Kepley, Vance 1991: 'The Origins of Soviet Cinema: A Study of Industry Development'. In Richard Taylor and Ian Christie (eds), *Inside the Film Factory*. London: Routledge, 60–79.

Kepley, Vance and Kepley, Betty 1979: 'Foreign Films on Soviet Screens 1922–31'. In *Quarterly Review of Film Studies*, Fall, 428–442.

Kinder, Marsha (ed.) 1997: *Refiguring Spain: Cinema, Media, Representation*. Durham, NC, and London: Duke University Press.

Lindeperg, Sylvie 1997: *Les Écrans de l'ombre*. Paris: CNRS Editions.

Maltby, Richard 1998: '"D" for Disgusting: American Culture and English Criticism'. In Geoffrey Nowell-Smith and Ricci, Steven (eds), *Hollywood & Europe: Economics, Culture, National Identity, 1945–95*. London: British Film Institute, 104–115.

Maltby, Richard and Vasey, Ruth 1994: 'The International Language Problem: European Reactions to Hollywood's Conversion to Sound'. In David Ellwood and Rob Kroes (eds), *Hollywood in Europe: Experiences of a Cultural Hegemony*. Amsterdam: VU University Press.

Michaels, Eric 1994: 'Hollywood Iconography: A Warlpiri Reading '. In *Bad Aboriginal Art: Traditions, Media and Technological Horizons*. Minneapolis: University of Minnesota Press.

Morley, David and Robbins Kevin 1990: 'No Place like Heimat: Images of Home(land) in European Culture'. In *New Formations*, 12, Winter, 1–23.

Neale, Steve 1981: 'Art Cinema as Institution'. In *Screen*, 22, 1, 11–39.

Nowell-Smith, Geoffrey 1968: 'Italy Sotto Voce'. In *Sight and Sound*, 37, 3, 145–147.

Nowell-Smith, Geoffrey (ed.) 1996: *The Oxford History of World Cinema*. Oxford: Oxford University Press.

Nowell-Smith, Geoffrey and Ricci, Steven (eds) 1998: *Hollywood & Europe: Economics, Culture, National Identity, 1945–1995*. London: British Film Institute.

Petley, Julian 1979: *Capital and Culture: German Cinema, 1933–45*. London: British Film Institute.

Petrie, Duncan (ed.) 1992: *Screening Europe: Image and Identity in Contemporary European Cinema*. London: British Film Institute.

Puttnam, David 1997: *The Undeclared War: The Struggle for Control of the World Film Industry*. London: HarperCollins.

Richards, Jeffrey 1984: *The Age of the Dream Palace: British Cinema and Society, 1930–1939*. London: Routledge.

Sadoul, Georges 1947: *Histoire générale du cinéma*, vol. 2: *Les Pionniers du cinéma, 1897–1909*. Paris: Editions Denoël.

Shohat, Ella and Stam, Robert 1985: 'The Cinema after Babel: Language, Difference, Power'. In *Screen*, 26, 3–4, 35–59.

Taylor, Richard and Christie, Ian 1988: *The Film Factory: Russian and Soviet Cinema in Documents, 1896–1939*. London: Routledge & Kegan Paul.

Thompson, David and Christie, Ian (eds) 1989: *Scorsese on Scorsese*. London: Faber.

Thompson, Kristin 1985: *Exporting Entertainment: America in the World Film Market, 1907–1934*. London: British Film Institute.

Thompson, Kristin and Bordwell, David 1994: *Film History: An Introduction*. New York: McGraw-Hill.

Vasey, Ruth 1997: *The World According to Hollywood, 1918–1939*. Exeter: Exeter University Press.

Vincendeau, Ginette 1988: 'Hollywood Babel'. In *Screen*, 29, 2, 24–39.

Vincendeau, Ginette (ed.) 1995: *Encyclopedia of European Cinema*. London: British Film Institute: Cassell.

Wagstaff, Christopher 1984: 'The Italian Cinema Industry during the Fascist Regime'. In *The Italianist*, 4, 160–74.

Williams, Alan 1992: 'Historical and Theoretical Issues in the Coming of Recorded Sound to the Cinema'. In Rick Altman (ed.), *Sound Theory, Sound Practice*. London: Routledge, 126–37.

Part II

Case Studies

1 *The Battleship Potemkin*
The massacre on the Odessa steps.

Bronenosets Potemkin/ Potyomkin (The Battleship Potemkin)

Birgit Beumers

Voted the best film of all time by an international critics' poll conducted in 1958, Sergei Eisenstein's *The Battleship Potemkin* (*Bronenosets Potemkin/Potyomkin*, 1926) was produced in the Soviet Union at a time when that country was pioneering a new form of social and economic order: socialism. In the nationalised Soviet film industry the state controlled film production, a situation which highlights the relationship between art and politics during the early years of the Soviet regime. Indeed, many Russian artists, especially those of the left-wing avant-garde movements of the 1910s, hailed the 1917 Revolution and actively supported its cause, some by taking up posts in the political structures, others by putting their art at the service of the new ideals. At this time the state also realised cinema's potential for agitation of the masses and for political propaganda. It is within this context that an analysis of *The Battleship Potemkin* must be located.

Cinema of the Soviets

The state took control of the film industry in 1919 and in 1922 Lenin declared: 'of all arts, the cinema is for us the most important'. However, as a consequence of the civil war, film stock was in very short supply at the time and future film directors like Lev Kuleshov (1899–1970) were reduced to experimenting in acting studios without actually filming. Sergei Eisenstein (1898–1948) had trained as a set designer before he studied with the theatre director Vsevolod Meyerhold (1874–1940) to become a director. Meyerhold's theatre was based on the idea that theatre would enlarge and enhance certain fragments or episodes from reality; for this purpose, he restructured plays into fragments and episodes and set his productions in Constructivist designs. He perceived theatre as having a social and political function and went out to factories to perform plays whilst closely monitoring audience response in order to heighten the comic and agitational elements. His actors were trained in 'bio-mechanics' (the science of rational movement), so that movements on stage would be choreographed and paced (rather than motivated by the psychological identification of the actor with his role) and bring man closer to a perfect, machine-like state. He thus created *types* rather than characters with psychological depth. Both the concept of fragmentation and that of 'typage' through body language and choreographed movement are important for Eisenstein's work in the cinema. For his staging of Ostrovsky's *The Wise Man* (1922) Eisenstein made his first film, a short called *Glumov's Diary*, which he used in the production.

Goskino (the State Committee for Cinematography) was established in 1922 to organise cinema matters centrally after the Treaty of Rapallo between Germany and the Soviet Union had, among other things, guaranteed imported supplies of film stock. With these incentives in place, many young artists were anxious to apply their experiences in theatre and the visual arts to the newer medium of film, and to devote their work to the socialist cause.

The Battleship Potemkin is Eisenstein's second full-length film, commissioned by the state in 1925 to commemorate the twentieth anniversary of the abortive 1905 Revolution. It was intended to create a positive image of the country's revolutionary past in order to justify the rule of the Bolsheviks at a time which followed prolonged suffering of the population during the civil war.

Eisenstein worked on the scenario and soon embarked on the filming of 'The Year 1905' in St Petersburg. When weather conditions made it impossible to continue, he and his film crew moved down to Odessa to shoot what was intended as a minor episode in the film, the mutiny on the battleship *Prince Potemkin*. The 'minor' sequence turned into an entire film, which was shot (to a modified screenplay) over three months in Odessa, partly on the *Potemkin's* sister-ship *Twelve Apostles* since the *Potemkin* itself had been dismantled. *The Battleship Potemkin* was officially premiered at a gala screening in the Bolshoi Theatre on 21 December 1925 and released in January 1926. During the twelve days of screening in Moscow in January and February 1926 it attracted almost 30,000 spectators, a number that had, at the time, only been achieved by American films. The film made a profit through export to Germany, France and the USA, enabling the state-run industry to purchase new equipment and film stock from the west, and it was to be promoted as the pride of Soviet cinema. Indeed, its immense success in Berlin in April and May 1926 played a particular role in its promotion both at home and abroad.

It was also in Berlin that the music for *The Battleship Potemkin* was composed by Edmund Meisel, the first violinist of the Berlin Philharmonic Orchestra. Meisel composed the music not as a mere accompaniment to the film, but – at Eisenstein's request – to stress moods, such as tension and triumph, and to echo the rhythm and noise of the engines in the last part of the film. This version is normally used in international distribution. A second version, restored in 1976, uses the score written by the Russian composer Dmitry Shostakovich, whilst the film itself has been re-edited by Sergei Yutkevitch to match this score.

In the years following the October Revolution artists thus put their art to the service of politics, while the state used (and later abused) its control over the funds needed for film production to finance films that would advance the ideas of socialism. Shortly after the Revolution, theatre directors had begun to mount mass spectacles in the streets in celebration of the event: *The Storming of the Winter Palace* (1918) marked the anniversary of the Revolution, involving 100,000 actors. Eisenstein's film *October* (1927), which commemorated the tenth anniversary, required a cast of 120,000 people although there had been far fewer people around the Winter Palace on 25 October 1917. In this instance, and in other films of the 1920s, historical facts were manipulated, certain events being 'magnified' and appropriated in order to glorify the Soviet regime. The cinema of Eisenstein played a key role in this approach to the past and constituted a crucial element of Lenin's propaganda policies for the arts.

Propaganda and Myth-Making

In 1928 Eisenstein and Alexandrov wrote: 'The first basic function of our films is to interpret the theses and decrees, to reveal them and make them infectious through a visual demonstration of their significance in the general cause of socialist construction' (in Taylor and Christie, 218). Eisenstein perceived theatre and film as means to convey a political message and to 'cinefy' the theses of the Party and the state. He used the devices of fragmentation and montage (discussed below) to construct worlds which would allow for parallels to be drawn between the past and the present. In his films of the 1920s, *Stachka* (*The Strike*, 1925), *The Battleship Potemkin*, and *Oktiabr'* (*October*, 1927), Eisenstein related history with the help of images which he cut, fragmented, edited, and reassembled, thereby creating a new text. By merging the past and the present, he created the perfect world of a socialist utopia.

The Battleship Potemkin clearly reveals the impact that the 1917 Revolution had on the subsequent assessment of Russian history. Since the reality of a country stricken by a civil war and struggling with new forms of economic management was far too grim, but since film-makers still wanted to support socialism, they represented history in an idealised way. In *The Battleship Potemkin* Eisenstein created the myth of a successful 1905 Revolution in order to re-affirm and consolidate the new Soviet regime, whereas what had actually happened in 1905 had been far from successful. This Revolution had failed but it was to prove a key event in the years leading up to the fall of the Romanov dynasty and was therefore to serve as a precursor to the Bolshevik Revolution of 1917.

The Battleship Potemkin portrays the 1905 Revolution in the light of the successful 1917 Revolution: the final success of the revolutionary ideals is more important than contemporary historical accuracy. The demonstrations of people petitioning for civil rights and equitable wages in St Petersburg on 9 January 1905 ended in a massacre: the Tsarist troops panicked, and over 200 people were shot on 'Bloody Sunday'. However, despite the failure of the 1905 uprising, the spirit of the Revolution spread. The event caused a wave of strikes and demonstrations all over Russia, among them the mutiny on the battleship *Potemkin*. The Revolution propelled Tsar Nicholas II to grant the right to establish a parliament, the Duma, but he was to remain in charge of the armed forces and to instruct them to crush the revolutionary movement. In June 1905, the Odessa uprising coincided with the mutiny on the battleship *Potemkin* just outside the port. The crew turned to the citizens of Odessa for supplies and deposited in the port the body of the martyr-sailor Vakulinchuk who had been shot during the mutiny. It was less the news of the mutiny (the citizens of Odessa were also hard up and suffered injustice from the regime) than the presence of the vessel which boosted the citizens' confidence. Growing civil unrest, combined with looting in the town, eventually led to a massacre when the Tsarist troops shot indiscriminately into the crowd. During the massacre on the night of 15/16 June the *Potemkin* failed to fire a single shot; it was only on the next day that the vessel fired some volleys into the air, missing the Odessa Theatre. The *Potemkin* was isolated among the fleet and later left for Romania for coal and supplies. This uprising, then, was anything but successful, and some historians have noted that a more active and forceful part by the *Potemkin* in these events might have led to the triumph described in the film and even triggered a revolution.

Eisenstein stops his version of the historical events at a convenient and advantageous point: 'We stop the event at this point where it had become an "asset" of the Revolution,' he commented (Eisenstein, in Taylor, 60). In the film the vessel's guns aim, fire and hit a target: the military headquarters located in the classical building of the Odessa Theatre. Eisenstein conflates two moments in time: the massacre on the night of 15 June takes place during the day (much more convenient for filming), and through montage he brings the gunfire forward in time to make it coincide with the events on the Odessa Steps. Other details also differ from factual accounts of the events. For example, Eisenstein neglects the fact that some crew members were agitators who belonged to the radical movement, preferring to locate their dissatisfaction in injustice rather than ideology. Instead of the battleship being left in isolation at the end, it is supported by the squadron, and there is no sign of unrest or looting in Odessa before the arrival of the vessel in the bay. In Eisenstein's rigorous construction of the film there is no room for any interaction among the opposing forces (the soldiers versus the people or the sailors), since he operates within a strict dialectical principle of opposition. All the action develops from the individual to the crowd, from the part to the whole (*pars pro toto*). The individual is never concerned with himself, but fights for the sake of others, excluding himself, and thereby annihilating himself as an entity. Eisenstein treats film form in the same way: he films not the individual but the people, and he edits the sequence of frames, not the individual frame. Eisenstein thus distorts historical fact through fragmenting and reassembling the fragments to create a new entity.

Stars or Types, Individual or Mass?

Eisenstein's emphasis is placed on the masses, not on individuals. 'The shot itself as star,' he wrote, '[w]e must look for the essence of cinema not in the shots but in the relationship between the shots, just as in history we look not at individuals but at the relationships between individuals, classes, etc.' (Eisenstein, in Taylor and Christie, 147). The revolutionary spirit of the people is seen as victorious in the light of the October Revolution and, as a sign of triumph, the soldiers on the battleship even raise a red flag, which was hand-coloured in each print of the black and white film. The masses are elevated to heroic status and only the agitators on both sides – Vakulinchuk, Matiushenko, the senior officer Giliarovsky, the captain, and the doctor – are individualised. The masses are portrayed heroically in their suffering and their sacrifices for the revolutionary cause in order to legitimise the October Revolution, an event which was started in the name of the people but was steered by one man alone: Lenin. The depiction of the masses as supportive of their leaders and agitators is an important feature in Soviet films of the 1920s, since it serves to justify the socialist principle of the rule of a leader over the masses.

Eisenstein used 'types', people with expressive faces and an interesting physiognomy, rather than professional actors. As in Meyerhold's theatre he utilised physical expression and choreographed movement for action rather than psychological motivation. While for some directors, such as Trauberg and Kozintsev, the movement and facial expression within the frame was important, for Eisenstein the emphasis at that time lay on the juxtaposition of different movements within one frame or within sequences, on choreography and (arranged) chaos, on the lines and circles of movement. In his famous sequence of the Odessa Steps the linear movement of the soldiers is juxtaposed to the unorganised, chaotic and elemental movement of the people, who were described by one critic as 'bouncing down the steps like cherry stones'.

In *The Battleship Potemkin* Eisenstein made his assistant Grigori Alexandrov play Giliarovsky, the priest was played by a gardener, while the doctor, played by a stoker who was working on the set, bears a striking resemblance to the great dramatist Anton Chekhov, who was a medical doctor by training. Villains are mostly portrayed with a touch of the grotesque, for example the priest pretends to be dead when he falls down the stairs yet he winks in the following shot, while the workers and sailors are shown in a realistic manner.

Eisenstein uses stereotypes in the characterisation of groups of society, so that the bourgeoisie are characterised by their fashion accessories, whereas the sailors are muscular and strong. Women usually endure and suffer (a mother is shot, a child is trampled on), while only men fight with weapons. There are also sexual implications in the imagery of the battleship's guns, filmed from above to stress their phallic shape. They fire only under the command of the sailors, implying that while the Tsarist regime is impotent and infertile, the energy and force of the sailors makes the guns potent.

Composition and Structure, Fragmentation and Montage

Eisenstein's contemporary Lev Kuleshov outlined, in 1917, how the director should approach film composition: 'The essence of cinema art lies in the creativity of the director and the artist: everything is based on composition. To make a picture the director must compose the separate filmed fragments, disordered and disjointed, into a single whole and juxtapose these separate moments into a more advantageous, integral and rhythmical sequence' (Kuleshov, in Taylor and Christie, 41). The film narrates the events in chronological order: the sailors on board the battleship *Potemkin* are discontented and protest when they are given rotten meat. When they are threatened with execution, the brave cry of the sailor Vakulinchuk makes the firing squad realise that they are about to shoot at their 'brothers'. This heroic deed costs Vakulinchuk his life: while the sailors seize control over the ship he is shot by the senior officer Giliarovsky after a decktop chase. His body is taken to the port of Odessa, where the citizens soon flock to the pier in mourning and begin to send supplies to the battleship. The Tsarist troops try to control the crowds gathering around the tent with the dead sailor, and, advancing from the top of the Odessa Steps, shoot at the citizens. The battleship's guns fire at the staff headquarters (the theatre) to defend the people of Odessa. The next day, the rebellious battleship is met by the fleet, which, after a period of anxiety about the fleet's attitude to the mutiny, supports the *Potemkin* by letting the vessel pass.

Eisenstein uses the classical structure of Aristotelian tragedy by dividing the film into five parts: Part 1: Men and Maggots; Part 2: Drama at Tendra;[1] Part 3: Appeal from the Dead; Part 4: The Odessa Steps; Part 5: Meeting the Squadron, with exposition, peripetia, and dénouement. Broadly speaking, he observes the unity of time, since the action takes place over twenty-four hours, and place, since it takes place in one location, and there are no sub-plots which would distract from the main story. He designs a rigid compositional principle of opposing images and moods within each sequence and within each part. The action within each of the five parts is very neatly organised in that each part contains a change of mood: (1) from quiet suffering (passivity) to declared dissatisfaction (active resistance); (2) from the fear of execution (submissiveness) to mutiny (aggression); (3) from mourning over the dead sailor (passive) to anger at the injustice (active); (4) from sending boats to demonstrate solidarity with the sailors on the ship (building bridges) to the slaughter on the Odessa Steps (destruction) that triggers the gunfire from the battleship (action); and (5) from anxiety over the fleet's response (passive, subdued, insecure) to triumph (safety, active response, red flag). Each part moves from passive to active, from subdued to triumphant, from submissive to aggressive, thus ensuring both the juxtaposition of opposing principles (thesis/antithesis) and the dialectical conclusion: progress (synthesis). This principle also determines the structure of the filmic sequences so that 'any two frames juxtaposed inevitably combine into a new concept' (Eisenstein, in Taylor and Christie, 145).

The appeal for solidarity ('brothers') resounds twice: as an appeal when the firing squad is about to fire and as a cry for solidarity when the fleet joins the battleship in its revolt. At these two points the film moves from the part to the whole, from the sailors to the other 'workers' on the battleship (the firing squad) and then from the battleship to the entire fleet. The spirit of the Revolution spreads first on the ship, then across the fleet. Yet it also spreads to Odessa when the body is taken there on a boat and the Odessans symbolically send their boats to the ship with supplies. There is a reciprocal movement from sea to shore and shore to sea, implying that the Revolutionary spirit of the citizens spurs on the sailors, and that the sailors will rush to the citizens' defence. The episode of the boats sailing from the port to the battleship and the sequence of the gunfire from the battleship at the theatre are therefore filmed from camera positions both on the shore and on the boat. The parallel between land and sea, city-dwellers and sailors, is enhanced by the split-level structure which can be found both on the battleship (upper deck and lower deck) and in the city (top of steps and pier, bridges and arches).

The neat symmetry in the composition is reflected in the creation of parallels and contrasts in the scene before the uprising, when the sailors, sleeping in their hammocks, resemble lumps of meat (which is the source of their complaint), whereas after the rebellion, they sleep on sofas and in chairs. Similarly, and continuing with the theme of parallels and contrasts, while the meat is infested by maggots, the officers later thrown overboard go 'down to feed the maggots'. During the rebellion the sailors are threatened with being hanged from the yard-arm, a threat which is visualised; later they are shown triumphant on the very same yard-arm. The priest strikes the cross with the same gesture as that used by the officer with his dagger and when the priest falls, the cross is thrust into the floor like a dagger. Both the priest's response to the rebellious sailors and the officers' response to the meat ignore the facts and aim only at maintaining the status quo, thus creating a parallel between military and religious oppression.

Such formal unity lends meaning to the film as a whole, while it destroys the fragments which are parts of the whole. Eisenstein's principle of a movement from the small cell to the whole is also expressed in the intertitle 'all for one, one for all', which appears twice in the film – when Vakulinchuk has died for the sailors, and when the battleship has scored a victory for the entire fleet. Since it is a silent film the narrative of *The Battleship Potemkin* is communicated not through spoken dialogue but through the five-part structure, through the intertitles which supply the most important parts of narrative and dialogue, and through the relationship between the contents of each frame. The way in which frames with different content are assembled is known as the principle of 'montage'.

Montage is the juxtaposition of images, usually of a contrasting nature, and it can imply conflict between two opposing principles. In Part 4, the chaotic movement of people on the steps is juxtaposed to the disciplined movement of the soldiers; the organised movement of many soldiers downward is countered by the upward movement of a single figure, the mother; the white uniforms of the soldiers are contrasted with the dark garments of the citizens, and the numerous bayonets of the soldiers are opposed by the single shot fired from the battleship's gun. Montage can also create the illusion of setting things in motion: the people on the steps, representatives of all classes – bourgeois, workers, beggars – are portrayed in a jump cut sequence (frame to frame without coherence) as though a static picture was being animated and set in motion through a gradual increase in the number of frames devoted to each single action. Society is fragmented, while the Tsarist forces move in unison, and their movement requires a greater number of frames. Montage can produce movement artificially, as in the three shots of the lions – sleeping, waking, rising – which not only give the illusion that a single lion rises, but also appear to make the lion roar, thus transgressing the boundaries of the visual.

Eisenstein later defined five types of montage: *Metric montage* determines the absolute length of a piece, and refers to the rhythm or pace of a sequence. In the last part, the number of shots per minute increases along with the battleship's speed. Similarly, in the 'Odessa Steps' sequence, the shots change more frequently as the chaos increases. Both sequences create the illusion of accelerated pace and enhance the sense of panic and chaos. *Rhythmic montage* refers to the movement within the frame, to its actual length. The 'Odessa Steps' sequence begins with a shot of the motionless citizens and the soldiers. The camera subsequently focuses on the feet of the soldiers advancing downward and of the crowd trampling over bodies, and finally we see a baby carriage rolling down the steps – a movement which in itself is faster than the steps of the soldiers or the running of the crowd. This gradation serves to create a crescendo, so again Eisenstein manages to cross the boundary of the visual, giving the impression of an outcry (sound) through images alone. This is achieved by the way in which visual images are punctuated by different movements and speeds so that when we see the woman scream as she falls, the lack of conventional soundtrack is not a problem.

Tonal montage refers to the choice of tone or colour, light or gloom, within a frame. On the steps the soldiers in their white uniforms and with their bayonets cast a dark shadow which pierces the figure of the mother before she is actually shot. The fog outside the tent reflects the doomed, gloomy mood of mourning and, as a final reference to Vakulinchuk's passing away, the light that penetrates the tent from outside is eclipsed by a passing vessel at the end of the sequence.

Intellectual montage implies the juxtaposition, or comparison, of one situation to another. When the battleship fires, the lion rises. The statues of the lions are not part of the architecture of the Odessa Theatre (they are pictures taken of the Tsar's palace at Alupka on the Crimea), nor do they belong in the narrative of the film; they are non-diegetic images (not part of the space or time of the narrative) which symbolise the beginning of the revolt. Similar examples can be found in other Eisenstein films, such as the sequence in *The Strike* when the features of human faces are compared to those of animals using shots of a monkey, an owl, and a fox which intersect the narrative to portray a character. Finally, *overtonal montage* is a synthesis of different forms of montage: in the Odessa Steps sequence the pace of the action increases both in terms of the length of the frame and in terms of the movement within the frame (metric and rhythmic montage), light opposes darkness and shadows (tonal montage), the movement of the soldiers is opposed to the movement of the crowd in its direction and in its quality (linearity/chaos) to render a sense of the conflict escalating. Eisenstein frequently uses the device of overlapping editing: he would shoot a sequence from different angles and overlap the frames in editing, thus prolonging the duration of the action. This is very clearly visible in the sequence of the sailor smashing a plate, where part of his movement is repeated to underline the thrust behind this gesture.

Eisenstein's principle of montage is complemented by that of 'attractions'. He had already elaborated on the concept of attractions during his time in the theatre:

> An attraction is any aggressive moment in the theatre,... calculated to produce specific emotional shocks.... These shocks provide the only opportunity of perceiving the ideological aspect of what is being shown, the final ideological conclusion.... Our present approach radically alters our opportunities in the principles of creating an 'effective structure' instead of a static 'reflection' of a particular event dictated by the theme... and this gives rise to a new concept: a free montage with arbitrarily chosen independent effects (attractions) but with the precise aim of a specific final thematic effect – montage of attractions. (Taylor and Christie, 87–9)

'Attractions' are scenes which shock the spectator, which are provocative, and may even be repulsive, such as the near-execution of the sailors covered by a tarpaulin, the maggots in the meat (enlarged through the doctor's pince-nez), and the slaughter of the innocent people on the steps. 'Attractions' thus challenge the spectator to take action and defend the unjustly treated. At the end of the film he offers another striking 'attraction' when the spectators appear to be bombarded by the battleship, whose keel splits the frame in half.

By creating 'attractions' (as in the circus) Eisenstein challenges the spectator intellectually rather than leading him/her into the illusion of a make-believe world as created in the traditional Hollywood plot. This device, known as 'estrangement' (*ostranenie*), was derived from Russian formalism and was to translate into German theatre theory as Brecht's *Verfremdungseffekt* (alienation effect). The estrangement or alienation from the usual is achieved by displaying the devices, reflected to a certain degree in Eisenstein's concern with montage, which can serve to make the spectator aware of the manipulation of images for the purpose of telling a story through images alone. The techniques of fragmentation and montage, of challenging the audience intellectually by juxtaposing images and concepts which propel them to act, of alienation and estrangement to ensure rational judgement, were common features for many avant-garde artists working all over Europe in different spheres during this period.

Avant-garde and Tradition

In the 1910s, artists across Europe had begun to fragment the world that surrounded them and reassemble it in a different way, in order to estrange the spectator from traditional, habitual ways of perception and to offer a fresh view. The stage of construction endowed artists with the power to create a world more perfect than reality; to make history more glorious in the light of subsequent developments and to build through their work the world that the socialist Revolution had promised. This allowed the artist to appropriate the past and conquer the future. However, the power to appropriate the past could also make artists servants of a particular ideology, and this was to degenerate into a totalitarian system under Stalin in the 1930s.

In *The Battleship Potemkin* Eisenstein stands between tradition and the avant-garde. The film offers continuity with tradition in its narrative, but a rejection of tradition in its formal fragmentation. Bearing in mind the techniques of montage discussed above, it is important to note that Eisenstein uses a classical five-part structure; he takes traditional shots with a largely stationary camera; he constructs a narrative through a series of intertitles; and finally, he relies on traditional vocabulary to formulate a revolutionary message. In his traditional story-telling Eisenstein is closest to the realism that would dominate Soviet arts in the 1930s, when he would succumb to the call for realism after the method of montage had came under fire in the late 1920s for being too formalistic, too intellectual, and too sophisticated for the masses. At this point, in order to be able to make films, Eisenstein had to bow to Stalin's orders for historical films which would legitimise the use of absolute power in certain moments of history.

The Battleship Potemkin was designed to serve the state and promulgate the Revolution first and foremost to Soviet audiences, yet its complex form meant that it did not appeal to the mass audiences in the Soviet Union. Abroad, however, the opposite occurred. The film enjoyed considerable success in intellectual circles, especially in Germany, and through its use of a new medium it created a lasting image of the new Soviet state for western audiences. Indeed, for years to come, Eisenstein's version of the 1905 Revolution and his use of cinema for an intellectual reflection on history were to dictate the manner in which Soviet history would be perceived.

References

Taylor, Richard (ed.) 1998: *The Eisenstein Reader*. London: British Film Institute.
Taylor, Richard and Christie, Ian (eds) 1994: *The Film Factory*. London: Routledge.

Suggestions for Further Reading

Aumont, Jacques 1987: *Montage Eisenstein*. Bloomington, IN: Indiana University Press.
Barna, Yon 1973: *Eisenstein*. London: Secker & Warburg.
Bordwell, David 1993: *The Cinema of Eisenstein*. Cambridge, MA, and London: Harvard University Press.
Eisenstein, Sergei 1949: *Film Form*. Edited and translated by Jay Leyda. New York: Harcourt Brace.
Kenez, Peter 1992: *Cinema and Soviet Society, 1917–1953*. Cambridge: Cambridge University Press.
Taylor, Richard (ed.) 1998: *The Eisenstein Reader*. London: British Film Institute.
Taylor, Richard 1979: *The Politics of the Soviet Cinema, 1917–1929*. Cambridge: Cambridge University Press.
Taylor, Richard 1999: *The Battleship Potemkin*. London: I. B. Tauris.
Taylor, Richard and Ian Christie (eds) 1994: *The Film Factory*. London: Routledge.

Note

1. This title is sometimes mistranslated as 'Drama on Quarterdeck'. Tendra is the place-name of a sandbank in the Black Sea to the south-east of Odessa.

Credits

Director	Sergei Eisenstein
Production	Goskino
Scenario	Sergei Eisenstein
Director of Photography	Eduard Tissé
Editor	Sergei Eisenstein

Art Director	Vasili Rakhals
Music	Edmund Meisel

'Mosfilm version' restored by Naum Kleiman and Sergei Yutkevich (1976), to the music by Dmitry Shostakovich

Cast

Alexander Antonov	Vakulinchuk
Grigori Alexandrov	Officer Giliarovsky

Sailors of the Navy, citizens of Odessa, actors of the Proletkult Theatre (Moscow)

Filmography

Stachka (*The Strike*, 1925)
Bronenosets Potemkin (*The Battleship Potemkin*, 1926)
Oktiabr' (*October*, 1928)
Staroie i novoe (*The General Line / The Old and the New*, 1929)
Que Viva Mexico! (1932)
Bezhin lug (*Bezhin Meadow*, 1935)
Aleksandr Nevskii (*Alexander Nevsky*, 1938)
Ivan grozni (*Ivan the Terrible*, 1943–6)

66

2 *The Lodger*
Expressionist imagery in *The Lodger* shows Hitchcock's debt to German cinema.

The Lodger
Sarah Street

The Lodger, a British silent film directed by Alfred Hitchcock, was produced in 1926 and released in 1927. It starred Ivor Novello as a mysterious young man who lodges in a London home at a time when a number of blonde-haired young women have been murdered in the city. It was one of the most significant British films of the decade, praised by critics who in particular appreciated Hitchcock's importation of German techniques which were used to create suspense and atmosphere. *The Lodger* was released when the British film industry was struggling to survive, and it represented a sophisticated response to the problem of producing distinctive film drama at a time when the market was more or less dominated by Hollywood's films. Hitchcock's adaptation of a popular story, based on the Jack the Ripper murders, can be linked to contemporary fears of, and ambivalence about, modernity and city life, and is distinctively British in its settings. As this chapter will also argue, it raises questions of gender identity which featured in many German films of this period (Petro, 1989).

For many years *The Lodger* was studied primarily in terms of its relation to Hitchcock's later, more celebrated films in Britain and America (such as *The Thirty-Nine Steps*, 1935; *The Lady Vanishes*, 1938; *Strangers on a Train*, 1951; or *Vertigo*, 1958), as evidence of his young talent, the beginning of a brilliant trajectory which was slowly ripening to maturity. British film director Lindsay Anderson expressed this view very clearly:

> Considered in relation to Hitchcock's subsequent career, *The Lodger* is particularly interesting. Its realistic settings, its lower middle class locale (presented without any false glamour) are those which were to form the background to Hitchcock's famous series of melodramas in the thirties. Most, indeed, of the later films' ingredients are here; the ingenious visual touches, the acute and sometimes caustic observation, the imaginative economical style, the long build up of suspense, the climactic violence. In all these *The Lodger* pointed forward to its director's great future.   (Anderson, in Manvell, 378).

Other critics argued that as an 'early work', *The Lodger* was blighted by the prevailing modes of silent cinema which foregrounded melodrama over realism:

> I do not think that the silent film, although it was photographic, was expected by its popular audiences to reconstruct the scenes and situations of real life.

The silent film offered you a fancy world, impressive but remote, the genuinely realistic films (*Birth of a Nation, Potemkin, Drifters* etc.) were outstanding because they were so exceptional. The silent images normally belonged to the fantasy of sentiment or of melodrama, and occasionally they produced their own genuine poetry. Their measure was not that of the street outside or of the crime columns of real newspapers; they derived mostly from the vagaries of lady novelists, or from the ingenious imaginings of the creators of haunted houses.   (Manvell, 378)

The quotations from Anderson and Manvell illustrate the prevailing critical orthodoxy of the 1950s when film critics privileged two dominant value-systems, the appreciation of the *auteur* and the praise of realism above melodrama. While Anderson's view reveals how an auteurist approach automatically demarks areas for analysis – the identification of 'visual touches', 'acute and sometimes caustic observation', 'economical style', 'suspense' and 'climactic violence' – the more dismissive view of Manvell reproaches silent films such as *The Lodger* for their lack of realism and their origins in 'the fantasy of sentiment or of melodrama . . . derived mostly from the vagaries of lady novelists'. This chapter aims to challenge both these critical approaches, arguing that *The Lodger* should be analysed in relation to other European and American films (as opposed to its evaluation solely in terms of Hitchcock's films) and in the immediate context of its release. The place of melodrama in British cinema will also be a focus of the analysis, interpreted not in Manvell's terms as an inferior mode to realism, but as an integral aspect of the address of silent cinema and the photographic emphasis of Ivor Novello's star persona.

The Lodger is related to a tradition of British cinema in the 1920s which drew inspiration from films from France, Germany, the Soviet Union and also from Hollywood. This eclectic mix of styles was an integral aspect of the economic and cultural aspirations of 'Film Europe' which was an attempt in the 1920s to promote co-operation among European film-producing countries to counter the domination of American films. Germany took the initiative, encouraging films to be made in a 'European' rather than a national style, and Hitchcock's first feature film, *The Pleasure Garden* (1925), was a British–German co-production shot in Germany. *The Lodger* was shot in Britain but stylistic homage to German expressionism, French impressionism and Soviet montage has been noted (Ryall, 24–30). Whereas many of the films made under the 'Film Europe' banner lost their sense of national identity in the spirit of co-production and internationalism (Bordwell and Thompson, 185), *The Lodger* managed to utilise a range of European and American techniques and at the same time preserve a sense of 'Britishness' which is located in its London story and setting, in its characters, and by featuring the top British box-office star of the period, Ivor Novello. A convincing case can therefore be made that *The Lodger* is both a European *and* a British film.

As far as the evidence for Hitchcock's familiarity with German expressionism is concerned, he had been to Germany in 1924 as a member of the production team of *The Passionate Adventure*, a co-production between Michael Balcon's Gainsborough Pictures and Germany's major film conglomerate, UFA. While in Germany, Hitchcock familiarised himself with the techniques of F. W. Murnau, director of *Nosferatu* (1922), and Fritz Lang, director of *Dr Mabuse, the Gambler* (1922), who were both associated with expressionism. Their films took inspiration from the reaction against nineteenth-century realism which was evident in painting and theatre from about 1908. Expressionist art aimed to convey inner emotional experience through distorted images and unrealistic colour. The films used studio-built sets to create an extreme sense of stylisation, for example the sets used in Robert Weine's *The Cabinet of Dr Caligari* (1920) created a *mise en scène* which expressed its characters' confused state of mind. Large, distorted structures appeared to blend in with the characters' costumes and gestural acting style. The purpose of lighting in expressionist films was not to create the illusion of realism but instead to convey dark moods, fear and foreboding. Hitchcock's first two films involved European settings (*The Pleasure Garden* and *The Mountain Eagle*, 1926). *The Mountain Eagle* starred Bernard Goetzke, a distinguished German actor who had been directed by Fritz Lang in *Der müde Tod (Destiny)* in 1921, and in this film Hitchcock experimented with lighting effects. But it was *The Lodger*, made in 1926 when Balcon and Hitchcock returned to London, which paid the most sustained homage to the themes and techniques of German expressionism with the construction of a three-sided house with narrow walls and ceilings to facilitate the varied lighting effects in the film.

Hitchcock's familiarity with European cinema also stemmed from his membership of the Film Society, formed in 1925 by left-wing intellectual Ivor Montagu and actor Hugh Miller to show imported art films and films which were not screened in London's commercial cinemas because of censorship. Private clubs could ignore the rulings of the British Board of Film Censors and bans effected by local authorities. In this way Hitchcock and other members of the Film Society saw banned films including *Nosferatu* and *The Battleship Potemkin*. Ivor Montagu, an admirer of the Soviet regime and of Eisenstein's films, re-edited some scenes in *The Lodger* after the film's distributors were concerned about its commercial viability. Montagu and the Film Society represented the trend of cultural modernism which also manifested itself in *Close-Up*, an art film periodical which reviewed many European films (Street, 150–4). So when Hitchcock returned to London in 1926 the film-makers he had studied in Germany were also being discussed and written about by those who wanted to promote European cinema as an artistic vanguard against the perceived commercialism of Hollywood.

As *The Lodger* reveals, however, Hitchcock was not as critical of Hollywood's methods and techniques as his modernist colleagues who wrote articles for *Close-Up*. He had always admired American films and his first film-related job was working as a title designer for Famous-Players-Lasky (an American film company which later became Paramount) at their Islington studios in London.

In the mid- to late 1920s Hollywood was interested in developments in European art cinema and several film-makers including Ernst Lubitsch (director of popular German comedies in the 1920s), Mauritz Stiller (a Scandinavian who had discovered Greta Garbo), Paul Leni (director of the expressionist classic *Waxworks*, 1924) and F. W. Murnau went to Hollywood to make films. There is much evidence, therefore, of stylistic cross-fertilisation between Hollywood and Europe in the 1920s and *The Lodger* demonstrates an appreciation of 'art' cinema and at the same time admiration for Hollywood's narrative techniques and acknowledgement of the need to entertain the film audience. In keeping with 'classical' Hollywood cinema, the narrative displays a clear trajectory organised around the principle of 'problem-resolution'.

The narrative of *The Lodger* is 'classical' in the sense that the film poses, and answers, a basic question: who is 'the Avenger'? The most obvious candidate is the Lodger (Ivor Novello), but there are also grounds for suspecting Joe (Malcolm Keen), who is associated with sexual banter with Daisy (June) and comments early on in the film 'I'm keen on golden hair myself, same as the Avenger is'. Like many films based on patterns of classical narrative the film introduces its 'inciting incident' when the Lodger arrives at the Buntings' house looking for a room to let. On top of the mystery already established about the murders, another crucial layer is added which presents us with the possible culprit, who has a strange reaction to the paintings of fair-haired women which are on the walls of his room. Further suspense is created when we know that fair-haired Daisy lives in the house and is therefore a potential victim for the Avenger.

The composition and structure of *The Lodger* would appear to be fairly straightforward. It consists of ten sequences which deal with murder number seven; the reporting of the murder; introduction to Daisy as she hears the news at work with other chorus girls; introduction to the Buntings and Joe; the arrival of the Lodger; the development of the 'love triangle' between Daisy, Joe and the Lodger; murder number eight; the Lodger is suspected; Joe closing in on the Lodger; the Lodger's arrest; followed by the final sequence of the Lodger and Daisy in their home after the discovery of his innocence. Despite this clear pattern there are, however, several layers of ambiguity which raise the story from a simple 'whodunnit'. The main site of ambiguity, especially for audiences watching the film in the 1920s, concerns the Lodger, who was played by Ivor Novello, a well known and loved star. Apart from our knowledge of his star persona and contemporary popularity he is coded completely differently from the other male characters. What might be construed as sinister about him can also be interpreted as sensitive, well-bred and attractive. Several incidents are puzzling – for example, what does the Lodger have in his bag and where does he go at night? These enigmas serve as devices to propel the narrative from one plot event to the next. Novello's star persona is discussed at more length below, but it is important to note here his ambiguous function in a narrative context.

The narrative uses various mechanisms to link particular incidents and themes, the most noticeable being associative and parallel action. In the first sequence we see not just the discovery of a murder but the introduction of the crowds who later play an important part in hounding the Lodger when he is mistaken for the Avenger. In the fifth sequence, when the Lodger is introduced, his arrival is intercut with a comedic episode with Mr Bunting standing on a chair to put money in the meter above the door because the light has gone out. The Lodger is startled when he hears a crash (as Bunting falls off the chair) and the light suddenly goes on again. The parallel action here serves two purposes: a comedic one which is consistent with the characterisation of the Bunting family as previously presented, and as a mechanism of suspense which becomes associated with the Lodger. The light is also significant in that it goes out just before the Lodger first arrives, cueing us to expect something sinister and setting up a key motif which recurs throughout the rest of the film. In the penultimate sequence, when the Lodger takes Daisy to a dark street, they sit on a bench under a lamp; he meets her again later at the same place when he has escaped from Joe. The light surrounded by darkness here serves to focus even more attention on the Lodger and Daisy in these two key scenes, when they appear to be vulnerable innocents who find the city threatening and dangerous.

Another narrative device is the way in which scenes progress into sequences (a sequence being made up of a series of linked scenes) by advancing from the general to the particular, establishing a state of affairs, developing the situation and ending with a particular event or suggestion. The second sequence, for example, which deals with the reporting of the murder on the wireless, in newspapers and by word-of-mouth, begins with a general shot of editors scanning a wire in the newsroom. It then progresses to the publication of the news in papers, in neon and via radio, and ends with the particular reception of the news by the crowds. Similarly, the following sequence, which shows how the dancers and Daisy learn the news, begins with their general discussion of the crimes and builds up to their particular reception of the news of murder number seven. Similarly, in the sequence which introduces the 'love triangle' theme between Daisy, Joe and the Lodger, a complex dynamic between the three characters is established by progressing from a general observation about Daisy and the Lodger's increasing friendliness and intimacy, to Joe's jealousy and symbolic linking of the murders with his plans to marry Daisy. Here the handcuffs serve as a symbol of sexual violence: when Joe catches the Avenger he will marry Daisy (a 'rope around the Avenger's neck' is equated with 'a ring around Daisy's finger'). Into the conventional mystery another layer of ambiguity is therefore inserted. As a character we are not encouraged to like Joe, who is less handsome and refined than the Lodger. The incident with the handcuffs associates his desire for Daisy with the violence of murder, which is given an extra sexual edge with the persistent use of the pulsating neon flashes of 'Tonight. Golden Curls' which recur throughout the film.

Narrative structure and *mise en scène* are used to explore the film's major themes of guilt and innocence, communication, the dangers of the city, and gender/sexuality. The identity of the Avenger is the major question posed by the narrative. It is important, however, to appreciate how the revelation that he has been caught (we never see him) reminds us that although we have been anxious to learn his identity we have been encouraged to suspect both the Lodger and Joe. In so doing we learn other things about them, which raises the question that either of them *might*, in different circumstances, have been capable of murder. On several occasions the Lodger is built up as suspicious: his dramatic, wincing reaction to the paintings of fair-haired women when he enters his room; the intertitle: 'Be careful, I'll get you yet' when he is flirting with Daisy in his room; his restless pacing in his room, which we see from the point of view of the Buntings from below (using the celebrated technique of the thick plate-glass ceiling); the coincidence of timing that the Lodger is out at the time that the eighth murder is committed; the discovery of the map, press cuttings and photograph in his bag and, finally, aspects of Novello's acting style and Hitchcock's visual composition of the actor in the frame.

These last two points suggest comparison with Murnau's *Nosferatu*. On several occasions Novello's slow, gestural acting style is reminiscent of expressionist acting techniques. His movements are deliberate and studied and his hand gestures reveal long fingers that are similar to those of the vampire in *Nosferatu*. When the Lodger has arrived at the Buntings' house and is installed in his room there is a shot of him from outside the window. As he looks out, the window pane forms a frame-within-a-frame around his face and the lighting effects create a streak of vertical light down his face. This image is very foreboding, particularly of the scene at the end of the film when the Lodger's handcuffs have got caught on the railings. In *Nosferatu* the vampire is also filmed so that his face is framed by window panes, his fingers are unnaturally long and the visual construction of his image shows consistent patterns of a trapped individual, contributing to the film's suggestion of sympathy for the vampire. Novello's white make-up also gives him a vampiric quality, while Daisy's instantaneous attraction to him is reminiscent of the classic representation of the vampire whom women are compelled to desire.

As previously noted, Joe is also a suspect although he is a policeman. His relationship with Daisy is coded with overtones of violence and fetishism (the handcuff incident) and his desire to capture the Avenger becomes acute when he realises that he can obliterate his rival at the same time by identifying him as the Avenger. The motif of the triangle is a plot device which links the murderer with the serial killings of the fair-haired women and provides clues for the location of the most likely spot for the next murder. Its other crucial function is to symbolise the three-way love contest between Daisy, Joe and the Lodger. When it becomes clear that Daisy is attracted to the Lodger, Joe becomes all the more intent on linking him with the killings, as we see from a montage of subjective shots which convince him that the Lodger is the Avenger. The inference is that patterns can be detected when you want them to be, and were it not for the news that the real Avenger has been caught, the film could have ended with the crowd lynching the Lodger, even though we (and Daisy) know about his sister via the two flashback scenes of the story of his sister's murder at a ball and of his mother on her deathbed. The fact that the film's ending is ostensibly 'happy' does not, perhaps, remove every doubt about the characters' potential to be violent.

The film contains many montage sequences of communication, communication systems and communication between people. The opening sequences deal with the murder and how the news spreads via modern technology (the wire and mass production of newspapers) and word-of-mouth. This provides an opportunity for some documentarist sequences that bear a close resemblance to images of modern technology in Soviet films. This representation of modernity as progressive and efficient was consistent with European modernism's fascination with machinery as a progressive force. Consequently, in the second sequence, we learn *how* the news is spread from the newsroom to the crowd. This montage is not strictly necessary for the advancement of the plot, but it provides an opportunity for yet another style to be incorporated into the film. The impression is of pace, but the machines which print the newspapers are lingered on for their aesthetic qualities, encouraging the spectator to admire not only their efficiency but also their beauty. Once the news reaches the crowds, however, its details are distorted, exaggerated and engulfed by the by-standers, who are both shocked by and fascinated with the Avenger's deeds. The inference is that although modern technology can make news travel fast it has no control over how it is received, what interpretations people will construct from its 'neutral' factual bulletins. The by-standers' discussion of the murders also permits an opportunity for humour, as in the scene when someone pretends to be the Avenger by pulling a scarf over the lower half of their face. When the chorus girls and Daisy's colleagues at the fashion house hear the news they devise schemes to thwart the Avenger by wearing dark wigs to disguise their fair hair. Their banter is fearful but excited, which contributes to the sexual theme that pervades the entire film.

The Lodger can be linked generically to films which portray the city as threatening and vice-ridden. While avant-garde cinema embraced technology it could often be critical of the structures which sustained modernity, including the city. Many films in the 1920s, such as the German *Strassenfilme* ('street' films), depicted the city as a dangerous place, and G. W. Pabst was one of the key directors who worked with this genre. Perhaps his best known film is *Pandora's Box* (1929), which succeeded *The Lodger* by three years but contains many of the same preoccupations, including the Jack the Ripper theme at the end of the film. As already noted, the scenes in *The Lodger* when Ivor Novello and Daisy (June) are under the streetlamp are reminiscent of many European images of the city as dense, threatening, in this case fog-ridden (which also has a metaphorical function), and mysterious. The city is represented as a dangerous place for women and the film's insistence on the Avenger's victims being fair-haired relates to the tradition of the *femme fatale* which was incorporated into American *films noirs* of the 1940s. This complicates the impression that the victims are innocent: the women we see discussing the murders are mostly young, attractive, and work in city-related occupations on the stage and in glamorous fashion houses. As in Murnau's *Sunrise* (1927), women who live in the city are portrayed as vulnerable, tempting and a source of male anxiety, anger and even violence; the neon-flashing 'Tonight. Golden Curls' encapsulates the impression of the city as full of promise but with a dangerous edge.

Related to the theme of women and the city is the broader issue of gender and sexuality. Ivor Novello's portrayal of the Lodger is tinged with sexual ambiguity. His appearance is somewhat androgynous: his hair is sleek, he has a pale face and dark eye make-up. He is the direct opposite of the rougher, more conventionally masculine Joe. Two intertitles intimate that the Lodger may be homosexual: 'I'm glad he's not keen on the girls' and 'Even if he is a bit queer, he's a gentleman'. Novello's portrayal of the Lodger also demonstrates a classic representation of gay male sexuality of the period: the sad young man who is a misunderstood outsider. Although Ivor Novello's own gay sexuality was not widely known at the time, the film's ambiguous narrative and the way the star is photographed in long, languorous close-ups which emphasise his good looks, large dark eyes, and hair, permit a reading which places sexual ambivalence at the centre rather than at the margins of the film. At the time, Novello was the most popular British male film star. As well as being an actor he was a songwriter and playwright and had acted in Hollywood in the early 1920s, returning to star in a successful film adaptation of his stage play *The Rat* (Graham Cutts, 1925). Audiences would have been familiar with Novello's stage and screen work and, according to Donald Spoto, Hitchcock could not end the film on an ambiguous note, leaving it unclear as to whether the Lodger was the Avenger or not because the distributors were convinced that Novello's fans would not tolerate him being depicted as a villain (Spoto, 85).

In terms of film style, *The Lodger* utilises many techniques of silent cinema at its most visual and graphic. The sparse, but adequate intertitles (in keeping with German films) were designed by McKnight Kauffer, a painter and poster designer. As the first frames of the film appear, the originality of the designs is striking and they continue to punctuate the narrative throughout. Other textual insertions are important: the repeated flashing in neon of 'Tonight. Golden Curls' creates a link between the murder of blonde women and the city which exploits them for sex. The news bulletin giving the details of the seventh murder provides the spectator with vital plot information. The film's *mise en scène* is employed to the full for the advancement of plot and suggestion of sub-plot. The triangle with 'The Avenger' written in its centre is a key plot device which also symbolises the three-way love contest.

Costume is used in intriguing ways to confuse our expectations about the characters. When we first see Daisy she appears to be a well-to-do woman dressed in a fur coat, emerging from a doorway. We then cut to a wide shot which reveals that she is in fact a model for expensive clothes in a fashion house. The Lodger's first appearance codes him as mysterious, dressed exactly as we would expect the Avenger to be, wearing a long, black cloak, dark hat and with a scarf covering the lower half of his face. The clothes we see him in later suggest to us that he is upper class, an observation which is later confirmed by the flashback of his sister's 'coming out' ball and the penultimate scene when the Buntings visit his palatial mansion. The Lodger's bag is important for the plot in that we see from very early on, when he first goes to his room at the Buntings, that it must hold something vital because he locks it in the sideboard. Later on, when Joe arrests the Lodger, the bag is opened to reveal maps, press cuttings about the murders, and the photograph of his sister. This condemns him in the eyes of Joe but vindicates him according to Daisy, who believes his story about his sister being the Avenger's first victim. Used here primarily as a plot device, the bag is nevertheless deployed in a way that is similar to how bags feature in Hitchcock's later films – as a character's private space where secrets can be hidden. While a bag is usually a woman's property, in this instance the nature of its use links it with the theme of sexual ambiguity. Novello is identified with 'the feminine' in the film – the way he is filmed, his association with sensitivity, his clash with the uncomplicated 'masculine' Joe, his inability to communicate his story – and this use of conventionally feminine *mise en scène* in connection with the Lodger is therefore not surprising.

Novello's acting style was typical of silent cinema. His melodramatic gestures and slow, deliberate movements are, however, rather different from those of the other characters. In *The Lodger* the Buntings' acting style is also melodramatic, but the camera singles them out less than Novello. As Christine Gledhill has argued, British cinema of the 1920s engaged with traditions inherited from popular late nineteenth-century stage melodrama in such a way as to adapt them to suit cinematic techniques. In stage melodrama, acting was non-naturalistic, typified by large, often slowish and languid movements to give presence to characters who were representing extremes of good and evil. While cinematic representation did not require the use of such grand gestures, acting traditions taken from the theatre were clearly present in early screen acting. The close-up, for example, could convey the dramatic equivalent of a fulsome melodramatic stage gesture and at the same time communicate a scene's emotional core. Thus melodrama had not disappeared in silent cinema but had simply been accommodated by the film medium, and Novello's style is therefore very appropriate for the camera in terms of both his physical movements and his suitability for close-ups.

It has been argued in this chapter that *The Lodger* engages with many styles and techniques which were prevalent in both European and Hollywood cinema of the 1920s. In what ways, therefore, is it a 'British' film? The traditions inherited from late nineteenth-century stage melodrama are important in that the film can be linked to a longer trajectory of British popular theatre. The film was an adaptation of a novel by Mrs Belloc Lowndes, written in 1913 about the Jack the Ripper murders, which had taken place in Whitechapel in the 1880s. A more direct source for the film was *Who Is He?*, a stage adaptation of the novel, which Hitchcock had seen. As well as its link with popular mythology surrounding Jack the Ripper, a sense of 'Britishness' comes mainly from the use of London settings in *The Lodger*. The lower middle-class milieu of the Buntings' house, the foggy street scenes and the scenes of communal activity (the street tea-dispenser, the pub) connote London life, as do the inter-titles of dialogue, particularly those conveying the colloquial speech of the crowds and the Buntings ('dearie'; 'the way that fiend did her in').

The film was a popular and critical success and was released at a time when the British film industry was being singled out as a candidate for state assistance to bolster production and counter American domination. The Cinematograph Films Act, 1927, stipulated that renters and exhibitors should handle and show a certain percentage of British films in relation to the total number they distributed and exhibited. *The Lodger* was highly praised as an example of a standard to which other British films should aspire. The trade paper *The Bioscope* even went so far as to suggest it was 'possibly' the finest British production ever made. *The Lodger* represents both the sophistication of silent cinema and the prevailing trends towards co-operation and internationalism which were cut short by the upheavals wrought by the coming of sound in the late 1920s. From this perspective it is a key film which illustrates the eclecticism of European film production and its accommodation with Hollywood.

References

Gledhill, Christine 1999: 'Taking it Forward: Theatricality and British Cinema Style in the 1920s'. In Linda Fitzsimmons and Sarah Street (eds), *Moving Performance: Theatre and Early Cinema in Britain*. Wiltshire: Flicks Books.

Manvell, Roger 1951: 'Revaluations'. In *Sight and Sound*, January, 378.

Petro, Patrice 1989: *Joyless Streets: Women and Melodramatic Representation in Weimar Germany*. Princeton, NJ: Princeton University Press.

Ryall, Tom 1986: *Alfred Hitchcock and the British Cinema*. London: Croom Helm.

Spoto, Donald 1986: *The Life of Alfred Hitchcock: The Dark Side of Genius*. London: Collins.

Street, Sarah 1997: *British National Cinema*. London: Routledge.

Thompson, Kristin and Bordwell, David 1994: *Film History: An Introduction*, NewYork: McGraw-Hill.

Suggestions for Further Reading

Barr, Charles 1997: 'Before *Blackmail*: Silent British Cinema'. In Robert Murphy (ed.), *The British Cinema Book*. London: British Film Institute.

Barr, Charles 1999: *English Hitchcock*. London: Cameron & Hollis.
Higson, Andrew 1993: *Waving the Flag: Constructing a National Cinema in Britain*. Oxford: Clarendon Press.
Low, Rachel 1971: *The History of the British Film, 1918–1929*. London: Allen and Unwin.

Credits

Director	Alfred Hitchcock
Assistant Director	Alma Reville
Producer	Michael Balcon
Production Company	Gainsborough Pictures
Screenplay	Eliot Stannard, from novel by Marie Belloc Lowndes
Editor/Titling	Ivor Montagu
Director of Photography	Baron [Giovanni] Ventimiglia
Art Director	C. Wilfrid Arnold, Bertram Evans
Title Designs	E. McKnight Kauffer

Cast

Marie Ault	Mrs Bunting
Arthur Chesney	Mr Bunting
June	Daisy Bunting
Malcolm Keen	Joe
Ivor Novello	The Lodger

Filmography (Hitchcock's British Films)

The Pleasure Garden (1925)
The Mountain Eagle (1925)
The Lodger (1926)
Downhill (1927)
Easy Virtue (1927)
The Ring (1927)
The Farmer's Wife (1927)
Champagne (1928)
The Manxman (1928)
Blackmail (1929)
Juno and the Paycock (1930)
Murder! (1930)
The Skin Game (1930–1)
Number Seventeen (1931)
Rich and Strange (1932)
Waltzes from Vienna (1933)
The Man Who Knew Too Much (1934)

The Thirty-Nine Steps (1935)
Secret Agent (1935)
Sabotage (1936)
Young and Innocent (1937)
The Lady Vanishes (1937)
Jamaica Inn (1938)

3 *La règle du jeu*
Christine (Nora Gregor) and Geneviève (Mila Parely) in fancy dress with Octave (Jean Renoir).

La règle du jeu
Jill Forbes

Filmed in the spring of 1939 and first released in July of that year, Jean Renoir's *La règle du jeu* is a magnificent summary of an era that was about to come to an end, both in the history of France and in the French cinema. When Renoir began the film he was at the height of his fame and fortune. His adaptation of Zola's novel *La bête humaine*, starring Jean Gabin and Simone Simon, had opened at the end of 1938 to universal acclaim and, with his brother Claude, his assistant director André Zwoboda, and several other associates, he had formed a production and distribution company called La nouvelle édition française, which he hoped would operate rather in the manner of the United Artists Company in the United States, promoting the work of its owners rather than the fortunes of the studios or big business. *La règle du jeu* was the company's first project, and an ambitious one, described by Renoir as 'a precise description of bourgeois people of our period' (Curchod and Faulkner, 10).

The film tells the story of the daring aviator André Jurieux, who flies the Atlantic, single-handed, for love of Christine, Marquise de La Chesnaye. But when he lands at Le Bourget airport, to the rapturous acclaim of the assembled crowds, he is not met by Christine, as he had hoped, but by her family friend Octave. And instead of behaving as the national hero the waiting crowd desires, he gives a radio interview, heard by Christine and her husband at home in Paris, in which he petulantly expresses his disappointment at Christine's absence. His despair is such that shortly afterwards he attempts suicide by trying to crash his car.

These episodes serve as a prologue which introduces us to Octave, Christine, her husband Robert de La Chesnaye, and Robert's mistress, Geneviève, a world of wealthy 'bourgeois' with useless aristocratic titles, innumerable servants, and assorted hangers-on. We accompany this group to a weekend house party given at the La Chesnaye country seat, La Colinière, and momentarily appear to be transported back in time to a world that was frequently represented in the comic theatre of the eighteenth and nineteenth centuries by playwrights such as Beaumarchais, Marivaux and Musset. The central preoccupation of all the characters, whether masters or servants, is an elaborate series of games, played, as the title of the film suggests, according to rules which everyone understands and which must not, under any circumstances, be broken. One of these games is hunting, which is depicted in an exquisitely beautiful and poignant sequence of the film, shot on location in the Sologne countryside; another is play-acting, in evidence in a series of gruesome music-hall turns performed by the hosts and guests at La Colinière for the benefit of the assembled household. Most of all, the game in question is that of love – conjugal or adulterous – in all its vagaries and permutations. But whatever the game, it seems that the form is more significant than the content and that the observation of the rules is an end in itself, an end which is more important than winning or losing.

This eminently theatrical and highly artificial setting, as well as the invention of characters whose concerns are apparently entirely frivolous and solipsistic, seemed an extraordinary subject for a film in 1939 and especially for Renoir, who was known both for the 'realism' of his films and for his support for left-wing causes. The political context was, indeed, sombre. In France, the Popular Front government, elected in 1936, had ended in failure, brought down by violent opposition from the extreme Right but also by a series of strikes by the Left, and in 1938 the Frontist Prime Minister Léon Blum had been replaced by Édouard Daladier. Outside France, events were moving with frightening speed. In March 1938 came the Anschluss, when Germany invaded Austria and annexed it to the Third Reich, clearly signalling that war was imminent. On 29 September 1938, Hitler, Chamberlain and Daladier met in Munich and signed the agreement which, Chamberlain declared, secured 'peace in our time' – or, at least, a breathing space – but in March 1939, as Renoir was shooting the first sequences of the film, Germany invaded Czechoslovakia. On 1 September Germany invaded Poland and on 3 September war was declared.

The principal characters in *La règle du jeu* seem blithely unaware of the impending conflagration and resolutely turn their faces against the realities of politics. The Marquis collects mechanical musical instruments, one of which he proudly demonstrates to his assembled guests; the General cares only about preserving appearances; the aviator cares only whether Christine loves him; Geneviève is preoccupied by the belief that Robert will leave her; Jackie cares only for André, who does not love her; and her mother seeks only to marry off her daughter. The servants, too, share their employers' preoccupations, mirroring their solipsism and introversion. There is, apparently, no character in the film who speaks for 'the people' or 'the common man' or who is capable of offering an outside perspective on this group determined to sink with their ship.

Understandably, Renoir was criticised from all sides. From the Right came the accusation that the film caricatured and ridiculed the very people on whom France depended for its defence. The Army is represented here by the General, who is an aimiable buffoon, while the Air Force is – at least potentially – represented by André Jurieux, who is totally unwilling to place his country above his personal preoccupations. Thus such military heroes as the film contains are decidedly unsatisfactory and, with hindsight, we may say that Renoir's view of the military capabilities of France in 1939 was more prescient than his critics on the Right admitted publicly. Perhaps this knowledge explains why the film came in for virulent attacks from the right-wing press and provoked violent incidents when it was screened. But from the Left, too, came criticism that was certainly more muted but which nevertheless expressed unease at Renoir's essentially sympathetic portrayal of the foibles of a group of people who were rich, idle and exploitative. During the 1930s, there was much criticism on the Left of the so-called 'two hundred families' who were said to be ruining France. *La règle du jeu* apparently depicts one of these in all its magnificent irresponsibility.

The strength of Renoir's films in the 1930s, and indeed the feature on which much of his reputation rested, was his humanism, his creation of sympathetic communities, the notion that runs from film to film of the nation as a collectivity in which each person has a part to play, and of the way that individualities contribute to a richly variegated totality. We see this in films such as *Le crime de Monsieur Lange* (1935), which rests on working-class solidarity, or *La Marseillaise* (1938) where the community is extended to the nation as a whole. *La règle du jeu* apparently conforms to this approach both ideologically and cinematically since it is a film without stars and without a principal character or characters. But the difficulty, at least for critics on the Left, was that the community in question, with its 'upstairs downstairs' relationships and its impermeability to outside forces, more closely resembled that of an eighteenth-century château than that of France in 1939.

Clearly, *La règle du jeu* was not what audiences in 1939 expected from France's most celebrated director. After its initial screening Renoir shortened the film in an attempt to make it more accessible, but even so its first run only lasted a few weeks. Thereafter, the turn of events removed it from commercial release for over two decades, leaving it to acquire an underground reputation which, if anything, reinforced its political impact. The film was banned under wartime censorship in 1942 and may have been banned as early as 1940 in the category of films considered 'depressing, morbid, immoral and likely to corrupt young people' (Curchod and Faulkner, 21–2). In November 1940, its director left France for the United States where he remained until 1952, while its negative was destroyed by Allied bombing in 1942. It was not until 1958 that the version we see today was pieced together by two devoted film scholars, and it was not until 1965 that it was commercially re-released. Though the present version is longer than the one released commercially in 1939 it is shorter than Renoir had originally intended, with the result that several episodes seem incoherent or unexplained (notably André Jurieux's suicide attempt and the intimacy of the relationship between Christine and Octave). But perhaps the most important effect is to alter the balance of the film, to make it appear less of a psychological drama which turns on the emotions of characters such as Jurieux and Octave, and to make the house party at La Colinière the structural centre and focus of the film.

The house party is a metaphor commonly used to signify a society in microcosm, enabling a cross-section of social types and interests to be brought together in one place. It was a particularly common device in boulevard theatre but its ultimate origins lie in the Aristotelian unities of time, place and action. The fact that La Colinière has become the centre of the film emphasises both its literary origins and its satirical import. While *La règle du jeu* depicts a weekend rather than twenty-four hours, it appears to achieve a dramatic unity: for a short period of time an assorted group of people, representing a microcosm of French society, are brought together under one roof. A carnivalesque atmosphere prevails in which it is difficult to distinguish servants and masters, and cases of mistaken identity occur – one thinks of similar revelries in Shakespeare's *Twelfth Night* or *A Midsummer Night's Dream* – until finally a dramatic action brings the crazy atmosphere to an end, order is restored and everything returns to 'normal'.

However, it was not just the theatre in general to which Renoir referred but specific literary sources. In order to see how this is explored we must return to the beginning of the film and its epigraph from *Le mariage de Figaro* (*The Marriage of Figaro*), a play by Beaumarchais (1732–99) first performed in 1784: 'Cœurs sensibles, cœurs fidèles/Qui blamez l'amour léger/Cessez vos plaintes cruelles/Est-ce un crime de changer?' (Sensitive hearts, faithful hearts/Who condemn fickle love/Cease your harsh complaints/Is it a crime to change?). The epigraph seems to anchor the film securely in French eighteenth-century culture, in the world of the *ancien régime*, ruled by an aristocracy which invented the concept of politeness and good manners and where sexual and social relationships were conducted according to strict codes of behaviour. We might also note similarities of title and plot to another eighteenth-century play, *Le jeu de l'amour et du hasard* (1730) by Marivaux (1688–1763), in which a noblewoman changes places with her maid in order to observe her suitor who, unbeknown to her, has changed places with his manservant for the same reason. This was not the first time that Renoir had evoked the eighteenth century on film. In *La Marseillaise*, in which he played the role of an artist, casting himself as the painter of the Revolution Jacques-Louis David, he explored the origins of the French national anthem by following a group of Marseillais as they travel to Paris to support the Revolution.

It seems fair to assume that Renoir's fascination with the eighteenth century was in part because it was a period of revolutionary change, the time when a corrupt aristocracy was overthrown by popular action rather as many had hoped would occur in 1936. But the eighteenth century had other attractions too: the formalism of its literature, its fondness for structural games and *mises en abyme*, and its reflexivity, all of which are also mirrored in *La règle du jeu*. However, the film was initially conceived as an adaptation of Alfred de Musset's play *Les caprices de Marianne* (1840), in which Marianne, who is married to Claudio, is having an affair with Octave, and in which Célio, who also loves Marianne, goes to a rendezvous in place of Octave and is killed on the orders of Claudio. This provided Renoir with part of his plot and the name of his own character as well as a further theme, embodied in the name Marianne, which links the exploration of the state of the nation – Marianne was the female figure of the Republic – with that of the role and status of women. What can we learn from this complex of intertexts which were and are extremely familiar to French audiences? And how do they reinforce the political impact of the film?

Perhaps the strongest theme to emerge from them is that of social satire. It is a commonplace of literary history to view *Le mariage de Figaro* as a prefiguration of the Revolution, which took place five years after it was first performed and which overturned the social structure it depicted. Beaumarchais subversively satirised the customs and habits of a declining aristocracy by showing the essential similarity between its behaviour and that of its servants. With hindsight, Beaumarchais appeared premonitory in exactly the same way as, with hindsight, Renoir appeared premonitory. The analogy works, provided one accepts that the France of 1939 was ruled by a kind of *ancien régime* which was swept away by the revolutionary forces of post-war modernisation, and it is an analogy that critics in the 1950s and 1960s were understandably eager to embrace in order to distinguish post-war France from the period of shameful appeasement and occupation in the 1930s and 1940s.

In French cinema we frequently find film-makers using the body of a woman to symbolise the body politic, and in wishing to adapt Musset's play about 'Marianne' it may well be that Renoir had something of the kind in mind. Women's inconstancy is often said to be the subject-matter of *Les caprices de Marianne* and, to some extent, *Le jeu de l'amour et du hasard* but a modern reading would probably emphasise that the subject is women's freedom of choice. Certainly, plays and film juxtapose inclination and duty, doing as you please and doing as you should, frivolity and seriousness, comedy and tragedy. However, it is interesting that Renoir's 'Marianne' is not French but Austrian, since one of the vital questions posed in the film is the nature of identity. What makes people what they are? Can they change? And can one judge essence from external appearances? Renoir's literary sources make great play with carnivalesque disguise and inversions of identity: in Beaumarchais the implication is that a servant can become a master; in Musset the *quiproquo*, or mistaken identity, leads to a tragic outcome. And in *La règle du jeu* such questions have a strongly political dimension.

A great deal of dressing up goes on in the film. This is of course most obvious during the evening's theatricals when Geneviève wears gypsy costume, Christine wears Tyrolean costume, and Octave puts on a bearskin. Perhaps these costumes are intended to reveal 'true' identity rather than to disguise. Octave, for example, seems stuck inside his bearskin, which turns him into a permanent pantomime character against his will and makes a mockery of his later confession of musical ambitions and his love for Christine. If so, what are we to make of the performances of the other guests at La Colinière and the songs they sing? One of these, *En r'v'nant d'la revue*, was a late nineteenth-century musical-hall song which became the anthem of supporters of General Boulanger who, in the late 1880s, attempted a military coup d'état against the

Republic. Is Renoir implying that the performers at La Colinière would support such an anti-Republican act and that they thought one was needed? Arguably, when Marshal Pétain became head of state the following year, that is exactly what happened, and such people did support him. The second song performed, *Nous avons l'vé le pied*, was a so-called music-hall 'patter song' and it is sung by Berthelin, La Bruyère, L'Inverti (the Homosexual) and the South American, disguised as office workers with enormous and clearly false beards. Its ironies are harder to interpret but Keith Reader has suggested that these are burlesque representatives of a class which is absent from the film, that of the petty bourgeoisie, whose social instability had proved the downfall of the Popular Front. By the time the ghosts and the skeleton come on stage to cavort to the music of Saint-Saëns, spookily provided by a piano that no-one plays, it is clear that the theatricals are not, or no longer, harmless play-acting, for during this performance the whole tone of the film shifts from the comic to the tragic. The intimate relationships in the household are reconfigured during the *danse macabre*, so that its placing gives it a premonitory function as it points forward to the tragedy that will occur. Renoir referred to French society, in the context of *La règle du jeu*, as 'dancing on a volcano' and perhaps that is indicated by this dance of death.

If the significance of dress and identity are overdetermined in the theatricals, they are also crucial elsewhere in the film. For example, Marceau the poacher is issued with a servant's livery and is transformed, at least in theory, commenting with what for the audience is heavy irony, 'I've always dreamed of being a servant'. The double case of mistaken identity is caused by nothing more complicated than coats: Lisette lends Christine her cape so that Christine is mistaken for Lisette by Schumacher and Marceau as she is embracing Octave; Octave lends Jurieux his coat in order for him to run away with Christine, so that Schumacher mistakes him for Octave whom he mistakenly thought had been embracing his wife. André's death is sacrificial, restoring calm and order and allowing everyone to return to their 'rightful' place and their 'true' identity.

However, true identity is not always as clear-cut as some of the characters might wish. Christine is Austrian – indeed, she speaks French with a marked accent – and is played by the actress Nora Gregor who was a real refugee from Hitler's Anschluss. Christine comes from a musical family (we learn from Octave that her father was a conductor), and we are reminded of the Austrian tradition he represented by the musical quotations of Mozart's *Marriage of Figaro*. It is a tradition quite different from the bellicose and predatory one symbolised by the Anschluss and embodied in Hitler, another Austrian. It is not clear whether Christine has put her Austrian origins behind her. Her assimilation into French society is initially imperfect and she does not understand the rules of the game Robert is playing. Above all, she does not know, initially, that he has a mistress. She is perhaps nostalgic, too, for her country of birth, because she likes to dress up in Tyrolean costume. In her person she therefore embodies the conflictual Austrian destiny: Hitler or Mozart, *Realpolitik* or music.

Her husband is not what he seems either. He has an aristocratic title but, as the General points out, 'his grandfather's name was Rosenthal'. The Marquis is a man of exquisite taste who knows how things should be done; he has immense style but he is, in the cook's words, a 'métèque' (that is, of mixed race). France was, and had been for over a century, a country that welcomed immigrants of all kinds and granted them civil rights, and this was one reason why the pre-war Jewish population in France was both numerous and assimilated. In addition to obliquely referring to Renoir's earlier, pacifist film *La grande illusion* (1937), in which Dalio, the actor who plays Robert, had played a character named Rosenthal, the remarks by the General and the cook reflect the anti-Semitism that was widespread in France across many social classes in the 1930s and that was to be allowed to flourish under the Vichy regime and the German Occupation. Indeed, during the Occupation a portrait of the actor Dalio, by now a refugee in the United States, was used to 'help' people identify Jews. But despite Renoir's evident critique of anti-Semitism, the character Robert also embodies some caricatural aspects of Jewishness, both in his wealth and in his exaggerated adoption of the outward signs of Frenchness. For Robert is an actor – his white make-up, it has been suggested, is clown-like – he performs the part of a host, a lover, a theatrical impresario, and an aristocrat, and Dalio's performance as the Marquis brilliantly and convincingly conveys the impression of inauthenticity, which the audience is free to interpret positively or negatively.

The final component of this international jigsaw is Schumacher. As an Alsatian he embodies the dual or split identity and divided loyalty which is common to many in the house. Alsace is the province in eastern France which had been a political football since 1870 when it had been captured by Germany. Its loss had been a humiliation for the French army and its recovery by France, enacted under the Treaty of Versailles (1919), had become a nineteenth-century patriotic *cause célèbre*. Alsace's 'dual nationality' is wittily referred to when Christine pronounces Schumacher's name with a German inflection in contrast to Robert's French stress. It is a double allegiance which is mirrored in Schumacher's status: he is both of the household and outside it; he is not quite a servant but not quite a master. He is said to like order, and indeed organises the hunt in a military fashion, suggesting a caricaturally Germanic trait; but he is a man of deep emotions, and everywhere he goes he creates chaos. Above all, perhaps, he is the agent of tragedy, as was the province he comes from.

Throughout the film Renoir calls attention to the artificial and theatrical nature of its contents and to his role as a film-maker in their production and *mise en scène*. This is signalled in the role of Octave, a wry but sympathetic portrait of the artist as a sometimes clumsy manipulator of events, someone who stands outside the main action, differentiated from the real players by his poverty and his class. Not for the first time, as we have seen, the role of the artist is played by Renoir himself and this serves to emphasise the degree to which the film is intended as an interrogation of his art.

In addition to the obviously theatrical numbers, Renoir establishes an important contrast between interiors and exteriors. During the hunting scene, nature is almost tangibly sensuous. We observe the shimmering play of light on the landscape, we hear the leaves rustling, we see the animals playing, the guests admire the antics of a squirrel through their binoculars in a shot which is held much longer than is narratively necessary in order to appreciate the beauty and grace of the animal. We also see the bloody destruction of this beauty as the beaters progress in grimly deliberate formation and the scene builds up to a crescendo of carnage while the camera lingers on the quivering bodies of dying rabbits and birds. The hunt sequence has rightly been called an anthology piece; a tour de force of sound, image, and movement; a palette of blacks, whites, and greys which confirmed Renoir's pre-war mastery of his art. But in the post-war, post-Holocaust Europe, its connotations have become sinister and have served to underline, once again, the political impact of the film.

There are other exteriors too, truncated in the final version of the film, which are far from being a poem to nature but are, rather, a hymn to the communications revolution of the 1930s: aeroplanes, automobiles and radio are evident in the crowd scenes at Le Bourget and the scene where André tries to crash his car. Cinema belonged to this revolution and Renoir had, in *La vie est à nous* (1936), assisted his communist friends in using the cinema for propaganda purposes. Thus in *La règle du jeu* we find juxtaposed the various uses to which the medium can be put: to convey the news, to influence the masses, to represent nature, and to offer entertainment in the form of theatrical spectacles. The latter are to be found in the film's interiors; unlike the hunt scenes, which were shot on location, these were filmed for the most part on an elaborate set at the Joinville studios in Paris (although the arrival at La Colinière was filmed at a stately home near Orléans). Here Renoir is participating in a debate which had raged in film circles since the advent of the talkies: had sound destroyed the naturalism of cinema and the essence of its art by requiring the use of studios?

Like many film-makers in the 1930s, Renoir inscribes the artificial and constructed nature of the set into the diegesis by filming the successive arrivals at La Colinière as a prologue, using a rainstorm to emphasise the contrast between the world outside and the space of the diegesis, and by reminding the audience, at intervals, that the events depicted are taking place inside an artificial space. This is clearly apparent in the scene where Octave, standing on a flight of exterior steps leading to the house, turns his back to the camera/audience and conducts an imaginary orchestra which would be situated inside the château. It is also to be seen in the closing moments of the film. André has been shot in the conservatory, a space which is half inside and half outside, half 'real' and half 'theatrical'. By interpreting this tragic dénouement as an 'accident' and inviting his guests to accompany him back into the house, Robert reassimilates the tragedy into the domain of the theatrical, defusing its impact and diminishing its significance. In this way Renoir asks what is the ultimate significance of spectacle, entertainment and performance when even death can be accommodated within it.

Above all, perhaps, Renoir seems eager to suggest that appearances, especially those offered by cinema, can be deceptive. *La règle du jeu* is a cinematic tour de force. In both the interiors and exteriors Renoir uses the deep focus which was later to be praised as such an innovative feature of Orson Welles's *Citizen Kane* (1941), to create an illusion of three-dimensional space – emphasised by aspects of the set design such as the chequered floor in the corridor of La Colinière, which is used to create an apparently distant vanishing point – and to heighten the naturalism of the hunt scene. Yet certain moments in the film indicate that we should not necessarily trust what we see, especially when it is shown to us by the cinema or other technologies of viewing. Thus during the *danse macabre*, in an extraordinarily long and fluid movement, the camera seems to be mirroring the quest of the guests as they seek out their preferred sexual partners, but just when they (and we) think they have lighted on the right person the camera shows us, instead, a reflection in a mirror. Even more tellingly, during the hunt sequence Christine changes the direction and focus of the binoculars she has been using to observe the squirrel, and brings into view a different kind of game – the figures of her husband and Geneviève embracing in the distance. Christine does not know that this is their farewell embrace and that the spy-glass has served to create another *quiproquo*. On the other hand, although the interpretation it allows her to place on their current relationship is false, it simultaneously allows her to make sense of the past in a way that would not otherwise have been possible. This extraordinary moment sums up the ambiguities of the truth of the spectacle we see, precisely by emphasising the beauty of the image and the satisfying character of the narratives it conveys. By posing questions about the nature of cinematic reality, by asking whether we can trust the products of the new technologies, by assimilating the traditions of eighteenth-century French culture into the cinema and using them to make a contemporary political statement, *La règle du jeu* has come to stand as the masterpiece of French cinema of the pre-war period.

However, Renoir owed much of his post-war reputation and celebrity to the critics of *Cahiers du cinéma* who were to become the film-makers of the New Wave. These critics and film-makers, and Truffaut in particular, adopted Renoir as a model and precursor of their own film practices. In fact Truffaut's film *Tirez sur le pianiste* (*Shoot the Pianist*, 1960) opens with shots of piano keys in tribute to *La règle du jeu*. Renoir's craft-based approach to film-making, his rejection of grandiose subjects and use of actors who were not stars, and his authorial control of his material, all differentiated him from the immediate predecessors of the New Wave and turned him into a suitable patron of its cinematic revolution. In *La règle du jeu*, Renoir uses many of the actors who had regularly appeared in his films and who had become part of his 'team' or his family, rather like British character actors in films of the 1950s. Here we see

Carette perform his 'turn' as Marceau the poacher with an accent that is improbably Parisian; Gaston Modot does his number as the impossibly rigid Schumacher; Paulette Dubost flounces her way through the film as Lisette the maid. Recurrent actors and roles were part of the appeal of cinema in the 1930s and such 'family' preferences were also to become commonplace in New Wave film-making as the same actors and actresses reappear from film to film.

Nevertheless, it is in some ways odd that *La règle du jeu*, which for the most part is highly theatrical and non-naturalistic, and whose sources are evidently literary, should have appealed so strongly to post-war audiences. The reason lies, perhaps, in the fact that it functions as a summum not just of French film-making but of a certain idea of French culture. It is a film which faces both ways. At the same time as it points to the future, it looks back over the 1930s with a degree of nostalgia, criticising both French society of the period and French film-making with considerable affection and assuming a cultural heritage which embraces the *ancien régime* as well as the new order.

References and Suggestions for Further Reading

Andrew, Dudley 1995: *Mists of Regret: Culture and Sensibility in Classic French Film*. Princeton, NJ: Princeton University Press.

Bazin, André 1971: *Jean Renoir*. Paris: Éditions Champ Libre.

Crisp, Colin 1993: *Classic French Cinema*. Bloomington, IN: Indiana University Press.

Curchod, Olivier and Faulkner, Christopher 1999: *La règle du jeu. Scénario original de Jean Renoir*. Paris: Nathan.

Faulkner, Christopher 1979: *Jean Renoir: A Guide to References and Resources*. Boston, MA: G. K. Hall.

Faulkner, Christopher 1986: *The Social Cinema of Jean Renoir*. Princeton, NJ: Princeton University Press.

Reader, Keith 1999: 'Chaos, Contradiction and Order in Jean Renoir's *La règle du jeu*'. In *Australian Journal of French Studies*, 36, 1, 26–38.

Sesonke, Alexander 1980: *Jean Renoir: The French Films*. Cambridge, MA: Harvard University Press.

Vanoye, Francis 1995: *La règle du jeu*. Paris: Nathan.

Credits

Director	Jean Renoir
Producer	Jean Renoir
Production Company	La Nouvelle Édition Française (NEF)
Screenplay	Jean Renoir, Carl Koch
Director of Photography	Jean Bachelet
Editor	Marguerite Houllé-Renoir
Art Directors	Eugène Lourié, Max Douy

Cast

Marcel Dalio	Robert de La Chesnaye
Nora Gregor	Christine de La Chesnaye
Jean Renoir	Octave
Roland Toutain	André Jurieux
Mila Parely	Geneviève de Maras
Paulette Dubost	Lisette Schumacher
Gaston Modot	Schumacher
Julien Carette	Marceau
Anne Mayen	Jackie
Pierre Nay	Saint-Aubin
Odette Talazac	Charlotte de La Plante
Pierre Magnier	The General
Georges Forster	Dick
Richard Francoeur	La Bruyère
Claire Gérard	Mme La Bruyère
Nicolas Amato	Cava
Eddy Debray	Corneille
Léon Larive	Cook

Filmography

La fille de l'eau (Whirlpool of Life, 1924)
Charleston (1927)
Marquitta (1928)
La petite marchande d'allumettes (The Little Match Girl, 1928)
Tire-au-flanc (1929)
Le bled (1929)
On purge bébé (1931)
La chienne (1931)
La nuit du carrefour (1932)
Boudu sauvé des eaux (Boudu Saved from Drowning, 1932)
Chotard et cie (1933)
Madame Bovary (1934)
Toni (1934)
Le crime de Monsieur Lange (1935)
La vie est à nous (People of France, 1936)
Une partie de campagne (A Day in the Country / Country Excursion, 1936/46)
Les bas-fonds (The Lower Depths / Underworld, 1936)
La grande illusion (1937)
La Marseillaise (1938)
La bête humaine (Judas was a Woman, 1938)
La règle du jeu (The Rules of the Game, 1939)
Swamp Water (1940)
This Land is Mine (1943)

Salute to France (1944)
The Southerner (1945)
Diary of a Chambermaid (1946)
The Woman on the Beach (1947)
The River (1950)
La Carrozza d'oro (*Le carrosse d'or / The Golden Coach*, 1952)
French Cancan (1954)
Eléna et les hommes (*Paris does Strange Things*, 1956)
Le déjeuner sur l'herbe (*Picnic on the Grass / Lunch on the Grass*, 1959)
Le testament du Docteur Cordelier (*Experiment in Evil*, 1959)
Le caporal épinglé (*The Elusive Corporal*, 1961)
Le petit théâtre de Jean Renoir (*The Little Theatre of Jean Renoir*, 1971)

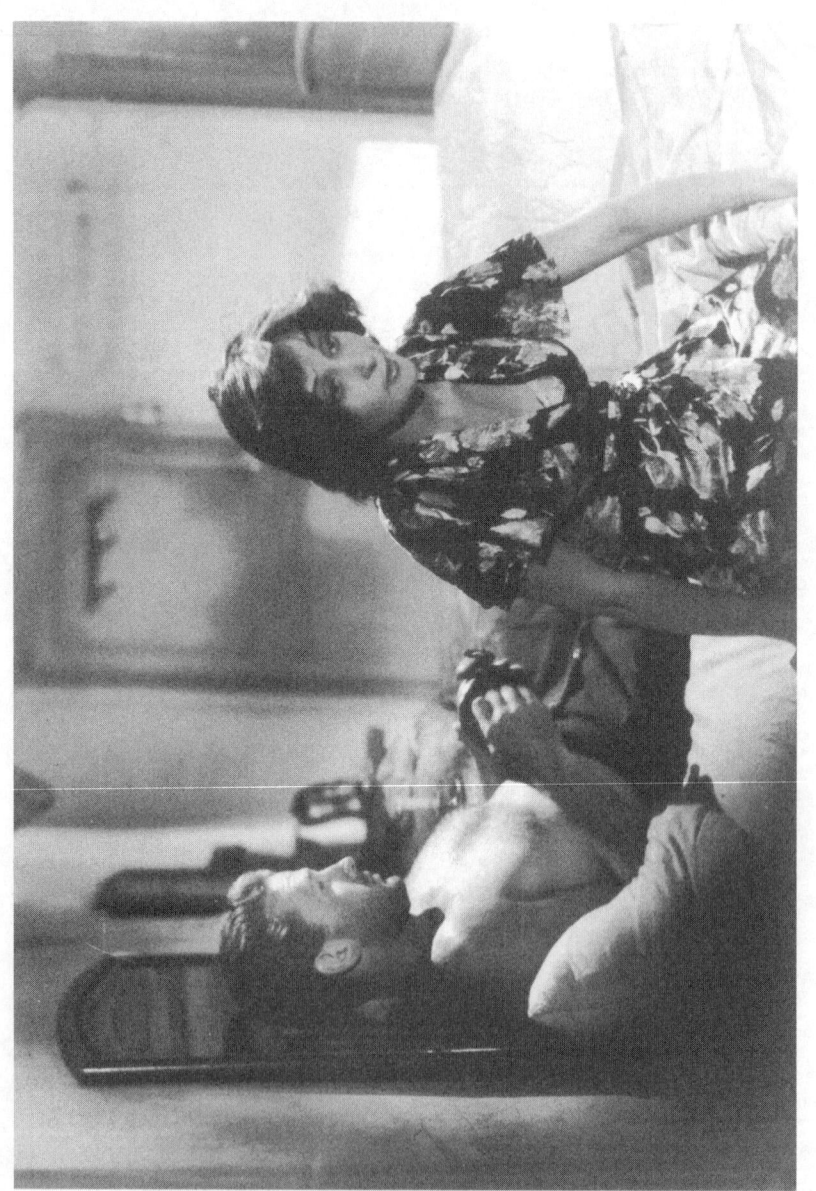

4 *Ossessione*
A dishevelled Giovanna (Clara Calamai) reflects on her life while her lover Gino (Massimo Girotti) looks indifferently on. Note the lighting of Gino's torso and face.

Ossessione

Derek Duncan

When Luchino Visconti's first film, *Ossessione*, was released in the spring of 1943, Mussolini had been Italy's head of state for twenty years and the country had been at war for three. In the summer of that year Mussolini's fascist government would be overthrown and the country torn apart by civil war. In retrospect, it is perhaps surprising that at this point Italy still had a thriving film industry. It is estimated that in 1942 no less than 117 feature films were produced and many had been made with government support. Mussolini's government had in fact promoted the Italian film industry throughout the 1930s in a variety of ways (Wagstaff, 160–74). Legislation was introduced that offered subsidies to the most successful film-makers, the network of film distribution was re-organised to favour Italian products, and restrictions were placed on the importing of films from the United States. Other initiatives such as the setting up of the Venice Film Festival in 1934, the creation of a film school, and the building of Cinecittà, the studio facility near Rome intended to emulate Hollywood, demonstrate the commitment of the fascist regime to the industry. Overall, these measures must be judged successful in significantly increasing the number of films produced in the course of the following decade. Although fascism operated a censorship policy the regime seems to have been more concerned with developing a profitable industry than with regulating the content of specific films. In general terms, this fitted in with the fascist economic policy of 'autarchia', or self-sufficiency, which proved disastrous in some areas of the economy but seems to have given the film industry a substantial and necessary boost.

While the regime sought to limit its influence, American cinema's financial success and technical proficiency along with its audience appeal remained a model. Italian films often imitated those of the United States; light comedies and historical costume dramas were popular, and Italian film stars copied the style of their American counterparts. Until the 1970s film critics derided the films made under fascism as either escapist nonsense or propaganda. Many films of that period have been destroyed but enough remain for more recent critics to have revised this purely negative assessment. While some films such as Giovacchino Forzano's *Camicia nera* (*Black Shirt*, 1933) clearly aim to show the regime in a positive light and others such as Carmine Gallone's *Scipione l'africano* (*Scipio Africanus*, 1937) offer a thinly veiled celebration of Mussolini's imperialistic forays into Africa in the mid-1930s, the political message of most was a low-key one of social conformity (Hay, 1987; Landy, 1986). Critics have also acknowledged certain technical innovations made by these film-makers such as the use of non-professional actors and outside locations, features often thought to characterise, and to have been invented by, the more celebrated neo-realist movement of Italian cinema in the post-war period.

Some of the most vociferous advocates of an autonomous national cinema in Italy were involved with the journal *Cinema*, which attracted a number of left-wing critics despite the fact that its editor was Mussolini's son Vittorio. These critics argued for a greater level of realism in Italian cinema, an argument that on the one hand drew on contemporary Soviet and French ideas about film, but also referred back to the realist tradition in Italian literature that sought, amongst other things, to portray accurately ordinary life. They believed style and politics to be closely linked. Visconti himself became involved with this group after returning from France where he had worked as a costume designer with Jean Renoir on *Une partie de campagne* (*A Day in the Country*, 1936). He had never worked in cinema before and the collaboration with Renoir proved decisive. He visited Hollywood in 1938 and was working again with Renoir on a film version of Puccini's opera *La tosca* in Rome in 1940 when Italy entered the war on the side of Germany and the left-wing French director was forced to leave the country. Renoir's influence was crucial in another respect for he had given Visconti a copy of the novel on which his first film would be based, the thriller *The Postman Always Rings Twice* (1934) by the American writer James Cain.

Visconti's choice of an American text as the source for his film is particularly interesting because of the complex and contradictory cultural position the United States occupied in Italy in the 1930s. The United States had attracted an enormous number of Italian emigrants earlier in the century and although tight immigration controls ended that era of mass emigration many Italians still believed it to be a land of opportunity and escape from the terrible poverty that affected much of the country. Left-wing writers such as Elio Vittorini and Cesare Pavese, perhaps surprisingly, viewed the United States positively as a new nation, full of possibilities. A very different version of the American experience is offered by the fascist writer Emilio Cecchi in the screenplay of *Harlem* (1943), a film that featured Massimo Girotti, the star of *Ossessione*, as an immigrant boxer whose dream turns into a nightmare in the streets of New York. In the 1930s, however, the United States was most commonly known through its own glamorised self-portrayal in films. Claretta Petacci, Mussolini's mistress, is reported to have had an American-style kitchen, indicating the appeal of the United States at every level of society, and the extent of its integration into everyday life. Even fascist concern about the representation of Italians as mafia criminals in American cinema of the period did not seriously damage its allure.

This story of adulterous and murderous passion was not Visconti's first choice of subject however. Originally, he had wanted to make a film based on a short story by the nineteenth-century realist writer Giovanni Verga. The short story itself was based on a newspaper item about a Sicilian bandit but the script was blocked by the fascist censor. Fascist censorship of the press was not solely directed at stifling political opposition but also suppressed the reporting of aspects of contemporary Italy that might reflect badly on the regime; censorship was as much about disguising the nation as about suppression. By drawing on a source that had few obvious links with what was going on in Italy, Visconti was able to elude the censors and develop his own critique of fascism, in turn masking the reality of what is represented on screen.

Cain's novel is set in California and is a contemporary tale of fatal passion, murder, and betrayal. The story is told by Frank, a rootless drifter who happens to turn up one day at a small restaurant run by Nick, a Greek-American, and his unhappy, frustrated wife Cora. Frank and Cora begin a passionate affair and they decide to run off together. Cora, however, changes her mind, unable to abandon the financial security that Nick gives her. A chance meeting brings Frank back into her life and the murder of Nick seems the only way out of their situation. Their relationship is finally destroyed through fear and suspicion, and Frank is charged with Cora's murder after she dies in a car accident, pregnant with their child. The first person narrative/voice-over turns out to be Frank's confession from his prison cell as he awaits execution. The Italian censor probably saw little to concern him in the way Visconti re-worked this melodramatic plot. The basic elements of Cain's novel remain; Gino, a young and handsome drifter, arrives one day at the trattoria run by Bragana and his wife Giovanna. Gino and Giovanna are immediately drawn together by a passion that will lead to the murder of Bragana and ultimately to her own accidental death. Yet within this familiar structure Visconti makes some subtle but significant changes.

In retrospect, Visconti said that he had wanted to make a film that was 'absolutely Italian' and that gave the audience a 'picture of Italy'. On the most superficial level, the story's setting is changed from California to the Po Valley, in the north of Italy. The flat river landscape features prominently in the film as do the cities of Ancona and Ferrara where some of the action is shot. In this sense, the film is recognisably Italian. Nevertheless, there is perhaps little in the film to locate the events in a country marked by twenty years of fascism. No direct reference is made to the political situation nor does the viewer see any evidence of it. There are, however, less obvious intimations of fascism's presence that contribute in no small measure to the film's unsettling effect. From the beginning, Gino and Giovanna use the familiar 'tu' form of address when they talk to each other, suggesting the commanding nature of their nascent passion. Later, when they meet in Ancona, the presence of Bragana demands that they appear less intimate. Rather than resorting to the traditional 'lei' form of address employed between strangers, Gino adopts the normally plural 'voi' form promoted by the fascist regime. Such details escape a foreign audience reliant on subtitles, but are resonant of the period. Similarly, apart from a brief glimpse of uniformed children towards the film's conclusion, there is no visual evidence of a regime that cultural historians argue was heavily dependent on spectacle and public ritual for its success (Gentile, 1996).

The image of Mussolini himself, which seems to have been omnipresent in fascist Italy, is absent. He figured prominently in the newsreels that accompanied every film-showing during the 1930s. These newsreels were used as propaganda to show how fascism had improved and modernised the country, and in addition, they attempted to instil a sense of patriotism in the Italian people. Like print journalism and film, what the newsreels did not show were images of Italy that in some way undermined the regime's wholesome and heroic image of itself. These images also provide one way of understanding the effect of Visconti's film when it was shown in Italy at that time; audiences left the cinema in uproar, and local party officials, often acting with representatives of the Church, succeeded in having the film banned, even though Mussolini himself was famously unperturbed by it. Compared with the Italy usually seen on the cinema screen *Ossessione* represented another country, and even without overtly criticising the regime, the fact that unsavoury aspects of the nation such as murder and adultery were shown at all constituted a challenge to how people were allowed to see Italy. Rather than holding a mirror up to a known reality, Visconti makes the spectator look again and question what passes for reality at the cinema, and also in the fascist nation.

While the novel's basic plot is retained, certain alterations to the way it unfolds provide an implicit critique of the fascist state. A large section of Cain's book deals with the role of the police and the legal system in the administration of justice. Visconti omits the courtroom drama that is central to the novel and also gives the police a less prominent and effective role. Although they are not convinced of the accidental nature of Bragana's death in the car crash, suspecting Gino and Giovanna from the outset, they are only able to act against them when two lorry drivers, who witnessed the incident, unexpectedly turn up at the police station. Gino is arrested after the second car crash, in which the pregnant Giovanna is accidentally killed as the lovers try to flee. They are punished by ironies of fate rather than by the order of law. The absence of an effective system of order and justice is a notable element of the film. Similarly, the Church lacks any moral authority; the priest, Padre Remigio, is primarily concerned with hunting and fishing, and when he is called upon to intervene in the irregular domestic arrangements of Giovanna and Gino after Bragana's death, suggests only a feeble, albeit pragmatic, compromise to their situation. Bragana, the patriarchal figurehead, is blustering and ineffectual, impervious to the needs of his wife and the threat posed by Gino, a slave to base carnal desire and infantile pleasure. This absence of any effective form of authority is an especially challenging element of Visconti's claims to be painting an authentic picture of Italy. Fascism prided itself on having restored law and order to the country and having established a strong regime with the figure of Mussolini as its symbolic and literal embodiment of authority. Not only is the iconography of fascism missing from Visconti's film but so too are many of the values through which fascism expressed itself and its sense of the nation.

Patriotism was one of fascism's key values. For Mussolini, fascism and Italy were synonymous, and the state tried to promote a positive sense of national identity in a number of ways. Often this was done through the organisation of mass public events and spectacles, or through impressive projects of public building. The education system had a crucial role in encouraging young Italians to identify with the nation, and was the hub of the youth organisations that combined the diffusion of nationalist propaganda with the pleasures of sport and subsidised entertainment. Such projects and activities appear wholly absent from the Italy of *Ossessione*. Yet, they do receive covert acknowledgement through the treatment of Bragana. Before he appears on screen, he is heard singing (rather well) a song from Giuseppe Verdi's romantic melodrama *La traviata*. His physical appearance belies the part of romantic hero, an irony that is taken even further with the motley range of competitors at the singing competition in Ancona. Implicitly too, the work of Verdi, considered Italy's national composer because of the symbolic importance of his work during the nineteenth century before Italy unified and became independent, is cast in an ironic light. Through its association with Bragana, and the indifference to it of the other main characters, it is turned into something comic and grotesque. Only Bragana demonstrates any attachment to the Italian state as his pride in having completed his national service in the 'bersaglieri' indicates. Yet his patriotism is merely an aspect of his buffoonery and discredits rather than enhances him. In Cain's novel, Nick, the husband, is mocked because of his Greek origins; Cora from the beginning is anxious to assert her pure American identity. Visconti manages to reverse the racism of the novel by making Bragana's patriotism the butt of humour whereas Gino, Giovanna, and the minor characters, lo Spagnolo and Anita, more marginal to the Italian state, are viewed with greater sympathy.

If, on a number of levels, the absence of fascist values characterises Visconti's film, the presence of unfamiliar elements equally threatens the image of Italy framed by fascism. As a political system, fascism had enormous ambitions to intervene in and transform the lives of the Italian people. This was nowhere more apparent than in its attempts to regulate aspects of sexuality and reproduction. The imperative to reproduce was most clearly directed at women; fascism saw women as mothers, reinforcing the traditional view of the Church (De Grazia, 1992). The family as an institution was in fact the key to the nation's development. Men were uneasily positioned within fascist ideas about gender; on the one hand they too were essential to the family, yet on the other, the fascist rhetoric of virility that developed round the figure of Mussolini himself suggested a more aggressive and adventurous model of male behaviour. This type of masculinity was also a common feature in Italian films of the period; Massimo Girotti, the star of *Ossessione*, in fact found fame embodying this sort of role where the emphasis was on action and on the actor's physical, rather than acting, prowess.

One of the primary mechanisms for the diffusion of ideas about gender at this time was the cinema, but there are limits to what this tells us about men and women of the period. Rather than showing cinema audiences what men and women were really like, films contributed in very powerful ways to creating an idea of what they perhaps should be like. Recent film critics have argued that while few Italian films of the time were overtly political, they were at their most reactionary in their portrayal of women. Women who obeyed society's rules were rewarded with a successful marriage and a happy family life whereas more independently minded women were invariably punished in some way. In this the Italian cinema of the period was noticeably more conservative than that of Hollywood, which did allow its female protagonists some measure of freedom (Landy, 72–117).

Visconti's film proposes representations of gender which were very different from those that commonly circulated under fascism; the manner in which the film is shot, the unfolding of the film's plot, and the casting of the actors, all contribute to an erosion of one of fascism's fundamental set of beliefs. The married couple so central to fascist ideology is parodied by the sham of Giovanna's relationship with Bragana. She married him to escape a life of poverty and semi-prostitution only to find herself trapped by the tyranny of domesticity and an old man whom she finds physically repellent. She abhors the idea of bearing his children but is trapped by her own need for the security he offers. If Giovanna is self-serving, Bragana is an oafish bully as far removed from the role of staunch patriarch as she is from that of loyal wife. Giovanna is immediately drawn to the handsome stranger, whose difference from her husband is quickly established; she comments at once on Gino's muscular body, underlining his desirability compared with her husband and drawing attention to the fact that it is Gino's body that will be on display throughout the film.

The casting of Clara Calamai and Massimo Girotti as Giovanna and Gino is very significant of the ways in which Visconti plays with accepted representations of gender. Both were established stars; Calamai was best known for playing the femme fatale in historical costume dramas and bourgeois comedies; as already noted, Girotti, a former swimming star, had starred in action and adventure movies. Calamai was also famous for being the first woman in Italian cinema to appear topless in a film, *La cena delle beffe (Joker's Banquet)* (1941). Her star persona was glamorous and sophisticated and she was not Visconti's first choice for the part. In *Ossessione*, however, she plays a character who goes against audience expectations of the familiar image of the female star. Here she is a working woman, worn down by a life of hardship and deprivation. Until she inherits Bragana's money, she appears down-at-heel and dishevelled. Her clothes are old and slightly grubby. After working hard all day in the trattoria she collapses exhausted, too tired to eat the plate of pasta she prepares for herself. Italian audiences were not used to seeing a star like Calamai stripped of her glamour. Visconti's exploitation of the ten-year age gap between the two stars also accentuated the dowdy desperation of her performance. Her acting style too contributes in no small measure to the effect of the film. Although the film contains many realistic elements it draws equally generously on the popular Italian tradition of melodrama. Calamai plays Giovanna in the style of a diva of the silent screen, a grand theatrical rather than smaller-scale cinematic style of performance – her exaggerated eye movements towards the camera point to a world beyond her tawdry provincial existence. Calamai herself was very distressed when she first saw herself in the role and it took her some time before realising how her unglamorous appearance added to her performance, and to the film's power.

The physicality of Girotti is as important however. In the opening scene, the bodily difference between the young, handsome Gino and the older, fatter Bragana, is immediately established. Gino is also more quick-witted and less self-satisfied. However, in some respects Bragana, initially at least, remains more attractive to Giovanna. On account of his relative wealth, he stands for security whereas, for his wife, Gino represents the precarious life she knew before. This is why she abandons their initial attempt to flee, preferring the material comfort her husband can provide to the erotic sustenance offered by Gino. Later, she sees the fulfilment of her passion for Gino in running the trattoria, but he resists such domestic confinement; the tension between freedom and the imprisonment by conventional ideals structures the film.

Gender and politics are thoroughly enmeshed in *Ossessione*. After Giovanna returns to her husband, Gino meets, again by chance, a character known only as lo Spagnolo (the Spaniard). He is the only character who has no parallel in the novel and originally, as is suggested by a name that alludes to the Spanish Civil War, was meant to embody the voice of socialism and personal freedom. Like Gino, he appears to be a drifter and they meet when he offers to pay the penniless Gino's train fare. They become friends, largely at lo Spagnolo's behest, and go on the road together until Gino's chance encounter with Bragana and Giovanna at a fair in Ancona. Most critics see lo Spagnolo as homosexual and even misogynist, for he tries to convince Gino that there is more to life than chasing after women. Yet perhaps it might be more tellingly argued that his attack is less on women as such than on a specific style of heterosexuality popularised under fascism, promoting the interests of the lower middle classes by means of the regulation of sexuality and reproduction. He contrasts with Giovanna, who accepts these values not because she is a woman, but because she identifies with certain class interests. This becomes clearest when she collects Bragana's life assurance policy; although she claims ignorance of its existence, Gino suspects that she used him as an accomplice. Her claims lack credibility because early in the film Bragana had referred to a document which would provide for her after he was gone, a fairly clear reference to the policy. This suggestion of betrayal has also been attributed to lo Spagnolo who is seen, at one point, in the police station. The episode is obscure yet it does not lead directly to the arrest of the couple, which occurs only after the chance arrival of the truck drivers and the second fatal accident. That Giovanna also contrasts with Anita, the dancer/prostitute whom Gino meets in Ancona, further indicates that Visconti does not simply associate femininity and heterosexuality with confinement, and male homosexuality with freedom. Unlike Giovanna, Anita gives herself freely and asks nothing in return, in sharp contrast to Giovanna who represents not femininity but the material values of a fascist lower middle class.

This tension between freedom and confinement also emerges through Visconti's treatment of space. He uses exterior shots (notably in Ancona where Gino and lo Spagnolo sit smoking on the sea wall, and later when Giovanna and Gino fall asleep on the beach) to indicate an absence of constraint and the positive enjoyment of the natural world. The ill-lit, dingy trattoria resonates with the claustrophobia of Giovanna's desires and Bragana's ignorant mean-spiritedness, a comment on the Italy that the two represent.

Such contrasts form a structure within which the narrative develops; the meaning of events emerges from the play of oppositions as much as through any narrative logic or motivation. Everything centres round the figure of Gino who does little to initiate events. His past is never fully explained and he remains enigmatic throughout the film, a screen onto which other people can project their fantasies. For most of the film it is Giovanna's desire that drives the plot. She sees Gino as someone who can rescue her from her predicament. After they make love for the first time, she describes the horror of her marriage to Gino, yet only the spectators are listening to her for he has ears solely for the sound of distant waves in a seashell he picks up in her bedroom, as she goes on to orchestrate the plan first to leave her husband and then to kill him. Similarly, she wants to stay and run the trattoria whereas all Gino wants to do is take the money and run. In the episodes involving lo Spagnolo and Anita, Gino again appears as a blank screen onto which they project their own desires.

In many respects, Gino is constructed by how others see him. This is best illustrated by the different ways in which he is seen by Giovanna and Bragana and how they interpret what they see as it suits them. Bragana sees Gino's tattered clothes and his muscular body as symptomatic of his status as a vagrant used to physical labour. For Giovanna, his physical vigour represents all that her husband lacks and he is immediately seen as an escape route. Bragana fails to see the threat Gino poses, and Giovanna fails to see that Gino cannot offer her the security she prizes more than anything. When, later in the film, Gino fails to live up to what lo Spagnolo sees in him the episode erupts into violence. Violence is in fact the end result of the failure to see the reality behind fantasy. Bragana and Giovanna both die violent deaths; the relationship between Gino and Giovanna had become violent in the wake of their mutual suspicion and resentment. That the problem of looking is an integral part of the film is suggested by the opening credit sequence shot from the front seat of the truck carrying Gino to the trattoria and accompanied by archetypally dramatic *film noir* music. Yet it is not Gino who is looking; he is hidden, asleep on the back. The significance of this shot emerges only late in the film when the police discover that the crime committed by Gino and Giovanna has been witnessed from the cab of a truck.

The suggestion that Gino is looked at yet never really seen is supported by the way the film is both shot and narrated. In the American version of the film, Frank (John Garfield) is also the film's narrator. His voice-over replicates the first person narrative of the novel. Everything is told and largely seen from his perspective. When we first see Cora (Lana Turner) it is from his point of view and the spectator shares his gaze as his eyes gradually move up her body to take in the effect of her statuesque and overwhelming glamour. This is almost an exact reversal of the parallel scene in *Ossessione*. At the beginning of the film, Gino is discovered hiding on the truck that pulls into Bragana's trattoria. In the exchange that follows between him, Bragana, and the truck drivers his face remains hidden. He enters the trattoria and the camera follows him from behind as far as the kitchen where Giovanna sits painting her nails. As she looks up in irritation and then desire, the camera angle changes and for the first time the spectator sees Gino sharing Giovanna's angle of vision. It is Gino, not Giovanna, whose body is the focus of the camera's gaze. Most often, it is his body that is lit in the scenes both with Giovanna and with lo Spagnolo. He tends to appear supine while the others (including the spectators) do the looking. This is clearly the case in the first bedroom scene with Giovanna where he sprawls languidly on the bed while she delineates her determination to alter a situation that has become untenable. Just as Gino does nothing to advance the plot, so too is he passive in front of the camera. Later when Gino is sharing a hotel room with lo Spagnolo, lo Spagnolo lights a match after the light has been switched out, the effect of which is to illuminate Gino's body. Gino's head is turned away from the camera; he is purely the object of the gaze. Throughout the film Girotti's torso and his torn vest are familiar sights and the camera lingers on them rather than on the body of the female star.

The prominence of Girotti's body poses a problem for critics. Some contend that it is simply a symptom of Visconti's homosexuality, and use the same argument to explain what they see as the rough treatment of Calamai. This view fails to pay due attention to the complexity and conventionality of how bodies are seen in the cinema, and is reductive in its assessment of how sexuality and artistic production might be linked. By inverting the spectator's expectations of what men and women usually look like on screen, Visconti successfully challenges commonplace ideas about gender. In particular he contests the very powerful ideals about gender roles and identity that circulated under fascism and found expression in Italian cinema in the 1930s and 1940s. He also, however, reveals something about how the technology of cinema encourages spectators to look at bodies in a certain way. It is in their effect on the spectator that Girotti and his vest are most disturbing for they constitute improper objects of desire in a medium that depends on the stability offered by the heterosexual, male gaze.

Ossessione is often viewed in terms of its contribution to how cinema developed after the war in Italy, yet spectators in the 1940s clearly could not see it in those terms, but they could appreciate how it differed from other films of the period. On one level Visconti's film works as a *film noir*, yet behind the melodrama the spectator can discern a cultural specificity that compels a historical reading. Visconti's film may not nowadays seem to be about fascism at all let alone to present an attack on it. However, *Ossessione* offered an alternative view of marriage and family life to the one familiar from fascist ideology, and also proposed a different sexual economy to that familiar from other films. This second point is important for it underlines the extent to which Visconti adapted cinematic conventions of the time. The values of American cinema and culture inhabited those of Italy under fascism, albeit always in concealed form. While directors in Italy had previously looked to the United States in order to imitate the models it offered, Visconti uses American culture as a malleable resource through which to articulate his own political critique. He transposes the darker, less optimistic face of the United States into an Italian context and shows the audience aspects of Italy that fascism pretended did not exist. Visconti's film re-works the cinematic forms of his time and as a consequence proposes new ways through which to represent the nation.

References

De Grazia, Victoria 1992: *How Fascism Ruled Women*. Berkeley, CA: University of California Press.
Gentile, Emilio 1996: *The Sacralization of Politics in Fascist Italy*. Translated by Keith Botsford. Cambridge, MA and London: Harvard University Press.
Hay, James 1987: *Popular Film Culture in Italy: The Passing of the Rex*. Bloomington, IN: Indiana University Press.
Landy, Marcia 1986: *Fascism in Film: The Italian Commercial Cinema, 1931–1943*. Princeton, NJ: Princeton University Press.
Wagstaff, Christopher 1984: 'The Italian Film Industry during the Fascist Regime'. In *The Italianist*, 4, 160–74.

Suggestions for Further Reading

Bacon, Henry 1998: *Visconti: Explorations of Vision and Decay*. Cambridge: Cambridge University Press.
Hay, James 1987: *Popular Film Culture in Italy: The Passing of the Rex*. Bloomington, IN: Indiana University Press.
Landy, Marcia 1986: *Fascism in Film: The Italian Commercial Cinema, 1931–1943*. Princeton, NJ: Princeton University Press.

Nowell Smith, Geoffrey 1967: *Luchino Visconti*. London: Secker and Warburg.
Overby, David (ed.) 1978: *Springtime in Italy: A Reader on Neo-Realism*. London: Talisman.
Sorlin, Pierre 1996: *Italian National Cinema, 1896–1996*. London and New York: Routledge.
Tonetti, Claretta 1987: *Luchino Visconti*. London: Columbus Books.
Wagstaff, Christopher 1984: 'The Italian Film Industry during the Fascist Regime'. In *The Italianist*, 4, 160–74.

Credits

Director	Luchino Visconti
Producer	Libero Solaroli
Production Company	Industrie Cinematografiche Italiane
Screenplay	Luchino Visconti. Mario Alicata, Giuseppe de Santis, Gianni Puccini
Director of Photography	Aldo Tonti, Domenico Scala
Editor	Mario Serandrei
Art Director	Gino Franzi
Music	Giuseppe Rosati

Cast

Clara Calamai	Giovanna
Massimo Girotti	Gino
Juan De Landa	Bragana
Dhia Cristiani	Anita
Elio Marcuzzo	Lo Spagnolo

Filmography

Ossessione (The Postman Always Rings Twice, 1942)
La terra trema [The Earth Trembles] (1948)
Bellissima (1951)
Senso (The Wanton Countess / Summer Storm, 1954)
Le notti bianche (White Nights / Sleepless Nights, 1957)
Rocco e i suoi fratelli (Rocco and his Brothers, 1960)
Il gattopardo (The Leopard, 1962)
Vaghe stelle dell'orsa (Sandra, 1964)
Lo straniero (The Outsider, 1967)
La caduta degli Dei (The Damned, 1969)
Morte a Venezia (Death in Venice, 1971)
Ludwig (1972)
Gruppo di famiglia in un interno (Conversation Piece, 1974)
L'innocente (The Innocent / The Intruder, 1976)

As co-director:

Siamo donne (*We, Women*, 1952)
Giorni di gloria [Days of Glory] (1945)
Boccaccio '70 (1962)
Le streghe (*The Witches*, 1966)

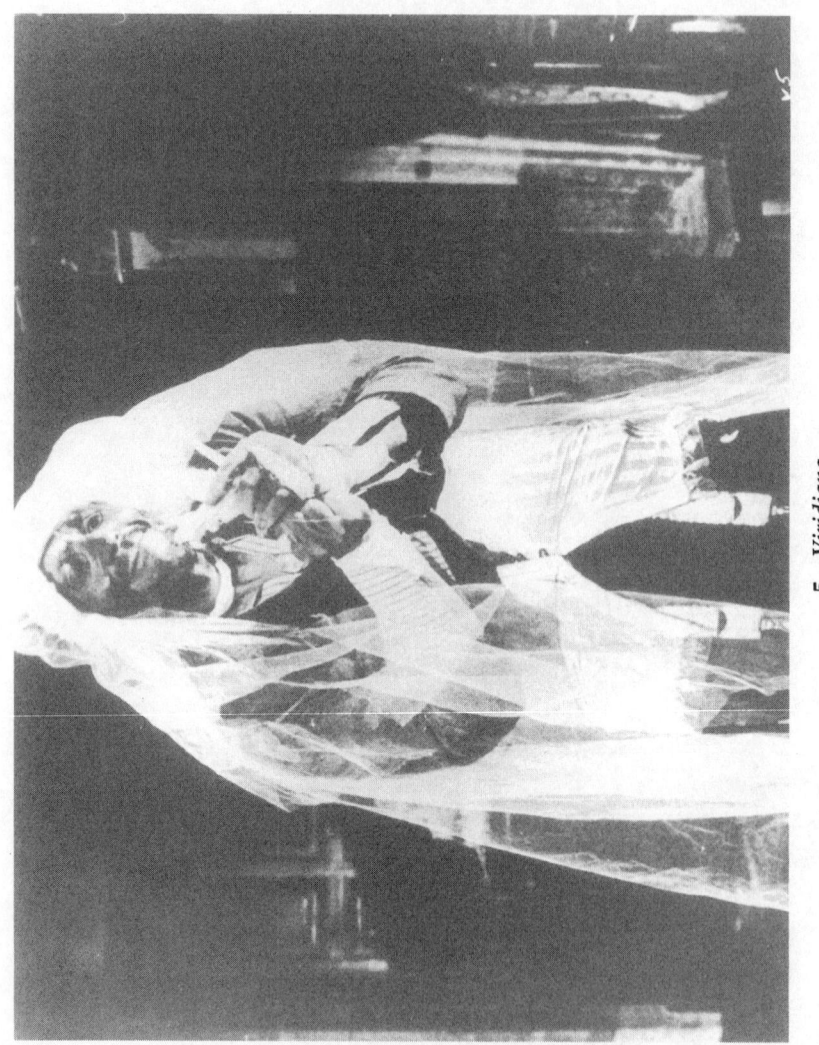

5 *Viridiana*
During the beggars' feast, the leper (Juan García Tienda) dresses in the bridal clothes of Don Jaime's dead wife and caresses a dead dove.

Viridiana

Annella McDermott

Derek Malcolm, the former film critic of the *Guardian*, chose *Viridiana* as one of the hundred great films of the twentieth century on the grounds that it 'caused the maximum annoyance to the type of people one is always glad to see offended' (*Guardian Supplement*, 1 April 1999, 12). It certainly gave great offence to the Franco government in Spain, where it was filmed in 1961 but promptly banned. It was, in fact, first released in New York in 1962, and was not seen in Spain until after the death of Franco in 1975, by which time it had been widely exhibited and was considered a classic, elsewhere in Europe and across the world. The film is a savage critique of the kind of right-wing Catholicism on which Franco's regime was based. The Spanish Civil War of 1936–9, one of the key historical events of the twentieth century – together with the Second World War, which it prefigured – began with a military uprising against the Republican government, and ended with the victory of right-wing authoritarian forces, led by Franco, who was to remain in power for the next thirty-six years. The Francoist state was anti-democratic, and opposed both to capitalism, which it considered materialist and decadent, and to communism. Basic freedoms were heavily curtailed; there were no political parties; all the media were subject to tight censorship; the Catholic Church exercised a great deal of influence, particularly through its privileged role in secondary education; laws had to conform to Catholic teaching, so that there was no divorce, for example, nor free access to contraception or abortion. Although Spain remained neutral during the Second World War, it was clear that the regime's sympathies lay with the fascist powers and, with their defeat, Spain found itself in an isolated position throughout the late 1940s and early 1950s.

Luis Buñuel, the director of *Viridiana*, was profoundly marked by the political events outlined above, which definitively altered his life and his directing career by forcing him into exile. Buñuel was born in 1900 into a wealthy middle-class family. His mother was a pious Catholic and Buñuel was educated until the age of eighteen by Jesuits. His early experience was of a highly traditional society, as he notes in his memoirs: 'In my own village of Calanda... the Middle Ages lasted until the First World War. It was a closed and isolated society, with clear and unchanging distinctions among the classes. The respectful subordination of the peasants to the big landowners was deeply rooted in tradition and seemed unshakeable' (Buñuel, 1984, 8). However, he moved for his University education to Madrid, where he lived from 1917 to 1925 in a college known for its liberal ideas, the *Residencia de estudiantes*, and met several other young men who would become radical figures in the intellectual life of Spain in the 1920s and early 1930s, particularly the poet Federico García Lorca and the painter Salvador Dalí. Buñuel developed an interest in film during a subsequent stay in France, and in 1929 he made a short film with Dalí, *Un chien andalou* (*An Andalusian Dog*, 1928), financed by Buñuel's mother.

This film, and a second film made in collaboration with Dalí, *L'âge d'or* (1930), are examples of surrealist cinema. Surrealism placed a high value on the products of the unconscious, as opposed to the conscious mind, giving great importance to intuition, dreams, trances, sleep-walking and other apparent manifestations of unconscious impulses, and being highly critical of the repression of these impulses by conventional morality, religion, or the institutions of the state. Buñuel writes with passion in his memoirs about the importance of his contact with surrealism, going so far as to say that it changed his life (Buñuel, 1984, 123).

Buñuel was invited by the Spanish Republican government in 1936 to work on their behalf in Paris, and he remained there until 1937, when he left for the United States. Like many intellectuals sympathetic to the Republic, Buñuel chose not to live in Francoist Spain, and he settled initially in the United States, then later in Mexico.

Spain's post-war isolation was attenuated by a Concordat signed with the Vatican in 1953, an agreement with the United States allowing the establishment of US military bases in Spain in 1955, and towards the end of the decade by a desire on the part of the regime itself to seek closer relations with the rest of Europe, which led to some flexibility in areas such as censorship in the arts. This explains why Buñuel, a prominent opponent of the regime, was able to take up an invitation from some young Spanish directors to shoot a film there in 1961.

Viridiana is a merciless attack on a certain kind of Roman Catholicism, one that expresses relative contempt for the needs of the body, as opposed to those of the spirit, and advocates the practice of charity as a remedy for poverty. Viridiana is an orphan, a novice in a convent, who shortly before taking her final vows is invited to visit her uncle, Don Jaime, whom she hardly knows, but who has paid for her education and maintenance and has provided the dowry which the families of wealthy aspirant nuns donated to the order which they would enter. Though reluctant to leave the convent, Viridiana is persuaded by her Mother Superior to agree to her uncle's request. From the moment of her arrival at his run-down estate, Viridiana's uncle shows a great interest in her, which is contrasted with the indifference, bordering on contempt, that she shows towards him. In the scene immediately preceding Viridiana's arrival there is a suggestion that Don Jaime is a sensualist, since he is shown gazing in pleasure at the legs of a little girl who is skipping with a rope he has given her. Viridiana, on the other hand, repeatedly shows distrust and fear of her own and other bodies.

As Viridiana and her uncle walk towards the house, he comments, to her evident displeasure, on her resemblance to his dead wife, her aunt. During

Viridiana's first night in his home, he is shown playing a piece of classical music on a small organ in his sitting-room, intercut with shots of the young woman undressing in her bedroom. Viridiana is played by a Mexican actress, Silvia Pinal, whose physical appearance is far removed from the classic dark Spanish type of beauty. She is blonde, pale and somewhat ethereal: as she rolls down her black stockings, we have a brightly-lit close-up of her long, smooth, white legs. The next shot shows Don Jaime, still playing his music, with a dreamy expression on his face. The maid, Ramona, who has peeped through Viridiana's keyhole, reports to Don Jaime that the young novice has prepared her bed on the floor, that she appears to have a crown of thorns in her suitcase, and is wearing a night-dress of very rough cloth; we then see Viridiana praying on her knees in her room, followed by a close-up of a cushion on which are laid the crown of thorns previously referred to, nails, a hammer and a sponge. For a Catholic, particularly a Spanish Catholic of the time, there was a perfectly acceptable, pious reason for the contemplation of these objects – to be reminded that Christ suffered on the Cross in order to redeem mankind (the hammer representing the one used to drive the nails into Christ's hands and the sponge being a reference to the sponge soaked in gall which was offered when Christ asked for water). However, for an audience distanced to some extent from this kind of religious practice, the bizarre appearance of these objects in a young woman's bedroom, and their juxtaposition with Viridiana's pale, vulnerable body, clearly carry the suggestion that Catholicism invites masochism by its insistence on repression and mortification of the body.

A related idea is suggested in a scene set on the morning following Viridiana's arrival, which begins with a close-up of a male farmworker's hand grasping a cow's teat, which has a comical resemblance to a flaccid penis. Viridiana is persuaded to try milking the cow, but she is clearly repelled by the feel of the teat in her hand and cannot milk effectively, even when the farmworker encourages her by clasping his hand around hers and urging her to pull hard at the teat and squeeze. Because the screenplay emphasises the fact that the farmhand is oblivious to the reason for Viridiana's squeamishness, it seems that Buñuel is suggesting that through Catholicism's attempts to suppress the practical realities of the body, perverse notions of transgression are introduced into otherwise innocent activities (Buñuel, 1969, 10).

The importance of surrealism to Buñuel's early film career has already been mentioned. Most commentators see its influence in this film also. Gwynne Edwards, for example, examines some statements by Buñuel about the lack of conscious planning of the film and concludes:

> Buñuel's account of the film's birth and development is one which, stressing its natural and spontaneous evolution and his own instinctive feeling for certain associations, juxtapositions and contrasts, underlines the importance he has always given, in his life as well as in his art, to impulse and the expression of the unconscious freed from the constraints of reason and moral dictates.

To this extent *Viridiana* is as much a product of surrealism as *Un chien andalou* and *L'âge d'or*.   (Edwards, 145)

This refers, of course, to the creative process. In relation to the film itself, there are a number of sequences that could be considered surrealist. In the sleep-walking scene, Viridiana carries out an enigmatic series of actions, entering the sitting-room, throwing her knitting on the fire and putting ashes from the fire into her work-basket, which she then takes to Don Jaime's bedroom, where she sprinkles the ashes on the bed. When Don Jaime tells her of the incident the next day, Viridiana interprets it by recourse to religious symbolism: ashes, she says, mean penitence and death (and this does foreshadow later events in the film). However, an audience familiar with Freudian ideas will readily see the sleep-walking as a symptom of repression or guilt, and will probably interpret her actions to mean that she has some feelings with regard to her uncle, which she has consciously ignored, but which express themselves when her unconscious impulses take over in the state of somnambulism. Despite her orthodox interpretation of her actions, she appears to be embarrassed by her conduct while asleep.

Don Jaime's behaviour also displays some bizarre elements. He has kept his dead wife's bridal clothes in a chest, and we see him get these out and try them on – a white satin high-heeled shoe that he perches on the end of his own huge foot, and a corset which he wraps round his own body, this ceremony being lent an air of sublimity by the music of Beethoven's *Ninth Symphony* issuing from his gramophone. Later, he tells Viridiana that her aunt died in his arms of a heart attack, still wearing those clothes, on their wedding night, hence his desire to see Viridiana dress in them, which she reluctantly agrees to do. Don Jaime is a fetishist whose erotic attention has become focused on these items of clothing, and when he asks Viridiana to marry him, we take it that his principal incentive is her strong physical resemblance to her dead aunt, whence her ability to transport him back to his wedding night by dressing in the bridal clothes. He is so obsessed by this possibility that when Viridiana indignantly turns him down, he enlists the help of his servant Ramona to drug Viridiana so that he can prolong the illusion of having his wife back. There is a suggestion, too, of necrophilia, as we see him arrange the unconscious young woman into the image of a corpse, with hands crossed on her breast as though prepared for viewing and burial. The screenplay indicates that he 'begins to perfect his masterpiece' with 'an artist's meticulousness' (Buñuel, 1969, 30). However, Don Jaime's fetishism and necrophilia are not blamed on religion; they are the product of the particular circumstances of his wife's death and the sensuality that is part of his character, and the audience may well find his behaviour touching.

There is some ambiguity in Buñuel's attitude to sexual repression. The main theme of the film is that sexual repression is unnatural and produces frigidity, distance and even cruelty in human relationships. On the other hand, the use of music in connection with sexual yearning, in both the scene in which Don Jaime plays the organ, and the scene of his handling his dead wife's clothes, seems to allude to the theory of sublimation – that art is the product of a displacement of sexual energy into another activity, and may thus be viewed as a positive outcome arising from repression. Buñuel also mentions in his memoirs the role of prohibition as a stimulus:

> I've often wondered why Catholicism has such a horror of sexuality. To be sure, there are countless theological, historical and moral reasons; but it seems to me that in a rigidly hierarchical society, sex – which respects no barriers and obeys no laws – can at any moment become an agent of chaos. I suppose that's why some Church Fathers, Saint Thomas Aquinas amongst them, were so severe in their dealings with the disturbing aspects of the flesh. . . . Ironically, this implacable prohibition inspired a feeling of sin which for me was positively voluptuous. (Buñuel, 1984, 14)

Don Jaime does not rape the unconscious Viridiana, although he is tempted to do so, and the next morning he initially pretends to her that he did, in order to try to prevent her from returning to her convent. When he sees the look of hatred on her face he confesses the truth, and hangs himself, presumably out of remorse, after she has left. However, before he does so he composes a document, which we will later realise is his will, in which he leaves his estate jointly to Viridiana and his illegitimate son Jorge. As he takes up his pen, he smiles and strokes his beard, a gesture which indicates he has thought of an amusing plan. We assume later that he realised that Viridiana would feel unable to take her vows when she learned of his suicide, and would come to live on the estate alongside Jorge. It is never made clear to us whether Don Jaime's pleasure in this prospect was malicious. His smile during the writing of the will may have been vengeful, or it may simply have indicated that he foresaw a positive outcome, as does Buñuel, to the enforced cohabitation of Viridiana and Jorge.

The film's critique of the practice of charity is mainly developed in the middle section, which deals with Viridiana withdrawing from the convent, and setting up a refuge for beggars on her dead uncle's estate. Buñuel's depiction of the beggars is resolutely unsentimental in that he rejects any idea that they are individuals who have been ennobled by poverty and suffering. They are sharply practical: when one of the women comments that Viridiana is a very good person, another woman replies: 'Very good but a bit of a simpleton' (Buñuel, 1969, 48). They are also cruel to each other, as shown by the blind beggar striking the bald one with his stick when the latter's intemperate language looks likely to jeopardize Viridiana's offer of charity. They show no charity towards the leper, as they call him, pretending to accept him while Viridiana is present but pulling a knife on him when she leaves, so that he has to go and sleep outside. He himself, while protesting to Viridiana that the sores on his arms are due to varicose veins, is evidently convinced that they are the result of a venereal disease, and he is accused by one of his companions of deliberately placing his arm in the holy water font in church with the aim of infecting others. Incidentally, the role of the leper is not played by an actor, but by a real beggar, and another of the beggars is played by a lottery-ticket seller. When Jorge, Viridiana, Ramona and the child have to go into town, leaving the beggars in charge of the house, the dialogue points up the brutality of the beggars' lives. The blind man urges Enedina to shut up her crying child, and she asks: 'You'd like me to kill them?', to receive the reply from another beggar: 'With the life that's ahead of them they'd be better off being sent to Paradise' (Buñuel, 1969, 84). At one point the blind man boasts of having turned in to the police a fellow-beggar who tried to cheat him out of his share of the day's takings. Sexual relationships among the beggars are portrayed as promiscuous and coarse.

It seems likely that Buñuel was a member of the Communist Party in the 1930s. John Baxter discusses the evidence in some detail and concludes that he was a Party member, probably from 1929 to at least 1945 (Baxter, 130–1). The depiction of the beggars in *Viridiana*, and the sceptical attitude the film displays towards charity as a response to poverty, have led many to see *Viridiana* as a communist film. Emilio G. Riera writes, for example: 'The beggars are monstrous because of their depraved profanity. Once and for all, Buñuel destroys the myth of purity cloaked in rags (which clearly identifies him with a Marxist line of thought)' (Riera, in Mellen, 222).

Buñuel clearly dislikes the paternalistic relationship charity establishes between donor and recipient. Viridiana is aware of the danger of spiritual pride inherent in her adoption of the beggars, as she shows by discouraging any compliments to the effect that she has the face of an angel. Yet she feels entitled to control the beggars' lives in return for her charity, separating the sexes and announcing that they are all to work (news which is greeted by a superb comic double-take from one of the beggars). There is a suggestion, too, that charity arises from a situation of privilege. Although Viridiana appears to have been virtually brought up in a convent, her manners are bourgeois. An example of this is the scene in which we see her hands in close-up, peeling the skin from an apple in one continuous strip, for in Spain, where fresh fruit is often served at the end of a meal, the ability to deal in a refined manner with skin and pips is a class marker. Unlike Viridiana, Moncho, the estate overseer, openly loathes and despises the beggars, and even Ramona's little girl, Rita, taunts the beggars with the fact that they are not to sleep in the house, but in the outbuildings, with the chickens. The beggars, for their part, despise Moncho because he is a servant. One beggar, told that in return for charity he must exercise self-restraint and humility, decides that he would rather take his chances elsewhere. He still asks for a handout, but only, as he remarks, because he is poor, that is to say, if he had the choice he would not submit to this indignity. The invasion of the house while the family is away demonstrates the naivety of Viridiana's assumption that the beggars will be content with a roof over their heads, plain food and hard work. On the contrary, they like lace tablecloths, porcelain, silver, roast lamb and good wine, just like everyone else, and help themselves to these luxuries at the first opportunity.

It is not, however, only Christian charity that is attacked in the film, but religious belief itself. One of the most famous scenes from the film is the freeze-frame when the beggars pose as though for a photograph. The composition of the shot imitates Leonardo's depiction of *The Last Supper*, with the blind man in the centre, like Christ, and the beggars grouped around him like the Apostles. The meaning of this parallel would seem to be that the goodness and altruism symbolised in the Last Supper are contradicted by the brutality and degradation of the lives of the destitute on earth. Depicting Christ as blind, a notion used again by Buñuel in his later film *La voie lactée* (*The Milky Way*, 1968), would seem to imply that there is an essential 'blindness' at the heart of Christian belief, which points up the principal theme of the film, Viridiana's awakening to reality from the dream or illusion of faith. The crucifix which conceals a knife-blade, found by Jorge among his dead uncle's possessions, seems to mock Christianity's claim to be a religion of peace. The beggars' orgy culminates in the leper's grotesque dance, dressed in Don Jaime's dead wife's corset and veil, during which he scatters feathers from the white dove we saw him capture earlier and which he has clearly killed. The importance of a white dove as a Christian icon hardly needs emphasising. Moreover, the dance is performed to the accompaniment of the Hallelujah Chorus from Handel's *Messiah*, a contrast which again appears to suggest that there is a radical incompatibility between the sublime beauty of religious music and the real behaviour of human beings, particularly those leading deprived lives.

It would be oversimplifying the film, however, to see it as providing a crude contrast between the religious impulse and reality, and forcing the audience to prefer the latter to the former. At one point, Buñuel uses a series of alternating shots of Viridiana and the beggars murmuring the Angelus under some almond trees, and workmen mixing cement, sawing planks, piling logs, and tipping stones out of a wheelbarrow. Clearly, the editing here aims to establish a contrast between Jorge's worldly practicality and Viridiana's adherence to ritual. For a Spanish audience, accustomed to a debate on tradition versus modernity that goes back to writers of the eighteenth and nineteenth centuries, the dry, dusty landscape of the neglected estate could easily be read as a metaphor for Spain itself, with Viridiana embodying archaic, obscurantist religious beliefs, and Jorge representing progressive modernity. Yet it is not entirely clear that the audience will find the scenes of construction more appealing than the prayers, murmured against a background of almond blossom. Moreover, although Viridiana strikes us in the first part of the film as cold and remote, this feeling vanishes in the second part, in which she is more relaxed and more appealing to the audience.

Jorge, in any case, suffers from his own form of blindness. He rescues a dog which has been tied to the back axle of a cart, but turns away and so m sight, clear to the audience, of another dog in exactly the same situatio a few seconds later, illustrating the point he himself made earlier to Viridiana, that charity extended to individuals is a drop in the ocean compared with the numbers of the deprived and abused. Nevertheless, his pragmatic attitude to human motivation enables him to save Viridiana from being raped when they return to the house and interrupt the beggars' dinner, by bribing the leper to knock out her assailant. It is clear, too, that Viridiana knows that she was overcome and would have been raped if it had not been for Jorge. We understand that this experience brings her face to face with the reality of human sexual impulses and causes the veil of illusion to fall from her eyes, so that she subsequently seeks out Jorge, presumably to initiate a sexual relationship with him.

Jorge is handsome, energetic, full of curiosity, laid-back and tolerant in his attitudes (and he is played by Francisco Rabal, one of Spain's most popular and attractive actors). Yet some doubt has been cast over the character earlier in the film, in a scene where he and the servant Ramona end up making love in the attic and where Buñuel uses an uncharacteristic metaphorical montage, involving a cat leaping on a mouse, to suggest that he is rapacious. When Viridiana goes to his room, at the end of the film, he is listening to a record of a song with English-language lyrics whose banality constitutes an ironic comment on the accommodation to reality that will presumably take the place of Viridiana's religious philosophy: 'Shake, baby, shake, shake your cares away'. There is a certain sadness for the audience in watching defiant illusion giving way to a resigned acceptance of reality. Viewers more sensitised to feminist issues than Buñuel or his audience in the early 1960s may also feel uneasy with the notion of attempted rape as the agent of Viridiana's liberation, or wonder why facing reality has to involve a sexual relationship with a man, particularly Jorge. Celibacy born of fear or distrust of the body is clearly negative, but celibacy freely chosen is an option modern audiences might like to see offered to the former nun.

Viridiana was Spain's entry at the Cannes Film Festival in 1961. It won the Golden Palm but was subsequently attacked as blasphemous and sacrilegious and banned in Spain, thus creating the unusual situation of a country refusing to screen a film which had won for it the most prestigious international prize in cinema. A number of commentators argued that the use of the term 'blasphemous' was inappropriate, because the film was the work of an atheist. This was the view taken by Riera in the context of Buñuel's Marxism: 'Not once does this movie-maker deride or insult God, which would be tantamount to acknowledging His existence. Buñuel never discusses God. What he discusses is man's conception of God, thereby revealing the strange, unpredictable role that religion plays in the subconscious of his characters' (Riera, in Mellen, 220).

Some Catholic critics argued, even around the time the film was made, that Buñuel was attacking attitudes and practices that were no longer current. An article first published in 1962 cites the view of a progressive Catholic layman, Jean Carta:

Whether the spectator is Catholic or not, he will be hard put to recognize the social doctrine of the Church in the actions of [this illuminated creature].... It will be even harder if one is aware of the immense current of social Christianity which has come into being and daily grown stronger during the last several decades... in this movement, a spirit of charity without lucidity, without the value of a collective perspective, without political commitment, cannot suffice. The half-blind bigotry, the absence of common-sense which Buñuel attributes to... the devout Viridiana, reign still, perhaps, in certain sectors of the Spanish Church, the most archaic in Europe, but it certainly does not pertain to the militant church around us.... *Viridiana* comes too late to convince us. (Seguin, in Mellen, 231)

In any case the attack on religion is unlikely to be a theme of major interest to the more secular audience, outside and inside Spain, of today. On the other hand, and perhaps rather unexpectedly, in the period since the 1960s, the sight of beggars, once confined to the 'backward' regions of Europe, has become commonplace in all our cities, and the concept of charity is once more a subject of debate.

Formally, *Viridiana* remains an intensely captivating film. Buñuel wrote the scenario himself, in collaboration with a young Spanish writer, Julio Alejandro. It is a highly literary script, reminiscent, for a Spanish audience, of the work of Spain's great nineteenth-century novelist Benito Pérez Galdós, both in its themes and in the rich, rather archaic, colloquial language given to the beggars. There are echoes too of the Spanish sixteenth- and seventeenth-century picaresque novel, in the depiction of the lives of beggars and tricksters; and Viridiana's awakening to reality from the illusion of religious belief is a modern reversal of a theme of awakening from delusion into belief that goes back to Spanish drama of the sixteenth and seventeenth centuries. Although these echoes are less evident to non-Spanish audiences, the latter will readily appreciate the pace and economy of the narration and, even through subtitling, the telling irony of much of the dialogue. The overall ironies of the theme are underlined by the repetition of visual details: the skipping-rope with the phallic wooden handles that we first see in the hands of Ramona's little girl, is the rope with which Don Jaime hangs himself, and is then used as a belt to hold up his trousers by the beggar who attempts to rape Viridiana. The shots of Ramona's legs and feet as she skips are echoed by Don Jaime's as he works the pedals of the harmonium, Viridiana's legs and feet as she rolls down her black stockings, Don Jaime's again as he hangs from the tree, and Jorge's as he bathes his feet in a basin after inspecting the estate on foot. Much of the film is visually very striking: the faces and bodies of the beggars, some of whom, as has been mentioned, were not professional actors; Don Jaime, and later the leper, dressed in the corset and veil of the dead bride; the flaming crown of thorns on the bonfire; the crucifix with its concealed knife-blade. These images have a power and originality undimmed by the years that have elapsed since the film was made.

References and Suggestions for Further Reading

Baxter, John 1994: *Buñuel*. London: Fourth Estate.
Buñuel, Luis 1984: *My Last Breath*. London: Fontana.
Buñuel Luis 1969: *Three Screenplays: Viridiana, The Exterminating Angel, Simon of the Desert*. New York: Grossman.
Carr, Raymond and Fusi, Juan Pablo 1981: *Spain: Dictatorship to Democracy*, 2nd edn. London: George Allen and Unwin.
Edwards, Gwynne 1982: *The Discreet Art of Luis Buñuel*. London: Marion Boyars.
Higginbotham, Virginia 1979: *Luis Buñuel*. Boston, MA: Twayne.
Mellen, Joan (ed.) 1978: *The World of Luis Buñuel*, New York. Oxford University Press.

Credits

Director	Luis Buñuel
Producer	Ricardo Muñoz Suay
Production Company	Gustavo Alatriste (Mexico) and Uninci Films 59 (Madrid)
Scenario	Luis Buñuel and Julio Alejandro
Director of Photography	José A. Agayo
Art Director	Francisco Canet
Editor	Pedro del Rey

Cast

Silvia Pinal	Viridiana
Fernando Rey	Don Jaime
Francisco Rabal	Jorge
Margarita Lozano	Ramona
Victoria Zinny	Lucía
Teresa Rabal	Rita
Juan García Tienda	Leper

Filmography

L'âge d'or (1928)
Un chien andalou (*An Andalusian Dog*, 1930)
Las Hurdes (*Land without Bread*, 1932)
Don Quintín, el amargao (*Embittered Don Quintín*, 1935)
La hija de Juan Simón [Juan Simón's Daughter] (1935)
¿Quién me quiere a mí? [Who loves me?] (1936)
España leal, en armas (*España 1936*, 1937)
Gran Casino (*Tampico*, 1946)
El gran calavera [The rake] (1949)
Los olvidados (*The Young and Damned*, 1950)

Susana (1950)

Una mujer sin amor (A Woman without Love, 1951)

La hija del engaño [Daughter of Deception] (1951)

Subida al cielo (Mexican Bus Ride, 1951)

Él (He, 1952)

El bruto (The Brute, 1952)

Las aventuras de Robinson Crusoe (Adventures of Robinson Crusoe, 1952)

La ilusión viaja en tranvía (The Runaway Streetcar, 1953)

Abismos de pasión (Wuthering Heights, 1953)

El río y la muerte (Death and the River, 1954)

Ensayo de un crimen (The Criminal Life of Archibaldo de la Cruz, 1955)

Celà s'appelle l'aurore [That is called the dawn] (1956)

La mort en ce jardin (Evil Eden, 1956)

Nazarín (1958)

La fièvre monte à El Pao [Fever mounts in El Pao] (1959)

La joven (The Young One, 1960)

Viridiana (1961)

El ángel exterminador (The Exterminating Angel, 1963)

Journal d'une femme de chambre (Diary of a Chambermaid, 1964)

Simón del desierto (Simon of the Desert, 1965)

Belle de jour (1967)

La voie lactée (The Milky Way, 1968)

Tristana (1970)

Le charme discret de la bourgeoisie (The Discreet Charm of the Bourgeoisie, 1972)

Le fantôme de la liberté (The Phantom of Liberty, 1974)

Cet obscur objet du désir (That Obscure Object of Desire, 1977)

6 *Alice in den Städten*
Framed? Alice (Yella Rottländer) takes a family snapshot of Winter (Rüdiger Vogler) in Holland at the beginning of their journey to search for her grandmother.

Alice in den Städten
(Alice in the Cities)
Stuart Taberner

'The old cinema is dead. We believe in the new' (in Elsaesser, 1989, 20–1). These words resonate at the close of the precociously self-confident manifesto signed by twenty-six up-and-coming West German film-makers at the 1962 Oberhausen Film Festival. The interlopers, who were inspired by the French New Wave, styled themselves as the 'Young German Cinema' and were exasperated by the way domestic theatres were dominated by Hollywood re-runs and the peculiarly German genre *Heimatfilme*, insipid depictions of sentimentalised rustic idylls. A decade later – once youth had mellowed into middle age – they would prefer to be known as the '*New* German Cinema'. Original signatories such as Alexander Kluge and Edgar Reitz had been joined by film-makers such as Werner Herzog, Rainer Werner Fassbinder, Margarethe von Trotta, and Wim Wenders. These film-makers gained international acclaim for their formal and thematic innovation and became leading intellectual figures in their own country.

Yet the story of the New German Cinema is a tale of glorious failure. In 1967 the *Board of Young German Film* was set up – partly in response to the clamouring of the Oberhausen directors – to pump-prime 'artistically worthwhile' projects. Semi-official support from the state and regional competitions furnished limited but indispensable funding for innovative film-making (although the parallel introduction of a tax on movie tickets favoured more commercial products, low-brow comedies, and soft porn). Making a virtue of necessity, directors transposed financial hardship into aesthetic gain. They exploited the unfinished appearance of their films in order to stress the open-endedness of the plot (and therefore of the social and political conditions they took as their themes) and to draw attention to the cinematographic process itself. Their films are often highly self-conscious and suspicious of the claims to omniscience made by Hollywood-inspired movies. Almost by definition, therefore, directors were celebrated for their creative input, but remained exiled in art-house theatres specialising in avant-garde 'European' pictures. In 1978, only 8 per cent of the West German film market was claimed by domestic production (Elsaesser, 1989, 36). It began to appear that the 'New German Cinema' was being kept alive by government subsidies, and, as such, had become a tool of the Federal Republic's foreign policy, designed to demonstrate to sceptical outsiders the extent of West Germany's post-war commitment to liberal values, cultural variety, and the toleration of criticism.

Wim Wenders, one of the few West German directors to pass through film school, has also been one of a mere handful whose films have succeeded in appealing to audiences beyond those of art-house cinema. Two films in particular, *Paris, Texas* (1984) and *Wings of Desire* (1987), have charmed large audiences; others such as *Der amerikanische Freund* (*The American Friend*, 1977) and *Bis an Ende der Welt* (*Till the End of the World*, 1991) have attracted more modest attention, but none the less appear successful by the standards of European film. Along with fellow West German directors Volker Schlöndorff and Wolfgang Petersen, Wenders has been able to negotiate the move to Hollywood that is necessary for major international recognition, although he has consistently returned to work in his home country. In his association with American studios he also has followed in the path of earlier German directors such as F. W. Murnau and Fritz Lang. At the same time, Wenders's attitude towards Hollywood has been ambivalent. In *Im Lauf der Zeit* (*Kings of the Road*, 1976), one character complains 'the Americans have colonised our subconscious', while *Der Stand der Dinge* (*The State of Things*, 1982) delivers a biting satire on the suppression of directorial autonomy by movie moguls, reflecting Wenders's experience of making *Hammett* (1978–82) in partnership with Francis Ford Coppola.

This uncertainty regarding Hollywood reflects both the reaction of European avant-garde film-makers in general (from the 1920s onwards, and intensifying after 1945) to the dominance of American movies and a more specifically West German sensibility towards the influence of the United States upon the shaping of its institutions, values and culture following the establishment of the Federal Republic in 1949. Wenders's generation admired the Americans as the bringers of democracy and liberation from Hitler's national socialism. They aped the carefree informality, openness and exuberance of American culture, and embraced rock and roll, jazz, and Hollywood movies as the expression of a nation at peace with itself (in marked contrast to their own country's tortuous relationship to its own past, and present existence). Wenders has often spoken of listening to rock and roll as a teenager, and jukeboxes and popular culture feature as leitmotifs in his films, including music by the Rolling Stones, Jimi Hendrix, Bob Dylan, The Kinks, Roy Orbison, Chuck Berry, and many other British, but far more frequently American, recording artists. These are passions he shares with Peter Handke, the Austrian novelist with whom he has often collaborated – *Die Angst des Tormanns beim Elfmeter* (*The Goalkeeper's Fear of the Penalty*, 1972); *Falsche Bewegung* (*Wrong Movement*, 1975); *Wings of Desire* (1987).

By the mid-1960s, however, this inherited affection for the United States had become far more problematical. Politically, the United States had damaged its reputation as the bearer of democratic values through its deepening involvement in the Vietnam War, and as a result of the mistreatment of black Americans campaigning for civil rights in the southern states (this theme is intimated at the beginning of *Alice in den Städten* in images highlighting black social exclusion).

Culturally, film-makers, writers and intellectuals were becoming perturbed by the American permeation of West Germany's self-understanding, and by Hollywood's increasingly hegemonic claim. By the early 1980s Edgar Reitz even considered it necessary to introduce each part of his TV serialisation *Heimat* (*Home*, 1980–4) with the words 'made in Germany' (in English) in order to reclaim his vision of German history (in this case, the story of a small village from the end of the First World War into the 1980s) from its appropriation by American movies. West German film-makers were particularly conscious of the way in which Hollywood had been allowed to define images of the country's fascist past, a feeling reinforced by the German screening of the American TV series *Holocaust* in 1979, and felt that movie representations of jack-booted Nazis threatened to deprive Germans of any meaningful relationship with their history.

Personal and national identity are paramount in Wenders's *Alice in den Städten* (*Alice in the Cities*, 1974). The link between the two is established by images, photography, and film-making itself, although for much of the story this (literal) medium fails to function, engendering rootlessness, disorientation and alienation in the lead character Philip Winter (acoustically similar to Wenders, especially when pronounced by a Dutch voice speaking through a loudspeaker at Schipol airport in Amsterdam). *Alice in den Städten* is the narrative of multiple journeys, or searches. The film opens with Winter on America's Atlantic coast, apparently watching a jet flying from West to East, predicting his own physical and psychic voyage back to his European (more accurately, German) origins. His subsequent return to Europe is linked with his efforts to reinvest images with meaning following their reduction to one-dimensionality by the American culture industry. Winter's sense of his Germanness thus depends upon his reclaiming of images from Hollywood's grasp. More specifically, Winter turns to photographs to give meaning to his own existence and to insert himself into more tangible relationships with other people, as a substitute father (to Alice), and potentially at least, as a partner in a monogamous union with a woman. The theme of masculinity, so powerful in some of Wenders's other films (such as *Kings of the Road*; *The American Friend*; *Paris, Texas*, and *Wings of Desire*), is here linked to the American cowboy and road-movie genres. In *Alice*, therefore, Winter finally breaks with the model of male behaviour (heroic isolation, rootlessness, and the refusal of commitment) established by Hollywood through figures such as Humphrey Bogart, who was a popular role model for many West German men in the 1950s, and internalised by a generation of German males lacking any 'intact' personal or national identity.

In *Alice in den Städten*, America appears as uncompromisingly foreign. It is not the character of Philip Winter that alienates the viewer – actor Rüdiger Vogler's wry smiles and appealing interiority generate sympathy – but the unemotional landscapes, impersonal motels, and uninterrupted commercialism that dominate at the beginning of the film. Diegetic music – that is, music 'within' the film, this time from Winter's car radio – reveals the failure of American popular culture (rock and roll, folk and country music) to imbue this landscape with warmth and emotion. Winter becomes frustrated by the constant interference of commercials, the multiplication of stations which merely replicate the lack of diversity, and by the inanity of the presenters' chatter. The viewer is alternately identified with Winter through point-of-view camera angles and distanced from him by face-on shots inserting a third person narrative perspective. This technique may reflect the incongruity between the character and his environment. Subsequently, Winter stays in a motel, watches a TV advert for a Negro College fund juxtaposed with publicity for a town in the west, and is irritated by the way in which these marketing slots interrupt his viewing of the John Ford film *Young Mr Lincoln* (1939). The idealism of Ford's film, promoting America's initial liberal promise, has, it seems, been corrupted by commercialism. The adverts distort the American dream of the land of opportunity into a business proposition. In addition, this sequence anticipates Winter's inversion of the Hollywood fantasy of travelling west towards freedom when he later returns east to Europe to begin his rendering of another Ford film, *The Searchers* (1956). Before he finally leaves, however, he must pass through New York, where he is forced to admit to his editor that he has been unable to write the script to accompany the polaroids he has taken of America.

New York is a city that has been reduced to iconographic status. The images the film offers of the metropolis, in a series of long takes, are so familiar that they have become clichéd, representations of America that overwhelm reality and that refer only to their own commodity value. They short-circuit meaning and are empty of content. Shots of the Empire State Building, the Chrysler Building, the World Trade Center, and of Greyhound buses are void of emotionality and human reference. They suggest Winter's disillusionment with the compelling power of images once they have become stereotypes. At the beginning of the film, he complains that photographs 'never really show you what you saw'. Unlike Peter Handke's novel *Der kurze Brief zum langen Abschied* (*The Brief Letter upon a Lengthy Farewell*, 1972), to which the film partly responds, Wenders demonstrates the impossibility of 'knowing' America. The discrepancy between the hackneyed images of American life popularised by Hollywood and western popular culture and what Winter actually encounters in the United States distorts the country beyond all recognition. He protests to his editor that he is unable to write the script to his photo-journey through the United States because 'the story's about the things you see ... about signs and images'. The implication is clearly that he has not yet discovered a means of narrating these images, or making sense of them, in words, as a coherent story. Later, in conversation with an ex-girlfriend in New York, he acknowledges that he has lost his bearings, thereby confirming that the crisis he is experiencing with regard to images and icons has shattered his sense of personal identity. Yet her suggestion that he had lost direction long ago may imply that his recent sensitivity towards the deceptions of American culture in fact reflects his disappointment with the substitute lifestyle he had adopted in the absence of any self-confident *German* identity. The Peter Handke book lying on her table, *Wunschloses Unglück*

(1972), recalls this young novelist's efforts to trace his mother's experiences under national socialism, and his subsequent questioning of national identity. At the same time, Winter's ex-girlfriend also alludes to his taking of pictures as 'proof, proof that you still exist'. Photography, and by implication film-making, continues to offer the possibility of anchoring oneself. What Winter needs to do is to liberate his images from cliché, from their appropriation by Hollywood, and to infuse meaning into the snapshots that he constantly takes of his surroundings.

Winter's quest to reconnect meaning with images corresponds to Wenders's intentions in making the film. In keeping with the principle of *Autorenkino (auteur* cinema) that informed the work of the New German Cinema, *Alice* is a highly personal, subjective, and often autobiographical work. Winter's return to the heavily industrialised Ruhr area of West Germany, after the initial sequences in America, takes him back to Wenders's own past. The picture enacts Wenders's engagement with the United States, and mirrors his efforts to establish his identity as a film-maker, integrating Hollywood influences into a distinctively European heritage. *Alice* is littered with references to John Ford and Nicholas Ray, American directors close to Wenders's heart, the former for his vision of the integrative potential of film, the latter for his undermining of this whole-someness (Ray in fact appears as a crook in Wenders's *Der amerikanische Freund*). John Ford's death is even acknowledged at the end of the film, in a newspaper obituary entitled 'Lost Worlds', an epithet that perhaps mirrors Wenders's perception of the mutation of a healthy tradition of American film-making into bland commercialism. Moreover, the cowboy genre refined by both Ford and Ray is adapted and transformed by the German film-maker to make it relevant to his own heritage. The road movie – the modern version of the cowboy story in which men roam *westwards* into the American wilderness to find themselves – is inverted. Winter travels *east* back to his European origins on a journey of self-discovery which takes the past as the starting point of identity, rather than a future in uncharted lands without history. American and German traditions fuse as the road movie becomes a *Bildungsroman*. Winter's automobile tour through the streets of West German cities is metamorphosed into a 'novel of self-development' in which the protagonist finally achieves maturity and social integration.

The allusion to the German *literary* heritage is significant, reflecting a typically European desire to raise the cultural status of film by association with the more prestigious medium. German films from the 1920s onwards have often had a distinctly 'literary feel', and from the 1960s onwards West German directors have often felt that it would be easier to attract state subsidies if they filmed classic works of fiction or otherwise blurred the lines between literature and film. More specifically, works of literature have been the inspiration for many of Wenders's films, including those by Peter Handke, and Nathaniel Hawthorne's *The Scarlet Letter*. The symbiosis of film and fiction sets images in a verbal context, replenishing the meaning they seem to lose when divorced from language. *Alice* attaches great significance to dialogue – a convention of nineteenth-century realist and naturalist novels – and especially to the discussion of pictures.

Wenders's debate with America does not only take place at the level of genre. The fabric of *Alice*, the way it is put together as a series of shots and sequences, also promotes a reconciliation of Hollywood conventions with European sensibilities. Establishing shots ensure that the viewer does not endure the deliberate disorientation typical of much European avant-garde cinema. Most of the dialogue sequences follow the Hollywood 'shot/reverse shot' pattern, stitching the viewer into the scene and creating the intimacy that Wenders requires if Winter is not simply to appear as a disaffected and unsympathetic outsider. The middle portion of the film, from Winter's arrival in Amsterdam to his abandonment of Alice at the police station, is highly conventional in its use of camera angles and cutting between scenes. Yet these tributes to Hollywood are blended with other techniques that establish an entirely different feel to the film than might be expected from an American director. Dissolves remove suspense, create a softer, more reflective focus, and erase the breaks between apparent oppositions. Winter's sojourn in America fades into his European odyssey, signalling the seamless merging of the two filmic traditions. Long takes and expansive panning shots perhaps repay a debt to Alfred Hitchcock, or Orson Welles, but they are endowed here with a new sensibility, especially in the last third of the film. The camera lingers nostalgically on antiquated houses soon to be demolished, and country landscapes encroached upon by industry. An obsession with social change and the erosion of familiarity underlines *Alice*'s European credentials.

If Wenders's aim is to marry America and Europe through cinematography, then Winter arrives at the same destination at the level of plot. The desire for rapprochement is present all along. Winter forgets to hand in his key for the American Skyway Motel and does not seem disconcerted when he happens across it back in Europe. After leaving Alice at the police station he attends a Chuck Berry concert and clearly enjoys experiencing American culture in a German context. On another occasion, he watches a young boy singing along to the rock and roll music playing on a jukebox and appears to feel an affinity. Yet the catalyst for his successful quest for greater self-awareness is Alice, the precocious child abandoned to Winter's reluctant care by her mother in New York. Alice reintroduces Winter to the passion for images from which he had become disconnected in America. She also inspires him once more to associate pictures with story-telling and thus to invest them with personal meaning. Finally, she helps him to resolve the crisis of male identity that derives, in part at least, from the rootlessness engendered by his inability to locate himself either in his German past or in the American present he had adopted as a substitute culture. The film closes with Winter's decision to travel with Alice to Munich, to share with her the views of the countryside outside their train, in an episode that signals his acceptance of the responsibility of the substitute father figure, his renewed pleasure in images, and his reintegration into the German landscape from which he had been alienated. The final scene points forward with Winter's decision to complete his story (we are not sure whether he means the script to his American photo-journey, or his travels with Alice). This resolution reverses his earlier insistence that the narration of images was impossible.

Alice in den Städten is not only about filmic representations – a self-reflexive excursus on cinematography and photography – it is also about its protagonist's self-image. Images become metaphors as Winter looks at himself in mirrors, unable to comprehend the person reflected there. The picture he receives from others reflects his adoption of the role of the libidinous predator in the company of the opposite sex. He appears to be attracted to Alice's mother and she fully expects him to want to sleep with her. The next day, of course, she abandons her daughter to his care in New York, thereby forcing him into a new role. The ex-girlfriend he visits in New York also feels it necessary to disabuse him of his certainty that he will be able to share a bed with her, despite his long absence and lack of communication. A woman in a bus on the way from Amsterdam to Germany smiles flirtatiously at him, probably responding to his initiation of eye contact, whilst Alice is left to play with another child at the back of the vehicle. Later, the woman at the open-air swimming pool he visits with Alice immediately understands his purpose in allowing the girl to engage in conversation with her. They spend the night together and Winter appears pleased by the implied lack of commitment. The next morning Alice disapproves and they leave the apartment before the woman wakes, in a scene that hints at her growing influence over his behaviour. His self-exculpatory remark that Alice had occupied the couch before he had been able to make his bed there appears defensive, patronising and devious in its attempt at concealment, and implicitly cedes her the right to comment on his actions.

Winter's disorientation throughout the first two-thirds of the film reflects his disaffection with the movies. He no longer empathises with the models of masculinity offered by Hollywood, and his playing of the male parts assigned to him appears correspondingly unconvincing. Alice prompts Winter to take an initial step towards self-knowledge when she induces him to narrate his anxiety – he admits that he is 'afraid of fear' – in their Dutch airport hotel at the beginning of their European trip, despite his insistence that he doesn't know any stories. Meaning is restored to images through story-telling, as the images of male identity that he has internalised from the movies are reworked into a tale of his own making. He improvises a parable of a boy who abandons his mother in the woods, crosses a river, comes across a man riding a horse, follows him to a road from the side of which he is picked up by a truck driver, only finally to arrive at the sea, where he is stricken by grief for the mother he had deserted. It is not difficult to interpret this sequence allegorically. Hauntingly nostalgic extra-diegetic music lifts the scene out of the flow of events unfolding within the linear narrative of the film, giving pause for reflection. Winter liberates himself from the stereotypes that previously determined his identity – his awareness of the clichés he lives by, but his inability to act otherwise – through his use of metaphor, imagery, and narration. The boy (clearly Winter) is initiated into masculinity via the archetypes of the cowboy figure and the road movie. The disavowal of the mother implies a repudiation of domesticity as the boy pursues the path of outsiderdom, heroic isolation, and freedom from obligation, mapped out by Hollywood. The rejection of the 'motherland' is intimated too, as the boy crosses the water in order to adopt new customs, leaving behind the woods (often associated with 'Germanness'), family, and community existence. America has colonised Winter's identity. The film promotes the idea that identity can be 'organic', that is, 'naturally' emerging from a national or, more often, regional affinity with a distinctive cultural heritage. The absence of an 'organic' concept of self consequently leaves Winter vulnerable to the images that threaten to engulf him.

At the same time, however, pictures and photographs offer the possibility of redemption. Soon after their arrival in Holland, Alice takes a polaroid picture of Winter, using his camera, and thereby turns his attempts to annex his environment through photography back on himself. He is forced to confront his own image and therefore his own confusion and disorientation. Significantly, Alice appears reflected in the shiny surface of the polaroid, looking over his shoulder, transforming Winter's representation of masculine detachment and self-isolation into a family portrait. Alice's presence 'completes' the picture, fills the gap, and gives it meaning as a transposition of intimacy, and of a human relationship. This meaning is formalised in a later scene when they pose together in a photobooth. Alice takes her lead from his expressions, alternately mock serious and comic, thus confirming her 'adoption' of him as a father figure. This sequence, in turn, provides the narrative solution to the episode in which Alice had asked the woman at the swimming pool whether she thought Winter was her father. On that occasion, he had betrayed the image that he and Alice had constructed of themselves, by exploiting the situation to seduce the woman. His response to Alice's implorings the next morning, however, signalled his growing awareness of the need to accept responsibility. Images regain a positive value in the subsequent photo-booth scene. Photographs create an identity – self-knowledge and mutual dependence – for Alice and Winter, institutionalising the father–daughter relationship that may not exist by virtue of blood ties, but which affection and their free choice substantiate.

Growing closer to Alice revives Winter's realisation that relationships with other people and an awareness of origins form an essential part of identity. He learns how to be a father to Alice and subsequently sets out to visit his own parents. His detour, symbolically, takes him across water, this time on a ferry, recalling the story he told Alice of crossing the river after having abandoned his mother, as well as duplicating his transatlantic passage to Germany from America. The entirety of Winter's journey through the Ruhr represents a pilgrimage back to his 'Germanness' and to the web of relationships that sustain it. Once again the role of images is vital. In an earlier scene, Alice had shown him a photograph of her grandmother's house and family snapshots, underscoring the concept that pictures can anchor identity. More generally, Winter chooses Oberhausen as the first town in which to search for Alice's grandmother. This pays a tribute to the original determination of signatories of the Oberhausen manifesto to create a national cinema. It also implies a healing of the wound exposed by the actions of the young directors who initiated the 'Young German Cinema'. The Oberhausen declaration was directed against 'Opas Kino', that is, against the film-making of their grandfathers, which they now pronounced dead. Significantly, fathers are missing from this formulation, reflecting a widespread feeling amongst Wenders's contemporaries that theirs was a 'fatherless' generation. War had robbed many of them of their real fathers. Complicity in national socialism, furthermore, had deprived them of role models and untainted artistic traditions. The alternative, it seemed, was to look to America for paternal influence and guidance.

All of the major themes of the film are united in the scene on the ferry. As Winter and Alice travel across the river, he aims his camera at a young woman with a small child. Alice appears in the background of the shot, completing, as usual, the family portrait. This time Winter's absence from the picture is legitimate. He takes on the role of father and photographer of a domestic outing. His perspective on a woman is, for the first time, entirely framed by children. The possibility of a monogamous relationship is implied, as is the resolution of his crisis of masculinity. The meaningfulness of images, moreover, is linked to human intimacy and this enables Winter to overcome the phobia of photography that had paralysed him in the United States. America, too, can be integrated into his newly established sense of identity. The woman is singing a song, an American rock and roll tune. Several words can be distinguished, including 'daughter' and 'son', evoking the theme of family relationships one last time, and juxtaposing this with the best of American culture – its non-conformist heritage rather than its commercialised mainstream – which is now seen as an integral part of a German identity rather than as a threat. Affection for America need not erase the individual's sense of self. Many influences, it seems, can co-exist and generate a fertile mix, both in film-making and in broad cultural terms.

Alice in den Städten embodies this fusion of cultures at all levels, in its plot, in its characterisation, and in the way it is shot. This is especially the case with regard to the pivotal relationship between Europe and America, and between the United States and Germany. More generally, the film shows that images can be filled with new meaning and spaces can be unlocked for new identities. Alice and Winter trace her grandmother's house with the help of a photograph, only to discover that the house is presently occupied by an Italian woman. In this case, pictures enforce an awareness of demographic change and invite the viewer to respond positively, if nostalgically. Later, we see shots of Turkish families. These images reflect the increasingly multicultural composition of West German society from the late 1950s, and particularly from the early 1970s, in a markedly reflective yet reassuringly unprejudiced fashion. *Alice* may be tinged with sentimentality – its lingering shots of pastoral scenes and its focus on old houses and new factories are evidence of this – but it also appears optimistic about social transformation, and refreshingly open to cultural diversity.

References and Suggestions for Further Reading

Elsaesser, Thomas 1981: 'A Retrospect on the New German Cinema'. In *German Life and Letters*, 41, 3.

Elsaesser, Thomas 1985: 'Germany's America: Wim Wenders and Peter Handke'. In Susan Hayward 1985: *European Cinema*, Birmingham: Aston University.

Elsaesser, Thomas 1989: *New German Cinema: A History*. London: Macmillan.

Kolker, Robert Philip and Beicken, Peter 1993: *The Films of Wim Wenders: Cinema as Vision and Desire*. Cambridge: Cambridge University Press.

Sandford, John 1980: *The New German Cinema*. New York: Da Capo.

Wenders, Wim 1991: *The Logic of Images: Essays and Conversations*. Translated by Michael Hofmann. London: Faber & Faber.

Wenders, Wim 1997: *The Act of Seeing: Texts and Conversations*. Translated by Michael Hofmann. London: Faber & Faber.

Credits

Director	Wim Wenders
Producer	Joachim von Mengershausen
Production Company	Filmverlag der Autoren
Screenplay	Wim Wenders
	Veit von Fürstenberg
Director of Photography	Robby Müller
Editors	Peter Przygodda
	Barbara von Weitershausen
Music	Can

Cast

Rüdiger Vogler	Philip Winter
Yella Rottländer	Alice van Damm
Lisa Kreuzer	Lisa van Damm
Edda Köchl	Edda
Didi Petrikat	Girl in bus
Ernst Böhm	Policeman
Sam Presti	Car salesman
Lois Moran	Airline assistant

Filmography

Summer in the City (1969–70)
Die Angst des Tormanns beim Elfmeter (The Goalkeeper's Fear of the Penalty, 1972)
Der scharlachrote Buchstabe (The Scarlet Letter, 1972)
Alice in den Städten (Alice in the Cities, 1973)

Falsche Bewegung (False Movement, 1975)
Im Lauf der Zeit (Kings of the Road, 1975)
Der amerikanische Freund (The American Friend, 1977)
Lightning over Water/Nick's Movie (1980)
Hammett (1982)
Der Stand der Dinge (The State of Things, 1982)
Paris, Texas (1984)
Tokyo Ga (1985)
Himmel uber Berlin (Wings of Desire, 1987)
Aufzeichnungen zu Kleidern und Städten (Notebook on Clothes and Cities, 1989)
Bis an Ende der Welt (Till the End of the World, 1991)
In weiter Ferne, so nah! (Far Away, So Close, 1993)
Arisha, der Bär und der steinerne Ring (Arisha, the Bear and the Stone Ring, 1994)
Lisbon Story (1995)
Lumière de Berlin (1996)
The End of Violence (1997)
Alfama (1997)

7 *Carmen*

The fight in the tobacco factory. Cristina (Cristina de Hoyos) taunts Carmen (Laura del Sol).

Carmen
Annella McDermott

Carmen is an excellent example of a particular kind of European film – intensely local, and displaying a preoccupation with ideas of national identity, yet appealing to a wider European and international audience. It is a dance film, a showcase for *ballet español*, a fusion of contemporary dance and flamenco. The main events in the film are the search for a principal dancer, followed by the rehearsals for a flamenco ballet based on the opera *Carmen*, by the French composer Bizet, itself based on the novel by Prosper Mérimée.

The opera is now one of the most popular in the classical repertoire, though it shocked audiences when it was first performed, with its portrayal of a free woman as the main character. Carmen is independent in an economic sense, since she works in a cigar-factory. She also claims the freedom to fall in and out of love as she chooses. In a quarrel, she stabs a fellow-worker and is arrested by José, whom she seduces into releasing her, thus sacrificing his army career. Despite her warning that love is a law unto itself, he is devastated when she leaves him for a bullfighter, and eventually kills her. In the film, the rehearsals of the ballet based on this opera are intercut with the story of an affair between Antonio, the director of the company, who is dancing the role of José in the ballet, and the dancer chosen for the role of Carmen. This 'real-life' relationship mirrors the relationship between the characters in the ballet, although the correspondence between the two levels of the film is not absolutely symmetrical: for example, in the 'real-life' story Antonio faces three rivals for Carmen's love, whereas in the ballet José has only one.

For a Spanish audience some of the meaning of the film derives from events in Spain in the years immediately preceding its making: the death of General Franco in 1975, the restoration of democracy and the monarchy after thirty-six years of dictatorship, Spain's re-application in 1980 for entry to what is now the European Union (Spain was finally admitted in 1986), and the election victory in 1982 of the PSOE, the Spanish Socialist Workers' Party. Spain had changed out of all recognition in the space of only a few years, and it was important to look again at national traditions and stereotypes in an attempt to decide which parts of the heritage were fake and which authentic, which parts had been contaminated by identification with the dictatorship, and which could be salvaged for the future.

Carmen dates from 1983, that is, the second year of the socialist government. During the Franco regime, Saura had been one of the leading exponents of a type of film that denounced the effect of authoritarian values and education on human psychology. His films of that period often had a strong autobiographical content, and they looked at middle-class Spaniards, in particular their family and personal relationships, in order to trace the effects of religious and social repression on behaviour. To overcome the problem of censorship, these films relied to a great extent on metaphor and allegory to make their points. The audience had to know how to read between the lines, interpret the allegory, and see its applicability to national political and social issues. For this reason, the films Saura made during the Franco years had difficulty finding an audience outside Spain, except among people particularly interested in Spain and Spanish politics. During those years, a standard judgement on Spanish films, Saura's amongst them, was that they were so preoccupied with Spanish issues, and were forced to deal with these issues in such an oblique fashion, that they did not travel well. With the transition to democracy, that particular subject-matter and that way of reading films were no longer relevant. This did not mean, however, that films ceased to have a specifically national character. Gwynne Edwards, in his preface to *Indecent Exposures*, a study of four Spanish directors, of whom Saura is one, insists that: 'the strength of Spanish cinema lies in its Spanishness: its concern with Spanish issues, its drawing on Spanish traditions, its essentially Spanish style' (Edwards, 10). What changed was not the national focus of films, but their accessibility to a wider audience.

Saura had always been very fond of music, which is a major feature even of his most political films. In the 1980s, he began a series of films about flamenco, an art form which is peculiar to Spain, and which embraces song, instrumental music, and dance. Naturally, the instrumental music and dance are the forms most likely to appeal to an international audience, since they involve no issue of spoken language. Saura has made five flamenco films to date. The first was *Bodas de Sangre* (*Blood Wedding*, 1981), filmed in black and white and purporting to show the dress rehearsal for a flamenco ballet based on a play by the poet and dramatist Federico García Lorca ('purporting to show', in that the ballet does not exist outside the film). *Carmen* is the second of these flamenco films. The third, *Love the Magician* (1986), like *Carmen*, is feature-length and in colour, a filmed version of a flamenco ballet by probably the best-known Spanish composer of the century, Manuel de Falla. All three films have been successful internationally, as well as in Spain. Saura has also made two documentaries on related topics: *Sevillanas* (1992), which illustrates the varieties of this particular dance form, and was made for EXPO 92 in Spain, and *Flamenco* (1995), which documents the main tendencies and exponents of flamenco music, song and dance.

The origins of flamenco are a matter of conjecture since there is a lack of documentation. It is generally considered to have originated in Andalusia, in southern Spain, though subsequent movement of workers from Andalusia to other parts of Spain has given flamenco a presence in other parts of the country. The type of scale used in the song, and certain movements used in the dance, suggest that it dates from the period of Muslim occupation of Andalusia, between the eighth and the fifteenth centuries, and is a mixture of Muslim, Jewish and Christian elements. It appears to have been taken up by the gypsies, who are said to be the descendants of groups of people who emigrated in successive waves from India from the eleventh century onwards, using two routes, one through Central Europe, the other via North Africa, settling in many places along these routes and reaching Spain probably in the fifteenth century. There is some controversy in Spain as to whether the gypsies should be considered a separate ethnic group from Andalusians in general. James Woodall, in his *In Search of the Firedance*, takes the view that the gypsies of Andalusia are a race apart, yet socially integrated. Nevertheless, he traces a history of persecution of the gypsies, from a law of 1499 to implement immediate banishment of gypsies without a certifiable occupation, through subsequent threats of forced labour in the galleys for those who remained vagabond, a prohibition on gypsies practising certain trades, prohibition of the use of the dress, name or language of gypsies, and laws denying the ancient custom of sanctuary in churches to gypsies, but ending with legislation in the late eighteenth century which removed legal obstacles to their plying any trade they wished, while requiring them to abjure their customs. Though integrated legally, gypsies nowadays live in what he describes as 'ghettos' and suffer from social discrimination (Woodall, 87). Despite the strong association of flamenco with gypsies, many of the leading exponents are non-gypsies. This is the case, for example, of the principal guitarist seen in the film, Paco de Lucía, who is considered one of Spain's best and most innovative flamenco guitar soloists.

There is some basis for considering flamenco a 'folk' form. It uses no system of notation for the style of singing and playing: like the dance, these styles are passed on by oral tradition, teaching and imitation (Paco de Lucía has never learned to read music). Saura's film emphasises the point that flamenco expression is not confined to performance: in the 'real life' layer of the film, Carmen invites Antonio to express his feelings for her by dancing a *farruca*, the key male solo dance in flamenco, and the birthday-party sequence shows flamenco being used spontaneously in celebration.

Needless to say, there is no necessary connection between flamenco and left-wing politics. Although the words of flamenco songs often reflect the history of persecution or discrimination outlined above, the protest is usually considered a-political. Indeed, a recent study by Timothy Mitchell, *Flamenco Deep Song*, accuses the form of expressing the misery of the singer, and the community he represented, in a way that allowed his listeners – the very people who were the cause of the suffering – to feel purged by pity from their burden of guilt (Mitchell, 107, 137). Mitchell, however, was speaking of a particular context in which flamenco song was performed – at private parties organised by members of Andalusia's elite landowning families. It does seem possible to argue that there is a connection between Saura's film and the coming to power of a socialist government in Spain after thirty-six years of dictatorship followed by eight years of the transition to democracy. The ballet that will emerge from the rehearsals is not, of course, a folk-form: it is choreographed, performed by dancers and instrumentalists who are mainly professionals, and is based on the 'high' art forms of literature and opera. However, one could readily see this ballet as a socialist project, since it combines these 'high' art forms with the popular art of a persecuted minority, one which includes Jewish and Muslim elements and therefore can carry notions of multiculturalism appropriate to the new, open and tolerant democracy. There is a history in Spain of attempts by leftist intellectuals to dignify flamenco, notably the festival of flamenco song organised in Granada in 1922 by García Lorca, who was killed by the rebel Nationalists in the first weeks of the Spanish Civil War, and the composer Manuel de Falla, who went into exile in Argentina at the end of the war. Saura can therefore be seen as re-initiating a project that had been interrupted by the Spanish Civil War and the dictatorship that followed.

It should be noted, however, that the Franco regime also promoted flamenco culture from a populist viewpoint, and Spanish film studios in the 1940s and 1950s produced a large number of musicals and melodramas set in Andalusia and using flamenco or flamenco-related music. Moreover, from the 1960s onwards Spain was keen to encourage tourism, which is a major earner of foreign currency, and flamenco dance was promoted as a spectacle suitable for tourist consumption. Saura alludes to this in the scene in the film where Carmen dances in a flamenco night-club full of Japanese tourists. While the dancers are performing, instead of remaining respectfully still, a waiter circulates, taking orders for drinks and delivering them to tables. The suggestion is that this is a commercial, soulless form of flamenco, in contrast to the flamenco seen in other parts of the film, which, it is implied, is more authentic.

Andalusia is one of the economically depressed regions of Spain, an area of high unemployment, from which large numbers of people had to emigrate, particularly in the 1950s and 1960s, either to more industrialised regions of Spain, such as Catalonia and the Basque country, or to other countries in Europe, especially France or Germany, to work in agriculture or industry. In all of these destinations, including the regions of northern Spain, they have experienced the discrimination and prejudice directed at those forced to emigrate to find work. It is thus ironic that a regional art from this neglected region has come to be seen as the typical manifestation of Spanishness, particularly since the nineteenth century, and particularly under the influence of French artists. Woodall has a chapter in his book entitled 'Andalusia Invented', in which he traces the origins of this process:

> In the twentieth century, many have been lured to Andalusia as it has represented the last refuge from the technological oppressions of modern life; in the nineteenth, for writers in particular, the region came to represent the embodiment of all the historical and cultural forces with which they felt their work needed to be infused, and which defined their imaginative universe. For the French Romantics, especially, Andalusia was what the Lake District

was for the first-generation English Romantics, with all the subsequent stereotyping effects the latter has had on Cumbria applying to Andalusia, and how it – Spain as whole – has forever been perceived.   (Woodall, 121, 125)

Saura's film, then, is clearly in part an interrogation by Spaniards in the new democratic Spain of external, particularly French, images of their country over the last two centuries (Woodall emphasises the French role in the construction of such images). The pre-credit sequence in the film establishes that Antonio is the director of a dance company and that he is looking for a principal female dancer with particular qualities, which the available dancers lack. He arranges to make a trip on the following day to Seville, one of the key sites in the history of flamenco, to find a suitable dancer, explaining to his lead guitarist that none of the women he has seen so far is a convincing Carmen. With the pronunciation of the name, which is immediately redolent of a particular stereotype of Spanishness, a chorus from Bizet's opera begins to be heard, sung in French, naturally, and the credits start to roll over a background of a set of drawings of typically Andalusian characters by the French artist Gustave Doré. At several points in the film, notably when Antonio first sees the girl who will dance Carmen, we hear voice-overs of Antonio reading from a Spanish translation of Mérimée's novel, and when he arranges for her to dance the part he gives her a copy of the novel, somewhat to her bemusement, saying that she is not obliged to read it, but will probably find it useful.

It is worth noting here that Spain's relationship with France over the last two hundred years or so has been a complex one. Although there was widespread popular resistance to the Napoleonic invasion of Spain in the early nineteenth century, and though *afrancesado*, meaning 'Frenchified', was used as a term of abuse, there was a current in liberal thought that admired the French and even welcomed Napoleon, in the belief that he would rescue Spain from the backwardness and obscurantism of feudal social institutions and clericalism. To some extent, Saura can be said to be following that current, in that the film is based on the premise that Mérimée, Bizet and Doré had, at the very least, something interesting to say on the subject of Spanishness. However, a significant sequence in this respect is the one following soon after the credits, in which Antonio is listening to a tape of an aria from the opera and tapping his fingers, clearly trying to work out how it can be choreographed. Paco de Lucía, the guitarist, listens intently for a few moments, tries a few notes on the guitar, then effortlessly transposes the aria into a flamenco rhythm. This sequence would appear to imply that Spain's elaboration of a new sense of identity does not require a wholesale repudiation of foreign images of Spanishness: what is acceptable in those images can be appropriated, transformed and recycled for Spain's own purposes.

Some moments in the film acknowledge the existence of tawdry or kitsch versions of flamenco. The scene in the tourist *tablao*, or flamenco night-club, has already been mentioned. In the scene where Antonio dances alone in the studio in the middle of the night, after Carmen has got up, dressed and gone home, he is thinking about costumes for the ballet. He ponders the possibility of Carmen using a fan, veil, and high comb, calling it a cliché, but wondering whether that is really a valid reason for rejecting it. As he speaks, Carmen appears, a figment of his imagination, though presented realistically. As though to confirm his suggestion that something can be rescued from cliché, she looks stunningly beautiful in black dress, veil, comb and fan. On the other hand, at the birthday party, Carmen gets herself up in a deliberately tacky version of flamenco dress and make-up. In these scenes, the film seems to be exploring the possibility of rescuing an acceptable version of flamenco from grotesque distortions growing out of right-wing populism and the tourist industry.

Carmen is a multi-layered film which deliberately blurs the distinction between reality and film, just as it blurs within the film the distinction between 'real life' and performance. On one level, Antonio Gades, Paco de Lucía and Cristina de Hoyos, an older dancer who is denied the part of Carmen because of her age, play characters who are indistinguishable from themselves as real people, at least so far as their surface characteristics are concerned. Within the film, there are a further two layers: there is a level of 'real life' which is represented by the gypsy singers and musicians, the dancers in the intervals between rehearsals, Antonio and Carmen in their off-stage affair, and Carmen's husband in jail and on his release. The third layer consists of the scenes from the ballet, which we see in rehearsal. The situation is further complicated by the fact that the majority of the film is set in a rehearsal room, one entire wall of which is a mirror. We often see actions first of all in a mirror, though we may only realise that fact once the camera pulls back. There are therefore pervasive metaphors in the film of 'looking in a mirror' and 'seeing a reflection', which can easily be read to imply that the dancers are like Spaniards seeing themselves in the mirror of foreign (and national) stereotypes.

The boundaries between these levels of reality are deliberately violated on several occasions. A good example is the scene involving a poker game which develops into a confrontation between Antonio and a man whom we initially take to be Carmen's husband. The confrontation is expressed as dance, which surprises the audience, since there has been no previous indication that Carmen's husband was a dancer (he was in jail for drug-trafficking); we probably assume that he has been co-opted into the performance, though we are also encouraged to interpret the confrontation as taking place in 'real life' by the facial expressions of the onlookers, who seem concerned. After he falls to the ground, the tension is held for some time, until Carmen smiles, and says: 'That's long enough, surely,' whereupon her 'husband' is revealed to be a dancer wearing a wig, and we revise our understanding of the scene to conclude that the poker game and fight are part of the ballet, though it remains clear that Antonio is expressing, in this sequence from the ballet, his murderous feelings towards Carmen's husband. Similarly, the confrontation between Antonio and the dancer taking the role of the bullfighter raises a doubt in our minds as to whether what we are seeing is 'real life' or a scene from the ballet, or a product of Antonio's imagination. Even when Carmen is murdered by Antonio, we initially assume that the act is taking place in 'real life', though clearly echoing the murder in the opera, until the camera pulls back and shows us the other dancers, unconcerned, implying that the scene did not happen in the plane of 'real life', but is simply a projection of Antonio's violent jealousy. There is thus a second pervading metaphor in the film, that of performance, which invites us to reflect on the extent to which national identity may consist of the 'performance' of roles created partly by foreign observers and partly by national producers of culture with a social or political agenda of their own.

Another function of this blurring of levels is to draw attention to similarities between the passions expressed in the opera and those experienced by the dancers, particularly Antonio, in 'real life'. He may not kill Carmen, as José does in the opera, but there is no doubt that his jealousy is violent enough for him to want to do so. Saura appears to be asserting that the stereotype of the domineering and jealous Spanish male corresponds to reality and has persisted into the new Spain. As a recent study of Spanish film remarks, *Carmen* 'engage[s] critically with such issues as the destructive attitudes and behaviour prompted by Spanish *machismo* and traditional constructions of male pride, jealousy, honour, etc.' (Jordan and Morgan-Tamosunas, 29).

The Carmen story lends itself relatively well to updating, since the nineteenth-century character is already a woman who is economically independent of men, because of the availability of work in the tobacco factory. If anything, the modern-day Carmen is less objectively independent, since she wants the lead role in the ballet and is therefore dependent on Antonio's patronage. However, the film does not interest itself in this casting-couch aspect of the relationship between the two. Carmen is depicted as strong and self-confident. In the scene in her dressing-room at the flamenco night-club, she reassures Antonio that her agent will not be a problem, saying that when she makes her mind up, she tends to get what she wants, and adding that she is stronger than he might think. She surprises him by being the one who gets dressed and goes home after lovemaking, with hardly a word of explanation, and she rejects his attempt to impose notions of fidelity on her. This is not to say that the character is presented as a model of womanhood. Even the modern audience may find her intransigent and careless of others' feelings. Nevertheless, there is no suggestion in the film that Carmen bears any responsibility for the final act of violence. The emphasis is on Antonio, who is on the one hand a steadfast romantic who falls in love at first sight, and on the other an authoritarian figure, accustomed to moulding large groups of mainly female dancers to his vision, and who, finally, would prefer to kill a woman rather than have her resist his will. Parallel to the sexual politics, the Spanish audience would readily see an allusion in Antonio to the still-recent dictatorship, and in Carmen, to the new democracy.

So far there has been a concentration on the film's meaning in relation to Spanish history and identity. This should not blind us to the fact that there is also a documentary intention to the film. Saura clearly wants to illustrate the various elements in flamenco dance, and he can conveniently do this by using the convention of rehearsal, where there is a plausible reason for concentration on individual elements such as the sinuous movements of the arms and hands, the particular posture of head, neck, torso and waist, the use of castanets, the sounds produced by finger-clicking, rhythmic clapping, drumming with hands on tables, drumming with walking-sticks on the floor and drumming or stamping with the feet. Antonio's search for a dancer to play Carmen takes him to a flamenco dance academy in Seville, which again provides an opportunity for a fairly detailed study of certain movements. It also suggests the community-based nature of flamenco dance in that there are children, amateurs and professional dancers, all studying together. Although ideas of discipline and technique are present in these scenes, the main emphasis in the film falls on the notion of flamenco as an art-form that comes from the heart, and demands passion and sincerity. While there are many close-ups, particularly of feet, there is also masterly use of middle and long shot to illustrate posture, and fluid, sweeping movements of the camera to convey the speed and exhilaration, particularly of the ensemble dancing.

The film, then, can be seen as a celebration of flamenco. Yet it could be argued that marrying flamenco to contemporary dance introduces elements, such as complex narrative content, that are alien to flamenco, and perhaps betrays a fear that raw flamenco would not arouse the same enthusiasm in the audience. The spectator may also feel that the *machismo* being denounced in the film is in fact inherent in flamenco dance since the form appears to depend on fairly rigid notions of gender separation, with particular types of posture and movement considered appropriate to each gender. This raises the question of whether flamenco is an outdated form, enjoyment of which is essentially conditioned by nostalgia, or whether it can in some way be updated to accommodate new visions of gender.

Considerations of genre are relevant to this film. *Carmen* is considered, in the British market at least, as an 'art-house' film, but clearly there are elements of plot, characterisation, theme, and setting to connect the work to the genre of dance movies from Hollywood and elsewhere. The figure of the authoritarian dance director has a particular resonance in Spain because of its recent history of dictatorship, but his search for a dancer with particular qualities, which are hard to define in words, but which he will recognise immediately he sees them, and the obsessive quest for perfection which leads him to harry his dancers, are familiar to an audience that has seen Hollywood dance movies like Alan Parker's *Fame* (1980) or Richard Attenborough's *A Chorus Line* (1985). Similarly, the theme of dance as an art that depends as much on feeling and sincerity as on technique, is one that this film shares with Randal Kleiser's *Grease* (1978), Emile Ardolino's *Dirty Dancing* (1986), the Australian Baz Luhrmann's *Strictly Ballroom* (1992) or the Japanese Masayuki Suo's *Shall We Dance?* (1996). The film has attracted some criticism in Spain on account of its perceived commercialism, when contrasted with Saura's more politically committed films of the Franco era (Jordan and Morgan-Tamosunas, 28). Yet it could be argued that within the framework of an accessible genre film, Saura poses questions about gender, about regional and/or national identity, and about high and low art, that are of real concern to his audience, and are political in a wide sense.

References and Suggestions for Further Reading

D'Lugo, Marvin 1991: *The Films of Carlos Saura*. Princeton, NJ: Princeton University Press.
Edwards, Gwynne 1995: *Indecent Exposures: Buñuel, Saura, Erice & Almodóvar*. Marion Boyars: London & New York.
Fiddian, Robin W. and Evans, Peter W. 1988: *Challenges to Authority: Fiction and Film in Contemporary Spain*. London: Tamesis Books.
Hooper, John 1995: *The New Spaniards*. London: Penguin Books.
Jordan, Barry and Morgan-Tamosunas, Rikki 1998: *Contemporary Spanish Cinema*. Manchester: Manchester University Press.
Kinder, Marsha (ed.) 1997: *Refiguring Spain: Cinema, Media, Representation*. Durham, NC, and London: Duke University Press.
Mitchell, Timothy 1994: *Flamenco Deep Song in Text*. New Haven, CT: Yale University Press.
Washabaugh, William 1996: *Flamenco: Passion, Politics and Popular Culture*. Oxford and Washington, DC: Berg.
Woodall, James 1992: *In Search of the Firedance: Spain through Flamenco*. London: Sinclair-Stevenson.

Credits

Director	Carlos Saura
Producer	Emiliano Piedra
Production Company	Emiliano Piedra
Scenario	Carlos Saura and Antonio Gades
Editor	Pedro del Rey
Director of Photography	Teo Escamillo
Art Director	Felix Murcia
Music	Georges Bizet, Paco de Lucía

Cast

Antonio Gades	Antonio
Laura del Sol	Carmen
Cristina de Hoyos	Cristina

| *Paco de Lucía* | Paco |
| *Juan Antonio Jiménez* | Juan/Husband |

Filmography

Los golfos (*The Hooligans*, 1959)
Llanto por un bandido [Lament for a bandit] (1963)
La caza (*The Hunt*, 1965)
Peppermint frappé (1967)
Stress es tres, tres [Stress is three, three] (1967)
La madriguera (*The Honeycomb*, 1969)
El jardín de las delicias (*The Garden of Delights*, 1970)
Ana y los lobos (*Anna and the Wolves*, 1972)
La prima Angélica (*Cousin Angelica*, 1974)
Cría cuervos (*Raise Ravens*, 1975)
Elisa, vida mía (*Elisa, My Love*, 1977)
Los ojos vendados (*Blindfolded Eyes*, 1978)
Mamá cumple 100 años (*Mama Turns a Hundred*, 1979)
De prisa, de prisa (*Faster, Faster / Hurry, Hurry / Fast, Fast*, 1981)
Bodas de sangre (*Blood Wedding*, 1981)
Dulces horas (*Sweet Yesterdays / Sweet Hours*, 1982)
Antonieta (1982)
Carmen (1983)
Los zancos (*The Stilts*, 1984)
El amor brujo (*Love the Magician / A Love Bewitched*, 1986)
El Dorado (*Eldorado*, 1988)
La noche oscura (*The Dark Night*, 1989)
¡Ay, Carmela! (1990)
Sevillanas (*Carlos Saura's Sevillanas*, 1992)
Dispara (*Outrage*, 1993)
Flamenco (*Carlos Saura's Flamenco*, 1995)
Taxi (1996)
Pajarico (*Little Bird*, 1996)
Tango (1997)

8 *Good Morning Babilonia*

In the film's final sequence the brothers Nicola (Vincent Spano) and Andrea (Joaquim de Almeida) stage and record their deaths for the camera.

Good Morning Babilonia
Derek Duncan

The extraordinary commercial and critical success outside Italy of *La vita è bella* (*Life is Beautiful*, 1997), Roberto Benigni's romantic comedy about the Holocaust, marks the culmination of a decade in which Italian cinema has re-established itself on the international scene. Films such as Giuseppe Tornatore's *Nuovo Cinema Paradiso* (*Cinema Paradiso*, 1987) and Gabriele Salvatores's *Mediterraneo* (1992) won Oscars for Best Foreign Film, and the established stars Sophia Loren and Marcello Mastroianni received similar Lifetime Achievement awards. This was not the first time, however, that Italian cinema had attracted world acclaim. Previously the type of Italian films to attract attention abroad had been strictly art-house, yet the films successfully exported since the late 1980s appeal to a broader market. They do not, therefore, represent a continuation of the experimental tradition of Italian cinema best known through the neo-realist cinema of the immediate post-war era, and the work of innovative film-makers such as Antonioni and Fellini in the 1960s and 1970s. Their appeal is more middlebrow, attracting an audience closer to the mainstream. This chapter will look at *Good Morning Babilonia* (*Good Morning Babylon*, 1987), an early example of this more recent trend in Italian film-making. Typically, these films are elegantly crafted, slow moving, spectacular epics. Set sometime in the recent past, they recall a lost Italy that nevertheless is in the compass of living memory. They are sentimental, occasionally humorous, films about men and masculinity, and their historical dimension is largely the backdrop for the exploration of intimate, but never sexualised, relationships between the male protagonists. In every respect *La vita è bella* fits firmly into this category. While some have hailed Benigni's treatment of the Holocaust as startlingly original, it is perhaps more accurate to see his film as characteristic, or indeed imitative, of this strand in contemporary Italian film production in terms of its aesthetic values, its thematic concerns, and crucially its marketability.

Good Morning Babilonia, directed by Paolo and Vittorio Taviani, is not the most successful, nor the best, of these Italian films but serves usefully as a compendium of their cinematic values. Set in the early part of the twentieth century, it relates the story of two brothers who leave Italy to make their fortune in the United States. They are able to utilise their traditional stonemasonry skills in the burgeoning Hollywood film industry, and although they die (in each other's arms) fighting in the First World War, they manage to film their deaths, providing a permanent record for posterity. The film was a joint production venture

securing finance from France and the United States as well as from RAI, the Italian
state television company (Sorlin, 162–4). Its cast included internationally
known stars such as Greta Scacchi and Charles Dance. Only in the opening
section set in Italy is Italian used; when the brothers are in America they speak in
(accented) English. Such factors indicate that the film was created and marketed
very much with an international audience in mind. In its content, however,
the film is decidedly Italian, tackling the very complex issue of Italian national
identity in the 1980s through an exploration of the immigrant experience earlier in
the century. The journey from Italy to the United States is not solely a geographical one for it brings to the fore a number of contradictory elements that com-
plicate what it might mean to be Italian, or indeed to become American. The
experience of immigration involves clashes of language and culture and asks
questions about the possible continuity of historical experience. The film sets
up a dialogue between cultures that is enacted through the personal stories of the
two brothers set against a period of momentous social, political, and artistic
change.

One possible way of approaching films such as *Good Morning Babilonia* is
through the admittedly contested category of 'heritage cinema' that has been
applied to other film cultures of the period. Andrew Higson's discussion of British
heritage cinema offers a useful starting point from which to consider similar
films made in Italy although there are inevitably crucial differences between
the two contexts (Higson, 232–49). Higson admits that there are difficulties in
trying to define what constitutes a 'heritage' film. The term seems most obviously
applicable to films such as the Merchant Ivory romantic epics *A Room with a
View* (1985) or *Howards End* (1992). These films, both based on classic novels by
E. M. Forster, look back to a glorious Edwardian past in which the upper
middle classes of England appear to be enjoying the last days of a reassuring
social stability. The aesthetic qualities of these films play an enormous part in
diverting the spectator's attention from a narrative that has the potential to
challenge such reassuring fictions. He notes that the preference in many of
these films for long and medium shots rather than close-ups, and a slow-paced
narrative not held together by tight editing, contributes to the creation of what he
calls a 'restrained aesthetic of display' (234). The past appears solely as spectacle.
They are, Higson suggests, 'intimate epics of national identity played out in a
historical context' (233). The past offers at least the illusion of a better way of
life; nostalgia functions as a form of indirect critique of the present.

Higson's argument cannot be transplanted wholesale into the Italian context.
Although the Merchant Ivory films were well received in Italy, attracting the
kind of audience they might have had in the UK, 'somewhere between the
art-house and the mainstream', whatever nostalgia they displayed was for
England not Italy. Nevertheless, in films such as *Mediterraneo*, it is possible to
see elements of a similar aesthetic at play although the historical setting is
clearly and necessarily different. The film's visual dimension is stronger than
its narrative, which serves largely to motivate the lingering camera-work. The

concept of a group of Italian soldiers setting up an idyllic community on a Greek island where they had landed as invaders offers a very benign statement on Italian national identity. Set in the Second World War, the narrative, however, longs for a more distant past as the values embodied by the soldiers are those of a lost pre-industrial age. The film's unfettered nostalgia is exemplified by its dedication to 'all those who are running away'.

Just as *Mediterraneo* avoids the trauma of the Second World War, *Good Morning Babilonia* barely investigates the upheavals of mass emigration that Italy experienced round the turn of the century. The film's historical dimension is supplied rather by cinema itself; its own historical development and its role in preserving/constructing historical memory. History and cinema, visual spectacle and political critique, have been constant preoccupations of the Taviani Brothers since their directorial debut with *Un uomo da bruciare* (*A Man for Burning*, 1962). In the early years of their career this project was informed by a Marxist perspective, yet although their sense of ideological commitment has since diminished (most notably in their 1996 adaptation of Goethe's *Elective Affinities*), their interest in exploring the past through the medium of film has remained. *Good Morning Babilonia* is their most self-conscious exploration of cinema's historical role and is also a commentary on the historical development of cinema.

Hollywood has not always dominated world cinema. Only in the 1920s did it become such a powerful force, building the robust studio system whose financial might attracted many of the most talented actors, directors and technicians from Europe. Until then, however, Italian film-makers had enjoyed world renown particularly for their grandiose historical epics. In 1915, when production was at its height, well over 500 films were made in Italy, while the rapidity of the industry's decline in the face of American competition is demonstrated by the fact that by 1930 only seven films are estimated to have been made there. Fascism's determination to halt the influx of films from the US stemmed largely from economic factors, and through the regulation of imports and the provision of financial subsidy succeeded in revitalising the Italian film sector. After the Second World War, however, the influence of the US on the economic, political and artistic life of Italy reasserted itself dramatically and has been a source of anxiety for both left-wing parties and the Catholic right ever since (Wagstaff, 89–116). In cultural terms these anxieties tend to focus on what is seen as the commod-ification of mass culture. From this perspective, cultural products are marketed and sold like any other; they are intended neither to educate, edify, nor induce intellectual contemplation, but simply to entertain. As an enormously popular form of mass entertainment, cinema has been the focus of much of this debate. Since the war American finance has had a critical effect on the development of film production in Italy, particularly the case in terms of distribution and mar-keting.

Italian audiences, like many others in Europe, have enjoyed a film culture that is American in origin rather than indigenous. Italy itself was a favoured location for American directors so that in the post-war period Italians often saw themselves represented on the screen through foreign eyes. On another level, Italian film-makers and actors adopted American styles of film-making and acting; Italian stars were often marketed as imitations of existing American idols. To the dismay of many, American values were purveyed as social norms, and were seen as the unwelcome agents of social change; the relative degree of autonomy granted to modern women is one example. Yet it is too simplistic to see American culture as a product imprinted on the Italian psyche in a direct manner. American culture as experienced in Italy was transformed and made into something else, mediated by the distinctive Italian context. An interesting example of this in the field of cinema is the practice of dubbing all foreign-language films. This has meant that while Italian audiences saw American stars, what they heard were Italian voices, which transformed the American landscape into something much closer to home and created a product that was neither purely American nor purely Italian but rather a hybrid mixture of the two.

The term 'hybridity' is one often used in current cultural debates on identity to refer to the unpredictable fusions that occur when cultures meet; what results is not a dilution but rather a dynamic mix of contrasting elements that is never assimilated, always remaining productively different. Such hybridity, however, challenges the attempt to write its history, for it is precisely a history of change and discontinuity that constitutes it. Nevertheless, identities and cultures often seek to affirm themselves through the creation of a history even if this history is largely the result of an imaginative reworking of the past rather than its scrupulous documentation. In *Good Morning Babilonia*, the Taviani Brothers attempt to piece together such a past, bringing together two apparently irre-concilable cultures and finding a way of giving them a common history. This they achieve through historicising the medium of cinema itself.

The film opens with a scene of astonishing luminosity, and indeed, the play of light and shade is one of the central motifs of the film. A group of workmen are completing the restoration of the façade of a Tuscan Romanesque cathedral. The canvas sheets are taken away to reveal the shining white stone and the intricacy with which the craftsmen have deployed their skills. Only one section remains covered where two of the workmen are putting the finishing touches to the figure of a white elephant seen in close-up. The workmen are Andrea and Nicola Bonanno, the youngest sons of the master-craftsman directing the restoration work. They work in the family business along with their five older brothers but are the most talented, and consequently favoured by their father. After his eulogy to the stonemason's art, praising the combination of the hands working with the imagination in a tradition that stretches back to the Middle Ages, the next scene sees the family seated around a large dinner table for what should be a celebration for the completion of the work. The father, however, announces the bankruptcy of the family business. At odds with their older brothers, Andrea and Nicola determine to buy back the firm. They leave for the United States, vowing to return only when they have made enough money to carry on the family tradition. Having received their father's blessing they set off.

The opening section of the film introduces most of the elements that will be developed later in the film. Most notably, it makes clear that it is a film about men; no women appear at all in the early part of the film. The skill passed on from father to son is part of a solely masculine tradition of craftsmanship. The names of the characters are significant in establishing this. Nicola Pisano was a thirteenth-century Tuscan sculptor whose most famous work is the extra-ordinarily intricate pulpit decorated with scenes from the life of Christ in the baptistery in Pisa. In the following century, the unrelated Andrea Pisano was responsible for sculpting the bronze doors on the baptistery in neighbouring Florence, the design of which he completed after having studied the baptistery doors in Pisa, which had been made some hundred and fifty years before by the sculptor Bonanno. Bonanno is the family name of the Tavianis' Tuscan craftsmen. Nicola and Andrea are considered to be two of the great masters of Tuscan art, bringing to sculpture the qualities Giotto brought to painting. The brothers are consequently situated directly in this illustrious Tuscan tradition, the various nuances of which the Tavianis exploit in the course of the film. A less subtle reference later in the film makes them the descendants of Michelangelo and Leonardo da Vinci, the great artists of the Italian Renaissance.

Although at this stage no mention is made of the cinema, a comparison is already being set up between the father and the American film director D. W. Griffith, who appears later in the film. Both are responsible for co-ordinating the work of skilled technicians and for producing great public art. Bonanno's request for a chair from which to contemplate the completed restoration, and the staged theatricality of the way in which the scene is shot, prepare the spectator for the parallel made more explicit later on. Similarly, the dinner scene in which the patriarch addresses his dependants anticipates a later scene in which the father and Griffith meet when the boys marry. The figure of the elephant and the form of the Romanesque church recur throughout the film as images that structure the narrative, providing a sense of continuity that transcends the limits of time and place. When the brothers first catch sight of America through the porthole of their ship, what they see is a stylised Manhattan sky-line whose glittering lights transport them back to childhood and a vision of the Christmas tree and its promise of future delight. The sense of place is constituted through imagination and longing. The representation of the United States as a land of opportunity is of course clichéd and will inevitably be revealed as false; the brothers will not make their fortune nor return home to live happily ever after. Nevertheless, the foregrounding of the fantasy through which America is imagined allows the Tavianis to explore the ways in which cultural representations, or ideas, vie with social and economic realities. The film goes on to examine the consequences of this myth of America but in doing so demonstrates that Italy is also a mythical place. It is this process of imagining place that the film recounts and shows.

For the two brothers the move from one culture to another causes the fracturing of their identities. The dream of America is short-lived as these skilled craftsmen are forced to earn a living as swineherds. Their struggle to speak English is a sign of their struggle to adapt to their new environment. By chance they encounter a group of Italian workmen on their way to San Francisco to work on the Italian pavilion at the World Exposition in 1915. They first of all hear them singing a piece from Verdi's *La forza del destino* and through the music are nostalgically transported to Italy. Music is often used in the film to evoke Italy, and the operatic tradition of Verdi and Rossini heard in America suggests the potent influence of Italian culture on the other side of the Atlantic. The Italian pavilion is a dazzling success and it is here that the American director D. W. Griffith sees the epic Italian film *Cabiria* (1914). He is so impressed by the quality of the craftsmanship displayed in it that he decides to employ the Italian workmen on the set of his new film. The brothers, who had only worked as day-labourers on the film, try to pass themselves off as foremen. They are caught out and accused of being shiftless liars, fulfilling the American stereotype of Italians. When they first meet Edna and Mabel, the girls they eventually marry, they are dismissed as losers because of their nationality yet they, too, pander to another stereotype by playing the part of romantic Latin lovers. The brothers are themselves trapped by America's own myth of Italy.

The brothers' identity is constructed largely through their work and the recognition of their skills. Eventually, they attract the attention of the famous director by building a model of an elephant for his film *Intolerance* (1916). The Tavianis probably overstate the impact of the Italian film on Griffith. Nevertheless, *Cabiria* was important in the history of cinema, noted especially for the grandiosity of its sets, and its development of the tracking shot. Griffith acknowledges his debt to Pastrone, the director of *Cabiria*, who used a model of a black elephant in his own historical epic. On one level this is an example of film quoting film as one director pays homage to another (a feature also of the Tavianis' work), but it also recalls the elephant carved by the brothers on the façade of the cathedral at the beginning of the film. By successfully redeploying their skills the brothers are able not only to ensure their livelihood in the present but also to effect a reconciliation between cultures and between eras through the continuity provided by their technical abilities. A historical narrative is made possible through the hands and the imaginations of the brothers.

The Tavianis are not interested simply in creating a narrative of historical continuity but seek to pay their own homage and acknowledge their own debt to the early cinema and to their own craft as film-makers. Much of the film's long middle section set in Hollywood serves only to recall the excitement of an era when film-making technique was still being honed. A greater dependency on natural light meant that shooting often took place in the open air, or was harnessed by crudely improvised means, as in the dance scene where Edna and Mabel are awakened by the sun's rays. A number of scenes simply recall the genres of the early cinema: the historical epic, the slapstick comedy, the exotic melodrama are revisited purely for the pleasure of their spectacle. The importance of cinema as a growing cultural phenomenon is reflected in the feverish questioning of Griffith by reporters anxious to know how he will respond to the challenge laid down by *Cabiria*; and the riots outside the cinema after the first screening of the anti-war *Intolerance* underline the role of cinema as a purveyor of ideas and an opinion maker.

Yet the Tavianis' view of the early cinema is not just nostalgic, for they also draw attention to the role of cinema in recording and preserving history for future generations. This theme is first introduced elliptically. Griffith is only able to see the elephant made by Andrea and Nicola because it was captured on film; their model having been destroyed by jealous rivals. This anticipates the film's conclusion where Nicola, having joined the Italian army to fight in the First World War, and nicknamed Hollywood, is given the task of regimental cameraman. By an extraordinary coincidence he bumps into Andrea on the battlefield. Both mortally wounded, they manage to record their deaths for their sons. As they raise their hands in blessing against the background of a Romanesque church, the spectator is transported back to other blessings, other churches seen earlier in the film. The act of filming allows the narrative both to return to the past and to be projected forward into the future. The imagery allows it to be circular and linear at the same time.

This sense of continuity stretches across both time and space. It is closely bound up with the film's representation of masculinity. The brothers' sense of identity is dependent largely on the recognition of their craft, which has been handed down from their ancestors. Their skill is an amalgam of creation and preservation; through it the cathedrals of the Middle Ages and the celluloid film of the twentieth century become historical archives. There is no place for women in this tradition just as there is very little place for them in this film. The conquest of Edna and Mabel is part of the brothers' process of integration into the United States; love changes Nicola to Nickie, for example. The romantic plot is an important element in negotiating cultural difference and the passage from a traditional to a modern way of life. As well as being exceptionally beautiful, Edna and Mabel are indelibly modern. Sexually liberated career girls, they embody the sense of opportunity and freedom from tradition that defined the myth of America. Their sexual liberation is, however, also part of the film's spectacle, as they undress for their lovers, and for the spectator, in a woodland setting that underlines the film's nostalgic pastoral longing. The narrative destiny of the girls is therefore at odds with their representation as independent women but entirely consonant with their passive eroticism. They cannot remain lovers but must become wives and then mothers in order to ensure the continuity of the male line. It is no coincidence that both women give birth to sons.

The death of Edna provokes a crisis in the film's construction of masculinity. Nicola refuses to bring up the baby alone, appearing therefore to refuse the patriarchal mantle. It is this crisis that brings him to return to his origins by enlisting in the Italian army (Andrea fights for the United States). Yet, the rejection of his son is motivated by the fact that his wife's death has made him unequal to his brother. Their relationship had been premised on their equality and the bond that this created protected them from the rivalry of their older brothers and the envy of their competitors in Hollywood. This doubling is also fundamental to the relationship between Bonanno and Griffith. Their meeting at the marriage of the brothers constitutes the film's central scene. The tableau takes place on the set constructed by Griffith for *Intolerance*, reconstructed by the Tavianis for *Good Morning Babilonia* and, like the rest of the film, shot in Tuscany. Placed at either end of a long table the patriarchs face up to each other like gunfighters. Their encounter, in which the urbane Griffith exchanges fire with the defiant Bonanno, concludes in an act of mutual recognition that confers their authority on the sense of continuity through change set up by the brothers. Women have no place in this exchange; their role as onlookers confirming their place in the masculine chain of reproduction. It is men who both make and maintain historical tradition.

One of the consequences of this mode of gender representation is that the challenges of modernity and cultural displacement are met and overcome by a reassertion of traditional values. These are asserted even in the final scene when the fairy tale's apparently tragic conclusion is salvaged by an ironic smile to the camera and to posterity. The film struggles with two contrasting ideas of time; the timeless mode characteristic of the fable, and linear time in which history is made. It is through the representation of space that this conflict is most apparent. The image of Italy created by the film is that of the tourist fantasy; the Tuscan farmhouse, the cathedral façade, the sun-drenched landscape evoke a sense of history that stands outside time. The United States does not, however, represent a historicised counter to this; brief glimpses of the metropolis and modernity give way to the fantastic space of Hollywood or the countryside. When modern space is represented (the hospital or the architect's office) it is a hostile environment threatening to the brothers. This may go some way to explaining the reference in the film's title to the biblical city of Babylon with its dual connotations of exile and sinfulness.

Good Morning Babilonia proposes a comforting historical model at odds with that suggested by the Tavianis' earlier films. *Padre padrone* (*Father, Master*, 1977) is a study in generational conflict set in rural Sardinia and is also a narrative detailing the transition from pre-industrial to modern society. Rural life is portrayed as harsh and unforgiving and patriarchy as brutal and oppressive; there is no anticipation of the bucolic idyll central to *Good Morning Babilonia*. Similarly, in *La notte di San Lorenzo* (*The Night of the Shooting Stars*, 1982) the Tavianis look back at the unresolvable conflict that splits a small Tuscan village during the Second World War; again there is no mechanism through which to render the past a more habitable place than the present even when viewed through the lens of fantasy and memory. Although both films share many of the production values of the later one, most notably the lingering camera-work on the natural landscape, their aesthetic dimension never displaces the historical enquiry of the narrative. However, it might also be added that their analysis is limited to the issue of conflict within a given society and culture, and does not address the perhaps more difficult questions involving exchange between cultures. In *Good Morning Babilonia* the Tavianis attempt to explore cultural and historical difference through the personal experience of two immigrants. It is an attempt to understand how such differences are inhabited and made sense of by those in the midst of the process of transition. The fairy-tale structure of the film and the sentimental emphasis of the narrative combine with the film's aesthetic to conceal the underlying political, social, and economic realities that motivate events. Yet what this reveals is the extent to which myth-making and the construction of specific histories form part of how cultural change is negotiated by those involved. The centrality of cinema as a cultural institution in the film is an essential element of this, for the Tavianis show how crucial the medium has been to the process of cultural interpretation and the construction of historical memory in the twentieth century.

It may be possible to relate the phenomenon of the Italian heritage film to broad social changes taking place in Italy during this period. The political consensus established after the setting up of the Italian Republic after the war had been broken in the 1970s and new political formations, most obviously those led by the media tycoon Silvio Berlusconi, were in the process of creating new alliances with unpredictable consequences. The divide between the prosperous north and the still impoverished south had fostered a climate of separatism and racist intolerance. The arrival, in large numbers, of economic migrants from Africa and Asia also forced Italy to reconsider its status as a First World power and to deal for the first time with questions of racial difference. The diminishing authority of the Catholic Church, and the rise of social movements, most notably feminism, in the wake of 1968, contributed to the reshaping and reconceptualisation of what it might mean to be Italian. To draw attention to these broad changes in Italian society is not simply to attempt to explain films such as *Good Morning Babilonia* or *Nuovo Cinema Paradiso* as merely the products of such change, but rather to indicate the hidden historical moment from which they look back.

Tentatively, it might be suggested that in Italian heritage cinema of the 1980s the longing for Edwardian England is replaced by a longing for a pre-industrial rural society which in the Italian imagination harbours similar connotations of national stability and integrity. Ultimately, however, what the Italian versions of heritage cinema may nostalgically yearn for is less the idealised picture of a pastoral nation than a form of masculine identity that stands outside history and society but, paradoxically, is seen as its motivator, and its agent of preservation and continuity.

References

Baranski, Zygmunt G. and Lumley, Robert (eds) 1990: *Culture and Conflict in Post-War Italy: Essays on Mass and Popular Culture*. London: Macmillan.

Duggan, Christopher and Wagstaff, Christopher (eds) 1995: *Italy in the Cold War: Politics, Culture and Society, 1948–58*. Oxford: Berg.
Higson, Andrew 1996: 'The Heritage Film and British Cinema'. In Andrew Higson (ed.), *Dissolving Views: Key Writings on British Cinema*. London: Cassell.
Sorlin, Pierre 1996: *Italian National Cinema, 1896–1996*. London: Routledge.
Wagstaff, Christopher 1995: 'Italy and the Post-War Cinema Market'. In Duggan and Wagstaff 1995: *Italy in the Cold War: Politics, Culture and Society, 1948–58*. Oxford: Berg.

Suggestions for Further Reading

Ferrucci, Riccardo and Patrizia Turini (eds) 1995: *Paolo & Vittorio Taviani: La poesia del paesaggio*. Rome: Gremese Editore.
Forgács, David 1990: *Italian Culture in the Industrial Era, 1880–1980: Cultural Industries, Politics and the Public*. Manchester: Manchester University Press.
Malavolti, Francesca and Katia Ugolini (eds) 1994: *L'utopia, la poesia, il silenzio. Il cinema dei fratelli Taviani*. Rovigo: Tipografia la grafica.
Sorlin, Pierre 1996: *Italian National Cinema, 1896–1996*. London: Routledge.
Taviani, Paolo 1987: *Good Morning Babilonia*. London: Faber.
Wagstaff, Christopher 1996: 'Cinema'. In David Forgács and Robert Lumley (eds): *Italian Cultural Studies*. Oxford: Oxford University Press. 216–32.

Credits

Directors	Paolo and Vittorio Taviani
Producer	Giuliani G. de Negri
Production Company	Filmtre/MK2 Productions/Pressman Film Corporation, in association with RAI, Films A2
Screenplay	Paolo and Vittorio Taviani
Director of Photography	Giuseppe Lanci
Editor	Roberto Perpignani
Art Director	Gianni Sbarra
Music	Nicola Piovani

Cast

Vincent Spano	Nicola
Joaquim de Almeida	Andrea
Greta Scacchi	Edna
Désirée Baker	Mabel
Omero Antonutti	Bonanno
Charles Dance	D. W. Griffith

Filmography

Un uomo da bruciare (*A Man for Burning*, 1962)
Fuorilegge del matrimonio [Outlaws of matrimony] (1963)
Sovversivi (*The Subversives*, 1967)
Putiferio va alla guerra (*The Magic Bird*, 1968)
Sotto il segno dello scorpione (*Under the Sign of Scorpio*, 1968)
San Michele aveva un gallo (*Saint Michael had a Rooster*, 1971)
Allonsanfan (1974)
Padre, padrone (*Father, Master*, 1977)
Il prato (*The Meadow*, 1979)
La notte di San Lorenzo (*The Night of the Shooting Stars*, 1981)
Kaos (*Chaos*, 1984)
Good Morning Babilonia (*Good Morning Babylon*, 1987)
Il sole anche di notte (*The Sun also Shines at Night*, 1990)
Fiorile (1993)
Affinità elettive (*Chosen Affinities*, 1996)
Tu ridi (*You Laugh*, 1998)

9   *Das Versprechen*

Sophie glimpses West Berlin for the first time, her expression full of anticipation or apprehension.

Das Versprechen (The Promise)

Stuart Taberner

9th November 1989 is etched onto the German national consciousness as the day on which the Berlin Wall fell. Televised images of the euphoria experienced by the inhabitants of this divided city, of their seemingly infinite delight and disbelief, provoked unprecedented sympathy worldwide for a people long respected for the economic success and political stability of the two states in which recent history had determined that they should live, but for whom few outsiders had been able to muster any real affection. The Wall had been erected on 13 August 1961 by the communist rulers of the German Democratic Republic (GDR), ostensibly to 'protect' their East German population against the 'imperialism' of the capitalist west. Berlin thus embodied the global division into two competing power blocs after the Second World War. The collapse of the Wall thirty-eight years after its construction inaugurated the final chapter in the Cold War following the 'velvet revolutions' that had swept across eastern Europe at the decade's end, and a new beginning for Germany, which was unified almost a year later on 3 October 1990.

Epochal events in national history seem to demand an appropriate response in national culture. Almost before the ink was dry on the treaty constituting their new state, Germans were clamouring for *the* novel, *the* drama, *the* work of art that would encapsulate their sensation of being present at the making of history. People needed to work through collective experience and to make sense of a forty-year period that appeared exceptional, even abnormal, from their new perspective. One art form above all may be particularly suited to this task. A film can foreshorten a lengthy chronology, its images can capture monumental events succinctly, provoking 'unmediated' emotional responses, and the medium's popularity means that a director may reach the entire nation. It is not surprising, therefore, that the release of Margarethe von Trotta's *Das Versprechen* (*The Promise*) in 1994 was eagerly awaited by a public impatient to see their experiences reflected back to themselves.

With its use of voice-over narration and documentary material in its introductory scenes, and its frequent recourse to imposing extra-diegetic music, von Trotta's film claims to be an authoritative response to the momentous occurrences it depicts. Yet *Das Versprechen* is just as much about the early 1990s, the time of its production, as about 1989, or even the long years of the Wall's existence. Contemporary affairs are investigated in equal measure with recent history. The film closes with an image of its female protagonist, Sophie, standing on a bridge linking East and West Berlin, surrounded by revellers celebrating the opening of the border. She is gazing at her former lover Konrad, who had remained in the east when Sophie escaped, separated from her by the Wall. Sophie contemplates Konrad (west inspects east), yet her expression reveals little elation, rather an uncanny failure to recognise someone who should be so well known to her. She makes no attempt to approach him, leaving the film's conclusion ambiguous. East and West Germans, a family riven for more than forty years (since the founding of the two states in 1949, and all the more so after the building of the Wall in 1961), are unsure whether they will get on once reunited, and still less confident that they will like one another, or have anything in common after such a long period apart. Indeed, the 'family' metaphor is used extensively in the film. Sophie flees west, but wants her mother to know that she still loves her. Konrad is also alienated, from his father, by his scepticism towards the East German state that his father helped to create. Sophie, on the other hand, blames her stepfather for the suicide in police custody of her real father, implying that an 'authentic' GDR patrimony has been supplanted by an unscrupulous successor. Later, Konrad concedes to Sophie that 'our break-up didn't kill me', much as she contemplated whether their cohabitation in Prague in 1968 would succeed: 'I don't know. We've never lived together'. In both cases, East and West Germans admit that family ties have loosened and that it is not certain that the grand reunion will flourish. The symbolism of the bridge (one of many images of bridges and trains in the film) may be an empty gesture as Germans continue to be divided by the 'Wall in the head' – an expression that has become shorthand for the many misunderstandings between *Ossis* and *Wessis* – by different value systems, cultural codes, and economic prospects. In a sense, therefore, the film suggests the failure of unification, and reveals the promise that stands as its title to be one that has been neither kept, nor fulfilled. Its final scene denies the classic cinematic pleasure of closure and refuses to deliver the happy ending that the audience might have expected.

More particularly, the film expresses the disappointment of the left–liberal social, political and intellectual consensus that had dominated West Germany's cultural sphere since the late 1960s, most often in implied, sometimes even explicit opposition to the conservative politicians who had ruled the country for much of its short existence. The attitudes of the writers, dramatists, and film-makers whose beliefs had been shaped by their participation in the student revolts of 1968 had always been ambiguous on the question of German division. On the one hand, they insisted that the carving up of the nation was just punishment for their parents' complicity in Hitler's madness. At the same time, they were critical of their own state, of the conservative nature of society and politics in West Germany, its materialism, unexpunged racism, social divisiveness, and inequality. They looked to East Germany, therefore, to realise their ideal of a fairer society, free of capitalism and of the dominance of one social class over another. In their minds the German Democratic Republic had always offered a potential utopia – in *theory*, at least – to be contrasted with the seeming corruption of their own state, which appeared to many of them as latently fascist, indeed barely reformed after national socialism. Intellectuals had been particularly disturbed by the ease with which ex-members of the Nazi party had risen to high positions in the West German economy and government. Yet the collapse of East Germany in 1989, followed by countless revelations of neighbours spying on one another, propitious political conversions, supposed dissidents collaborating with the state secret services, and ubiquitous social disintegration finally revealed the emptiness of the promise that the GDR had long embodied for West German intellectuals. They could no longer believe that the country's geriatric totalitarian leadership had been an aberration, the corruption of a dream that had none the less remained alive within the population as a whole, and which ordinary East Germans would rush to accomplish once they were free to do so, in 1989/90, and a whole range of writers, intellectuals and film-makers, including Margarethe von Trotta and Wim Wenders, were forced to look again at their previous attitudes towards both East and West Germany.

The realisation that they had been wrong to trust in the GDR's ability to reform itself and fulfil its potential led to a crisis of confidence amongst the mainly left-leaning West German cultural aristocracy that had held sway since the late 1960s. This was compounded by their powerlessness to resist the march towards unification between November 1989 and October 1990. They were forced to acknowledge that – far from desiring to introduce 'true' socialism in the GDR – the majority of East Germans, as proved by elections and demonstrations, wanted only to join West Germany as quickly as possible in order to enjoy a standard of living of which they had only been able to dream previously. The call with which the revolution in the GDR had started, 'We are *the* people' – interpreted by West German intellectuals as the demand of ordinary East Germans for self-determination, democracy, and social justice – had given way to the more insistent, and rapacious, 'We are *one* people'. Access to the affluence taken for granted by West Germans had become the major impetus for unification.

This condemnation of *eastern* materialism features strongly in *Das Versprechen*. The young East Germans who escape to the west with Sophie shortly after the building of the Wall in 1961 are portrayed as acquisitive. They joke about Sophie's aunt, asking whether she lives in a villa, and about her uncle, demanding to know if he owns a castle. On emerging from the sewage system into West Berlin, one of the youths exclaims: 'I love Fords', thereby embracing American-style consumerism from the moment he arrives. Even Sophie is seen to partake in the fashions and comforts of the west, especially in later years, when her sophistication is contrasted with the 'impoverishment' of Konrad's life in the east. In a memorable scene, shortly after her arrival in West Berlin, Sophie is pictured at a fashion show with the ruins of the church built in memory of the Emperor Wilhelm in the background. This places her on the Kurfursten-damm, West Berlin's most elegant shopping street, and allegorises the links between West German consumerism, West Berlin landmarks, the repression of Hitler's war, and even the First World War (Kaiser Wilhelm's war). More frequently, however, the film engages with questions of complicity, conformity, and opposition in the GDR, interrogating Konrad about the compromises he makes with the regime in order to pursue his career and personal happiness. The attention paid to Konrad in fact highlights the film's lack of balance in its almost exclusive focus on the East. *Das Versprechen* thus serves a dual purpose: education about East Germany, and condemnation of those in the GDR who failed to reform a corrupt communism. Significantly, perhaps, von Trotta's production was partially funded by the Ministry of the Interior of Helmut Kohl's conservative government – that is, a government that was against both the GDR and the dominance of the intellectual left in West German culture.

One of those who played a major role in the conceptualisation of *Das Versprechen* as co-writer was Peter Schneider, an established author and critic of West Germany's social and political conservatism since the 1960s. Schneider's novel *Der Mauerspringer* (*The Wall Jumper*, 1982) had attracted much attention for its vision of a shared German culture, and more particularly for its suggestion that the imagination might occupy the (literal) no-man's land between the ideological positions of the two states. The border zone of the Berlin Wall where Schneider's characters meet on their fantastical journeys from east to west and west to east creates a realm where the potential inherent in both Germanies – distorted by the Cold War – might be realised, if only in fiction. In 1990, however, Schneider was forced to concede that even this might be too much to ask. In a collection of essays published in that year, the author outlines the need for those on the West German left (including himself) to recognise the folly of their identification with the aims and ideals of what they mistakenly saw as the 'real' GDR, that is, 'true' socialism, equality, and solidarity as opposed to the corruption of the leadership.

Schneider's participation as a writer in the making of *Das Versprechen* is reflected in the fact that its 'message' is conveyed in the dialogue and narrative progression. The participation of Margarethe von Trotta is perhaps more puzzling. Von Trotta's interest in recent German history had been apparent in almost all of her previous work, and she has often commented that she cannot imagine making a film that does not bear directly upon the situation in Germany. Likewise, her concern with the fate of liberal values, the humanist heritage of the Lutheran Church, and her anti-fascist and pro-peace agenda are as evident in *Das Versprechen* as in her previous work, as is her concentration upon the family as a microcosm of society. Yet, above all, von Trotta is a feminist film-maker, who has been concerned more with the oppression of women than with German division. She has been at the forefront of 'women's film' (an ambiguous but perhaps inevitable term) in West Germany since the emergence of the feminist movement in the early 1970s gave it its initial impetus. Women directors focused on abortion, patriarchy, and female identity, often favoured a documentary style, and engaged with issues of spectatorship (who is looking at whom, and the question of audience). A creator of more conventionally narrative cinema than other women directors, von Trotta soon established herself as a leading feminist film-maker in a country in which the existence of television stations interested in social themes and film subsidies had brought more women into film production than anywhere else in the world.

The fact that *Das Versprechen* does not focus on matters of particular relevance to women, in contrast to von Trotta's earlier films, may mirror the transformation of West Germany's film culture in the early 1990s. Once again, therefore, *Das Versprechen* reflects upon the historical circumstances of its own production. In the 1970s, various types of 'women's film' (as befits the ambiguity of the term) had emerged in response to the feminist movement and to the perception that women (who had previously made up the majority of audiences) were no longer going to the cinema. Hence, at the same time as innovative film-makers such as von Trotta, Helma Sanders-Brahms, and Helke Sander were exploring female identity in an avant-garde fashion in their films, male directors such as Rainer Werner Fassbinder and Alexander Kluge were responding to the demand for female autonomy by scripting women protagonists. Hollywood, more cynically, aimed to appeal directly to a potential female audience in movies such as Scorsese's *Alice Doesn't Live Here Anymore* (1974), in which a woman escapes male domination and begins a new life.

By the 1990s, however, the market for women's cinema had changed. A decline in interest in both 'highbrow' women's films and the Hollywood variant of the genre had coincided with the emergence of a 'post-feminist' sensibility. At the same time, German culture has undergone a 'normalisation' since 1989, that is, it has become more similar to the patterns in force across the western world. Unification, and the arrival of a new generation of writers, artists, and film-makers, has led to the substitution of the 'traditional' themes of West German culture – the national socialist past, German identity, and the divided nation – for the issues that dominate the 1990s in other western countries. In common with film culture elsewhere in Europe and America, German films, and especially those by female directors, have been examining the legacy of feminism, and redefining it in the context of a wider debate on gender and sexuality. Romantic comedies for 'thirty-somethings' have scored incredible successes in a way that would have been improbable only a few years earlier. Sönke Wortmann's *Der bewegte Mann* (*Maybe . . . Maybe Not*, 1994) thus features a man, thrown out by his girlfriend after an affair, who finds refuge in the gay scene as a straight object of desire. Gender and sexuality confusion follow with comic alacrity until the woman takes him back, creating new ground rules for the relationship, reuniting men and women, and conceding her need for his love. This need for male affection is also central to Katja von Garnier's *Abgeschminkt!* (*Makin' Up!*, 1993), as the tomboy protagonist reconciles her desire for independence with her attraction for a partner who combines a 'fundamental' masculinity with a 'new man' attitude towards women.

In the context of these developments in German film, *Das Versprechen*, with its focus on history and the theme of national identity, seems to belong to a pre-1989 cultural paradigm. Von Trotta avoids the issue of gender relations almost entirely, perhaps in acknowledgement of changed market conditions, perhaps because it is not central to her theme of divided Germany. Yet another aspect of the film's production reveals a rather more astute understanding of the transformation of the film scene. *Das Versprechen* is a German–French–Swiss co-production filmed in the Berlin Babelsberg studios (ironically the former home of the East German DEFA film company). This internationalisation reflects the increasing trend towards co-operation between European television stations with a more 'art-house' and less obviously commercial remit, such as Channel Four Films, or Canal Plus, with European financial assistance. This has raised questions about the extent to which films made in Europe can still be divided into 'national cinemas', even as it has enabled European directors to compete with Hollywood. The scale of *Das Versprechen*, as well as the conventionality of its cinematography and plot (a standard, perhaps even trivial love story), may imply a new confidence in European film's ability to survive alongside its American rivals.

Das Versprechen discloses its debt to America not only in its wholesale adoption of Hollywood film techniques (such as the fact that at key moments the camera imitates the conventional Hollywood romantic two-shot), but also in its recognition of the centrality of the United States to European culture, particularly in West Germany. The 'Americanisation' of the western part of the country is integrated into the film's theme of the divided nation. Sophie's son Alexander lives with his mother in West Berlin, separated from his father Konrad by the Wall. He is thoroughly 'American', and is typically seen wearing a baseball cap turned backwards on his head along with a bomber jacket. He emerges as sophisticated and cosmopolitan, especially in contrast with his half-sister, who lives with their father in East Berlin. The theme of national identity, or its absence, is implied by Alexander's appearance and attitudes. The fact that he is indistinguishable from American youths of his age suggests the saturation of West German identity by American popular culture.

West German society is criticised for its materialism, consumerism, and superficiality, traits that are believed to have derived from the wholesale adoption of American values. On its few excursions to West Berlin, the film is determined to insinuate the social disintegration, anomie, and inequality typically associated with American-style capitalism. When Konrad visits Alexander in West Berlin, for example, the symptoms of urban decay are obvious. They walk past youths stripping down an abandoned car, and Alexander appears unsurprised by what is clearly an everyday occurrence in his district. Konrad's brother-in-law Harald is later expelled from the GDR by the authorities (a favoured means of exporting 'awkward characters') and deposited in the Zoologischer Garten railway station, a West Berlin location in which drug-pushers, beggars, and prostitutes infamously gather. Harald is overwhelmed by the depravity of the west and effectively commits suicide by attempting to recross the border illegally. His bewildered reaction highlights the relative absence of 'western' social ills in East Germany, partly as a consequence of generous welfare provision (concealing problems such as structural unemployment and homelessness through subsidies), and partly resulting from the authorities' ruthlessness in stamping out criminality.

To a large extent Sophie embodies the unease felt by the makers of *Das Versprechen*, and by the intellectual left in general, with regard to West Germany as a capitalist state within the economic, military, and political system of the west. Unlike her fellow escapees from the GDR, she never feels entirely at home in West Germany. She represents the intellectual conscience of the divided nation, made uncomfortable by the superficiality of the west, but shocked by the denial of freedom in the east. Her reluctance to celebrate the opening of the Wall suggests her disillusionment with the materialism that came to dominate the drive towards unification in 1989/1990 and her regret at the missed opportunities made manifest by the failure of East German socialism. This sense of rootlessness is expressed on a number of occasions during the film, most notably when Sophie responds to questions about her departure from the GDR with the revealing words: 'I left but I don't really know if I got anywhere', and later with distinctly lukewarm enthusiasm, in Prague in 1968, to an enquiry from a Czech friend as to whether she is from West Germany: 'I lived there'.

During her stay in Czechoslovakia in 1968, Sophie admits that she has never felt at home in the west. The Prague Spring, in fact, is given great prominence in the film, reflecting the profound impression it made upon intellectuals in both East and West Germany. The efforts of Alexander Dubcek's reformist government to liberalise Czech politics, to achieve a degree of independence from the Soviet Union, and to steer a 'third way' between capitalism and communism – summed up in the rallying call 'socialism with a human face' – generated immense sympathy amongst those West German intellectuals who disapproved of their own country's reliance on the United States, and who were disappointed by the GDR's failure to realise its utopian potential. Many East German intellectuals also watched developments in Prague with passionate interest, hoping that the example might spread to the GDR. For Sophie and Konrad, however, the Prague Spring is but a brief interlude, time snatched together on neutral territory in a place where they might both feel at home. The film's images of the arrival of Soviet tanks in the dead of night and of courageous, yet futile, Czech resistance possess an almost ritual quality. The rumble of the tanks' engines shatters window panes, protesters are beaten off by heavily armed Soviet troops, and western press photographs are used by the authorities to identify the 'culprits'. The fact that the film is able to offer no new images of Prague in 1968 may suggest the collective trauma of those intellectuals in east and west whose hopes were destroyed by the crushing of the Czech experiment. The failure of the Prague Spring remains a stumbling block in the psyche of the left that cannot be overcome nor revisioned in aesthetic terms other than those that have dominated since the events themselves.

The outcome of 1968 marked a turning point in the history of the GDR. In *Das Versprechen* East German troops are rumoured to be part of the Soviet

force. Intellectuals in both parts of Germany were horrified by the apparent
complicity of German infantry in the demolition of Czechoslovakia less than
thirty years after Hitler's brutal conquest (in fact no GDR soldiers were directly
involved in the Soviet invasion, but this was not clear at the time). For East
Germans in particular, the failure of the Prague Spring made it painfully clear
that reform was impossible in their own country. The choice was stark, therefore,
between conformity and opposition. Yet this could never be an easy decision.
Konrad's professor, mentor, and friend, signs the denunciation of the Prague
Spring that is required of him by the East German authorities, thereby com-
promising his earlier commitment to improving the communist state from
within. Individual history, the fact that he chose the GDR over what he saw
as the resurgence of fascism in the West after 1945, means that Konrad's boss
is emotionally linked with the GDR, despite its imperfections: 'I'm part of this
fucked up country'. Biographical ties, idealism, and personal identification made
it difficult for many East German intellectuals to cross over into direct opposition.

Notwithstanding the effort required to overcome previous identification with
the founding ideals of the GDR, von Trotta's film interrogates its East German
protagonists as to the motives for their continued conformity after the crushing
of the Prague experiment in 1968. By implication it also asks whether West
German intellectuals were naive in their refusal to abandon their utopian vision
of the 'other GDR', that is, of the resistance offered by supposedly 'ordinary'
East Germans to the state in their pursuit of 'true' socialism. In doing this, the
film also addresses the key post-unification debate on the question of whether
GDR socialism can be compared to national socialism. This is a vital issue. If
East Germany and the Nazi state can be equated, then the failure to resist
GDR totalitarianism constitutes a 'second guilt', a repeated dereliction of the
moral imperative to oppose evil. As Konrad says to his professor: 'It's because
of people like you that tanks decide'. East Germany, moreover, drew much of its
legitimacy, and even its appeal, from the claim that it alone represented the
anti-fascist tradition in German history. Many of the film's East German characters defend their state, and its occasional excesses, as the only alternative to
West Germany, which is seen as the successor state to Hitler's Third Reich.
Konrad's father, for example, initially justifies the building of the Berlin Wall
as a necessary evil if the communist cause is to counter the threat posed by a
'fascist' West German state. Later in the film, Konrad's secret police chaperone,
Müller, claims that he joined the security services because he was so incensed
by Nazi barbarism as exposed in early East German didactic films.

Müller represents the distortion of the anti-fascist ideals that underpinned
the founding of the GDR into the reality of intrusive state surveillance and social
control. Yet the analogy between East Germany and the Hitler regime is most
pointed at Konrad's trial for refusing to add his name to the condemnation of
the Prague Spring already signed by his professor. His father is refused entry
to the courtroom and comments bitterly that even under Hitler his own parents
had been allowed to attend his hearing. The implicit analogy, suggested by

a member of the founding generation of the GDR, a victim of fascism for whom the new state had initially represented the redemption of Germany's Nazi past, almost goes unnoticed by the official on duty: 'well, we no longer live in the...did you say "Nazi days?"' The hesitation perhaps implies that the comparison is less scandalous than it might at first appear. The point is well made for an audience accustomed to self-recrimination for their national socialist past. Here is another legacy that must be confronted in an ongoing investigation of an apparent historical propensity for acquiescence and complicity.

Shortly after Konrad's trial, his father dies, a broken man, disaffected from the state he had helped to create, and urging his son to flee west to be with Sophie and the child that she had conceived in Prague. The fact that the possibility even exists for Konrad to attend a congress in Stockholm (where he plans to abscond with Sophie) raises questions, however, about the extent to which he has sacrificed the principled stand he took with regard to the Prague Spring, for the sake of personal gain. It is clear that he must have signed the denunciation of the Czech experiment required of him, or otherwise compromised with the state, in order to get permission to travel in the west, since this was a privilege reserved only for the most trusted servants of the regime. In many ways, Konrad's duplicity here merely confirms his ambivalent attitude towards the state from the very beginning. At the start of the film he stumbles whilst trying to tie his shoelaces and is left behind by Sophie and their friends who escape through the drainage system from East into West Berlin. He subsequently fastens them on the orders of the party official who interrogates him. Konrad's son Alexander unwittingly alludes to the 'shoelace motif' much later when standing with his father near the East Berlin manhole through which Sophie had escaped. Alexander jokes about escaping and kneels down to tie his father's laces.

Throughout the film, in fact, doubts are raised as to whether Konrad was ever committed to leaving the GDR. He accepts promotions, adjusts to the limited possibilities that are open to him in order to realise his scientific talent, and consistently gives in to the state's efforts to coerce him into conformity by threatening to deny Alexander permission to enter the country. Konrad's single act of rebellion when he strikes Müller has less to do with resistance to an oppressive regime than with his inability to contain any longer the frustration that has been accumulating within him for years. The uprising of 1989, embodied by Konrad's explosion of anger, is thus dismissed as a rather uncharacteristic – and belated – gesture of almost immature defiance by an otherwise passive GDR population. Konrad may be reading a book entitled *Das neue Denken* (*The New Thinking*), but he has insufficient presence of mind to grasp that a neighbour's cry that the wall has come down refers to the Berlin Wall.

Margarethe von Trotta's *Das Versprechen* responds to contemporary concerns on a number of levels. It belongs to a pre-1989 pattern in its final reckoning with the themes that traditionally dominated cultural practice in West Germany – national socialism, German identity, and national division – but which, since unification, have gradually given way to the issues of sexuality and personal identity that have shaped the postmodern 1990s throughout the western world. In its recognition of the internationalisation of European film-making, however, it also embodies the transformation of the film market. More specifically, *Das Versprechen* addresses the debates that have been raging in the new Germany about the nation's most recent past. It alludes to the questions of whether GDR socialism can be equated with Hitler's Germany, whether left-wing intellectuals in the west were naive to cling on to their idealistic assessment of the GDR's ability to realise its potential, and whether ordinary East German citizens were complicit for too long in tolerating an oppressive state. The film implies that there is always a choice, and that the majority of people decide for personal security rather than moral integrity.

In an intentional echo of the controversy surrounding court cases brought against former GDR border guards who had carried out the state's shoot-to-kill policy, Konrad is shown early in the film practising bayoneting techniques in preparation for his own service at the Berlin Wall. Another soldier refuses to countenance the murder of fellow citizens desiring to escape and is dismissed. Konrad, on the other hand, continues with his training, perhaps hesitantly, but none the less certain this is the only way to achieve his ambitions of university education and a career as a scientist. Unlike his sister, whose activities as a protestant pastor bring her into constant conflict with the state (and with the Church authorities, who were keen not to antagonise a regime that tolerated religion only with the greatest reluctance), Konrad remains in the country not because of any idealistic notion of transforming socialism, but because he is comfortable there. Ultimately, he is 'at home'. We may imagine that he, unlike his sister, will prosper in the new Germany. The church groups, grassroots political organisations, and various pressure groups that had fought so courageously against their own hierarchies and the state to bring about the amelioration of the GDR, disappeared after 1989, rendered insignificant by the numbers of people favouring affluence over meaningful political change. The determination of Konrad's sister to make a difference in East Germany is mocked by the masses crossing the bridge to the west. For the overwhelming majority the consumerist paradise on earth proved to be preferable to the heavenly promise that the protestant pastor, along with fellow intellectuals in east and west, had hoped the GDR might help to realise.

References and Suggestions for Further Reading

Knight, Julia 1992: *Women and the New German Cinema*. London: Verso.

Elsaesser, Thomas 1987: 'Public Bodies and Divided Selves: German Women Film-makers in the 80s'. In *Monthly Film Bulletin*, December.

Elsaesser, Thomas 1988: 'A Retrospect on the New German Cinema'. In *German Life and Letters*, 41, 3.

Elsaesser, Thomas 1989: *New German Cinema: A History*. London: Macmillan.

Fulbrook, Mary 1991: *Germany: The Divided Nation*. London: Fontana.
Fulbrook, Mary 1995: *Anatomy of a Dictatorship: Inside the GDR, 1949–89*. Oxford: Oxford University Press.
Sandford, John 1980: *The New German Cinema*. New York: Da Capo.
Schneider, Peter 1992: *The German Comedy: Scenes of Life after the Wall*. London: I. B. Tauris.

Credits

Director	Margarethe von Trotta
Producer	Eberhard Kunkersdorf
Production Company	Bioskop-Film, Munich; Odessa Films; J. M. H. Productions, Lausanne; Westdeutscher Rundfunk; Babelsberg Studios; Canal Plus; Centre National de la Cinématographie; Fonds Eurimages du Conseil de l'Europe; Bundesministerium des Innern
Scenario	Margarethe von Trotta, Peter Schneider
Editor	Suzanne Baron
Director of Photography	Franz Rath
Art Director	Martin Dostal
Music	Jürgen Knieper

Cast

Meret Becker	Sophie 1
Corinna Harfouch	Sophie 2
Anian Zollner	Konrad 1
August Zirner	Konrad 2
Susann Ugé	Barbara 1
Eva Mattes	Barbara 2
Pierre Besson	Harald 1
Hans Kremer	Harald 2
Christian Herschmann	Alexander 1
Jörg Meister	Alexander 2
Otto Sander	Lorenz
Udo Kroschwald	Müller 1
Hask Bohm	Müller 2
Tina Engel	Sophie's aunt
Jean-Yves	Gaultier Gérard
Dieter Mann	Konrad's father
Ulrike Krumbiegel	Elisabeth

Filmography

Das zweite Erwachen des Christa Klages (*The Second Awakening of Christa Klages*, 1977)
Schwestern oder Die Balance des Glücks (*Sisters or The Balance of Happiness*, 1979)

Die bleierne Zeit (The German Sisters, 1981)
Heller Wahn (Friends and Husbands, 1982)
Rosa Luxemburg (1981)
Drei Schwestern (Three Sisters, 1988)
Rückkehr (Africana / Return, 1990)
Il lungo Silenzio (The Long Silence, 1993)
Die Frauen in der Rosenstrasse (1994)
Mit 50 Küssen Manner Anders (1998)

10 *La haine*

Vinz (Vincent Cassel), Saïd (Saïd Taghmaoui), and Hubert (Hubert Koundé) try to get into Astérix's flat.

La haine

Jill Forbes

Since its initial screening at the Cannes Film festival in 1995 where it was awarded the director's prize, *La haine* has become a cult movie inside and outside France, attracting large audiences and generating websites and electronic discussion groups – a success which is based on its ability to appeal to widely different audiences. Its subject-matter is parochial, but it addresses all those who live in large, cosmopolitan conurbations; it appeals to generational solidarity beyond distinctions of race, gender or nationality; it refers to the traditions of French cinema and culture and depicts a social context which is French, but its citation of American filmic and musical material gives it an international dimension. It is a highly wrought and meticulously planned work of art, but it looks like a television current affairs or documentary programme. Like Godard's *A bout de souffle* or Blier's *Les valseuses*, *La haine* is a *zeitgeist* film which sums up the mood and preoccupations of a particular time and place, but in a way that is internationally appealing.

The film depicts twenty-four hours in the life of three unemployed young men, Vinz, Saïd and Hubert – a Jew, a Beur (child of North African immigrants) and a Black – who live on a housing estate called the Cité des Muguets (lilies of the valley) and who hang out together. It is distantly inspired by events in April 1993 when the seventeen-year-old Makomé (Mako) M'Bowole from Zaire died in custody, allegedly as a result of police brutality. In *La haine* the fictional Abdel Ichaha is in a coma in hospital because of a police blunder (*bavure*) and the inhabitants of the Cité have protested by rioting, causing a great deal of damage to property and totally destroying the gym where Hubert used to train.

La haine is divided into segments, each representing roughly two hours, by digital time-checks flashed onto a black screen. These are accompanied by a ticking sound, as though the film were a countdown to an explosion, which builds up dramatic tension and creates a powerful teleological movement. As in so much French newspaper and television reporting of 'les quartiers chauds' (problem districts), the Cité is presented as a powder keg made up of a lethal mixture of drugs, unemployment, racism and police brutality. At the beginning of the film we see the image of a Molotov cocktail hurled at a globe and breaking into flames, prefiguring the lethal outburst of violence at the end. The image is given an allegorical dimension by a parable, heard first in voice-over at the beginning, and repeated twice, about a man who jumps from a fifty-storey block of flats and who, as he falls, repeats to himself 'so far so good', with the punchline 'what's important isn't the fall but the landing'. What propels *La haine* is the irony and creative tension which derive from this contrast between the film's structural purposefulness and the aimlessness of the protagonists' lives, between the inevitability of the explosion of violence and the friends' essential innocence and naivety.

The unemployment, racial tension and rioting in several large cities, which contributed to the rise of the extreme-right National Front in France in the 1980s, provide the film's social backdrop. Under electoral and media pressure from the Front, the right-wing government of the late 1980s tried to enact new nationality laws which particularly targeted Beurs like Saïd and required them to 'prove' that they were worthy of being French. This gave rise to a national debate about citizenship, integration and multiculturalism which set the French tradition of 'universalism' (whereby immigrants are seamlessly incorporated into the national community through an education system which does not recognise ethnic, religious or racial diversity) against a 'multiculturalist' tradition, seen as originating in America. The three protagonists were all born and brought up in France but because they all belong to minority religious or ethnic groups, it would be customary to refer to them as 'immigrés' even though they are not technically 'immigrants' at all. Though they reject the cultures associated with their families – Vinz's grandmother complains about him not attending synagogue – they have not been integrated into the national community in a way that community accepts. Their language is 'verlan', a kind of backslang that has become the fashionable dialect of young people, rather than the standard French heard on the television, and their values are those of homosocial, cross-race, generational solidarity. Whatever the public rhetoric about universal values, these young men are excluded from the national community by unemployment and poverty and by their geographical relegation to a housing development outside the narrowly defined boundaries of central Paris.

La haine seizes brilliantly on a metaphor which is a commonplace in French novels and films about the city, and re-interprets it for the 1990s. From the nineteenth century onwards many writers, such as Baudelaire whose blown-up image adorns a wall of the Cité, embroidered on the distinction beween Paris and the surrounding area, known as the 'zone', which was supposedly populated by gangs of criminals and prostitutes, and was richly invested with imaginative possibilities. One was that the bourgeois inhabitants of Paris could visit the outlying areas as tourists in search of visual or sexual thrills; another was that the denizens of the outlying districts, the 'zonards', might invade the city and cause havoc of one kind or another. This notion was exploited by many of the French reviewers of the film who described how hordes of young people from 'la banlieue' were swarming into Paris to see themselves represented on screen. Axiomatic to this convention was the idea that the rules and codes of conduct of one area did not apply and, indeed, were often inverted in the other, just as the 'verlan' used in the Cité inverts standard French; and this can be seen in the films of Marcel Carné or Jacques Becker which are the distant ancestors of *La haine*. *La haine* uses the relationship of inversion between the city and its outlying districts as a structuring trope and combines literary and filmic convention with contemporary social discourse that is itself influenced by such clichés. The latter are evident in the gallery owner's comment on the friends' behaviour as the 'malaise des banlieues' ('housing estate' sickness) as well as in the stream of slogans and proverbs the friends cite, with some irony, to pass the time before they can go home. In this way, the friends' trip into Paris and their adventures in the city, which occupy most of the second half of the film, combine social comment on the difference between the values of the *banlieue* and those of the metropolis, a critique of the exclusion of one group from the centre of culture and civilisation, a critique of that civilisation, and a calculated evocation of artistic conventions which are based on the distinction between Paris and the zone. *La haine* succeeds in espousing the values of the outlying districts, keeping the viewer's sympathies firmly with the three friends, even when they are shown behaving badly, whilst at the same time transforming their adventures into spectacle and entertainment for bourgeois consumption by the use of recognisable conventions of French literature and cinema.

The credit sequences are a telescopic montage of most of the themes and techniques in the film. We see a Molotov cocktail thrown onto a blue globe which explodes in flames that change from colour to black and white, marking a transition from the high-gloss world of the advertising hoarding where the globe originates (as we discover later in the film), to the gritty reality of documentary film-making. A man in overalls with his back to the camera shouts to a distant line of armed police that the workers' only weapon is stones. Shots of CRS riot police fitting metal screens over the windows of their vehicles alternate with footage of demonstrators in central Paris. We then see the police lined up in riot gear, confronting young people dancing in the streets. Gradually the images of confrontation become more violent: the police fire tear-gas grenades and flares; the demonstrators overturn and set fire to a car, break the windows of shops, hurl stones at the CRS. Finally we see the neon sign of a shopping centre illuminated by a conflagration. The Bob Marley song *Burnin' and Lootin'* is dubbed over these images, replacing the original soundtracks attached to the footage, and it is not until the end of the sequence that sound and image finally coincide when we see glass being broken and hear it as well. As the song ceases, a female newsreader's voice reports the riots in the Cité and we cut to her face on the TV screen. We realise that this montage is a brief history of urban protest which has taken us from the relatively peaceful student demonstrations of May 1968, through the hippy street parties of the early 1970s, to the gradual importing into France of race hatred and police brutality – it is implied, from America. One poster reads 'Don't forget the police kill'; another 'Remember Mako'. The sounds of violence and what the Marley song calls 'the music of the ghetto' come together to underline and problematise the coincidence of art and reality.

The use of the newsreader is an economical way of informing the viewer about what is happening and it also introduces a major theme of the film, which is the power of the media. The friends depend on television to know what is going on in their community, and hope to see themselves 'making the news'. Vinz tries to watch the news when in Darty's store, as does Hubert when he calls in at home, and it is while they are sprawled in front of a giant, silent TV screen, waiting for the first train to take them home, that they learn from a newsflash that Abdel has died. But in the Cité communications are distinctly low-tech, the televisions don't work properly and when Saïd wants to get in touch with Vinz he shouts up to an open window. In Paris, on the other hand, Astérix's flat is entered via a high-tech intercom and video screen and all the hoardings and screens in the metropolis convey their messages with smooth efficiency, exacerbating the sense that the Cité is dispossessed. The film criticises the patronising approach of much television reporting of 'la banlieue' and the way television seeks to sensationalise confrontations between the police and young people. Thus the friends accuse a TV crew, who are too frightened or too lazy to get out of their van, of treating them like animals in the safari park at Thoiry, dangerous beasts to be looked at from the safety of a car. At the same time, they long to see themselves on television because it is a form of legitimation, a confirmation that they exist for the world outside.

In this society it appears that people are constantly being filmed. This can be for security reasons (Astérix's flat), for comic effect (Saïd's brother's virtually incomprehensible story about the candid camera), or because of an almost prurient curiosity about how the other half live (the TV crew). At various points the film asks who owns images, how images relate to reality, and how they take on symbolic significance. Vinz mimics Travis Bickle, the hero of Scorsese's *Taxi Driver*, leading the audience to wonder if he will adopt Bickle's gun-crazy persona. Hubert's image as a boxer appears on a poster for a match, perhaps recalling that of De Niro in Scorsese's *Raging Bull*, but its implied violence is at odds with Hubert's reflective, sober and essentially non-violent character. Abdel, who is, ironically, the only member of the community to achieve the legitimation of television, has ceased to be real and has become an image on countless TV screens and a symbol of police brutality.

In general in the film, the media transform reality into theatrical spectacle. They dramatise events such as the riots, or the loss of the policeman's gun, which turns into a suspense narrative that requires a tragic dénouement. Theatricality is emphasised by the three-part structure of the film, which might be thought to emulate the protasis, epitasis and catastrophe of Greek or Racinian tragedy. Television transforms the Cité into an entertainment in which people do not act naturally but perform predetermined roles which inevitably lead to a final, tragic shoot-out.

Against this we are given glimpses of more spontaneous or authentic creativity in the apparently irrelevant story told by Grunwalski in the toilet, or the various forms of expressive activity open to the friends. Vinz is an actor and dancer, or would like to be; Hubert is a sportsman; Saïd is an artist who embodies the anarchic spirit of the Situationists by spraying graffiti on a police van or altering the message on a billboard. By leaving his mark in this way and changing the slogan from 'the world is yours' to 'the world is ours', Saïd is momentarily able to repossess the public sphere which is otherwise regulated by strenuous but pointless efforts to dominate the people by physical or ideological means.

An immediately striking aspect of *La haine* is the very minor role women play in the film. The central characters are male, the police are almost all male, the children hanging around the estate are male and almost all the people encountered in Paris are men. Women are referred to with a combination of exaggerated respect and contempt, and put in only brief appearances as sisters, mothers and grandmothers. Hubert, Vinz and Saïd discuss women so as to valorise their masculinity, but in practice they are bossed around and often intimidated by their female relations in a manner which underlines their disempowerment. Vinz, for example, is verbally abused by his sister, and is scared of his grandmother's reaction when he brings red peppers rather than green ones back from the shop. Likewise Hubert's mother asserts her dominance of the domestic space by chasing him from the kitchen. On their rare appearances outside the home, young women, in pairs or in groups, are not impressed or intimidated by the boys' aggressiveness. Saïd is teased by his sister and her friends as he tries to police her sexuality, while his attempt to chat up two girls in the art gallery in Paris falls extremely flat since they had expected an intellectual rather than a sexual approach.

The virtual elimination of women from the action emphasises the fact that space in the Cité des Muguets is divided on gender lines. The exterior belongs to the men, who compete to dominate the available space: the roof where the barbecue takes place is a prized vantage point which the young men, the security guards and the plainclothes police all fight to control with a degree of primitive territoriality; the walkways and piazzas are places where Vinz, Hub, Saïd and their contemporaries wander freely, as do the male children. The interiors are dominated by women, who are shown in the stereotypically female pursuits of cooking and sewing. The women uphold traditional moral, educational and social practices reflected in child-rearing (Hubert's mother is pregnant), domestic labour, and religion (Vinz's grandmother's attachment to synagogue), which are all the domain of the females on this estate.

Spatial relations are initially disrupted by the riot. Saïd puzzles over how a car managed to get inside the gym, transforming the interior into an exterior. Surreal moments, such as Vinz's vision of a cow, or the literal flight of fancy over the rooftops which is apparently induced by a sound-mix of rap and Edith Piaf, turn into acute disorientation when the trio arrive in Paris. Their sense of dislocation on arrival is underscored, for the audience, by a shot that combines a dolly-in and a zoom out, flattening the perspective and distorting the relationship of the planes of the image. Such spatial *dépaysement* is echoed in the polite behaviour of the Paris policeman who, to Saïd's astonishment, treats him respectfully.

In Paris the friends find that they cannot map gender onto space as they can, for the most part, in the Cité. The simple and easily understood spatial relations in the first part of the film gradually turn into a metaphor for exclusion as the friends attempt to enter various spaces and find either that their presence is not acceptable, or that the space is not decipherable, or that the spaces become prisons of one kind or another. The Astérix episode is a case in point. 'Astérix' is an ironically assumed French identity (Astérix the Gaul); he does not own the apartment, he has borrowed it; his gestures and body language are aggressive not because he is male but because he is on drugs, and his sexual preferences are ambiguous since it is implied that he is attracted to Saïd. The loin cloth he is wearing also contributes to the uncertainty about whether this space is inside (female) or outside (male). One of the girls in the gallery is a Beur but she has more in common with the gallery owner than with Saïd; another is sporting an extravagant decolleté which, like Astérix's clothes, creates confusion about interior and exterior space and which Saïd misreads as an invitation to seduction. This confusion is compounded by the gallery owner, who is not only precious in speech and manner but also sides with the girls instead of with Vinz, Hub and Saïd, as male solidarity ought to have dictated. Other spaces are equally difficult to decode. The shopping mall is half interior and half exterior (unlike the shop on the estate in which Vinz does not feel at home and which the queue of women codes as interior); the hospital is an interior which the friends cannot penetrate, while the police station is an interior that they enter literally at their peril. Sometimes only violence will force a way inside, as when Vinz sees, or imagines he sees, a Black trying to shoot his way into a nightclub. The culmination of this confusion is the way Paris itself becomes a prison. By deliberately holding Hub and Saïd too long in custody the police make the friends miss the last train home, with the result, as Said puts it in another graphic inversion, that they are 'enfermés dehors' ('locked in outside').

Just as the music is a montage of reggae and French rap, so the cast of characters in *La haine* provides a *métissage*, or mixing, which derives from a complex set of references to both French and American film traditions. The threesome is a dramatic device used in films as various as Truffaut's *Jules et Jim* (1961), Blier's *Les valseuses* (*Making It*, 1974) and in the more farcical *Tenue de soirée* (*Evening Dress*, 1986) or Balasko's *Gazon maudit* (*French Twist*, 1995) to explore heterosexual rivalry and homosocial attraction. *La haine* differs from such films in having no 'love interest', but it shares this characteristic with many French films of the 1990s which centre on friendships among young people, women as well as men, but are not based on the heterosexual romance which was the staple of New Wave films about young people in the late 1950s and early 1960s or the homosexual version that became popular in the 1970s and 1980s. The French vogue for films about men can be traced back to the 1970s, but the friendship and solidarity that links Vinz, Hubert and Saïd is more directly reminiscent of American buddy movies and gangster films.

In some respects, therefore, *La haine* appears to have an answer to French intellectuals such as Pierre Bourdieu or Alain Finkielkraut who denounce multiculturalism as a form of American imperialism, appearing to consider it an attempt to dilute the principles on which French republicanism is based. The giant TV screen which announces that Abdel has died defaults to an image of the old France associated with the traditional 'blue, white, red' tricolour and the slogan 'liberté, égalité, fraternité'. It is a motto Vinz, Hub and Saïd quote ironically when hanging out in the shopping mall, and their trio is clearly meant to exemplify a 'new tricolour' of 'black, blanc, beur' – one that was on display in France's victorious 1998 World Cup team – an ideal *métissage* which might be France's response to the multicultural challenge.

On the other hand, the film also shows that young people – or at least young people from this social background – are profoundly influenced by American culture, even in details such as how they cut their hair. The police gun Vinz acquires is compared to the gun in Donner's *Lethal Weapon* (1987) while the final Mexican stand-off parodies Tarantino's *Reservoir Dogs* (1992) which, itself, parodies shoot-outs in innumerable gangster films and westerns. In interviews about the film the director has stated that in Brian de Palma's *Scarface*, Al Pacino as the 'guy who comes from the ghetto, is stuffed full of drugs, and who dies a violent death but only after he has reached the top' (Rémy, 23) serves as a powerful role model. Indeed, the billboard slogan 'the world is yours', altered by Saïd to 'ours', is a quotation from *Scarface*. According to Kassovitz, *Scarface* is one of the few films people like those in the Cité des Muguets will have seen, and they believe it depicts reality in the United States. Tales of American gangsters are as compelling, and have the same degree of reality, as other narratives, like Hubert's story about the man falling from a block of flats, or Saïd's brother's tale about the candid camera. More worryingly, perhaps, the specifically European shaggy dog story about deportation told by the elderly Jew encountered in the public lavatories in Paris, whom Kassovitz said he modelled on his own grandfather, is seen as 'pointless'.

But above all, *La haine* is influenced by Martin Scorsese. Vincent Cassel's febrile performance and obsession with guns inevitably recalls Robert de Niro as Johnny Boy in *Mean Streets*, while De Niro/Travis Bickle's solipsistic 'Are you talking to me?' routine enacted in front of a mirror in *Taxi Driver* is mimicked by Vinz. Scorsese's semi-indulgent, semi-critical attitude towards the Italian immigrant community and his invention of autobiographical personae for De Niro are echoed in Vinz's attitude towards his immigrant background and the way in which Vinz, actor and Jew, is cast as a representation of Kassovitz (who himself plays the skinhead). Indeed, Kassovitz has said that *Mean Streets* is the film he would most like to have made. As influential as the detail of characters and settings, is Scorsese's aesthetic – the brilliance with which he combines the realistic and the poetic, the rational and the irrational, the everyday and the fantastic, not least in the soundtracks of his films which are extraordinary montages of music, dialogue and street noises. Like Scorsese, Kassovitz contrives to achieve a synthesis of traditions of urban film-making so as to combine the documentary/realist representations familiar from television with the poetic representations of the city in French films from the 1930s onwards. Thus the gag about turning off the lights on the Eiffel Tower is lifted, inter alia, from Eric Rochant's *Un monde sans pitié* (1989). But one of the most powerful intertexts, perhaps, is Marcel Carné's *Le jour se lève* (1939) with which *La haine* shares a 24-hour time frame, opened and closed by an explosion or gunshot, a setting in the outlying districts of the city, and a powerful tragic teleology. And just as its star, Jean Gabin, served as the symbol of the French working man in the 1930s, so Vinz, Hubert and Saïd collectively embody the dispossessed of the 1990s.

La haine rapidly became a media phenomenon in a way that might appear ironic for a film which criticises the media's tendency to turn any spectacle, however gruesome or violent, into entertainment. Its success depended on extremely skilful marketing and its release was accompanied by various tie-ins. For the bourgeois audience there was an exhibition of production photographs and an accompanying book by Gilles Favier and Mathieu Kassovitz entitled *Jusqu'ici tout va bien* (so far so good). For the younger audience there was a CD of the soundtrack which combined reggae performers like Marley with rap music from French bands like NTM. For film buffs there was a video edition of the 'director's cut', about thirty minutes longer than the version released on screen. And when it was released in the United States, the subtitles deliberately drew comparisons with race violence in America, referring, for example, to 'Rodney King'. In this way, Kassovitz ensured that a film about the difficulty of crossing boundaries owed its success to its ability to cross such national and generational divisions.

However, in France there was another dimension to its success. By forgoing the romantic plot and the attractive young actresses, like Emmanuelle Béart, Julie Delpy or Sophie Marceau, who are usually central to the international sales of French films, and by deliberately making its actors appear ugly – even Vincent Cassel, who plays the romantic lead in other films such as Mimouni's *L'Appartement* (1996) – the film gained credibility as a slice of life and as a warning shot, a 'pavé dans la mare' (hence the image of the exploding Molotov cocktail). Kassovitz's criticism of police brutality is serious, especially when it is set alongside the relative triviality of the friends' misdemeanours. It is true that they try to steal a car, but it turns out that none of them knows how to drive. It is true that they steal a credit card but they cannnot find a taxi driver who will let them use it to take them back home. *La haine* takes a strongly opposing view to Bertrand Tavernier's contemporaneous *L 627* (1992) which attempted to depict the police as heroes in the struggle against drug-related, immigrant-perpetrated crime. By slightly modifying the opening parable from 'it's the story of a man' to 'it's the story of a society', the lines with which the film closes, and by ending the film with the sound of an explosion over a black screen as Saïd shuts his eyes in terrified anticipation, Kassovitz appears to wish his film to convey the message that a generation of essentially decent young people is being forced into violent and murderous action by a society that is unwilling or unable to acknowledge their predicament. In this way he seems to suggest that the role models offered by American cinema, in the characters played by actors such as Al Pacino, Robert de Niro or Spike Lee, are likely to move out of the realm of art and enter that of real life.

Reference

Rémy, Vincent 1995: 'Entretien avec Mathieu Kassovitz'. In *Télérama*, 31 May, 19–24.

Suggestions for Further Reading

Alexander, Karen 1995: 'La haine'. In *Vertigo*, Autumn/Winter, 45–46.
Bourguignon, Thomas and Tobin, Yann 1995: 'Entretien avec Mathieu Kassovitz'. In *Positif*, 412, 8–13. Translated in Ciment, Michel and Herpe, Noël 1999: *Projections 9: French Film-makers on Film-making*. London: Faber, 183–93.
Chambers, Ross 1999: 'Interesting Circumstances: Queerness, Cruising and the Parasocial (Thoughts on and around Kassovitz's *La haine*)'. Unpublished article.
Darke, Chris 1995: '*La haine*'. In *Sight and Sound*, November, 221.
Favier, Gilles and Kassovitz, Mathieu 1995: *Jusqu'ici tout va bien: Scénario et photographies autour du film* 'La haine'. Arles: Actes Sud.
Rémy, Vincent 1995: 'Entretien avec Mathieu Kassovitz'. In *Télérama*, 31 May, 19–24.
Trémois, Claude-Marie 1997: *Les Enfants de la liberté*. Paris: Éditions du Seuil.

Credits

Director	Mathieu Kassovitz
Producer	Christophe Rossignon
Production Company	Les Productions Lazennec
Screenplay	Mathieu Kassovitz
Director of Photography	Pierre Aim
Editors	Mathieu Kassovitz Scott Stevenson
Art Director	Giuseppe Ponturo
Music	Bob Marley, Tony Joe White, Roger Troutman, Expression Direkt, Cut Killer, Etan Massuri, Solo, The Beastie Boys and others.

Cast

Vincent Cassel	Vinz
Hubert Koundé	Hubert
Saïd Taghmaoui	Saïd
François Levantal	Astérix
Peter Kassovitz	Gallery Patron
Vincent Lindon	Drunk Man
Mathieu Kassovitz	Skinhead

Filmography

Cauchemar blanc (1991)
Assassins (1992)
Métisse (*Café au lait/Blended*, 1993)
La haine (*Hate*, 1995)
Assassin(s) (1997)

11 Trainspotting

'Hollywood come in please . . . your time is up'. *Trainspotting* at odds with Scottish heritage.

Trainspotting

Sarah Street

Trainspotting was released in New York in July 1996, ten months after its UK première. It took $262,000 on its opening weekend and continued to attract audiences, earning $12 million at the US box office after eight weeks. By Hollywood standards this is not a large sum – in seven weeks Roland Emmerich's *Independence Day* (1996) grossed $285 million – but *Trainspotting*'s career abroad exceeded expectations, it 'travelled' well, receiving excellent reviews and high-profile publicity in Europe and the USA. As a low-budget, parochial film which certainly did not exemplify the conventional virtues and values of Britain, utilising broad Scottish accents (some dubbing was necessary for American release) and dealing with risqué subject-matter, it would, at first sight, appear to be destined for short theatrical domestic release followed by a video career. John Hill has argued that:

> [T]he most interesting type of British cinema, and the one which is most worthy of support, differs from the type which is often hoped for – a British cinema capable of competing with Hollywood and exemplifying the virtues and values of Britain. A different conception of British cinema recognises that its economic ambitions will have to be more modest. However, its cultural ambitions can, and should, be correspondingly more ambitious: the provision of diverse and challenging representations adequate to the complexities of contemporary Britain. (Hill, 18–19)

This chapter will consider *Trainspotting* as an example of the sort of cinema John Hill would like to be considered as 'British' and discuss the reasons for its success at home *and* abroad. It will argue that the film is representative of contemporary hybrid forms associated with generic fluidity and cinematic 'flow' which are conducive to exportation while at the same time retaining an acute sense of national identity.

Registered as British, *Trainspotting* falls into the category of British films that seek to challenge dominant notions of 'Britishness'. As Hill points out, this does not disqualify them from being British, it simply locates them within a dissident, but significant, tradition. By this I am referring to 'oppositional' films such as those directed by Derek Jarman which, as I have argued elsewhere (Street, 181–4), subvert the iconography of 'Britishness', such as can be seen, for example, in archive film of the Second World War, by placing it in a more contemporary context. Similarly, one of *Trainspotting*'s most recurrent strategies is to take a particular image or idea, and subvert it by suggesting an alternative scenario by visual or aural counterpoint. This technique originates in the theories and practice of classic Soviet montage and is assisted by the film's energetic pace, verve and wit. It is this quality, combined with the particular subject-matter, which renders *Trainspotting* both British *and* exportable, for it operates within a tradition of British films which appeal to European and American audiences.

Indeed, *Trainspotting* is a film which contains a sense of national specificity 'without being either nationalist or attached to homogenising myths of national identity' (Hill, 16). In an interview, the producer Andrew MacDonald argued that although it is set primarily in Scotland it is nevertheless 'British' in the sense that it appeals south of the border with its context of life in the Thatcherite 1980s: 'We set out to create a world that could be anywhere – pubs, estates and dole offices' (*Premiere*, 61). The film could well have been set in any major British city and the drug culture it describes transcends national boundaries. The film contains observations about being Scottish in the 'United' Kingdom, or, as Renton puts it, living as 'the lowest of the low' in a 'colonised' country; but, as will be suggested below, the film's strategy of counterpoint and refusal to conform to generic fixity works to broaden rather than limit its address.

One compelling aspect of the film is its narrative and the degree to which it breaks with conventional closure. Will Self's review of *Trainspotting* criticises the film for adopting a linear narrative which, he argues, is littered with incidents that lose their pathos by selling-out to neat comic pay-offs (the examples he gives are the 'worst toilet in Scotland' incident when Renton dives down the toilet to recover opium suppositories which he has evacuated, and Tommy's funeral). On first examination the narrative would indeed appear to be linear – it introduces us to Renton and his friends; charts Renton's attempts to get 'clean'; the subsequent resumption of his heroin habit, court appearance and overdose; his resolution to 'find something new' after seeing Tommy in a state of HIV-infected degradation; his move to London; Tommy's funeral and Renton's involvement in a lucrative drugs deal with Sick Boy, Begbie and Spud which takes them back to London; and Renton making off with the money at the end. Yet the narrative works in a more complicated way than this brief outline would suggest, and as a more detailed analysis shows, contains room for ambiguity and a refusal of closure on several occasions.

This strategy is signalled from the arresting opening sequence of the film, when the main characters run down a street, being chased by police. The opening serves as a signal for the film's style and content: we are simultaneously being introduced to the characters, prepared for a later story event and at the same time exposed to the film's major technique of counterpoint between and within the visual and aural. The visual style is of stasis and disruption: the first shot is a low camera angle showing shoppers walking slowly, viewed from behind. Renton runs into the frame with the camera in the same position and the next series of shots alternate between medium and long shots of Renton and Spud from the front. The sequence follows their dash through the crowds until Renton's path is halted by a car coming around a corner, when he tumbles across its bonnet as it halts to avoid hitting him. This gives time for a brief pause as Renton looks directly at the camera and his introductory caption appears in freeze-frame: 'Renton'. Far from being a strictly linear opening, this comes from the middle rather than the beginning of Renton's story. We see the same shot of him on the car bonnet later on in the film, just before the courtroom scene and his overdose. While we are seeing this fast-paced, urgent sequence we also hear Renton's voice-over: 'Choose life, choose a job, choose a career, choose a family, choose a fucking big television, choose washing machines, cars, compact disc players and electrical tin openers.' The soundtrack plays 'Lust for Life' (Iggy Pop), creating a pulsating beat which matches the images and establishes a contrast with Renton's sardonic, ironic listing of consumer purchases that are supposed to be essential for modern living.

The rest of this opening sequence is divided between two locations – Renton's room where he has just 'shot up' heroin, and the introduction of his friends on a football pitch. As with the introduction of Renton, each of the main characters in the film is singled out by freeze-frame with his name in caption, reminiscent of the opening sequence of the 1960s cult television series *The Monkees* and utilising devices like the jump-cut in reference to Richard Lester's Beatles film *A Hard Day's Night* (1964), which was a world-wide success. These two locations are in stark contrast: while we see Renton alone, smoking, his movements slow and the camera static (first in medium shot and then a long shot), the voice-over invites us to 'Choose good health, low cholesterol and dental insurance. Choose fixed interest mortgage repayments, choose a starter home, choose your friends' (at which point we cut to a shot of his friends, gathered in goal as for a football-team photograph). The football scenes are quick, jaunty and fun but as Renton is hit on the head by a football we hear him again say 'choose life', and we revert to shots of Renton at home. He falls to the floor and the camera follows his body slowly, at a low-angle. The sequence makes clear that he *didn't* 'choose life' but instead opted for drugs: 'who needs reasons when you've got heroin'. In just a few minutes the film-makers have managed to convey some essentials about *Trainspotting*: that image and dialogue are often at odds with one another (the incongruity of the running figures and Renton's catalogue of consumer durables); that the main characters in the film are five young males; and, via voice-over, that Renton is the central character.

Renton's agency as a central character is crucial in ensuring that the audience maintains a more intimate relationship with him than with the other characters. This is in contrast to the Irvine Welsh novel on which the film is based, which permits a variety of characters to have a direct 'voice'. The film is, in many ways, *Renton's* story, from drug addiction to lucky break and upward mobility in London. Possessing the voice-over usually endows a film character with a degree of control over the narrative, often encouraging us to see things from her/his point of view. Renton acts as our mentor, our guide through his world of addiction and theft. The comic, ironic spin on his voice-overs, however, also single him out to us as more intelligent, more street-wise and, eventually, more successful than his friends. At the end of *Trainspotting*, when Renton has stolen the money, he explains in voice-over that Sick Boy would have done the same and that the violent Begbie deserved to be swindled. We see him leave some of the money for Spud to recover, thereby making us appreciate the gesture and accept the theft more readily.

Although voice-over and image can sometimes be in conflict with each other, on most occasions Renton has the last word, as in the scene when Tommy (not yet a heroin addict) wants them all to go for a walk when they visit the Scottish hills. Tommy has gone on ahead and calls to the others to join him. The shots of him with the hills in the background are much brighter, with sunshine and billowing clouds, than the reverse images of his friends, each of them reluctant to take to the hills. The landscape behind them is dark, the sky is cloudy, linking them with a bleaker, more dangerous Scotland than the one that appears in holiday brochures. For a moment it seems as if Tommy's more idyllic background will persist in the memory, but when he calls to them, 'Doesn't it make you proud to be Scottish?' Renton delivers a classic riposte which undermines Tommy's (and our) enthusiasm: 'It's shite being Scottish, we're the lowest of the low, the scum of the fucking earth, most wretched, miserable, servile, pathetic trash that was ever shagged into civilisation. Some people hate the English – I don't – they're just wankers. We, on the other hand, are colonised by wankers – can't even find a decent culture to be colonised by. We're ruled by effete arseholes. It's a shite state to be in Tommy and all the fresh air in the world won't make any difference.'

The above sequence typifies the film's attitude towards conventionality – it cocks a snook at accepted notions of representation – in this case of the Scottish tourist industry – and replaces them with a dissident view. When an unwary American tourist asks to use the pub toilet at the start of the Edinburgh Festival, Begbie leads the troupe of angry Scottish friends in pursuit, with the intention of beating him up. Again, this is a blatant rejection of an established element of Scottish heritage. The film also critiques the genre of American films which perpetuate stereotypical notions of Scottish heritage, including Vincente Minnelli's *Brigadoon* (1954) and Mel Gibson's *Braveheart* (1995).

As a film not just about national identity, or feeling estranged from a sense of traditional nationalism, *Trainspotting* dares to draw attention to itself by refusing the realist cinematic traditions which one would have expected to spawn a film about drug culture in the 1980s. Instead of delivering a didactic message against drug-taking, *Trainspotting* claims to know what it is like to be an addict, avoiding a heavy-handed 'message' approach which would undoubtedly have alienated many cinemagoers, and instead daring to represent some of the pleasures of heroin, particularly in the scenes of ecstatic release experienced by Renton when the drug is first administered. The avoidance of didacticism is a major strategy utilised by the film-makers even though, ironically, the audience is encouraged to admire Renton's ability to rise above the mundane, conquer his addiction and, in Thatcherite fashion, apply himself to money-making in London and be the major beneficiary of the drugs deal at the end of the film. As the credits roll we are tempted to speculate: has he swapped one dubious way of life for another?

The inclusion of surrealist, fantastical elements enables *Trainspotting* to deal with issues and scenes that would have been particularly harrowing in more conventional realist form (even if there is a risk, in so doing, of trivialising the incidents). Thus the scene when Renton dives into the toilet to recover the suppositories begins in realist fashion as we see him put his hand down the bowl, desperately trying to avoid retching at the same time. The surrealism begins when his whole body disappears down the toilet, emerging into an underwater location in which he appears to be diving for pearls on the bed of the sea. Combining realism with this imaginative conclusion to the scene serves the purpose of conveying both the desperation of the drug addict and something of his elation when the drugs have been recovered. To Renton they are like valuable pearls and there are clearly no lengths to which he would not go in order to retrieve his lost treasure. Far from trivialising the incident the scene achieves an impressionist conclusion by encouraging the audience to understand Renton's psyche and how his quest for drugs blinds him to the revulsion we experience from a more realist perspective.

The use of music also serves as effective counterpoint. In the sequence after Renton has been given a suspended prison sentence for theft on condition that he undergoes a monitored detoxification programme, the pressures build up as he craves a 'hit' of heroin. He visits 'Mother Superior' for a fix 'to get me through this long day'. After a comic scene between the two in which they role-play a rich customer and a waiter, Renton lies back in relief once the drug has been administered, much as we have seen him react before in an ecstatic haze of pleasure when the heroin kicks in. We hear the beginning of Lou Reed's *Perfect Day* and in a break with realism we see Renton disappear through the floor. The languid tones and lyrics of the song continue as background to this serene moment but we gradually realise that he has, in fact, overdosed and is rapidly descending into a coma. 'Mother Superior' drags him out to an empty street where a taxi rushes him to hospital. The song then becomes completely ironic as what started out as a scene in which Renton's desperation, depression and loneliness is 'cured' by heroin, ends up as a nightmare of near-death, anything but a perfect day.

Trainspotting's stylistic break from realism facilitated its export, and the rest of this chapter will discuss how the film's success was in part due to its marketing and reception by reviewers, many of whom debated the film's relationship with previous traditions of British cinema. Reviews commented particularly on the celebrated, unexpected surrealism of the 'toilet' scene, creating an expectation of sensationalism – British films do not normally do this sort of thing. Many American reviews pointed out that the film was a far cry from the films of Mike Leigh or Ken Loach, instead comparing it with previous 'cult' successes like Stanley Kubrick's *A Clockwork Orange* (1971) and the films of Scorsese and Tarantino. It is somewhat ironic that these last comparisons go some way towards explaining its success in America, although this should not imply that it was not appreciated as a British film. It was understood primarily in terms of its relation to British cultural icons. References to The Beatles encouraged its 'cult' status: the Internet Movie Database website, for example, compiled a list of 'trivia' points which occur within the film, including reference to a scene where store detectives chase Renton down a street that is reminiscent of a scene in *A Hard Day's Night* where the Beatles are pursued by fans, and a scene towards the end of *Trainspotting* in which the four friends cross a road in similar fashion to the front sleeve shot of The Beatles on their album *Abbey Road*. The film's focus on the men's friendship and involvement in counter-culture is reminiscent of the way the Beatles are pitted against the Establish-ment in *A Hard Day's Night*, particularly in both films' use of 'in-joke' humour as a discourse which is reflective of, in their different contexts, their appeal to the youth market. As a result of Sick-Boy's obsession, the film also contains many references to James Bond films, another example of its preoccupation with British cultural icons from the 1960s.

Filmic intertexts are also referenced when Renton arrives in London. Boyle creates an ironic montage of 'famous signposts/sights' which are reminiscent of British 'Swinging London' films of the 1960s, in which the capital was repres-ented, in films such as John Schlesinger's *Billy Liar!* (1963) or Richard Lester's *The Knack* (1965), as an escape from small-town life, parochialism and stasis. As in many of these earlier films, the city in *Trainspotting* is depicted as ruthless, in the midst of the 1980s boom, with Renton working at a property agency, saving his money and living in a squalid bed-sit. Despite the film's energy the prognosis is bleak: the only way out is to make money but what you should spend it on is unclear. Renton's suggestions – drugs, 'life', or consumer durables – are not presented in a positive light. The only scenes of 'ordinary' life in the film come across as stultifying, and in the case of Begbie's alternative of addiction to alcohol, violent and dangerous. The scenes of the four friends in London at the end of the film serve as a reminder of Britain's regional diversity as they struggle to profit from their big deal, appearing as strangers to the London drug-dealing scene, amateurs in a world of organised crime.

Contrary to accepted opinion, the British films which have done best in the USA are not pale imitations of Hollywood epics, 'international' films that are devoid of national identity. Rather, they are precisely those, like the Ealing comedies or the satirical, surreal Monty Python films, which do engage with 'Britishness' in an intriguing way. From this perspective it is not at all surprising that *Trainspotting* should have been so well received outside the UK, and most of the American reviews placed it in the tradition of slightly surrealistic, satirical humour, particularly in relation to its noted resemblances to *A Hard Day's Night*. What would appear to be a paradox – a 'small', parochial British film breaking out of the domestic market – is not, therefore, an exception. It is the result of an intriguing combination of a fresh look at national identity with an arresting cinematic visual style which delivers that much sought-after quality: world-wide critical recognition *and* box-office success.

Along with a refusal to conform to expectations of British social realism, *Trainspotting* is also difficult to locate in generic terms. While this can often have the effect of producing a confused, unfocused impression of a film prior to release, it can, if handled astutely, maximise interest. Reviewers found it hard to place in terms of genre, alternating between discussing its comic merits, its 'cult' status, links with 'Britpop' music, intertextual relations with *A Hard Day's Night* – 'the boys shoot up and fall down in pleasure, and sometimes they jump about Edinburgh, chasing down streets like The Beatles in *A Hard Day's Night*, romping in and out of bars or just sitting around making preposterous jokes' (*New York*, 12 August 1996) – and comparing it to *A Clockwork Orange*, Scorsese and Tarantino films, and to the loosely-defined genre of 'drug' films including Abel Ferrara's *Bad Lieutenant* (1992), Ulrich Edel's *Christiane F* (1981) and David Cronenberg's *Naked Lunch* (1991). In many senses, *Trainspotting* is all these things. As an example of the contemporary hybrid film its negation of fixity allows discussion to involve the production team, the stars, the themes, the style and soundtrack in a fluid, intertextual fashion. One feature most reviewers agreed on, however, was the film's ability to communicate energy: 'There's no escaping its bluster and commotion... Even when there is nothing to it but noise and colour, it still has swagger and style, and it feels very rowdy' (*Première*, March 1996). The art direction, by Tracey Gallacher, is excellent, making it a visual spectacle that contains many qualities of contemporary European and American independent/art house movies, for example Jean-Pierre Jeunet's and Marc Caro's *Delicatessen* (1991) or the Coen brothers' *Barton Fink* (1991). Much of *Trainspotting* was shot in a large disused cigarette factory in which thirty of the fifty locations were built. The camera was often at a low angle to create a sense of space and the colours of the rooms were blues, oranges, reds and purples, similar to the bold stylistic approach that had been adopted for *Shallow Grave* (1994).

Steve Neale (1990) has observed the inherent mutability of generic film forms and the importance of a film's publicity campaign in creating a climate of expectation in the potential audience's mind before they see the film. In the case of *Trainspotting*, the 'narrative image' was rather a 'stylistic image' that relied on visual spectacle, the charisma of the performers, and the 'event' of the soundtrack release. This would appear to take the film back to the realms of the 'cinema of attractions', a phrase used by Tom Gunning (1986) to describe early cinema's appeal to the senses as a display of technological artistry which drew the spectator in for its own sake rather than as an adjunct to narrative.

These many qualities were evident from *Trainspotting*'s marketing campaign (by Polygram in the UK and Miramax in the USA), which in turn influenced reviews. This aspect of the film's success was crucial, enhancing its status as a 'must-see' film and pitching it at the youth, 'cult' market with the assistance of a distinctive 'Britpop' soundtrack. From this perspective, people were familiar with the *idea* of *Trainspotting* before the film's release, especially if they had read Welsh's novel, first published in 1993. In February 1996 the British press was full of comment about the novel and the forthcoming film. The production team and cast, particularly Ewan McGregor, who was a familiar name as one of the main actors in Danny Boyle's earlier film *Shallow Grave* (1995), were available for interview and contributed to a precise and well-organised publicity campaign which heightened audience expectation for a film that was different, hip and visual. The posters, produced by design company Stylo Rouge, were distinctive in their singling out of the characters in monochrome, with orange type which was influenced by the wording on drug packages and British Rail signs. The production team's previous success with the stylish *Shallow Grave* served to augment anticipation of another new and exciting British cinematic experience. The poster which declared 'Hollywood come in please...your time is up' characterised the film's brazen and confident attitude in no uncertain terms.

Although the seriousness of heroin addiction was also discussed, some reviewers took exception to the apparent contradiction between the energy and pace of the film's style and its deathly subject-matter:

The film is governed by the sort of indiscriminate regard for the Spunky Spirit of Renegade Youth that you usually only find in building societies worried about their image, or television executives worried about their age. Imagine *Mean Streets* re-made by Janet Street-Porter and you're halfway there. Add some street poetry ('It wasn't just the baby that died that day...'), the likes of which you won't have heard since the last Hanif Kureishi effort, and some finger-snapping editing, the likes of which you won't have seen since the TSB last got hungry for young money, and you have *Trainspotting*: the film about drugs that likes to say 'YES!'   (Shone)

I'd have hated to be a using heroin addict in London over the past week. In fact I'd hate to be a using heroin addict at all and anywhere. But this past week in London, I would've been subjected to a continual taunt from hoardings advertising the listings magazine *Time Out*, and by extension, the film, *Trainspotting*. The taunt is a line from the film extolling the virtues of the hit of heroin: 'Take the best orgasm you've ever had, multiply it by a thousand, and you'll still be nowhere close.'   (Self)

Indeed, it is this aspect of the film which attracted most controversial comment – the possibility that the sequences of ecstatic relief when a heroin-filled needle is inserted into the vein might not be cancelled out by their binary opposites, the sequences showing the agonies of 'cold turkey'. As an example of the contemporary hybrid film, *Trainspotting* delivered its promise of excitement, colour, wit and energy. In cinematic terms, the refusal to allow conventional realist representations of drug addiction to dominate the film opened it to a wider audience at the risk of trivialising the subject of heroin addiction. As has been argued, however, the film's open-ended narrative events and strategies of visual and aural ironic counterpoint achieve a sense of complexity which would have been impossible from a more overtly didactic perspective. Indeed, *Trainspotting* chose cinematic 'life' as a means of producing 'diverse and challenging representations adequate to the complexities of contemporary Britain' (Hill, 19). On the strength of *Trainspotting*, the Boyle–Hodge–MacDonald team managed to obtain finance for a subsequent project, *A Life Less Ordinary* (1997), although it did not attract the same degree of critical acclaim or box-office success, while the film also established Ewan McGregor as a major British film star who went on to work in a variety of films including Peter Greenaway's *The Pillow Book* (1996), Mark Herman's *The Rise and Fall of Little Voice* (1998) and George Lucas's *Star Wars (Episode 1)* (1999). Probably the closest generic inheritors of *Trainspotting* were Kevin Allen's *Twin Town* (1997) and Guy Ritchie's *Lock, Stock & Two Smoking Barrels* (1998), films which displayed similarly inventive formal structures, lively cinematographic styles, wit, pace and verve. Above all, the legacy of *Trainspotting* has been a greater tolerance of cinematic difference and the opening up of new perspectives on national identity(ies) for world markets.

References

Gunning, Tom 1986: 'The Cinema of Attractions: Early Film, its Spectators and the Avant-Garde'. In *Wide Angle*, 8, 3–4.
Hill, John 1992: 'The Issue of National Cinema and British Film Production'. In Duncan Petrie (ed.), *New Questions of British Cinema*. London: British Film Institute.
MacDonald, Andrew 1996: 'It's Such a Perfect Day'. In *Premiere UK*, March.
Neale, Steve 1990: 'Questions of Genre'. In *Screen*, 31, 1.
Self, Will 1996: 'Trainspotting'. In *Observer Preview*, 11–17 February.
Shone, Tom 1996: 'Trainspotting'. In *Sunday Times*, 25 February.
Street, Sarah 1997: *British National Cinema*. London: Routledge.

Suggestions for Further Reading

Caughie, John 1990: 'Representing Scotland: New Questions for Scottish Cinema'. In E. Dick (ed.), *From Limelight to Satellite*. London: British Film Institute/Scottish Film Council.

Petrie, Duncan 1996: 'British Cinema: The Search for Identity'. In Geoffrey Nowell-Smith (ed.), *Oxford History of World Cinema*. Oxford: Oxford University Press.

Credits

Director	Danny Boyle
Producer	Andrew MacDonald
Production Company	A Figment Film in association with Noel Gay Motion Picture Company Ltd for Channel Four
Screenplay	John Hodge, based on Irvine Welsh's novel
Director of Photography	Brian Tufano
Editor	Masahiro Hirakubo
Production Designer	Kave Quinn
Art Direction	Tracey Gallacher
Music	No original music

Cast

Ewan McGregor	Renton
Ewen Bremner	Spud
Johnny Lee Miller	Sick Boy
Kevin McKidd	Tommy
Robert Carlyle	Begbie
Kelly Macdonald	Diane

Filmography

Shallow Grave (1995)
Trainspotting (1996)
A Life Less Ordinary (1997)
The Beach (2000)

194

12 *The Barber of Siberia*
McCracken (Richard Harris) in front of his invention, the Barber of Siberia.

Sibirskii tsiriul'nik
(The Barber of Siberia)
Birgit Beumers

While the first Russian film discussed in this book, *The Battleship Potemkin* (1926), ranks among the world's best films, *The Barber of Siberia* (*Sibirskii tsiriul'nik*, 1998) is one of the most expensive feature films ever made outside Hollywood ($49 million). While Eisenstein had a hand-painted red flag in his film, emphasising the triumphant spirit of the Revolution and turning its success forward in time, Mikhalkov turned time backwards by having the red stars, symbol of Soviet power, removed from the Kremlin towers to allow for the film's setting in pre-Revolutionary Russia. While Eisenstein constructed Soviet history, Mikhalkov remembers Russia's past values with nostalgia. The temporal axes of the two films are thus diametrically opposed, although both film-makers look towards the future in their reassessment of the past. They represent in their spirit the beginning and the end of the Soviet era, and of a century of film-making.

The Barber of Siberia is a rare film in its combination of English and Russian dialogue, its production history, its use of star actors from Russia, the USA and the UK, but, above all, because of the director's aim to provide a model of direction and to offer moral guidance to an audience at a time when the mainstream of Russian film-makers portray the bleakness, the abyss and the degeneration surrounding them. Mikhalkov's *The Barber of Siberia* shapes the values of the future by telling a story about Russia's past, which elevates the traditions of the east above those of the west, tells a fairy tale without a happy ending, and stands in both form and content aloof from Hollywood expectations.

It is more than surprising that such a film should come from a country like Russia, shaken by economic crises and trying to define its national identity after the collapse of the Soviet Union. The Soviet film industry had been state-controlled and state-managed, so that film-makers could work almost independently of audience taste, but were subjected instead to ideological control. The industry almost collapsed after 1991 when the country entered the free market which forced producers to raise money in a system that offered no tax incentives to investors in the arts. To make the situation worse, the cinema infrastructure was outdated and video piracy undermined any chance of recouping production costs. Mikhalkov's successful collaboration on earlier film projects with the French producer Michel Seydoux secured him a business partner for the project who could raise two-thirds of the funds. The film is a co-production between TriTe (Russia) and Camera One (France), shot at the Barrandov studios in Prague, in Moscow, Kostroma and Nizhny Novgorod (Russia), and in Portugal.

The film brings together stars from American and British cinema, as well as from Russia's film and theatre scene. Julia Ormond plays Jane Callaghan, while Richard Harris is cast as the eccentric inventor McCracken. Oleg Menshikov, a major star of Russian cinema who has become known internationally since *Utomlennye solntsem* (*Burnt by the Sun*), plays Andrei Tolstoi, and Alexei Petrenko, Elem Klimov's Rasputin in *Agonìa* (*Agony*), stars as Radlov. The director of the film, Nikita Mikhalkov, plays Tsar Alexander III, the 'father' of Russia, which is a significant choice because the pre-publicity and release of the film coincided with Mikhalkov's real-life political interests in the run-up for the next presidential elections, and amidst ongoing speculation about his candidature. Mikhalkov's daughter Anna plays Dunia, his son Artem plays the cadet Buturlin, and his daughter Nadia (the little girl Nadia of *Burnt by the Sun*) appears in an episode at the fair. Almost the entire Mikhalkov family features in the film, continuing the director's preoccupation with the themes of fatherhood and family which have been evident in almost all of his films.

The film is shot almost equally in English and Russian. While Jane and McCracken speak only English and Tolstoi converses with them in English, the rest of the dialogue is in Russian. Jane's narrative through her letters to Andrew is also in English, with a voice-over for the Russian version narrated by the film's director. The title of the film echoes that of Rossini's opera *The Barber of Seville*, which is also concerned with money as a motivation for people's actions, and with role-play to achieve a set goal, two key themes which dominate Jane's actions. The choice of the name Tolstoi for the male protagonist will, of course, suggest to international audiences a parallel to the ninteenth-century writer Lev Tolstoi, whose novel *Anna Karenina* Jane is reading on the train. Tolstoi was also the name of the Minister of Interior Affairs under Alexander II. Mikhalkov's approach to dialogue, casting and story-line make the film viable for an international market. Russian habits are unfamiliar to Jane, a foreigner to the country, and through her they are explained in an unpatronising form to an international audience, a strategy which does not necessitate special editing of the film for its international release.

Nikita Mikhalkov is the son of Sergei Mikhalkov, a writer of children's stories, plays, and of the text of the Soviet national anthem (1943). Mikhalkov's elder brother, Andrei Konchalovsky, is also a film-maker who left for Hollywood in the 1980s. Nikita Mikhalkov began his career as an actor before completing his studies as a film director, and he rose to international fame with the Italian co-production *Dark Eyes* (1987) and the Oscar-winning *Burnt by the Sun* (1994). He occupies many influential positions in Russian cultural politics: in 1990 he became adviser to the Prime Minister on cultural issues, and in 1993 he was elected president of the Russian Fund for Culture. Since 1989 he has run his own production company, TriTe, which also has a publishing arm that has published archival material relating to Russian history.

In December 1997 Mikhalkov was elected chairman of the Film-makers' Union in a vote of trust. In his speech to the Congress of the Union in May 1998, Mikhalkov proposed the creation of an extra-budgetary fund to support the film industry, to be created from fees collected from licensing video retail, which would then be invested in the reconstruction of cinemas, the production of new films, and the renovation and maintenance of the Union's properties, significantly suggesting forms of assistance based on those within other European film industries rather than looking to Hollywood as a model. In his speech, Mikhalkov argued strongly that the task of a national Russian cinema should be to instil hope in the cinema audience by re-creating the myth of a Russian national hero in order to regain a spirit of patriotism that had bonded the Soviet Union in the past, a spirit which Mikhalkov believes to exist in contemporary America, encouraged by the Hollywood 'myth' factory. Thus for Mikhalkov, cinema is capable of projecting a lost sense of national identity, inspiring the people to have hope in the future while the political reality is void of any direction or ideology. The means by which this can be achieved, he argues, are by encouraging the growth of a financially sound film industry and by producing popular films which inculcate a coherent sense of national identity. Using the example of the US film industry, whose success, he suggests, lies in the creation of positive heroes with whom the American nation identifies, Mikhalkov neglects the fact that America is also proud of its industry because it makes $3.5 billion profit per year.

The evolution of the script for *The Barber of Siberia* spans the period of belief in the reform of the political system under Gorbachev, the collapse of the Soviet Union, and the emergence of the new Russia. The script was written in 1987–8, published in Russia in 1992–3, and filmed between 1995 and 1997. Because of the economic crisis that hit Russia in August 1998, *The Barber of Siberia* could not be launched in ten Siberian cities before its Moscow première, as had been anticipated, but it was eventually premiered in lavish style in the Kremlin Palace of Congresses on 20 February 1999, the first film to be premiered there in over twenty years.

The publicity campaign around the film was carefully co-ordinated. Banners and posters were positioned all over central Moscow, and a new brand of vodka, 'Russian Standard', was launched as well as a new perfume range, 'Cadet No. 1' and 'Cadet No. 3'. Mikhalkov appeared for over a week on almost all television shows, with several channels screening retrospectives of his films, and the première brought together Moscow's VIPs and beau-monde in the Kremlin Palace of Congresses, specially fitted with a Dolby Stereo Surround system and a new projection screen for this purpose. Moreover, the campaign connected Mikhalkov's role in the film to his political programme, which gave rise to speculations about his candidature during the forthcoming presidential elections. The linking of art and politics, however, together with the media hype around the film, drove journalists to review the film in negative terms as a political manifesto rather than as an artistic product. The nationalist ideas of the film-maker had been a thorn in the flesh of most journalists, if not since Mikhalkov's takeover of the Film-makers' Union, then certainly after his failed attempt to position the director of his studio in the vacant ministerial chair at Goskino, the State Committee for Cinematography.

The Barber of Siberia tells the story of Jane Callaghan, an American woman who travels to Russia in 1885 in order to assist the Irish-American inventor Douglas McCracken in securing funding for his machine, the 'barber', which is designed to chop down the Siberian forests. McCracken has run out of funding and, under pressure from his creditors, has hired Jane to charm General Radlov, the head of the Military Academy, in order to gain through him the support of Grand Duke Alexei. Jane achieves this task by pretending to be McCracken's daughter and flirting with the self-conscious and vain General who proposes to her. In her business-oriented approach to life Jane offers her ability to charm for hire, and sells her body when necessary, since she was abused in her childhood by her stepfather and was forced to fend for herself at an early age. Then she meets the cadet Andrei Tolstoi, who falls in love with her. As a cadet, Tolstoi has very high moral values: he defends his feelings for Jane in a duel, he humiliates himself when he proposes to Jane in front of the General, and he is prepared to sacrifice his career for Jane. She, on the other hand, continues her intrigues in which Radlov plays a key role, in order to fulfil her contract and get the papers which McCracken needs to be signed by the Grand Duke. Unwilling to sacrifice her scheme for the sake of love, she spends a day with the General at a Shrovetide fair and encourages him to drink, seeking to compromise him. When he sees Jane flirting with the General in the theatre just after she has spent the night with him, Tolstoi attacks his rival with a violin bow during a performance of *The Marriage of Figaro* in which Tolstoi is singing the part of Figaro. The production by the Military Academy is taking place in the presence of the Grand Duke, and Radlov swiftly accuses Tolstoi of an attempt upon the Grand Duke's life. Thus Radlov secures promotion for himself by 'preventing a terrorist act'. Tolstoi is found guilty and sent to a prison camp in Siberia, without ever attempting to defend his actions.

Ten years later, Jane has married McCracken so that her son (Tolstoi's child) will have a father. On the occasion of the launch of McCracken's 'barber' Jane travels to Siberia. As the machine begins the massive destruction of the Siberian *taiga*, Jane finds the house where Tolstoi, who now earns a living as a barber, lives with his wife Dunia (formerly a maid in the Tolstois' house in Moscow) and their children. Jane then leaves Russia.

The love story of Jane and Andrei Tolstoi is embedded in a narration by Jane, who, in 1905, writes a letter to her son, Andrew, a recruit at a US military base. Time and again, we see her writing the letter, while her voice reads parts of it, and we see Andrew at the US base, as stubborn as his father and upholding values and principles which he defends with his life. A key example of this is when he stands up for his veneration of Mozart by refusing to repeat a phrase denigrating the composer. Rather than do this he wears a gas mask for more than twenty-four hours because he refuses to repeat commander O'Leary's remark, 'I don't give a shit about Mozart'. Finally, when Andrew's endurance wins out, O'Leary accepts that 'Mozart is a great composer'. As the commander is shouting this phrase across the barracks, Jane drives up in a car to visit her son and she shows the commander a portrait of Andrew's father, the former Russian cadet Tolstoi, suggesting that Andrew's Russian roots explain his behaviour.

The film's narrative stretches over twenty years. Each part (Jane's retrospective narrative, the episode at the US military base, and the love story) develops chronologically, and the three story lines are joined up at the end. The way Tolstoi behaved towards Jane parallels the stubborn insistence upon principle displayed by the recruit Andrew. The Jane who reflects on the past does so with hindsight, but is still unable fully to understand Russia, underscoring the notion that Russia cannot be grasped by reason alone. Jane and McCracken represent a world that is largely deprived of any spiritual ideals, while the Russian cadets are endowed with a sense of honour and love for the Fatherland. The western characters acknowledge only success in business or the achievement of goals, while most of the Russian characters surrender to a fatalistic vision of their life, accepting suffering and solitude.

Almost all the characters lack a happy family life. Jane comes from a broken family: her father died, her mother remarried, and she was abused by her stepfather who then left her mother. She was never loved by her mother, and was destroyed by her stepfather; she has nothing to believe in, nothing to live for, and has never experienced love. She has abandoned herself, reduced herself to selling her services, physical or social. When she spends the night with Tolstoi she realises his devotion to her; yet she continues to play her game in order to fulfil her contract, for her financial benefit. Jane is gambling, thinking she can both fulfil her contract and achieve happiness with Tolstoi, but the stakes are too high. She never really understands Tolstoi's pride and honour; instead, she interprets his behaviour as that of an immature boy. Their relationship does not come across as one endowed with love. The love-scene happens off-screen and remains unconvincing, with a lack of genuine emotion between the characters. Tolstoi's family too is broken: his mother has an affair with his uncle. Both the military men in the film, the General and the Captain, are bachelors. Love fails on a human level across all classes of society: neither Jane's nor Andrei's families were happy, and even the Tsar would have had no children if things had gone the way his wife, the Empress Maria Fedorovna (Dagmar of Denmark), had wished. The only love acceptable for a military man is the love of the Tsar, and when Tolstoi places Jane above the Tsar he betrays the 'Father' of the nation.

Tolstoi and the cadets have high moral values and are bonded by a comradeship that transcends the boundaries of everyday life: the cadets Polievsky and Tolstoi fight a duel, but later it is Polievsky who fetches Jane so that she can visit Tolstoi in hospital after the duel, and who summons her to the railway station when Tolstoi is sent to Siberia. Set in a time when ideals were high, the film also displays the cadets' absolute belief in the Tsar, while their encounter with him strengthens their love for the Tsar as their father. Their captain, Mokin, often assumes the role of a father-figure when he covers up for some of the cadets' adventures. Both Captain Mokin and Commander O'Leary at the US military base are strict, but they are ready to listen to their cadets. Both are ultimately concerned with more than discipline and are ready to admit when they have been wrong, and to defend 'their' soldiers. In this way, despite its discipline, life in the military is endowed with human concern and the military is idealised. The Tsar is the ideal father, and the only person worthy of love. In the absence of intact family life and genuine father-figures, the military community replaces the family, while the Tsar substitutes for the father who is also represented on a lower level by the military commanders. In Mikhalkov's vision the whole of Russian society is transformed into one large family with a patriarch at its head.

Tolstoi seems confused in his behaviour and his words. While he serves and loves the Tsar he allows a terrorist to escape. He also confuses his love for the Tsar with his love for Jane and defends a woman who is a liar. The director's intended portrayal of a positive hero is hampered by the naivety of the young cadet, who is easily fooled, shows a high level of human compassion and who follows ideals unquestioningly. Tolstoi's personality is not suited to the discipline required for a military career but his acceptance of his sentence is indicative of his sincerity because he accepts his imprisonment and exile as the price to be paid for following a false ideal.

The love intrigue in the film draws a subtle distinction between the passion and foolishness of Tolstoi and Jane, and the love displayed by Dunia, who shares her remaining money and follows Tolstoi to Siberia. Jane seduces Tolstoi in his moment of weakness, when the naive, inexperienced, but devoted cadet faints. Jane discovers that love is possible for her, despite all her negative experiences in the past; yet she destroys their relationship, sullying the pure feeling of the cadet, Tolstoi, with her intrigues. The film uses a historical setting for this romantic plot, with a positive hero to transport the moral values of the past into the present. Even Jane can, and will, find her place in life and follow the path which everybody must find for themselves. High moral values, ideals and principles may have a price, but they will triumph: Mozart *is* a great composer. Andrew is the spitting image of his father, with the same principled outlook on life.

The film is set in the Russia of Tsar Alexander III (ruled 1881–94), a world into which an American woman and an Irish-American inventor intrude. The reactionary and nationalist Tsar Alexander III is portrayed as a benevolent ruler who loves children and takes his son Mikhail on horseback to the parade. The Tsar is endowed with human rather than god-like traits, covering Mikhail's mouth when the boy wants to shout a second greeting to induce a reply from the cadets, a game he would like to play. As the cadets stand to attention, the camera captures a sparrow at the cadets' feet and closes up on the small creature. Mikhalkov never neglects the small at the expense of the grand. The Tsar is thus presented as an ideal father, for his child as well as for the nation. Such a portrayal is important in the light of the absence of a father-figure in so many contemporary Russian films of the post-Soviet period, such as Sergei Bodrov's *Kavkazskii plennik* (*The Prisoner of the Mountains*, 1996), in which soldiers no longer know what they are fighting and dying for.

In the publicity leaflet for the film, Mikhalkov wrote: 'I hope that our film will help the spectator to feel again pride in the genuine merit of his Fatherland,' suggesting that the moral values of the young Russian cadet Tolstoi are a model designed to help contemporary audiences value and love their fatherland. The film promulgates the standards of nineteenth-century Russia: honour and the readiness to stand by ideals irrespective of a potential risk to life. These were echoed in the launch of the vodka brand 'Russian Standard' and the competition initiated among the students of the Film Institute to make short films on the five components of the Russian character – creation, trust, perfection, experience, and patriotism. As the critic Lidia Maslova observed (*Kommersant*, 23 February 1999), the film is itself a commercial for the 'product Russia'. The campaign for Russian values on both commercial and cinematic levels also underscores the film's fusion of past and present, and film and reality.

The film pinpoints the divergence between the traditions of the east and the west. Russia has always sought to define its identity by reference to its allegiance to eastern or western cultures, or as having the unique mission to act as a bridge between the two. This is reflected in the long-standing debate between the 'westernisers', who considered Russia a backward part of European culture, and the 'slavophiles', who glorified Russia's native institutions and traditions. In this controversy, Mikhalkov's position is on the side of the slavophiles since he idealises Russia and portrays some western features, such as the business-oriented approach discussed above, in derogatory terms, even though the film is designed for western as well as Russian audiences.

Russian traditions are portrayed in great detail in the script. The rituals of 'Forgiveness Sunday' and the Shrovetide celebrations in the week before Lent take up a substantial, and costly, part of the film. Mikhalkov films, at length, scenes at the Shrovetide fair which show people drinking together and fighting each other, only to seek forgiveness the next day. The scenes also show us a theatre of Lilliputians re-enacting Napoleon's battles, factory workers engaging in fist fights on the ice, and a fireworks display. It is as if the world turns, temporarily, into a theatre in which social and class boundaries are broken in the true spirit of carnival, and 'man behaves like a beast while animals drink like people'. The spectator is presented with this image of Russia through the eyes of a foreigner, Jane, who is capable only of imitating Russian habits without ever comprehending the concepts behind them. In Russia, she remains a 'nobody', not allowed to see Tolstoi in prison, not taken seriously by Tolstoi's mother, and unable to travel within Russia. When she writes the letter to her son in 1905, she pretends to be a different Jane and claims the old Jane is just a 'friend'. Jane has played so many roles in her life that she just sheds one role and becomes a new person. Her roles and her history change so fast that one is never quite sure what to believe, and she appears to adapt her story to each changing situation very swiftly. She pretends, for example, to be McCracken's daughter, but then admits she is not. On another occasion she tells McCracken that her husband drowned in the Nile, while Radlov is told that he died in battle. Another 'fiction' emerges when we realise that in reality Jane was never married.

In breaking with her character Jane does nothing of substance to save Tolstoi. She explains her behaviour to him speaking through a closed door when he has already left the room. She is uninventive and cannot think of a role when asked at the prison gate what relation she has to Tolstoi; instead she offers herself to Radlov to try and save Tolstoi, prepared to soil their relationship by betraying Tolstoi's feelings. Dunia, on the other hand, is ready to strike Jane with a sickle when she comes into their house in Siberia to take Tolstoi away with her. Conversely, McCracken has an ideal he believes in, to such an extent that it dominates his life and he forgets everything else, takes no interest in the world around him, and is prepared to die for his ideal, trying to hang himself when funding is uncertain. The machine that embodies the meaning of his life, that conquers nature and makes him its master, is also a machine which destroys nature and causes long-term damage to the environment. Here the film-maker draws a parallel with Stalin, another dangerous, utopian dreamer in Soviet history, who attempted to conquer territory and master nature.

The values upheld in the film are typical of the nineteenth century, which Mikhalkov connects to the beauty, and the deep sense, of Russian folk traditions at a time before these were destroyed by the Soviet regime. The heroism displayed by Tolstoi is possible only in a setting of the previous century; contemporary Russia has no room for such heroism. *The Barber of Siberia* instils nostalgia in the spectator, not for the Stalinist and Soviet past as so many contemporary television programmes do, but for the Tsarist, pre-Revolutionary Russia, related to the present through the historical event that dominated 1998: the laying to rest of the remains of the last Tsar and his family, the Romanovs, in St Petersburg in July 1998.

Since the film's title plays upon the opera *The Barber of Seville* and includes a performance of Mozart's *The Marriage of Figaro*, we need to consider briefly the role of music. *The Marriage of Figaro*, the opera performed by the cadets, stands at the centre of the film. Tolstoi is singing Figaro's aria when he attacks Radlov, but Tolstoi is not as lucky as Figaro: Figaro wants to marry Susanna, but Count Almaviva tries to seduce the bride before the wedding. In reality, Tolstoi sees Jane 'seduced' by Almaviva–Radlov and takes fate into his own hands instead of leaving it in the hands of the fictional opera libretto, which would have secured a happy end: the Countess Almaviva discovers her husband in the garden trying to seduce Susanna – who is nobody else but the Countess herself in disguise. Though it has been suggested above that the only love acceptable was that for the Tsar, the film-maker allows one exception, which is the love of Mozart. In using the composer to represent the rejection of national (political) values in favour of artistic ones, Mikhalkov is making a political statement that politics does not matter when placed alongside a taste for great art or music.

Tolstoi first sings Figaro's aria 'Non piu andare' (from Act I) on the train; later he sings it instead of the cadets' March, that is to say, he betrays his love for the Tsar. On the train with all the convicts, in reply to the call from 'Susanna', the part the cadet Nazarov played in the production, he sings the aria again so that the cadets can find him among the convicts on the train. The portrait of Mozart – the visual, rather than musical representation of the composer – dominates Andrew's life as a recruit in the US Army. The typically Russian character is shown as stubborn, proud and ready to suffer. These qualities are also the outstanding characteristics of Andrew, and single him out from the other recruits who all, sooner or later, take off their gas masks and give up their defence of Mozart as a great composer.

Tolstoi plays the part of Figaro, and addresses the phrase 'Count, you seem to like my wife' to Radlov in the scene immediately preceding his attack. He snatches a bow from a violinist and hits the General, injuring his ear in a fashion which is not unlike that of a bad barber, as if he has 'shaved' the General's ear off. Tolstoi later works as a barber in Siberia where he has a place in the world and has found his path in life, which is humble but honest. While he cuts hair, the 'barber' wreaks destruction on a larger scale. Indeed, hair plays an important part throughout the film. Tolstoi has his head shaved before he is sent to Siberia, while Andrew's head is half shaven before the incident where the commander criticises the portrait of Mozart that hangs over Andrew's bed (mistaking the composer for a 'dame') and makes the recruits put on gas masks, which will be removed only if they agree that they 'don't give a shit about Mozart'. Radlov has problems with his thinning hair; he even consults a hair implant specialist, which is actually a trap set up by Jane to compromise him in case she cannot charm Radlov into supporting McCracken in front of the Grand Duke, but to no avail. His baldness is a sign of his vanity, though, and does not have the same implications as the shaving of heads. It is also, in his case, associated with impotence, which he tries to disguise through wearing a wig, and socially covers up by having Tolstoi read his proposal to Jane. The cutting of hair is an unnatural procedure, as is the cutting of trees by the 'barber'. In the context of one of the reforms in Peter the Great's programme of westernisation, which required the shaving of all civil servants' long beards, shaving may be seen as particularly 'unnatural' to Russians, who advocate instead the growth of hair, beards, and forests as a question of 'nationalist' pride.

The space of the city consists largely of the interiors of houses, while external views of streets normally show enclosed architectural spaces such as fences, courtyards and the Kremlin walls, which reveal the oppressive atmosphere of the city. This cityscape contrasts with the vast, open space of the Siberian forests, filmed from an aerial perspective and providing a visual frame for the film at the beginning and the end. The entire plot is set in Moscow, rather than in St Petersburg, the capital of the Russian Empire, with the exception of the final episode in Siberia and the interludes at the US base. It was in Moscow that foreigners like McCracken were developing new inventions for Russia. Life in the city offers distractions, and is characterised by social activity. It contrasts sharply with the wide forests of Siberia. In the end McCracken takes his invention to the provinces: to conquer Russian lands, to destroy Russian nature, just as Jane had destroyed Tolstoi's life. In the final analysis, Jane has destroyed the possibility of her own happiness as well as Tolstoi's life, and McCracken has 'wasted' ten years of his life on a machine that brings destruction and scares the inhabitants of the *taiga*. Characters are contrasted, though these contrasts are not simply black and white, but complicated and differentiated. The theme of the destruction of nature offers a larger dimension to the intrusion of Jane's values into Tolstoi's life. Destruction begins on the level of human values and ends with ecological disaster. Thus Mikhalkov moves from a concern with the individual to a larger scale, investigating the significance of human actions for the world at large and thereby creating a link between the individual and the global, the urban and the provincial, east and west, past and present.

The Barber of Siberia offers a moral statement in asserting the necessity of having principles, and it presents a positive hero with the potential to instil hope in contemporary Russian audiences. The film is also a commodity for export, designed to boost the image of Russia as a nation with high ideals, unwilling to compromise, and with a strong leadership. By using national and international stars, and by breaking the linear development of the plot through Jane's narrative voice, the film provides room for development and reflection, love intrigues and comedy, the portrayal of national rituals along with a foreign response to them. The film is simultaneously past and future, objective and subjective, national and international, a film that attempts to create a myth for audiences at home and abroad in a manner modelled on that of Hollywood. In a speech to the Fourth Congress of Film-makers in May 1998, Mikhalkov said:

> Have many of our fellow countrymen been in the USA? I imagine some five per cent; maybe even less, three per cent. Yet do many people know about the USA? Almost everybody does. But they know the America that the cinema has shown them. America has forced the world to perceive it through cinema. (In *Iskusstvo kino*, 8, 1998)

In *The Barber of Siberia* he is clearly striving to offer an idealised view of Russia to foreign audiences and to create a 'myth' on similar lines.

As a political manifesto the film contains a strange nationalistic statement for the future of Russia, envisaging the resurrection of absolute rule and discipline which would reinstate a value system and thus benefit the Russian population. This has struck a chord with Russian audiences who love the film. As a commercial product this 'Russian *Titanic*' attempts to sell to western audiences the 'product Russia' as a country which may have strange traditions, but has sound principles of trust, honour and reliability. As an artistic product, it bears comparison with epics such as *Gone with the Wind* (1939) and it is filmed by Pavel Lebeshev, one of the most talented cameramen in Russia, in a brave attempt to market a Russian film in western style, and to show the world what a beautiful country Russia is.

References and Suggestions for Further Reading

Attwood, Lynne (ed.) 1993: *Red Women on the Silver Screen: Soviet Women and Cinema from the Beginning to the End of the Communist Era*. London: Pandora.

Berry, E. and Miller-Pogacar, A. (eds) 1995: *Re-Entering the Sign*. Ann Arbor, MI: University of Michigan Press.

Beumers, Birgit (ed.) 1999: *Russia on Reels: The Russian Idea in Post-Soviet Cinema*. London: I. B. Tauris.

Condee, Nancy (ed.) 1995: *Soviet Hieroglyphics: Visual Culture in Late Twentieth-Century Russia*. Bloomington, IN, and London: Indiana University Press.

Freidin, Gregory (ed.) 1993: *Russian Culture in Transition*. Palo Alto, CA: Stanford University Press.

Horton, Andrew and Brashinsky, Michael 1991: *The Zero-Hour: Glasnost and Soviet Cinema in Transition*. Princeton, NJ: Princeton University Press.

Kelly, C. and Shepherd D. (eds) 1998: *Russian Cultural Studies: An Introduction*. Oxford: Oxford University Press.

Lawton, Anna 1992: *Kinoglasnost*. Cambridge: Cambridge University Press.

Shalin, D. 1996: *Russian Culture at the Crossroads*. Oxford: Oxford University Press.

Credits

Director	Nikita Mikhalkov
Producer	Michel Seydoux
Production Company	TriTe (Russia) and Camera One (France)
Screenplay	Rustam Ibragimbekov, Nikita Mikhalkov
Editor	Enzo Meniconi
Director of Photography	Pavel Lebeshev
Art Director	Vladimir Murzin
Music	Eduard Artemiev

Cast

Julia Ormond	Jane Callaghan
Oleg Menshikov	Andrei Tolstoi
Richard Harris	Douglas McCracken
Alexei Petrenko	General Radlov
Vladimir Ilyin	Captain Mokin
Marat Basharov	Count Polievsky (cadet)
Nikita Tatarenkov	Prince Alibekov (cadet)
Georgi Dronov	Nazarov (cadet)
Artem Mikhalkov	Buturlin (cadet)
Daniel Olbrykhsky	Kopnovsky (McCracken's assistant)
Marina Neelova	Tolstoi's mother
Avangard Leontiev	Uncle Nikolai
Anna Mikhalkova	Dunia (maid)
Robert Hardy	Professor Forsten
Nikita Mikhalkov	Alexander III
Isabel Renault	Maria Fedorovna (Empress)
Filipp Dyachkov	Prince Mikhail (their son)
Evgeni Steblov	Grand Duke Alexei Alexandrovich

Filmography

Svoi sredi chuzhikh, chuzhoi sredi svoikh (*At Home among Strangers, a Stranger at Home / At Home among Strangers, Alone among Friends*, 1974)

Raba lubvi (*A Slave of Love*, 1975)

Neokonchennaya pyesa dlya mekhanicheskoovo pianino (*Unfinished Piece for a Mechanical Piano*, 1977)

Pyat' vecherov (*Five Evenings*, 1978)

Neskolko dnei iz zhizni I. I. Oblomov (*Oblomov / Several Days in the Life of I. I. Oblomov*, 1979)

Kinsfolk (1981)

Bez svidetelei (*A Private Conversation / Without Witnesses*, 1983)

Oci ciornie (*Dark Eyes*, 1987)

Autostop (1990)

Urga (*Urga: Territory of Love / Urga: Close to Eden*, 1991)

Anna 6–18 (1993)

Utomlennye solntsem (*Burnt by the Sun*, 1994)

Sibirskii tsiriul'nik (*The Barber of Siberia*, 1998)

Notes on the Contributors

Birgit Beumers is Lecturer in Russian at the University of Bristol. She is an authority on Russian cinema, theatre and culture post-1945, author of *Yury Lyubimov at the Taganka Theatre* (1997) and editor of *Russia on Reels: The Russian Idea in Post-Soviet Cinema* (1999).

Derek Duncan is Senior Lecturer in Italian at the University of Bristol. He has published widely on issues of gender in twentieth-century Italian fiction and is co-editing a book on European travel-writing. His book *Masculinity and National Identity in Italy* will be published soon.

Jill Forbes is Professor of French at Queen Mary and Westfield, University of London. She is an international authority on French cinema and author of many publications in the field including *The Cinema in France: After the New Wave* (1992) and *Les Enfants du paradis* (1997).

Annella McDermott is Lecturer in Hispanic Studies at the University of Bristol. She has wide-ranging interests in the fields of Spanish cinema and literature and has recently published, with Margaret Tull Costa, *The Dedalus Book of Spanish Fantasy* (1999).

Sarah Street is Senior Lecturer in Film and Television Studies at the University of Bristol. A distinguished authority on British cinema, her publications include *Cinema and State: The Film Industry and the Government, 1927–84* (1985, co-authored with Margaret Dickinson), *British National Cinema* (1997) and the forthcoming *British Cinema in Documents* (2000).

Stuart Taberner is Lecturer in German at the University of Leeds. He has published on Günter Grass, Uwe Johnson, Martin Walser, Monika Maron and Stefan Heym, as well as on German film, and is currently working on the writing of younger German authors in the years since unification in 1990.

Index of Film Titles

General Index

Adjani, Isabelle, 46
Alejandro, Julio, 117
Alexandrov, Grigori, 13, 31, 45, 55, 57
Allen, Kevin, 191
Almodóvar, Pedro, 41, 43
Anderson, Lindsay, 21, 67
Andreotti Act, 1949 (Italy), 19
Angelopoulos, Theo, 22
Anglo-American Film Agreement, 1949
   (UK–US), 18
Antonioni, Michelangelo, 20, 21, 37, 44
Ardolino, Emile, 140
Arletty, 46
Arliss, Leslie, 44
art cinema, xii, 20, 37–40, 42
Askoldov, Alexei, 14
Attenborough, Richard, 140
audiences, 21, 32, 38, 147

Balasko, Josiane, 176
Balcon, Michael, 36, 69
Barber of Seville, The (opera), 196, 202
Bardem, Juan Antonio, 13
Bardot, Brigitte, 39
Barnet, Boris, 9
Barrault, Jean-Louis, 47
Baur, Harry, 47
Baxter, John, 114
Beauvoir, Simone de, 34
Beineix, Jean-Jacques, 43
Belmondo, Jean-Paul, 46
Berlanga, Luis García, 13, 41
Berlin Wall, fall of, x, 23, 24, 28, 157–66
Berlusconi, Silvio, 22, 153
Berri, Claude, 24, 40
Berry, Jules, 47
Bertini, Francesca, 46
Besson, Luc, 28, 43, 48
Bizet, Georges, 133, 137
Blier, Bertrand, 171, 176
Blum, Léon, 82
Bodrov, Sergei, 201
Bogart, Humphrey, 123
Bolshevik Revolution, 1917 (USSR), 28
Boothby, Robert, 17

Bordwell, David, ix, 37, 39
Borelli, Lydia, 46
Bourdieu, Pierre, 176
Boyle, Danny, 183–92
Brasseur, Pierre, 47
Brecht, Bertholt, 62
British cinema/film industry, xiii, 4, 7,
   11–12, 16, 17, 22, 23, 32, 42, 44, 45,
   46, 47, 67–78, 183–92
Buñuel, Luis, 28, 34, 38, 109–19

Cahiers du cinéma, 39, 89
Cain, James, M., 13, 96, 98–9
Calamai, Clara, 100–1
Calvert, Phyllis, 47
Canal Plus (France), 23
Cannes Film Festival, 20, 21, 116, 171
Caprices de Marianne, Les, 4, 85
Carné, Marcel, 16, 44, 178
Caro, Marc, 189
Carroll, Madeleine, 11
Catholic Church/Catholicism, 12–13, 99,
   109–10, 115, 147, 153
censorship, xi–xii, 11–14, 17
   Britain, 11–12
   France, 11, 13–14
   Germany, 11
   Italy, 11, 13
   Soviet/Russia, 12, 13, 14, 39
   Spain, 11–12, 14
Chabrol, Claude, 21, 34
Chanan, Michael, 24
Channel Four (Britain), 22
Chaplin, Charlie, 13, 28, 31, 38
Chekhov, Anton, 37
Chevalier, Maurice, 32
Chiari, Walter, 47
Chiaureli, Mikhail E., 15
Christie, Ian, ix, xi
Clair, René, 28, 31, 35
Clouzot, Henri, 16
Cold War, The, xi, 19
Commission on Educational and Cultural
   Films (UK), 27
Cook, Pam, ix

212

From the Depths of the Ghetto to Soaring
Corporate Heights . . .

The Chains

"Bursting with vitality, vivid characters and uncomfortably believable history, this saga by the author of the bestsellers *The Last Angry Man* and *To Brooklyn, With Love* and of the TV series *Holocaust* features three generations of brawling, semicriminal Chains, a Brooklyn Jewish family . . . It's a passionate, violent story, streetwise and rich in authentic detail, a lesson in social history delivered from the barrel of a gun—and it grips at every point."

—*Publishers Weekly*

"Green at his most honest and unadulterated . . . a solid, lively . . . bet."

—*Kirkus Reviews*

"Sweeping across the years 1910 to 1960, this dramatic epic follows three generations of fearless men and fiery women who climb and claw their way from Jewish ghetto to corporate boardroom."

—*Literary Guild*

Bantam Books by Gerald Green

THE CHAINS
HOLOCAUST

THE CHAINS

Gerald Green

THE CHAINS

*A Bantam Book / published by arrangement with
Seaview Books*

PRINTING HISTORY
Seaview edition published April 1980
Bantam edition / June 1981

ISBN 0-553-13419-1

Published simultaneously in the United States and Canada

*Bantam Books are published by Bantam Books, Inc. Its trade-
mark, consisting of the words "Bantam Books" and the portrayal of a bantam, is Registered in U.S. Patent and Trademark
Office and in other countries. Marca Registrada. Bantam
Books, Inc., 666 Fifth Avenue, New York, New York 10103.*

PRINTED IN THE UNITED STATES OF AMERICA

0 9 8 7 6 5 4 3 2 1

For Marie,
wife, companion, and inspiration

THE CHAINS

1960
Myron Malkin's Notebook

A smallish man, Mr. Martin B. Chain, but not at all dainty. About five-nine, hundred and forty pounds. Whippet-lean, muscular hands. He moves like a tricky backcourt man or a wide receiver. I can see him on the tennis or squash court—tireless, intense.

The face is dark and secretive. It gives you nothing. Long straight nose, high cheekbones, slightly slanted black eyes, long lashes, heavy eyebrows, thick straight black hair. And well tanned in November. A dark, foxy face.

The suit is Oxford gray and vested. Not the style you'd expect on a thirty-six-year-old who inherited a fortune. Made his multimillionaire father look like a cheapskate. Chain Industries. Chain Pharmaceuticals. Chain Distilleries.

Chunks of gold gleam on his trim figure. Cuff links that could be artifacts from a pharaoh's tomb. A Piaget watch as thin as a communion wafer. A wide wedding band. A class ring, Dartmouth? He's got his diplomas framed on the wall—Choate, Dartmouth, Harvard Business. An honorary degree from Brandeis.

"I'm quite busy, Malkin," he says. Low soft voice. Unlocatable accent. No need to shout. "The only reason I agreed to see you is, well, your uncle."

My late uncle, Dr. Samuel Abelman, delivered Mr. Martin B. Chain. And also his kid brother, Davey, and his sister, Iris. On Haven Place in Brownsville, Brooklyn. Quite a leap to a Park Avenue office. Before the family moved to their twenty-room mansion on Ocean Parkway. Long before young Martin moved to Fifth Avenue and Armonk with seasonal pads in Barbados and Klosters.

"I appreciate it, Mr. Chain. I know you have a lot on your mind."

No acknowledgment. He doesn't need a dingy reporter to remind him that he is very rich, very powerful, very social, and has a great deal on his mind. Our financial editor tells me that Martin inherited the empire, trebled its book value, turned it into one of the postwar industrial giants. And not just with whiskey.

The New York Times of Wednesday, May 18, 1960, is on his desk. The eight-column banner is about the collapse of the Eisenhower-Khrushchev meeting in Vienna:

SUMMIT CONFERENCE BREAKS UP IN DISPUTE;
WEST BLAMES KHRUSHCHEV'S RIGID STAND;
HE INSISTS ON EISENHOWER'S SPYING APOLOGY

"Quite a mess out there," I say. I'm a news junkie. I've already read the *News* and the *Times*. I'll read matchbox covers and box tops if there's nothing else. Martin stares at me over peaked fingers. Then I notice he—someone—has circled a smaller headline in red:

KENNEDY SWEEPS
MARYLAND'S VOTE

Gets 70% of Total in Routing
Morse for Sixth Straight
Primary Triumph

"That seems to have interested you, Mr. Chain."

"What?" Careful, careful. Not too close, Myron. We're about the same age. Born on the same street in Brooklyn. But that doesn't mean I can get comfy with him.

"Kennedy's primary win."

"He'll get the nomination and he'll be elected. No one seems to understand that his Irish Catholicism will win for him. It'll keep enough Democrats in line. People keep saying it's a drawback, but it's his biggest advantage over Nixon."

"The Chains are backing the senator?"

"Not a question of backing. We've given generous support to both men. They're both adequate. Kennedy is more conservative than people think, and Nixon is more liberal."

On reflection, I see he's right. Everyone drifts to some amorphous *center* sooner or later. And not just in politics.

"Why are you smiling, Malkin?"

"I was thinking of your late grandfather, Benny Otzenberger. The boss of Brownsville. If he didn't deliver at least ninety-eight percent of the vote for the Democrats, he cried. What would he say knowing his grandson was giving money to a Republican?"

"He'd understand."

I laugh weakly. Old Benny. Illiterate grocery wholesaler.

Commissioner of weights and measures. A walrus-mustached blimp, one of my uncle Doc's first patients. Fixer, job getter, rogue, personal friend of FDR. Otzenberger's daughter Hilda was Martin Chain's mother.

"Benny used to say it was Tammany Hall or no hall at all. He meant the union hall, I guess."

Martin Chain isn't buying my cozy recollections of Brownsville. "Malkin, you aren't here to discuss politics. I don't think you care about my grandfather."

"But I do. The other one. Jacob Chain."

He stiffens. The vulpine face pulls back a bit. I realize he's quite handsome in a dark, domineering way. "I see. Some tired old stuff about Crazy Jake? Sunday-supplement garbage? What was justice in this case?"

"I want the story on Crazy Jake Chain. The king of the *shtarkers.*"

"He's been dead a long time."

"Lincoln's been dead longer. They write about him."

Patiently, I explain it all again. I have already interviewed a flunky at his public-relations firm, his vice-president for PR, his secretary, and other people to whom he's shunted me.

Credentials again: I'm a reporter for World News Association. I free-lance magazine articles. I'm fascinated with the Chain saga.

"Do you have a publisher?" Martin asks. He walks away and studies the Dow-Jones ticker. I'm reminded of a marvelous scene in *Citizen Kane*. Everett Sloane making the same move and saying to a reporter: *"It's not hard to make a lot of money—if that's all you want to do...."*

No publisher yet. But I'm sure I can get it in print—as a magazine series or a book. The Chains are national names. I point to some photographs on the wall. Martin with Eisenhower, Martin's father, Mortimer, getting a plaque from Ben-Gurion. Martin and Mortimer, son and father, seated on a dais with Cardinal Spellman, John F. Kennedy, and Mayor Bill O'Dwyer.

"We won't cooperate," he says. There's iodine in his voice. No Brooklyn intonations. No dentalized *T*'s. Choate, Dartmouth, and Harvard have endowed him with a generalized Eastern Seaboard accent. He sounds a bit like a reformed rabbi in Scarsdale.

"I'd like to convince you it's in your interest to help me."

"Is that a threat? Forget it. My loyalty to Dr. Abelman for bringing me into the world has limits."

"Heck no, Mr. Chain. This can be a fascinating book."

"When we want it written, we'll hire Allan Nevins."

Not bad, not bad. The official biographer of the big pirates. The Chains will go first-class.

"Mr. Chain, the *real* story is much better than the bland stuff you let out. I saw that article in *Town and Country*. Four pages of color photographs. Horses. Rare books. Vintage wines. Black-tie dinners at 1030 Fifth Avenue. Hunt-club breakfasts in Armonk."

"What are you trying to say?"

"The true story of the Chains is richer. From horses to horses in three generations."

There's a glint in his onyx eyes. It isn't friendly. "What does that mean?"

"Jake Chain was a seltzer-wagon driver. What Jews call a *balegolah*—a low type. My aunt and uncle remember him with his old horse. Before he became—ah, what shall I say? A union offical?"

"It has its charm, Malkin. But we will *not* give you any help. In fact our lawyers will make it tough for you. You'll regret it. Stay with your job at World News—incidentally, I'm a squash partner of the chairman—and forget about this."

I'm getting it all. *Lawyers. Squash. Board chairman.* Even his twenty-dollar cologne is getting to me. I'm supposed to be intimidated. Screw him. I know the house where he was born. Puerto Ricans live there now. Forty of them in seven rooms.

"Let's not try to con each other, Martin," I say, astonished at my *chutzpah*. "Your grandfather was a strong-arm man. Crazy Jake, the one-man mob. It's nothing to hide. Americans love a tough cookie. That's the beautiful thing about this story. In 1910, 1911, 1912, your grandfather was beating up scabs and foremen. Torching pants factories. Today you endow research centers. If you can't see the drama in that—"

"You're warned. We'll stop you."

"I know something about the laws of libel and the rights of the press. You'd be surprised how thoroughly *The New York Times* covered your grandfather's career. Crazy Jake was great copy. Your father gave them more front-page stuff. The mysterious Mort Chain, baron of Rum Row, king of the Brooklyn bootleggers."

I start fumbling in my briefcase. I've made photostatic copies of some ripe articles from old newspapers. The New York Public Library, for modest fees, has duplicated dozens of columns about Crazy Jake for me. And even more newsprint about his son.

In my haste, clippings litter the two-inch blue velvet carpeting. I grab at a spread from *Vogue* I clipped recently. *Martin and DeeDee Chain, New York's dazzling young do-gooders and good-timers* . . . DeeDee Grau Chain. Emma Willard, Wellesley, Junior League, a Hoch-Deutsch princess of impeccable lineage. I doubt that among her department-store antecedents you'll find a fellow who set fires in lofts. Can't this stiff-ass see how funny it is?

As I'm gathering up the clippings (Chains Dedicate New Wing at Cancer Center; Chain Industries to Absorb Elm & Elm Factories; Justice Department Drops Suit Against Chains—Cites Lack of Witnesses), Martin is on the phone. He's talking to DeeDee. And glaring at me.

"Yes, dear. I'll try not to be late. I know it's an important dinner. You'll have to defend Jack Kennedy by yourself if I'm not there."

By the time I've gotten my papers together, he's buzzed for his secretary. She's a broad-beamed, white-haired woman who suggests an outside linebacker. "Miss Fleet, please show Mr. Malkin out."

I dig out a scrap of paper, a Xerox of a *Times* front page. "Care to hear about this price list, Mr. Chain?"

He's at the Dow-Jones machine with his back to me.

"This way, please," Miss Fleet says.

"Five dollars for a broken nose, ten dollars for a broken arm, twenty dollars for throwing a man down a flight of steps, fifteen dollars for a woman—"

"What are you babbling about?" Martin Chain asks. "Miss Fleet, if this man refuses to go, call Hayward."

I met Hayward on the way in. He guards the front desk. A uniformed Nubian.

"Funny you never knew about your grandfather's price list."

"This way, please," says Miss Fleet, the human enema.

"Is Eva Heilig alive, Mr. Chain? Do you know where I could reach her?"

"She's alive. I'm warning you, Malkin. If you keep after this, you'll regret it. Keep your nose clean. Maybe there'll be a job for you in our public-relations department."

He's a Chain. Charm, threat, bluff, promise, bribe. Uncle Doc always said that about them. And yet he liked them. Especially the old battler, Jake. I'm not so tolerant. Martin Chain may be worth over a hundred million dollars, but to me he's a spoiled, handsome punk. Or am I jealous?

PART I

1910

Chapter 1

On the fiftieth anniversary of the collapse of the Baum Building, a reporter for the *Daily Forward* recalled that, when it fell, the noise could be heard ten blocks away. For five seconds it was as if Niagara Falls had cascaded over Brownsville.

A rush, a roar. Then an eerie echo. Screams, sirens, shouts of people running to Van Dam Street, struggling to break through police lines.

A plume of dust (the writer remembered) rose a hundred feet into the crystalline blue summer sky, feathery dusty gray, suggesting death and mutilation and shame.

The building was a landmark in Brownsville. Four stories, red brick and granite. It housed the K & R Bathrobe and Kimono factory. The initials honored the brothers who owned it, Kalman and Reuven Baum, German Jews who lived on Riverside Drive and came to work everyday in a chauffeured Oakland touring car.

The Baum brothers were equally famous for charitable activities and their refusal to deal with unions. They had, the old reported reminisced, "fixed" every politician and police official in Brooklyn so that investigations of the disaster were derailed, frustrated, and ultimately abandoned. To this day (he wrote), no one knows the reason why twenty-seven immigrant girls were crushed to death in the avalanche of masonry, bricks, plaster, twisted metal, splintered wood.

Of course, it was never a secret that the floors were overloaded with heavy machinery. Isaac (Ike) Brunstein, president of the Bathrobe, Kimono, and House Dress Workers Union, Local 37, made the charge repeatedly. Cracks in the walls. Sagging floors. Weird creaking noises when the sixty machines were humming. As if the vibrations were aggravating strains in the old bricks.

Later it was proven that judges had been bought, witnesses bribed, state legislators persuaded that the accident was no one's fault.

"An act of God," intoned Francis Fagan Dullahan, state assemblyman and Brooklyn Democratic boss. " 'Tis a tragedy beyond doubt, and my heart grieves for those poor ladies and

9

their dear ones, but there is no blame to be affixed, and 'tis best let alone."

"Even in the hour of our death," Eva Heilig had shouted at a hearing in Albany, "we girls were robbed of our dignity!"

She referred to the body searches by a woman foreman, a cousin of the Baums'. Seconds before the south wall slid away in a rush of dust, Mrs. Reich was peering into shirtwaists, skirts, corsets, and bloomers for stolen goods. Girls were herded in groups of four into the fetid ladies' room, forced to show that they were not stealing.

"Have they no shame?" Eva Heilig had cried out. "Have they no mercy? In seconds my fellow workers would be dead! And their feminine privacy was being violated for—*what?* A yard of flannel?"

On the steamy morning when the building collapsed, Jacob Chain had just unloaded a dozen cases of blue seltzer siphons at the Little Hungary restaurant.

Emerging from the restaurant, picking his teeth with a gold toothpick, was Benny Otzenberger, a whale in a white pongee suit. Otzenberger had just dined in imperial fashion, as befitted a rising political figure. He watched Jake Chain, in soiled undershirt and stained black trousers, heft the cases. The fat man admired the thick muscles on the driver's arms and back. What a brute! A regular Jeffries!

"*Nu,* Jake," Otzenberger teased. "You wouldn't want to be a prizefighter? I'll manage. You'll train at Fein's gym. You could be another Joosh champeen."

"I ain't a fighter, Benny."

"Not from what I heard. Reds Mulqueen says he seen you lay out three wops with two punches. Look at them arms. Better than shlepping seltzer. You'll change your mind, talk to me. Joosh prizefighters are a good item."

A heavy-boned, flat-faced man in his twenties with smooth ruddy skin and a mop of straw-blond hair, Chain said no more. He hefted another case and started through the open cellar door. Then he stopped. A wild rushing noise roared through his ears. Benny Otzenberger was frozen, staring at the source of the thundering sound. A few blocks away, a column of dust rose above the tenement roofs.

Jake climbed aboard his wagon and hefted Benny to the seat. Then he slapped the reins on the mare's back. "Go, Kotchka, go!" he shouted.

People were running alongside the wagon, out of tenements, out of side streets. Jake saw Doc Abelman racing from the direction of Haven Place. He was coatless and carrying a black satchel, his legs pumping vigorously. Jake could remember him as a summertime gym teacher in the schoolyards, before he hung out his shingle.

Callery, a policeman from the 71st, leaped onto the step of the wagon and shouted at Jake: "Baum's place! Explosion or something. Look at that smoke!"

Now they could hear shouts, shrieks, the sounds of—what? Rocks falling? A loud sliding sound.

"My wife works there," Jake said.

"*Oi vay*, your wife. And my son. Heshy, my heart." Otzenberger's son, Heshy, age twenty, was an assistant foreman.

A horse-drawn ambulance, with an intern standing on the wagon seat and clanging a bell, almost collided with Jake's mare. He drew the reins sharply. Kotchka reared, whickered, and pawed the air.

They were engulfed by the mob. Old Jews in yarmulkas, women in babushkas, barefoot street brats in torn caps, sweaty workmen, peddlers in the standard uniform—black derby, black vest, collarless white shirt, black trousers. Jake could see Dr. Abelman muscling his hard body through the mob.

It was impossible to go further with the wagon. Jake spotted Sal Ferrante, the fifteen-year-old kid who sold lemon ice and hokey-pokey from a cart. He was rushing toward the disaster. Abruptly Sal's cart was unable to move. Jake leaped down and handed the boy the reins. "Mind my wagon, Sal," Jake said. "I'll give you a penny."

Ferrante nodded. His older brother, Luigi, who had once boxed with Jake at the gym, ran past them. "The whole wall," Luigi shouted. "The whole *sfaccim'* wall fell down. Our sister's in there! Thersea's in there."

Patrolman Callery leaped from the wagon. Benny Otzenberger rolled off the other side; the pavement shuddered as his bulk hit the bricks. Jake helped him to his feet and raced off. With long hard arms, the legs of an athlete, he cut through the screaming mob. And gasped with his first look at the disaster.

It was like a doll's house, with the front removed, that he had once seen in a window on Pitkin Avenue. Open. Exposed. Sections of the upper two stories were standing—machines, benches.

Below, hidden in a cloud of dust, masonry, and dirt, was a pile of smoking rubble. How could anyone be alive under

11

that mass of junk? The front wall of the building had tumbled entirely, a mountain of plaster and brick, twisted machines. He saw an arm waving feebly. The rest of the body was buried. A shoeless foot protruded from a mound of pulverized bricks.

Otzenberger (the police knew him well) was allowed past the line of officers. The fat man was bawling. Tears soaked his moustache. "My heart, my Heshy," he wailed. "Wait, wait, I'll fix those Baum bastards."

A hundred feet from the building one could see the wreckage more clearly. Wires and cables dangled like jungle vines from the upper stories. An entire bank of sewing machines, hanging from heavy tables, were tilted crazily on the top floor. Boards creaked and sagged. Blocks of plaster and random bricks fell from side walls. A cornice of granite shivered and broke away. People screamed and ran for cover. The chunk of stone exploded like a bomb on the pavement. A fragment broke the leg of an old man in vest, yarmulka, and *tsitsith*. He fell as if shot by a cossack's bullet.

In front of the collapsed wall, firemen in rubber coats were carrying out more bodies. Jake saw bloodied heads; arms and legs in positions not normal for anyone's arms or legs. Feet were pointing where they weren't meant to point. Heads were turned around. People gasped as half a torso—legs and groin—was removed. One girl had been stripped of her clothing. Shreds of petticoats clung to her dust-coated body. Her stockings and shoes had been stripped clean. A woman's body, so misshapen that it was impossible to imagine it had once lived, was wrenched free from a steel girder.

"Good God," Abelman gasped. "Hit them like a volcano." He ran into the schoolyard, following another ambulance and two interns in whites.

A fireman stumbled and picked up the body of a tiny woman whose face was crimson mush. Yet she was breathing. Calling for someone named Chayim.

In the schoolyard (where his son Mutteh played kicketycan and Chinese handball), Jake, numb, looked for his wife. Stethoscope in ears, Abelman joined the doctors from Saint Mary's. "Dead," Jake heard Abelman say. "No heartbeat. Didn't give them a chance. The bastards won't let you live."

Jake wandered amid the dying and the mutilated, their screams sailing the air.

Abelman dusted the plaster from a woman's face. Eyes opened in terror. "My arm hurts. It hurts, doctor." Jake saw

Abelman stroke her forehead and reach into his bag for a syringe.

(*"Nightmares all my life,"* Abelman said years later. *"I never forgot the look on their faces. The living worse than the dead. . . ."*)

No sign of Sarah. Jake helped Abelman move a dead woman to another part of the schoolyard. Pink bubbles formed around her mouth. Her eyes were staring. The physician closed them and wiped her face. A doctor from Saint Mary's shouted at them to leave the bodies where they were.

"Dry up, sonny boy," Abelman said. "Dead on one side, those who have a chance on the other. Come on, Jake."

"My wife—my Sarah," Chain said. "You seen her?"

"No, Jake."

The police line sagged and broke. Relatives and survivors rushed to the building. A pall of dust covered the street. Chunks of plaster continued to topple from upper stories.

Against the wall of a grocery, Heshy Otzenberger was sobbing out the story of his miraculous escape.

"We heard it on the ground floor in Baum's office," Heshy bawled. Unlike his balloon of a father, he was stick-thin and round-shouldered, with a sallow sneaky face and a mop of dark brown Brillo rising over a low forehead.

"So you ran out, thanks God," Benny said.

"Me and the girls in the office and the Baum brothers. We heard it. Like cracking. Splitting. I seen this funny thing in the wall, like a line running up. So fast it happened."

Jake thought: Heshy and the Baums were safe. What about the girls locked in the workrooms? *Locked.* Bolts on the doors. Cloths over the clocks so they wouldn't waste time. Stairways blocked.

Luigi Ferrante, dark as a *shwarzer,* banana-nosed, ran to Jake. "Onna side, Jake, onna side of da building. I seen Theresa and ya wife."

Jake and Luigi ran around the corner. A section of the lower wall facing an alley had fallen away. The walls above did not look secure. Nothing seemed to be supporting them except a single steel beam.

Astonishingly, Theresa Ferrante was unhurt. Her clothing was filthy, her face smeared with plaster and blood, but she walked firmly, and flew to Luigi's arms. She was a dark girl, long-legged and graceful.

"Ya awright?" Luigi asked. "Bastards. I catch the *sfaccim'* what done this, they'll be sorry."

13

He put his arm around the girl and led her away.

Jake wondered: *What will you do, Luigi, you and Sal and your five brothers? Throw bricks at the Baums?*

He saw Sarah. Small, dark, weak. Jake vaulted over mounds of plaster. They had set Sarah on the pavement. No sheet. Nothing. A rush of guilt made him shiver. Six days in the factory. Five nights a week of work in the "outside place" for their landlord, Feigenbaum. What did Jake give her? Ten dollars a week from driving the wagon. The animals in the Prospect Park Zoo lived better.

Most of the dead and injured were in the schoolyard. More ambulances had arrived. Casualties were rushed to Saint Mary's or Brownsville Jewish. He could see Abelman helping girls onto stretchers, moving from one to another, taking pulses, listening to hearts.

"Sarah, it's Jake," he said. "Can you talk?"

Patrolman Mulqueen tugged at his shirt. "Jake, get outta here. The side wall is comin' down any minute."

Whistles shrilled. The crowd eddied, groaned. Mulqueen and Callery started clubbing people away from the alley.

"I can talk, Jake. But my legs. I can't walk."

"What else hurts?" He kissed her soiled forehead. Stared at her terrified eyes, her narrow face. A woman who never understood she was pretty. Black hair, piercing dark brown eyes. Too busy struggling to live. Others mocked her when she married Jacob Chain, a bum with no family, a man who could read neither Yiddish nor Hebrew nor English, a lummox good only for hauling boxes.

"I don't know—the legs, the knees—I tried to get out of the place—I fell—Jake, I'm dying."

Above him he heard a soft roar. *God in heaven, the upper wall.*

He lifted Sarah. She screamed. On a runner's legs he sprinted out of the passageway to Van Dam Place, battled his way through screaming women and howling men, a gauntlet of police billies. Soon he was in the sanctuary of the schoolyard.

"Doc, my wife, my Sarah!" Jake shouted. "Look at her!"

Abelman said something, but it was as if he lost speech. His mouth moved. Jake heard nothing. They were stricken deaf by the roar. The side of the factory rumbled to earth, crushing everything in its path, creating a new mountain of junk, ruined machines, jungles of wires and tubing.

"Her legs," Jake screamed. "She can't walk."

14

"Easy," Abelman said. "On the stretcher. Don't touch her legs."

Sarah's knees were crazily angled. One pointing out, one in. Her shoeless feet, with torn stockings exposed, were flattened and shapeless.

"Something's sticking in my leg, Jake." She wept. "Something sharp in the left leg."

Abelman called for one of the interns. They gave Sarah morphine pills. She gagged and struggled to rise. Her eyes flooded. Spittle depended from her mouth. Jake knelt and held her forehead.

"She got to go to the hospital, Doc?"

"Looks that way, Jake. Give us a hand."

They lifted the stretcher. Another ambulance arrived. A smoky pall hovered over the yard. The fallen walls exhaled a miasma of filth and death. Gritty powder settled on weeping families, stricken girls, the dead.

Abelman and Chain guided the stretcher into the ambulance. Jake kissed Sarah's cheek.

"Does it hurt, little bird?" Jake asked. He smoothed her dusty hair.

"In my legs, dear husband. Like iron in them. Someone pushing it in. I can't move. I'm sorry I'm crying. I shouldn't make trouble for you."

She was born to apologize, to regret everything she did. *I am whole and strong,* Jack thought, *and she is broken and in pain, and yet she is sorry, she is unhappy that she is making me hurt. . . .*

The intern began to close the ambulance door. Jake embraced his wife, kissed her again. Within his iron chest, he prayed for forgiveness for his failure to do more for her and for Mutteh. *Bet ya five cents, Crazy Jake, ya can't lift anudda box, ya horse!*

"Twenty-two stiffs, forty hoit," he heard a cop telling a reporter. "And there's more they ain't found yet."

Jake shouted after the ambulance: "I'll come, Sarah, with our son."

People rushed by him. The mob was assaulting the Otzenbergers. Cunningly, the Baums had driven away to their apartment in New York. Let the assistant foreman and his father take the blows.

The punches were soft and ineffective. Hair pulled. Behinds kicked. The clawing and biting of people who did not know how to fight.

"Help, *police!*" shrieked Benny. He struggled like a gaffed

15

whale until he and Heshy were hustled into a police van for their own protection.

A soft lavender sky settled over Brownsville. The mob broke through the flailing clubs and charged the police van. They hammered with weak fists at the side. Jake watched with contempt.

"You and me, Doc," he said in a cold voice. "If we wanted, we could turn it over. Scare Otzenberger and his kid. How come he's alive and the girls are dead?"

Arms flapping, Ike Brunstein came racing down the street. His pince-nez flew behind him. They were attached to his lapel with a black ribbon. Brunstein's mop of curly brown hair seemed a yard behind him.

"Outrage! *Outrage!*" Brunstein shouted. "Where is the police commissioner? The fire commissioner?"

Frustrated in its attempts to reach the Otzenbergers, the mob turned on the union president. Hands clutched him. Tearful faces howled for revenge, help, an explanation.

"You could have been here quicker, Brunstein," an old man wept. "My daughter—gone—my angel—my light . . ."

"Workers, we will not tolerate this!" Ike cried.

"Too late, Ike," Dr. Abelman said. "It's done." He wiped his hands on a bandage and sighed.

Brunstein flew at a sergeant. Would arrests be made? Would an inquiry be held? Were officials notified?

The cop shoved him away rudely. Ike, flustered, squinted at his badge number and began to write on a small pad.

The patrolman ripped the memo book from Ike's hand. The two began to wrestle for it. Raised from the sidewalk, Ike was shaken mercilessly. His pince-nez flew from his nose. His trousers sagged, ready to drop.

Another officer measured Ike's head with his club.

"Cossack," Ike wheezed. "Enemy of the workingman."

Jake Chain saw that Ike was about to be crowned. He ran between the club and the union man's head. As the club descended, Jake caught the officer's wrist and twisted it. The billy bounced to the sidewalk. The cocobolo wood clanked resonantly.

"Another smart kike," the cop said. He bent over for the club.

Jake grabbed his arm, spun him around, and held him at arm's length. The cop gasped. He recognized the huge flat-faced man. The hebe who once wrestled kegs for Mulqueen's father. His grip felt like the iron bands they put on kegs.

"Brunstein didn't do nothing," Jake said calmly. "He asked you a question."

The cop found his billy and raised it again. "You try askin' one, Izzy." The policeman moved forward a step.

Jake stood his ground. He had learned a long time ago, as a child on the piss-smelling immigrant boat, later in the Hebrew Orphan Asylum and on the streets of Brownsville, that a man never showed fear. Take a blow, give one. But never show fear.

"I didn't want you should hit a guy who can't fight," Jake said.

The policeman hesitated. The big man—Christ, he was a strong mocky—was standing with his arms apart, palms out.

"Smart kike, huh?"

"Lay off, buddy," Doc Abelman said, moving next to Jake. The unaccented English, the Indian face gave the officer pause. Why push it? Jews didn't fight. They didn't know their way around a saloon. They were mush, cowards, *shit*. Why start with a sheeny sawbones?

"That's a nice fella," Abelman said. The cop hung the club on his belt. He eyed Brunstein like a hawk cheated of a field mouse. Then he turned away.

Chain walked off. With his rotton luck, someone had probably stolen the horse and wagon.

Brunstein flew around the wrecked building looking for witnesses. It was no easy job. The survivors had left. The police patrolled Van Dam Place, the alley, the side street. No looting, Francis Fagan Dullahan had decreed by phone. The Baums' property was to be protected. Bad enough they'd lost a factory. (Dullahan was well greased by the Baums. The money came every month via Benny Otzenberger in a brown bag.)

Ike located a man from the *Brooklyn Daily Eagle* and another from the *Jewish Daily Forward*. They found two girls who had survived the disaster.

One of the women talking to reporters was Eva Heilig, the union secretary. Eva was twenty-four, small, shapely, with a cloud of curling blond hair rising over a carved white face. Stealing a pinch, Heshy Otzenberger would call her *Die Gibsoneh*—after Charles Dana Gibson's idealized beauties. But Eva was no lissome *shiksa*. A distant cousin of Jake Chain's, she was an activist, a street-corner orator. Now she had an audience and she was letting the reporters, and a group of girls and their relatives, hear her vibrant voice at its most outraged.

"No fire escape," Eva Heilig was saying. "The doors were bolted. God forbid a person wanted a breath of fresh air. Girls were inspected like cattle. They were warned if they didn't come in Sunday, they should stay away Monday. Cheating on paychecks. Charging us for needles, for machine oil, for any wasted cloth! A penny a day for lockers! You see how we are forced to live? And now this—this—"

"Twenty-two victims," Ike said as he came alongside her. "Blood on the hands of the Baums."

"A Red," the Eagle reporter said. He began to ask Ike and Eva about their association with the Jewish Trade Unions. Radical outfits? Bunch of foreigners? Guys with beards and accents?

Eva's pale green eyes widened. She was distractingly beautiful. The lustrous pile of golden hair, the fair skin (even though dirtied now with streen grime), short nose, firm cleft chin, slender neck, ivory throat. The man from the Eagle had difficulty envisioning her as a Red. Brunstein was more like it. Dark suit, floppy tie, mop of hair, beard, pince-nez, built like a clothes tree. As if the long-legged goop were an actor trying to look like Trotsky.

"Quite a cookie, that Heilig," the Eagle reporter said when Eva and Ike had taken their leave. "What's she doing on a sewing machine? With that sweet ass, she could work at a lot of other things."

The man from the Forward (a socialist veteran) shook his head. A decent enough boy, his fellow journalist, but a goy in his heart. Women like Eva Heilig he would never understand.

When she and Brunstein had walked about a block, Eva saw her cousin Jake giving a coin to Sal the hokey-pokey vendor.

"Thanks, kid," Jake was saying. "Your sister okay?"

Sal Ferrante had a face as brown and as narrow as a piece of belting. He nodded. Theresa was cut and bruised. But she was okay. One dead lady, Angela Colucci, was an aunt or something. Lived with the Ferrantes. They didn't know much about her.

Eva listened. The unfathomable misery of the poor. And yet, Eva reflected, they had strength, resilience. Jews and Italians, poorest of the poor. They would not give up. What impelled them to struggle? The answer was evident. They worked or starved.

Eva watched Jake untethering his horse and climbing into the seat. The boor, the dumb ox of the family. Eva's parents and brothers treated Jake with indifferent contempt. But Eva had always nurtured sympathy for the crude man with his flattened face, his athletic grace, the stoic manner in which he accepted a brutish life. There was something to be admired in the man's affection for his birdlike wife and runty son.

"Jake," she called. "Sarah, is she all right?" She ran to the wagon.

Chain showed no emotion. "Both legs broke. They took her to the hospital."

"I'm sorry, Jake. Can we help? Ike, what can we do?"

"The union will raise a fund for the workers injured at K & R," Brunstein said. "Benefits will be small but they'll help. Burial expenses also."

Eva began to weep. She held a hand out to Jake. He took it clumsily, thinking, *Maybe I am too dumb to cry.* In his heart there was an ice pick. But the tears would not come. When had he last cried? Years ago. As a child in the orphanage when he learned that his father had betrayed him. Sent him off, and would never come to America for him, was unable to raise money for passage. The letter. He had saved it for years, burned it after he married Sarah Klebanow. His mother was long dead of typhus in the farmhouse in Glebocka.

"I'll bring supper for you and the boy," Eva said.

"It's all right. I have food. You were hurt?"

"I was lucky. I was in the office arguing with Heshy about the clocks. When the noise started, he dragged me out. I'll come with food."

As he snapped the reins and drove off, he prayed she would come. More beautiful than he could believe. Of his blood. How in the same family?

The blood relationship was frail (his mother was a second cousin of her mother) and the Heiligs had no interest in pursuing it. They were ambitious people, Eva and her two brothers. Eva went to night school and lectures. She was reading her way through the Watkins Avenue branch of the public library and attended Mrs. Abelman's poetry classes at the YWHA.

A plodding man, Chain knew one thing. Something he admitted to no one. Something he tried to stifle within his oak-hard chest: *He loved Eva Heilig.*

It was a sin, he was certain, thinking of her face, her body, what she would look like unclothed, when his wife was lying in a hospital with her legs smashed. A sin to think such things about a cousin.

Once he had had to punch Label Kuflik after the driver had read an article in the *Forward* about Eva. There was a photograph also—mass of blond hair, white face, wide eyes. The article was a tribute to the courageous working girls. Eva had earned a name among them: *Die Goldeneh Shtimmeh*— The Golden Voice.

At the end of the article, Kuflik sniggered: "But it don't say how she *shtups* for Brunstein."

A right fist had sent Kuflik sailing across Kolodny's stable into a pile of manure. Warning enough: Kuflik never mentioned Eva again.

I love her, Jake thought, *and it is hopeless.*

Jake drove into Kolodny's stable. He unharnessed the mare and went into the bottler's dusty office with the cash and receipts for the deliveries. Before his boss asked about Chain's wife, he scolded him for failing to get a receipt from the Little Hungary.

"I'll get it tomorrow. I had to drive away when we heard the building falling."

"No excuse, Chain," Kolodny said. "What do you got for brains? Horse piss? No wonder they call you Crazy Jake."

Kolodny was a hunchback. A bald-headed gnome. Squint-eyed, foul-tempered.

"I'll get the receipt on my way to the hospital. Mr. Kolodny, could you advance me a dollar? Who knows when my wife will be paid? And who knows if she can work again?"

"No advances. It says in the Talmud that the workman is like the ox in the field—"

"I'm too stupid to know if it's the truth or you made it up."

Kolodny's face twisted itself into a smile. He needed Jake Chain, a man who could handle horses, haul crates, work long hours, and, if necessary, give a competitor a *klop* on the mouth that could send him back to Chelm.

In the stable, Jake borrowed a half-dollar from Label Kuflik. Kuflik, a bulky man whose fleshy face was constructed around a swollen, pitted nose, had a heart of sorts. Jake thanked him.

There are people worse off than me, Jake thought. *But not many.*

Chapter 2

Old man Pasquale was playing the hurdy-gurdy as Jake approached. Children were holding hands in a circle and singing.

They formed a ring around the hand organ. Girls in wide skirts and high-button shoes, barefoot boys in loose-hanging knickers. Jake saw his son, Mutteh, a scrawny seven-year-old, pushing his way between two older girls. The children swung their arms in time with the ratchety music.

> *Who wants to come to the sisters' meeting?*
> *To the sisters' praying.*
> *Who wants to come, who wants to come?*
> *Who wants to come with me?*

The oldest girl, Kalotkin's daughter, formed the children into two lines and they began to "go in and out the window." Mutteh was the runt of the group.

Bernie Feigenbaum, the landlord's son, a fat, bespectacled kid, yanked Mutteh's cap off. Mutteh, a head shorter than Bernie, left the entwined arms and raced after his tormentor.

Bernie held the cap out of Mutteh's reach and taunted him. He fended wild swings with one chubby arm. "You be the nigger Johnson and I'll be Jeffries, okay?"

"Gimme my hat, fatso."

"Ya call me fatso, ya never get it. C'mon, you be Johnson."

"I ain't no nigger. You be Johnson."

"I'm Jeffries. A white guy can beat a nigger, 'cause niggers are yellow."

Mutteh grabbed the cap and jammed it on his head. The boys squared off boxer-style, jabbing and feinting. Mutteh was swift and lithe but so skinny he was barely visible when he turned sideways. Bernie's tits juggled under his shirt.

21

Jake did not interfere. He had a rule: Let Mutteh fight. He had taught him long ago. Fight fair. But if the other guy is dirty, use a stick, a stone, your teeth, your feet, your head.

Aaron Feigenbaum, landlord and sweatshop operator, leaned out the window. He crossed his woolly arms on the stone sill. He was walleyed and gray-bearded, a wraith of a man who mercilessly drove a family of eight and his part-time workers like Sarah Chain.

"*Nu*, Jake? Your wife's hurt?" Feigenbaum asked.

"Her legs are broke."

"A pity. A scandal and an outrage. How you'll pay the rent?"

"I'll work double shifts for Kolodny."

Feigenbaum demanded twelve to fifteen pairs of kneepants in a twelve-hour workday. The entire ground floor—dark, damp, floorboards piled with cuttings—rattled with the hum of sewing machines. Sarah worked as a "finisher"—buttons and buttonholes. No one was unionized in the "outside" shop. Six dollars a week for a full-time worker. Three for Sarah, who sewed until ten at night after her work at Baums'.

Old Pasquale passed the hat. Pennies descended from the windows. Jake also tossed a penny.

Bernie threw a right at Mutteh's bobbing head. Mutteh ducked under it and drove a fist into "Jeffries's" paunch.

"Johnson's a nigger," Mutteh said. Bernie doubled over and hollered foul. "But Johnson won, right, papa?"

"Right, Mutteleh. He murdered Jeffries."

"Niggers fight dirty." Bernie gulped. He wiped tears from his eyes and looked around for a missile.

The children followed the hurdy-gurdy down the littered street. Jake could hear the sweet voices.

> *Nan-nan-nanny goat!*
> *Sew, sew, sew,*
> *Sew my petticoat, no, no, no!*

"Ya got a penny for me, papa?" Mutteh asked. His bright eyes stared at his father's strong face. "A penny for a piece of candy?"

"Later, Mutteh. Son, mama is hurt. She got hurt in the building that fell down."

"She'll be better? She'll be all better?"

"Dr. Abelman said so. But you and me, Mutteh, we got to take care of the house. In September you'll go to school. So you'll not be dumb like your father."

"You ain't dumb, papa. Can I have a penny?"

Jake stroked his coarse black hair. It grew in stringy strands around his dark neck and ears. Sarah trimmed it once a month with a scissors. Jake had a terrible awareness of the boy's smallness. A crippled mother and a stupid father. What life for him?

"They told me mama was dead," Mutteh blurted out. He began to cry. "Bernie and some other kids. They said she was dead. They said her legs was cut off."

"Lies, Mutteleh."

Mutteh pressed his head against his father's sweaty shirt. Chain's chest was like a slab of concrete. Jake kissed the boy's head. It made him think of a bird's egg.

They walked to the corner. Streetlights blazed. Halos of night insects hummed around them.

"Hey, it's Aunt Eva," Mutteh said.

Jake saw his cousin approaching. She was carrying a blue enameled pot. As always, she was beautiful, graceful.

Mutteh ran from his father and buried his head in Eva's thigh. She gave the pot to Jake and kissed the boy's head. The boy sniffed her soapy sweet odor. He never understood why he liked it so much. A different smell from his mother. It excited him. Made him think funny things. Sometimes he thought he loved Eva more than he loved his mother.

Eva said to Jake, "We had more than enough to eat. Compliments of my parents."

Jake smiled. He knew Eva's mother didn't care for him. Eva's father, Avner Heilig, the eccentric "Uncle Sourmilk," had no feelings one way or another. A mathematician, he was preoccupied with proving the Triumph of Socialism Through Mathematics.

"Sour milk?" Jake asked.

"Mushroom-and-barley soup. I'll heat it for you."

She studied his blunted broad face. A handsome face. Wide cheekbones, strong chin, a nose slightly squashed from an old fight. His eyes were a clear staring blue. The shock of blond hair was a surprise.

They walked back to Feigenbaum's tenement. Bernie ran behind Mutteh, goosed him, then tripped over his own feet as he dodged Mutteh's swing.

Leaning on the windowsill, Mrs. Feigenbaum observed the visitor. That blondie, Eva Heilig. *That Red*. A shameless one who went to meetings with men, argued with men, hollered at girls to defy the bosses, and talked back to cops.

23

"Better you shouldn't come in," Jake said. "It's dirty inside. Your parents don't like when you visit."

"I do what I want. Go on, Jake. Mutteh, no more fighting." She wagged a finger at Bernie Feigenbaum. "You're twice his size. Let him alone."

"I c'n fight him, Aunt Eva," Mutteh said.

It was hot and malodorous in the basement. The stained walls shuddered with the rattling of Feigenbaum's sweatshop. There was a gas ring and a cracked sink. They used a toilet on the second floor. Once a week, Jake, Sarah, and Mutteh went to the public bathhouse. It was inconceivable to Eva (hardly a wealthy girl) how people could live so miserably. No one had earned such punishment.

With the soup, she had brought buttered rolls. Jake and Mutteh sat in the tiny room, eating noisily, saying little. He found it hard to thank her. Why did she do this? She owed him nothing.

Mutteh finished his dinner and flew from the room. The summer street beckoned—adventure, exploring empty lots, hitching rides on wagons, kickety-can, Johnny-on-the-pony.

"Jake, you have to look ahead," she said. "If Sarah can't work . . . Listen, you *must* learn to read and write."

"I'm fit only for a horse," Jake said. "Kolodny told me."

"Don't listen to a boss. They want to keep us stupid." She patted the back of his hand and felt the taut muscles. "Jake, you owe it to your son. Do something for yourself. I know you're angry. You've had a rotten life. Go to school. If you're embarrassed, I'll go with you the first day."

He laughed. "Like a mother taking a kid to class? The drivers would make fun of me. They'll say, Look, he can lift four crates on his back. He can lift a wagon. He's the guy who beat up three Italians. Why does an animal need to write?"

"Don't say that about yourself!"

He tried not to stare at her white shirtwaist with the dainty collar and muttonchop sleeves. Small mounds where her breasts showed. The tightwaisted pleated black skirt. High-button shoes and black stockings.

"You better not stay," he said. "Your father don't like it. That *yenta* Feigenbaum, she'll talk."

"Ridiculous. I'm your cousin." Eva smiled at him. Impoverished, unlearned, a strange Jew raised in back of a saloon, he had a stolid dignity.

He spoke her name, halted. Something more than his gratitude for the food was on his mind. His limpid blue eyes stared at her, suppressing emotion. She knew he loved her. He could not hide it. She did not want him to experience more pain than he was suffering at the moment.

She rose to leave, and he walked out to the street with her. The street teemed with people. Groups lounged on stoops, in front of pushcarts and stores. Many discussed the disaster at Baum's. A stout woman wept uncontrollably, rent her dress, tore at her hair. Two daughters dead, *dead*. On the corner, an orator—one of Brunstein's radicals—had drawn a crowd. Several police appeared.

"We welcome the police," the young radical cried. "We welcome our brother workers in uniform, for they, too, are exploited by cruel bosses. . . ."

Unmoved, the cops began to clear the street corner. "Okay, Moe, climb down," one said. "Enough revolution."

Eva shook Jake's iron hand. "The union will get Sarah a job. I promise you. And you promise *me* you'll go to school."

"I could become a professor. I'd be sixty years old before I'd be smart enough. Thanks for the soup." Jake held her hand, sensed the thrill of touching her flesh. He did it as naturally as breathing, walking. Some joke. A handshake. He squeezed the palm gently.

She looked at his street-hardened face. He deserved better of the world. Who knew if Sarah would survive? And what would become of the boy and of Jake himself? In her family, people studied, attacked books with a vengeance, availed themselves of every scrap of knowledge available in the new *Medineh*. For Jake Chain, it was all a cheat.

She kissed his cheek. She walked off. Jake watched her, full of cold pain. He had to go to the hospital; had to forget Eva.

In the hallway, Jake glanced into Feigenbaum's "outside" factory. All of the landlord's family, penniless greenhorns, and a few strays. Operator. Baster. Finisher. Presser. Girl for sewing buttons. Girl for sewing buttonholes. Bushelman. Fitter. Delivery boy.

A world of cloth, scissors, thread, weary fingers, bent backs, foul air. A hotbox in the summer, freezing in the winter. One filthy toilet. One sink. Four months of the year there was no work. Feigenbaum collected rents and waited for the next orders.

Maybe I'm better off with my strong back and arms, and the horse, he thought. At least I'm in the open, and I like the animal's stink, and the stable, and I am freer than they are. . . .

He dimly recalled a boyhood of deprivation and cruelty. Yet something sweet stuck in his memory. Meadows, a muddy barnyard. Chickens and geese. Fruit trees and a field of green vegetables. A carp pond. His father's place. Once men came with papers. There was an argument over who owned the land. His father, a big blond man like himself, was crying, then fighting with the Lithuanian policemen. His father's head was covered with blood. He was clutching at black boots. A man in a fur-collared coat gave orders.

Long ago. Later he was on a freezing train, tagged, a ticket in his pocket. A smoky, noisy city. Hamburg, someone said. And the hold of a ship, slippery with vomit, urine, crap. He had survived the passage—for what?

"She'll walk," Dr. Abelman said. "But she won't be the same."

The doctor was standing with Jake outside a ward in Brownsville Jewish Hospital. Outside, the dusk obscured the street, the maples and poplars.

"A cripple."

"Compound fractures of both legs. It'll take a long time, Jake. A wheelchair. Crutches later. She might never get off the crutches."

Jake folded his arms. A nurse walked by, wheeling a shriveled old woman. Sarah in ten years.

"No hope? An operation maybe?" Jake detested his ignorance. He felt guilty bothering Abelman. He did not charge for hospital visits; it was assumed this was part of his care. Office visits were a half-dollar. A house call cost one dollar.

"Jake, maybe it would be better if I died," Sarah said when she saw his face. "I won't be a bother to no one anymore. A woman with crippled legs. Maybe I'm better dead."

"Don't say it. You will live."

"A cripple. In a wheelchair. I know what Dr. Abelman said."

Abelman waved his right hand, smiled. "No, Sarah. You can walk again. You'll need help, but people use their legs again."

She wept apologetically, ashamed of adding to their misery.

Chapter 3

Jake approached Kolodny's bottling plant to load up his morning deliveries. It was a humid mid-September day, three weeks after the collapse of the Baum place. Trees beyond the soda-water factory were orange and red and purple. Colors Jake could not believe existed. He paused to look at them. Strange how people thought Brownsville was a slum. In 1910 it was also fields and meadows and farms.

Mutteh was in first grade. The smallest boy in P.S. 144. But he was enjoying the challenge of lessons and the daily fight. He came home with a blackened eye, a cut lip, never cried, did his homework. After school he hunted for soda bottles or tied old newspapers in bundles for Junkman John. The pennies he earned he kept.

The stable door was closed. An oak two-by-four was jammed into the wooden arms. Label Kuflik was standing in front of the door. His hairy arms were folded on his chest.

"So?" Jake asked. "It's a Jewish holiday?"

"Don't go in."

"Kolodny locked us out? That's all I need. With a sick wife and debts up to my belly button. Come on, open."

A scream emanated from the stable doors. Then another. The noise sickened Jake. He had been in enough fights. He knew the sound. Someone was being beaten.

"The boss," Kuflik said.

"He's hitting someone? That hunchback?"

"He's getting hit. You know Moishe Nigger?"

"The Horse Poisoner."

"He's inside with his boys. They killed two horses. Your Kotchka. Rafaelson's horse. By the time they're finished beating Kolodny, he won't have a hump on his back. It'll be in his throat."

Jake knew about the racketeers. Years ago when Benny Otzenberger had tried to make Jake a "prelim boy," he had met them at Fein's gym. Nifty dressers. White celluloid collars. Striped shirts. Box-toed shoes. Derbies. They extorted, terrorized, beat up storekeepers, threatened factory owners and organizers. They ran "hoo-er" houses and sold booze.

Kolodny howled again.

"I'm going in," Jake said.

"Don't be a shlemiel," Kuflik said. "Your horse is dead. You got no job. Bunchik, the Nigger's fella, gave me a dollar to watch the door. My horse they won't poison."

"Get out of my way, Kuflik."

"Wake up. In America a horse is worth more than a Jew."

"Kuflik, shove Bunchik's dollar up your nose. In a month you'll have a nose full of dollars and you'll be rich. Out of my way."

The driver backed off. "You'll be sorry, Chain. I got orders you shouldn't—"

Jake seized Kuflik by the shoulders and hurled him into the dirt. He lifted the beam and shoved the creaky doors apart. Shafts of morning light slanted into the stable. A horse whickered and stomped.

The hay and the horse odors smelled fresh and wild. Like the countryside of his lost youth in Lithuania. What was to fear? He had so little. Nothing to lose. Sick wife. No job. Anyone who stole bread from his mouth would have to be taught it was wrong.

A pale young man with a beaked nose and pimpled cheeks was guarding the side door that led to the bottling plant. He wore a white straw boater, a green-and-pink striped shirt, and bright green suspenders. As Jake entered, the youth, Bunchik by name, pointed an ax handle at him.

"*Out!* Kuflik, whaddya letting people in for?" he shouted.

Jake walked across the dung-strewn floor. Kotchka was lying on her side in the stall. The mare hadn't been much, but she'd been part of his life. A pile of manure rested under her tail. Even when they die they crap, Jake thought.

"Hey, jerk-off, get out," Bunchik called. "Moishe, a guy walked in."

A hoarse voice called from a stall: "Hit him in the head, Bunchik."

"He's too big."

In the last stall, Jake found Menasha Kolodny and his tormentors. Naked ass up, the bottler was doubled over a water trough. His pants and long underwear had been yanked down. He had a small wrinkled ass. It was covered with bloody welts.

A fat, broad-chested man, dark as a mulatto, dapper in a pearl-gray derby and striped orange shirt, was standing over Kolodny. He had a buggy whip in his hand. A second hoodlum, very short, in a checked beige-and-brown suit, was holding Kolodny's body down. The Nigger's assistant, Little Mendel, had a froglike face with a wide mouth and jellied green eyes.

The short man grinned at Jake. *"Putz,* get adda here. Beat it."

The man in the derby was Moishe "Nigger" Pearlberg. He shouted, "Bunchik, tell Kuflik if he lets anyone else in, he'll get his ass whipped also."

Moishe Nigger cracked the whip across Kolodny's buttocks. The owner screamed. Another red welt blossomed.

"Chain!" Kolodny screamed. "Go to the police! They killed two horses! They'll kill me! Get the cops! This is Moishe Nigger and his gang—"

Crack. Jake winced. Kolodny wailed like a starving baby.

Bunchik came back from the outer door and leaned against the stall.

"Who are you, Polack?" Moishe Nigger asked.

"I'm one of his drivers. Chain."

"Drive yourself out of here. Keep your mouth shut, or you'll get your ass whipped also."

"He looks like a toilet chain." Bunchik laughed.

Jake didn't move. "Me it won't help to whip, Mr. Nigger. I'm a poor man without ten cents. You could whip all day I couldn't give a penny."

"But you got a mouth," the froggy man squatting on Kolodny said. "You open your mouth you'll get worster. Right, Moishe?"

"Right."

Jake paused. He knew about Moishe Nigger.

"Look," Jake said softly. "All I understand is I lost my job. It isn't fair."

"This is fair," Moishe Nigger said. He cracked the whip against Kolodny. The bottler screamed. He wailed to be let up. He was ready to meet the Horse Poisoner's terms. They could discuss business in the office.

Bunchik jabbed Jake in the kidneys with the ax handle. "What do we do with the Polack, Moishe?"

"I ain't a Polack. I'm a Jew like you."

"You're too big for a Jew," Little Mendel said. "Your mother got it from a Polack policeman."

Jake let his arms hang limp. His fingers flexed, unflexed.

Blowing snot from his nose, Kolodny pulled up his suspenders and buttoned his fly. He walked gingerly.

"For ten dollars a week you needed this?" Moishe Nigger

asked. He put a thick arm around Kolodny and patted the hump. "For good luck, Kolodny. Now we're partners."

"Please, don't talk. I'll pay."

Moishe's sallow face, bulbous nose, and low brow gleamed. "Kolodny, it's a good thing you're a Hungarian like me. If you was a Litvak or a Galitzianer I wouldn't be so kind."

"Mr. Kolodny," Jake said. "The horse—my deliveries—"

"I got no deliveries for you, Chain."

Bunchik and Little Mendel laughed and slapped their thighs.

The hunchback wept. "Chain, don't torture me. Tell Kuflik he ain't working neither. I don't know when you'll be back."

Moishe Nigger held the door open. He bowed to let his new client enter.

"What about this bum?" Bunchik had the ax handle pressed against Jake's kidneys.

"Let him shovel shit," the Horse Poisoner said, and followed Kolodny through the door.

"Pick up a shovel," Bunchik said. "You heard what Moishe said. Shovel drek." Bunchik dug the handle sharply into Jake's left kidney.

"No funny stuff," Mendel said. He walked away from the trough. A snub-nosed revolver was in his hand. He leveled it at Jake's midriff. "You got a hard belly, Chain. But it won't stop bullets."

"Where should I start?"

"Right here." Little Mendel, keeping the gun trained on Jake, threw a shovel at him. "Into the barrel. Maybe we'll ask you to climb in with it."

Jake walked to the stall where Kotchka lay on her side. Clouds of angry green flies buzzed around the dead horse.

"Start," Bunchik said. He sat on an upturned pail and lit a cigarette. As he did, he let the ax handle drop. Mendel kept the pistol pointed at Jake.

The flies nipped wickedly at Jake's arms. He worked slowly.

The gangsters smoked and chattered. When Jake moved to the next stall, they followed him.

"Listen, Chain," Bunchik said. "You see my shirt? Six dollars in Kossow's on Pitkin Avenue. *Silk*. The pants are from Jaffe's and the shoes from Siegel's. Only the best. I got silk drawers on. You got clothes like that?"

"No. I only got bad luck."

"Listen, Chain," Little Mendel said. "With those arms and

hands, you could get a job with Moishe. He likes strong boys."

"Nah, nah," Bunchik sneered. "He's too dumb to be a *shtarker*. He'd hit the wrong guy. He'd hit his cock."

The flies swarmed around Jake. They were vicious and hungry. Like Moishe Nigger and his mob.

Bunchik tossed his Sweet Caporal away and stuck a fresh one in his mouth. He walked from behind Jake toward Mendel to borrow a match. Mendel reached in his back pocket.

"Tell us about your wife," Little Mendel said. "She's a Polack like you? A big blonde with tits like balloons?"

Jake watched from the corner of his eye. Bunchik struck the match on the sole of his box-toed shoe and lit up.

Chain moved around the dead horse. Suddenly he swung the shovel blade with all the power in his arms. Mendel tried to duck and caught half the force of the blow. The gun fell from his hand. He toppled senseless.

The wide arc of the shovel caught Bunchik in the face. The skinny man collapsed with a whoosh of air, as if a giant's palm had slammed him. The two-fell, bloodied and unconscious.

He tossed the shovel aside. He enjoyed the summery quiet of the stable. A horse neighing and stomping. The buzzing of swarms of flies. Trickles of water from the tap. But there was no point in hanging around. No horse, no job. The bottler had surrendered to Moishe Nigger. And Jake had made an enemy of the liver-lipped thug.

More bad luck, Jake thought. A man with nothing to lose. That was why he had slammed the shovel against Mendel and Bunchik. They would come and look for him. It did not matter. Sarah was doomed. Mutteh would end up in the orphan assylum. And him? Maybe they'd shoot him in an alley some dark night.

When the King of the Horse Poisoners called for his lieutenants, he got no response. He waddled into the stable and found Mendel and Bunchik struggling to rise from the floor. Their faces were mashed and bloodied.

"The big guy," Moishe said. "You let him do this? You ain't worth the money I pay you. Who *was* that big bum?"

Chapter 4

"Socialism must triumph," Avner Heilig proclaimed (at regular intervals) to family, friends, and visitors. In proof he would produce stacks of dog-eared ledgers in which he had, through a series of involved computations, demonstrated that Marx was right.

Bundists, Social Democrats, Socialists, Anarchists, assorted left intellectuals came to visit Heilig. They studied his notebooks with the endless x's and y's and concluded he was a harmless nut.

Ike Brunstein, president of the Bathrobe, Kimono, and House Dress Workers Union, Local 37, thought Avner Heilig a fool. But Ike kept his opinions to himself. He pined for Avner's daughter, Eva. He hoped to marry her.

Visiting the Heiligs was always an exhilarating experience for Brunstein. A disciple of the legendary Barondess—orator, political figure, and union leader—Ike enjoyed status in Brownsville. Yet in the Heiligs' noisy apartment on Haven Place, three doors down from Dr. Abelman's house, he was not especially esteemed and often ignored. An ironist, Brunstein was amused. All the Heiligs were talkative, optimistic, and vigorous. They were a family bound together with love of one another and hatred of sour milk, the *Lactobacillus acidophilus* that Papa Heilig forced on his three children. Indeed (Ike noticed), sour milk was even urged on the scores of greenhorn "relatives" to whom the generous-hearted Matla Heilig, Eva's mother, offered a temporary haven.

At this moment, a young couple and a child, cousins so distantly removed as to make the tracing of bloodlines a job for Burke's Peerage, were seated in a dim corner of the kitchen drinking Uncle Sourmilk's cure-all. The man was shriveled and round-shouldered. He had Eva's green eyes and light brown curling hair. His wife was tiny. A black wig covered her shaved head. She cradled a howling infant in her arms. No sour milk for the child, she had evidently decided. But the two immigrants sipped it as if in payment for lodging in the Heilig ménage.

"New ones?" Ike asked Avner Heilig. Eva's father was making notations in a ledger.

"Yeah, yeah. From whose side of the family I'm not sure. I lose track, we have so many. They'll sleep in the living room until they find a job. Extra mouths we can always feed. Besides, with sour milk, other foods are unnecessary."

Avner's wife, Matla, a chirpy woman, as blond as her daughter and with Eva's clear green eyes, poked her head in from the kitchen. She and the younger Heilig son, Sol, were drying dishes. "So where is all *your* energy, Uncle Sourmilk? Who runs the candy store fourteen hours a day? Who shops, cleans, and cooks? Me! I *hate* sour milk. And you sit in a chair all day making fly tracks in a book."

"That also takes energy!" Avner Heilig shouted. "More energy! Recent studies in neurology bear me out. Every question in my analysis of the victory of socialism derives from mental gifts endowed by sour milk! Brunstein, don't smile."

No one took Avner Heilig seriously. He had not done a day's work in twelve years. Matla, a robust woman, ran the candy store with the help of her sons, Sol and Abe. When not assisting in the store, the boys worked at odd jobs—carpentry, electrical repairs, anything that would bring in a dollar.

Ike Brunstein admired the family. Not only were they his hoped-for in-laws, they were ambitious, undefeated, generous, full of good humor. The stew of his gloomy nature needed the spice of their laughter. Most of all he craved Eva. So lovely, so strong-willed, with her noble bearing and heavenly face.

She appeared in the door to the living room. Ike battled vertigo.

"I'm ready," she said. "Let's go, Ike. I don't want to get to the meeting too late."

Brunstein tried to keep his face from turning crimson, his hands from shaking. Eva had put on a tight blue skirt, a wide-brimmed blue hat. Her face, freshly scrubbed, was like a cultured flower. Her green eyes were shining.

Abe, a City College student, entered the room and tossed copies of the *Forward* (the socialist paper) and the *Wahrheit* (its anarchist rival) on the table. "There you go, pop. For once the two papers agree. Somebody's got to be punished for the *shonda* at Baum's." Abe kissed his mother, winked at Eva, waved at Ike. He was eighteen, intent on becoming a physician. He barely stopped, marched to the kitchen for a late dinner. Nobody moved slothfully or without purpose in the house except the head of the family.

Uncle Sourmilk leaped up and followed his daughter and Ike to the door. "Heed Maimonides," he said. " 'Anticipate charity by preventing poverty, assist the reduced fellowman, either by a considerable gift or a sum of money or by teaching him a trade or by putting him in a way of business.' Like our *landsleit*. In helping them, we follow the Talmud and Maimonides."

Ike said, "It isn't Maimonides we're dealing with, Uncle Sourmilk. It's cheating employers, rotten politicians, and corrupt police."

"And our own frightened members," Eva added.

They had not walked a half a block when Ike proposed marriage (for the fourth time that week) to Eva.

"United, we will be an even more potent force," Brunstein said. "Think of it, Eva. A husband-and-wife team running the union. Who could prevail against us?"

Her beauty rendered him weak-kneed. It created quiverings in his gut, caused him to speak breathlessly. Oh, he was not alone. Beauty and brains, old Meyer Flugelman, the union theorist, said with a poignant leer, a woman in a million. *And what courage!* Behind all the male admiration, Ike knew, men craved her. The fine face, the glowing green eyes. And what else . . . ? Beneath the layers of clothing . . . ?

Stop, stop, Brunstein! he had to tell himself. You are a beast, a monster of sexual appetites!

"Eva, my darling," he pleaded. "I want to marry you. Don't you reciprocate my respect and admiration?" His voice shook. "And my love?"

"Respect and admiration, yes. I don't know what love is. It's a myth invented by poets."

"I believe in the myth."

She laughed, cocked her head. "Oh, Ike. Go read poetry."

"Don't make fun."

"I've told you a hundred times, Ike. Emotions and the class struggle are a bad mixture. You keep appealing to my social conscience to entice me into marriage."

They approached the Jewish Fellowship Hall. It was a gray stone building plastered with handbills. Under insect-hazed streetlights, animated groups had gathered. Survivors, relatives, union members, candidates. Boys raced up and down the steps, slid down bronze banisters, flew in and out doors.

Sal Ferrante peddled his hokey-pokey—shavings of unsanitary ice doused with a choice of syrups that suggested Paris green, Prussian blue, sulfurous yellow.

Bernie Feigenbaum bought a double scoop of the concoction. With a lamprey's mouth, he sucked at the purple-stained ice. Mrs. Feigenbaum shrieked, pounced on him, knocked the paper cup from his hand. She yelled at Sal: "Gedda odda here, you poisoner! Those *fekokteh* syrups they make from worms! You could die from such *chazerei!*"

"No it ain't," Sal said. "It's pure."

Susan Stofsky arrived in a wheelchair pushed by her brother. People applauded and made way. Another girl came on crutches. Eva watched with wrenching pity. Jake's wife, Sarah, would not be there. Her legs would be in casts a long time.

As Eva and Ike entered, a pudgy man in a soiled black suit, soft shirt, and black musician's tie jostled Brunstein. "So, Brunstein, more useless gestures?" the man asked. He was in his sixties—frazzled, short-bearded, gray, pouches the size and hue of small eggplants under popping eyes.

"Mosherman, please. Your anarchist manners are not in order tonight. For a change, join us."

Across the street in a Chandler phaeton, Francis Fagan Dullahan, political boss of Brooklyn, viewed his Hebrew constituents with keen Celtic satisfaction. Florid and fat, bald as a stone, Dullahan was an aging fox observing chickens.

With Dullahan was his Man in Brownsville, Benny Otzenberger. Two hundred and eighty pounds in a gray linen suit with black velvet lapels, Dullahan managed to make Benny look undernourished. A pair of marauding sea creatures they seemed—black whale, white whale. Benny was spiffy in white linen, a white panama.

Dullahan gave Otzenberger a fistful of dark Coronas. "For the boys, Benjamin. Too bad we have to do this, but Brunstein is a menace."

"Brunstein couldn't start a revolution in a men's room, Mr. D. He won't even get a strike vote tonight."

Like an old turtle, Dullahan blinked his eyes and said nothing.

Heshy Otzenberger approached the phaeton. His father gave him the cigars and a manila envelope. "Take care of them," Benny whispered. "Tell the Nigger and his mob to do it fast and run."

"The cops?"

"They ain't gonna be around."

It took fifteen minutes for Ike to get the meeting organized. People drifted in late. Bundists argued violently with Socialists. Mosherman the anarchist detested everyone equally. An angry group of Labor Zionists got into the debates. The old story, Ike told Eva—two Jews, three synagogues.

Ultimately it was Eva, with her assertive voice and her commanding eyes, who restored order.

"Disgraceful!" she cried. "Stop this bickering, this fighting of Jew against Jew! Take a lesson from our Italian sisters in the working-class movement—they sit quietly, determined, mannerly, and wait for the meeting!"

A girl with her arm in a sling got to her feet. "It ain't easy, Eva. The bosses find out you pay union dues, or go to a meeting like this . . ." She looked around fearfully. "So you're the first one fired."

A few girls left. The Italians looked fretful. Lose a job? *Santa Maria,* the end of their world!

"Yeah, yeah," Susan bawled from her wheelchair. "I got a union card. I pay dues. What did I get for it? Crippled. No chance for a husband or children."

A strange wailing arose from the audience. It was a moaning, undulant noise, begun by the parents of the dead.

"Our daughters, give us our daughters."

"God in Heaven, Lord of the Universe, give us our children, our daughters."

Brunstein flapped his arms. "It's hopeless. They can't be controlled. They won't listen. They wail."

Eva's eyes were angry. "I'll *make* them listen." She moved Ike away from the lectern. "All of you stop crying!" she shouted. "Sit down. Dry your eyes. Blow your noses. Act like proud human beings!"

Vibrant and clear, her voice silenced the stuffy hall. Girls snuffled quietly. Bereaved parents held hands.

"There is *one* answer," Eva said. "Listen to me. Susan Stofsky, stop crying at *once.*"

The girl in the wheelchair buried her face in a handkerchief.

"I say there is one answer," Eva said. "Strike! Strike! Strike!"

Two blocks from the Jewish Fellowship Hall, Heshy Otzenberger conferred with four men in the schoolyard of Public School 168. The men chewed on Dullahan's cigars, blew clouds of smoke.

Heshy was terrified of them. Especially Moishe "Nigger" Pearlberg in his gray derby and stiff collar. It was said he could bend a silver dollar in half between thumb and forefinger. Once he gouged a rival mobster's eyes from his head.

"My chest hoits, Nigger," Bunchik said. "I ever catch that bastard Chain, I'll mopolize him."

"Me too," Little Mendel whined. "You got to let us get that big bum, Nigger."

Heshy tried to suppress a smile. His pointed ears twitched. So. It was Crazy Jake who had done such a job on these animals. Mendel's face was a mass of red scabs, welts, and lumps. Bunchik looked lopsided. One eye was covered.

"Chain done this? That bum?" Heshy was grinning.

"Whaddya smiling for, *putz?*" Mendel asked. He took a pistol from his belt and jabbed it in Heshy's ribs. "Whaddya think, it's funny?"

Moishe counted the money in the envelope. "It ain't enough, Heshy. Twenty for me, ten for each boy?"

"My father says it's the first time you *shtarked* a union meeting," Heshy said. "Besides, it's almost all girls."

The fourth man, a youth with wide shoulders and a narrow waist, was dancing around the schoolyard, throwing combinations. He wore a heavy black sweater, black drainpipe trousers, and gym shoes.

"Who's he?" Heshy asked.

"Otzenberger, you never read the sports section?" Bunchik asked. "That's Duffy Plotkin, the next welterweight champeen."

Gevalt, Hesky thought. Why am I mixed up in this? A professional boxer to beat up factory girls?

A globelike figure, mincing on dagger-toed shoes, short arms pumping, porky face sweating, approached Moishe Nigger. "Ready, boss. The Saratoga Avenue Meal ticket himself."

"Cops?" Moishe Nigger asked.

"Fixed," Heshy answered.

Little Mendel asked, "Could maybe an honest cop come by?"

"So what?" Heshy asked, "The judge takes his orders from Dullahan. You'll get medals for being patriotic Americans. Congratulations for *klopping* Reds."

Heshy peeked through a side window of the noisy hall. He knew the girls. Scared like mice. Afraid they'd be blacklisted. Now Eva Heilig had created an army of screaming warriors.

"Strike!" they shouted.

Eva shouted back: "Why wait? What do we fear? They have murdered our comrades! Twisted our sisters' backs, broken their legs, fractured their heads! We are persecuted, hated, exploited, and we—will—not—surrender!"

They were on their feet. Roaring, applauding.

Strike, strike, strike!

It was time to call Moishe Nigger.

Heshy whistled from the corner. Moishe led his troops. The Saratoga Meal Ticket walked delicately on small feet, twirling his cane, two paces ahead of Bunchik and Mendel. Each of the latter had brass knuckles in one hand, a bicycle chain in the other. Around them, ducking, bobbing, Duffy Plotkin threw punches. The Jewish Ketchell.

Fifty feet from the hall, the Nigger bought hokey-pokey for his boys from Sal—toxic looking cherry, pineapple, raspberry, orange syrup poured over street-filthy ice.

"For you, you don't gotta pay, Mistah Pearlberg," Sal said. He smelled trouble.

Moishe let his gang suck at the flavored ice for a minute or so. The chanting of the girls surged out of the hall, wild and exhilarated.

The inside of the hall was bedlam. People stood on benches. They wept, embraced, shouted, laughed. Sal entered, found Theresa with two other Italian girls. He grabbed her arms. "Papa says you gotta come home." He dragged his sister to the door and raced down the steps, almost colliding with Plotkin.

Up the steps clattered Moishe Nigger's thugs. The Saratoga Avenue Meal Ticket, spinning on pointed feet, smashed his cane against an old man's astonished face. It turned crimson. His wife shrieked. They staggered down the steps. *Cossacks!*

Moishe Nigger led the charge into the hall, punching and kicking women, swinging a lead pipe. He dragged a fat woman by the hair from her seat, kicked an old man, spit in the face of an Italian girl.

Duffy Plotkin punched a man in the gut, grabbed another by the collar and threw him over a bench, hurled a third against a window and shattered it. A professional, he would hit only men. People screamed, hid, fled for the doors.

"Stop! *Stop!*" Eva shrieked. "We are your own people! What we do is for you also!"

"Oh, my God!" cried Brunstein. "They hired gangsters. Flugelman, somebody, call the police!"

Meyer Flugelman, veteran of a thousand discussions on Marx, Engels, Lassalle, and De Leon, his mind honed to an intellectual fineness that was the envy of every Socialist in Brownsville, shuffled to the rear door.

Bunchik, an apparition in bloodied bandages, cracked Flugelman across the kidneys with his bicycle chain. The theorizer howled.

"Stay there, ya bum," Bunchik said. "Ya holler copper, I'll beat ya brains out."

Eva hurled herself at Bunchik, clawing at what was left of his face, her arms beating at his chest. The hoodlum wriggled free and slapped her across the face. She came at him again. He hit her in the chest with his brass knuckles. She gasped. "Blondie bitch, stay away," he said. "We don't wanna hoit no one. Clear the hall."

"Reds, anarchists!" Moishe Nigger croaked. "Outta here! This here meeting is outta order." He grabbed two women by the hair and dragged them to the door. Mendel shoved them down the stairs, spun on an attacking brother, and hit him in the nose with a lead pipe.

Blood streamed down Eva's face. Her blouse was ripped. She ran back to the stage, "Workers! Do not be frightened! We have sent for the police! Don't let them scare you!"

The Meal Ticket pirouetted away from a girl who lay screaming on the floor, and grabbed Eva's skirt. He dragged her from the stage. She landed on him, swinging and scratching. The fat man grabbed her thighs, squeezed them until Eva shrieked with pain, lifted her, and threw her against Brunstein.

"Fight them!" Eva screamed. "Chairs, tables! Workers, don't give in!"

Seeing the Meal Ticket kicking an Italian girl, Eva pulled a pin from her hat, leaped from the stage, and jabbed it into his buttocks. He howled and straightened up. She stuck him again. He screamed, turned, and was confronted by her flaming eyes.

"I will kill you, murderer," Eva said. "I am not afraid."

The Meal Ticket's eyes glistened. Not a dame to muss up, but a dame to *shtup*. A piece of sweet candy.

"Stick me, huh?" the Meal Ticket asked. He bounced toward her. Ike leaped between them and struggled helplessly with the thug. Eva was pulled away by Bunchik. He pinned her arms behind her back.

"The skinny shmuck fighting with the Meal Ticket," Moishe said to Duffy. "He's the boss. Work him over and we'll go."

Brunstein was borne aloft by the Meal Ticket and the boxer Plotkin. A screaming Eva was restrained by Bunchik. Mendel and the Nigger chased stragglers from the wrecked hall. The Meal Ticket and the boxer carried Ike to the steps, one holding his legs, one holding his arms.

Tossed into space, Brunstein felt himself floating, airborne. He landed on a pile of sweepings.

"Meeting's over," Moishe Nigger yelled. "Duffy, stop. Bunchik, Mendel, Ticket. C'mom."

They did not look back.

Weeping, Eva sat on the steps of the wrecked hall. Blood trickled from her nose. One of the Marrotta sisters, her eye closed and purpling, sat with her and sobbed.

A police van pulled up. Sergeant Ahearn, Patrolman Mulqueen, and two other men walked out.

"Yez are all under arrest," Ahearn said. "Incitin' to riot."

"So," Eva said. "They bribed you. Someday you'll learn." Bone-weary, she got up. The blood dripping from her nose gave her strength. She licked at it with her tongue.

"I'm arrested also?" Angelina Marrotta asked. She was in shock. She had gone to the meeting in defiance of her parents.

Mulqueen and Ahearn shoved them into the Black Maria.

Eva, Ike, Flugelman, and Angie Marrotta were arrested, along with an old man selling knishes who was looking for his daughter.

Chapter 5

Three weeks after her discharge from the hospital, Sarah Chain hobbled on crutches. She had lost weight. To Jake, her body seemed to have shrunk. She was always a small woman, but now she was bent at her waist as if fearful of a blow. Her legs, with casts removed, were skeleton-thin. Her thighs had shriveled. Her breasts were two flaps. She needed help dressing and undressing. Mutteh had to be sent out of the basement when Jake assisted her.

But Sarah was pleased to see how clean the apartment was. Jake and Mutteh had swept and scrubbed in anticipation of her return. She was ashamed that she could not help them. It was a woman's job. People would laugh at Jake when they heard.

"Let them laugh," the big man said. "Only they shouldn't cheat me of money."

She needed medicine and food to build her up. Luckily, Kolodny kept Jake on the job. At first he was fearful that Jake's rude handling of Moishe Nigger's soldiers would make him a marked man. "Chain, I'm grateful what you did to those *manzerim*," the hunchback said. "But suppose they blame it on me?"

"They know I did it. You pay protection money every week. That's all the Horse Poisoners wants."

Surprisingly, Moishe and his gang did not come looking for Jake. The Nigger was a shrewd businessman. He did not believe in pursuing vendettas that had no cash value.

Kolodny gave Jake an "inside" job, stacking, hauling, bossing the work crew inside the plant. Landlord Feigenbaum mercifully allowed Sarah to work a half-day for three dollars a week. She finished buttonholes on kneepants. Mutteh was employed after school as a delivery boy. A wiry runt in tattered blue cap, baggy blue knickers, and high sox, he lugged piles of trousers taller than he was.

Dr. Abelman thought that Sarah would soon be able to walk without crutches. Two canes, maybe. But he gave no assurances. She needed exercise. But how? Half-days at the machines. One day a week off.

"It's wrong you should have to work," Jake said to her. They were in bed on a warm September night. Mutteh slept on the cot in the corner of the musty room.

"We have to eat. We have to send the child to school."

"But you're hurt. You should have time to go to the hospital and get exercise and get better."

There seemed no way out. She would hobble forever, Jake suspected.

Their sexual attachment was unraveling. Jake discovered she could not move her legs. The desire was in him. But although she functioned below the waist, the legs were immobile. The effort embarrassed both of them. She wept.

Once when Jake had succeeded in making love to her, she cried and pushed him away.

"I hurt you? I won't do it no more."

"No, Jake. It's wrong I should enjoy anything."

Nightmares, she sobbed to Jake. She would have nightmares for the rest of her life. In the midst of deep sleep, she could not catch her breath. She was suffocating. Her mouth and her nose were stuffed with plaster. Lucia, the girl who worked next to her, was screaming in her ear, but Sarah could not hear the screams. She saw Lucia's brown face with the red mouth open and no noise coming out. Then the two of them, covered by a gray cloud. A heavy cloud shoving them down. Something bursting their ears. She would awaken shivering, cold, unable to forget Lucia's face.

"I am no good to you," she said. "You can't do with me what husbands must do."

"I want you to feel better."

"It will make my cry again. My body is broken. Like a bird with broken wings. If you do with me what men do, what a husband should do, you'll become weak like me."

"It's not true." He put his arm around her. She trembled.

He could see Mutteh's eyes glinting at him from the floor. Jake stared at the boy. The eyes closed.

Sarah worried continually. She never smiled. The work for Feigenbaum was too much for her, hefting herself on crutches. ("One day I'll have to get rid of the *kolyaka*, the cripple," the landlord told his wife.) She worried about Mutteh. How could he stay in school? There was no one to give him a meal when he came home.

Her timid parents looked at her with dumb despair. What good was she to anyone? Her father, old Klebanow, a pushcart peddler, was in trouble again. Shakedowns from the cops. Unable to pay the five-dollars-a-month protection money. He could not help with their bills. He barely made enough for his rent. Speaking no English, Jake's father-in-law had not understood when the police ordered him, with flat smiles, to "come to Limerick." He learned soon enough after three arrests for loitering.

"We are no better than my papa," Sarah cried. She nestled in Jake's arms for protection. "Will Mutteh be better? Jake, what will happen to him?"

Ike and Eva got nowhere over the disaster at the Baum place and the attack on the meeting. The city received their appeals with the icy smile of officialdom. Even Jews in places of power had little patience. Trouble-makers. Agitators. *Reds.*

Hauled into court for "illegal assembly," Eva, Ike, and a half-dozen girls were bailed out by Leo Glauberman, the union lawyer. Judge Younghusband, an austere Brooklyn Episcopalian, lectured the accused on "acts against God, society, and humanity."

"These people are fighting for their lives and livelihood, Your Honor," Glauberman argued. "Perhaps God and society are on their side. They should not be standing here on trumped-up charges. The gangsters who attacked them should. The police who failed to protect them. The owners who abused them—"

"That will be enough. I dismiss the case but I warn you against any further meetings or demonstrations that may incite violence."

Eva could not control her temper. "We incite nothing! We met peacefully to discuss rights! We were attacked. Look at the bruises on my arms! Hoodlums with chains and clubs—and we are the ones accused?"

Younghusband pounded his gavel. No further outburst would be permitted. Mr. Brunstein and Miss Heilig should consider themselves lucky.

Outside, Glauberman, a chunky man who looked like Teddy Roosevelt, told them that Benny Otzenberger's fat hand was at work in the dismissal. Benny knew he could not antagonize large segments of his constituency. Garment workers make up a large part of the Brownsville population.

"You'll still strike?" the lawyer asked. "Now that you've been freed?"

"The Strike Committee has voted for it," Eva said. "We will not be intimidated."

"They'll break the union," Glauberman said ominously.

Jake Chain, on his way to the bottling plant, saw Eva handing out "strike benefits." A dollar and a half a week, doled out from a metal box.

He did not greet her. Arms folded, shivering in the morning air, Jake watched his cousin, and felt a surge of love for her. Love. And all the other things.

Eva climbed to the hood of a Dodge car. It bore a sign on the side: DEPARTMENT OF HEALTH. Cops watched with cold eyes. Jake heard one say, "Sheeny bitch. Do they screw like other women?"

A policeman started to drag Eva down from the car.

"Hands off me!" Eva shouted. "I want to talk to the girls!"

"City property, lady. Ya creatin' a distoibance."

The officer clutched at her. Eva would not move. There was a surge in the picket line.

Jake felt the old urge to *hit*. He looked at the cop—fat, puffy. He could lay him out, with or without the club. But there were seven policemen on duty. The patrols had increased. Prices had gone up for police protection, yet the owners paid willingly.

"Don't touch her!" Angie Marrotta screamed.

A tall woman in a black straw hat and a gray uniform got out of the car. She carried a black satchel. Jake moved closer and listened.

"It's all right, officer," the woman said. "I am Mildred Halstead of the Visiting Nurse Service. The mayor's office asked me to visit the picket line. I have no objection to this young woman standing on the car."

Jake looked at the nurse. Eyeglasses. Long straight nose. Plain hair. Very *goyisha*. He had to hand it to her. The police knew class when they saw it. They drew back. Eva continued her speech.

Miss Halstead joined Eva on the running board. She told the girls that if any were suffering bruises, cuts, headaches, or any other ailment, she would be glad to minister to them from the car, as soon as Miss—what is your name, dear?—finished her speech.

Angelina Marrotta, a minuscule girl, slumped into a dead faint. Miss Halstead helped Rachel Goldstein, the picket captain, carry Angie to the side of the building. Briskly the Visiting Nurse opened her bag, pulled the stopper from a green bottle, and waved it under her patient's nose.

Angie twitched, shook her head, and rubbed her eyes. The girls left the line and watched gratefully.

"Disgraceful," the nurse said. Her accent hinted at Bryn Mawr or Mount Holyoke. "This girl is undernourished. Look at her skin. Her wrists are like sticks."

Jake Chain watched. Life was a hard road. As Doc Abelman used to say in his tirades against city, employers, crooks, swindlers, and galoots, *The bastards won't let you live.* Jake tucked his lunch under his arm and walked away.

Kalman Baum shouted from the window: "Tell 'em to stop with this strike, lady! Then they won't starve! They want to starve, let them starve!"

The girls shouted back at the bathrobe king.

"Bloodsucker!"

"Thief!"

Mildred Halstead gave Eva a card. "Miss Heilig, I've read about you. If you ever need help, call me at my office. I'll drop by twice a week."

"You mean the politicians are *worried* about us?" Eva asked. She looked about nervously. Something distressed her. The police had vanished.

"You would be surprised, Miss Heilig, how many influential women admire you."

Eva's face manifested her gratitude. "I didn't know *anyone* was for us except our relatives. But why should you take time from your job to look after us? The judge said we were on strike against God."

Heshy Otzenberger, in a green-checked suit and orange shoes, was greeting the trolley car at the corner. It came to a clanging stop. Wild kids leaped off the back. From the door of the tram emerged four dark girls. Heshy led them toward the side entrance. He moved swiftly, prodding his new scabs in Yiddish and Italian. One was an older woman, slow-moving, in layers of black skirts and petticoats.

"Stop!" Eva shouted. *"Stop!* You are taking the food from our mouths! We are your sisters!"

"Per favore, non lavore qui!"

"Yiddishe maidlech, geh nicht arein!"

Eva led the charge around the factory to the side entrance. Pickets followed her.

"Please!" Eva cried, as the pickets surrounded Heshy's recruits. "We are your sisters in work! If you take our jobs today, you'll suffer tomorrow!"

The older woman tried to fight her way through the surrounding strikers. Her children were hungry, she wept.

Two girls tried to hold the stout woman back. They tore at her shawl, pulled at her arms. She stumbled and fell.

Panic overwhelmed scabs and strikers. Women shrieked, yanked at hair and clothing.

In Baum's office, four men waited. Kalman opened the door. "Go ahead, but don't hurt no one too bad," he said. "Chase those *kurvas* away."

Moishe Nigger tilted his derby and yanked at his suspenders. He led his gang across the factory floor to the side door. Bunchik picked up a two-by-four. The Saratoga Avenue Meal Ticket polished his brass knucks. Duffy Plotkin threw punches. Little Mendel had been left at home. His head bothered him. That gorilla Chain had fixed him for a long time.

Eva was trying to draw her girls away from the melee. She saw Moishe Nigger's grinning face as he charged from the door.

"Adda my way, adda my way," the King of the Horse Poisoners shouted. "Anybody gets in my way it's her own fault!"

He grabbed the sign from Angie, jammed the stick into her ribs, sent her sprawling. The Meal Ticket hit Rachel Goldstein in the teeth with his brass-covered right fist. Blood spurted from her mouth. She fell slowly. Girls screamed and ran.

Heshy shouted to his scabs: "Follow me, girls! Nothing to be afraid of!"

"Baum, you are responsible for this!" Eva shouted. She saw Bunchik raising the two-by-four to strike at Esther Levy. Eva flew at him and dug her nails into his face.

"You hoo-er," Bunchik said. "I'll loin ya." He swung the board again and hit Eva a grazing blow on the hip. She swayed, smothered the pain, righted herself. Bunchik was under attack from four girls. They ripped his raspberry-colored box coat, tore at his green drainpipe pants.

Moishe cracked a girl across the nape of the neck, punched another in the chest. Duffy Plotkin picked up Esther Levy and hurled her down the cellar steps.

Reuven Baum watched from the window. "*Oi, oi,*" he moaned. "Too much, Kalman. Broken bones, bloody heads. This I didn't want. Just to scare them a little."

Eva kicked the Meal Ticket's shins. He did a one-legged dance, spun like a ballerina, caught her left arm, jabbed a finger in her eye, spit in her face.

"You scum, you filth!" Eva shouted. "You are a Jew, Wesselberg. How dare you!"

"You should talk, hoo-er. Shaddap and get adda here."

A half-dozen girls were bloodied. Others had run off screaming for the police. Two lay where they had fallen. Miss Halstead, using her satchel as a shield, dragged them to the shade of a candy-store awning and ministered to them.

"Nigger, Nigger," Kalman cried from the window. "Enough."

Ten of Eva's pickets fled. Dresses ripped, stockings loose, some shoeless, other hatless, they scattered. Esther Levy stumbled up the cellar steps. She was hysterical and kept pointing to her left wrist. "Broke," she cried. "Broke. I can't move my hand."

Eva led her to the shelter of the awning. Miss Halstead peered over her rimless glasses. "Miss Heilig, go into that store and phone for an ambulance at once. Mention my name at Saint Mary's. They know me."

Esther groaned. "Eva, it's wrong we should have to stay on the picket line. We ain't protected."

Rachel nodded her dark head. Blood gushed from her lips. Teeth had been knocked loose from her jaw.

Enraged, Eva began to tremble. *Her* girls.

A siren wailed. A police van was approaching.

The nurse pressed a gauze bandage to Rachel's mouth. It turned crimson in a second. Angie became hysterical, shaking, banging her head against the brick wall.

Mildred Halstead shook her head. She watched the police park outside the factory. Moishe Nigger and his friends had disappeared as swiftly as they had attacked. The carnage had lasted less than three minutes.

Sergeant Ahearn jumped out of the van. Two policemen followed him. Miss Halstead got to her feet. She had been winding a bandage around Esther's wrist.

"Officers, these women were attacked," Mildred Halstead said. "I demand that your men look for the criminals who beat them."

Ahearn's eyes were cunning and secretive. He surveyed the beaten girls. The blond Heilig cookie, the Red.

"Yez are all under arrest," he said.

Chapter 6

Blaufox, a dapper lawyer in a cocoa-brown suit, represented the Baum brothers. Impeding legally hired workers. Obstructing the workings of a factory . . .

The city, with a sleepy assistant district attorney named Curtis presenting the case, was going to bring another suit. Violation of picketing regulations, inciting to riot.

Judge Younghusband yawned prodigiously. One slim girl in a torn shirtwaist, blond hair flying like a Medusa's, capable of all this? It was something to laugh at. But he owed people favors. Dullahan had nothing against working people—hell, he'd been a ditchdigger himself, a foundry worker. But this dame was a pain in the ass. Besides, the bathrobe makers had given him two thousand dollars to break the strike.

Eva had spent the previous night in a lockup. She was allowed no calls. Uncle Sourmilk and Abie came to the precinct and were turned away. Ike Brunstein could not get past the desk sergeant. Eva sent word out that she was all right. She was lecturing two prostitutes on Marx.

In the morning light, with Ike and lawyer Glauberman present, the judge listened dolefully as Eva protested.

"Your Honor, where are the gangsters who attacked us? Where are the hoodlums who broke Angie Marrotta's ribs, knocked the teeth from Rachel Goldstein's mouth, fractured Esther Levy's wrist?"

If not deaf and blind, justice was indifferent. Not a cruel man, Judge Younghusband nevertheless knew where the power rested. He said nothing.

Glauberman reviewed some points. They had a permit to picket. They had been peaceful. They were attacked.

Sergeant Ahearn disputed him. These women, led by the defendant, had obstructed the rights of other women to earn a living. The Heilig woman, using her picket sign as a weapon, had led the attack.

"But," Eva said, "you weren't *around* when it happened, if it happened at all. You and your policemen disappeared. You left us to the mercies of gangsters!"

The judge banged his gavel. "Silence, miss. Case seems

clear to me. If you waive the right to trial, Miss Heilig, you will be fined a thousand dollars and released."

Eva whispered to Ike, "What do we do?"

"We haven't got four hundred dollars in the union treasury," he muttered.

"Your Honor," Eva said, "can't you see we are fighting for our lives?"

"You are guests in this country," he said. "Behave like good citizens. The police assure me that your pickets started the violence. A one-thousand-dollar fine to be paid now or a trial. The trial will go hard with you. I may ask the district attorney to open an investigation of this entire matter. I am sick and tired of violence in front of factories. Property owners have rights also."

Eva was allowed to have a conference with Ike and the lawyer. What could they do?

"We're doomed." Ike said,

"Ike, I'll be happy to go to jail. Why don't we refuse to pay and see what they'll do? The girls will be out on the lines again."

The judge summoned Glauberman to the bench. "Counselor?"

"My client is of a mind to ask for a trial."

"I will then set bail at *two* thousand dollars."

Eva winked at Ike. "I'm not afraid," she said.

Mildred Halstead, accompanied by a slender, bespectacled man in a severe black suit, entered the courtroom. She had come, unbidden, to testify in behalf of the girls. The man with her was her brother, a freelance journalist for the *Brooklyn Eagle*.

The Halsteads walked forward. No court attendant sought to stop them. They possessed command presence. The woman in dark gray uniform, the man in a black suit and high white collar, his light brown hair parted neatly in the middle, advertised their status: old-line New York Protestants.

"Your Honor, if I may," Mildred Halstead said, "I am with the Visiting Nurse Service. I was at the Baum factory when the fighting took place. Miss Heilig's version of the events is correct. She and her pickets were beaten by riffraff."

The man at her side nodded. He stared at Eva.

Brunstein and Glauberman turned to look at their new allies. Aliens, people from another planet.

Respectfully, Younghusband asked Mildred Halstead her name. She responded and identified herself as a city employee. "This gentleman is my brother, Mr. Garrison Halstead. He is employed by the *Brooklyn Daily Eagle*."

"You are related to Garrison Halstead, Senior?"

"He is our father," Mildred said.

"Your version of the events differs from that of the police," the judge said.

"The police were not present when the events occurred," Mildred said. "I saw a young woman beaten and thrown down stairs, other outrages. I should like, Your Honor, to locate the people who employed gangsters and confront *them* with the evidence."

Eva smiled at the Halsteads. The tall man with the lantern jaw and ruddy face smiled back. He seemed much more elegant than any reporter she had ever met—pressed suit, gleaming black shoes, a black leather briefcase under one arm.

"The fine must stand," Judge Younghusband said amicably. "I will drop the charge of incitement to riot and will not pursue any further investigation. But the union must pay the fine for obstructing other workers."

Brushing back his Teddy Roosevelt hair, Glauberman protested. "A thousand dollars? For getting beaten up?"

"Our treasury will be bankrupted," Ike said. "We have to feed hungry children, Your Honor."

"You should have thought of that when you disobeyed the law."

Mildred's brother stepped forward. "If it please the court, Your Honor, I'm also an attorney. I know this is irregular, but what law of society does Your Honor refer to?"

"Mr. Halstead," the judge said, "I wish to enter into no argument with you. I was speaking about the orderly processes of society. These strikes, this agitation by radicals, are threats to the fabric of our lives."

Halstead rubbed his jaw. He had pale gray eyes, Eva noticed, so pale as to almost make him appear eyeless.

"I have no desire to pursue philosophical arguments, Your Honor," Halstead said. "Can we not end this by my paying the fine? I am sure that the defendant's union will reimburse me."

Younghusband agreed at once. It solved everything. Keep the Halsteads on his side. Satisfy Baum and the manufacturers. And get that blond tigress off his back.

"That is acceptable," the judge said. "Give my regards to your father and your uncle. I had the pleasure of representing Halstead and Halstead on some matters when I was a young lawyer."

A clerk took Halstead aside and made the arrangements. No question about accepting a check from Mr. Garrison Halstead.

"All charges are dismissed?" Halstead asked.

"All," the judge said.

Ike sighed. Was this a way to advance the class struggle?

On the steps of the courthouse, introductions were hesitantly made. Eva, Ike, and Glauberman expressed their gratitude. Ike insisted on giving Garrison Halstead a written receipt for the thousand dollars. He would be paid when the union could afford it.

"Why did you do this for us?" Eva asked.

Halstead smiled. He had long white teeth. "My sister and I are interested in the trade union movement. You and these gentlemen must think it strange."

"Strange?" Glauberman asked. "No insult, Mr. Halstead, but, lawyer to lawyer, we didn't expect help from—from—"

"Bloated capitalists?"

The lawyer said, "Let's say the other side of the fence." Glauberman doffed his hat and excused himself. Ike departed with him. They had papers to file, appeals to make. The introduction of the gangsters was an increasingly frightening element in the strike.

"Why did you put up the money?" Eva asked Halstead when the other two had gone.

"In the interests of journalism."

"And justice," added Mildred. "Garrison and I are supporters of the unions. We worked with the cloakmakers last year. Garrison may do a book on the subject."

"I see," Eva said, "Observing us?"

"With a sympathetic eye and understanding heart, Miss Heilig," Halstead said.

Mildred left them. She had calls to make. Halstead invited Eva to dine with him. It was a bit early for dinner, but they could sit and chat in Gage & Tollner's.

Eva brushed her hair back. "I'm hardly in condition to be seen in a fancy restaurant, Mr. Halstead. My hair is a mess. My blouse is torn."

He took her arm. "Miss Heilig, you are one of the most attractive women I have ever seen. You need make no apologies for your appearance."

51

They walked down Fulton Street to the restaurant. Trolleys clanged by. Storekeepers lounged on the pavement, trying to "pull in" customers. Lawyers and courthouse flunkies stood on the curb and made deals. They discussed Mayor Gaynor critically and paid tribute to F.F. Dullahan.

As they walked, Halstead questioned her about the union. Eva told him of the difficulties organizing the girls. Especially the Italians. They trudged home after an exhausting day on the picket line and often suffered beatings from their fathers. *Not work? Talk back to the boss?* That was for troublesome Jews, not for good Italian girls who had to get married and have children!

"My goodness," said Halstead as he opened the restaurant door for her, "those men should be given a lecture on Garibaldi and Mazzini. They have a great revolutionary tradition and they must be made aware of it."

"The families need every penny the girls earn, Mr. Halstead."

"May I ask that you call me Garry? And may I call you Eva?"

She smiled. "Of course."

The caramel-colored headwaiter, in high apron and black jacket, studied her a moment—he knew Halstead well—and was offended by the tattered shirtwaist, the undone mass of blond hair. Garrison Halstead with a hooker? Impossible.

"A quiet table, Everett," Halstead said.

"Certainly, sir."

Halstead became uneasy when the headwaiter brought menus. "Goodness, I hope you don't observe dietary laws, Eva," he said. "I should have thought—"

"Don't worry. My family isn't observant. My father is a Socialist. We pay some respect to our origins. The intellectual and ethical traditions. But we never let a good meal be impeded by dietary laws."

Halstead asked her if she wanted a drink. She accepted a glass of red wine. He ordered whiskey.

"I have been told by some of my Jewish friends in the reform movement," Halstead said, "that they view socialism as secular Judaism. An interesting concept. How do you feel?"

"Mr. Hal—"

"Garry."

"I don't concern myself with theories. I am a working woman. I'm interested in improving the conditions under which people work. I don't want them to be afraid and uneducated. Whether it's socialism, or Judaism, or anything else doesn't bother me."

"You are a pragmatist."

"I don't know what that means."

Halstead sipped his whiskey. Eva tasted the wine. Not sweet and thick, like the wine they drank on holidays, but with a warming musty flavor.

"It means you are practical, that you do what is useful and productive."

"I suppose I am that way."

"You are also staggeringly beautiful. You must have a dozen beaus. I noticed the way Brunstein was studying you. I can't blame him. I envy him if he is indeed your lover."

"You are presumptuous, Mr. Halstead."

She had a slight accent, Halstead noted, a bit of ghetto singsong in her voice. And the word "presumptuous" amused him. A laboring girl?

He asked her, as the waiter served grilled lamb chops, potatoes au gratin, and crisp salad, about her family and her education. How did a working girl learn to speak so well?

With humor and verve, Eva told him about her head-in-the-clouds father. The renowned Uncle Sourmilk who swore by the life-prolonging power of *acidophilus*. A self-trained mathematician, he insisted on his sons attending college. Abe, her older brother, was already at CCNY. Sol, the younger, helped their mother in the store, but he, too, would be college educated.

"But you chose to do the meanest work available?" Halstead asked.

"I got involved in the union movement when I was young, and I did not want to desert my girls."

"*Your* girls?" Halstead realized she had a considerable ego.

"Ike says if we win the strike I'll work full-time for the union."

He marveled at her. Halstead, a socialist journalist (he was not fully employed by the *Eagle* but free-lanced for them), a nonpracticing graduate of Yale Law School, heir to the Halstead fortune, had never met a woman like Eva Heilig. His notion of a union official was some drab, unhappy man. She was exquisite and vivacious, an enchanting optimist.

"I'd like to see those galoots get theirs someday," she said. Eva ate with gusto, eager to try Gage & Tollner's blueberry pie on Halstead's recommendation.

"Galoots?"

"It's a word our family doctor uses. Those hoodlums who

attacked us. It isn't fair. We know who hired them." She clenched her tiny fist. "Someday there'll be justice. You know something, Garry? Those brutes who beat our girls are Jews also."

"You are an innocent, Eva. There is a history of racketeers preying on their own people."

"On the East Side maybe. Not in Brownsville. We've tried to make it a better place."

He took her hand. "I'm sure you will, Eva."

"Please. We hardly know one another. I don't know what I'm doing here with you."

She changed the subject. Was he a journalist? Then let him write about the strike. The English-language press depicted them as Reds and criminals. Employers and police were never criticized. If he was truly interested in her, let him spend a day on the picket line or inspecting the worst of the factories.

"My education starts today. You may keep me after school any day, Miss Heilig."

"You mustn't be too forward with me. What do we have in common? I speak with an accent. My mother works fourteen hours a day in a candy store."

Outside, Halstead took her arm. The evening was soft and warm. This time she did not pull away. "You ask what we have in common, Eva. We believe in justice. I admire your people. Poor and despised, coming here with nothing more than hope. Am I being sentimental? They work and raise children, and like your brothers—who I am sure I would like—they strive to make a better life for themselves. I am astonished by Hebrews."

"You'll get tired of hanging around the poor. We can drive you crazy. Bickering, battling, bargaining, everyone against everyone else."

"That makes life exciting. Among my people, everyone is proper and in agreement on all matters. That's why my sister and I are considered eccentrics."

"Garry, I don't think so. Your sister is a marvelous woman."

"And her brother?"

She suppressed a teasing smile as she looked up at his sun-reddened face, the gold-rimmed glasses, the long jaw of the aristocratic, the light brown hair parted in the center. "I appreciate your sympathy for us. But you must assume nothing. Let's view each other as a journalist and his source of information."

"That is all I have in mind." He flashed his teeth. "For the time being." Halstead had parked his Oldsmobile a few blocks away. He had paid two boys a dime each to "watch" it.

Eva climbed in, trying to suppress her astonishment at its elegance. In glass vases, set in brass brackets, fresh flowers nested. The seats were covered with soft black leather.

The car created a sensation on Haven Place as Halstead wheeled it slowly toward the Heilig house. The only other car on the block was Dr. Abelman's Dodge. The Olds drew a crowd of admiring, staring children.

Halstead wanted to meet her parents. She told him she preferred that he not come out. Later, perhaps. No, she was not ashamed of her family. He assured her she had no need to be. He had already explained his admiration for Jews.

Eva could see her father sitting on the stoop, reading the *Forward*. Abie was visible in the ground-floor window, his eyes boring into a textbook. Resting against the cast-iron railing in front of the house were two of her battered picket captains, Rachel Goldstein and Angie Marrotta. They looked weary and miserable.

"Two of my front-line soldiers," Eva said. "Thank you for dinner, and for paying the fine, which will be returned. Goodbye."

Halstead wanted to kiss her. Impossible, of course, given the audience. Smudged white faces leered at him. Small Hebrews crowded on his running boards.

"Where can I reach you?" Halstead asked.

"On the picket line. Goodbye, Mr. Halstead."

Rachel and Angie had come to Eva's house to tell her there had been a riot at the union office where the milk and bread were being dispensed. They had run out of milk. Women had gone berserk, tearing apart the office, ripping Ike's coat, screaming that their children were hungry. *Union this! Union that!* They were ready to take anything the bosses offered.

"Where do we get the milk?" Eva asked.

Angie said it came from Greenbaum's dairy. He was selling it to them at a penny below his usual price. Still, Ike had been unable to pay the bills.

"And the bread?" Eva asked. "Karp's bakery?"

"They also ain't been paid," Rachel said. Her drooping dark eyes and melting nose were the essence of defeat.

"We will visit both those gentlemen *now*," Eva said.

"They'll *have* to trust us a little longer. If they won't, no union member will buy their products when the strike is over. You two come with me."

Rachel looked at Angie. They got up and limped after Eva.

Chapter 7

Beyond Greenbaum's dairy and Kolodny's bottling plant, eruptions of industry on the bucolic outskirts of Brownsville, there was a meandering brook known as Amsterdam Creek. Some early Dutch settler gave it its name. No more than ten yards wide, it was fed by an underground stream and supplied water to farmers. On Rosh Hashanah, the Jewish New Year, it was the custom of Orthodox Jews to gather at the stream in the afternoon and perform the ceremony of *tashlik*.

A few days after Halstead's meeting with Eva, a half-dozen Orthodox Jews, prayer books under their arms, walked across the humming meadows to observe *tashlik*. Meyer Flugelman (himself a nonobserver) accompanied his ninety-year-old father, a white-bearded, straight-backed ancient, an honored holder of a seat on the eastern wall. In a trembling voice, the old man explained the prayers at the river's bank.

"According to midrashic interpretation of the holy books, when Abraham was on his way to sacrifice Isaac, Satan appeared to him as a river overflowing the sands of the desert."

"So why the prayers?"

"We discard our sins into the waters. On the New Year we ask the stream to take our sins."

Morris Kuflik, the father of the driver Label, agreed. "You're right, Flugelman, but there's more to it than that. There is an injunction in the Bible itself. The prophets tell us to pray by the waters."

Flugelman marveled: a learned old man with ignorant sons.

There were several groups of black-clad Jews standing alongside the stream. Sunlight sparkled on the winding waters, on bright stands of goldenrod. Strange, the way much of Brownsville was "country." No wonder Jews who remembered tiny villages and farms and open fields had been drawn

56

there. Not all Jews were urban dwellers. Meyer Flugelman reflected that he might write an article for the *Forward* on "Early Days in Brownsville."

Old Asher Flugelman halted beside the waters. Yellow daisies and bluebells bloomed along the banks. The black earth, nourished by Kolodny's horses and Greenbaum's cows, was rich and soft.

He opened his prayer book. "Micah Seven, verse nineteen, children," he said. "And then psalms thirty-three and one hundred and thirty."

On a knoll shaded by poplars and maples, some distance from the praying men, Jake Chain sat with his wife and son. Mutteh waded in the clean stream, picked flowers, and made mud pies. Sarah, now able to maneuver on crutches, was cheerful. They munched hard-boiled-egg sandwiches and watched Mutteh roll down the green hillside.

"Praying," Jake said. "The old men."

"We never pray," Sarah said. "If we could read . . ."

Jake laughed. "Hebrew, I had a few lessons in Glebocki. The teacher beat me with a stick and I ran away. That's all I remember."

"Mutteh will go to *cheder*," Sarah said.

"If we can afford. I suppose he should be a good Jew and go to shul."

He held her hand. She was seated on the grass, her back against a maple trunk. She smiled into the sun. She had combed her hair, tied it with a blue ribbon. She had patched and stitched her coat, polished her shoes.

Jake tried to suppress pity. Feeling sorry did not help. They did not sleep as man and wife. She could not accept his body. He was repelled by her dead limbs. She cried a great deal.

Yet they survived. Jake had a chance to become an assistant foreman at a new plant Kolodny was planning. The hunchback owed Jake a great deal. Moishe Nigger still collected blood money, but he did not raise the weekly tribute.

Jake put an arm around his wife. She drew close. "I am bad for you," she said. "I cannot be a wife any longer."

"It don't matter." He knew it did. His loins were burning. His manhood was starved. How change it? He was a vigorous man. Somehow he would have to be gratified. Whores? Behind the curtained windows of one of the gangsters' "beer halls" where hoodlums kept *nafkas?* A joke! He could not even afford a visit!

Eva. He craved Eva. No good, no good. The man who married her, who knew her body, would win an unearthly reward. Brunstein was no man for her. Never. For all his revolutionary talk, he was the kind of radical who feared the sight of a cop, shrank from a blow, would not even cross the street against a red light.

Mutteh scrambled up the hillside. Jake realized with shame that he loved the boy more than he loved the broken woman sitting beside him. Mutteh gave his mother a bouquet of wild-flowers. "Here, ma. I picked myself."

She kissed his head and held him close. He must, he *must,* she told herself, go to school, go to *cheder,* be a better American, a finer Jew, than they ever were. *It is no good to be poor, but it is the worst to be poor and stupid.*

"Mutteh, when you learn to read and write, you'll maybe teach your mother and father," she said.

"I hate school. I'll run away."

Jake grabbed him and tousled his head. "*Mozzik.* Imp. You'll learn."

Asher Flugelman started reading from his prayer book. The others joined in. ("Every man for himself," Doc Abelman used to joke. "It's not for each other's benefit. It's between them and God.")

Old Flugelman rested on his son's arm and savored the holy words:

He will turn again, he will have compassion upon us; he will subdue our iniquities; and thou wilt cast all their sins into the depths of the sea. . . .

At the edge of the stream, Mutteh watched, wondering why they talked so fast. He didn't understand the religion. But he knew it was a "sin" to tear a page in a Hebrew book and a "sin" to eat certain things or put on a light on Saturday.

Flugelman turned pages with a shivering hand. Others joined the worshipers. Three yeshiva students with curling earlocks and shaved heads appeared. They were shepherded by a frail redheaded teacher.

Rejoice in the Lord, O ye righteous, for praise is comely for the upright; Praise the Lord with harp; sing unto him with the psaltery and an instrument of ten strings. . . .

None of the praying men noticed four rough-looking youths drinking from pint bottles, stumbling along the edge of the brook fifty feet away. The newcomers halted and stared at the Jews.

. . . the eye of the Lord is upon them that fear him; upon them that hope in his mercy. To deliver their soul from death and to keep them alive in famine . . .

The first stone struck the carpenter Levine in the chest.

"Sheenies," one shouted. He was fat and freckled, no more than seventeen.

"Go away," Meyer Flugelman said. "We are praying."

"Pray on my ass, mocky," the young man shouted.

A weedy half-drunk boy of sixteen threw another rock. It struck the red-bearded Hebrew teacher.

Asher Flugelman behaved as if nothing had happened. He had survived cossacks, Lithuanian police, Okhrana agents, and was alive at age ninety. God would protect him on Rosh Hashanah.

Mutteh ran up the hill. He was terrified, his mind full of questions. Why did Jews let themselves be hit with stones?

"Ignore them," Asher Flugelman said. "Psalm one hundred and thirty."

The youths picked up sticks. A third stone sailed into the group and bounced off the curly head of Kalotkin the roofer. Kalotkin was no weakling. He folded his book and took off his coat.

"Papa," Mutteh called. "Those guys, they're picking on the people by the river."

Jake squinted across the meadow. He got to his feet and saw a hail of rocks descend on the Jews.

Out of the depths have I cried unto thee, O Lord. Lord, hear my voice, let thine ears be attentive to the voice of my supplication. . . .

But there is forgiveness with thee, that thou mayest be feared.

I wait for the Lord, my soul doth wait, and in his word do I hope . . .

They attacked Kalotkin first, four of them, shoving and punching the roofer. Kalotkin, dropping his prayer book, his new derby sailing off, landed in the muddy stream with a splash.

"Help, police, help!" screamed the yeshiva teacher. "Boys, run, run!"

The gang began pummeling Levine the carpenter. They ripped the book from his hand and threw it into the field. Then they lifted him up and hurled him into the creek. Water-choked, gasping, Levine and Kalotkin struggled to climb the slippery bank.

Flugelman kept praying. His son tried to drag him away.

My soul waiteth for the Lord more than they that watch for the morning; I say more than they that watch for the morning. . . .

Meyer Flugelman pleaded in terror: "Papa, they'll kill us."

"No, my son. I must finish *tashlîk.*"

Let Israel hope in the Lord; for with the Lord there is mercy, and with him is plenteous redemption. . . .

The fat boy had a moonlike face awash with nickel-size freckles. He seemed an apparition as he picked up the teacher and began to pummel him.

"Help!" Meyer Flugelman howled. "Someone!"

Jake Chain was racing down the hill. *I'm dumb and I can't pray,* he thought, *but I can fight.*

Jake leaped down the incline and cocked his fists.

"Please mister," Asher Flugelman said. He closed his book. Prayers had ended. Sins had been cast into the stream. "Please, mister," he said to Jake, "you shouldn't get them mad."

The attackers were pushing the teacher back and forth, tugging at his earlocks.

"Watcha got under the beard, Moe?"

They shoved him to the ground and kicked him. His students fled.

Blinded with mud, Kalotkin helped Levine out of the creek. Levine staggered away. Kalotkin could fight but he did not like the odds. Then he saw Chain.

"Chain, Chain, help!"

Jake said nothing. He charged for the fat boy who was yanking at Flugelman's beard.

"Ding-dong," the fat boy said. "Ding-dong, you old kike."

Jake grabbed the boy's collar and yanked him off his feet. A trick he had learned working for Mulqueen. When he dropped him, he slammed his left fist against the side of the youth's head, watched his eyes cross, heard the breath *whoosh* from his mouth, drove his right fist into the soft gut, an inch above the groin. The youth collapsed into the muddy bank. Jake kicked him into the stream.

The intruders stared at Jake. Who was he? Where did he come from? No beard. No black hat. No prayer book.

The thin boy brandished his stick. "C'mon, sheeny. Wanna fight?"

Kalotkin, rubbing mud from his eyes, lined up with Jake. "Chain," the roofer said. He peeled off his serge jacket. "I'm with you." Kalotkin raised his fists. He nodded at Jake.

The two sailed into the hoodlums, warding off blows with their arms and fists. One youth circled Jake, got his hands on his throat. Another started to punch at Jake's stomach. Jake reached behind and, with hands like an iron clamp, squeezed the strangler's balls. The boy screamed and let go. Jake grabbed the other, punched him twice on the nose, dropped him with a short blow of his palm against his gut.

Kalotkin pinned another youth and began to lecture him. "We are praying, understand? This is a holy place. What right do you have to do this? We don't do bad things to your church."

Stick to roofing, Jake thought.

"Let him up," Jake said. "They want to fight some more, I'll fight. Who is next? You? You?" Boxer-style, he held his fists up the way he had learned in the gym when he was sixteen. "Anyone?" Jake asked.

"Jewboy."

Sarah had struggled to her feet, picked up her crutches, and was limping down the hill. She screamed at Jake to stop.

Jake called to his awestruck son: "Mutteh, go to mama. Stop her. I'm all right."

Kalotkin got to his feet. He let his victim lie in the mud. "Enough?" the roofer asked, standing over the boy.

"Sheenies!"

Jake lifted the boy from the ground and held him over his head. The youth wriggled and spit curses.

"You won't pick on old people," Jake said. "You want to fight, fight me. You want to go in the river again, boy?"

Jake dropped him, yanked him close with one hand, and shook him a few times. Then he punched him in the throat. The boy doubled over and howled.

"Awright, Chain," Kalotkin said. "They learned a lesson."

Taking advantage of the fight—shades of Old Testament warriors, Meyer Flugelman thought—the worshipers halted at the path alongside the dairy. Flugelman watched in awe. Socialist, altruist, he was learning something. This Chain. This stupid man with no fear. None. Fists like cast iron. Was there a lesson? Something not in Marx or the Talmud?

The more Meyer Flugelman thought of it, the more the idea appealed to him. At a strategy meeting at the union office, he waited his chance to bring it up.

Eva, Ike, and the picket captains—Rachel Goldstein and the Marrotta sisters—were discussing the current situation. There had been two more attacks on picket lines. Moishe Nigger and his gang were so brazen that they now brought their girlfriends along.

"These dirty women, these *hoo-ers,*" Rachel said. "They come in a taxi. They lean out the window and they cheer when those bums hit the girls."

Angelina looked at the floor. She remembered the whores laughing as she fell. Screaming as he twisted her ears and slammed a hand against her nose and made her weep. Women with piles of curls, red rouge, lipstick. One of them stuck a black-stockinged leg out of the taxi door, pulled up her skirt, and showed a ruffled red garter to the pickets.

"We cannot," Ike said, with a glance at Eva, "count on socialites like Mr. Halstead raising bail or paying fines forever, Eva."

"Ike, stay on the subject," Eva said wearily.

He'd been furious when she told him that Halstead had taken her to dinner at Gage & Tollner's. A traitor to the cause and her class! Halstead was slumming. Looking for a story for the *Eagle.* He would use her, Ike said. His class always did.

Meyer Flugelman made a circle around the office, listening to the interminable arguments.

"Flugelman, stop the parade," Brunstein cried. "You want to help, sit down."

Meyer raised a hand. "There is a solution, if we have the courage."

They looked at him. To this point, he had been their resident philosopher.

Flugelman said that Jacob Chain might be a help. Did they know the big man?

"He is my *landsman,*" Eva said.

"A *grub ying*—a stupid man," Ike said.

"I saw this fellow Chain destroy four bums who were tormenting Jews."

"So?" Brunstein asked.

"Why are we always meek? Why do we turn the cheek?" Flugelman asked. "I am talking about the time when I watched my aged father pelted with rocks. They pulled his beard. They threw Jews into the water on the observance of *tashlik*. But this ignoramus they call Crazy Jake came down like Joshua ben Nun—"

"Please, Flugelman," Ike interrupted. "Now, in the matter of benefits, I propose we—"

Eva got to her feet. "Meyer is right. Our own protection. Men who aren't afraid of Moishe Nigger."

Brunstein frowned. "Hmm. It's a bit irregular—"

"Brunstein!" Flugelman shouted, recalling his youthful days in the Beth Midrash. "Brunstein! Was Joshua irregular? The Maccabees? Simon Bar Kochba? Brunstein, Chain is a warrior!"

The union stalwarts were silent a moment; Flugelman had convinced them.

Chapter 8

Mutteh was sitting on the stoop of the Feigenbaum house doing his "homework." He had a ruled notebook on his lap. His teacher, Miss O'Neill, had neatly written his name and grade on the cover: MORTIMER CHAIN 1A3. In a neat hand, Mutteh was writing capital and lower-case letters. He did nine sets to a page, three-by-threes, licking his stub of a pencil, admiring his penmanship.

Eva kissed his head. "You like school, Mutteh?" she asked.

"Yeah. The kids pick on me 'cause I'm little. But I knocked two guys out yesterday."

Bernie Feigenbaum discharged a mouth fart from the window. But he was wary of the squirt. He had lost his last two fights with the newly christened Mortimer Chain.

"Papa's home?" Eva asked. She wanted to speak to Jake alone. Sarah would never permit him to take the job Eva intended to offer. Besides, the crippled woman made Eva nervous. Sarah had become a whiner, a woman drowning in ignorance.

"He went to the ice dock. They had a job for him."

Jake was picking up odd jobs. Working nights.

She thanked the boy, complimented him on his neat slanting *C*'s, and left.

Eva found Jake hauling blocks of ice from a wagon to the murky interior of the icehouse. He was barechested and bareheaded. An old burlap sack covered his back to keep the slabs of blue-white ice from bruising his skin. He carried the tongs as if they were tweezers.

She watched him a moment. *What strength!* A Negro on the truck slid the four-foot blocks toward Jake. Jake caught them with the tongs, spun them, set them against the tensed muscles on his back, and walked into the cold darkness.

Was she doing the right thing asking him to endanger himself? The union had been wary of doing what some of the East Side unions had done. They had fought fire with fire. She had read the names in the papers. Big Jack Zelig, Pinchy Paul, Joe the Greaser, Dopey Benny Fine. Horrid men.

Jake hauled the last of the ice from the truck and waved at the black man. He noticed Eva standing at the entrance to the icehouse. Ashamed of his nude chest, he put on a stained blue shirt. He tugged a frayed cap over his mop of yellow hair and approached her.

"You came to watch me haul ice?"

"You do it like an expert."

"Icehouse Sammy pays me a dollar two nights a week. It helps with Mutteh in school." He sounded proud of his son.

"I went to the house. He was doing homework. You should encourage him."

"We try. I'm ashamed Sarah had to work also. Tears all the time."

They walked down the darkening street. Peddlers, finishing a fifteen-hour day of hawking wares, pushed rickety carts. An old man wheeled a homemade cart with an oven inside. He was selling *haisa arbas*—hot chick-peas. Eva bought a bag for each of them.

"You shouldn't spend money on me," Jake said. "You haven't worked in six weeks. I heard the judge wanted to send you to prison."

"But I'm free. Jake, would you have rescued me from jail?"

"By myself." He knocked a fist against one palm.

They sat in a playground. It was deserted except for a

drunk sleeping on a bench. Eva could remember as a child learning folk dancing and games with hoops and a basketball from Dr. Abelman when he was a medical student. Summers, Abelman had been the playground instructor.

She told him what the union had in mind—men to protect the pickets. They would be paid. They would see to it that the hoodlums would not terrorize the girls again.

Jake grinned. "You want me to be a *shtarker*."

"I hate that word. It sounds like a bad person."

"It's a bad business. But that's what you want. A *shtarker*, a strong one. Not like your friends who drink tea and talk about a revolution."

"All right, a *shtarker*."

"How do I live? What about my job?"

"What does Kolodny pay you?"

Jake was amused. A new side to his beloved cousin! She was always a goddess to him, lovely, bright, courageous. Now it seemed she had a head for business.

"Eleven dollars a week. I work inside now—load, stack, shlep. No more with the horse and wagon. Kolodny's cheating me. He fired an inside man and I do the work for two."

"The union will pay you fifteen dollars a week."

"What happens when the strike is over? When there's no more girls to protect?"

"We'll find work for you. I will insist that you learn to read and write."

"It's too late. I'm stupid."

"No!" She punched his shoulder. It was like hitting the poplar tree in front of Abelman's house. "If you're ashamed to go to night school, I'll get Abe to teach you. I don't want you hauling crates of soda forever. You've had a terrible life. I know how your father threw you away. No family. You ran away from the Hebrew Orphan Asylum and slept in back of Reds Mulqueen's bar. Hauling beer barrels when you were twelve."

"I learned to fight."

"But that can't be your whole life, Jake."

"How do I start?"

"I'll talk to the union."

Jake looked at her eyes. Clear green, with pinpoints of pale light. "I'll need other men," Jake said.

"Find them. We'll make you the subcontractor." Eva laughed. "Jake, you'll be a businessman."

He shook his head. He wanted to embrace her, inhale her sweet-soapy odor, crush her yellow hair with kisses. Never. It would never happen. He was a *bulvan*, a hardfisted tramp.

"What are you staring at, Jake?"

"You're so beautiful. I always—always—"

"No, no, that isn't what we're talking about. Beauty is nothing. An accident. It's what you *do*, how you *live*, that's important."

"Not when your wife isn't a wife anymore. And you are not a man."

"I'm sorry, Jake. Maybe we can get help for Sarah."

"Abelman says this is the best she can be." He got up, stretching.

He held Eva's elbow with a gentle touch as they crossed Sterling Place, and he was tempted to put an arm around her. He could not. If he touched her, he would want more. He knew himself. The streak of violence, the strength hidden by the solid exterior. Never, never. His love for her was like a high fever, making him dizzy, weak.

Garrison Halstead knocked at his sister's door and entered at the sound of her low voice.

Mildred was wearing a blue smock. She held a jar of poster paint in one hand and a brush in the other. Against her bed were four white cardboard rectangles. Halstead smiled as he read them.

NEW YORK WOMEN'S LEAGUE
SUPPORTS AND ENDORSES
THIS STRIKE

FELLOW WORKERS! DO NOT
CROSS THE LINE! IT IS YOUR
FIGHT AS WELL AS OURS!

He stroked his chin. "*Your* fight, Mildred? You and your friends haven't been treading the pavement for a ten-dollar week. I haven't heard of any of your Mount Holyoke friends being charged twenty-five cents for a locker or docked a week's pay for a broken machine."

"You're only mildly amusing, Garrison."

"You really intend to march on the picket line with the strikers?"

"I have organized a committee to support them."

She checked a notebook for names. Halstead was astonished. A Belmont, a Morgan, a Vanderbilt, other daughters of the ruling families. There were Quakers, Unitarians, and a defector from a rich Catholic family.

"You may get beaten and jailed for your efforts."

Mildred applied a final dab to a poster.

ORGANIZE! JOIN! WE ASK
ONLY A LIVING WAGE AND
HUMANE CONDITIONS!

"Why not? It will teach us about life. I would prefer, Garrison, that you not tell our parents of this enterprise. If you keep my secret, I'll keep yours."

"What's mine?"

"Your newest romantic interest. The Heilig girl."

"What makes you think I give a tinker's damn if they know? I suspect father is sympathetic to the strike. Mother will never budge from her conviction that they are in rebellion against God."

Mildred sat on the edge of the bed. She inspected a new pair of brown Coward's arch-supporting shoes. She would wear them when she and her friends joined the girls on the picket line. A grand joke there! Special uniforms for special pickets. She'd advised Dorothy Van Horn and Peggy DeWitt to do the same—flat heels, loose clothing, and a wide-brimmed hat in case of rain.

Garrison sat at her desk. In the light of the Tiffany lamp, he glanced at the *World*. "The free press is marvelous," he said. "It's always the strikers who start the violence. Never a word about the thugs who intimidate them. I may write a letter to the *Times* when I finish my piece for the *Eagle*."

Mildred cocked her head, "If I know you, Garrison, neither will be finished. Your career as a free-lance journalist, now that you've decided law bores you, will be impeded by your bent for procrastination and moodiness."

"I listen to a different drummer."

Mildred had to agree. At Yale he had refused to join a club, failed to attend his graduation, angering his father and causing his mother to break into tears. Garrison had decided it was a farce. He had always been an outsider at Yale, Snob, intellectual, radical, contemptuous of athletes and aesthetes. What had saved him from *their* contempt was his wealth and his success as a Lothario. Riches had its own aura. The bearer of riches was permitted eccentricities, departures from the norm.

The lesson had not been lost on young Halstead or on his older sister. She had graduated from Mount Holyoke, worked at Bellevue, gotten her accreditation as a registered nurse, and gone to work for the city. He, leaving a Wall Street law firm, was determined to be a crusading journalist, to work with reformers, challenge the Tammany Tiger, cleanse the city of corruption.

"Tell me about Eva Heilig," Mildred said. "She's extremely pretty."

"A fascinating girl. In a torn shirtwaist and a soiled skirt, she was the most elegant person in the restaurant. She may have a Yiddish accent, but she has natural grace and dignity."

"And courage."

"Yes, that too."

"And how much of your interest in her is political and how much is personal?"

"I can't quantify my feelings."

Halstead lit a cigar, blew smoke toward the lofty ceiling. It was decorated with gold ormolu curlicues. They dined on Rosenthal china, ate with vermeil knives and forks. These hallmarks of great wealth reflected their mother's attitudes: Wealth demanded a certain seemly display within the confines of one's home. Their father was a different breed. He rode the elevated train to Wall Street, shined his own shoes, and owned three suits. Brooks Brothers affairs, durable and plain. He was a Quaker, a descendant of the Greenes of Rhode Island, and could trace a shadowy line to General Nathanael Greene.

"I can't dissemble with you, Mildred," Garrison said. "The woman fascinates me. She's without much more than a high-school education, but her native intelligence is high. She takes night courses at the Labor Lyceum. A Socialist, a pacifist, deeply involved in the union movement. And no despair in her, no solemnity."

"And she is beautiful."

"Quite beautiful. Don't misunderstand me. You know I am without prejudice. But she is not your typical heavy-featured Jewess. There's something Slavic or nothern in her face. They tell me that, over the centuries, Jews frequently intermarried with Poles and Russians."

Halstead lifted one of Mildred's picket signs. "How do I

look, Mildred? Do you think my Deborah of the streets will think better of me if I join?"

Mildred took the sign away. "It's a woman's job, Garrison. Don't get too intimate with the girl. Don't hurt her. You haven't hesitated in the past."

Halstead flicked ashes into a cloisonné tray, waved at the air to dissipate the smoke. Mildred was tolerant. Their mother forbade smoking downstairs. "She appears to me the kind who knows how to take care of herself," he said. "Neither police, nor hoodlums, nor crooked politicians seem to have gotten the best of her. Why should she fear a Yale man?"

Mildred shook her head. Garrison had long had the reputation of a rake. He had bedded down, Mildred knew, with chambermaids, nurses, and waitresses. "Why indeed, Garrison."

"I'd like to be on hand when you and your sisters of the elite take your place on the picket line with Eva Heilig's Jewesses and Italians."

"Are you mocking us?"

"By no means. But no fair showing up just to get your names in the papers. You'll be expected to put in a full day of marching, chanting, and, if necessary, getting clubbed and bloodied."

"We are quite ready for that."

Garrison, before leaving for his evening chess game with his father, shook his finger at her. "Mildred, bear in mind that we are of the unarrestable class."

"There is no such word."

"There is such a word. I looked it up in Webster's. There is not only such a word, there is also such a condition of life, and we are exemplars of it."

Chapter 9

Kolodny was sorry to lose Jake. He told him he'd never get the job back. Business was lousy. He'd make do with a nigger. So what was Chain going to do? Who would hire such an ox? J. P. Morgan?

Jake shrugged. He knew enough to keep his mouth shut.

Some new work, was all he said. By the way, he asked Kolodny, what had happened to Kuflik, the fat man with the potato nose?

Jake found Label Kuflik at the "Pig Market," the corner of Pitkin Avenue and Strauss Street where unemployed laborers gathered to pick up odd jobs as draymen or pick-and-shovel workers.

Kuflik's nose had gotten bigger and more misshapen since his unemployment. Jake seemed to see two Kufliks—the nose, and what was behind it, a burly man in a ragged jacket. With Kuflik was a man almost a head taller. He had a mashed, furrowed face. A kind of animal dumbness was etched in the low brow, the squashed nose.

"My cousin," Kuflik said. "Yussel Kuflik. I got to look after him. He ain't smart."

Look who's talking, Jake thought. "So? You got work?" Jake asked.

"A little here and there," Label said.

The giant Yussel nodded. "Yeah. Here and there."

"You want a job?" Eva had not specified how many men to hire. But he knew enough about street brawling. Five men should be sufficient.

"Chain, you're a boss now?"

The giant Yussel laughed, exposing a mouth of rotting teeth.

Jake explained in words that the Kufliks understood. They were to be *shtarkers*. They were to protect the girls on the picket lines. The would have to *klop* and get *klopped*.

"No thanks," Label said. "You see this nose? Who could resist hitting such a nose? How much it pays?"

"Fifteen a week, Kuflik. Tha same for this gorilla."

"Thanks, I accept," Kuflik said. "Him also. I know a little from this. We'll need lead pipes, bicycle chains, knives and one pistol. Chain, you're the big shot. You can carry the pistol."

Jake shook his head. "Not until we need it."

Two more men.

He thought at once of the Ferrantes. Ever since he was a kid he had gotten along with Italians. With Irishers, the first words out of their mouths were always *sheeny*, *kike*, *hebe*, *mocky*. An Italian might call you that sometimes, but really

70

didn't care one way or the other. Also, you never saw an Italian drunk in the gutter. And they kept secrets.

The Ferrantes seemed the logical place to start recruiting. Salvatore was only fifteen, but Luigi, he knew, was out of a job. He'd also met the eldest of the seven brothers, Frankie. He might be willing to join the "guardians," as Eva called them. With two Ferrantes and two Kufliks, he would have a good gang of *shtarkers*.

He found the Ferrante boys pitching pennies against the side of the tenement in which they lived on Pacific Street. The block was a Neapolitan enclave in Jewish Brownsville. Jewish boys and girls were warned to avoid the street; the *tolyinns* would pounce on them and steal their money. Jake had never had any trouble with them. Maybe because of his size.

"Eh, Crazy Jake," Luigi said. "*Come va?*"

Frankie, cross-eyed, pudgy, with oily black hair parted in the middle, looked suspiciously at Jake. "Whaddya want, seltzer man?"

"To talk."

Sal rested against the side of his hokey-pokey cart. He was sampling his own wares—a cup of shaved ice dripping with purple syrup. A drunken black stumbled by and bought a bottle of deadly green syrup. Makes his own at home, Jake figured. Salvatore screwed him on the change, Jake was certain.

"You talk, Chain?" Luigi asked. "Come on."

Theresa leaned on the windowsill. She was pretty—long-nosed, wide-eyed, with a cap of black curls. She had pouting crimson lips, broad cheeks splotched with blushes of red on muddy skin. Next to her was a younger sister, Iolande. She was even prettier. Like an actress, Jake thought.

"Mistah Chain, wanna see my feet?" Theresa laughed.

"Feet?"

"Yeah. From walkin' the picket lines. Look."

Theresa lifted a long slender leg, displayed her right foot wrapped in a bloody bandage.

"Eh, put ya leg down," Frankie ordered. "You ain't no tramp." He squinted at Jake. "We don' want her to picket no more. She got sores on her feet."

Old man Ferrante, the patriarch, puffing a pipe he had bought to celebrate Garibaldi's entrance into Rome in 1870, said nothing. He was a sedate barber, who spent evenings in a cane-back chair on the sidewalk. Handlebar moustache, pompadour in the manner of King Umberto, a red-white-and-green medal on his breast pocket. His wife rarely appeared in the street. Bundled in black layers, she mourned lost children, a dead sister, a departed aunt.

"Come across the street, ya wanna talk," Luigi said. He preferred conspiracy, even though the only ones within hearing distance were his relatives. Frankie, belly overhanging his belt, joined them.

They sat on a bench in front of the Santa Lucia Mutual Association, a store with dusty green curtains in the window. Inside, old men played cards, smoked guinea-stinkers, drank red wine.

"I hear you guys ain't working," Jake said.

"I been laid off," Luigi said. He was chunky and resembled Frankie but was more muscular. It was rumored he had once choked a man to death in the Pig Market. The man, a drunken laborer, had made the fatal error of lifting Theresa's skirt.

Sal left the cart and joined them. He leaned against a lamppost, lithe, darker than his brothers. His goatlike face absorbed everything.

"I got work," Jake said.

From the Santa Lucia Mutual Association came the soupy sounds of a clarinet, the strumming of a mandolin. A few more Ferrantes, Vince and Baggie (Biagio), warming up. The brothers worked part-time as musicians.

"What kinda work?" Luigi asked.

"A buck more a week that you get pouring concrete or bricklaying."

K & R Robes, The Baum brothers' new factory, was chosen as a testing ground. Next to Finemaster's Fine Bathrobes, theirs was the biggest "inside" place. The Baums were in trouble. But they hung on grimly.

In a savage late October rain—it had turned cold and windy, and the poplars on Haven Place were denuding—Eva sent her pickets out early to prevent the entry of scabs. She had gotten a tip from a girl who remained "inside" and tolerated Heshy's pinches and kisses.

This morning, the girl said, Baum was bringing in a truckload of goods—bolts of flannel, cotton, and velvet. "The Nigger," Heshy said to Eva's spy. "The Nigger's gonna get it through the gate." Already the pickets had forced one truck to turn back.

On the picket line that morning, marching fore and aft of

Theresa, were her brothers, Luigi and Frank Ferrante. Each had hidden a lead pipe in his belt.

Across the street, Sal lolled against his cart. He had a vat of hot water. A wood fire kept it boiling. In it floated ears of husked yellow corn. "Hot corn," a penny apiece.

Jake and the Kufliks—Label and Yussel—waited in a rain-flooded doorway near the "hotcorn" cart. Sal complained that business was lousy. The rain kept putting out the charcoal fire.

Jake yanked his torn jacket around his neck. Maybe nothing would happen.

"*Nu?*" Label asked. "This is a way to spend a morning?"

Jake peered through the slanting rain. Gray street, gray factory. An old warehouse that the Baums had converted. They were two tough cookies. They were also running a secret factory in Jamaica, hidden in the meadows around the bay.

Jake could see Eva handing out raincoats to her girls. One girl began to cough. Eva led her to the shelter of a doorway. They often came to the picket lines with only a cup of tea sloshing in empty stomachs.

A Ford police van puttered by slowly. Maybe Baum was paying the police to escort the truck. It would mean that the gang probably would not show up. Jake understood the rules. He and his mob would not dare confront cops. Moishe Nigger's gang was a different matter.

The van slowed down. A cop jumped out, walked over to Eva, and asked to see her permit. Eva showed it to him. The cop nodded and climbed back into the van.

Another officer got out. He helped himself to four ears of corn from Sal Ferrante's boiling vat. He did not pay, laughed as he climbed back into the paddy wagon. Jake and the Kufliks retreated down the hallway, out of sight.

"Eh, ya lousy *polizia*," Sal said to the rain.

"Here it comes!" Rachel Goldstein shouted. "Here it comes! Girls, form a line!"

The police van vanished and a truck rolled into view.

Jake understood. The cops were leaving the field to Moishe Nigger.

"A line, a *line!*" Eva cried.

The girls locked arms in front of the factory gates. Already the scabs had been spirited in—side doors, back doors. The pickets formed a ragged line. In the center stood a rain-soaked Theresa Ferrante. On either side of her were her brothers, Luigi and Frankie. The girls threw their signs down, locked arms and yelled at the driver to turn around.

Instead he inched the truck forward.

"Now?" Label asked Jake.

"Not yet. He hits anyone, we drag him outta the cab." Jake squinted through the pelting rain. He recognized the man at the wheel. It was the boxer, Duffy Plotkin.

"Get ready," Jake said.

"Don't move, don't move!" the girls chanted.

"No goods for the bosses!"

"Turn around!"

Plotkin inched the truck forward. Heshy came running from the front door. He stopped in the flooded courtyard and waved at Duffy to move ahead. A few scabbing men stood behind Heshy.

"Girls!" Eva shouted. "Comrades! Do as I do!"

Jake and the Kufliks watched in amazement. Eva had hiked up her skirt, yanked her hat down over her mass of hair, and had fallen onto the soaked pavement. She stretched her body in front of the truck, daring Plotkin to drive over her.

"Join me!" she screamed. "Join me!"

Rachel Goldstein and Esther Levy imitated her. They fell down, oblivious to rain and cold puddles, and lay alongside Eva. Theresa and Angie followed. Soon there was a row of drenched, shouting women in the courtyard.

"Bestids! Hoo-ers! *Nafkas!*" Kalman Baum was shoving Heshy forward. "Get rid of them! They got no right! They are taking bread from my children's mouths! Otzenberger, what do we pay your father for?"

"I can't," Heshy mumbled. His voice drowned in the downpour. "Too many . . . Plotkin . . . do something. . . ."

The boxer leaped out of the cab. But instead of attempting to drag the women away (he was deterred by the sight of the Ferrante brothers standing over the girls), he ran to the rear of the truck and undid a chain. The tailgate fell with an echoing clang.

Moishe Nigger jumped out of the rear. The Saratoga Avenue Meal Ticket, Bunchik, and Little Mendel followed. Each carried an ax handle.

"One side, one side, hoo-ers," Moishe Nigger growled. "Plotkin, ya shoulda runned them over."

A half-dozen screaming girls fled through the open gates. They yelled for police. There was not a cop within three blocks of the Baum factory.

The hoodlums began flailing at pickets, striking at legs,

backs, breasts, and heads. The women shrieked, covered their drenched bodies.

"The ones in front!" Moishe Nigger yelled. "Beat the hell outta the ones trying to stop the truck. Get the blonde!"

Methodically the Meal Ticket and Mendel began to thwack the legs of the prostrate girls. Howls reverberated across the street, where Jake's crew awaited his signal. They could see Theresa being yanked to her feet. Plotkin punched her in the stomach twice. Luigi and Frank went for him.

Jake said, "I want the fat guy. Let's go."

Label Kuflik pulled the leap pipe from his belt. "What if they got guns?"

"We'll find out," Jake said.

A great calm had come over Jake Chain. Hitting and getting hit. It had been his life. It gave him a sense of relief. Bloodied lips and loose teeth and cut ears did not please him. But he had learned to accept them as part of his existence. There was always an exhilarating feeling of release. The satisfying thrill when you hit back.

Jake said, "I got the fat guy. Label, grab the prizefighter. Yussel, go for Moishe Nigger. Luigi and Frankie got the little guys."

Jake's gang raced across the flooded cobblestones.

The Meal Ticket was tearing at Eva's skirt, trying to yank it off. Her white petticoats were soaked and soiled. She kicked, struggled to rise, slammed at him with her picket sign. He kicked her ribs. "Hoo-er," the Meal Ticket said. Jake could see the agony on her wet face. But no tears.

Yellow shoes, Jake thought. Fancy as a pimp. What Doc Abelman would call a cake-eater. Chain rushed at the Meal Ticket with his long arms apart. He grabbed the velvet lapels with his left hand, slammed the lead pipe across the fat man's face with the other. Eyes, cheek, mouth slid softly to one side. The Meal Ticket had half a face. Blood spurted from the lips and the button nose. The Saratoga Avenue sport sat down in the wet. Like a buddha, he squatted in the rain, holding a hand to his mashed face, shaking his head. He was finished.

Luigi wrestled Mendel for his ax handle, twisted it out of his hands, cracked him across the chest with it. "Lay offa my sister," Luigi said.

Mendel yanked a knife from his belt and bent low. He had a reputation as a knife fighter. It was rumored he had cut off the tip of a prostitute's nose and made her chew it.

"*Sfaccim',*" Luigi said. With this tribute, Luigi, hard as the cement he poured, cracked the pipe against Mendel's knees. Mendel crumpled and joined the Meal Ticket.

Frankie tackled Bunchik. The latter and Duffy Plotkin were racing for the cab of the truck. The motor was running. The girls were on their feet. Some ran. Some clawed and scratched at their attackers, swarming around the Meal Ticket and Mendel.

Yussel lifted Moishe Nigger off the ground, threw him into the rear of the truck, slammed the tailgate, and hooked the sides. The Nigger knew when he was in a losing fight.

"Chain, you bastard," Moishe Nigger roared. "For this you'll die."

Frankie dragged Bunchik from the truck door and hit him in the teeth. He ran faster than any of the girls. Box-toed shoes and lollipop-stick shanks splashed through the street. He vanished. Memories of the way Crazy Jake had slammed a shovel against his head haunted him. And the big Polack was looking to kill someone.

The Kufliks tried to drag Duffy Plotkin from the cab. He was a tough nut—hard, fast, quick with his fists. He came out of the other side of the cab, with a wrench in his fist, Once he feinted, then he smashed it against Label's enormous nose. The nose turned purple and a waterfall of blood poured out. Tears clouded Label's eyss. Plotkin hit him across an ear. Label fell.

Plotkin feinted again with his left. With the wrench in his right hand, he cracked it against Yussel Kuflik's right wrist. A bone snapped. Yussel bent double. "Get him, get the bum!" he cried to Jake. Jake had just kicked the Meal Ticket in his mountainous ass as he tried to rise.

Kalman Baum was shrieking into a telephone for police. He shoved Heshy and his brother Reuven out of side doors. "Get the cops! Get them!"

Moishe Nigger crouched in back of the van, shouting to Duffy to drive off. Plotkin stood his ground, wielding the wrench, sneakered feet dancing on the paving stones.

Jake circled him. Girls fled. Eva pulled others away.

"Jake, Jake!" Eva shouted. "Tell him to go!"

"You heard her," Jake said. "Get in the truck and beat it."

"C'mon, ya bum," Duffy said. He had no nose. Forehead, nose, chin were in a perpendicular line. His brains were mashed, people said. Too many losing fights, too many blows to the head.

He swung at Jake with the wrench, ducked Jake's arms, swung again, caught Jake on the upper left forearm. The pain was like an electric shock, zigzagging up the muscle into shoulder and neck.

Jake got a right hand on the boxer's left elbow, tried to spin him, ducked again, caught the iron wrench on his right shoulder.

The Meal Ticket stumbled to his feet and tried to tackle Jake. Yussel clubbed the fat man with his pipe. The Meal Ticket collapsed again.

"Ye wanna fight, *fight*," Plotkin taunted. "Ya a boxer, Chain? Ya got a jab?"

Brains muddled, eyes crossed, Duffy hit Jake three more times with the wrench, twice on the arm, once on the hand.

Moishe Nigger crawled through the rear of the van, shoving aside the bolts of cloth. He wriggled into the cab.

"I'll kill ya, Polack," Duffy snorted.

Jake grabbed the right wrist. Plotkin struggled free and cracked the wrench again. Jake's arms were a mass of welts and bruises. *Next time I grab, he won't have time to hit*, Jake thought.

Moishe Nigger was pointing a black .38 out the window of the van. The hoodlums had never fired a shot in their assaults on pickets. It was an unspoken edict from employers. No shooting. No guns. Who needed guns against a bunch of girls?

"Jake!" Luigi shouted. "Watch out! The gun!"

Eva, shepherding girls across the street, also saw the gun. "In the truck, Jake!" she screamed.

The Nigger squeezed off a shot. It flew past Jake's tattered cap, richocheted off the side of the Baum factory, and fell harmlessly.

The King of the Horse Poisoners again aimed the stubby pistol. This time it jammed. He shook it as Jake and the boxer wrestled, cursed, grunted, and fell to the wet stones. Jake had torn the wrench from his hands.

Sal Ferrante knew about guns. They had four of them in the house. Italian Army relics.

Sal shoved his pushcart of "hotcorn" with its red-green-white umbrella across the street. He rammed it against the flank of the truck, opposite the bloody wrestling match between Duffy and Jake. Their bodies rolled in the water, thrashing, legs and arms locked. Duffy was trying to gouge Jake's eyes out.

Distantly a police siren wailed.

"We gotta beat it!" Luigi shouted to Jake. "Cops. Baum'll get me arrested. Me and Frankie are going. Let the stiff go."

Moishe Nigger unfouled his gun. Once more he leveled it

at Jake. Plotkin had belted Jake on the cheek and opened a red gash. Chain tried to throttle the boxer, but Plotkin wriggled like a live carp in a fish tank.

The Nigger aimed the gun.

"The hot water," Sal said to his brothers.

Luigi understood. He and Sal lifted the vat of boiling water from the charcoal burner. The two of them counted to three, then leaped to the running board. As Moishe Nigger found his target and was ready to squeeze a shot, they hurled the scalding water at him. He screamed and dropped the gun. The derby protected his bushy head, but the hot water, richly scented with sweet corn, boiled his sallow face, his ears, his nose, his nigger-lips.

"Oi, oi, murder, murder!" he screamed. "Help! *Help!*"

The sirens were louder.

At the iron-barred window of his office, Baum was screaming for police.

Hearing Moishe's shrieks, Duffy turned. Jake hit him across the neck. Plotkin's head wobbled. He fell against the door of the cab and slid to the ground.

"Basta, Jake," Luigi said. "Let's go."

Jake looked at Eva and her girls. "You go also," he said. "Tell the girls to run."

Horrified by the bloody battle, the girls retrieved signs, gathered up hats and purses, and hurried away. The rain came down in drowning sheets. They could hear Moishe Nigger howling inside the truck.

Jake, Luigi, and Frankie raced down a side street. Sal did not run. All innocence, he hefted the kettle to the stove, picked up a few ears of corn, tossed them in, and pushed off. Every penny counted.

"Hotcorn! Hotcorn!"

Chapter 10

"It's wrong, it's wrong, it can only get us in trouble," Brunstein moaned. "Eva, don't you see where this will lead?"

"To victory. For once those scoundrels *ran.* For once we showed the bosses we wouldn't take their punishment."

It was a few days later. They were seated in the office of

the attorney, Leo Glauberman, the toothy man with the spectacles and roached hair. Glauberman was a Socialist, but of his own design. He believed; he didn't believe.

The office was shabbily furnished and was located in a second story on the corner of Pitkin and Rockaway avenues. Below were the boarded-up ruins of the Jenkins Trust Company that had failed in 1907. Glauberman knew about bank failures. He had invested in three financial ventures and seen his money evaporate three times. Jenkins Bank, Union Bank, Allied Bank. A realist, he decided that union work was more stable. He listened with interest to the account of the battle royal.

"We are using armed hoodlums," Ike said. "We are no better than *they* are."

"Ike has a point," the lawyer said. "The fighting can't go on forever. But it's a warning to the bosses. You'll note, not a word in the newspapers. Baum and his friends were afraid to report it."

Glauberman's secretary went to the door in response to a buzzer. She opened it. Jake Chain walked in. He had his torn cap in his hand. The left side of his face was a swollen purple-crimson lump. He held his right arm close to his side, winced when he moved it.

"Our conquering hero," Brunstein said sarcastically.

Eva got up. The men remained seated, wary. Jake Chain was not their kind of Jew.

"Jake! Did you see Dr. Abelman? Are you better?"

"No doctor. It's just a few bruises."

Meeting Eva in front of these educated men reminded him of his lowliness.

"Jake, you know Ike, don't you? And this is Mr. Glauberman, our lawyer."

"Nice job, Chain," Glauberman said. "You were Hairbreadth Harry to the rescue. Got the girls off the railroad track before the train hit them."

Ike got up. "The less I know about this whole affair the better. God forbid it should get into the newspapers."

Jake sat uneasily on the edge of a chair, cap in his hands. He found himself staring at Eva. She winked at him, as if to say: *We won.*

"Wait till next time," Ike said as he walked to the door. "The papers were against us before this—this—development. When is there a good word written about us? That's all we need, hiring gangsters."

"Mr. Brunstein," Jake said gently, "I ain't a gangster."

"Hmmm? I guess not. Coming, Eva?"

Eva walked to the door. "A good job, Jake. It was fun seeing *them* catch it for a change. Mr. Glauberman wants to talk to you."

Jake stood up and nodded. Reds Mulqueen had taught him to stand up when a lady entered or left the room. But make sure she's a lady and not a hoo-er, Reds said. Eva was surely a lady.

When they had gone, Glauberman offered Jake a cigar, lit it, and took a bottle of Old Overholt from his rolltop desk. Glauberman said they should drink to further successes.

"You mean they want I should do this again?"

"That was the understanding."

His body ached from the blows from fists, from Plotkin's wrench. His right arm felt as if it would never be able to move properly. He had to grit his teeth as he crossed his legs.

"They gave you pretty good, Chain?"

"I gave them better."

Glauberman was appraising the big man the way a housewife studies a side of kosher beef. This was better than kosher, the glinting spectacles observed. The big bum was *glatt kosher,* a superior grade-A item. There was cash value in this hulking brute.

"Chain, listen to me. I am a lawyer, and I understand the human mind. You follow me? Never mind, don't answer. You've spent most of your life smelling horse farts. There are opportunities for a man like you. I know about you from Mulqueen. There isn't anything you're afraid of. Any man who could take on the Nigger's gang is a man for me."

"For you or for the girls on strike?"

"You're not so dumb, Chain. Why did they call you Crazy Jake when you were a kid?"

Jake found the whiskey warming his insides, soothing his bloody bruises. The cigar smoke was pleasant, hazy, making him loose, more talkative.

"I was twelve years old. Three Italian guys tried to steal a keg of beer from Mulqueen. I beat up two of them, and ran after the third. He almost killed me with a lead pipe. Reds said anyone who'd pull such a thing had to be crazy."

Glauberman folded his hands on his vest. "There are easier ways to make a living than hanging around picket lines. Or fighting battles royal with Dago Johnny or the East Side bums they'll be bringing in. Chain, this is a life-and-death struggle."

The lawyer got up. His Teddy Roosevelt face looked out to Pitkin Avenue.

"Who needs fights in the street? Find the man who is giving us trouble and *klop* him a little," Glauberman said. "Make him worry."

"I should *klop* Baum? I should just grab Kalman Baum on the street and *klop* him?"

"Too big. Some pisher first. Maybe a scab from the Pig Market. Or you and your friends could get inside a factory and make a fire. Jewish lightning."

Jake gulped another shot of booze. He was giddy. He wished at times like these he were smarter. Why had Eva and Brunstein left him? Then he understood. Glauberman was handling the dirty end for them.

"All this for fifteen dollars a week?"

The grin sliced Glauberman's robust face in half laterally. "Let's take each job as it comes. Know the end of the trolley line by the brewery?"

"Yeah."

"Across from the brewery there's a small inside place. No sign. Gottlober's. The son of a bitch is going full blast with scabs. Too far for us to send pickets."

"So?"

"Supply him a little heating."

Jake hesitated. This was different from protecting Theresa Ferrante and Rachel Goldstein.

"For fifteen dollars? I should risk going to jail?"

Glauberman handed him an envelope. "From now on, we pay by the job. At fifteen a week you are a bargain. Take a look in there. Figure out how you'll pay off your employees."

There were ten ten-dollar bills in the envelope. Jake had only seen that much money when Mulqueen or Kolodny cleaned out the cashbox.

"Let me suggest ten for each of your friends and you keep the rest," Glauberman said.

He'd need only Yussel Kuflik, Luigi and Frank. Thirty bucks. He'd keep seventy. *Seven weeks' work!* For a half-hour of dirty work.

Jake said, "Who is Gottlober? Why should I do this to him?"

"Don't worry about him. Here's a diagram of the place. You smash a window in back, reach in, and open the door."

"What happens if I get caught?"

"Do it fast and run. When you throw the match, keep in mind how your wife got crippled at Baums'."

Years later, when he was Jacob Chain, "labor consultant," Jake often thought of that job he pulled at Gottlober's factory. It was ridiculously easy. If you wanted to frighten a man, there were many easy ways to do it. It was, he told himself, the reason he rose so fast, made so much money, grabbed so much power.

Luigi borrowed a truck belonging to a contractor he worked for, a cement-caked Dodge. Yussel brought two cans of gasoline. Frankie Ferrante brought a supply of tools—crowbars, axes, sledges, wrenches.

Sarah complained when Jake left. He lied to her: an emergency at the bottling plant. But wasn't he quitting to work for the union? A last job for Kolodny, he said. She was afraid of being alone. He assured her she'd be all right. Mrs. Feigenbaum would come downstairs and give her "eat."

Leaving, he would see Mutteh's gleaming eyes fixed on him. Mutteh knew about what his father's gang had done to Moishe Nigger. It was becoming Brownsville legend.

Gottlober's two-story brick place went up in a cone of orange flame. The gasoline-soaked bolts of cloth burned like giant wicks. Jake's gang wrecked a dozen machines before they spilled the gas, and Yussel tossed matches. They raced through the rear door, climbed into Luigi's truck, and sped down Liberty Avenue to Brownsville.

In the garage, Jake paid them off.

"The big boss," Jake said, "says ten bucks for each of you, but I'm giving you fifteen, because it was the first job."

Fifteen bucks! A week's work of bricking or pouring cement! *More* than a week's work of shlepping cases of oranges! Jake doled out the bills. He would retain fifty-five dollars instead of seventy. But he would have the loyalty of the men.

The fire at Gottlober's created a sensation. Police interrogated Ike, Eva, Flugelman, and the picket captains. They knew nothing about it. But Ike and Eva knew where the orders had come from. They were paying fees to Glauberman. He had promised to end the strike, one way or another.

Benny Otzenberger invited Ike to lunch at the Little Hungary and pleaded with him not to let matters get out of hand.

The Baum Battle was a bad sign. Gangsters, a bloodbath. And now Gottlober—ruined. Everyone knew it was Ike's local that did it. Better settle with the bathrobe manufacturers.

"And get rid of the whole damn shootin' match," Benny said, between mouthfuls of stuffed veal roast.

"Otzenberger, my workers had nothing to do with the fight at Baums', which was instigated by Moishe Nigger's gang." Brunstein sounded nervier than usual.

Benny belched loudly enough to be heard in Williamsburg. So much for Brunstein's professions of innocence.

"Just tell your new associate Mr. Chain to watch out," Otzenberger said. "One bullet is enough to stop even the biggest bull."

Jake could not lie to Sarah forever. He told her he had a new job. With the union. She was puzzled. He had no skills. He could not operate a machine or cut cloth, sew buttons. Odd jobs, he said. Eva asked him to help distribute milk and bread to the strikers, to "help" the pickets.

They were celebrating his new "job" with a roast chicken. It had unborn "chickie" eggs inside its golden carcass. Mutteh ate greedily. *Chicken in the middle of the week?*

Sarah, dragging herself about, had made dumplings, gravy, sweetened carrots. A feast for the Chains! Mrs. Feigenbaum sniffed unaccustomed aromas wafting up from the basement. She had her suspicions.

"So all this is from handing out food?" Sarah asked. "For watching that Esther and Rachel don't fall down?"

"I lay chiggy in case somebody is coming to make trouble," Jake said.

"Eva got you into this?"

"Eva?" He feigned innocence. "She and Brunstein and a few others."

"Eva. That blondie. They say she's like a man. She smokes cigarettes and drinks beer."

She is like no man, Jake thought. In deference to his wife's crippled legs (though she looked prettier lately), he said nothing.

"Papa," Mutteh said. "There's this kid in my class?"

"So?"

Mutteh swallowed a mouthful of white meat, gobbled the last of the "chickie" eggs. "This kid's name is Irving Bunchik?"

"He got tough with you?"

"Nah. Nobody gets tough with me. I sock 'em—pow, *pow!*

Irving says guys are gonna kill you. He said you was all kinds of dirty things and his father was gonna break your arms and legs. He's lying, ain't he, papa?"

Jake lit a cigarette. The first decent meal they had had in months. God, what a difference a few dollars made! And more to come. *Much more.* Glauberman had plans for a man who was not afraid.

"What's he talking?" Sarah cried. "What is this, men will break your legs? It can't be true."

"It's not," Jake said. "You tell this boy your father ain't worried about anyone. You think these people scare me?"

"No, papa."

"Give a feel." Jake peeled back his shirt sleeve and flexed his right arm. The biceps thickened and swelled. The cords on the forearms were like strips of harness leather. "Go on, feel, kid."

The muscles danced and writhed.

"Show-off," Sarah said. "You do this for Eva Heilig when you're watching the girls?"

"No," Jake said. "Only for my son."

Fascinated, Mutteh pinched the hard flesh of his father's arm. Let Bunchik's father try something. Nobody was as strong as his papa.

Sarah laughed. "Thank God you are strong for all of us. Even if I'm not sure what you're doing. Jake, don't tell me no more."

The envelope with the fresh hundred dollars felt comforting inside Jake's shirt pocket. He wore a heavy-knit dark blue sweater, like a boxer's pullover. He had bought it on Pitkin Avenue with money he had earned from Glauberman. The money always felt good, as if giving off heat, feeding his body.

He had talked to Sarah of looking for a new apartment. Maybe in a better neighborhood. Haven Place or St. Mark's Avenue. She protested: How could she get to work? As awful as the basement was, she had to climb but one flight of stairs to get to the shop. No more sweatshops, Jake said. Soon she would not have to work. She could look after Mutteh, cook, clean, be a good housewife.

Waiting in the early morning chill on a street near the Brooklyn Bridge, Jake felt a distinct joy in the job awaiting him. He had learned the lesson quickly: There was money, lots of money, to be made with fists and clubs. Eva assured him it was all for "a good cause."

There were rumors that the manufacturers were getting ready to make a deal. A fifty-hour week, a two-dollar wage increase. No more charges for needles, oil, lockers. But no recognition of the union, no closed shop. They were enraged and terrified. How dare the union resort to strong-arm men! It was a *shonda* and *a khoppa*—a scandal and an outrage. Intellectuals like Isaac Brunstein and Meyer Flugelman employing such monsters?

"Of course," Eva told Jake, as he poured over the alphabet with her brother Abe, who was teaching him to read, "of course we'll end this when we win the strike. I don't like what's happening any more than Ike does. We've left it to Glauberman."

Jake nodded, copied neat *M*'s and *N*'s in a notebook.

"Good work, Jake," Abe Heilig said. "I mean your letters."

Every morning at six, Glauberman said, a wagonload of scabs crossed the Brooklyn Bridge. Greenhorns from the East Side. Jake was to stop them.

"Women?" Jake asked. "I got to hit women?"

"*Scare* them," Glauberman said. "One look at you, they'll run. The wagon says Brumberg's Pickles."

Resting in the doorway of a closed grocery store on Adams Street, Jake yawned and wondered if he was doing the right thing. He was not a cruel man. Tough, crude, unthinking. But to hit women? Not a nice idea. Yet it made a difference when Glauberman counted out the bills. He could buy Mutteh a suit for Chanukah. A dress for Sarah. A pair of special shoes for cripples. Then they would move to a decent apartment.

The wagon was a flatbed with wooden rails on the side. It was open on top. A sign read:

BRUMBERG'S KOSHER PICKLES
QUALITY & TASTE

On the bed of the wagon stood a dozen barrels. The wagon was pulled by two spavined horses. In the icy morning air, their snorts formed clouds like the gusts from a pressing machine. There was a bearded driver wearing a black derby and a long black overcoat. Next to him was an enormous man in a leather jacket and leather cap. He carried four feet of two-by-four. A section had been chipped away to form a handle. The man seemed half-asleep. His lumpy red face suggested he was half-drunk.

"Where's the dames?" Luigi asked.

"In the barrels," Jake said.

Chain pondered their move. The street was deserted. He wanted to frighten the girls but not hurt them. A painful job. The battle at Baums' had been a pleasure. Even putting the torch to the Jamaica factory was fun. But to *klop* women?

"Yussel, grab the horses," Jake said. "I'll go for the guy with the club. Luigi and Frank, you hear me?"

They nodded. Unshaven, red-eyed, they evoked terror by their very appearance. "Yeah, Jake." Luigi yawned.

"Pull off the tops from the barrels. Roll a few off the back. Holler at them. They'll get scared and run. Don't hurt."

The wagon approached the corner. The horses stopped for a moment. One farted and dropped steaming road apples. The other bucked and whickered.

"Get them," Jake said.

Yussel lumbered in front of the horses and grabbed the bridles.

"Hey" the man in the derby said. "Beat it. Get away from the horses."

"Police," Yussel boomed. "Ya got no license to transport persons."

"This is pickles, *putz*, not persons."

Luigi and Frank climbed on the back of the wagon and yanked the lid off a barrel. Two terrified women in ragged coats and shawls crouched inside. Like canned cherry peppers, Luigi thought.

"Get out and beat it," Luigi shouted. "Against the law."

He grabbed a woman's arm. She screamed. Luigi and Frank pulled at her and kicked the barrel to one side. It knocked over the adjacent barrel, and the lid fell off. Two more women were exposed.

The giant next to the driver stood up, roaring and swinging his club. Jake dodged it. "Hey, fathead, it's me, Crazy Jake Chain. Ya heard of me? No scabs allowed in Brooklyn."

The fat man clambered into the rear of the wagon, swinging his club at the Ferrante brothers. The barrels toppled, rolled, and the women crawled out, screaming, falling from the flatbed.

"Stay, stay!" the driver shouted. "It's the lousy union. Get him, Yankele!"

Jake grabbed the driver by the coat and hurled him out of

the seat. The horses reared and whinnied. Yussel held them firmly.

The guard, seeing he could not stop the unpackaging of his cargo—girls were screaming and falling from the wagon—swung his club at Jake, missed.

"Go home, go home!" Frankie yelled at the women. "Don't break no strike. G'wan, beat it."

The women needed no second warning. They scurried toward the bridge.

"Bestid," Yankele said. "I know from you." Jake was about to take the reins in the driver's seat when the man brained him. The club struck Jake at the base of his head. Only the thick collar of the knitted sweater, bunched at the neck, saved him from a fractured skull. The blow stunned him and knocked him out of the seat, onto the rearing horses.

Frankie and Luigi went for Yankele, twisted the club from his hands, ripped his jacket, and threw him off the wagon.

"Get Jake," Frankie shouted to Yussel.

The horses bolted, dragging Yussel, pulling an unconscious Jake, tangled in harnesses and braces. Dead to the world, his mind in a black cloud, Jake's feet bounced against the cobblestones. A shoe came loose. Frankie Ferrante grabbed the reins and stopped the horses a block from Borough Hall.

A policeman came running up. "Trouble? What the hell you guys doing?"

"Deliverin' pickles, officer," Frankie said. "The horses bolted."

They hauled Jake aboard the flatbed. Brumberg's pickle wagon could serve as an ambulance. By the time Yankele and the derby-hatted driver had explained to the cop what had happened, the wagon was gone.

"Concussion," Doc Abelman said. He palpated the back of Jake's head with his hand. I don't think there's a fracture. But, boy, what an egg somebody laid there."

Jake lay on the black leather examining table in Abelman's office. The physician had been awakened at seven in the morning. He was accustomed to emergencies.

"Fell off a wagon," Luigi said. "We was loading sacks, Doc, and Jake fell."

"On the back of his head? It looks to me like somebody tried to brain him."

Jake stirred as the doctor washed the area with iodine and

looked for a break in the skin. Semiconscious, Jake struggled to get up.

"Take it easy, Jake. Who am I?"

"Dr. Abelman. It hurts."

"That's a good sign. You can feel pain. At least not everything is scrambled inside. You guys turn him around."

Luigi and Frankie—Yussel was reporting to Glauberman on the pickle-barrel affair—hefted Jake and sat him upright. Abelman held up three fingers. "How many?" He said.

"Three. I ain't seeing so good. Like there's two of you?"

Doc shook his head. "Go home and rest." He scrawled a prescription. "Take two of these every four hours. A big galoot like you should get over a bump on the head. That's all I get lately. *Shtarkers*. You know a guy named Morris Pearlberg?"

The Ferrantes and Jake expressed ignorance. Silence. Never. Never heard of him.

"Hefty guy in a gray derby. They call him Nigger. Came in here with a pistol stuck in his belt."

"Maybe I seen him around, Doc," Frankie said innocently.

Abelman scratched. He looked from Chain to the dark brothers. Something going on here.

"This Pearlberg's face and arms were boiled pink. The guy looked like a lobster from Lundy's restaurant. I asked him what happened. He wouldn't say, but he said he was going to kill the bums who did it to him. Took his pistol out and counted off the shots. A bullet for every one of the guys who cooked him."

Jake was in bed three days with the concussion. Sarah wailed. She was certain he was involved in dirty business. She begged him to stop, to ask Mr. Kolodny to give him back his job.

She became a scold, weeping, limping around the basement on her cane, cursing their terrible life. Bad dreams troubled her. She saw monsters, demons, frightening animals that looked like people, or people that looked like animals, attacking her.

Jake silenced her with twenty-five dollars. She could not believe the money. When her brown eyes were as wide as they could get, he gave her twenty-five more.

She tucked the money into her corset top. *Fifty dollars!* And she had seen more. A roll from which he had peeled the bills. She limped upstairs to the sweatshop. She feared for Jake. She knew what he was doing. No secrets in Brownsville.

Already he was becoming a hero to the working girls and the union people. Feigenbaum looked at him with wonder and fear. Sarah noticed that the sweatshop operator was more solicitous of her. Mrs. Feigenbaum offered her a glass of tea and a cookie every morning.

This is what comes of hitting, Sarah thought bitterly. Greeted by smiles from Boss Feigenbaum, she understood the power, the new money, the future that had to be better. She would quit the job and be a housewife the way Jake wanted. Her father could sell his pushcart and open a fruit-and-vegetable store.

Below, Jake moaned and took his pills. He dreamed of making love to Eva. All naked. The two of them. No shame. He would love her all over. He would make money on top of money, dress her in satins and furs, like the fancy New York women in the newspapers.

Chapter 11

"No fire this time," Leo Glauberman said. "Just wreck the place."

"How much?" Jake asked.

The two were alone in "Teddy Rosenfelt's" second-floor office. On windy Pitkin Avenue, the Ferrante brothers waited in the truck with Yussel the Bear. They amused themselves whistling at women shoppers.

"Two hundred," Glauberman said. "Chain, a lot of this money I borrowed from the bank. It ain't the union's."

"Not enough. I want three hundred. Last time I got a terrible *klop* on the head, I could be dead."

Glauberman turned sideways and jiggled his pince-nez. A month ago, Jacob Chain had been a thickheaded horse.

"Take more than that to kill *you*, Jake."

"You ain't answered, Mr. Glauberman. Three hundred dollars to wreck a place? Whose?"

"Finemaster's."

"The price just went up to four hundred."

They haggled for ten minutes. Glauberman suffocated his Rooseveltian rage at this placid giant. They compromised on three hundred and fifty dollars, the highest fee to date.

89

Jake told the lawyer that his head was feeling better. He had come into the office with terrible aches and pains. It was a miracle how the lump went down when they agreed on three hundred and fifty.

It took Jake and his gang a half-hour to wreck Finemaster's factory.

The guard, an unarmed drunk, was tricked into approaching Sal Ferrante's "hotcorn" cart, hit on the head by Luigi, and lugged into the basement.

Yussel and Frankie clipped the lock on the front gate. Jake smashed a window. Jake, Yussel, Frank, Luigi, and little Sal smashed machines, threw acid on the cloth, broke the elevator cables, and tossed a stink bomb in the furnace.

"No cops," Jake said, as they rode off in the Ferrantes' truck.

"They been paid off," Sal said in his scratchy voice. "I heard Otzenberger hollerin'. He says the union is gettin' as smart as the bosses. They're also payin' the cops."

They stopped at Mulqueen's bar, where Jake gave each "soldier" twenty dollars. That left him with two hundred and seventy for himself.

They came out of Mulqueen's, Jake looming in their midst. The word had gotten around. Pimps, thugs, and shakedown artists stared at him. This was Crazy Jake Chain, chief *shtarker* for the union.

In beige tweed cap a size too big for him, Little Mendel came out of a car and shuffled toward Jake.

"Don't hit, Chain, don't hit," Mendel said. He had a white scar running across his forehead where the shovel had almost taken his head off.

"Who's hitting?" Jake asked. "And who's in the car?"

"Mr. Morris Pearlberg, who is in the same business you are in."

"What does he want?"

"To talk."

"I can't talk. Later, maybe."

Little Mendel shook his head. "It ain't my business, Chain, but you're making a mistake. What you done to Finemaster's, everyone knows. Better make a deal with Pearlberg so we can work together."

"I don't know from Finemaster." Jake looked at the Ferrante brothers and Yussel. "You?"

"Who the hell is Finemaster?" Luigi asked. "We been drinkin' beer all night."

Mendel crossed the street to the parked car. "You had your chance, Chain," he called. "You got a head could be broken, a heart could be stabbed. And a wife and a kid. And that blond bitch Heilig."

Jake started to cross the street. Blood pumped in his head. He'd kill them. On the street. Luigi and Yussel grabbed his arms. Frankie and Sal clung to his legs. He struggled in rage, finding no words, spitting at the car as it pulled away.

Moishe Nigger pointed a pistol at them. The gun clicked harmlessly a few times.

Yussel took Jake to a *weisbierstube* on Belmont Avenue. The owner was a one-eyed woman named Tante Bella Botkin. Yussel said it was a safe place. Moishe Nigger never went there—Aunt Bella was too tough. She was protected by another mob, the Belmont Bulldogs. Her son, Bulldog Botkin, was the boss.

"So what happens here?" Jake asked. He rarely drank. He did not play *shtuss* or poker; his mind could not follow the action. What he craved was knowledge, deciphering letters and numbers. He felt he was getting rich. Money on top of money. Tomorrow he would open an account in the East New York Savings Bank. Glauberman was a good fairy, a wizard.

He nursed a beer at Aunt Bella's and watched Yussel get into a *shtuss* game. In a half-hour the Bear lost the twenty Jake gave him.

"Want some fun, Chain?" Yussel asked.

"A woman?"

"It's all right. No one'll know except you and the hoo-er, and me and Tante Bella."

Jake felt his neck turn scarlet. He had always been hesitant with women. Strange, sweet, soft creatures. Vague memories of his mother—a soft breast, hands that stroked him. Long ago. Carried in her arms. So young he could not walk. The farm, the trees. A field of yellow flowers.

Sarah had been beautiful once. Lithe, dark, like a forest bird. And Eva. More beauty than he could envision. He could never stop imagining her naked, glowing, waiting for him.

"Come on, Chain," Yussel said. "Bella knows you're a big

shot. She saved the best for you. For two dollars, what can you lose?"

He would have asked God to forgive him, if he believed. If he could pray. If it mattered. Sarah would not know. What harm?

Over the saloon were three small rooms. In each were a cot, a shaded lamp, a table, a basin, and a pitcher of water.

Yussel, with a throaty roar, blundered into the first room and greeted a woman. He spoke Russian.

The girl in the next room was fat but pretty. She had a small beaked nose, painted red lips, a mass of curling black hair. Her cheeks were round, rouged, and puffy, and her eyes were black and slanted, suggesting a strain of Hungarian.

"Hello, Jake Chain. My name is Minnie Fassbender."

"You know me?"

"You're famous. I used to make fun for Moishe Nigger at another place. The girls who work there told me you boiled him like a chicken. So what are you staring?"

She had taken off her green satin kimono. Jake gawked, intrigued with the round flesh. She bulged the laced corset, the ruffled blue silk drawers, red garters, black stockings. His hands trembled. His throat turned to sandpaper. If Moishe Nigger and the mob caught him now, he'd be dead in a minute. Helpless on his belly. He would not have the strength to lift a fist.

"Whaddya lookin' at, Crazy Jake? Ya like me?" She snapped a garter, turned, and showed him her blooming cheeks.

"I love you." His voice drowned.

"Oh, sure. C'mon. Don't stand there shaking. Let's see if you can love as good as you fight."

He fell to his knees and embraced the silken hips. He could not stop his hands from shaking.

When it was over, he was as drained as any empty seltzer siphon. He did not feel shame. He felt elated, rewarded. He gave her five dollars instead of her usual two.

"Come back, Jakie," she said. She wiggled fingers in his ears, kissed his thick hair, ran her tongue over his face. "Ask for Minnie."

Aroused again, he craved her. They made love again. He gave her five more dollars.

He watched her pulling on the stockings, tying the strings on her underpants, standing in front of a cracked mirror and painting her lips. She combed her hair. A plain girl. *Tsatski'd* up with makeup, perfume.

He grabbed her from behind, cupped her breasts, and bit her neck with his lips.

"Enough. Twice is enough."

"I'll be back."

"I'll be here."

Reaching between her legs from the rear, grasping her lower parts in one hand, he was gentle and possessive. This, too, came with money, fame, and the terror he was learning he could arouse in people. He had been faithful to Sarah for one reason: poverty.

Chapter 12

A week before Chanukah, the bosses were ready to settle.

Moishe Nigger's mob was no match for Jake Chain's *shtarkers*, although the parboiled Nigger counterattacked. Frankie Ferrante was ambushed and beaten up by Duffy Plotkin and Bunchik. They clipped off a third of his left ear and smashed his nose. Undeterred, Jake, Luigi, and Yussel intercepted a wagonload of scabs on Fulton Street, unhitched the horses, and drubbed the driver.

The Baum brothers and Finemaster contacted Brunstein. Enough was enough.

"Not enough scabs, gentlemen?" Ike asked loftily. "You have learned something of proletariat solidarity. Not a worker in Brownsville will scab for you."

They sat in the Little Hungary restaurant—Kalman Baum, Finemaster, Ike, and Flugelman. The union men sniffed victory with the beef goulash and stuffed cabbage.

Kalman, who had lost ten pounds, sipped bitter seltzer. "Solidarity my ass, Brunstein. It's the gangsters."

"Gangsters? How dare you!"

"Never mind," Baum said. "The Heilig woman, that Red. Some citizen you turned out to be, Isaac Brunstein. Your father was a Hebrew teacher and look at you. Not only a Socialist but hiring criminal scum."

Finemaster's voice trembled. "Eight thousand dollars' equipment wrecked in my place. The insurance companies hear Brownsville and they run. You did it to us, gentlemen."

Outside they could hear chanting. All four men, napkins

tucked in shirt collars, went to the window. A waiter complained. So what was new? The unions again.

A strange procession. First, two mounted policemen. Then a butcher's wagon. A policeman rode on its rear platform. What was he guarding? Then two more mounted police. Behind them a funeral procession. There were at least forty people, most of them girls on strike. They carried black candles. Rachel Goldstein and Esther Levy bore a sign: RIGHTEOUSNESS SAVES FROM DEATH. Eva Heilig was leading the parade.

"They're crazy," Baum muttered. "All of them."

"Not so crazy," Ike said. "Inside that butcher truck are twenty scabs for your factory. But they'll never get there. We shamed them into refusing to work and they are being escorted back to Manhattan."

Flugelman nodded. "You'll notice, gentlemen, police protection. A change in attitude in City Hall. Mr. Otzenberger understands where votes come from."

Baum gritted his teeth. *Damn that bastard Chain!* Flugelman, Brunstein, the Heilig woman, they could yap forever about union solidarity. But when it got down to cases, it was Jake Chain who had ruined them.

From his second-story window, Glauberman watched the "funeral cortege." His idea. Escort the handful of remaining scabs back to the bridge. And police yet! Otzenberger was seeing the light.

Jake stood next to him. He wore a heavy blue serge suit, a stiff white collar, a dark blue tie. He had been barbered, shaved, and powdered. His enormous freckled hands hung clumsily from the starched snowy cuffs.

"It's over, Jake," Glauberman said. "By tonight the bosses will settle. Fifty-hour week. Ten-percent wage increase. Time off for the toilet, lunch, sick leave. Shop stewards to mediate infractions. Jake, you don't seem interested."

It was lost on him. What the hell was an infraction? He had twelve hundred dollars in the East New York Savings Bank. Sarah was going that night—in a taxi!—to buy a fur coat. In a few days, they would say goodbye to the basement. Jake had rented the lower floor of a house on Haven Place—three big rooms, a kitchen, a spotless bathroom.

Jake could see Eva leaving the procession. She was talking to a man in a fur-collared greatcoat and a black homburg. A young-looking man. Something *goyish* about him.

Jake edged closer to the window. Snow was swirling, an early dusting on a dark December day. He could see Eva's round fur hat, the long heavy coat. Shamed, he thought of his visits to the "hoo-er." Did it matter? He went there to fill a need. Sarah could not supply it. And he would not dare think of Eva sleeping with him. When he went to the noisy, crowded, overheated Heilig house for his lessons and sat at the kitchen table with Abie, spelling words, he could not stop staring at her. She was always in motion, always talking. The Heiligs had had a telephone installed. She was on it forever. Picket captains. City Hall. Ike. Support from the Jewish Trade Council. An article in the *Forward.*

"Now the strike's over, what do you need me for?" Jake asked. He wondered about the new apartment on Haven Place. Mutteh was asking when they could buy an automobile.

"Strikes or no strikes," Glauberman said, "you'll be needed. I am getting into the union myself. Not just as their attorney but in a more direct way. You can help, Jake."

"How?" He was wary of something cunning, secret, in Glauberman. The lawyer had changed in the past few months.

"The labor movement is going to need help. Chain, there are wet-wash workers, butchers, kneepants makers, cloakmakers, bakers, carpenters, all kinds of working people who need help. It's good you're learning to read and write. You could be an executive."

To celebrate the end of the strike, Garrison Halstead invited Eva to dinner at Luchow's. It was a snowy, crisp evening, a few days before Christmas.

Eva was no longer a mere worker. Ike, Flugelman, and the others had decided that the union would pay her as full-time "vice-president for organizing." She was a find. A natural. Old Socialists swallowed their chauvinism. When she spoke, workers listened. Her tiny figure, the mass of blond hair, the intense green eyes, the assertive chin, disarmed (and sometimes frightened) employers.

Halstead congratulated her on her new job. He lifted his glass of Rhine wine. She smiled and did likewise. A gypsy orchestra played Strauss waltzes. The restaurant, with its penumbral walls, stuffed stag heads, obese waiters bearing trays of golden beer and gargantuan portions of veal Holstein and hasenpfeffer, filled her with a vague dread. It was not only terribly Christian. It was barbaric, savage, something out of northern forests. She looked in vain for a Jewish face, listened for a snatch of Yiddish. Nothing. But plenty of *Deutsch*.

"To your new eminence," Garrison said.

"Don't make fun of me. This wine is too *sour*."

"It's called *dry*, Eva."

"You see my ignorance? How can you be interested in me?"

She looked around the smoky, tumultuous restaurant. The gypsies had retired in favor of a German *oompah* band in leather pants, embroidered suspenders, and green hats with feathers. Jew-killing after the roast goose, she thought. Or roast Jew?

"You're the most beautiful and intriguing woman here," Halstead said. "My sister tells me that even on the picket line when you're screaming at the girls, you're beautiful."

Eva blushed. His sister Mildred was too generous. Eva had told Halstead to thank her for the support Mildred had gotten from her friends. They had raised money, marched with the girls, allowed themselves to be arrested in a show of unity.

"Look around you," Garrison said. "These are women of wealth, actresses, some *horizontales*."

"*What?*"

"Fancy prostitutes. Don't look shocked. You're a Socialist and a realist. You know how the rich arrange things. Eva, there is more beauty in your freshly soaped face than in all of these lazy pampered women. See that man staring at you? The bald one? My father's associate in real-estate dealings. Mr. Ten Eyck. He knows quality when he sees it. His Dutch brain is wondering right now: Who are you? What am I doing with you? How in God's name did I find someone so beautiful?"

"The wine is sweeter every second."

"If those Tyrolean nincompoops would stop blaring, I'd tell you I love you."

His voice was drowned out by a thumping, bleating chorus of "Watch on the Rhine." She was unable to read his lips.

"What did you say?" Eva shouted. She held her ears.

"I'll repeat it outside. I want us to be alone when I tell you."

She confessed she was enjoying a taste of the high life. Quite a change from Brownsville. But the barbaric "Christianness" (as she put it) of the restaurant frightened her. The soaring Christmas tree was like a glittering green monster.

The wind made her light-headed, happily giddy. She realized she was beautiful. It gratified her. Men stared. Women whispered. Hardly like meetings in drafty factories, in Ike's grim headquarters—interminable arguments over tactics, procedures, dues, benefits.

"This is fun," Eva said. "But why do I feel strange? The wine? Because Christmas isn't my holiday?"

"Now, my dear," Halstead said, taking her hand. "We are both Socialists, correct?"

"Yes."

"And atheists?"

"Yes."

"So none of this means anything to us, except having a good time. There could be a crucified Christ on the wall of the restaurant in place of that stag's head, or a Virgin Mary in place of the evergreen, and it would mean nothing to either of us. Statuary. Neither fear in you nor respect from me. Isn't it heartening that we can feel the same way?"

"I guess so." She hiccuped. The fried veal, covered with bread crumbs and a shiny egg, was more than she could manage. The egg stared at her her—the eye of a troll. The sweet-and-sour red cabbage clogged her nose. She drank more wine. "But you have a head start. You can make fun of Christmas because you were raised with it. I am a child of the ghetto. Christianity means what? Hating. Killing Jews. The fear is natural, even though my father says there'd be no anti-Semitism if everyone studied algebra."

"A wise man, your father. I look forward to meeting him."

The *oompah* band paraded around the restaurant. Christmas carols boomed in the smoky air. A bespectacled man in a tuxedo came by to whisper in Halstead's ear. It bothered Eva. Garry did not introduce her, although the man stared at her with an impertinent smile.

"You see?" she said when the man left. "You can't overcome your class, Garry. No introduction?"

"You're too good for him. Horace Vermont. Formerly Grunberg. Spoiled, rich, haughty, ashamed of his Jewish origins. He asked who you were."

"What did you say?" The wine made her giggle.

"I told him you were a dangerous anarchist. I knew him at Yale. A bad lot. No one is meaner about Jews than a rich Jew who tries to hide it."

When the music subsided, Halstead tried to coax her to

taste a vast apple pancake, big enough, Eva thought, to feed half the Hebrew Orphan Asylum. As she pecked at it, he asked her about the strike settlement. The pretext for the dinner had been his need for a story for the *Eagle*. The editor was aware that the burgeoning Jewish population in Brownsville was educating itself, learning English, becoming politically active. Why not try to win them as readers?

As they sipped coffee, Halstead confessed his ignorance of labor matters despite his avowed socialism. It was astonishing the way the employers had acceded after such a bitter battle. They had used all their resources—thugs, politicians, police, courts, scabs.

Eva said, "We have much work ahead of us. We will not stop until they recognize the union as bargaining agent and give us the union shop."

Halstead laughed. His pince-nez jiggled, his reddish face turned a shade darker. *What teeth he had!* she marveled. Each one a snow-white work of art. The rich had superb teeth. And ruddy complexions, and neat hands, and graceful feet, and, very often, long narrow jaws.

"Why do you laugh?" she asked.

"Eva, when you are declaiming your dedication to the cause—and I mean no offense—you're even more beautiful. It is as if a Botticelli angel were to start quoting from *Das Kapital*. I love you for it."

She tried to stop his praise. It embarrassed her. She did not know how to respond. So she asked that he interview her on how the strike was won. In responding to his questions, she said not a word about Jake Chain.

Halstead was no fool. The police at headquarters had told him of a mob of gangsters the union employed. (A police captain found it amusing. "Sheeny against sheeny, Mr. Halstead." Captain O'Connor laughed. "The kike bosses started it, and the kike strikers copied them. Hired some big hebe to scare them out of their skullcaps. I bet a few beards got pulled.")

Later they strolled along Fifth Avenue. They walked past the brownstone mansions. They paused in front of the First Presbyterian Church. Garrison asked if she wished to go in; the stained glass was stunning and there were enchanting Christmas decorations.

"I think not," Eva said.

"My atheist? Why not look at it as art with no religious connotation?"

"I can't help it. We don't go to synagogue and we regard all these things as distractions—"

"So do I."

"It just makes me nervous."

"I didn't think anything did."

"Garrison, I'm brave enough on the picket line or at a meeting or facing a boss. My voice scares them. But—I'm afraid."

"Of me?"

"No."

Christmas worshipers in furs, muffs, high hats, and greatcoats emerged from the Gothic church. Halstead nodded at a few. It was not his family's church. They were Episcopalians.

They walked uptown on Fifth Avenue. He took her arm.

"I guess it's the old ghetto fear," Eva said. "It doesn't leave you. Always waiting for the next blow. That's why my father retreated to mathematics. My brothers are intelligent. Much more so than I. They'll escape. And I fight my way through the labor movement." She stopped and cocked her head. He adored her at that moment, snow flecking her mass of hair. "They call me the leader of our 'burning Jewish maidens.'"

Halstead smiled and tapped his cane in the snow. "Really? How delightful. How does it sound in Yiddish?"

"Unsere verbrente Yiddishe Maidlech."

"My burning Jewish maiden," he said. Halstead embraced her. He kissed her gently on the lips, the cheeks, the closed eyes. "My beloved Eva. I intend to marry you."

She shoved him away with firm gloved hands. No one had ever kissed her in that manner. "No, Garrison. That is nonsense. Your father does not want in-laws who run a candy store. We are poor Jews."

"I shall marry you. In fact, we are going to make love before the wedding. You and I, Eva, are free souls."

"Maybe *you* are. You're rich and you can do what you want. I can't. You must remember. All my Jewish radicalism is based on a code of ethics. I can't abandon it overnight. I'm sorry, but that is how it is, Garry."

"I have an apartment on Gramercy Park. Let's stay there awhile. We'll sit by the fire."

"No, Garry. I know I sound ridiculous. A liberated woman who will not let her passions be liberated. I am fond of you. But the more we get involved with each other, the worse it will be someday."

"Nonsense. We need never see my family again if they reject you."

"It's not that. *You'll* reject me at some point. My accent. My Jewishness."

"I only know that you are the bravest, loveliest, most desirable woman in the world. You've taught me of the potential in women. Not just beauty and grace, but courage, sense, dedication. Please come with me, Eva. I do love you."

She shook her head, then rested it against the thick beaver collar. "No. No. I won't."

Halstead kissed her forehead. "Thy cheeks are comely with rows of gold," he whispered. "Thy neck with chains of gold."

"Garry, don't try to make me give in by quoting my ancestors' love songs. I'm a long way from the queen of Sheba."

The snowflakes on her hair and face, he thought, are like the rows of gold. A natural beauty, this descendant of desert wanderers and warriors.

"A bundle of myrrh is my well-beloved to me," Halstead said. "He shall lie all night between my breasts."

"*I* am supposed to say that, but I won't. Good night, dear friend."

"You will sleep with me, Eva. I will marry you."

"Garry, don't speak about things that can't happen."

He summoned a cab for her and kissed her again as he helped her in. "They will happen, if your parents think I'm good enough for you. Your lineage is more distinguished than mine, Eva."

Watching the horse-drawn carriage depart, thinking of her small figure snug in the cab, the blankets drawn over her, he shivered with desire. She would be his wife.

"I don't understand," Sarah Chain said. "This work for the union. It's over now that the strike is settled. How will you live? How can I quit my job?"

"You'll quit. There's plenty work for me."

Snow whirled in light gusts, spreading a cleansing dry powder over Haven Place. Jake helped Sarah out of Glauberman's Oakland. He had learned to drive. The lawyer had lent him the car for the day. On the last day of 1910 they would move into the house on Haven Place—the entire ground floor for themselves. A living room, a kitchen with a gas stove, a separate bedroom for Mutteh, a larger room at the rear for Jake and Sarah.

She refused to believe their good fortune, refused to believe it could continue. Frightened, subdued, she was wary of reaching too far.

"Jake, I'm afraid," she said. She limped on her cane around the large empty rooms. They would need furniture, rugs, curtains, Mutteh raced from room to room, sliding on the waxed parquet floors.

The landlord, who kept the flat immaculate, lived upstairs. He was named Aaron Rimkoff. An Orthodox Jew, an elder with a seat on the eastern wall of the synagogue, he owned a prosperous dairy store in the indoor market on Haven Place. He employed only Orthodox Jews. Rimkoff and his colleagues deplored his younger son, a scrappy lightweight and pool shark named Bobby Rimkoff.

Jake had signed a year's lease and paid three months' rent in advance. He didn't care. The money was sitting in the bank. There would be more to come.

"Work, work," Sarah said sadly. "I know what you're doing."

They were in the middle room. The house was attached to identical houses on either side. The interior rooms and hallway were dark.

"You *know*," he said with annoyance. "Don't talk about it."

"You are a *shtarker*. You hit people. You burned a place. You wrecked Finemaster. Everyone knows."

He took her in his arms. She was still pretty. She set her hair and used perfume now. "Don't be afraid. No one can hurt Jake Chain."

"The people at Feigenbaum's say the bosses will get you. They'll pay Moishe Nigger to kill you. They won't let you do what you do." She began to weep.

"Never. Glauberman says I'm a labor consultant. You hear, Sarah? A consultant, your husband."

She hobbled away from him into the rear room. This was nicer. A big room with two windows and a door to the kitchen. There was a view of a backyard. Earth, trees, open ground. Maybe in the spring Mrs. Rimkoff would let her plant vegetables and flowers. Window boxes with yellow daisies. No more basements, no more damp floors, toilets on the second floor. They would live in light, with fresh air, dry walls, a stove that worked, beds fit for human beings. It was wrong for her to *kvetch* at Jake.

"Wow, a yard!" Mutteh shouted. He was dancing in front

of the rear window. "Look, Papa—trees! I can build a snow-man!"

Jake joined his wife and son at the window. Maybe he was moving up too fast.

Chapter 13

"Say hello to Mr. Harris Tsipkin," Glauberman said, grinning. "Mr. Tsipkin, the famous Jacob Chain."

"Famous I don't know. Others things I know."

Harris Tsipkin was not quite five feet tall. His feet barely touched the floor as he sat in a cane-back chair. He kept his long *kaputa* buttoned. Only the lower half of his face peeked from a derby a size too big. Orthodox, he refused a shnapps, explaining to Glauberman that it wasn't the refreshment he feared but the unclean glass.

"So we'll get you a paper cup," Glauberman said.

"No thanks. A man never knows how they manufacture such *chazerei* in *America Gonif,* where all kinds magic things can happen."

Jake remained silent. He wore a dark gray vested suit, a stiff collar, a striped blue tie. But the massive hands gave him away: the hands of the *shtarker.*

"Let me explain Mr. Tsipkin's problem. He is the acting president of the Jewish Painters Guild—or as Mr. Tsipkin would say, *paintners.*"

Glauberman went on. Tsipkin and his colleagues were craftsmen, he told Jake. There was a building boom in Brownsville. Houses springing up all the way to the Queens county line. Yet they were having difficulty getting work. When they did, it was always below the union wage. Why? Because the crafts unions—painters, carpenters, electricians, bricklayers, masons, and plumbers—were controlled by gen-tiles.

"They won't give you a card?" Jake asked. His flat eyes were expressionless.

Tsipkin said, "For a hundred dollars, a hundred fifty, they'll give a temporary card. But next comes a test in En-glish words. Who understands it? My members know to mix paint, to put on sizing, to scrape, to clean, to patch a hole with plaster, to put up wallpaper. But examinations? So the unions take the hundred dollars and goodbye job."

Glauberman gave Jake a slip of paper. "Here is the address of the United Painters Guild of Brooklyn, Local Seventy-two. The president of this guild is Mr. Otto Lentz. You should arrange to have his office redone. After the redecorating job, I will call him on Mr. Tsipkin's behalf."

"I ain't sure I like this," the painter said. "No one should get hurt."

"What's to like or not like?" Glauberman asked. "It's how things get done."

Tsipkin scratched his short beard. "I have a wife and seven children to feed. I have union brothers who ain't working. Mr. Glauberman, whatever this man Chain does, keep it secret."

"Silence is our watchword. Mr. Tsipkin, you will give us a three-hundred-dollar deposit. When the work is done, another three hundred."

With a paint-stained hand, Harris Tsipkin obliged.

The wrecking of the United Painters Guild office on Bushwick Avenue would have gone more smoothly had not Mr. Otto Lentz and his secretary chosen to stay late.

Jake, Luigi, and Frank entered on rubber-soled shoes. They were masked. They surprised Mr. Lentz with his pants off, on top of Miss Margaret Mulhouser, on the office couch. She was a stout, big-boned woman. Even in the semidarkness of the December dusk, Jake and the Ferrantes could see that Mr. Lentz had to work extremely hard. In the flickering light of a coal stove, Jake could see a rose-colored petticoat on the frayed rug. Otto Lentz labored like Hercules atop her. He barely saw or heard the invaders.

She screamed as the men entered. But she followed orders, retrieved her underclothing, and allowed herself to be locked, sobbing, in the ladies' room. Mr. Lentz was bound and gagged, tied to his swivel chair. Jake, Frank, and Luigi methodically destroyed files, records, furniture, typewriters.

Halfway through their work, the union president tried to stumble toward the door. Jake hit him once with the flat of the hand. "It ain't personal," Jake said. "It's only my job. You'll get further instructions."

After a talk with Leo Glauberman, Otto Lentz decided that certain qualified craftsmen could be accepted as new brother unionists. Jobs opened for them at once. Harris Tsipkin forked over another three hundred, and each newly employed "paintner" now paid Leo Glauberman five dollars a month.

Before entering Reds Mulqueen's saloon (a place where normally he would not set foot), Ike Brunstein saw the Ferrantes' Dodge truck rumble by. Jake Chain, like a stone monument, was standing in it, with one of the Ferrante boys. They were holding together a pyramid of furniture. The lummox was moving to Haven Place, five doors down from the Heiligs, six from Dr. Abelman. The street with Abelman's beautiful trees. Two-story houses. Respectability. Ike shuddered. In wondrous ways did the revolution advance. He hated himself for letting Eva, Flugelman, and others convince him that Chain was needed.

Inside Mulqueen's, Benny Otzenberger, in a raccoon-lined coat and a plug hat (he was on his way to the mayor's New Year's party at City Hall), was drinking beer on the house. Ike, in his black cloak and flowing tie, felt like a mouse in a cage of snakes. Otzenberger was one of the few Jews who frequented Mulqueen's. It reeked of beer, cigar smoke, heavy farts. Sawdust floor, posters of busty actresses. *Where Jake Chain had grown up,* Ike reflected. *While I was disowning my faith for Marx. Which of us was more of an apostate?*

Benny wished Ike a Happy New Year. "You win, Brunstein. Who said I ain't for the workingman? Heshy tells me everything is hunky-dory now that the *tsatske* Heilig quit her job and is doing union business."

"You will kindly not refer to Eva Heilig as a *tsatske.*"

"No offense. Beer, Brunstein? Whiskey?"

"A glass of red wine will do, thank you."

Mulqueen looked the union president over with a gummy gray eye. Bomb thrower. Red. But scared of his own shadow.

"So what did you wish to tell me, Mr. Otzenberger?" asked Ike.

"Your friend Chain."

"What about him?"

"He's making it bad for everyone in Brownsville. He's in with Glauberman. Between the two of them, nobody'll be able to make honest graft anymore. Brunstein, the world has to go on. Unions, bosses, manufacturers, they all have to live, give, take."

In his haughtiest manner, Ike reminded the politico that Chain was not his responsibility. The big man had merely supplied protection for the harassed girls. A one-shot affair. Ike had no connection with Chain.

"No, but the *tsatske*—excuse me—Miss Heilig does. She's his cousin. It's no secret he's in love with her. He's got a thing in his pants the size of a salami for her and he'll listen to any—"

"You disgust me, Otzenberger."

"Forget any personal remarks. I'm warning you. Since they did a job on the painters' union, I ain't heard the end of it. Me, they blame. I'm supposed to keep Jews quiet."

"We got rid of Chain as soon as we won the strike."

Otzenberger shifted his elephantine ass and blew foam from his stein. "He's building a mob, Brunstein. Those greaseballs the Ferrantes. There's so many wop brothers, even the father, the barber, don't know. He's afraid to smack a kid in the street because it might be his. I see what's coming and I don't like it. Brownsville is respectable. So far I've run things pretty good."

"Mr. Otzenberger, it is no secret you sided with the bosses in every single strike until our girls stood up to you. Your son was the most notorious contractor for scabs in Brooklyn."

"I warned you, Brunstein. Wait, it'll come the turn of the tuxedo makers, the cloakmakers, the building trades, the bakers, the kosher butchers. Brunstein, talk to your fellow union-niks. You asked a puppy into your house to be a watchdog, right? It can grow up into a wolf and eat you."

Brunstein finished his glass of wine. He put his wide-brimmed black trilby on. "You seem to be in favor of hoodlums, so long as they work for the bosses. When we defend ourselves, it's un-American. Your son hired bullies to beat up women. Why the double standard?"

Otzenberger's piggy eyes were half-shut. He did not respond. He knew Ike spoke the truth. And he was on the spot. How to jump? Each side had its mobsters. All were dangerous. And there were votes from the workers who were swiftly becoming citizens.

"Tell Miss Heilig to warn her cousin Chain. He's looking to get himself in a cement mixer."

The Ferrante truck lurched up to 1667 Haven Place, came to a clanking halt. It was bitter cold. He and Luigi wrestled a new purple brocade-covered sofa off the back of the truck.

Jake had covered it with brown paper. Sarah loved the new furniture. Especially the dining-room table. Solid oak. Carved legs. Yes, Jake thought as he and Luigi hefted the sofa up the stone steps, it would be nice if they could have a real sabbath on Friday nights. Lights, *chalah*, wine. Like others in Brownsville. Mutteh—now Mortimer—could go to Hebrew school and learn to pray.

Frankie of the clipped ear followed. He bore two ornate brass lamps with green parchment shades. Jake had gotten a "special-for-you" price from the owner of the big furniture store on Rockaway Avenue. The Chain reputation had spread. It was amazing the way people wanted to do favors for him.

Jake rested his end of the sofa on the cast-iron balustrade. He searched his pocket for the key to the front door.

The landlord, Rimkoff, peered out the upstairs window watching his new tenant move in. Fancy furniture. More stuff piled on the Ferrante truck—overstuffed chairs, cabinets, dismantled beds. Rimkoff nodded sagely. So that's what came from being a *shtarker*, a man unafraid to use his fists. The landlord couldn't complain. Chain had paid up, flashed a thick roll, showed him his passbook from the East New York Savings Bank.

His hands freezing, Jake inserted the key and opened the front door. There was an enclosed vestibule between the street door and the door to the foyer. Stairs to the left led up to the Rimkoff apartment. Often Jake could hear Bobby Rimkoff, the future "champeen," doing laps or skipping rope when his father was not at home.

A second key opened the inner door. Luigi held the outside door open with a foot, allowing Frankie, the lampbearer, to enter. Outside, smoking a cigarette, Sal lounged against the truck, watching the rest of Jake's possessions. Snow settled on his dark, wraithlike figure.

"Wait, wait," Jake said. "The light on the wall. I paid rent already. Rimkoff should have the electric on."

He fumbled for the switch, found it, flicked on the yellow-gray hall light. The walls were newly painted—cream and chocolate brown. He pointed to the right, the front room, through which they could carry the couch.

Jake leading and the Ferrantes following, they maneuvered the sofa around the sharp corner into the barren room.

"Through the sliding doors," Jake said. "I'll open them. Put the couch down. Slow. Sarah will get sore if it gets scratched."

Luigi and Frank waited in the gloom. Business must be good for Jake, Luigi was thinking. Not bad for them either. They worked part-time for him now. The rest of the time they laid brick, poured cement.

"Door's stuck," Jake said. He lit a match. The lighting fixtures were missing in the front room. Something had wedged the door. He crouched, trying to pry the sliding doors apart with his hands.

The doors creaked open on dry runners.

Later he remembered only the first few shots. But the guns started shooting immediately when his huge figure was visible to the shadowy men in the center room.

Jake saw the orange-yellow flashes. Bursts of flame in the wintry dark. The noises were not as loud as he had expected, popping sounds, like firecrackers. His scalp was hot and wet; his legs rubber.

Behind him, he heard one of the Ferrante brothers screaming. The other shouted and ran.

Bullets ravaged Jake's head, his arms, his chest. He stumbled forward. "Bastards, fight," he said. "Throw away the guns."

No one was in back of him. Frankie Ferrante would no longer be ashamed of his clipped ear and bent nose. He was dead. A .38 slug had passed through his left eye. Luigi, winged on the left arm, holding a broken bone, raced to the street screaming for help, police, shouting at Sal.

Blood streaming from his scalp, his cheek, his hands, Jake plodded forward. He saw the two figures—derby, short coat on one; the other a fat man in a checked coat, a big cap. A fat man who moved on little feet, making gestures with little hands emptying his revolver.

Hit him again.
No use, I emptied both guns, the bastard's still coming.
He gotta be dead. He gotta.
I think we got one of the wops.

Doors slammed. Hard heels clattered on the parquet floor. There was a rush of icy air from the rear door. Sounds of huffing, a door closing, then silence.

Jake brushed blood from his eyes. He tasted blood, choked on blood, felt himself drowning in it. Wet and warm. A funny taste. Like iron. He hit the floor, thinking that it was one hell of a way to spend the first day in his new home.

Chapter 14

"He's made of iron," Dr. Abelman said to the young intern. "Twelve bullets."

Jake lay in Brownsville Jewish Hospital. He was covered with bandages. They had counted twelve holes in him. Scalp, cheek, jaw, both arms, chest, groin, legs. And not one of them fatal—unless hemorrhaging started or he developed an infection. Abelman and the resident had found eight of the lead pellets.

The ward held six patients, one of them dying noisily with gasps, moans, and delirious curses.

Abelman, brushing back his shock of Indian-black hair, shook his head in wonder as he looked at Jake's morphine-dulled body. Incredible. Apart from considerable loss of blood, a possible jaw fracture, and the new orifices opened in him, Chain was going to survive. The worst of the wounds, in the groin, had passed through, missing vital organs. Creased scalp, a hole in his cheek, a somewhat askew jaw, assorted other wounds—and alive.

"Your patient?" the intern asked.

"Yeah. Strong as an ox."

"Somebody really wanted to get rid of him."

Bandaged, splinted, covered with splotches of iodine and bloody stains, Jake slept soundlessly. His huge chest rose and fell. A rock, Abelman thought, indestructible. He knew Jake Chain was involved in dirty business. He'd heard stories of some not-so-nice things Chain and his buddies had done. But he had always liked the man—plain, honest, paying his bills on time.

At the entrance to the overheated ward, two detectives appeared. Sergeant Flannery approached the bed. "This Jacob Chain?"

Dr. Abelman nodded. The intern left.

"Can he talk?" Sergeant Pope asked.

"Usually," Abelman said. "But not with twelve holes in him and enough morphine to put a whale to sleep."

Flannery clucked admiringly. "Big bastard. Look at them

arms and legs." He squinted at Abelman. "Some dago with him was shot dead. Guy named Frank Ferrante. Another guinea got clipped, his brother Luigi. Know any of them?"

"I only know Chain. He won't be in condition to talk for another twenty-four hours. Loss of blood. Shock."

"Whaddya know about him?" Flannery asked.

"He's learning to read and write. Maybe he'll write you a letter when he learns the alphabet."

"Muscleman," Flannery said to his partner after Dr. Abelman had left. "His partner is Glauberman, the shyster. They teamed up a few weeks ago. Union rackets."

"I never heard of him."

"You will. If he lives much longer."

A bawling and shivering Sarah came to see Jake. She left Mutteh in the care of the Feigenbaums. It would terrify the child, she thought, to see his father all bloody. The incident had scarred her mind, filled her with fears, tremors, a desire to run, hide.

Incredibly, Jake was sitting up in bed. His jaw had been wired and he could barely speak. He took nourishment through a glass tube. Liquids would be all he could manage for a while. He was hungry and angry.

"Jake, everyone in Brownsville knows. Gangsters tried to kill you. Because you are a gangster too."

"Nah, nah," he mumbled. "I'm in business. Don't worry." Mashed, distorted, he sounded like a retarded child.

"I'm afraid. We paid for the furniture. The rent on the apartment. New clothes. Now what? You won't be able to work. You, my husband, you are almost dead."

Wailing, she tried to embrace him, but he cautioned her. Full of holes. Some of them still open. If she needed money, Leo Glauberman would take care of her. They had an agreement. In fact he wanted her to make sure the lawyer paid for Frank Ferrante's funeral.

Sarah told him she was afraid to go to the new apartment. The police had taken her there and asked questions. The floor was covered with blood, pools of it, where he had fallen in the center room, full of hot lead and holes.

"The furniture is okay?" he mumbled. "They didn't ruin the couch or the lamps?"

"Who cares about couches and lamps?" Sarah sobbed.

"I do." He tried to smile. He thought his jaw would come

apart. Wincing, he asked for her hand. "We'll move in, dear wife. Our new place."

"They'll try to kill you again."

In the night he bled copiously from the wound in his groin, developed a fever, became delirious. He thrashed in the narrow bed—too short for his giant frame—and stained the sheets crimson. The nurses took turns quieting him, changing bandages. But he did not appear weaker to them. To their amazement, running a fever of 103°, bleeding, in pain, he tried to climb out of bed.

"I got to get them," he said. "Nobody kills Jake."

It took two nurses and an intern to subdue him.

Awakening, he saw Eva standing at his bedside with a tall woman in a gray uniform and a straw hat. The city nurse who took care of the pickets at Baum's.

Eva had brought him hothouse flowers and a box of chocolates (which his wired jaw could not tolerate and he gave to the nurses) and fifty dollars in an envelope. This had been Meyer Flugelman's idea.

Ike had objected to giving money so blatantly to Chain. The newspapers were full of the story. The hoodlum Ferrante dead. The boss mobster Chain filled with bullets. A scandal. A disgrace. Rabbis and other respected members of the Brownsville community denounced the affair. *The union's fault! Bringing hoodlums into labor dealings! Using scoundrels like Crazy Jake Chain!*

The woman in the gray straw hat was Mildred Halstead, Sarah told Jake. Mildred was making sure that he got the best of attention. The Halsteads carried a great deal of weight in city hospitals.

"Thanks, lady," Jake said, through semilocked teeth.

"Twelve bullets," Eva said. "Jake, how awful. We were afraid we'd never see you again. We'll get those men. Rimkoff gave a description of the two who ran into the backyard."

"I know who they are. I'll take care of them myself."

He told Eva that until he got out, he wanted protection for Sarah and his son. They were to be moved into the new apartment.

"The police also say you know who shot you," Eva said. "But they said you aren't cooperative."

"What does that mean?"

"You won't tell them anything." Eva looked at his smashed, discolored face. A crude and hard man. But he had a primitive sense of justice.

"The cops can ask me a hundred times. I won't tell them."

Mildred Halstead cocked her head. What a strange man! (Really, she thought, what a strange *Jew*.) He was huge, muscled, fair. A Viking warrior recovering from wounds of pike and sword.

"Why won't you tell them?" Eva asked.

Through the miasma of alcohol, iodoform, disinfectant soap, he smelled Eva's sweet scent. He would love her all his life. "Because, Cousin Eva, it's my fight. I'll get them."

If you are not killed, she thought.

Garrison Halstead appeared in the doorway. Halstead had talked to other reporters. Gang warfare. The respectable Jewish community shaken by gunfire, a murder, dreadful acts of vengeance. And here was the cause of it all—Crazy Jake, cousin of his beloved.

Halstead did not enter the ward. Jake saw him. A tall man in a fur-collared black coat, eyeglasses on a black string. The long jaw and white teeth. He knew about him. This man also loved Eva. Jake had heard stories. The two of them at fancy restaurants, the Broadway theater.

Eva kissed Jake's bruised forehead. As soon as he was stronger, Dr. Abelman said, they'd start pulling the rest of the bullets out of his body.

That night, under morphine, Jake dreamed of making love to Eva. Bleeding, suppurating, his mind muddled, he had to battle the surge of sexual desire that elevated his fever, inflamed his wounded groin.

Eva questioned Bobby Rimkoff about what he had seen that night. The Ferrante brothers—Luigi, Sal, Vince, Baggie, and the others—had no interest in her investigation. They would "take care" of the men who killed their brother in their own way. Besides, she was a woman, and it was none of her business.

Rimkoff was a slow-talking youth, forever shadowboxing, snorting through a mashed nose, unable to string sentences together with much sense. Some thought him retarded. But he told her (as his Orthodox parents wrung their hands and threatened to have Sarah evicted) that he had seen two men climbing the rear fence after the shooting.

"I seen 'em," Bobby said. "One was a fat guy, I 'member,

'cause he couldn't climb the fence. He got his pants tore. The guy in a derby pulled him over."

Moishe Nigger and the Meal Ticket.

Armed with this knowledge, Eva walked into the 71st precinct and demanded to see Captain Hanratty. In front of the red-haired officer, she made Bobby repeat his eyewitness testimony. The young pugilist did so. If a bit awed by the captain, promptings by a determined Eva jogged his memory.

Hanratty winked at a sergeant. Freckles scattered as he grinned.

"What does that mean, captain?" Eva asked. "What's so funny?"

"Miss Heilig, it sounds like you've coached your friend. Besides, he isn't exactly a witness. Punchy. Cuckoo. How long you been in school, Rimkoff?"

"I finished fourth grade. I ain't neither punchy."

"That has no bearing on his testimony. Captain, a man was murdered on Haven Place. Mr. Chain took twelve bullets in his body and might have been killed."

"Let's be honest, Miss Heilig. It was scum versus scum. I can't go arresting people on the testimony of this half-wit."

Captain Hanratty whispered something in the sergeant's ear. The latter retired to a rear room and phoned Francis Fagan Dullahan. Both officers knew who had killed Frank Ferrante and made a clay pigeon of Chain.

Dullahan gave the word to the cops: *Lay off.* Morris Pearlberg and Herman Wesselberg were a pair of ticking bombs. If ever *they* opened their traps, the political structure would be in trouble. The sergeant was given his orders: Softsoap the Heilig bitch, warn Rimkoff to shut up.

Captain Hanratty got the word in whispers. He turned on a charming smile and used his softest Sligo accents. "Well, then, we'll look into it. A man in a derby? A fat man? That should narrow our suspects down to about a million, Miss Heilig. A grand challenge it is."

Eva's eyes burned. "You know who they are. The same men who attacked our pickets."

"There's no evidence, Miss Heilig. If I were you, I'd forget it. You too, pinhead."

Not unexpectedly the executive board of the bathrobe makers union was of the same opinion. Let well enough alone. Too bad the Italian—what was his name?—died. Be grateful Chain was alive, but he was an embarrassment any way you looked at it. *Shtarkers* had been used as a desperate measure. Now that things were settling down, why start up?

"Life means little to a bum like Chain," intoned elegant Boris Chachkes of the Jewish Trades Council. "We have no obligation to seek justice. That is the civil authorities' job. Such members of the *lumpenproletariat* can be discarded when they outlive their usefulness."

Eva raged at him: "You ingrate! You arrogant know-it-all! Chain saved your necks! He put the fear of God into the bosses! Now that he's dying, you won't help find the people who tried to kill him?"

Chachkes blew white smoke to the ceiling, played with his ivory cigarette holder. The less said about Crazy Jake the better. No union officer should *in any way* hint at a relationship between the labor movement and savages like Chain.

"Mr. Chachkes is right," Ike said. "It's the only way." He was less eager to placate Eva these days. He knew he had lost her to Halstead.

"You are cowards, hypocrites, and mealy-mouthed schemers," Eva said. "And you will not stop me from what I intend to do."

Several days later, an interview with Eva under Garrison Halstead's byline appeared in the *Eagle*. In it Eva charged that Frank Ferrante and Jacob Chain had been attacked by Morris Pearlberg and Herman Wesselberg of the notorious "Moishe Nigger Gang." The headline read:

BATHROBE UNION OFFICIAL CHARGES
NEW YORK HOODLUMS KILLED FERRANTE

****

Enemies of "Crazy Jake" Chain
Named by Eva Heilig as Gunmen
Who Shot Him Twelve Times

Leo Glauberman also gave Halstead a statement. The lawyer's intuition told him to remain silent, but he admitted to Halstead that there had been bloody threats from Moishe Nigger ever since he had been parboiled. It was no secret that Pearlberg hated and feared Crazy Jake.

"I know," Glauberman told Halstead after Eva had convinced him to speak out, "that Chain is no angel. But that hardly justifies murder. Justice must prevail, or the labor movement will become an arena for fraternal carnage."

The *Eagle* article was like an explosion from one of Jake's gasoline bombs. Phones buzzed. New York papers called Eva. Old police reporters with underworld connections found Moishe Nigger in his *shtuss* house on the Lower East Side. Pearlberg denied it. He was out of town that day. The Meal Ticket was visiting his mother in Hartford the night Ferrante and Chain were shot. Chain was crazy, a liar, a killer.

F. F. Dullahan and Benny Otzenberger, disturbed by Eva's interview, held a meeting in the boss's red brick mansion in Brooklyn Heights.

"Tell Hanratty to move his ass," Dullahan said. "Get the New York cops to haul those tramps in, question them, confirm their alibis, and turn them loose. Benny, they are grand fellows, the Nigger and the Meal Ticket. But we must make sure they keep their mouths shut."

Pearlberg and his fat aide were taken in and questioned for an afternoon by the police. They were turned loose for lack of evidence two hours later.

Again, Garrison Halstead wrote a long article on the Chain-Ferrante affair, and again Eva was quoted.

"These killers have no right to roam the streets," the Golden Voice said. "The police and the politicians are protecting them. I will not be silent until they are brought to justice."

Chapter 15

January's icy wind howled through the Abelman house. A hell of a way to start 1911, the doctor thought.

Unable to sleep, he nevertheless muttered his usual litany of curses when the doorbell buzzed at one in the morning.

"Bastards won't let you live," Abelman said. He got out of bed, his feet searching for the scuffed slippers. It was frigid in the house; the basement coal fire had been banked.

"I'll go, Sam," his wife said.

"Nah, nah. It's my job." He was young, strong, undeterred by night calls. In a snowstorm two days ago he had rented a horse and sleigh and toured Brownsville like a grim Santa Claus.

Ableman walked through the darkened house to the front

window and threw it open. January air rushed at him and made him catch his breath.

The buzzing had not stopped. He stuck his head out, holding the pajama collar around his throat.

In the half-light of the snow-covered street he saw a woman standing on his top step, face upturned. She was crying.

"Dr. Abelman—please—help—"

"I'll be right down."

The physician hurried down the stairs, went through the foyer into the vestibule (the house was a replica of the Chains' and the Heiligs'), turned the lock and opened the bolt.

Eva Heilig, her face bloodied and bruised, collapsed in his arms. "Doctor—please—take me inside. They did this—hurt me. . . ."

(Years later, Abelman would recall that even battered and half-conscious, Eva Heilig had shown little fear. He marveled at her. Iron in the girl. She was a woman he would never forget, long after she had left Brownsville.)

Mrs. Abelman—a dignified woman who taught poetry at the Lyceum—came down to help.

Eva gasped out the story. Two men had grabbed her when she left the Utica Avenue subway station and was walking down Park Place. They had dragged her into a hallway and stuffed cloth in her mouth, punched her repeatedly.

"You didn't shout for help?" Abelman asked. He lifted her eyelids. No sign of internal bleeding. But she had an enormous purpling welt under each eye. The upper lid of the left eye was twice its size.

"They said they knew me," she said. "That they wanted to talk to me—" Eva covered her face and sobbed.

Abelman said to his wife: "Make some hot tea. With a shot of brandy."

Eva talked. The doctor wiped the blood from her face and she winced. She was coming home from a lecture she'd given at the Young Socialist League. A lot of talk, plans, theorizing. (She was getting a reputation. She was in demand as a speaker. The beautiful girl who had won the bathrobe strike.) She could find no cab. Tired of waiting for the St. John's Place trolley car, she began to walk. Arctic air invigorated her.

"You knew these galoots?" Abelman asked.

She shook her head. Strikebreakers, thugs. She had tangled with them before. She covered her face and sobbed in great convulsive heaves. Abelman patted her head like a father.

Eva took off her dress. The physician looked for fractures, internal bleeding. There was a severe bruise on her upper back, across the shoulder blades. The skin was scraped as if she had fallen heavily.

"They threw me against a radiator in the hall," she said, wiping her nose. "Hit my back on it, punched my eyes."

"The bastards should have their hands cut off. Anything special hurts?"

"This wrist. I fought with them. One of them twisted it."

Mrs. Abelman returned with the brandy-laced tea, kissed Eva, and left. Did she want to call her parents?

"No, please. Not yet."

"The police?" asked the doctor.

Eva shook her head. "They know me from the other side of the law," she said. "The Red, the agitator. Oh, that hurt when you touched my wrist. I twisted it again trying to get away."

"The wrist may be broken, Eva," Abelman said. "I'll put a cast on it. We can have it X-rayed tomorrow. Lie down and tell me anything you want."

He began to soak plaster-caked strips of cloth in warm water. She cried softly and he gave her something for the pain.

"Dr. Abelman—they did to me—they . . ."

"What? What did the galoots do?"

"They tried to rape me."

Abelman breathed deeply. "I'll have to examine you. You know what I mean."

"It's all right."

Abelman locked the door. Gently, he conducted the examination, trying to be detached, to suppress the anger in him that said: *Go out and kill the villains who did this.*

He found bleeding but no sign of penetration. He did not have the heart to ask her anything further. She would weep, sniffle, wipe her face, and then, with a courage that astonished him, would stop. Analytically, detached, she began to question him. Was it—could she have children? Would a husband know . . . ?

"You're all right," he said. No rupture of tissue. "You must have fought like hell."

She sat up and buttoned her chemise. "I scratched one of them so he'll have marks on his face a long time."

"They didn't do what they wanted to, Eva," the doctor said. "You're what you were. I know it isn't easy to accept, and it's easy for me to make speeches. But you aren't hurt that badly. It's the broken wrist we have to fix."

The doctor wrapped layers of plastered gauze around her wrist, reducing the fracture by manipulating and extending her arm.

She began to sob again, racking, gulping noises, as if she could not suck enough air into her lungs. She rested her aching head against the doctor's chest and would not stop bawling. They must have hit her fifty times, he thought. But she had fought back. He wondered why they had let her go before finishing their dirty work. The noise may have awakened people. Someone entering the building. Miraculously, she had walked two long blocks.

When she was dressed, he let her rest and finish the tea. He wrote a prescription for her pain. He had some morphine pills in his medicine cabinet, ointment for the bruises. These would tide her over, help her sleep.

At the door she made him promise to tell no one about the attempted rape. And until she decided what she wanted to do, she would not name the men who attacked her.

"I will use it for political advantage, for the *cause*," she said. The Heilig chin thrust forward. The eyes were dry, eager for a fight. "I don't mean a thing, Dr. Abelman. But what I'm fighting for does. I'll use this to destroy our enemies. What happened to me is our secret."

"I'll walk you home if you wait a minute."

"You're in your bathrobe, and it's cold and dark outside."

The physician laughed. "I'm tough, Eva. Remember when I ran the summer playground and taught you gymnastics?"

She smiled. The doctor put on overshoes and a heavy coat. He called to his wife that he'd be gone a minute, and escorted Eva to her house. Brave girl, he thought. Too brave.

Her parents reacted with hysteria, Brunstein and Flugelman with fear, Halstead with Protestant indignation.

Avner and Matla Heilig and her brothers Abe and Sol were all for a full report to the police, a demand that the ruffians be apprehended. Eva, her broken wrist in a bright red sling, her bruised eye closed, dissuaded them. Abe and Sol swore vengeance, but only halfheartedly. They were scholars, not brawlers. She lied that she did not know her attackers. Two strange men.

Brunstein and Flugelman wrung hands, feared for themselves, worried about her: She talked too much, talked back, challenged people unnecessarily.

"But the union is not recognized!" she said. "We don't have a union shop!"

Ike said he would bear more of the burden.

"Eva, you must not be on the barricades," Flugelman said protectively. "You must be careful. You are a woman."

"It had nothing to do with my union work, Meyer. It was a robbery by criminals."

Halstead proposed an article for the *Eagle*, kissed her battered face and her immobilized wrist, suggested that his father's political connections—more awesome than Dullahan's —be utilized. Obviously the bosses' thugs had done this. Revenge. The Chain business. They feared him. Having failed to kill Chain, they were warning Jake to lay off. If they could not murder him with twelve slugs, Halstead said, they would go after an unprotected woman.

"I am not weak and I do not feel unprotected," Eva said. "I will walk the streets at night. I will make speeches and I will challenge the oppressors."

"My darling, lower the red flag. You're too good to be shedding blood for it. You should be Mrs. Halstead."

She mocked him. "We could have the wedding reception in my mother's candy store."

He kissed her. They were in his apartment on Gramercy Park. She would not let him make love to her. She feared that she had been damaged. She suspected Abelman may have lied to comfort her. But she did not *feel* different. When they had spread her legs, punched her, tried to force their way into her, her struggles had been so intense that now she barely remembered what happened.

"Let me love you," he said. "I've never loved anyone. Anyone. Eva, my exotic Oriental."

"Stop, Garry. I'll laugh at you. And don't kiss my wrist again. It hurts."

On a warm February day Jake Chain learned the truth about the attack on Eva Heilig, from the "hoo-er" Minnie Fassbender.

He was dressing, moving slowly—the wounds had healed, but his muscles and bones were sore—when Minnie began to prattle about a visit she'd had recently with Moishe Nigger.

"Pearlberg?" Jake asked, buttoning his fly. He winced. The bullet had passed through his groin, missing vital parts, but the stitching and repair work—"the plumbing," as Abelman called it—left him with pains, the itching and strain of the healing process.

"Yeah, him. The one you boiled."

"I thought he was out of Brooklyn."

"I went to his place in New York. A big party on Washington's Birthday for the Morris Pearlberg Benevolent Association. He wanted extra girls. He ain't as good as you, Jake."

"So what did Pearlberg say?"

"Wouldn't *you* like to know." Minnie stuck her tongue out at him. She wrapped a kimono around her fat body. Nowadays, when he was finished with her Jake always felt a mild disgust. He came to her once a week; each visit satisfied him briefly, but left him empty and frustrated. Yet he needed the release. He and Sarah were strangers at night. He had bought twin beds, spent nights away from home, playing cards, visiting prostitutes, sometimes eating at the Ferrantes', where there was always a dinner setting for their *goombah* Jake.

"Tell me."

"When I told him how good he was, he give me an extra twenty dollars. And he said . . ." She stopped talking, walked to the mirror, and in the rose-colored light began painting her face.

Jake studied her overstuffed behind. "Hey," he said. "What did Moishe Nigger tell you?"

"Nothing, Jake. Nothing."

He twisted her arm behind her back. The green kimono opened, revealing her pink thighs, the gartered black stockings. She cried.

"The Nigger said he and the fat guy screwed Eva Heilig," Minnie said. "Jake, don't say I told you."

"He said this?"

"They got her in a house on Park Place. When she got beat up? I seen her with her arm in a sling. I wondered what happened."

"What else did he say?"

"He said they beat her up good so she wouldn't hire people like you no more and then they . . ."

"What else?" His voice was distant, an echo.

"He said if they couldn't kill a horse like you, they would kill *her* someday."

His blood was thundering. The old street anger. Different from the time he fought the men who tried to steal the keg of beer. Different from all the times he had thrown foremen down steps, battled Moishe's gang on the picket lines, scattered wagonloads of scabs.

This was something else. Now he understood why Eva was so secretive about the "robbery." Why only a halfhearted report to the police had been made.

"I don't like how you look, Jake," Minnie whimpered.

He jammed his cap on his head, paid her, and walked stiffly to the door. He did not hear her appeals.

"Jake, please, don't let them find out I told you. They'll kill me!"

In the street, he gasped for air, watched kids playing stickball under the streetlights, tried to control the rage in his chest. They could not kill him. So they had turned to an easier victim. They would pay.

Chapter 16

Jake told only one person, Luigi Ferrante. And he told him little. "Just find out for me," Jake said, "where the Nigger lives, where he goes, what he does at night."

A few days later, Luigi and Baggie scouted Moishe Nigger's territory. They learned he was separated from his wife and lived in a walk-up on Rivington Street. Usually he spent evenings at his *shtuss* house and came home late with his bodyguard, Duffy Plotkin. One or two o'clock. He drank little, carried a gun, talked about killing Crazy Jake Chain someday.

Jake and Luigi visited the street where the Nigger lived. A lively place—tenements, pushcarts. Less so in the winter. Late at night it would be deserted. Laboring Jews, peddlers, housewives, and students went to bed early and rose early. Some of them journeyed halfway across the city to jobs. Only people like Moishe stayed up late, gambling and whoring.

"The chicken market," Jake said to Luigi. "Down from where he lives?"

"Three stores down."

"Pick the lock for me the night I go."

"I want to work on him also."

Jake shook his head. "It's personal. Just break the lock."

Jake heard at Dannenfelser's poolroom that Plotkin was fighting in Boston on Saturday night. Good chance the Nigger would not go. Duffy was washed up, a bum who took tank jobs. Bobby Rimkoff had knocked him out in two rounds.

Sarah asked where he was going so late at night.

"Business meeting," Jake said.

"Eleven o'clock? Jake, you're starting again. Full of holes, almost dead . . . Don't go."

"It's nothing. Night shift in a hat factory in Queens. The workers need advice."

"Where? What Queens? You never went there."

"Glauberman asked me to go." He kissed her cold forehead. She was always cold, even in the overheated apartment. "If anyone asks, I was home all night. *All night,* you understand, dear wife?"

"Jake, come to me. We'll try again. Like a man and a woman who are married."

"Maybe some other time. I'll be back late."

Luigi drove him to the East Side and dropped him two blocks from Moishe Nigger's home. If necessary, Jake was prepared to come back night after night to find him.

He waited in the alley next to the chicken market. Luigi broke the lock on the side door and vanished. Jake fingered the open latch and stuck his head in once. No lights. No watchman. It stank of chicken shit and chicken blood. The doomed birds huddled in the cane cages. Some life, Jake thought. Not much different from the way people were treated. Food, crapping, a slit throat.

He hid in the angle that the poultry mart formed with the street and watched two cops walk by. A drunken Irish laborer rolled into the gutter. With surprising vigor, he came alive and started to punch when the cops tried to drag him off. They clubbed him mercilessly. He spat at them, cursed, fell, was dragged to his feet again. They clubbed him all the way to the corner.

Sorry, buddy, Jake thought. The busier cops were with drunks, the better for him.

Two weary prostitutes ambled by, handbags slung over their shoulders after a hard night's labor. A peddler shoving an empty cart—where was he going at such an hour?—creaked by.

Close to one o'clock, when he was bone-chilled, half-paralyzed, suffering pain from the healing wounds, he saw Moishe Nigger.

The Horse Poisoner was alone. No bodyguard. But armed, Jake was sure. After all, Pearlberg was extorting money from a hundred East Side businessmen. Anything from pushcart peddlers to factory owners. He looked fatter and huskier. He seemed sober, whistling between his teeth, jaunty. Pearl-gray derby, beaver-collared gray coat, gleaming black shoes. He was puffing a Havana. Near the market he stopped, tossed the butt in the gutter. Then he opened his fly and urinated against a garbage can.

Like a dog, Jake thought. And he'll die like a dog.

Jake came out of the alley and walked behind the Nigger. He grabbed him by the throat with his right arm while he cranked the Nigger's arm behind his back.

The victim writhed. Gurgling noises issued from his throat. Once he tried to reach behind him—Jake's old trick—and grab Chain's crotch. Jake almost broke his hand. There was less and less strength in Moishe's arms.

"Ch—Chee . . ."

Pearlberg was trying to say Jake's name. Chain's right forearm pressed tighter against Nigger's neck. No words issued from the mobster's mouth. Pearlberg lurched, kicked, strained his muscles. Their legs entangled and they rolled in the gutter. Jake would not release him. He could feel the heavy body going limp. But he did not want him to die in the street.

With an effort that made him gasp, caused the wounds to scream, Jake dragged Pearlberg to his feet. He hit him in the neck with the edge of his right hand. The Nigger wheezed, coughed, lumbered toward Jake. He pulled a pistol from his belt. Chain grabbed his right arm. The gun fell from his fingers. Jake kicked him twice and pulled him into the alley.

"Chain, don't be crazy," the Nigger croaked. "You and me, we can work."

"You tried to kill me."

Something had happened to the Nigger's voice, something had been crushed and deformed in his throat. "My guys will get you. A hundred bullets this time."

At the door to the chicken market, Pearlberg tried to reach for a second revolver, but it had slipped inside his belt and was resting on his left buttock. Jake saw the floundering right hand and smashed it. He yanked the pistol from the Nigger's belt, stuck it in a side pocket.

"Heeelp!" the Nigger screamed. "Murder! Heeelp!"

Spinning Pearlberg around, Jake brought his forearm and fist to the hoodlum's throat, squeezed it until Moishe made gargling sounds. Like my old horse dying, Jake thought.

Jake kicked the door of the chicken market open and shoved Moishe Nigger inside. His gray derby had fallen off. The pomade on his kinky black hair clotted Jake's nostrils. Did Eva, he wondered, sniff the fancy goo when the Nigger and the Meal Ticket forced her legs apart?

"Lay off, Chain, lay off—we'll make a deal—"

"Tell me about the deal you made with Eva Heilig, Nigger. It felt good when you raped her?"

"I didn't—it was Meal Tick—"

"It was you, you bastard. For that you have to die, Nigger."

There were no more appeals from the mobster. He lived in violence; he would spit defiance.

"Can't keep her mouth shut. I shoved it in her. Me and the Meal Ticket—took turns—good. You shmuck, Chain, you'll never even see it. You like what I'm saying?"

Jake braced a knee in Moishe's back and shoved him toward the center of the chicken market. Mashed odors clogged his nostrils—chicken shit, chicken feed, chicken blood, street dirt.

A steel drum stood amid the cages of clucking, jittery birds. The drainings from the slashed necks of hens finished off by the ritual slaughterer, the *shochet*. In bloodstained smock, with sharp steel knife, he dispatched them. Jake had often heard the screams, seen the knife flash.

"This is how a dog like you has to die, Nigger," Chain said.

"I screwed her," Nigger wheezed hoarsely. "You never will, you dumb bastard."

"But I'm alive and you're dead."

With his left fist, he punched Pearlberg at the base of the skull. Then he lifted the heavy body and dumped it head-down into the drum. He listened awhile to the gurgling, bubbling noises. One iron hand kept the frizzy hair and dark face immersed in blood. Jake watched bubbles rise to the surface and burst. The bubbles got smaller and smaller. Then they stopped.

Moishe Nigger's ass and legs dangled over the side of the drum. A big hen. A fat chicken for some East Side housewife.

In the alley Jake found the gray derby. He dusted it carefully, the way he had often seen Moishe Nigger do it, and returned to the market. He sailed the derby into the drum of blood.

The nifty hat floated on the surface like a child's boat.

1960
Myron Malkin's Notebook

She's sitting half in shadow, half in sunlight on the glassed-in porch. The edges of her face glow with gold but the fine features are shadowy. In profile, with summer brightness filtered through the green glass, she looks astonishingly young and beautiful. One of the most beautiful women I have ever seen. By my computation she is now seventy-four years old.

We're alone on the porch. Outside, the steely blue Atlantic beats at the lifeless gray sands of Long Beach, New York. A handful of bathers on the beach. Sun too hot, air too humid. But inside the Star of Zion Nursing Home it's frigid. Mechanical iciness. I wonder whether it's good for the old bones and sagging bodies of the frail residents.

The chill doesn't seem to bother Eva Heilig Halstead. Although she is crippled and anchored to a wheelchair, she's alert and talkative, smiles at my jokes and flashes healthy teeth. There's sparkle—damned near flirtation—in her green eyes. I understand now why men fell in love with her. Why the immigrant girls braved the picket lines at the urging of "The Golden Voice."

"Of course I know you," she says. She turns her face to accept the glow of the sun. Her skin is a bit wrinkled, but it has a healthy sheen. No makeup. Mass of snowy hair piled high. As raffish as a Gibson girl's. "You are Dr. Abelman's son."

"Nephew, Mrs. Halstead."

"I don't use my married name. I'm Eva Heilig again. For a few years it was important to be Eva Halstead—when I wrote, when I lectured. But it was really fake. Married, yes. But a Halstead? Never."

"I looked up the old newspapers. It was quite a shocker. Jewish girl from Brownsville marrying rich New York WASP."

"Oh, yes. Quite an event."

I show the old woman a clipping. *"New York Times.* June

4, 1912. Want to read it? About the minister. And the way your family and your union sisters mingled with the Four Hundred in Sag Harbor."

"Yes, yes. You know, young man—what's your name?—it ended rather early, all that storybook romance."

I know, I tell her.

She's a legend. Not too well known anymore. She's been ill and out of action a long time. Paget's disease, a weakness and softening of her bones. Her legs are extended in metal braces. Her spine is askew. But the softening has not affected her face. The lines are firm, the forehead and cheekbones elegantly formed, the chin as determined as it was when she rallied the working girls.

"*Die Goldeneh Shtimmeh*," I say. "The Golden Voice. You're in the books about the American labor movement."

"Am I? I've lost interest. Tell me, how is Dr. Abelman and your aunt, that lovely woman who taught poetry."

"Uncle Doc died five years ago. A heart attack. My aunt is fine."

"A wonderful man. He was the Heilig family doctor. My brother Abe swore by him, my brother Sol, all of us. A temper and a bad tongue, but he cared about people. Abe became a doctor because of him. You know Abe?"

I do. A. M. Heilig, M.D., is chief of surgery at a New York hospital.

She keeps derailing me with questions about Uncle Doc and about Brownsville. How is it today? she asks. Black, I tell her. The poplars on Haven Place that my uncle planted? Dead. Stripped bare by wild *shwarzer*s. They come and go, the poorest, the dispossessed.

Abelman, Heilig, Chain. We lived on the same street.

"The Chain family, Miss Heilig. Can I ask about them?"

"Dr. Abelman's nephew can call me Eva. What about the Chains?"

I explain my notion. A magazine piece. Maybe a book. An American story. From a founding father who was a street hoodlum to a grandson who endows a medical school.

She laughs. "Myron, what a nice idea. The irony of it. Have you spoken to Martin?"

Yes, I think to myself, I've met that sleek, smart, dark young man. He wants no part of my article. *Town and Country* is fine. Black-tie evenings. Charity balls. Presidential commissions. Forget about the way it started. How a talent for busting heads grew into one of the hugest fortunes in America.

"Martin is a good boy," Eva says. "Oh, his wife, DeeDee, gives him fancy ideas. But they're happy. And so rich. They take care of me. I'm penniless, you know. I never asked Garrison Halstead for a nickel. I never earned much with my lectures and writing. An old broken-down Socialist."

Memories muddle my mind. The two-story attached homes of Haven Place. Old Brownsville. I recall Morty Chain, Crazy Jake's son, driving up to my uncle Doc's office in a black LaSalle. He'd moved his family from Haven Place to Ocean Parkway. A red brick mansion with a Spanish-tile roof and green-shuttered windows. My aunt said there were twenty rooms in the house, including a servants' wing. And an armed bodyguard, a big black, on duty. The second-generation Chain was getting shot at like his father. It ran in the family, this talent for becoming a moving target.

But nobody shoots at Mr. Martin Chain.

The old lady seems to be reading my mind. She asks me again about Martin—industrialist, real-estate king, adviser to governors.

"He was polite but not helpful. He says if he wants anything written about the Chain empire, he'll hire a professor to do it."

"And how can I help you?"

The loose green housecoat disguises the cruel curving of her spine. Now, shifting her slender body in the wheelchair and fixing those luminous eyes on me, I see the warmth and the spirit that made men love her. Garrison Halstead had not hesitated to leap across centuries of tradition to marry her.

"You're part of the Chain saga."

"Am I really? My daughter ended up fighting them."

"But you were related."

"Distantly. *Landsleit*. Does it matter anymore?"

"People say Jake Chain was in love with you."

"I suppose he was. That poor ox. I know, the newspapers called him a hoodlum, a gangster, a murderer. But . . ."

"What about the early days? How did Jake become your *shtarker*? The tough guy who'd protect your girls?"

She tells me an involved story that I can't quite follow. Something about Jews praying at a stream on Rosh Hashanah. A gang of toughs attacking them. Jake scattering the hoodlums.

"And Jake never went to shul, he couldn't pray." She laughs. "He learned to read and write when he was twenty-five! My brothers taught him. Did you know that?"

"Sol? The prosecutor?"

"Sol and Abe both. I can see so clearly the parlor in our house on Haven Place. Jake, so huge, with arms like a Greek statue's. Ashamed because he thought he was stupid. Sol used to go over his spelling.

"The Chains. They were a force of nature, Myron. The ambition was in their blood. *America Gonif*, where miracles occur, was invented for them. I liked Jake. A crippled wife. No education. An orphan. But there was tenderness and honesty in him."

"But Eva, he was a *killer*. It's no secret. He did away with people. He was never convicted, but from what I've read there's little doubt that he—"

"I don't condone it. He lived violently. But we helped create him. He was our *golem*."

"And his son?"

"Mortimer? Mutteleh? Oh, he was a *chuchem*, a *kluger*. You know what that means?"

"Clever."

"I'm sure you have plenty of clippings from the papers. Bootlegging was not my business. I was a Socialist. Birth control, pacifism, abortion, women's rights, rights for black people. Name a cause, I was part of it. Who cared about bootlegging?"

"And Martin?"

"How can I dislike him? He supports me. A thousand dollars a month to keep me in this kosher jail? Surrounded by ghosts, people I can't talk to? Who in this place knows about dialectical materialism? Anyway, I'm grateful. I've had Paget's disease for six years. A bad way to die, Myron. But I should not complain. Martin is—well, he's *Martin*. His younger brother, Davey, lives in Israel. He writes once a year. Iris, the sister, is in Hollywood. Martin got all of Mortimer's money. Believe me, Myron, it was *money*. Tens of millions, more. So much they never know."

"I admire him for helping you out."

"I'm nothing to him. If he doesn't come to see me, neither does my own daughter."

I consult my notebook. *Lillian Halstead, lawyer, Department of Justice, Washington, D.C.* I ask about her.

"Lillian? She was closer to me than she was to Mr. Halstead. I think he loved me so much he could not love our child. Do I sound conceited?"

She's crying. A film of tears on her exquisite eyes.

"I'm sorry," I say. "I didn't mean to revive so many memories."

"Oh, I'm enjoying it. So few visitors. No one to shmooze with. You know what it is to shmooze?"

"In the garment district. They stand in the street and talk on the lunch break. Politics, the union, business, sports."

"I was a good talker, Myron."

"And a marvelous woman. You still are."

"I wish Dr. Abelman were alive. I'd tell him what a nice nephew he has. I hope you write the book."

"But the Chains . . ."

She looks as puzzled as I do.

"What made them go?" I ask. "Where did they get the nerve, the ambition, the energy, the brains? Jake was a hoodlum. But he was rich when he died. He had the unions scared out of their wits. Look at Mortimer. Eva, he was so powerful during Prohibition, even the Italians and Irish, with all their murderers, couldn't touch him. They'd try, and *they'd* end up dead. And Martin. He's on the society or business page three times a week. How?"

"It was there for the taking, Myron. Some old Bolshevik once said Lenin found power lying in the street and picked it up."

"And the Chain family?"

"Something like that. The money was there. Ways to make money. Ways to grab power. They grabbed it."

I kiss her goodbye. Nearby, the Atlantic beats against the bleached sand. Eva Heilig smells sweet, clean, and young. I would have fallen in love with her myself fifty years ago.

I turn for a last look at her. She is nodding faintly as if reminding herself of her tenuous hold on life. The late-afternoon sun forms another edging of gold on her profile. The white hair is touched with glory.

I wish Uncle Doc were alive. I'd ask him about Paget's disease. He knew everything. He might have told me what kind of course it runs. What her prospects are. And surely he would have visited her.

But I have the feeling she doesn't want to see people. She was holding back. Unwilling to talk too much about her past or about her rogue relatives the Chains.

PART II

1922

Chapter 17

"A little shnapps, gentlemen?"

Leo Glauberman removed a fifth of Mount Vernon from his desk, found three shot glasses, turned the bottle of booze so the sunlight sparkled on the brown glass.

"The real thing. You see what the practice of law does for a man, Mr. Wallowitz?"

Jake Chain was seated in a corner of the law office. He was rubbing the long white scar in his awry jaw, watching the byplay. Glauberman was warming up a new client. Ike Brunstein, seated next to the client, maintained a hands-off attitude. Ike was prematurely gray. His scruffy moustache drooped, his slouch was more pronounced, and he looked shrunken inside his sleeveless cloak of black alpaca. Once a theorist and visionary, he had abandoned much of his idealism in favor of bread-and-butter issues—wages, hours, working conditions, pensions. Although he regarded Jake Chain as a criminal and Leo Glauberman as worse, his success in staying afloat in union waters was due in no small part to his access to them. Slightly ashamed of the tactics of Glauberman & Chain, Labor Consultants, he had nevertheless brought Mr. Wallowitz to the Pitkin Avenue office for help.

Hyman Wallowitz was a new fish. Walking delegate of the Wet Wash Laundry Workers Union, a struggling, underpaid group, he had come to Ike in desperation. Wallowitz was a cadaverous man suggesting a ruined Lincoln—long limbs, hands boiled out of shape by hot water. He was sunkencheeked, tufted-browed, and hollow-eyed. He sat on the edge of his chair and listened. During the last strike he had been drubbed by Duffy Plotkin, who punched three teeth out of Mr. Wallowitz's mouth. The gaps in his jaw muffled his speech.

"Prohibition, my *tuchas*," Glauberman said. "So they passed the amendment two years ago. All those dumb Baptists. *Goyim* who feel up women in the church pews, ministers who screw the ladies in the choir. But God forbid a human being should desire a shot. Enjoy, Wallowitz. You too, Ike."

"Good booze, Mr. Wallowitz?" Jake asked gently.

"You're excuse me," the ravaged Lincoln said, "but normally whiskey I don't take. Maybe a little for my heart now and then."

"So your pickets have been beaten up?" Jake asked, prodding him.

"Three times. Look at my teeth."

"The owners won't talk?" Glauberman asked.

"Only to tell us we'll get *worse*. They got nonunion Italian ladies. In laundry hampers. They bribed a shop steward. A lousy five-dollar raise and he quits the union and he's bringing in scabs for Metzinger's Wet Wash."

"The gentleman's name?" Glauberman asked. Teddy Roosevelt was in action, scribbling notes on a yellow pad.

"Who?"

"Who is sneaking in scabs?"

"Shikey Frummer. But, please, don't start with him. He got a brother, Futka, a gangster, a murderer."

In anguish, Brunstein stared at the ceiling. Ideals! *Ideals!*

"Who's doing anything?" Jake asked. He got up, huge and broad-shouldered in a vested gray tweed suit, and put a hand like a canoe paddle on Wallowitz's shoulders. "You ain't a client yet. Nothing happens until you sign up."

The gaunt man looked at Brunstein. "So? You brought me here."

"Wallowitz, I don't like this any better than you do. But sometimes harsh choices must be made. If the union treasury can afford it . . ."

Wallowitz blinked. "The cops arrested a picket line yesterday. Twenty men. My wife was threatened on the street by a fat man in a checked suit."

Jake laughed. "Wesselberg is back, Mr. G."

"Tell him about your services." Ike sighed.

Jake picked up a leather folder with a celluloid envelope within. It resembled a menu holder. Inside the transparency was a typed list. Jake read haltingly. He was no longer the illiterate workhorse of twelve years ago. At the age of thirty-seven he was a man of substance.

"For me and Mr. Glauberman, thirty dollars a day each," Jake said. "A bargain. That's basic expenses, whether we work or not, or whether a job is done or not. For each man we have on duty, seven and a half dollars a day. That's cheap. It ain't easy to hire *shtarkers*."

Ike covered his eyes. He was mortified.

"Why is that?" Wallowitz asked. "Business should be good."

"There's better jobs in booze." Jake raised his shot glass. "We got to compete on the labor market. Not like wet wash, where there's always cheap labor."

"Seven-fifty a day to have a man standing around?"

"Wallowitz," Glauberman said, "if our associates don't stand around, you'll have pickets with bloody heads and in jail." Glauberman leveled his specs at the gaunt man. "So a Shikey Frummer arranges for scabs. Futka brings them in. Next time they may stink-bomb your office. Or beat up your little boy on the way home from school."

"I got no boy. Only three girls, God bless them."

"*Worse*. What people like the Frummers do to girls I can't mention."

Jake resumed reading from his folder. "Wrecking a small factory or laundry or storeroom, two hundred dollars. The price can go as high as seven hundred and fifty, depending on the size of the place. Metzinger's is pretty big. You want a full job on it, dyes in the vats, acid in the pipes, stink bombs, the electric burned out, it might go as high as a thousand."

"A down payment of fifty dollars is required," Glauberman said.

"It's usual," Ike said.

The wet-wash delegate unfolded five creased ten-dollar bills. Hard-earned dues from his members. He put them on Glauberman's oak desk. "Why?"

"Expenses. Remember, Mr. Wallowitz." Glauberman leveled the pince-nez at him. "Any of our employees gets jailed, you must put up bond for him."

"And tell the whole world we're in with you?"

"The money can be given to this office," the lawyer said. "There is one final thing."

"In enough trouble I am. What else can happen?"

"Leo Glauberman, yours truly, will be elected executive vice-president of the union."

"Impossible," Wallowitz said. "Brunstein, tell them—"

"That's how it works," Ike mumbled. "You want to win the strike? The bosses started it with Pinkertons and gangsters. I don't care for this any more than you do."

For the wet-wash job, Crazy Jake imported four anonymous *shtarkers* from Jersey City. They were dock workers, Italians, recruited by Luigi Ferrante. Luigi and his brothers Baggie and Vince were the nucleus of the new mob. Sal sometimes helped out. Yussel Kuflik, the Bear, did odd jobs, specializing in arson and stink bombs. Label Kuflik had been shot to death in a poolroom brawl over a bet on the Willard-Johnson fight.

Jake's free lancers started by dropping Metzinger's foreman down an elevator shaft. He suffered a broken leg, a broken arm, and pangs of conscience. He found it difficult, from a hospital bed, to truck scabs to Brownsville. Metzinger's office was wrecked with a grenade. Two of his trucks were overturned and the drivers beaten.

In two weeks' time, the Wet Wash Association had settled with Wallowitz's union. Glauberman was installed as executive vice-president.

A week after the contract was signed, Jacob Chain, in new blue serge suit, white straw boater, and stiff collar, visited four other laundries. He was accompanied by Luigi Ferrante. A stubby .38 peeked from Luigi's belt.

With barely audible protest, the owners agreed that it was a splendid idea to pay Glauberman & Chain fifty dollars a week to ensure that no more violence was unloosed on their laundries and that workers remained uncomplaining.

Chapter 18

Eva could see Garry coming down the gravel path from the main house. He carried tennis rackets and a reticule filled with new balls. He walked like all the Halsteads—an odd short-gaited, knock-kneed walk, as if the legs were a bit underdeveloped. Inbreeding? she wondered. Mildred walked that way. So did Mr. Halstead, Sr. As if their slender limbs and narrow feet avoided maximum contact with the common clay of this world.

I can understand it in my father-in-law, she mused. But Garry and Mildred have touched earth many times and I love them for it. So why can't they plant their feet *firmly* on it?

She jotted down her speculation in her *Book of Personal*

Thoughts. She was seated in the gazebo of the Halstead summer mansion in Sag Harbor on Gardiner's Bay. Sailboats skimmed by. Screeching gulls wheeled and dipped. Terns chased schools of bait fish. Above the slow rise of golf-green lawn bordered with formal hedges—azaleas, yews, ilex, forsythia—rose the clapboard "cottage." She laughed when Garrison first took her there before their marriage ten years ago. Some cottage! Twenty-seven rooms, stables (converted to a five-car garage), outbuildings, a greenhouse, vegetable gardens, a tennis court, and a landing dock.

Eva liked the gazebo best. She had a writing table installed there by Harms, the Halsteads' mulatto groundskeeper (there were six in help), and she often worked on her articles and lectures in the white latticework structure. Cardinals and yellow warblers twittered about the feeders Harms kept filled. A tiger swallow-tail butterfly settled with tremulous wings on lavender phlox.

Mr. Garrison Halstead's Brownsville Butterfly is a delicate and lovely creature rising from the fetid slums of Brooklyn. She did not seem at all fazed by the luxury surrounding her....

She cherished the newspaper reports of the wedding. The social sensation of the year. A Halstead marrying a Jewish immigrant girl. The papers had started reporting their romance with a mocking tone. *Two Socialists?* Worlds apart but finding love in their dedication to reform? After the reporters attended the wedding—the service performed by the groom's uncle, the Reverend Isaac Yates of Saint Matthew's—they stopped sniggering.

Mrs. Halstead wore a gown of white lace tulle and a corsage of pink orchids attached with a bright red ribbon. She also wore a white lace headdress edged with bright red. When asked why she had chosen the scarlet accoutrements, the Cleopatra of the tenements smiled and said: "To remind all here that the revolution is yet to be won."

They had been married in 1912. It was two years after Halstead had first seen her in magistrates court, a woman accused of violent acts and disobeying a police order. She had to laugh. She recalled Garry putting up her bail. Her gray champion, as in the Hawthorne story. Only Garry had no gray hair, then or now. But her champion.

She had taken her notebooks and scrapbooks with her that morning. *Liberty* was interested in an article about their married life. A storybook romance, the editor said to her. After ten years, the well-nigh unbelievable Heilig-Halstead union was functioning, stronger than ever. No children, to be sure, but a happy marriage. Why not publicize it?

"You aren't going to indulge that fool of an editor?" Halstead asked. He had entered the gazebo on sneakered feet, kissed her neck, glanced at the clippings on the table. She was more fragrant than the meadows and flowers that surrounded her.

"I thought I might try it a different way, Garry. Forget all the society nonsense, forget my ghetto origins, and do a story about two people working for good causes."

"It won't satisfy them. They want to know if you use the right fork at formal dinners."

"We hardly ever go to any."

"They'll assume you do. They want to hear that the Brownsville beauty drinks from the finger bowl."

Eva laughed. "But I did once. On our honeymoon at that place in Bar Harbor. I was *thirsty*. You people drink so *much*. Liquor, wine, beer. I'm sorry if I was raised on sour milk."

Eva had rejected Uncle Sourmilk's panacea when she was twenty. "Poor papa," she mused. "Bloating himself with sour milk and dying at age fifty-five of influenza."

"It's possible the bacillus was contraindicated for influenza."

He looked at his wife's notes. Another lecture. He could not decipher her scribbles on the yellow pad. She had taken a course in shorthand and typing when she began to work as a union organizer.

"We Jews have that problem." Eva said. "Wrong bacilli, wrong choices, wrong politics. I don't believe our friends in Russia are backing the right people. A day of reckoning will come."

"Trust Lenin, my love."

Eva laughed so hard she had to cover her mouth. "Oh, my precious husband! In your tennis outfit from Abercrombie and Fitch! With your racket and tennis balls! On your Long Island estate, you tell me—*me!*—to trust Lenin!"

She almost fell from the wicker chair. Halstead caught her, kissed her open mouth. He stroked her breasts. It was astonishing. The longer they were married, the more he craved her. In bed he was tender, possessive, insatiable. *Stop, Garry, stop, you are wearing me out, I'm weary, I can't again. . . .*

Often distant and walled-in, Halstead conceived of himself as the weaker member of the marriage. Except in the dark privacy of the bedroom. There, his male needs, his gentile sword, conquered the Semite daughter, descendant of prophets and priests. Sometimes, he whispered to her. he felt like a soldier of the Tenth Roman Legion, taking his reward for the burning of the temple. Or perhaps a crusading knight with Godefroy de Bouillon raping a Jewess in the slums of Acre.

Reserved, at times unresponsive, she knew she was a disappointing sexual partner. Her radicalism preoccupied her. In demand as a lecturer, a writer, the voice of New American Women, she was a well-known name. Eva Heilig Halstead, organizer, labor executive, Socialist. More than once Garry had been referred to as "Mr. Heilig." At the Yale Club they joked behind his back about his Hebrew whore. The story came back to him and he resigned with an angry letter to the president.

"Who are you playing with today?" Eva asked.

He mentioned the names of neighbors—a broker, a banker. She could not tell them apart. They all appeared a great mass of pink healthy faces, strong white teeth, lean muscles. She refused to learn to play tennis, yet envied the women who did. They accepted her but did not understand her. *Garrison's little Jewess.* Most of them understood that if her origins were humble, her ambition was great. She wrote. She was published. She spoke to cheering crowds on pacifism, disarmament, equal rights for women, race prejudice, child labor. And now a new crusade—against the ravages of union racketeers.

"Work in progress?" Halstead asked. He got up from the bench that lined the interior of the gazebo.

"Gangsters in the unions."

"Ah, back to Brownsville."

"I promised the Labor Lyceum three speeches a year. They are one group that will never have to pay to hear me. Besides, I haven't seen my family in a long time."

"I'll go with you. What's all this about mobsters in unions? I thought all of that ended."

She showed him a *New York Times* article. One Herman Wesselberg had just been elected chief executive officer of the Bottlers and Soda-Water Wagon Drivers. A notorious criminal, tried for murder and acquitted. Twelve arrests. Her old enemy, the Saratoga Avenue Meal Ticket.

"Mr. Wesselberg and his kind were known to me when I was in charge of pickets," Eva said. "He's back, stronger than ever. Listen to this. 'Other notorious hoodlums, most of whom began their careers working for legitimate unions or employers, are moving in on positions of power in the labor movement. Captain Eric Stutz of the Seventy-first Precinct in Brooklyn reports that six unions in Brooklyn are currently dominated by underworld elements. He named the Wet Wash Workers, the Dairymen, the Furriers, and the Water Bagel Bakers. "Once they're in the house," Captain Stutz said, "it's hard to get these lice out. They frighten the workers as well as the bosses and extort money from both." ' "

"Would that include your cousin Mr. Chain?"

Halstead had heard stories about Crazy Jake and his mob. How they forced the bosses to give in by paying them back in kind. She had lost touch with Jake the past few years.

"Jake would not be a part of that," Eva said. "He's no angel, but he worked only when we needed him, and only for us."

He kissed her again.

Eva looked forward to the visit to Brooklyn and her family. She missed them. Her indefatigable mother, Matla, ran a prospering stationery store on Sutter Avenue. Abe had hung out his shingle on Pennsylvania Avenue and was on staff at Beth-Moses Hospital. During the dread influenza epidemic of 1919, when Uncle Sourmilk died, Abe and Sam Abelman had climbed hundreds of tenement stairs, leaped across roofs, worked a twenty-hour day trying to save lives. They had become good friends.

Her younger brother, Sol, was practicing law with two friends from Brooklyn Law School in a modest office on Court Street. Sol was in politics. There was talk that he might run for the state assembly. A strange fish, Sol, a *Republican,* coming out of Brownsville, where Socialists and Democrats prevailed.

There would be dinner at her mother's on Haven Place, then the ride in Abe's new Oakland, with Abe's sniffish wife Leah (daughter of the medical pioneer Aaron Lamkau), to the Lyceum. Garrison mingled with her old friends and family without discomfort. In his books *New Ghetto* and *Jewish Pioneers* and in articles, he had written about these energetic, talkative, intelligent hardworking people. It was, he noted, as if they were so in love with their adopted country that they were working overtime to pay off a debt. When they said *America Gonif*, it was uttered not as an insult but as a subtle term of approbation. Turn on an electric light? *America Gonif!* Admire a new Ford? *America Gonif!* They would be part of America, make no mistake, he wrote. And the nation would be better for their presence.

Garrison kissed her again now and went off to his game. Soon she could hear the distant *thwack-thwack* of tennis balls. There was no denying the beauty of the place. Still, she preferred their townhouse on Tenth Street. There they had only a maid, a cook, and a man-of-all-work, and they had been taught to keep their distance from the woman of the house. Eva wanted to hear nothing about menus, broken lamps, window cleaners. She wanted to immerse herself in her work.

"Married in a church?" Sarah Chain, walking with a cane, had asked when Jake had haltingly read the account of the wedding in the *News*.

Jake had read the description of the ceremony, the bridesmaids, the procession of cars and carriages from the white church in Sag Harbor to the estate.

A hoo-er, a *nafka*, that Heilig woman. Sarah and her neighbors on Haven Place (except for the dignified Mrs. Abelman) agreed as they haggled over the price of chicken in the open market.

Now that Jake was a "labor consultant," Sarah had her hair bobbed and slicked down. She wore bright stylish dresses from Loehmann's and purchased orthopedic shoes that minimized her limp. She smoked cigarettes incessantly. But she could not read. She learned to play cards and was an avid participant in penny-ante poker games.

Whenever Eva's name came up, memories of the daughter of Uncle Sourmilk, there were exchanges of narrow glances and arch comments over the ladies' poker table. Sadie Levinson and Molly Bauer and Rose Cohen knew. Jake Chain had been in love with his cousin. And maybe he still was. Who could blame him with a crippled wife who had developed a sharp tongue?

Chapter 19

"No fat," Minnie said. "If you were a chicken, I wouldn't buy you. But in a man. Oh, boy."

The prostitute ran her fingertips over Jake's naked body. He was like leather. Tough, resilient, scarred with the bullets that had cut him down in 1910. "Can I count them, Jake?" she asked.

Minnie had not aged. The first time Jake had made love to her she was eighteen—pudgy, round, cherry-lipped. There were old men in Brownsville, in fur-trimmed hats and long coats, who refused to believe that Jewish girls could be whores. Jake knew otherwise.

Her soft hands fluttered over his iron body. She excited him, but he did not kid himself. She was a substitute for his lost Sarah, for Eva. A man was like a machine. He had to be oiled and fueled. Minnie, with the soft, sluggish body of a girl who ate too much and hated work, was no real substitute.

Entering her, discharging his passion, he was filled with images of Eva. A stolid, uncomplaining man, who wasted no time on lost causes, on what could not be, he could not eradicate Eva's face, her voice, from his mind. Feared, hated, a power on the fringes of the Brownsville underworld, he had a reputation. People wanted to do favors for him. But the favor he craved, Eva's love, was one that no one could grant him. And he did not delude himself. No one ever could.

Twelve healed wounds. Twelve bullets from Moishe Nigger and the Meal Ticket. Wesselberg was still around, a big man in union rackets. When the Nigger drowned in chicken blood, when the Ferrantes made a torch of Little Mendel in Canarsie, the fat man inherited their illegal trade.

"On your jaw," Minnie said. "The long white mark. And a little mark on your head, where the blond hair grows over it. Thank God, Jake, *this* one didn't hurt you, or I'd be sad." Minnie stroked his crotch, probing the indentation to the left of his member. The bullet had ripped through hip and thigh. The two slugs that had bitten into his right leg bothered him more. Two others remained in him, one lodged against a bone.

"The man they couldn't kill," Minnie said. She stroked him to rigidity and played with him as if he were a gearshift. "Everyone's a-scared of you, Jake."

"Why? I'm a puppy dog."

Minnie maneuvered. "Neutral. First. Second. Third. Reverse is all the way over here. You didn't know I could drive? When I get outta here and don't have to work for Bella, I'll get a car. Jake, if you married me, I could have a car. A house in Crown Heights. I wouldn't have to be a hoo-er."

"I'm married."

"Some marriage. That *yenta*. I'm sorry, I'm sorry. Don't hit. You're a big man, Jake. You'll be rich someday. I could dress fancy, learn in night school, be a good wife. Then people wouldn't call me a hoo-er. It's no fun. Ten years with men I hate. You're the only one I love."

"Sorry, kid. I got Sarah and the boy. Maybe I don't sleep with my wife but I owe her plenty."

"What? A barrel of guilt? Like a keg of herrings in the appetizing store?"

"When we didn't have what to eat, she worked. She made buttonholes. She dressed Mutteh for school. I'm sorry, Minnie."

With an athlete's grace, he turned, naked as a carp, and entered her.

"Good," she said. "Only for you I do it for real."

He dressed quickly. A cut rate from Bella the madam. She knew a friend when she saw one. If Jake Chain was your friend, it was unlikely that Futka Frummer or his brother Shikey would come around for "protection." They avoided Crazy Jake's friends. The underworld knew what had happened to Moishe Nigger.

On the corner near the Lyceum, where Eva was to speak, Jake saw his son Mutt standing with Benny Otzenberger's daughter Hilda.

The boy was no longer Mutteh, or Mutteleh, but plain dumb-sounding *Mutt*. Miss Condon, his first-grade teacher, had decided that his name was Mortimer. And so it was entered in the school records. But to his friends he was *Mutt*. At eighteen he bore both names proudly. He signed himself Mortimer J. (for nothing) Chain. But to the young toughs, the hustlers, the smart kids around Dannenfelser's poolroom, the up-and-coming boxers, he was Mutt Chain, Crazy Jake's son.

Mutt was lean and stringy, three inches shorter than Jake. He had a sharp dark face, pointed ears, solemn brown eyes, a nose like a blade, and a taut mouth. A fox's face. Sarah's face, Sarah's dark skin and near-black hair, parted slickly in the middle. He did not smile often, but when he did, the effect was disarming. A handsome kid, intelligent. He had dropped out of Thomas Jefferson High School in his last year. It bored him. Besides, Kolodny the hunchback (now mixing bootleg hooch) had offered him a job as a "salesman," handing out cards to speakeasies, private customers, restaurants.

"*Nu*, Mutt?" Jake said. "Hello, Hilda."

Mortimer J. Chain sized the old man up. Just had his piece of ass. He knew. The kid knew everything. He knew his parents never made love. Jake slept in the front room on a sofa. Under the purple brocade slipcovers were three bullet holes from the shooting. It was as if Jake, a giant of the streets, renewed his strength on the wounded couch. Sarah slept alone in the middle room.

"Mama says don't come home too late," Mutt said. He smiled slyly. "She says she worries when you're late."

"You told her where I was going? To the Lyceum to hear the talk?"

"She didn't believe me. Until I said Cousin Eva was speaking."

Hilda Otzenberger, the most delectable of local beauties, was a moon-faced, raven-haired girl with a wide mouth, a snub-nose, and darting black eyes. She took Mutt's hand and pressed her warm thigh against his. She laughed softly.

How an ox like Benny Otzenberger could produce such a beautiful daughter eluded all of Brownsville. People expected a small whale, a fat shapeless girl. Hilda was exotic and lush, suggesting harems, biblical temptresses.

"Your cousin Eva is *famous*," Hilda said to Jake. "Honest, Mr. Chain. All the time in the newspapers. Once we even heard her on the radio."

Jake surveyed Hilda's inflated bosom, the luxuriant ass. Good for Mutt, he thought. And not a bad marriage, if it developed. Political connections would help now that he and Glauberman were expanding. Not that they didn't have Benny's blessing already.

"Papa, you haven't been to the Labor Lyceum in how long?" Mutt asked. He was taunting the old man.

"I don't listen to speeches," Jake said.

He watched the chattering crowd enter. Eva always drew them. They remembered The Golden Voice, even if she deserted Brownsville for a swanky *goy* husband.

Jake saw his father-in-law Klebanow and his wife entering. Klebanow was no longer the ragged peddler of twelve years ago. Using his mounting earnings as a "labor consultant," Jake had bought him a fruit-and-vegetable store on Prospect Place. Klebanow had prospered, almost seemed to have grown an inch or two. It was amazing what a little money did for people.

"There's grampa and grandma," Mutt said. "Since when do they go to lectures?"

"To hear Eva Heilig, everyone goes."

Mutt told him about Kolodny's plans. Bootlegging, the hunchback said, was the best racket. People wanted booze. It didn't matter what kind or how you got it. Maybe his father wanted to talk about it?

Jake smiled. No, the labor business was fine. Let Mutt be careful. He should always look around in dark places, never turn his back on an enemy.

"So far all I do is hand out cards."

Hilda Otzenberger listened, suspicious. What was all this talk? Speakeasies, bootlegging, merchandise from Canada. What did it mean? And who cared?

Mutt showed his father an embossed card.

HAPPY TIMES SPIRITS
PRESIDENT 4-4889 CALL ANYTIME, 10 AM—MIDNIGHT
FULL STOCK, FAIR PRICES, DELIVERIES

SCOTCH—RYE—GIN—BRANDY—CORDIALS—WINES

"Kolodny built a new place, papa," Mutt said. "Next to the old bottling plant. Bricks, cement, a big garage for trucks. And a separate part for the booze. He isn't so dumb."

For this my son dropped out of Thomas Jefferson High School? Jake wondered. He failed to understand his own role in shaping Mutt's life.

Chapter 20

"But there seems to be a mistake, Mr. Chain," Simon Baum said. "I've already signed a contract with the Glaziers Union."

Simon was the son of Kalman Baum, the old bathrobe tycoon. Simon was in his late twenties. Sleek raven hair parted at the side, pale oval face, piercing brown eyes, a waxed black moustache. He was one of Brownsville's leading builders, and his lavish office testified to his success. His current project was an enclosed market in East New York.

"I know you signed," Jake said. "But because I was just elected vice-president of the Glaziers, they wanted me to review the contract."

Simon Baum looked at his father's old enemy. Hoodlum. Bum. Seltzerwagon driver. The bastard who had broken the bosses' united front, ruined factories, forced employers to give in. Nothing had been the same since. Young Baum found it convenient to forget that it was his father and his uncle who had unleashed hoodlums on women strikers in the first place. To Simon, Crazy Jake was no avenging angel of the unions but a ruffian, an extortionist, a liar, and probably a murderer.

There were stories. Chain had been interrogated and released twelve years ago after the murder of Moishe "Nigger" Pearlberg. Probably guilty as hell, Baum thought. And those reptiles, the Ferrante brothers. One of them, Luigi, stood at the door, trimming his nails.

"Elected, Mr. Chain? Or did you and Glauberman force the Glaziers Union to accept you? What is your experience in collective bargaining?"

Jake tilted his chair back and hooked thumbs in his vest. He was wearing his spiffy straw boater in the office. It was pushed forward on his flat face. Baum studied the hard cheekbones, the blunted nose, the scar on the jaw. The Nigger should have killed him.

"How many windows you got installed in the East New York market?" Jake asked.

"Ninety."

"Call up your foreman on the job, Baum. He'll tell you you got only fifty windows. Half of them got broke while we were talking."

Baum hunched his shoulders. *Bastard, bum, hoodlum.*

"Very nice, Mr. Chain."

"The union says that the price for replacing the windows is double." Jake's half-shut eyes never left Baum's face. Let him suffer. The collapsed factory. Sarah crippled for life.

"That's a violation of the contract," Baum said.

Luigi Ferrante pared his nails with a four-inch blade. He wore a brown box-backed jacket, beige slacks. His yellow cap fell over the side of his head like an artist's beret.

"Maybe, maybe not," Jake said. "Unless you and me can come to an agreement, there'll be ninety busted windows in the market."

Baum picked up the phone and said to his secretary, "Tell Mr. Heilig to come in."

Sol Heilig entered, chubby, rumpled, smiling. He had Eva's fair coloring but none of her grace. He was a political comer, everyone said.

"Hi, Jake," Sol said. "Hi, Vinnie."

"Luigi," Luigi mumbled.

"Of course. Vinnie's got an ear missing."

"That's Frankie and he's dead." Luigi was hurt.

"Sorry. Anyway, I know Sal. He catered the booze for our New Year's party. Poison from Kolodny's warehouse."

Baum was getting impatient. "Can't we get down to cases? Mr. Heilig is my lawyer. He knows you are threatening me. He knows you are in violation of my contract with the glaziers."

"What violation?" Jake asked. "I'm acting as vice-president. They want an extra five dollars per window. Hazardous work."

"My, my, Jake, *hazardous*," Sol said.

Jake doffed his straw hat to Sol. "A credit to you, Solly. Remember when you and Abe learned me English?"

"Jake, we *taught* you, not *learned*. Anyway, what do you want?"

Jake twirled the straw hat on one finger. "Mr. Baum needs protection."

The phone rang. Baum took the receiver off the hook, listened, grunted as if he'd been kicked in the stomach. He hung up. "Ten more windows smashed. Your friend, counselor Heilig? Your relative?"

Jake yawned. "I have no idea who done such a thing."

"*Did* such a thing, Jake," Sol corrected.

"God in heavens, they're destroying me, and my lawyer is giving grammar lessons."

"How much do you want, Jake?" Sol asked.

"Fifty dollars a week. We'll make sure not a single window gets broke. No extra charge from the glaziers for fixing busted windows."

Heilig lowered his head. The *golem* was devouring everyone.

"I'm ashamed of you, Jake. You shake down Mr. Baum for protection, which means your people won't destroy his buildings. Then you cheat your own union members. You make both pay off."

"I won't stand for it," Baum said.

"Take thirty dollars a week," Sol Heilig said to Jake.

"Forty," Jake said.

"Thirty-five."

"A deal. First payment right now."

Baum shook his head. Where would it end? Tomorrow, next week, Jake Chain and his mob could ask for fifty, then a hundred.

"Jake, get out of it," Sol said solemnly. "This is no good for you."

Jake pocketed the bills. Luigi frowned. Hardly worth the threats. But he knew why the boss had gone easy on Baum. After all these years, Crazy Jake still had hot pants for the Heilig dame. He'd murdered the Nigger because of her.

"Listen, Mr. Baum," Jake said, "you got a bargain. Futka Frummer would charge seventy-five."

Chapter 21

Canada.

It sounded mysterious to Mutt. He drove his Chandler taxicab expertly, shifting gears on hills, handling the clutch, the wheel, the brake like a professional. Sal Ferrante, in the taxi ahead of him, warned him with brake lights when to slow down, used his left arm to signal turns. Sal drove an Essex. It was his own cab. He had purchased it with the profits from his fleet of hokey-pokey carts.

At twenty-seven, the youngest Ferrante was an entrepreneur. The kids who pushed the carts sold shaved ice for a penny or two cents and paid tribute to Sal. He disdained his brothers' careers as masons and strong-arm men for Chain. Sal was determined to be in business for himself. The wheezing Essex taxi was a common sight in Brownsville. It was rumored that a few of Chain's enemies, in need of education, had taken unwilling rides in the back seat. Like a neat housewife, Sal always washed away the stains.

But he did not care for the work, even if it meant a five-dollar tip from Jake. The day Prohibition went into effect and Reds Mulqueen's bar closed, Sal sighted a bigger pot of gold than *shtarking*. Booze.

His new career started in a lunatic way. Cruising downtown Brooklyn, he was flagged by a white-haired drunk in a pale blue suit and a floppy white panama. The gentleman staggering out of the Original Joe's was named Brian O'Toole, a political lieutenant of Francis Fagan Dullahan.

"Lousy rotgut, drugstore alky," Mr. O'Toole blubbered at Sal. "Take me to Canada, kid. Need some real stuff."

"How far?" Sal never wasted words. He had achieved much by listening, waiting.

"Goddamn near four hunnert miles. Turn off the meter and I'll give you fifty bucks."

After inspecting Mr. O'Toole's roll of bills, Sal helped him into the back seat. In a good week he was lucky to clear forty dollars with the taxi. It sounded like a profitable deal.

Arriving in Montreal, under Mr. O'Toole's guidance, Sal purchased a case of Canadian whisky for ten dollars. Mr. O'Toole bought four cases. *Thirsty.* He was always thirsty, he explained. Border guards were no problem. They waved the cab in and waved it out.

Back in Brooklyn, Sal sold his case of bonded Canadian rye to a speak-easy owner of Fulton Street for a hundred dollars. He did not need anyone to tell him that he had cleared *ninety dollars' profit* at the cost of a couple of tankfuls of gasoline.

A week after that first trip to Canada, Sal approached eighteen-year-old Mutt Chain and asked him to join him on a second trip.

"It's easy," Sal whispered. He hissed through his teeth. His eyes had developed a strange habit of looking into corners, past the person to whom he was talking. Arrested five times for vending without a license, three times for carrying a weapon, twice for breaking and entering, he had never been convicted. People did not like to give evidence against a Ferrante. And they were made queasy by his dancing eyes.

"Easy?" Mutt asked. He was working out with barbells in Futcher's Garage while his own taxi was getting a grease job. Futcher owned a dozen cabs. Mutt drove for him, ran errands in the cab for his father, for Otzenberger, for Mulqueen, for Kolodny.

Jake had wanted Mutt to go to college like the Heilig brothers. But Mutt was street-wise, tough, impatient. A wild hair up his ass, Otzenberger said. Lean like his mother, he had his father's strength. His hands seemed to belong to a man twice his size. And his temper was far worse than that of lethargic Jake. He had a glib, quick tongue.

"Get the cab from Futcher for a couple days," Sal said. "We drive up to Montreal, load up, and come back."

"What if we get caught? A Jew and a guinea? They'll hang us."

"Never. The guards let you in and out without lookin' at what you got."

"Even in a taxi?"

"Especially. Taxis go in and out alla time."

Sal told him of his trip to Montreal with O'Toole. Nothing to it. He lied about the profits. A ten-dollar case of booze could be sold for sixty, Sal said. He'd handle the sale in Brooklyn. Okay?

Mutt rubbed his chin. "If it's such a good thing, why just a case in the trunk? Why don't we take along a lot of valises, bags, crap that people on vacation carry? We can buy a real load."

Sal liked the idea. But it disturbed him a little that this punk had wised up so fast.

It took little to convince Mr. Futcher to lend Mutt the Chandler. *A pleasure, Mortimer.* Jake Chain provided "protection" for Futcher's Garage. He saw to it that Futcher's cabs got the best stations at the Utica Avenue and Sutter Avenue stops of the IRT. He made it easy with the hack bureau when licenses ran out. If Mr. Futcher got caught with phony meters that registered hastily, Jake Chain knew how to fix it.

It then occurred to the inventive Mutt that if they were lugging all those valises and trunks to Canada, a "passenger" would help.

Mutt had the answer. Ripe Hilda Otzenberger, two years older than Mutt, his steady girl, could play the part. Of course Benny would take some convincing. Luckily, Hilda was one of the few people in the world—perhaps the only one—to whom he could not say no.

"Ah, come on, pa." Hilda pouted. "Morty is a nice kid. Sal is just on the trip to show the way."

"And tell me, Hilda dollink," Benny asked, "for what is this shlep to Canada?"

"To see Niagara Falls."

"That's the other end of Canada. That much I know even if I can't read. Montreal is the other direction, where people talk French."

"Mort says we'll see Niagara Falls on the way back."

"A long trip. You'll sleep in different rooms, please."

Benny knew what you could get in Canada. *Real booze.* Friends of his were already looking into prospects. Leave it to that ginzo Salvatore. And now Jake Chain's son was in with those Ferrantes.

Now Hilda sat in the front seat of Mutt's rattling Chandler, dodging his exploring hand, slapping, teasing, letting him know just how far he could go.

"Lemme see your garters," Mutt said. They had left Albany and were headed north on the state road.

"Fresh."

"One garter."

"Okay, but that's all."

She raised her black serge skirt, revealed black stockings, a heavy alabaster thigh. A frilly pink garter pinched the soft flesh. Mutt reached across the gearshift to snap the elastic. She cracked his hand. "I said *no.* And we ain't sleeping in the same room. You can sleep with that wop."

"But I love you. You're the most beautiful girl on the block."

"Block? Boy, what a compliment. Hands off. I mean it."

Leaving Saratoga, he reached around her shoulder and began to massage one cushiony breast. She was wearing a hard corset. It made contact difficult, but elevated her bosom endearingly. Hilda got bored with his hand and pinched it.

"When I say no, it's *no.* Drive."

The road was bumpy and endless. At Glens Falls the scenery became more interesting. Pine forests. Lakes. Mountains. Mutt could recall going to a *kuch-alein*—a bungalow in the Catskills where his mother cooked in a tiny kitchen. It was after Jake had been beaten up by the Frummer brothers, the heirs of Moishe Nigger's gang. It was a warning. *Lay off*. His father was *shtarking* for the Carpenters Union, beating up scabs, wrecking nonunion shops.

They had broken Jake's nose, fractured his left arm, covered him with welts and bruises that would have sent any other man to a hospital for weeks. The next day Crazy Jake was back on his feet. guarding pickets. Three days later he was escorting wife and child to the mountains.

Doc Abelman had suggested he get away. It was wartime. Doughboys, parades, Liberty bonds. Bobby Rimkoff, the landlord's son, had enlisted in the Rainbow Division. He was not only divisional lightweight "champeen," but a hero of the battle of Saint Mihiel. There was talk of naming a street for him (a short one, to be sure, as befitted a lightweight) in East New York.

In Brownsville, a heavy demand for uniforms had the shops working overtime. Unions were in battle not only with bosses but with each other. The Bolshevik Revolution had split labor leaders eighteen different ways.

Mutt nurtured memories of bond rallies, a parade on Eastern Parkway. Rimkoff coming home a hero, challenging any welterweight around. (They'd start him with old stumblebums like Duffy Plotkin and Negro shoeshine boys before getting him a bout in the Garden.)

There was excitement in the air. He was sorry his father had not been part of the AEF. Jake would have made a natural first sergeant, people said. But he was so full of bullets, so scarred and bruised, that he would never be allowed to shoulder a rifle. Plenty of Brownsville boys enlisted or were drafted. Mutt envied them "over there."

It was over as soon as it began, it seemed to Mutt. He was fourteen, a kid in corduroy knickers and a "beanie" cap made from Jake's old brown fedora, when he stood on Eastern Parkway and watched the victorious army parade.

The war over, his father's "business" grew into a big-time operation. Everything was booming—building, needle trades, food processing, trucking. Glauberman & Chain, Labor Consultants, grew with the times. For a long time Mutt was not certain what Jake did. But he understood that his father was feared. People deferred to him. They wanted to do favors for him. The way Futcher had donated the taxi for the ride to Canada.

"I got to pee," Hilda said.

"You were supposed to go at the gas station in Saratoga."

"I can't help it. All that orange soda I drank for lunch.

Listen, I'm your passenger. I'm the rich girl going to visit her family in Montreal, right? I need two cabs to get me there, I'm so rich. So you gotta do what I say."

He honked three times, a prearranged signal to Sal, who drove like a madman, turning corners on two wheels, passing double lines, running lights. It surprised Mutt. Sal had a cautious manner—forever scheming and figuring. Mutt filed the knowledge. It was always good to know these things about people.

For identification at the border, Hilda had a copy of her birth certificate. Mutt and Sal showed registration papers from the New York hack bureau. The Customs and Immigration guards at Rouse's Point could not have cared less about the concocted story. Miss Otzenberger was en route to Montreal to visit her family. They looked at the trunks and valises filling the cabs and assumed she was a rich lady who always traveled with luggage.

"I tol' you," Sal said when they stopped for lunch. "Nobody knows what's going on here. They act like it's nothin' for a guy to ride a taxi in and outta Canada."

The lessons were not being lost on Mutt. Lie. Bluff. The law was blind, dumb, and uncaring.

It took them an entire day to load up with liquor. They were able to pack eight cases each of scotch and gin into the cabs, using the trunks, the seats, and even the roof of the Essex, on which they improvised a rack. The scotch had gone up slightly in price, eleven dollars for a case of twenty-four bottles. The gin was ten dollars the case. All told, they spent one hundred and sixty-eight dollars, saving just enough for gasoline and food for the return trip.

They stopped at a garage run by a friendly Breton. In French-accented English the mechanic said, "Plenty Americans come here with cab, right? Good booze, good business. You need partner?"

No, not a partner, Sal said. But a friend in Montreal wouldn't hurt. The garage owner's name was Louis Lamotte. He gave Sal a card. Glad to oblige an American. Business would be booming.

Later, Sal and Mutt settled accounts. Sal had laid out the cash for each purchase. Now, he told Mutt he was a "third" partner and thus owed him fifty-six dollars.

"Whatddya mean a *third*."

"A third, a third. It was my idea." Sal's eyes flitted left, right.

"Bullshit."

"That's right," Hilda seconded. "Bullshit."

The three were seated in a shabby truckers' diner a mile north of the border crossing. People were speaking French. Sal and Mutt had parked their taxis where they could keep wary eyes on the liquid treasure. They sipped coffee and ate cheese sandwiches. Mutt had done some fast mental arithmetic. The alcohol in the cabs was worth almost a thousand dollars.

"A third is all you get," Sal said. He looked creepy. Creepier than Mutt had ever seen him. He was slumped in his seat as if he had a flexible spine.

"He's cheatin' you, Mutt," Hilda said in a singsong. She took Mutt's hand. Suddenly she was afraid of Sal. She could remember him when she was a little girl. Sal the hokey-pokey man. Never smiling, rattling pennies in his soiled apron. Always something scary about him.

"Take it or leave it," Sal said. His eyes jumped—ceiling, counter, window.

"The way I figure," Mutt said, "is *I* should get two-thirds and you only a third."

"Eh, Mutt, don't be a *stroonz*." Sal did not smile.

"*Stroonz* yer ass," Mutt said. He spoke softly. "I brought Hilda and her valises and trunks. We're a team—two of us, *one* of you. I brought a cab of my own. So we should get two-thirds."

Mutt held Hilda's chubby hand. Nervy girl. One you could love. Benny would scream bloody murder if Jake Chain's son, a cabbie, asked for his daughter as a wife. Some son-in-law! Benny and his wife wanted doctors and lawyers, not a squirt like Mutt Chain.

"Hilda, go to the toilet," Mutt said. "Sal and I got business to talk."

"No. I wanna hear. I'm part of this deal. Anyway, what am I getting out of it besides my father will holler on me for running off? He woulda hit me if he could run faster."

"Go on, sweetie," Mutt said.

They watched her ample figure swivel to the ladies' room. The behind was big, the hips full, the legs nicely shaped. The cook also stared at Hilda's behind. It was of a shape and lilt that would attract stares when she was in her fifties; not just big, but wonderfully constructed.

"Ya get into her pants yet?" Sal asked.

"None of your business."

"Dry runs and jerk-offs?"

"I'm warning you, Sal, lay off. This is business. I want half the profits of everything. I'm giving you a break."

"Whaddya gonna do if I say no?"

"Beat the shit out of you. I'm not afraid of your gun."

Sal, for the first time, smiled. His beady eyes looked at the parked cabs. Big business beckoned: *trucks*. It was easy. So easy. All you needed was nerve, contacts, dependable partners. To be tied in with Crazy Jake and Benny Otzenberger had advantages.

"Okay, halfies," Sal said. His voice was dead.

"And no double-crossing. I'll go around with you when you sell the stuff."

The john door opened and Hilda emerged, crinkling her nose against the reek and smoothing her skirt.

"You big shots got it all settled?" she asked.

"You bet," Mutt said. "Finish your coffee."

At the border crossing they ran into trouble.

Cars and trucks were backed up fifty yards on the asphalt highway. It was a hot spring day. Engines were overheating. Cars were pulled off the road with their hoods up. Cursing men in shirt sleeves were repairing blowouts and steaming radiators.

Ever cautious, Sal stopped the Essex before he got to the waiting cars. He got out and stood on the running board.

Mutt braked the Chandler. It groaned and creaked under its load.

"What's wrong?" Hilda asked.

Sal gestured to Mutt to follow him to the roadside. The backup was a bad sign. Usually autos were whisked in and out.

A rangy man with a mop of Brillolike red hair saw the taxis parking and approached Sal. He was a thick-shouldered, unshaven rube with a checked green cap pulled to one side of his head. Although his blue work shirt and trousers were soiled, he wore a green satin bow tie.

"Runnin' booze?" he asked Sal.

"No. This lady is coming back from a week with her family in Montreal. She hired us to carry her stuff."

The redhead winked. He stuck his head in the window of Sal's cab. "You got an awful big load, mister. It ain't the Canadians stopping cars. It's the American Customs. They got tough a couple or three days ago. That's the holdup. Making people open trunks."

Mutt got out of the Chandler and walked to Sal's cab. The redheaded man was pointing west.

"Got fifty bucks? I'll get you out of here on a logging road. It's rough, but you'll end up near Malone, which is New York State. If your axles is strong, you'll make it."

"Fifty bucks?" Sal asked. "Just to show the way?"

"Or else you get searched." The redhead pointed to the queue of cars. It had gotten longer. Men were cursing and mopping their faces. Small boys urinated at the side of the road. A woman held an infant girl over the grassy shoulder to let the child pee.

"I'll give you twenny," Sal said.

"Make it thirty."

"Okay."

"Glad to help a couple of Yanks. Name's Bradford. I'm no lousy Canuck. You can depend on Emmett Bradford. I've hunted every acre around here. I know the roads."

"Get in." Sal said. "I have to talk to my partner."

Sal and Mutt walked to Mutt's cab. Sal opened the door and told Mutt to get in. He pulled a .38 from his pocket and gave it to Mutt. "I don't trust that redheaded guy," Sal said. "You know how to use this?"

"Sure."

"Now we got two. I always carry an extra."

Hilda gulped. "I don't wanna go along. Let me cross over on foot and I'll meet you somewhere." She was sweating. Her ripe body gave off a perfumy odor. It seemed to come out of her loins, her breasts.

"Nothing'll happen," Mutt said. He had his father's pride in getting jobs done, a cold view of the world. *Them or us.*

Sal returned to his car. Following Bradford's instructions, he made a U-turn and headed south. A mile down the road they turned left through an open wooden gate and clattered onto a red dirt road. It led through stands of giant pine and fir. There was no sign of habitation. Not a house, not a farm.

"Lumber company land," Bradford said. "I used to work it. Know the logging roads. How much you boys carrying? Big load? My God, I never knowed Americans were so thirsty. How much?"

"Enough."

They rode for ten minutes. Sal maneuvered the bone-rattling cab over pits and rocks, stopping now and then to move a fallen tree. The road was single-lane and followed the natural contours of the terrain.

In the car behind, Hilda bounced on the hard leather seat. Bruises blossomed on her tender buttocks. She grabbed the meter for dear life. With the other hand she braced herself against the door, ready to throw it open if they fell off a cliff or into a marshy pond.

The forest thickened, vast stands of commercial trees. They jounced past eerie bogs and dismal swamps peopled with dead stumps.

"I hate this place and I hate this ride," she wailed. "Morty, what's this all about?"

"We got to save the booze. The guy said the American Customs are inspecting cars."

"I hate your lousy booze and I hate this trip."

He assured her that after a few more trips he'd be rich enough to marry her. Benny might settle for having a successful bootlegger in the family. Mutt saw great possibilities. A great future for an eighteen-year-old who'd dropped out of Thomas Jefferson High.

The winding road was like a rust-colored scar in the green forest. Once they forded a shallow stream. Hilda blubbered as the Chandler sunk to its hubcaps in water. The engine coughed and died. It took a great deal of coaxing to get it started again. Mutt had to shout to Sal to wait. Then he got out and, knee-deep in water, hand-cranked the motor.

A half-mile beyond the stream. Bradford cut a wire fence, pulling apart the strands. It looked to Mutt as if he had done it many times. He did not trust the big man with the orange hair and green bow tie. He was glad he had Sal on his side and that both were armed. A certain exhilaration suffused his chest. He was his father's son.

Don't act yellow, his father told him, *don't move back, and when you're in a corner, keep swinging. And don't show the gun or the shiv unless the other guy does.*

The woodlands thinned. Mutt could see through the hazed green cover a distant lake—cool, clear. Nice to take a swim, relax, to admire Hilda's "built" in a bathing suit. But they had goods to deliver. A lot of money was waiting for them in Brooklyn.

Sal signaled Mutt to slow down. His Essex was turning right, following the red dirt track. Mutt could see a faded gray house with a broken porch. A rusted wreck of a Ford stood in the front yard, surrounded by oil drums and piles of firewood.

The Essex stopped. Bradford got out. Three men in rough clothing were waiting for him. They were pitching horseshoes, but halted when they saw the taxis. One of them, a full-bearded man with a vast paunch, shaded his eyes and peered into the rear of Sal's cab.

Sal did not get out. Bradford was talking to the other two men. They kept their horseshoes in their hands. One, a starved, chinless man, picked up an ax. They kept their backs to Sal.

Mutt stopped the Chandler. He smelled trouble. His Chain blood told him when things weren't kosher. Too many times Jake had been shot at, beaten, ambushed. *Always watch yourself,* his father warned him. *When there's money involved, a shakedown, a swindle, a bribe, watch out.*

"I don't like those guys," Hilda said. "I'm scared." Her voice quavered.

"They just want a cut for getting us through."

Bradford picked up a two-by-four. He left his friends and was talking to Sal.

"New York State's right ahead, son." He turned and smiled at the bearded man. "Got us a couple of smart city boys here with a load of bonded. Not just in the car trunks. But all them big valises."

"Open the trunk," the bearded man said to Sal. He had a weary voice.

"It's stuck."

"You a smart Jewboy? Or a wop? Come on, skinny, open it." He slammed a horseshoe against the lock.

"You'll bust it worse," Sal said sadly. "Mutt? Pull up, huh?"

Mutt shifted into low gear and aimed the nose of the Chandler at the fat man's ass.

On the slanted porch a guant woman in a stained dress puffed a cigarette.

"Thirty bucks, you said, for getting us here," Sal said sorrowfully. "And here it is, Mr. Bradford. A deal's a deal."

Mutt could see Sal handing bills to the redheaded man through the window.

"That's okay for me," Bradford said, "but my family here, they tell me it ain't nearly enough for helping two cars past Customs."

"I guess you're right," Sal said. "Can I ask my partner?"

Bradford grinned. "Sure."

"Mutt? Can we pay a few dollars more?" Sal called.

Mutt nodded his agreement. His car was a few yards behind Sal's. He drew the .38 from his belt. Hilda gagged, slid toward the door. Mutt grabbed her wrist. "Duck down when we go. Don't be scared. Put a handkerchief over your mouth."

"Whaddya want?" Sal asked stupidly.

The bearded man had opened the rear door and was inspecting valises. Luckily, the two bags stacked on the seat were extremely heavy and were wedged against the seat. He yanked at one and could not budge it. He shouted at the chinless man to help him.

"Half the load, son," Bradford said. "If it's real good stuff, maybe two-thirds."

"That ain't fair," Sal said. "You said thirty bucks to get us across. I'll give you fifty. Please. sir."

Bradford laughed and slapped his thigh. The bearded man and the chinless one began to tug at a wicker trunk. They grunted, worried the handles, trying to yank it through the narrow door.

Bradford lifted the two-by-four and aimed it, as if batting, at Sal's face. "Don't move, youngster. I'll ram this through your nose."

Sal turned and, with his darting eyes, signaled to Mutt—a wink, a flicker of the lids. The woman was trudging through the mud toward the Chandler. She carried a crowbar.

Mutt gave Hilda the .38. "It's cocked. Just point it and pull the trigger. I got to handle the wheel."

"I c-can't. I'm scared."

"You'll be dead if you don't."

"Gimme the keys to the trunk, son," Bradford said. "I know it's full of booze. Turn that engine off before you get a mouthful of pine splinters. Ever eat a two-by-four?"

Bradford was yawning, displaying rotten teeth, when Sal squeezed a single shot from his .38. The flame scorched Bradford's astonished mouth. The bullet entered between his tongue and upper teeth. Bradford's eyes popped, offended and outraged, and he walked backward, blood and brains spouting in a pink cloud from the back of his head. Then he sank slowly. He appeared to be praying before he fell on his face in the mud.

The woman shrieked. The bearded man grabbed one door, the chinless man another.

Sal gunned the engine, picked up speed. and dragged them along. Mutt followed him, bouncing over holes, ruts, rocks. The woman smashed the rear windshield of the Chandler with her crowbar. Glass splattered inside the taxi. Hilda screamed and ducked. But she was no coward. Otzenberger's daughter had *gedarim*—guts. She fired twice through the broken glass. Both shots missed, but the pursuit stopped. The woman howled and ran to Bradford's body. She embraced him in the mud, screamed at him to wake up.

The bearded man had gotten both feet on the running board of the Essex. He was clinging to the half-opened door. Sal turned and fired again. But the man was hunched low, protecting himself. Sal's .38 missed.

Mutt could see the man clearly—patched blue coveralls, flowing whiskers, a belly like a basketball. He was taking a wrench from his rear pocket.

Both cabs burst onto a tarred dirt road. They had left the logging road. A sign read: PLATTSBURGH.

New York State. Past the Customs. And a corpse left behind, a dead crook. Hilda was oyster gray, hysterical. She put the gun on the seat and began to have an attack of asthma.

"For chrissake," Mutt said. "Put the gun on safety. One jolt and it'll go off." He knew about guns. Jake kept a few in the house.

She was too shaken to obey him. He reached across her lap and put the safety on. Jesus, his first rum-running and a man was dead. What if those hicks had taken the plate numbers? Mutt realized his immediate problem was the bum clinging to Sal's running board.

"Hang on," Mutt said. "I'm gonna bump that fat guy."

"No more shooting," she bawled. "Mutt, no more!"

"Just a shot in the keester."

He honked loudly at Sal. Sal waved him on. The road curved and rose between pine forests. Not a car in sight, not a house. Least of all a cop.

It was funny (Mutt thought later) the way he and Sal had understood each other. Hated each other's guts sometimes, never trusted each other. They could guess the other guy's mind. Maybe because they were alike in many ways.

Sal understood. He slowed down and moved to the center of the road so Mutt could get a clear shot at the man hanging on to the running board, swinging the wrench every few seconds, then ducking to avoid the pistol.

Too late, potbelly saw what was coming. With raging eyes he turned his bushy head, trying to make up his mind whether to hand on and keep trying to kill the driver or save his own life.

Mutt rammed him broadside with the bumper and radiator

of the Chandler. The fat man roared curses. His insides turned to mush. Bones cracked and splintered in his legs. He unloosed his grip and rolled into the dirt, tried to stand, and walked on his knees several yards before collapsing.

Sal stopped the Essex. He shifted into reverse and backed up. Then he aimed the car at the crawling monster. He was going to run over him.

"Jesus, no, Sal, no!" Mutt shouted. "He can't do no harm."

The fat man flopped like a beached codfish, spattered the dirt with blood.

"Screw him, he's through," Sal agreed. "But you shoulda killed him."

The taxicabs sped toward Plattsburgh with their alcoholic loads. Hilda stopped crying and nestled against Mutt. She worried: What if they were found out? *What if . . . ?*

Chapter 22

Mrs. Wallowitz was gaunt and shabbily dressed. A poor woman, she was nonetheless mannerly and not without a certain dignity.

She was leaving Dr. Abelman's office on Haven Place when she spotted Jake Chain getting out of his shiny black Hupmobile. A tall woman with a haggard face, she lurched toward him.

Sarah Chain, sporting a tightly curled permanent and wearing a smart royal-blue dress from Loehmann's, sat on a cane chair on the stoop, gossiping with Mrs. Rimkoff. They were discussing Bobby Rimkoff's rising career as "The Brownsville Belter." He was ready to fight the number-one challenger. Mrs. Rimkoff didn't like the idea, although her Orthodox husband said he would let Bobby keep fighting "until he lost." Apparently, there was a talmudic precedent.

Jake paused under the poplar tree and looked at the kids in loose knickers and beanies playing stickball. Years ago he could belt a rubber ball two and a half "sewers." But he'd never had much time to play. He'd always had to work to keep bread in his stomach.

"Mr. Chain, please," Mrs. Wallowitz said.

"Yeah?"

Sarah and Mrs. Rimkoff watched. Sarah pouted. This one was obviously not one of his "hoo-ers." The woman was plain and poor. Mrs. Rimkoff had similar thoughts but said nothing. Everyone knew the pain Sarah Chain suffered. But at least she had money, a car, nice clothes, and new furniture. So her husband had *nafkas*. What else did anyone expect from a gangster?

"I'm the wife of Hyman Wallowitz."

"So?"

"This morning on the way to work they broke his legs."

Jake had spent the day in Queens, checking a local of the Glaziers Union. He had succeeded in getting boss and workers to agree to a "sweetheart" contract neither of them liked. It included a fee for Glauberman & Chain. It had gotten so that the very presence of labor consultant Jacob Chain produced cooperative feelings on the part of adversaries.

"You are supposed to protect him," she said. "I was by Dr. Abelman just now. My husband is in Brownsville Jewish. Maybe he'll be crippled." Mrs. Wallowitz glanced at Sarah as if to say *like your wife*.

"I don't know nothing about it," Jake said.

"My husband is an honest workingman. All his spare time he gave to the union. Then you and Mr. Glauberman came in and you got a contract. But ever since then . . ."

She began to bawl. Her shoulders heaved. Rocks had been thrown through their windows, she said. Her daughter found a dead cat in the airshaft of their apartment. And now this! Two men, Italians, breaking his knees with baseball bats! What kind of protection was that?

"I'll find out," Jake said. "Don't cry, don't cry."

When she left, he walked up the steps and kissed Sarah. He tried to dismiss the Wallowitz incident. He had bought a new Zenith radio, a huge mahogany set, complete with earphones. It was the envy of the neighborhood. A little music after dinner. But the attack on Wallowitz gnawed at him. Disturbed, he left his house and drove to Glauberman's.

Leo Glauberman lived in a yellow brick mansion on President Street, as befitted a successful attorney and union official. He had escaped Brownsville for the luxury of Crown Heights.

"What about Wallowtiz?" Jake asked his partner.

"What about him?"

They were in Glauberman's study, a walnut-paneled room with a high carved ceiling and a view of a greenhouse. The curtains were dark green velvet. The lamps on Glauberman's desk were also dark green. They gave his Teddy Roosevelt face a sinister greenish tint. The pince-nez had no eyes (it seemed to Jake), just two glasses glinting green.

"Who broke his knees?" asked Jake.

"Guess."

"Not my people. I learned about it from his wife."

Glauberman blew air from puffed cheeks through his cupped hands. In a nearby room Jake could hear a scratchy Victrola.

> *Yes, we have no bananas,*
> *We have no bananas today!*

"Wallowitz was a troublemaker. He made a deal with us but he was welshing."

"How?"

"Listening to grievances from his people. Some of them didn't like the settlement we got for them. So he began to complain also."

"Maybe they got a right to complain. It was a sweetheart job."

"Jake, forget your noble past. There are no more Eva Heiligs. These are just a bunch of ungrateful crybabies."

"Working people."

Glauberman got up. He drew the blinds so the view of the greenhouse was obliterated. "It's business. We took over the local. We also get paid by the owners. Metzinger is giving us a hundred bucks a week to keep things quiet. Wallowitz refuses to be quiet. Because the *putz* looks like Abraham Lincoln, he thinks he's freeing slaves."

"You didn't have to break his knees. Who did it?"

"Futka's mob."

Jake spoke slowly. "The deal was that we get rid of Shikey and Futka Frummer. We promised the wet-wash workers we'd protect them."

Something was bothering Jake. Some old loyalty, some sense of who was right, who was wrong. It had been simpler twelve years ago when he was beating up hoodlums. He understood things better then.

"Right! When we hit Wallowitz, we were protecting him from his own foolishness."

Jake shook his head. His starched collar felt too tight. The checkered vest bothered him. He wasn't meant for fancy clothes. "Who decided Wallowitz had to get beat up?"

"The court."

"What court?"

"Five of us meet every few weeks. People with contacts with the police and politicians. We figured you might not like the idea of hitting Wallowitz, so we asked Futka to handle it."

"Brownsville is my territory, not the Frummers'. Leo, you done me a lousy trick."

"Jake, the big money is working *both* ends. We *are* the unions. So what are we doing different than Brunstein or Flugelman, those socialist farts? We get the workers a living wage. We keep the bosses happy. Don't become a Red on me."

"I ain't no Red, Leo. At least we should do something for Wallowitz," Jake said. "The hospital bills, benefits. We should make out like we didn't have nothing to do with it."

"Fine, take care of it." The TR head leaned back. Sightless eyes, gleaming teeth, brush cut tinged with green. "Don't get sentimental, Jake."

Mrs. Glauberman, a busty blonde in a black silk dress and pearls, smoking an oval cigarette, knocked on the door. Oh, it was Mr. Chain? Would he like to stay for tea? Mr. Otzenberger was dropping by. And Judge Nitkin and Assemblyman Franzese . . .

Jake thanked her and refused. Too fancy company for him.

From his hospital bed, Wallowitz told Jake that he did not recognize the men who had waylaid him on Ralph Avenue. They had dragged him into a car and smashed his knees.

"The pain, the *pain*," he muttered. "Mr. Chain, what did I do? You and Mr. Glauberman are supposed to protect us."

"What did they look like?"

"Who knows? It was night. One was fat, round. The other I don't remember."

The Meal Ticket? Jake wondered. Herman Wesselberg, meet Hyman Wallowitz.

Troubled, Jake left the hospital. Why had Glauberman gone to East Side mobsters? The answer was clear. Jake Chain, soft of heart, an old hero to workers, could not be trusted to *klop* a union man. For that they needed a real son of a bitch, a *paskudnyak* like Futka. It was a different game. He had been too dumb and too greedy to realize it.

Jake drove across the Brooklyn Bridge, past pushcarts and delivery vans, and parked in front of the Cayuga Social Club on East Houston Street. He had been there before. It was the Frummers' headquarters. Jake could recall a meeting there a year ago when they had agreed to divide up the city.

A dingy tan curtain masked the window. Kids played stoopball next door. Others wrestled on the dirty pavement.

"Ya fadder's ass!"

"Ya mudder's twat!"

Jake found two of the biggest boys and gave each a nickel. "Watch the car," he said. "A nickel more for each of you when I come out."

Inside the clubhouse he found Shikey and Futka Frummer playing *shtuss* with two of their associates.

"Chain, pull up a chair," Futka Frummer said. He was short, round-headed, and jug-eared, a natty dresser. The late Moishe Nigger's aides had joined his gang.

Shikey was a respectable "front man"—labor negotiator, contractor. Younger than Futka, he was also small, with soft shiny skin. He was freshly barbered and powdered. Black hair, slicked down. Shikey had a spiked moustache and wore three rings. Futka was tougher, meaner, a loan shark and policy banker.

"So, Chain?" Futka asked. "All the way to Houston Street?"

"What about Wallowitz?"

The game stopped. Men in striped shirts, suspenders, and straw hats leaned back and stared at Jake. He was really *crazy*. The madman from Brownsville. The giant who boiled Moishe Nigger and survived twelve pieces of hot lead. (And, rumor had it, drowned the Nigger in chicken blood.)

"The scar on your chin, Jake," Shikey said. "It's getting bigger. Maybe it needs one on the other side?"

"I asked about Wallowitz." Jake sat down. He knew that he was safe. So long as he had Glauberman, and Glauberman owned judges and politicians, the brothers would not dare work him over.

"Ask Mr. Glauberman."

"So it's true. You broke his knees."

"Chain, you were one of the first to do this. A man breaks his word, what else can we do? Who cares if he was a union officer or a nigger who cleans toilets? Don't look so innocent. You started this with your price list."

163

"What did you get?"

"Fifty for each knee."

"The Meal Ticket around?" Jake asked. "I hear he *shtarks* for you sometimes."

"He had to visit his aunt in Jersey," Shikey said. He ordered one of the punks to deal. "Chain, don't become a boy scout in your old age. A lot of *shtarkers* don't trust you. Your trouble is you think only the jerks on the picket line deserve a break. Wrong. Whoever pays gets service."

Jake declined the offer of a drink. Real booze that Shikey was running in from the Bahamas. He walked into the noisy street. The kids were waiting for him. As he was about to enter the car, he saw Herman Wesselberg rolling toward the clubhouse. The Meal Ticket had gotten rounder and fleshier. But he was still light on his feet. He wore a high-crowned fawn homburg, beige tie, a chocolate box-backed suit, two-toned brown shoes. *You got off easy*, Jake thought. *I owe you.*

There was an alley crammed with garbage cans to the right of the clubhouse. Jake pulled his straw hat over his face and left the car. With a swift move, one that almost made it appear he was summoning a friend, he grasped Wesselberg's lapels and spun him into the alley. No one noticed. The kids were matching baseball cards.

"Christy Mathewson!"

"Walter Johnson!"

"Joe Dugan!"

The Meal Ticket gasped and sailed off his pointy feet like a rising balloon. Jake pinned him against a brick wall on which was scrawled in chalk: HOUSTON STREET TIGERS.

"Chain. Whaddya want, jerk? Whaddya doin' in Manhattan? This ain't your place."

"Brownsville ain't yours, Wesselberg."

"Leggo. I'll holler. Futka'll finish what we done to you twelve years ago. Bullet number thirteen."

"Meal Ticket. This is for Wallowitz. One for each knee." And, he wanted to add, for Eva.

Jake's arms worked like pistons. Two blows to the soft gut. A right, a left, below the navel, digging deep into the soft belly. The Meal Ticket's eyes crossed. Breath whooshed from his mouth in a long airy wheeze. He slid to the soiled pavement. "Don't hit, Chain. Don't hit no more."

Sometime after midnight, while a floor nurse dozed and a resident was summoned to emergency, a man sneaked into Brownsville Jewish Hospital and put a bullet through Wallowitz's forehead.

The gunman left no trace. Mr. Wallowitz died in his sleep, deep in morphine. He was mourned by his wife, his four children, and the members of the wet-wash workers local.

Chapter 23

For weeks Hilda Otzenberger had nightmares of the trip to Canada. She'd shrieked all the way to Plattsburgh, babbled, fainted once, clutched at Mutt. *That bastard Sal. That crazy wop.* Now the cops would be after them.

She kept calling Mutt when her parents weren't home. What if the cops came after them? Couldn't those farmers have written down license plates? Two New York cabs? Would they be so hard to find? *And oh, God, God in heaven,* Hilda wept, *the way the blood and all that white stuff came out of the back of his head* . . .

Mutt told her to shut up. Say nothing. Those men were crooks, stealing whiskey from honest American bootleggers. They weren't the kind who went to cops. It could ruin their own business. They didn't give a shit if one of their gang lived or died. Bradford was dead, maybe the bearded man. Nobody would care.

But he was frightened himself. Already he was planning ahead. He'd get an airtight alibi from his boss Futcher. Sal would get one also. Benny Otzenberger had friends in Albany. Mutt calmed Hilda and made plans for another trip with Sal.

They had sold their sixteen cases for sixteen hundred dollars, more than Sal's phony estimate. With deductions for gasoline and minor repairs to the cabs, they each came out with a clear profit of almost seven hundred dollars. As Mutt had insisted, the deal was fifty-fifty. He knew Sal had lied about the sale price, but did not call him on it. Why louse up their future? Mutt reasoned.

"We need trucks," Sal said as they divided the cash inside

his cab. "Cabs are too small. Maybe some drivers we can trust."

They had sold the booze to Reds Mulqueen's brother Babe. Babe ran an elegant speakeasy on Fulton Street, near the courthouse and Borough Hall. He had a blond chorus girl mistress and drove a Cadillac. His place was a well-known watering spot for thirsty politicians. Babe was grateful for, and a bit stunned by, the good stuff that two young punks in greasy caps had brought him.

"See this?" Babe Mulqueen asked. He showed them an empty green bottle with a fancy black-and-gold label. The label read: OLD McCULLOCH SCOTCH WHISKY, *Distilled and Blended in Glen Glarney, Scotland, U.K.*

"Who got ya that?" Sal asked. He spurned the "green" beer Babe offered him.

Babe arched tufted eyebrows. Silent, absorbing everything, Mutt stared at the bottle and at Babe's cunning eyes. He knew Babe trusted him. He was Jake Chain's son. Reds Mulqueen vouched for all of the Chains. When Reds's bar closed in 1920, Jake got him a job as foreman at Kolodny's.

"What's the empty bottle for?" Sal asked.

Babe Mulqueen picked up the corked and sealed bottle of eighty-six-proof scotch that the boys had taxied in from Canada. "See this stuff you sold me?" he asked. He appeared regretful. "One-third goes into the Old McCulloch bottle. Plus one-third water from the Brooklyn Water Company. Plus one-third grain alcohol neutral spirits. Presto, change-o! We get three times as much scotch as what you brought me. Same with the gin. For that I got a fancier bottle."

Mulqueen reached under the counter of the walnut bar and showed them another empty. A clear glass bottle with a flat shape and a red-and-blue label: UNION JACK GIN, *Distilled and Bottled in Wolverhampton, England, U.K.*

"Pretty neat," Mutt said. "You get three bottles for every one we sell you. How much is each worth when you sell shots to your customers?"

"A fortune, lads, a fortune. Now that I shown yez the tricks, don't get smart on me. I know all the Canadian brands and I want sealed bottles in unopened cases. You kids got a good customer in me, so don't screw me up. Understood?"

"Big Irish donkey," Sal muttered as they walked to their cabs. "Cheated us."

"No he didn't," Mutt said. "We learned something. Next time it'll be a hundred and *sixty* bucks a case. If he doesn't like it, there's lots of other speaks'll buy from us. Or maybe we can cut it ourselves."

That afternoon they made down payments on two used trucks. Luigi, an ace mechanic, tested the motors and found them sound. One was a Reo, the other a White. They came with slatted sides and canvas "tarpolions." Sal and Mutt invested in old mattresses and quilts, and several hundred yards of rope. They were ready to go into business in a big way— bribes, secret roads, protection.

Two days after the Wallowitz murder, Jake was picked up for questioning. He and Sarah had just come back from the movies at Loew's Palace. They had seen Milton Sills in *The Sea Wolf*, three short comedies, an "Out-of-the-Inkwell" cartoon, a newsreel, and a "serial."

As they approached the Hupmobile, two city detectives halted him. Would Mr. Chain mind joining them for a talk? At first Jake objected. What had he done? The Wallowitz case, one of the cops said.

Wallowitz's murder had been front-page stuff in the papers. Sarah had asked him about it. Wasn't Mrs. Wallowitz the skinny *yenta* who was bothering him last week?

"What did my husband do?" Sarah asked.

"A half-hour is all," the detective said. "At the Brooklyn D.A.'s office. You don't mind, do you, Mr. Chain?"

"My wife is crippled. I got to drive her home first. What do you want from me? Wallowitz was my friend."

"Then maybe you can help."

Sarah started to tremble. The cops agreed to follow Jake back to Haven Place in their car and give him a few minutes at home.

At the house he told her not to worry. She wept. She knew what he was doing. What he was up to. Why? *Why?* Did he kill Wallowitz?

Lean and sweaty in an undershirt, Mutt was sitting in the kitchen adding up figures. In one trip they could handle a hundred cases. Fifty to a truck. A hundred cases could bring in as much as *twelve grand!* Babe Mulqueen or some other speakeasy owner would welcome them with a pile of hundred-dollar bills. More money would mean more trucks and more drivers.

"What's the matter, papa?" Mutt asked. He looked up from his blue notebook.

"Nothing, Mutt. Tell your mother to stop crying. The cops want to talk with me about Wallowitz."

Mutt had no idea what his father had to do with it. But he did not fear for him. There was something bred in the Chains that obliterated fear.

The assistant D.A. was a smooth-cheeked baldish young man named Wayne Ordell. He wore a striped suit and a black tie and fussed with a briefcase a great deal. The detectives stayed in the room. One took notes while the other guarded the door and answered phone calls.

Jake knew the man guarding the door—a rock-fisted dick named Vorstadt. During the war, Jake had him on the payroll. Ten bucks a week to look the other way while Jake and the Ferrantes "settled" a strike at a pants factory with stink bombs. Vorstadt had showed up during scuffling on the picket line. Jake had lost no time lining him up.

Chain had learned the wisdom of the underworld adage "The store is open." Translated, it meant the cops and courts and politicians were fixed and the swindle or scam or roughhouse could start.

Assistant D.A. Ordell did not look like a man whose store could be opened.

"Jake, about the Wallowitz murder," Ordell said. "Did you know him?"

"Of course. I was an officer of the union."

Ordell looked at papers on his desk, studied mug shots. He held up a fuzzy profile and full-face of the Meal Ticket. "Know this man?"

"Sure. Herman Wesselberg. The Saratoga Avenue Meal Ticket."

Vorstadt stood in back of Jake. He cracked the flat of his hand against Jake's neck. It was like hitting an iron post. Coloring crimson, Jake barely moved.

"Talk, Jewboy," Vorstadt said. "You started *shtarking* in 1910. We got such a file on you, you couldn't read if you had ten years of Jew holidays."

Jake rubbed his neck. It stung a little. A hide like one of his horses, Kolodny used to say.

"That's enough of that, Vorstadt," Ordell said. "Mr. Chain will be truthful with us. How many times have you been arrested since 1910, Jake?"

"Twice, three times maybe."

"Your record shows eleven arrests in twelve years, Jake,"

the assistant D.A. said. "Charges dismissed every time. Carrying a concealed weapon three times. Assault and battery twice. Breaking and entering twice. Extortion twice. Bribery once. Burglary once."

"All frame-ups," Jake said. "Not one stuck. Mr. Ordell, I'm no criminal. I'm in a rough business."

"But who killed Wallowitz?"

"I don't know. But if I catch them, you won't get a chance to give them a third degree. I'll handle them myself."

Ordell reviewed the facts. Wallowitz had agreed to a new contract drawn up by the firm of Glauberman & Chain. Further, he had invited them to be "officers" of his local. But wasn't it true Wallowitz's workers didn't like the deal? Was it not true that an East Side hoodlum named Shikey Frummer had broken the man's knees? Why?

Jake's face revealed nothing. Glauberman had let the Frummers do the dirty work. Get rid of Wallowitz. And Glauberman's hands would be clean.

Or was it *his* fault? He had gone to Futka and warned him to lay off his fellow officers. In a rage he had beaten the Meal Ticket. Craving revenge, the Meal Ticket had then murdered Wallowitz. A helpless cripple in a hospital bed.

Glauberman would do nothing, for he had made a deal with Shikey and Futka, Jake knew.

"So, Jake?" Ordell asked. "Is it true you visited the Frummer boys' club and had words with them?"

"A social visit."

"But you hate their guts," Ordell said. "You kicked Shikey out of Brownsville, the way you—let's see . . ." Ordell consulted notes.

A file on me like a *megillah*, Jake thought. They know a lot, but they had never made a charge stick. There was always Otzenberger to bail him out.

". . . just the way you tangled with a gang led by Morris Pearlberg . . ."

"Moishe Nigger," Jake said.

" . . . and forced him out of Brownsville years ago. Sent him back to the East Side. A year later someone drowned him in chicken blood."

Vorstadt said, "Crazy Jake Chain, Mr. Ordell. The man they couldn't kill. How many slugs did you take, Jake?"

"Twelve. Four still in me. On rainy days they hurt."

Vorstadt circled the chair and put a hand on Jake's shoulder, thinking, the big bastard is made of *cement*. "Something'll hurt you worse if you don't talk to Mr. Ordell. You and Glauberman know who killed Wallowitz. What are you guys doing? Double-crossing your own union members?"

"I never did nothing that was against a worker. Look at my record. So I'm no angel. So I did some rotten things. But only for poor people."

Ordell was summoned by a secretary. When he was gone, Vorstadt taunted Jake with his .38. He ran the barrel across Jake's neck, over his forehead. Jake did not move. Vorstadt didn't scare him. A man you could buy was a man who had no balls.

Ordell returned. "You're to be released, Jake," he said. "Somebody from the mayor's office called. You can go."

A few days later, a Prohibition agent came to Benny Otzenberger's clubhouse and queried the district leader about a trip his daughter had made to Canada with two young men.

Benny now spent virtually all his time in the clubhouse office or touring Brownsville in a chauffeur-driven air-cooled Franklin. He had turned his wholesale grocery business over to his nervous son Heshy. Heshy was a skilled factory foreman, but things were getting rough in the garment trades, what with Jake Chain and his gang extorting money from unions *and* bosses. That rat Glauberman (Benny knew) was the power behind it, but what could he do? Glauberman took care of him to the tune of a thousand dollars a months to keep judges and cops happy.

Otzenberger could neither read nor write, but he always carried a *New York Times*. In the olive-green Franklin, strolling down Pitkin Avenue, seated in his thronelike chair in his clubhouse, the paper was always under his chunky arm or spread in his lap. Evidence that he was a learned man! Often he could be observed, thick glasses on his nose, "reading" the *Times* upside down. He would stroke his thick moustache, like a talmudic scholar pondering marginalia. ("Benny's problem," Dr. Abelman said, "is he can't tell the white from the black. He isn't sure which part he's supposed to read.")

It was thus that the snooper found him. Benny's beady brown eyes were studying a front-page story about President Harding's grief over the suicide of his pal, Jess Smith, the head of the Veterans Administration. *Some pal!* A bunch of crooks, with their oil leases, their payoffs. *Thanks God,* Benny thought, *all Republicans.* (Benny could not read, but one of his young clubhouse lawyers always circled the important stories and gave him a verbal précis.)

"Canada? Why my daughter should go to Canada?" Benny asked the snooper. "She's a girl who stays close to home. And with two men? What two men?"

When the snooper persisted, Benny calmly offered him fifty dollars wrapped around a bottle of "real stuff"—eighty-six-proof McCulloch Glen Scotch. It was part of the last shipment that Mutt Chain and Sal Ferrante had trucked in from Canada. This time they had gone without Hilda.

The snooper was deeply grateful.

"Forget it, Mr. Hutchins," Benny said. "This is from a personal friend. My daughter Hilda is pure as the snow, a daughter in a million, a sweetheart. For what would she want to take rides to Canada?"

Hutchins, a retired fireman from Queens, hired in the mad rush to enlist agents, knew when he had a good thing. He had heard about Otzenberger's power. And he didn't care too much about the daughter. It was two smart kids he was after. Jake Chain's son and one of those guinea Ferrantes. Italians were running alky cookers in their homes and garages all over Brooklyn. You could smell the mash stewing and vaporizing over half of Pacific Street. One of the Ferrante brothers was into something big, he'd been told. A company had been formed—F & C Cereals. Buying trucks. Paying off local cops.

"Your word is good with me, Mr. O," the snooper said. He pocketed the fifty and put the bottle in his briefcase. If he ever caught up with those two wise kids, it would cost them more than fifty bills.

Chapter 24

Mutt decided, after they had made their first run with the trucks and unloaded the cases of gin and scotch to Babe Mulqueen for a profit of eleven thousand dollars, that they were selling themselves cheap.

Sal had similar thoughts. Babe had paid them well for the truckloads, but he would make a fast *hundred grand* before he was finished serving it watered down in shot glasses to his parched customers.

As Mulqueen counted out the money in the back of his

speakeasy, he'd bragged about the manner in which he would rebottle the booze, cutting the liquor with water and grain alcohol.

"And a little caramel coloring, lads, and a touch of fusel oil for flavor, so's the customers don't wise up," the speakeasy owner said. "Jesus, it's a grand game. Glycerin helps to give the booze a 'bead.' Remember who your friend is. And don't get shot by a snooper or some big crook. Melvin Schonkeit likes to think the Canadian run is his. Look out for his fellows."

Melvin Schonkeit was a shadowy gambler, fixer, and money man. He was a king bootlegger and loan shark. He stayed out of sight, out of the newspapers. It was rumored he could fix anything. He was a department store of crime, a genius known as the Paymaster.

"Screw Melvin Schonkeit," Mutt said.

"*Fongool* Schonkeit," Sal added.

"Listen to them," Babe said. His eyes vanished in a piggy grin. "Crazy Jake Chain's son, right? Afraid of nothin', Mortimer? Isn't that the square handle, Mortimer J. Chain? Or is it Morris or Morton or Myron?"

"*Mortimer*, Mulqueen. And you're right. Chains aren't afraid of nothing."

After Mutt had deposited his share in the Dime Savings Bank—under the eyes of a stunned vice-president—he met Sal and Hilda in an Italian restaurant on Atlantic Avenue. They munched pizza and sipped cream soda. Sal objected to her presence. It was supposed to be a business meeting.

"She's in on it," Mutt said. "She made the first trip with us. Besides, we're getting married."

"Since when?" Hilda asked. "Honest, Morty."

Sal's eyes found the ceiling. "Ya supposed to leave dames out of it."

"You know, you can be a real creep?" Hilda said to Sal. "Why don't you look someone in the eye for once in your life?"

Sal said nothing. He disliked the girl. But she, like his partner Mutt, was part of the scheme of things. They needed Benny Otzenberger. They would need him even more now.

"We're *rich*," Mutt said to Hilda. "We're getting married. Sal can be best man."

"Hah! They wouldn't let him in the synagogue. My father would *plotz* if he showed up."

Mutt snapped her garter, nuzzled her neck. Let Sal stew. His sneaky partner never seemed interested in women. His brothers were all married, turning out mobs of small Ferrantes. Sal remained single and secretive.

"Some way to propose." Hilda pouted. "In a Nitalian restaurant over a lousy pizza. With Smiley here as a witness. Honest, Morty, even if I wanted to marry you—"

"You'll marry me, kid. I love you. Right, Sal? Didn't I always say I loved her? When we went to Canada?"

"Yeah, yeah," Sal said. Hilda was a stiff pain in the butt to him. She'd get in the way, and he and Mort had big plans. They had decided to screw Mulqueen. But they weren't sure how to go about it.

Over coffee and cigarettes, the youthful partners decided to buy Kolodny's bottling plant. He was a small-timer. And he was sick, coughing his guts out. A little convincing from Jake Chain's son would help in the negotiations.

"Whaddya gonna do?" Hilda asked. "Go back to peddling seltzer. like your old man?"

Mutt ignored her. They needed a warehouse. A place they could lock at night, a secure plant to mix and rebottle their own booze. A place to park trucks. To hell with Mulqueen and the other chiselers. Why should they make all the profit? Already Mutt was planning on buying two more trucks. But instead of selling the good whiskey to middlemen, they would rebottle it themselves. Mutt was going to see a printer in New York who specialized in labels. The guy designed them himself—reds, golds, and blacks, anything you wanted. Invent a fancy English or Scotch name, print as many as you needed. Also government tax stamps.

"Bottles also," Sal said. "Corks. Maybe bottles you can't fill again so no wise guy can use our old ones."

"I get it," Hilda said. "Oh, I get it."

"Keep ya mouth shut," Sal said. "Ya never heard us."

"Creep."

Hilda entered the conversation with gusto. She was full of ideas. She had taken a two-year course in stenography and bookkeeping at Pace Institute. Why didn't she go to work for them? She could be the office manager for F & C Cereals, Inc.

Sal frowned. In his family women were kept ignorant of business dealings. Cook, clean, have babies.

Mutt thought it was a great idea. "Hey, yeah. We put Hilda on the payroll. Office manager, bookkeeper. A nice-looking dame to talk to customers."

The deal was looking better and better. Kolodny's warehouse and bottling plant. A supply of phony bottles and fake labels. Four or five trucks running booze in from Canada, past Customs guards and Prohibition agents. Payoffs to whoever needed paying off—cops, judges, feds. Benny would help.

"All we need is the alcohol," Mutt said. "Lots of it. We got to get a steady supply. It ain't easy."

"Government warehouses are full of it," Sal said. "But try to get it out. Guys get killed going after it."

"You scared?" Mutt asked.

"I ain't a-scared of nothin'."

"Wanna pull a heist? There's a government warehouse out in Ozone Park."

"No," Hilda said. She grabbed Mutt's hand. "No. No funny business, Morty. I'm in the company now. You two *shmendricks* think you're hot stuff. I know what Mulqueen told you. Look out you don't get Schonkeit sore at you. Five trucks, six trucks, so what? You're just kids. He'll kill you both."

Mutt smiled at her. He kissed her nose. Sal cringed, looked at the door, the waiters, the menu stained with tomato paste. He wished they'd do their smooching somewhere else. Not in front of him. The notion of a woman, a twenty-year-old dame, knowing about their operations rankled him. Deep in his Neapolitan soul, he knew women were the devil, *sfaccim'*, bad luck. He grabbed his balls to ward off the evil eye.

"I need a haircut," Sal said. "I'm gonna see my old man."

The three of them left together. On Pacific Street they paused outside old man Ferrante's barbershop.

In the window was a row of hair-tonic bottles. Lucky Tiger. Westphalia. Attar of Roses. Vitalis. Something clicked in Mutt's mind. He was always full of new ideas, angles.

"*Hair tonic,*" Mutt said.

"Whah?" asked Sal. Sometimes he couldn't figure Mutt out.

"*Hair tonic.* It's fifty percent alcohol. Some guy on Belmont Avenue went blind drinking it. But the alcohol is okay. Or you can make it okay."

Sal blinked. "Whaddya wanna do? Strain them bottles through white bread like the niggers do?"

Mutt squinted, thinking. "No. But maybe your old man sets himself up in business. Ferrante's Hair Tonic. Or some fancy name—Pacific Breeze Hair Tonic. Get it? Then we could get alcohol from the warehouse."

Sal shook his head. The Ozone Park warehouse? Impossible. It was guarded. No windows. Steel doors. Armed guards.

"Ever hear of a Permit of Withdrawal?" Mutt asked.

"What the hell is that?"

Hilda listened, stunned by Mutt's knowledge. He was eighteen!

"The government gives them out if you got a legitimate business," Mutt said. "Also if you got a friend or someone to bribe." He looked at Hilda. "Your old man must know someone."

"What legitimate business?" Sal asked. "We gonna tell them we need their grain alky to cut booze? Oh, boy. You're a *chooch*, Mutt."

"We set up the Pacific Breeze Hair Tonic Company. Your old man is president. He gets stationery, bills of sale, a card. He needs alcohol, right? To make hair tonic. Let's talk to him. C'mon, I need a haircut also. Hilda, I'll see ya tonight."

Hilda sighed, swiveled her hips, walked away. She decided she was in love with Mutt. But she wished people would call him something else. Mortimer wasn't much of an improvement. Mort. *Morty.* If they got married, she told herself, he would be her Morty, and she would demand that everyone else call him Morty.

Old man Ferrante, veteran of Garibaldi's campaigns, wasn't quite sure what his son Salvatore and Chain's son had in mind. But he agreed. His own hair tonic! *Pacific Breeze.* He'd need coloring agents, essential oils, a preservative, and, of course, alcohol. Mutt would supply bottles and labels. They'd sell the hair tonic in the store and peddle it to barbershops all over Brooklyn. Luigi could be a traveling salesman.

The barber, with his roached white hair and Umberto moustache, his drooping face, listened. Then he said, "Salvatore, no fool the old man. You want alcohol to make booze. Okay, I am partner. But also got to make hair tonic, so if cops ask question, we got hair tonic in bottle to sell. *Capisci?*"

A week later, Mortimer J. Chain and Salvatore Ferrante paid Benny Otzenberger a thousand dollars to get them a dozen Permits of Withdrawal. These testified that Papa Ferrante, barber and manufacturer, of Pacific Street, Brooklyn, was the sole owner and operator of Pacific Breeze Hair Tonic Products. That same week they bought out Kolodny and installed fireproof steel windows and doors.

On a summer afternoon, Sal and his father, with Mutt riding on the truck bed, backed the Reo up to the loading dock at the bonded government warehouse. There, Sal paid fifteen hundred dollars for two thousand gallons of neutral grain spirits. Clear liquid treasure in government bottles, crated and insulated with straw.

The custodian of the government warehouse, Mr. Phil O'Connor, was paid off with five hundred dollars. He did not seem to mind. "Dumb donkey," Sal sneered. "He coulda got a grand if he had any brains."

The alcohol was stored under twenty-four-hour guard in Kolodny's warehouse. Two small signs were nailed to the metal doors that had replaced the old wooden door to the stable:

PACIFIC BREEZE HAIR TONIC PRODUCTS
F & C CEREALS, INC.

No one (the police least of all) was curious as to why a hair tonic company and a cereal firm shared a former bottling plant. No one asked. A week after the first shipment of alcohol arrived, Mutt saw to it that twelve patrolmen, two sergeants, and a captain went on a monthly payroll. His father's old adversary, Sergeant Pope, was appointed bagman.

Mutt learned from his father that "the store had to be open." A price list. A firm schedule of payments, Jake said. Ten bucks for flatfoots, twenty for sergeants, fifty for the captain. Plus extras at Christmas.

"You got any trouble," Jake told his son, "ask me." He was delighted by Mutt's enterprise.

An unemployed pharmacist named Charlie Goldsturm was hired to do the "mixing," set up an assembly line, supervice cutting, flavoring, and bottling.

Mortimer J. (for nothing) Chain and Salvatore Ferrante studied their first bottle of Highland Cream Scotch. The label assured the buyer that it was bottled in bond by master distillers in the Scottish highlands. It had won two gold medals! Eighty-six-proof blended whiskey. Actually it contained a third of the scotch trucked in from Canada, a third Brooklyn tap water, and a third of the "purified" alcohol destined for old Ferrante's hair tonic.

The "factory" produced six cases of real hair tonic a week. One bottle was displayed in the office that Mutt and Sal used, and a case was kept handy for the police to observe in the "showroom." Mutt had an artist get up an elaborate display card, a Rudolph Valentino type dousing his head with Pacific Breeze.

Hilda was put on payroll as a receptionist, bookkeeper, and secretary. She took orders on the phone, handled the accounts, and flirted with customers. Mutt decided that for sales to *individuals,* one case was the limit—at two hundred dollars the case. Big buyers like Mulqueen and the downtown speakeasies got a twenty percent discount.

Goldsturm proved to be a genius. He put in a store of burnt sugar, prune juice, oils of bourbon, scotch, and rye, juniper flavoring, glycerin, fusel oil, creosote, iodine, and several barrels of charred wood chips, for "aging."

So long as they could keep the Canada run operating, and get "Permits of Withdrawal" via Benny's friends, they were in business. Luigi and Baggie quit their construction jobs and were hired as drivers and handlers.

But F & C Cereals, Inc., and Pacific Breeze Hair Tonic remained wholly owned by the young corporate visionaries who had founded the firms, Salvatore Ferrante and Mortimer Chain. Each owned fifty percent.

So busy were the partners, collecting vast sums of cash, watching bank accounts inflate, contacting new customers, supervising the Canada trips that autumn, that Mutt found he was neglecting Hilda.

It was still his intention to marry her. He loved watching her in the office. Somehow, the simple dark skirts and severe white blouses, the plain pumps, the pencil stuck in her luxuriant hair made her even sexier.

One evening, when "Professor" Goldsturm, as Mutt had nicknamed him, had closed up shop after "purifying" a batch of denatured alcohol and cutting it into a hundred gallons of drinkable spirits, Mutt found himself alone in the bottling plant with Hilda. She was rolling her stockings, straightening the seams, smoothing her skirt in front of the mirror, when Mutt, redolent of the foul bourbon and scotch "essences" that permeated the plant, seized her from behind.

"I waited long enough," he said. "I'm nuts about you."

"No, Morty. No. After we're married." She was as cool as an icehouse.

"What's the difference?"

For all of Mutt's shrewdness and brashness, he had treated Hilda like a princess. Benny's daughter was no one to mess with. And he was a mobster's son, two years her junior. On the trip to Canada, a few feels, strokes, tweaks were all he attempted. And all, he knew, she would permit. Now, he embraced her, hugged her soft body, let his young rod press against her abdomen. His hands cupped her breasts. Handfuls! She sighed and surrendered. Her father would kill her, she said. Her mother would throw her out of the house.

Protesting as Mutt sought her mouth, kissed her lips, glued his tongue to hers, she let herself be wrestled to the abraded leather couch, a relic of Kolodny's day.

"It's the first for me," she said breathlessly.

Never, never, never was it so good, Mutt decided. And never would it be so good again. He told Hilda afterward, as they lay panting in the gloom, in the silent, fruity-smelling office, that he loved her forever, as no man could love her.

He watched her go to the bathroom and return. She wore a pink lacy slip that could not hide (indeed emphasized) her billowing breasts and delicious hips. Again she nestled close to him.

Once more they made love. Mutt understood at once. He would never be able to love a woman as he loved Hilda. Others would come to him, to seek out the king bootlegger, to be impressed by his power and wealth. But Hilda would be supreme. His first, his best.

"You used something?" She asked.

"No. I was too excited." The rusting tin of Peacock Lubricated Reservoir Ends had remained unopened in his trousers.

"Oh, God. Oh, God." She began to whimper. "What if you gave me a baby? My God, Morty. You're a kid, eighteen. What if you, you know . . . ?"

"It doesn't matter. We're getting married. You won't get no baby."

He held her close, joined to the soft, loving body. Something comical about it, he couldn't help feeling. His pants on the floor. Her clothes all over the place. But the best thing in the world. In the midst of a third round of love—neither seemed capable of tiring—he felt a profound pity for his father. Tied to a crippled, bitter wife. He knew they never slept together. All that strength in the old man, that power, going nowhere—except to hoo-ers.

"Again, again, again," Hilda moaned. "Oh, Morty. I'll love you my whole life."

Chapter 25

"It has gotten out of hand," Ike Brunstein said angrily to Eva Halstead. "It is a curse, a crime. Eva, we need help."

"Tell me. I want to help."

They were seated in the sunny parlor of Eva's brownstone on West Tenth Street. Prematurely gray, his moustache drooping, Ike sat opposite his lost love. Eva sat at her desk. Her mass of yellow hair was bright with afternoon sunlight. Two pencils were jammed into the thick curls around her tiny ear. She wore a short-skirted green silk dress. Her crossed legs were shod in dark Parisian silk. On her delicate feet were expensive black pumps, with heels a bit higher than Ike ever recalled her wearing.

Her desk was an antique rolltop, piled helter-skelter with books, clippings, magazines and photographs. A huge new Woodstock typewriter squatted on a wheeled table. Telephones rang incessantly. Finally, in deference to Ike, she took them off the hook. One was for private calls, she explained, the other for business.

He could see a blackboard above the desk, with a list of her engagements.

> *Sept. 7—Cleveland—Women's Rights, etc.*
> *Sept. 10—Cincinnati—Birth Control*
> *Sept. 12—Pittsburgh—Disarmament, For'n Affairs*

On the wall around the blackboard were photographs of the late Uncle Sourmilk, of Dr. Abraham M. Heilig, his wife and children, and her younger brother Sol, the lawyer whom Ike often worked with on union matters. There was an old family photo, faded sepia, in a gold frame: her parents, young and smiling, and the three handsome children. Eva must have been five. Golden, minuscule, dainty in a pale ruffled dress. A heartbreaker, exquisite and desirable, even as a little girl. Sorrow withered Ike's heart.

"I wish Garry were here," Eva said. "It sounds like something for the police and he has good contacts. Not all judges are corrupt, Ike."

"I am beginning to wonder."

The labor movement needed her, Ike said. Things were falling apart. Yes, he had joined the Communist party. They seemed to him more effective, more disciplined.

"Then you don't need me. I sympathize, Ike, but I'm afraid I'm old hat to the labor movement. The Golden Voice has been stilled as far as the rank and file is concerned."

She was right, he supposed. She was a lecturer and writer. In the newspapers every week. The marriage to Halstead had elevated her from an obscure radical to an object of curiosity, a valuable by-line.

She agreed that the situation in Brownsville was a disgrace. All New York was being plagued by the gorillas who were terrorizing unions, brazenly taking them over, extorting money from members, selling workers out.

"The Communists won't stand for it," Ike said.

"What will you do?"

"Hire our own *shtarkers*. It's the only answer."

"What an answer! More force? More terror? Really, Ike."

"We aren't afraid to use force. Revolutions aren't made by gentle people. I had enough theorizing when I was a Socialist. Look at Debs. Jail, convictions. An idiot like Harding had to save his neck. No more accommodation with capitalists. We'll make a new world like they're making in the Soviet Union."

Laughing, Eva covered her mouth. She leaned back in the swivel chair. Ike was mortified. Her joyous face was a mockery and a goad. *Oh, to have her naked and at his mercy!* But he never would. Breasts like rosebuds. The tiny waist. Cheeks like lilies. The rest, the secret golden filaments . . . He gagged slightly.

"Ike, if you Communists are so tough, why do you have to hire hoodlums? You should have lots of brave young men who'll drive the gangsters out."

He tried to strangle the desire to grab her, tear the green dress from her. When she moved, he got a glimpse of a green lace slip. He wanted to bury his face in her, enter some kingdom of delight known by few mortals. But he was grubby Brunstein, a starveling radical.

"You know as well as I do," Ike said. "What are we? Ghetto intellectuals sitting in dingy rooms arguing about Marx. There's not a knife or a gun in a crowd of fifty of us. Eva, our Communists are the most law-abiding people in the world. Dogs scare us. And we're starting a revolution? In the privacy of my misery I laugh at myself."

"So you're going to find your Jake Chain."

"You did. You didn't have to look far."

She leaned on one hand and smiled at her old comrade. "Ike, you complain that the gangsters are taking over, and what are you going to do? Hire your own mob to make a revolution!"

"We're talking to Melvin Schonkeit."

"Worse than Jake Chain. Much worse. You'll regret it, Ike."

"No choice, Eva."

Without knocking. Halstead entered the room, greeted Ike, and kissed Eva's cheek. Tall and straight, with his lantern-jawed face, finely tailored suit, and stiff collar, he seemed terribly alien to Ike. Brunstein studied him with envy and awe. The thought of this *langeh lukshen,* this quintessential *goy,* caressing, kissing, and entering his beloved dismayed him. Religious and racial backgrounds, Ike always felt, meant little. Brotherhood of Man. Jew, gentile, poor, rich. Character was what mattered. But it was no assurance to him as he watched Halstead talk casually with Eva, exchanging bits of household talk, discussions of their work. He was chairing a committee to force the British to free Gandhi.

"Nonviolence, noncooperation?" Ike asked. "He'll never succeed. The British will shoot his workers down."

"I'm afraid I disagree, Ike," Halstead said. "Gandhi is the model for future revolutions."

"Not in America," Ike said bleakly. "Try nonviolence in the garment district and see how far it will get you."

After mentioning a brief trip he was taking for *Scribner's* to do a piece on the Ku Klux Klan, Halstead left. Another gentle kiss planted on Eva's serene forehead, a loose handshake for Ike.

"How come you have no children?" Ike asked when he'd gone. "After ten years married?"

"I have my career. I like children, but they'd be a burden." She appeared irritated by his nosiness.

"I'm no one to talk. I'm not even married. I only loved you. I still do."

Ike pursued the point of his visit. He wanted Eva to talk to Jake, to plead with him to stop playing the double game, to stop sucking the blood of the unions, to stop double-crossing workers, terrorizing poor people. Jake had served a function once. But he was a parasite now. He and Glauberman and the Ferrantes, the criminal scum of Brooklyn, were monsters who had run amok.

"I see," Eva said. "But it's all right for you to hire Schonkeit's mob to achieve the revolution?"

He looked miserable, his head drooping, his figure slumped. Never a Trotsky. Not even close. He could never organize the Red Army from a military train. He needed Schonkeit's sinister power to battle the bourgeoisie. Eva was right. It was scandalous.

"I'll talk to Jake. But he won't listen. He's becoming a rich man."

"He'll listen to you, Eva. The way all of us do."

Listening to Ike Brunstein, the party leaders decided that fire would be fought with fire. The Communists were no mean force. They had members, money, contacts with segments of the Yiddish press. It was unfortunate that the social awareness of the proletariat was not "mature" enough to comprehend the need for revolution. Not at this point, anyway.

Thus, in Melvin Schonkeit's twelve-room duplex on Central Park West, a humble Brunstein and his comrades met with the great fixer. For ten years Schonkeit had spread his web over every form of criminal activity—narcotics, bootlegging, loan sharking, numbers, and, increasingly, union affairs. In the early days, reputable labor leaders had come to him for help against the bosses, as they had come to Jake Chain. A man to be trusted, Melvin Schonkeit. He came from a prosperous family. His father was considered a saint; he was a reader of the Talmud, a supporter of charities. The son, slender and handsome, married to a redheaded Follies girl, was a different plate of borsht.

"The key to the problem is this fellow Chain," Schonkeit told the Marxist delegation.

"Well," Ike said. "Chain and others."

"He is unpredictable," Schonkeit said. "That makes him dangerous."

Schonkeit's wife passed among them. Lissome and redolent of French perfume, she served "the real thing," scotch imported from the Bahamas on one of the host's rum-running boats. She twitched her shapely silken ass, dispensing eroticism with the whisky.

Ike sipped it warily. Dreadful taste. What did *goyim* see in such poison? Why all the fuss to kill, bribe, fight, cheat, to drink such mouth-searing *drek*?

"The price for getting rid of Jacob Chain," Schonkeit said carefully, "will be three hundred thousand dollars."

Brunstein gulped. He looked goggle-eyed at his aides, an old Marxist named Caplow and a young firebrand named Yodelman.

"We don't have it," Ike said.

"You'll raise it. Assess your membership. You control seven unions, Mr. Brunstein. You want to get rid of Jake Chain? You want to dominate the labor movement? These things cost money."

"There'll still be Glauberman," Yodelman said. "He's the brains. And those bloody Italians, Chain's pals."

Schonkeit stared at the ceiling. Jake had never seen such a ceiling. Gold curlicues in the corners, a painting of Greek gods in the middle. Everything in Schonkeit's living room was heavy and dark, full of texture, smelling of money. The Paymaster lived well. A wonder at age thirty-five.

"So who will protect us? Who'll be on our side during the next negotiations, the next strike?" Ike asked.

"My people."

"Who? *Who*, Mr. Schonkeit?"

"What's the difference, Brunstein? So long as we get rid of Chain. If you must know, the Frummer group. Shikey, Futka, Wesselberg."

Ike looked again at his comrades. Help! *Help!* Was this a way to make a revolution?

"This Herman Wesselberg," Ike said. "They call him the Meal Ticket? Mr. Schonkeit, twelve years ago when I led the strikes in the needle trades, this man was the vilest, rottenest strikebreaker. Chain was an angel alongside such a monster. And he'll be our protector now?"

"Times change, Brunstein."

"Can we—can we—keep all of this secret?" Ike asked.

"That is the way we operate."

"There's Glauberman," Yodelman persisted. "You get rid of Chain, please don't tell me how, Mr. Schonkeit, but Glauberman has power. . . ."

Schonkeit tinkled a copper bell. His leggy wife opened a sliding door, winked at someone in the study. Into the carpeted room walked Leo Glauberman.

"Gentlemen, meet my new partner," Schonkeit said. "Mr. Glauberman is in accord regarding our plans for Jacob Chain."

Wrong, wrong, wrong, Ike felt. Betrayal. Blood on his

hands. Chain was a thug, yes. But was Ike now delivering his hardworking members, the *revolution itself*, to people far worse? Yodelman drained his scotch and gagged. Caplow shook his bushy head. He would say no more. He wished he had not come.

"Ends justify means, gentlemen," Glauberman said. He grinned his Teddy Roosevelt grin.

Chapter 26

Jake parked his Hupmobile on lower Fifth Avenue. He got out and stretched in the early September sunlight. Washington Square Park looked lovely, inviting. He wondered why he never went to the city anymore. More and more he seemed locked into Brooklyn—Brownsville, Williamsburg, Gravesend, Flatbush. He had a yearning for his youth, when he and Sarah and little Mutteh took trolley rides to parks, meadows, the zoo. No more.

He was ashamed of his dullness, his slavery to a life of violence. A movie once a week. The radio. Hanging around Glauberman's office. Out in the street, in factories, speakeasies, restaurants, making deals with union officials, bosses, politicians. Usually he would sit silently, a big strong man, staring at his watch, flexing his massive hands. Glauberman or Otzenberger did the talking. Jake's presence was a warning. A show of strength. People understood his power.

Under the green-yellow dappled leaves, near the stone arch, Eva was waiting for him on a slatted bench. She wore a maroon silk dress falling loosely around her slender form. A string of amber beads, a tortoiseshell comb in her hair. She had taken to wearing it piled high, tucked behind her ivory ears. Small pearl earrings, a pearl brooch.

She was feeding pigeons. They flocked to her, as if aware of her beauty, Jake sensed. *Bushwah*, he reflected. They get fed, they come. They would as soon flock to the drunken Mary Sugar-Bum who staggered from bench to bench begging for pennies if the hag fed them.

Kids played hopscotch in the leafy park. Small boys in beanie caps flipped baseball cards. Others played "war" with checkers on a chalk battlefield drawn on the paving stones. Two kids chased each other on homemade scooters—orange crates nailed to a board, old roller skates bolted to the bottom. Jake recalled making one for Mutteh when the boy was ten.

"Hello, Jake," Eva said.

"Eva, how are you?"

"Tired."

"It's not a long walk. You live—what? Two blocks away?"

He had never been invited to the brownstone on West Tenth Street. Even now she preferred to meet him in the park. Very few of the old Haven Place crowd visited her there. The word was she had become snooty, famous, rich. Eva Heilig and her *shagitz*, with his banker father. Some friend of the working girl!

"I love to walk. But I've been working hard. I lectured last night at CCNY. We're starting an inquiry into the murder of the pickets in Rhode Island."

He had no idea what she was talking about. She explained. Strikers shot down by police in Pawtucket. Private police outside a struck mill fired without provocation. The state and the owners were covering up, bribing witnesses, refusing to prosecute. She and Garrison were heading a committee to investigate the outrage.

"Sounds like they need Crazy Jake," he said.

He sat close to her. Her face was a bit lined, with smudges under her eyes from too much reading. But the eyes were as clear and dazzlingly green as ever. Her perfume dizzied him. The maturity, the lines at the corner of her mouth, gave her a new serenity, a gentleness.

"The old Jake. The defender of the pickets."

"I'm still around."

"So I'm told. Ike Brunstein visited me."

"He's with the Communists, right?"

"I was annoyed with him, and I told him so."

Jake stretched his legs. Who cared about these political shmucks? In the long run, all of them depended on the same things—the fist, the club, the gun. And the bribe, the fix.

Eva asked about Sarah and Mutt. What was he called now? Mortimer? Morty?

Jake shrugged. Not much change with Sarah. She limped, needed a cane. She refused to go to night school, but he had taught her a little, enough to struggle through the *Daily News*. They both laughed—not at poor Sarah, but at the way the Heilig boys' educational efforts with Jake had trickled down to Sarah.

And Mutt? Morty? she asked.

"What a kid," Jake said. "Eighteen years old. He could have been anything he's so smart. An accountant, a lawyer, gone into business. But he quit high school. He's driving a truck."

"That's a pity," Eva said. "I always thought he was intelligent. Send him to see me. Maybe I can convince him to do something better."

"Mutt is his own boss. He's happy. He and one of the Ferrante kids—you remember them—they got a trucking business, a warehouse."

He knew damned well what they had. He had visited Kolodny's old place, walled with cinder block, steel-doored, guarded. A cereal storehouse? Hair tonic? *Hah!* Every flatfoot in Brooklyn knew what was going on inside. Professor Goldsturm's magic. But why tell Eva? Why upset her? Every problem in the world seemed to be hers, Jake reflected. No wonder she and Halstead had no children.

She came quickly to why she had asked him to meet her. Ike was distressed. So were other union officials. Decent workingmen, honest union officials were at the mercy of hoodlums who claimed to be benefiting them but sold them out to the bosses. Those who did not accept gangster rule were eliminated. What did Jake know about a man named Hyman Wallowitz?

"They shot him dead in the hospital."

"Who?"

Jake professed ignorance. Wallowitz was his client. A good guy, not a Red, not a crook. Maybe it was a personal grudge.

Eva said Ike had told her otherwise. Chain & Glauberman had represented the man and his workers. But the rank and file charged they were sold out. They complained to Wallowitz, and he in turn had asked that negotiations be reopened. Did Jake know about that?

From anyone else in the world Jake could have accepted the challenge. Played dumb. A film of innocence over his flattened Slavic face. Nothing. Not his doing. And in a sense it wasn't. He had not killed Wallowitz. He knew who had. The Meal Ticket on the Frummers' orders. A warning to Jake Chain not to get too big. And, Jake suspected, done with Glauberman's connivance. He'd heard rumors. Paymaster Schonkeit was running things from his Central Park West apartment. The gangsters would, as the kids playing marbles said, "divvy up" the unions.

"What do you want from me, Eva?"

"Get out. Stop what you're doing, Jake. I am ashamed of you."

"Were you ashamed when I boiled Moishe Nigger? When I wrecked factories for you? When I beat up scabs so you could get a contract?"

She lowered her head. Sunlight gleamed on the piled golden hair. He loved her so painfully he thought he would faint. Or grab her, there in the crowded, noisy, sunny park, and crush her to him.

"I accepted you and what you did."

"You asked me to do it. I did it. Why? Not for the money, not for the glory. What was glory in clipping a *manzer's* ear off? Eva, I did it because I—" Hesitant, he grasped her hand. "Because I loved you. I still love you. For you, Eva, there is nothing Jake Chain won't do. I knocked over wagons, beat up foremen, set fires. A bum, a mobster. Another Pinchy Paul, a Jack Zelig. I was the scum, the filth of the Jewish community. A scandal to decent people. Rabbis called me names. But you won the strikes."

"Yes, we won." She studied his pale eyes, the ruddy skin, the nose beaten flat in a hundred fights, the lopsided scarred jaw. There was a Grand Canyon, a continent, separating this crude hard man from Garrison Halstead—let alone an Ike Brunstein. And she had to respect him. When they'd needed strength, when the downtrodden had needed a defender, he was there.

"I shouldn't tell you this," he said. Passion inflamed him, rose like a fire from his groin, engulfing his gut and his chest, infusing his face with a scarlet glow. She could almost feel the heat.

"What is it?"

"What those guys did to you, I know."

She shuddered and closed her eyes. "Nothing. I was beaten up, robbed."

"No, I know the truth. I found out."

Eva's eyes, rimmed with tears, looked at his peasant face—fair, fearless. On the surface, a man lacking in emotions. Clod, horse, wagon driver. Hauler of ice, crates, beer kegs.

"The men who did it. I took care of one of them."

"I don't want to hear."

Why was he telling her this? Having opened the subject, he was now uncertain. He was saying in his fumbling way, This is the way Jake Chain operates. This was how I avenged you. And now you come to me, to give up my livelihood? New suits from Jaffe's, a new car, fine furniture, a fat bank account. People wanted to be Jake Chain's friend.

He was telling her that his fists and his courage and his anger had punished the monsters who had hurt her. *Know it, Eva, understand it.* It is not easy for a lout to change. And were he less of a *shtarker*, a man who could hurt, who could *kill*, they might strike back. Shut her golden mouth forever.

"You, Jake. I suspected. Oh, how awful."

"Pearlberg. He won't hurt women no more. Not with his fists or . . ." Gagging, he forced the words out: ". . . or anything else, God curse his rotten soul. Yes, Pearlberg. With my hands."

"I heard he died drunk, an accident."

Jake held up his massive hands. "Drunk, yeah. With these. Maybe he was practicing to be a kosher butcher. He got too close to where they kill the chickens and fell in. Someday I'll finish the fat guy. I know, Eva. In Brownsville I know everything."

Horrified, she touched her lips, drew away from him. "It was wrong. Yes, they hurt me, but not as bad as you think. Look at me, Eva, I'm alive, strong, happy. You shouldn't—God, Jake . . ."

"I did it because I love you. No man can do that to you. I killed Moishe Nigger, you hear?"

"Stop. I won't listen."

A rubber ball bounced between them. Jake fielded it, flipped it to a kid in kneepants. "For you, Eva. So no man could hurt you. Someday, the other one also. He'll find out what it is to hurt Jake Chain's—Jake's—"

"Don't say it."

"—the woman I always loved. I never talk like this to no one. Oh, *they* talk. *Yentas.* Bums in the poolroom. But they don't know how I feel. In my heart. When Sarah was hurt, I remember you came with food for me and the boy. In your long skirt and shirtwaist. Covered with plaster and dirt from the building. Your hair all messed. I can see you. As if you're walking across this park. Small, angry. Your friends were dead. But dinner for me and Mutteh. Why?"

"I felt sorry for you. You are of my blood. My family always felt an obligation to you. Abe and Sol always ask about you." She smiled. "When they read in the paper how you've been picked up for questioning again."

"Tell them Jake Chain is all right. The police never got me. I don't need help anymore. I didn't want help from your family. I wanted you."

"No, Jake. I can't bear to hear this."

"It's true. I'll love you until I die. People look at me—Chain, the bum, the killer. They don't know I started in the roughhouse business because you asked me. And if you asked again I'd do it. For you, Eva, anything."

He shut his eyes, ashamed of his confession. Not the kind of words that Jake Chain uttered. Pigeons skittered, pouted, waddled around their feet. A squirrel chased them, claimed prior rights to the corn kernels Eva had thrown about. The way people chase each other for a dollar, Jake thought.

"Then do what I ask. Get out of the rotten business."

"You think it will make a difference? There'll still be gangsters."

She squeezed his hand. Iron, hardwood. "You could cooperate with the district attorney. Tell what you know. Garrison can arrange it."

"Eva, you don't know me. Chain a squealer? When I was in the hospital with twelve holes in m body, I wouldn't tell. So why now, when nobody's got anything on me? Besides, I'd have to tell how you hired me. I won't talk."

"Jake, we're in different worlds."

"No, Eva. The same world. Like a man and a woman. What you do, all the good things you want for people, I'm not sure I understand. People want—what? Money, power, an easy life. That's all I understand. And I want you more than any of that, but I know it's useless."

"Jake, stop what you're doing. Leave Glauberman. Talk to the district attorney. You can do it secretly. Tell them what you know about the way gangsters are taking over the movement. Give them names."

Jake's eyes were half-shut. He stroked her arm. The thrill unnerved him and loosened his tongue.

"Ask Brunstein, Eva. He knows. I heard he's gone to Schonkeit for *shtarkers*. Good luck."

"How did you know that?"

"It's our business to know."

"All the more reason for you to get out. To find other work. I'm afraid for you."

And staring at him, long-bodied, the power evident in the arms and legs that seemed to burst the tan linen suit, the corded neck and impassive face, she realized she truly cared for him. She could never love him. To her family he had been an oddity, a freak, a matter for minor shame. Like the half-witted relative who, every Friday night, showed up for dinner at the Abelmans' house, was fed, thanked no one, and vanished. . . .

"Don't worry about Crazy Jake," he said.

"I worry about you all the time." She hesitated. "And I feel guilty. Ike and I started your career."

"Don't be sorry. It made me a rich man. Better than living in a basement and driving a wagon. Sarah's going to have another operation. The doctors say she could walk without a cane. You should see how fancy my wife is. A fur coat. Dresses from Loehmann's. Thanks to you and your union-niks."

"And you're never afraid? All that violence? And what they may try to do to you?"

"Afraid? Who'd touch Jake Chain? Glauberman and Chain are friends with every precinct captain, every judge in the city. They're on our payroll."

Halstead, with his knock-kneed walk, came across Washington Square Park. He seemed daintier to Jake. The pince-nez jiggled on his long nose. Funny thing about these *goyim*, Jake thought. They float, they're on air.

"Hello, Jake," Halstead said. He extended a soft hand.

Jake got up. His powerful body seemed to uncoil. He was four inches taller than Eva's husband. "Mr. Halstead, how are you?"

"Please. Garry. You're family. What does Eva say? *Machutonim?*"

"*Machutonim.*" Jake laughed. "In-laws. I'm not one you're proud of, I guess."

"Eva is worried about you. We hear disturbing things. The governor can't permit it. Your Jewish civic groups are furious. I have access to the Seligmans and the Schiffs and the Loebs and other important people in the Hebrew community. They are distressed."

"Give my regards to Mr. Schiff and Mr. Loeb." Jake's eyes were merry, sly. "I'm a Litvak. We don't talk to German Jews."

Halstead looked puzzled.

"Garry, Jake is pulling your leg."

"What? Oh. Oh, I see. Of course. The Schiffs and the . . . Yes, you wouldn't really . . ."

They were dining with the Roosevelts that night. Halstead reminded his wife. They had to dress, arrive early for cocktails.

"Hmmm. Same as Brownsville. Everyone has booze."

Jake walked a brief distance with them.

Halstead said, "Prohibition can't last. The country can't tolerate these killings and gang wars and violations. I agree with the wets. Repeal the damned thing."

"Not too fast," Jake said, enjoying his role as rogue. "Give my son a chance to make his fortune. He's got a good business going."

Eva pecked Jake's cheek. Halstead patted his back warmly. He regarded Chain as a source of comical stories, a troglodyte from some netherworld.

Jake watched Eva and Halstead leave under the arch and start uptown on Fifth Avenue. Two beautiful, graceful people. One could think her a fair Protestant daughter of wealth, graduate of a fancy college. She had lost her accent, eradicated the singsong cadences in her speech. Her legs were elegant and silk-shod, and her figure as lean and shapely as it had been when she was a girl on the picket lines.

The hunger gnawed at his insides, filled him with lost hopes, passions that would never be satisfied. He and Brunstein, he decided, should start a club. No one—Halstead, Ike, no man—could ever have loved her with body and spirit the way he could have.

Hungry for Eva, driven by visions of her body, the limbs and breasts, belly and hips he would never have, Jake went to Bella's in late afternoon. He telephoned Sarah. Business. A late meeting with Glauberman. Sarah sulked. There was a Clara Bow movie at the Palace. Could they go later? Maybe, he said. She tried to keep him on the phone. She was worried about Mutteh, all that business with the trucks in Canada . . .

"He's a big boy," Jake said, calling from a phone booth in Pomerantz's drugstore.

"Oh, sure. Eighteen years old. Jake, what is he doing? New suits, new shoes. Where he gets such money?"

"The trucking business is good. I'll be home in time for the movies. But I won't eat. I ain't hungry."

Brooding, silent to the prostitute Minnie's pleas for a gift—she needed a watch—he emptied his passion into her.

Drained, he sensed that it had given him only marginal relief. It was no substitute for Eva. Only in the heights of passion, the speedy climax, the loud exhalation of breath, the release of desire, was he relieved. Five minutes later the hunger was in him. But not for Minnie Fassbender.

He gave her twenty dollars. A sport, Jake Chain. A few seconds after he had put on his jacket and left, she ran to the telephone.

Hanging up, Minnie began to sob. She could see his huge figure getting into the Hupmobile. "Oh, God. Oh, God in Heaven, I'm sorry for what I do. They forced me, they made me do it. . . ."

He'd be late getting home. Cold dinner, sullen wife. Maybe they'd have time to catch the movie. Always, after emptying himself into his "hoo-er," he felt a surge of guilty loyalty to Sarah. Not a bad woman.

An unsubtle man, he understood that what a man's body needed and what his spirit yearned for were quite different. The surge of power in his loins, the craving for flesh, was at times unbearable. Hence, Minnie. But shreds of love and pity, a sense of partnership, were what he felt toward Sarah. Eva was his only love. Unattainable, distant. Fading, fading further from him with each year of his life. He wondered, as he parked the car and entered Fishman's Bakery on Belmont Avenue, if he had been educated, rich, respectable, and dignified, a man of the world, would Eva have accepted him?

The bakery was crowded with early evening shoppers, workers coming from the shops, peddlers, housewives, students in yarmulkes, Hebrew books tucked under their arms. Jake towered over them—blond, rugged, an alien presence. Some knew him. Two women whispered: *the gangster.*

Hirsh Fishman, the owner, flour dotting nose and neck, hairy and muscular in white undershirt and white apron, a spotless paper cap on his head, heard Jake's voice and came out of the oven room. Jake ordered a whole corn bread, bialys, onion rolls, a pound of aromatic *mohn* cake, Sarah's favorite. And for Mutt, the businessman, danish with nuts and raisins for breakfast.

Fishman came out from behind the counter, entangling himself in the string that unwound from the overhead spindle. He cursed, spread a trail of flour, intercepted Jake as he was about to pay the girl. "For you, Mr. Chain, a present. Forget it."

"Why? My money's good."

The baker pulled Jake's hand away and steered him to a corner of the store. "Listen, I know it's good. A man in business needs friends. You, I trust. I respect you. Enough? I can't talk too loud. Some young tramps are asking protection for my window. But if they know I'm a friend of Jacob Chain, maybe they won't suck my blood."

"I understand, Fishman. You got trouble, come see me. But I got to pay you." He was getting tired of people fawning on him. For what? For his fists and his power?

"All right, all right. You're a *mensh*, Mr. Chain. But at least take an extra from me for your wife. A fresh pumpernickel, the best. Like Russian health bread. Delicious." The baker tossed the huge loaf into a brown bag and forced it on Jake. He now had two large bags to carry to his car, which was double-parked across the street and surrounded by pushcarts. "Remember, Mr. Chain, anything special your wife wants—a birthday cake, catering—drop by. For you, special prices."

"Thanks, Fishman."

Jake crossed the garbage-littered street to where his car was double-parked. Remnants of wooden crates, cardboard boxes, rotting vegetables, newspapers. He liked the bustle and noise of the place. It was alive, bursting with good food, talk, money changing hands. His father-in-law's prospering fruit-and-vegetable store was just a block away. Business had never been better. Around the corner, Eva's mother, the diligent Matla Heilig, always in her green smock, puffing Fatima cigarettes, ran the best stationery store in Brownsville.

Disturbed, he saw himself as apart, isolated. When Rabbi Piltz denounced gangsters and parasities from the pulpit in Talmud Torah Tiphereth Hagro last Passover, without mentioning names, Jake knew whom he was talking about. But how could he explain to the rabbi that he had begun innocently twelve years ago, protecting young girls?

A cartload of bananas approached Jake's Hupmobile. Piled high with bunches of green-yellow fruit, it was pushed by a squat Italian in a ragged coat. Behind the pushcart, a Dodge sedan honked angrily.

"Move, ginzo," someone called from the car.

"He blocka me," the vendor said, pointing to Jake's parked car. "Pleez, mist'."

"Hold your water, banana man," Jake said.

Balancing the two bags of bread, Jake tried to open the door of his car. Always alert, gifted with a sense of danger, he realized he was too late. For one thing, he never carried a gun. Assistant D.A. Ordell had warned him: We catch you on a violation, Chain, we'll throw away the key.

No gun. Arms loaded with bags of bread.

The stumpy wop had stopped pushing the bananas. He opened his old coat—it looked like army issue—and was leveling a revolver at Jake's head.

Pops of orange fire, a cracking, small noise amid the shouts of vendors, the cries of *I gotta apple, pear, grapes* . . .

Jake ducked his head behind the bags. Some old instinct prevented him from dropping Fishman's over-warm bread and cakes. It saved his life.

Six shots were fired. The Dodge sedan backed away to the center of the street. Pushcarts scattered. Jake fell. Hit? Missed? He could not tell. So close was the gunman that he could smell burning powder. Women were shrieking. Peddlers and shoppers were flying toward the stores, falling into doorways. Oranges fell from a cart, bounced and rolled.

The gunman stumbled to the sedan. Hands dragged him in. Honking, knocking over carts, the car sped down Belmont Avenue. A hand emerged from a rear window firing a second fusillade at Jake.

Old gutter fighter, the animal who smelled death, Jake rolled under the Hupmobile, slithering on rotten tomatoes and wilted lettuce. *A salad,* he thought. *With my blood for dressing.*

Fishman was screaming to call a cop. He had seen it all. With floury eyes he watched Jake Chain crawl on hands and knees from the garbage, still clutching his bags of bread.

"Cops, an ambulance, help!" the baker screamed. "They tried to kill Chain! I seen it!"

Jake was on his feet. His head was soaked in blood. Eyes unseeing. People shrank from him. The peddlers flanking his car fled their carts and hid in an appetizing store. He was known to the merchants. The sinister giant. The man they couldn't kill.

Chapter 27

His head had been creased. The first shot, Doc Abelman said, had cut a path through his mop of blond hair, leaving a bloody path on the scalp, splitting the skin. Blood had poured down his face and his shirt and blinded him. Relieved, Jake realized it was the only bullet that had found a mark.

Sergeant Vorstadt and a plainclothesman had taken over Abelman's waiting room, chasing an elderly couple out, warning Mrs. Chain and Morty to wait until the doctor was finished treating Jake.

"He's my father," Mort protested.

On the doctor's waiting-room table, next to his tray of calling cards, Vorstadt had emptied the brown bags from Fishman's Bakery. "Hold your water, Chain," the detective said. "Be glad your old man is alive."

"Beats me." The other cop stared at the mangled loaves. "Saved his goddamn life. He used them as a shield."

Mr. Fishman's iron crusts and thick doughs had absorbed the impact of four slugs. One had missed completely. Two misshapen chunks of bullets nestled in the corn bread like iron raisins. Two more had made their journey through the giant pumpernickel, battered harmlessly against Jake's left arm, and left bloody welts.

"He's got more luck than he has brains," Vorstadt said. "Saved by two loaves of Jew bread."

Abelman opened the green-shaded office doors. Jake came out. He wore a blood-stained bandage around the upper half of his head. He was unsteady on his feet.

"Had to shave his head," the physician said. "Fourteen stitches, but only the scalp was split. I always said pumpernickel was made with a little cement."

Sarah flung herself at Jake, limping with her cane, weeping in convulsive gasps. She had dolled herself up for the movies—a permanent, makeup, a new short-skirted blue dress. He felt guilty. Whorehouses, lying.

He put an arm around her. He felt wobbly from loss of blood and sat in one of Abelman's oak-and-leather chairs. Sarah fell to her knees, rested her head in his lap.

"You okay, pop?" Mort asked. He lifted his mother to her feet.

"Terrific. Ask Doc."

Abelman nodded his head. "Nothing like last time. Maybe he should carry a few pumpernickels around with him. Better than a bulletproof vest."

Mort looked at his bawling mother and his stoic father. A strange pair. But she wasn't as weak as she appeared. Now she was dabbing at her eyes, pleading with Jake to tell the police what he knew.

"How about it, Jake?" Vorstadt said. "Who was it?"

"Some wop selling bananas."

The detective shook his head. They had witnesses. A Dodge car. The gunman had been hauled into it. Someone fired at Jake after he fell. Who? Did he recognize anyone?

"Strangers. Why would anyone want to knock me off?"

Vorstadt blew air out of his cheeks. Tough cookie, Chain. No emotions. A slab of muscle. But how smart was he, getting shot at all the time? The word was out in the underworld—he was *marked*.

At the breakfast table with her husband, Eva adjusted her eyeglasses and read the front-page account of the attempt to murder Jake. She read aloud, distressed, and did not appreciate Halstead's mocking smile.

UNION MOBSTER SHOT AT AGAIN
GUNMEN FAIL TO KILL CHAIN

Jacob Chain, 37, notorious labor racketeer, was gunned down today by rival hoodlums in the Belmont Avenue pushcart market in Brooklyn. He survived with a severe scalp wound.

Chain, a so-called labor consultant and a well-known "shtarker" or enforcer, has been the target of several murder attempts, earning him the sobriquet among New York police of "The Clay Pigeon."

Witnesses said that as Chain emerged from Fishman's Bakery, a gunman posing as a banana peddler opened fire. Miraculously, only one bullet found its target. The others missed, or were stopped by loaves of bread the victim was carrying.

Police said the would-be assassin fled in a black sedan

from which additional shots were fired. No clues were found on the banana cart.

Chain would say nothing, observing an underworld vow of silence.

A much-feared figure in the Brownsville section of Brooklyn, Chain got his start wrecking factories in 1910. He has, in interviews, claimed to be "for the working-man." But police sources said that he now sells his services to the highest bidder. . . .

Eva read on. Hints of disaffection in Chain's mob. More important and more powerful people out to get him. A series of charges being drawn up by the district attorney.

Halstead laughed. "For what? Endangering life and property by showing himself in public? My God, the man draws fire the way honey draws flies. Why are you so concerned about him?"

"He helped me once."

"His time has passed. He's an anachronism, an abysmal brute, as Jack London would say. Honestly, were it not for your blood relationship, I'd think—"

"What?"

"Perhaps you had a girlhood crush on him. Stupid and brutal as he is, he *is* a handsome man."

"Nonsense. I feel guilty, Garry. We used him. We encouraged him. He'll be killed someday. Blasted to bits by people far worse than he is. And who'll be to blame?"

"Not you, Eva. Chain is a product of his time. Forget about him."

She adjusted her glasses and tried to shut Jake from her mind by reading the rest of the front page. Gandhi was in jail again. More scandals in Harding's White House. Investigations into oil swindles. Off Montauk, the captain of a rum-running vessel had shot and killed a bootlegger.

The newspaper, propped amid the gleaming silver and imported china in the sunny breakfast room, dismayed her. What a gulf between the real world and hers. Did she deserve all this? For being beautiful, aggressive, someone who had caught a rich man's eye?

Halstead got up. He kissed her neck, cupped her breasts.

She sighed. "I don't give you all you need. I lack something."

"Never, my lover. The sight of you gratifies me."

When he had left to visit an editor and discuss a book on

the future of American socialism, she telephoned Jake's house. Sarah was cool and unfriendly. Jake was sleeping. He had pain. The doctor had given him pills to sleep.

"Can I come to see him?" Eva asked.

There was a pause. "Listen, Mrs. Halstead, better you should stay with your friends in New York."

She could not blame Sarah Chain for her bitterness. She surely knew how Jake felt about Eva, the temptress who first inveigled him into using his fists to make a living.

"I understand, Sarah. Please tell him I called. And if I can help in any way, you know I want to."

"You, Mrs. Halstead, you can't help him anymore."

In her study Eva tried to finish a speech against child labor she was to make at Cooper Union that night. She had trouble focusing her mind. Someday, she sensed with a tremor, Jake Chain would not be so lucky. Why, she wondered, did he not give up his brutal life? And she knew the answer. It was all he knew.

Chapter 28

"Meet Professor Goldsturm," Mutt Chain said. "Charlie Goldsturm, this is my father.

The bald, pint-sized pharmacist, in starched white smock, flowing black tie, gold-rimmed glasses, let his tiny hand be swallowed by Jake's mitt. "Ah, the famous Jacob Chain." Goldsturm's eyes twinkled behind the fancy cheaters. "Years ago, Mr. Chain, when they called you Crazy Jake—"

"They still do."

"Yes, the old-timers. Anyway, years ago—mind you, I don't hold it against you—some of your boychicks threw a brick through my drugstore window because I wouldn't cough up five dollars a week."

"Impossible," Jake said. "Breaking a window I never did for less than ten bucks."

"Anyway, it's a pleasure. Imagine, now I'm working for your son and Mr. Ferrante. It's better than filling prescriptions."

Mutt had brought his father to the old Kolodny place, now the warehouse and "cutting plant" for the Pacific Breeze Hair

Tonic Company and its mysterious associate, the F & C Cereal Co. Inc. The gloomy plant had expanded, added a great deal of stock, varied its line.

Recovered from the stitching in his scalp—he still had a few attacks of dizziness and double vision—Jake decided he wanted to see what his eighteen-year-old son had been up to. Jake wore a rakish brown plaid cap to cover his shaved skull.

He was impressed. Kolodny's office had been enlarged. There were two girls on the phones. keeping books, sweet-talking customers, handling contacts with buyers and suppliers. One was steamy Hilda Otzenberger, whom Mutt had already told his father he intended to marry. The other was Sal's older sister, Theresa, dark, low-voiced, quite beautiful, with her long Arabic nose, cap of black curls, Greek olive eyes.

Some years ago Theresa had taken a course in shorthand and typing, determined never to go back to a sewing machine. Jake could remember Mutt's telling him how her father and her older brothers had threatened her with a beating if she dared to improve herself, dared to go to a commercial school. She was to get married, have kids, cook, and wear black for the dead Frankie.

Young Sal, however, had visions, big ideas. He would need a front-office girl someday. Who better than his sister? Sal prevailed over family objections. Theresa looked spiffy, Jake thought. A tight lavender blouse bulged by her big bazooms. She wore a short black skirt. He could see the edge of her rolled stockings. Long, thin legs.

Jake could hear Hilda's nasal voice on the phone. "That's right, Mr. Hochstadt. Scotch is up to a hundred and ninety dollars a case. Listen, it's a bargain. We got bigger expenses. What? A dozen cases? Which, Highland Cream Special or Old MacDougald?"

Mutt was getting rich. The kid had never told him much. But he knew about the bank accounts. Sarah knew. As a minor, Mutt had to have someone cosign for him when he opened the accounts. Jake, rarely at home, checking on factories, meeting with union officials and bosses, had become a stranger to the boy. Then, while convalescing from the shooting at the bakery, Mutt had casually shown Jake a passbook from the Dime Savings Bank. Mortimer J. Chain had squirreled away a cool forty grand—*just in that one account.*

There was a rotting fruity odor in the "factory." It permeated everything, emanated from Professor Goldsturm's white-smocked figure. Beneath the smock, Goldsturm wore a tweed vest and trousers. A chain with a fancy gold insignia dangled over his tiny paunch. From time to time, the professor consulted a railroad man's watch attached to the chain. Jake liked him. Class. Brains. Even if he smelled of cheap booze.

"The big vats are for the mixing," the professor explained.

There were six giant copper kettles in the middle of the sawdust-covered floor. The walls had been plastered to double their original thickness. Racks and shelves had been extended. Jake noticed the steel doors. He had a memory of the day Kuflik tried to keep him out of the stable, and how he had damn near killed Bunchik and Little Mendel with a shovel. The old stalls, where the Horse Poisoner had done his dirty work, had been bricked up. Steel beams and steel lolly poles supported the roof. Two trucks were parked in what had been the stalls. From one, Stroonz Rizzo (a Ferrante cousin) and a fat black man named Buster Twine were unloading cardboard crates.

Jake shook his head in wonderment.

"Fresh stuff," Mutt said. "From the Canadian run. The new big truck holds about a hundred and eighty cases. Ten or eleven bucks a case in Canada, but that doesn't count gasoline, repairs, and payoffs."

Rizzo squinted at Mutt and his father and hefted a case of eighty-six-proof Bellows into the cutting plant. "And gettin' shot at," Rizzo whined. "Mutt, next time I wanna partner with a shotgun. Maybe Bobby Rimkoff can go with me."

"They got shot at?" Jake asked.

"He's exaggerating."

Mutt explained that two other trucks were headed north right now, to make purchases in Canada. He and Sal had a contact there, a liquor dealer to whom they paid an extra fee to keep them supplied, help them through Canadian Customs, and guide them over back roads. But the competition was getting tough. Schonkeit was financing his own mob of bootleggers. They were probably the ones who had taken potshots at Stroonz and Buster.

"Gentlemen, please," Goldsturm said. He motioned them from the doorway leading from the cutting plant to the garage. The chemist was intensely proud of his work. People praised his cut booze. *The real thing.* The alky from Pacific Breeze Hair Tonic, barkeeps and customers agreed was terrific. A real *bead.* A wallop. Good taste. You could feel it in your toes. It conquered thirst. O'Toole, O'Connor, Casey, all the regulars from the Brooklyn courthouse crowd, had become devotees of Highland Cream and other decoctions sold by Mortimer Chain and Sal Ferrante.

"The cider is for applejack," Goldsturm said, "but we don't get much call for that. Some of the hicks out in Queens, a few *shwarzers*. On the racks behind you, Mr. Chain, empty bottles, made special to order, all with our own labels. Notice the fancy one for our top-line scotch. It says blended and bottled under His Majesty's Government supervision. And it won the gold medal at the St. Louis Fair. Who can prove it didn't?"

On a long messy slate table, to one side of the malodorous vats, were Goldsturm's magical ingredients. He showed them off to Jake with professional enthusiasm.

"Creosote for scotch flavor. Distilled from the best wood tar. Go ahead, Mr. Chain, *shmeck*. Almost like scotch, no? It can't hurt. But don't try it straight. It'll take the enamel off your teeth."

Jake smiled.

"Iodine is also good for scotch," the professor went on, "but you got to be careful. Too much gives it a stink. It's good coloring for any brown booze. Prune juice is better. See? From the finest prunes. In the big jugs on top. I also got oil of juniper, oil of bourbon, oil of rye. And fusel oil for a clear color."

Jake sniffed the opened neck of a slender dark brown bottle. He got dizzy at once, slightly nauseated. There were hundreds like it on the shelves, labeled, neatly arranged. The odor was appalling. Like rotting garbage. *This was bourbon?* The "oil of rye" was worse. Like the vilest laxative or cough syrup.

Goldsturm showed off the rest of his equipment. Barrels filled with charred wood chips for "aging." Drums of pure ethyl alcohol drawn from the government warehouse with fake "Permits of Withdrawal." Drums of denatured alky, which the professor "purified" as needed.

Jake nodded. "I thought you used only pure alky. Didn't you say so, Mutt?"

"Both, papa. We get the denatured stuff legally. We don't even pay a tax. But we also got an arrangement with the storekeepers and gaugers. The poor shmucks get paid four bucks a day. So for a grand a month they give us an equal amount of *pure* ethyl alcohol."

"Like this," said Goldsturm. The chemist held up a jug of clear fluid. "Finest ethyl. For use only in hospitals and pharmacies. This is beautiful stuff. Just mix with water, whiskey, and a little coloring and fusel oil. Out comes our top product. Old Highland gets only pure ethyl. For the lower-priced brands we use the *drek*. I get most of the crap out of it, but it isn't easy, Mr. Chain. The government is full of tricks. Would you believe the wise guys have eighty different ways of poisoning good alcohol which people could otherwise enjoy? Pyridine, benzene, sulfuric ether, ammonium iodide! People less honorable than your son sell that *chazerei*, and customers die, go blind, go lame, go crazy. Your son will not countenance such disgusting practices."

Inspired by his own oratory, Goldsturm pulled a dark green bottle of Highland Cream from a case. Proudly he displayed the fake Canadian seals, the fake government stamps, the phony label. He held the bottle high to the overhead light and rotated it.

"The *bead*," he said. "Look at the bead. The way it shines, clear, brilliant. No poisons. We have a certain competitor who when his scotch drips on the floor it eats a hole in the rug. In the kitchen it dissolves the enamel from the sink. I am not joking."

Mutt showed his father stacks of filled orders, paid for in cash. Goldsturm waddled off to supervise the cutting of a shipment of gin. Juniper oil, water, ethyl alcohol, plus thirty percent English gin purchased in Canada.

Jake was feeling prouder of his son every minute. The old dreams he and Sarah had entertained—a lawyer, an accountant—seemed trivial.

"We're also working on reconsignments," Mutt said. "I got a connection with a dispatcher at the Long Island Railroad in Jamaica. We pay off the railroad guy to reroute the stuff to us. Then we pay off the paint or varnish people who bought the alky. They don't care. They make more dough selling us ethyl alcohol than they can manufacturing paint. We'll unload at the East New York station."

"You had any trouble from competition?" Jake asked.

"Some. Your name helps."

"I thought it would. They know who your old man is."

Winking, Mutt led his father past the shelves stacked ceiling-high with cartons ready for shipment. "Some guineas came around. They make their own stuff on alky cookers in their homes. Sal and I only buy from his brothers. But these other wops distill it from anything—garbage, potato peelings, rotten vegetables. The only reason I buy from the Ferrantes is they're old friends, and they work for us. Besides, the old man is an officer of the hair-tonic company. That's how we got our first alcohol."

They paused outside the office, where Theresa and Hilda, ripe dark fruits of the Mediterranean, labored. Theresa was making entries in the books. Three sets of books. One for Pacific Breeze; one for F & C Cereals; and a third secret set.

"Wine?" Hilda shouted to Mutt. "We handle wine?"

"Not yet," Mutt called back. "Who wants it?"

"Friend of Hochstadt's. He needs six cases of red wine."

"Tell him to call back in an hour. I'll think of something."

Jake was getting an education. He looked into the factory. Professor Goldsturm was supervising Stroonz and the black man, Buster, in an odd maneuver. They were immersing cases of cut scotch in a metal vat.

"What's that?"

"Seawater," Mutt explained. "We let it stain the cases. It stinks from sea salt. The suckers are convinced it's the real stuff from Long Island. A guy complains it's cut, we say to him, smell the seawater on the label."

The steel garage door groaned on its rollers. Sal and Stroonz were pushing it open. One of the trucks from Canada was inching in.

In broad daylight, Jake marveled. They had to be paying everyone off. It was surely easier than *shtarking*. No worry about Communists, union officials, Wallowitzes—people Jake did not want to harm. Mutt, Sal, and the professor supplied a *need*. Everyone cooperated. Everyone took a cut.

"How'd it go?" Mutt asked the driver. It was Baggie Ferrante.

Baggie pointed to four round gouges on the metal door of the cab. "Shot at us again," he said. "Me and Vin were lucky to make it."

"Shonkeit's mob, or the hicks in Canada?"

"Feds guarding the lumber road. I think maybe we busted a couple cases."

"Gentlemen," Goldsturm said, approaching Mutt and Jake with a bottle. "To mark Mr. Chain's recovery. Newly mixed, fresh from the vat, my deluxe line for the new label. Aberdeen Dew. Go on, have a snort."

He passed the bottle to Mutt, who declined and gave it to his father. Even good whiskey nauseated him. Mortimer J. Chain was a cream-soda and celery-tonic man.

Jake took a swig. His eyes popped, his throat constricted. He felt as if the wound on his scalp would be blown apart.

Staggering backward, he shoved the bottle of "Aberdeen Dew" at its creator.

"A little strong, Mr. Chain?"

"It tastes like horse piss, professor."

"We can't make enough of it." Mutt laughed.

In the office Jake could hear Hilda taking another order. *Ten cases of Highland Cream, six cases of Parliament Gin, six cases of Kentucky Meadow Bourbon . . .*

Goldsturm let his lips touch the mouth of his new creation, blinked a few times, exhaled. "I'll soften it with ethyl. The stuff we get from the backyard stills has too much potato peel. It gives it a stink."

Jake looked at his pocket watch. He had a meeting with Glauberman. His first since the banana man tried to kill him. A lot of things were bothering him. The lawyer was trying to run the whole labor show—Communists, right-wingers, Jewish unions. Cut the unions, cut the bosses, make everyone pay. Jake wondered about the attack on him.

"Pop," Mutt said, at the door. "Join the business. Enough with *shtarking*. This is better."

Jake shook his son's hand. "Only if I can help, Mutteh. No free ride for Jacob Chain."

Mutt smiled. The dark foxy face was full of intelligence, a face that understood the power his father radiated, the respect his name evoked. It would mean dividing the profits. But Mutt saw that the business was growing faster than they could control it. Extra hands, extra brains, extra courage would be needed.

The following Saturday night, Sarah's parents, the fruit vendor Shimen Klebanow and his minuscule wife, Leah, came to the Chain house for dinner. Mutt was not there. Saturday nights were his to court Hilda. They were off to a vaudeville show at the RKO Albee and a trip to Coney Island. A power in his own right in Brownsville, Mutt, finished with the menial work of cabdriving, had access—in exchange for a bottle of "real stuff"—to the unlimited use of Futcher's yellow cabs. Hilda complained about being hacked around Brooklyn in a taxi. Mutt assured her that he was eyeing new cars. A Buick or a Chandler.

Shimen Klebanow was Orthodox. Now that he was a prosperous merchant, thanks to Jake's generosity, he was afforded a better seat in the synagogue. He made contributions to the building fund, toward the purchase of a new Torah, to the Hebrew school. A shy man with a full gray beard and curling earlocks, who wore a black homburg and a black "alpaca" coat on the sabbath, he regretted his daughter's ignorance and his son-in-law's shadowy pursuits. But he rarely expressed an opinion.

His wife, Leah, withered at fifty-five, looked to be seventy. Yet she worked a twelve-hour day, running the cash register and keeping the books. Their store was famous for the quality of its fresh melons, excellent vegetables, and luscious fruits.

The sabbath having just ended with an evening service which the Klebanows had attended, the four settled down to a meal of brisket of beef, cholent, carrots and prunes from the Klebanow store, and a noodle pudding laced with raisins and cinnamon.

Jake ate sparingly. His head ached. He had been told by Doc Abelman that he might have sustained a concussion. Rest, get away, no exertion, the doctor said. Abelman had arched his eyebrows as if to say, "And no more *shtarking.*"

Jake admitted to himself he was in trouble. Glauberman was proving a pain. He was always busy or in New York, or downtown at the courthouse. Jake didn't like getting the runaround. About all he had to cheer him up, apart from his son's booming business, had been a phone call from Eva. The fluty voice made him shiver. He told her not to worry about him. It was nothing. The *gonovim* who were after him were such cowards they had to hire a dago with a banana cart. Better he should have tried to hit him with bananas than fire bullets. Lousy twenty-twos, at that, Jake said as Eva gasped. They couldn't kill with a thirty-eight years ago. . . .

Eva began to cry on the phone. *"Get out, get out,"* she pleaded. The D.A. knew her husband. He had warned Halstead that the day of labor racketeers was ending. The governor would not tolerate it. . . .

When she hung up, Jake sensed the old hunger for her. Worse than ever. He would die craving her.

Dinner did little to relieve his gloom, except for one aspect that amused him, and then intrigued him. Klebanow had brought a bottle of legitimate kosher wine from a New York State distillery.

"Pop, where did you get this?" Jake asked. He sipped it. Sweet. Pure. Not like the poison Professor Goldsturm had forced on him.

"Rabbi Piltz made me a present."

"Where does he get it?"

"For rabbis they got a special arrangement." The fruit vendor spoke a Romanian-Yiddish. Jake had trouble following the explanation. But he absorbed enough of it, ignoring Sarah's interruptions.

Since wine was obligatory in synagogue services and in the sacraments performed in the home, rabbis and priests were given a monthly allotment of wine drawn from government warehouses. The wine was sold to members of the congregation at cost—a gallon of wine a year for each adult member of the family, up to a total of five gallons.

Jake was fascinated. A new one on him. Something called a "Permit of Withdrawal" allowed the rabbi to procure the wine. The rabbi would present a list of his congregation and an estimate of their needs. No questions were asked.

"Just like that?" Jake asked.

"Just like that."

Sarah and her mother, bored with the talk about wine, cleared the table and went into the kitchen to clean up. Sarah had promised her mother an evening of listening to the new radio. Beautiful music, she said, a treat.

"Listen, papa," Jake said. "I got an idea. You want to help me and my son?"

Klebanow shifted uneasily in the dining-room chair. He knew all about his son-in-law. A gangster. A man who killed. Hardly an admirable Jew. Rabbi Piltz, a revered Vilna scholar, would never mention Jacob Chain's name in or out of his shul. He tolerated Shimen Klebanow as an honest man, a *gelernter* and a donator. But his son-in-law! A scandal and an outrage!

"Papa, get me from the rabbi's office some sheets of his stationery. What he writes his letters on."

"Why?"

"I'll explain later. When he ain't looking, grab a bunch of papers."

Klebanow feared his son-in-law. But what was S. Klebanow before Jake had set him up in a store? A peddler shoving a pushcart through Brownsville. Getting up at four in the morning to shlep the cursed cart to the wholesale market, haggling over carrots and potatoes and onions with heartless merchants. Now they came to *him*, delivering fresh-from-the-farm tomatoes and soup greens and asparagus. Klebanow's Fancy Fruits and Vegetables was no cheap operation. And he had Jake to thank for it. Rabbi Piltz would not miss his stationery.

"One other thing, papa," Jake said.

"Please, I can't steal the rabbi's prayer books."

"Meet me by the Kolodny place on Monday morning with three of your friends, and the stationery."

"What kind friends?"

"The older the better. Beards, black hats, long coats, *tsitsith*. Like rabbis."

Chapter 29

The show at the Albee was terrific, Mutt and Hilda agreed. Eight vaudeville acts! Plus a Charlie Chaplin short, a newsreel, an episode of *Tarzan*, and a western movie. On the stage a man juggled bread knives, a "tramp band" had them in hysterics, and a woman in a green velvet evening gown sang arias from Italian operas, while two stooges smoked through her act.

In the balcony, Mortimer Chain, bursting with desire, slipped one hand under Hilda's skirt and inside her green silk bloomers. She locked her thighs and trapped him. With the other hand he massaged her left breast. She protested, wriggled away from him, punished him with ineffectual slaps on his hand. They seemed to him more like invitations than protests.

Later, they parked on Surf Avenue near Pallini's restaurant. Hilda staggered from the taxi. Mutt had taken her on a wild careening ride through Brooklyn. She had tried to make him slow down. They'd get a ticket, for sure, she shouted, they'd be stopped by cops. And she knew that he always carried a "sample case" in the trunk of the taxi.

"Morty, you're crazy," she had cried. "Right through a red light! On Ocean Parkway!"

"It was changing."

"You'll see, wise guy. A cop'll stop you. He'll look for the booze. It still smells in here from a broken bottle."

"I'll hand him a sawbuck and a bottle of Highland Cream and he'll let me go. C'mon, sit closer. I wanna touch you."

The construction of Mr. Futcher's Yellow Cab presented

problems for traveling lovers. There was no seat next to the driver, just a dusty grease-stained black pit, for change box, rags, tools. Mutt had improvised a seat of sorts—a cane-back chair with cut-off legs and a soft kapok-filled cushion. On this unsteady throne, Hilda had sat, clinging for dear life to the meter, her body jolted black and blue as the rattling Checker bounced toward Coney Island.

"Hands off," Hilda said. "Honest, I never saw anyone with such hot pants."

"Because I love you. I mean it."

Hilda believed him. A kid, a *shnook*. Two years her junior. But already the "Boy Wonder" of booze. Her astute father was awed by the aggressiveness and ambition of Mortimer J. Chain. He was making his old man Jake look like a tinhorn.

In the middle of the spaghetti with red clam sauce (Hilda shied away at first because she had never eaten a clam), Mutt decided to contract business. He left her dipping crusty bread in the clam sauce, lugged his sample case from the trunk of the cab, and went into the kitchen to talk to Dominic Pallini. Dom was an old associate of the Ferrantes'. Who was the leading retailer in the Coney Island area? Mutt asked him. Did Dom sell booze? What about speakeasies? Coney Island had to be loaded with them.

"You kiddin'?" the pot-bellied man in an undershirt and sauce-stained apron asked. "You can buy booze in any store onna block. The drugstore. The barbershop. The candy store. *My* jernt. Any other restaurant. Any candy store. There's an undertaker around the corner sells wine in the back room. Some days the stink from hooch is so bad you can't smell the ocean."

Mutt absorbed this. He took out a sealed bottle of his chemist's latest achievement—Aberdeen Dew, guaranteed eighty-six-proof, Distilled and Blended in the Scottish Highlands under the Supervision of His Majesty's Government. The handsome black-and-gold label displayed two medallions—First Prize, St. Louis Exposition; First Prize, Paris World's Fair.

"Try this, Dom. We also got gin off the boat from the islands, real Kentucky bourbon, anything you want."

The restaurant owner stirred a frypan full of sizzling veal, peppers, and mushrooms, added a bit of garlic, then opened the foil cap, tore away the "revenue stamps," and yanked the cork out with his teeth. He wiped his mouth—"Get the garlic taste out, or it'll ruin the scotch," Mutt advised—and took a long draft of Goldsturm's elixir.

Dom Pallini was an experienced taster, a retailer who knew his booze. And although he had a generous capacity for alcohol, he was never drunk. Aberdeen Dew watered his eyes, turned his cheeks as red as his tomato sauce, and left him gasping. He reeled backward.

"Jesus. Jesus, it's got a kick like a *sfaccim'* Mack truck. I'll take a case."

"We don't sell less than six cases, Dom. Ten-percent discount for twelve cases. A bargain. A hundred and eighty bucks a case. The real item, right from Canada. You can see the original seals yourself. Just the way they bottled it in Scotland."

"Let's try it again."

Pallini took a second swig from the bottle. He was seized with a fit of coughing that almost blew out the gas jets under the simmering veal. He bent double, grabbed his diaphragm, straightened up, and said, "Boy, that's *prima* stuff, kid. It got to be from the other side. Whadda kick! My customers been complainin' the scotch I get is too watery, you know? I'll take the twelve."

Pallini was turning pea green. Sweat issued from his swarthy face and dripped into the veal cacciatore.

"Good stuff, kid. Kicks like a *chooch.*"

"Sale?" Mutt asked.

"You got it."

Mortimer Chain smiled. This *proved* it was real stuff.

Returning to the table, Mutt found Hilda pouting. "What were you doing in there so long? Honest, Mutt. Business, business, business."

"I made a big sale. A new customer."

"Is that all you ever think of?"

"One other thing. I love you, babe. Let's get married soon, huh?"

"You're eighteen."

"But I'm a man, right? What about all those guys who wanted to marry you? The lawyer, and the accountant, and the guy with the drygoods store. I'm better than any of them."

"Well, you're *nice*r." She tossed her hair, looked out at the surf and the gray beach. "My father doesn't care for your family, Morty. He says I'm asking for trouble. He doesn't even like that I work for you and Sal."

Mutt lit a cigarette and passed one to Hilda. "Your old man is scared I'll get shot at. Is that it? Or blown up? Never.

My father's coming into the business. A partner. Nobody messes with Crazy Jake. Tell that to Mr. Otzenberger."

"Oh, my God," Hilda moaned. "Worse and worse. Papa'll never let me marry you. He says your father is on a *list*. They'll get him someday."

Mutt paid the bill, helped Hilda up, and guided her into her topcoat. It was mid-October, cool near the ocean. "Nobody gets the best of the Chains, Hilda. Tell your old man. Know why? 'Cause we ain't afraid of anyone."

They turned a breezy corner. The sea wind swirled Hilda's dark green skirt. She giggled and held it down. Mutt drew her close. They walked toward the boardwalk. The concessions were boarded up; a lone sign for "Skee-Ball" rattled in the wind.

"Morty, I'm scared," Hilda said.

"What are you scared of?"

"I know what happens. I went to Canada the first time with you. When that creep Sal—when he— Morty, I still have nightmares about that red-headed guy. Someday the Canadian cops, or his family . . ."

"Nobody messes with the Chains."

"And the trucks that come back with bullet holes. I hear what you and the Ferrantes talk about. Schonkeit. And the Customs guards, with guns. Morty, I love you, even though your hands are all over me. I don't want you to get hurt."

His hands were, indeed, caressing, kneading, stroking her back, her waist. Soft and full. She wore no corset. The feel of her flesh, even beneath layers of clothing, inflamed him.

"We're getting rich," he said. "Nobody can hurt us. We're getting married."

They heard the beating of the surf. A mysterious sound. Mutt could recall his father telling him about the first time he saw the ocean. From the rail of a ship leaving Hamburg. So much water, so much to fear. Jake was alone, in patched clothing, carrying a sack of torn underwear and darned socks. A passport was sewn into his ragged coat. A tag with the name Yankele Schoen was tied around his starved neck. He had been given a paper bag of hard bread, sausage, and rocklike cheese to last him for fifteen days at sea. That and water had kept him alive. For ten days he remained unclaimed at Ellis Island, until the Hebrew Orphan Asylum took him.

"I'm freezing," Hilda said. "Let's go back to the car. I don't know what's worse, freezing here or getting bounced around in that taxi."

"I'll make you warm."

Mutt spread his jacket on the sand. He pulled her down with strong hands and fell on top of her.

"Ouch. Ouch. Don't hurt."

His moves were so swift, so expert, so coordinated that she barely gasped when he entered her.

"Oh, Morty. We're one person again."

"Forever, kid."

The following Monday, Hilda was still finding sand in her shoes, her skirt, her coat—indeed, in the most personal parts of her body.

Mutt teased her. "Hey, Sandy," he said. "That's your new nickname. Like the dog in 'Little Orphan Annie.' Say 'arf,' kid."

"That isn't funny. And not so *loud*."

Theresa Ferrante entered the office. The girls got to work early. Both complained to their bosses. There was more work than they could handle. They needed a third girl to help with phone orders.

Mutt tickled Hilda's neck and kissed her ear.

"You two better stop necking in here," Theresa said. "I'll snitch to someone."

"To who, Theresa?" Mutt asked. "Hey, Theresa, we're getting married. First thing next year. You're invited. You and all your brothers."

"It's true," Hilda said.

"So where's your ring?" asked Theresa. "Or at least a watch?" The rule was strict among Italians. Watch first, when the engagement was announced. Ring when the wedding date was announced. And a schedule for shopping for bridal clothing, furniture . . . Mutt and Hilda were different. Maybe because Hilda had no mother, Theresa thought. Besides, with her politician father and Mutt's money—*the fortune that punk was making!*—they would have no problems.

Sergeant Pope of the 71st Precinct appeared with his monthly checklist. Grumbling and rubbing his eyes, Sal joined Mutt. They did business with the bagman on the hood of one of the new White trucks. The list was checked carefully. Sal gave the officer a thousand dollars in twenties in a tan envelope.

"We're getting two more trucks," Sal said. His eyes never met Pope's. "In a few weeks we're knockin' a wall down and adding garage space for two more trucks. We'll get permits. We just don't want no trouble from cops when the work starts."

"*Eight* trucks?" asked Pope. "That may mean a little extra."

The Reo pulled into a bay and began unloading home-cooked alcohol in glass jugs labeled "Adirondack Mineral Water." Sal had bought a supply of jugs and labels and distributed them to the cottage cookers.

The home distiller, a squat Italian with a handelbar moustache, was helping Buster unload. Sal walked up to him and in a menacing voice began berating him in Italian.

"What's one wop saying to the other wop?" Pope asked Mutt.

Mutt had picked up some Italian. "Cockroaches," he said. He smiled at the officer.

"Hunh?"

"Cockroaches. Those damn guineas use anything to cook alky. Bugs get into the mash. We had complaints about Juniper Tree gin. It's the cheap line, so what's a few dead bugs?"

Sergeant Pope gagged. He'd been drinking Juniper Tree since last month's payoff. "I'll take Aberdeen Dew this time."

The cutting plant and the loading bay were always busy on Mondays. Several Ferrante brothers were on hand, as well as Professor Goldsturm, Buster, Stroonz, and the girls.

Officer Pope, carrying a three-pack of scotch sewn into a "burlock," walked out of the steel door. He bumped into Jake Chain as he stepped onto the pavement.

"Well," Pope said. "If it ain't the proud daddy of a grand businessman. No wonder nobody hijacks them. They know who they'd have to fight."

Jake did not smile. "Me? I scare people? That's funny, officer. I ain't *klopped* no one in years. *Years.* Give my regards to the people at the Seventy-first. I remember them from the old days on the picket lines. How come you were never around when Moishe Nigger hit girls?"

"I remember the time we picked you up after the Nigger went under for the third time."

"A pity. He thought the chicken blood was the Betsy Head Park pool. Imagine. Swimming in the middle of the night."

Politely, Jake held the door of the prowl car open. "And a good day to you, sir." He doffed his checked cap as the car pulled away. "Lousy donkey," Jake said softly. "You'll be on somebody's payroll all your life."

He waited in the autumn sunlight, enjoying the mild day. He hadn't yet seen Glauberman to tell him of his decision to quit. By now he was convinced the banana peddler had been hired by Schonkeit, maybe with Glauberman's consent. But since he was alive, he'd give Leo another chance. They would part amicably.

Shimen Klebanow, accompanied by an older and tinier man, came shuffling down the street. Both wore black alpaca coats and undented homburgs. The little man had a beard twice as long as Jake's father-in-law's. It was creamy white, tinged with a becoming yellow around the edges. His eyes glinted with old intelligence.

"Good morning, papa," Jake said respectfully to Klebanow. "Your friend? Only *one*? I could use two or three."

"Mr. Gelb. Retired. A cutter for the furriers, sixty-two years."

Ancient Gelb grabbed Jake's hand. "You I remember. Jake Chain. In 1912 you stuck up for us against the bosses. I was on strike twenty-eight days."

"Let's see," Jake said. "At Koppelman's Furs? Blake Avenue?"

"That was me. I was a kid sixty-five years old, a first-class cutter. The boss tried to bring in scabs. Mr. Chain, you turned over a truck and started a fire. We all cheered. I'm right?"

Jake grinned. "You're right, Mr. Gelb."

Klebanow fidgeted. If Mr. Gelb knew what his son-in-law was up to (the fruit vendor himself wasn't certain), he might not be so overjoyed at the reunion. *Oi, those Chains.*

"Come in, gentlemen," Jake said. "Take a seat in the office and we'll get to work."

The oldsters followed Jake into the warehouse, past Professor Goldsturm's aromatic vats and stained tables, past the shelves of cases and bottles. Klebanow had been there before. He was used to the odor. Old Gelb sniffed and licked his cracked lips. "I could use it at night a little drink myself sometimes. For my heart."

You'll get a drink and more, zayde, Jake thought.

In the office Mutt joined them. "Hey, grampa, whaddya doing here? Grandma's by herself in the store?"

"Monday is slow," the old man said.

"You got the rabbi's stationery?" Jake asked.

Klebanow handed him a manila envelope. Jake extracted a half-dozen large white sheets. At the top was the name of the

213

synagogue, its address, and in smaller letters, in Yiddish and English characters: *Rabbi Leb Benjamin Piltz, Graduate of the Vilna Yeshiva.*

"Pop, what's going on?" Mutt asked.

"I heard you needed wine. Watch how your father knows a few things. First, we'll need a lot more copies of this. I can't keep sending grampa into the rabbi's study to borrow stationery."

"I got a printer can make all we need," Mutt said.

"Hilda, you ready?" Jake asked.

"Sure."

"Type me two letters. How do you say it? To the person in charge? To the warehouse? What?"

"To whom it may concern."

"Nice. Then say, 'The bearer of this letter is my associate, Rabbi Shimen Klebanow—' "

"I'm no rabbi."

"Me neither," said Mr. Gelb.

"It wouldn't hurt to say you are. You're so religious, you're *almost* rabbis."

"Hilda? You listening?" Jake asked. She nodded, taking shorthand notes. "Rabbi Shimen Klebanow, who is my associate, presents to you a list of his congregation, and their needs for sacramental wine. Then say something nice, like he thanks them for their consideration, whatever you say polite at the end of the letter. Then another letter to introduce Rabbi—what's your first name, *zayde?*"

"Schmul."

"Rabbi Schmul Gelb, an associate who presents a list of his congregation and their needs for wine."

Mutt was laughing. "Pop, you think this'll work?"

"Watch me, sonny. Now we need lists. Theresa, go through the Brooklyn telephone book. Make two separate lists. Only Jewish names from Brownsville and East New York. Mix it up, like every other one gets two gallons, then a few with three gallons, and some for four and five."

"Just names outta the book?" Theresa's eyes were as round as the glass dishes in which Goldsturm mixed fusel oil.

"Sometimes two in the family, anything up to five. Each person gets a gallon, but five is the most."

Mutt said, "Pop, you'll need the Permits of Withdrawal. We fill in everything except the amount. Better be ready to grease the guy. All this trouble for a hundred cases of kosher wine?"

Jake winked. "You could give them to your professor, and it could come out *three* hundred cases, right?"

Jake shepherded his bearded friends into his Hupmobile. Buster Twine, the black workman, was to follow him in the Reo truck. Two hours later the Reo was groaning and rattling under the weight of one hundred and eighteen gallons of genuine Concord grape wine.

The scheme had worked like a new Ford motor, humming, purring, all the parts in order, Jake reflected as he returned to his son's warehouse. The storekeeper, a rat-faced clerk named Curtis, had surveyed the two "rabbis" with mean eyes. Jake slipped a fifty-dollar bill in with the papers.

"Pair of beavers," the man said to Jake. "Them old hebes really guzzle sweet wine."

"For religious purposes only."

Curtis assumed that all old Jews in black coats and long beards *had* to be rabbis. The lists were nothing new. He'd seen dozens of them. Assured he was dealing with honest men, he did not bother to check the congregations. It was lucky, Jake thought, that he hadn't. Theresa, prodded by Jake to hurry up, had included several Italians, a few Irish, and a Methodist minister from Ridgewood.

After Buster and Jake loaded the trucks—he could still put in a day's work—Jake returned to Curtis.

"I was wonderin'," Curtis said. "Who are *you*? How come the old guys didn't come by themselves?"

"I'm in charge of the Hebrew school. Helping out because my English is better, Mr. Curtis."

Curtis eyed the muscular man in the expensive tweed suit and the gray checked cap. "You look familiar. I seen you around? At the Otzenberger's clubhouse?"

"Possible. You'll excuse me, I got a class this afternoon."

O'Connor, the warehouse superintendent, came out of his office. He caught a glimpse of Jake ushering his "rabbis" into the Hupmobile.

"Who'd that horse say he was?" O'Connor asked. He was a ruddy curly-headed man, pale as bleached dog turds.

"Hebrew teacher."

"The hell he is. That's Crazy Jake Chain. One of them kike gangsters."

* * *

As far as Mutt was concerned, Jake had proved himself. There was no question that he had imagination, the guts to go along with his awesome reputation. He was a born bootlegger.

Jake gave Glauberman the news a few days after he had brought in a third truckload of kosher wine. He was finished with *shtarking*. He didn't like the way it was going. Goodbye, Glauberman, Glauberman & Chain, Labor Consultants.

The lawyer's face sliced itself into two sections with a toothy grin. The moustache bristled, the roached hair rose like a ridge on a dog's back.

"Getting soft, Jacob?"

"Never, Leo."

"The banana man? I don't blame you."

"Maybe I blame *you*, Leo."

Glauberman's square face turned sideways. He licked his moustache. Had to be careful with his partner. Illiterate, thick-headed bum. He had been the club, the gun in Glauberman's hand. Now that the firm had a half-dozen unions in its pocket, and was getting juicy fees from others, he didn't want trouble. But orders had come down from Schonkeit: *Get rid of Chain.*

Leo realized he had made the mistake of depending too much on Jake, on the terror he inspired, on his reputation as a defender of workingmen. There was an ample supply of strong-arm men available—unemployed kids out of the army looking for work, uneducated stiffs.

Schonkeit, knowing about Jake through his police contacts, understood as soon as he entered the unions rackets that Chain was a menace. The man had a strain of noble hero in him; he believed the crap about protecting the poor. Such a man was useless to the crime empire the Paymaster was building.

Glauberman, also, had grander notions. With Schonkeit's backing and Frummer mob, he was now specializing in "strike insurance," exorbitant initiation fees, and illegal "work permits." Schonkeit had taught him to work on a fixed eight-percent graft on all contracts, all salaries, all fees. Ike Brunstein, trying to install Communists in positions of power, had learned the lesson soon enough, Schonkeit said. His frightened Lenins of the sewing machines were soon siphoning off union funds to the Paymaster's hoodlums. Glauberman would be Shonkeit's man in Brooklyn.

"Okay with me, Jake," Glauberman said now, ignoring

Jake's pointed remark. "Whatever I owe you, you'll get. I think we're even."

"Even, yeah. Except for five grand for the job we did last month for the restaurant owners' association."

"I'll have the girl send you a check."

"Cash. Before I leave."

"Impossible. I don't keep that kind of cash around."

Jake got up from the leather chair. He walked to the mahogany desk and lifted the lawyer out of his swivel chair by the lapels. Glauberman was a heavy man. Jake handled him as if he were a child. He slammed Glauberman against the semicircular window with the gold lettering: GLAUBERMAN & CHAIN.

"Easy, Jake." The lawyer's voice shivered.

"Five grand and we're even. I know you're playing ball with Schonkeit, that pig who wants to eat everything in the city. His bums tried to kill me. The guinea with the pushcart and the guys in the Dodge. You finger me for them?"

"I don't buy in Fishman's Bakery."

"But you know I go to Bella's place."

"Nonsense." He squirmed. Jake held him in an iron grip. His hands were anchored to the blue serge lapels. He nailed Glauberman to the window.

"If you didn't finger me, you gave the okay. Schonkeit wouldn't try to knock me off without telling you. He knows you got Otzenberger's ear. Connections with judges."

"Jake, let go of me. You've been listening to idiots like Sol Heilig and his reform crowd. And his sister. Your old sweetie—"

The back of Jake's right hand, like a sheet of steel, cracked across Glauberman's cheek. The pince-nez flew from his nose and smashed against the window.

"Shut up, shyster. Don't talk about Eva Heilig. Five thousand and I'm out of the business. I'm going into bootlegging with my kid. You can have all the union *drek*. It's where you belong. I won't suck blood from workers anymore."

"Take your hands off. I could have you—"

"What? Assault and battery? With what I could spill to the D.A. about you? What I know about us?"

"You'll get put away before I will, Jake."

Jake slammed him against the wall, but did not go after him again.

The lawyer retrieved his fragmented pince-nez. He walked to the safe in the corner of the office. He had a lot more than five thousand dollars in it. Payoffs in cash were part of his daily transactions.

"Good luck running booze, Jake," he said as he counted bills. "The labor business isn't for you anymore."

Glauberman tried to be fatherly. But he was shaking. His insides had turned to jelly. God help the bootleggers once Crazy Jake was turned loose.

"Listen to your former partner, Jake," Glauberman said at the door. "Nobody's safe anymore. Nobody's honest anymore. Your friend Brunstein, he's with Schonkeit. We all need the Paymaster. Ike is like the fella in the Hasidic story. The devil talked him into giving him a finger. Then a hand. Now the devil has Brunstein's arm, and he's getting ready to eat him."

"I ain't Brunstein. I ain't got the brains to go with Schonkeit. I'm a horse, remember? Chain, the *bulvan*."

"You got guts, Jake. I enjoyed working with you. There aren't many around could do a job like you could."

"So long, Leo. If anything happens to me, the Ferrante brothers will know where it came from."

He jammed the checked cap on his head and left Glauberman's office for the last time.

Glauberman at once phoned Melvin Schonkeit. The union rackets had seen the end of Jacob Chain. A blessing, the lawyer thought, an end to a dangerous nuisance.

Chapter 30

"Sherry," Goldsturm said to Jake. "Next time you go with the rabbis to make the pickup, ask for a few cases sherry."

"That ain't kosher wine. Even those idiots at the warehouse, Curtis and O'Connor, know that."

"Tell them it's for a reform congregation. Get a young fella in a frockcoat and plug hat like a rabbi from a rich temple in Crown Heights. They'll believe."

"They'll believe if I give them a hundred bucks apiece. Why sherry?"

"The fusel oil is bad quality. Sherry gives a nice color for scotch and rye."

Mutt and Sal came out of the office. They were so backed

up on orders that they had rented a truck to make the Canada run. The Brooklyn Democratic Club was having its annual beefsteak dinner. Benny Otzenberger had arranged for F & C Cereals, Inc., to be sole purveyors of liquid refreshments.

"Nobody drinks like Democratic regulars," Mutt said. "But if we fill the order, it'll clean us out for a week. We got to get an inventory."

Goldsturm began to complain to the partners. The last batch of counterfeit government stamps was awful. The cross-hatching was blurred. Any agent could spot them as phonies. The customers didn't care, but a snooper might. Could Mortimer please see about getting a new printer or telling the current one to hire a better engraver?

Jake listened, smiling. *This was business!* Better than union rackets. It supplied a need. Everyone cooperated. The public admired an honest bootlegger. A man had status and respect when he could furnish unlimited cases of Highland Cream, Aberdeen Dew, Juniper Tree gin, Kentucky Sweetwater.

"The stuff from the alky cookers stinks," the chemist whined. "Sal's relatives got to replace the copper coils. They're patched with tin and the alcohol comes out gray. Then it turns black after I mix it. Nobody'll drink black booze. And for God's sake, they should spray their places with Flit. Cockroaches, bedbugs, spiders!"

"Get on their ass, Sal," Mutt said.

Ferrante nodded.

Jake watched them. Clearly his kid was taking over. The partners split profits, but Mutt came up with the new ideas. Mutt had connections. Moreover, he was a born salesman. Sincere, well spoken, polite. People liked and trusted young Mortimer J. Chain.

Sal was shaking his head. "Schonkeit hijacked the Reo last week, that's why we're short. I tol' our guys not to shoot back. He's too big for us. We're gonna have to get more alky out of the warehouses and get more fun from my *goombahs*."

Mutt looked solemn. He stroked his long nose, craned his neck to catch a glimpse of Hilda crossing her legs. A flash of thigh. Ah, tonight. In back of the new Chandler.

"We gotta have more real stuff to make the fake," Mutt said. "But I don't like fighting with Schonkeit either."

Recently a truck from F & C, loaded with Montreal scotch, had run into trouble. Buster Twine had been driving, with Baggie Ferrante riding shotgun, and they had done all the right things. Bribes to the Canadians. Bribes to the Customs guards.

But outside a diner in Plattsburgh, in broad daylight, two dagos had shoved a .38 into Baggie's left nostril while Buster was checking a tire. Buster fielded a sap with the back of his head and was left for dead. (It proved to be a mild concussion.) Then Schonkeit's hoodlums drove off with the truck and its load. The state police found it in downtown Albany, empty.

"How'd you know it was his guys?" Jake asked.

"They bragged about it," Mutt said. "The Paymaster wants it all. He picks on guys like us because he thinks we ain't tough."

"You got *me*. Maybe I can help. When's the rented truck going up?"

"In an hour. Buster says he's okay. He'll drive. Baggie's sick. Vince'll ride up front."

"And me."

"You, pop?"

Sal's eyes vanished. Nothing scared old man Chain. Baggie had come back from the hijacking in Plattsburgh shaking like a woman. He'd turned yellow. Luigi said maybe Baggie was finished with the truck run. You needed guts. Maybe they could find a safe job for him in the cutting plant.

"Jake, there's only room for two guys inna cab," Sal said.

"On the way up Vinnie can ride in the back," Jake said slowly. "On the way back, leave out a few cases. I'll ride there."

"It's a rough ride, pop," Mutt cautioned.

"I got an iron *tuchas*."

Jake drove him in the October sunlight, past kids playing "salugi." The poplars on Haven Place sparkled green and gold. Doc Abelman was on his stoop, talking to Rabbi Piltz.

Poor old Piltz. He never suspected that his stationery had gotten the Chains into the wine business. The rabbi was a stiff-backed man with a full black beard. Jake was wary of him. Piltz denounced "gangsters, *gonovim*, and Jewish *tromboniks*" regularly, and once even mentioned Jake by name. Jake had been hurt. Someday, Jake thought, F & C would make a contribution to the synagogue.

Sarah was in the kitchen preparing a roast. She sulked

when he told her he was going on a trip. Just upstate, to make a few sales, collect money for Mortimer. He'd be away overnight.

"Jake, I don't like what he's doing, or what you're doing. You shouldn't encourage him."

He kissed her cheek, patted her shrunken hips. Guilt and shame ate at him. They had not slept together in years. Yet, oddly, she did not object. Her legs were atrophied, but she managed nicely with a cane. It was as if the expensive clothes, the well-supplied kitchen, the radio, the car, made up for the lack of sex. Poor, hungry, lonely as a child, she relished their prosperity.

"I'll be back tomorrow, *ketzeleh*," he said.

"I worry."

"Never. I'm finished with *shtarking*. I quit Glauberman."

"But what you're doing is maybe worse?"

"Safe, safe. Everybody gets paid off. Everybody is part of it. The people need it."

In the bedroom he found a blue-black police .38, a gift from the Ferrante brothers on his thirty-fourth birthday. Jake loaded it and took a box of cartridges. The patch pockets on his gray jacket accommodated gun and bullets.

He walked upstairs and buzzed the Rimkoffs' apartment. Bobby, feinting and ducking punches, came to the door. Nose busted five times, ridges like leather over his eyes. *He'll be a contender when he is forty,* Jake thought.

"Bobby, boychick," he said. "That stuff you brought back from the army? The bayonet, the helmet? In the trunk?"

"Yeah. Watcha want?"

"Just to look."

Bobby ducked, belted the air with a right cross. "I'm fightin' Paco Gomez next week. I'll kill him."

"Good luck, kid. You'll be a champ someday."

In the bedroom were two photographs of the boxer. They were half lifesize, fuzzy black-and-whites, tinted with watercolors. One was Bobby at age eighteen. Crouched, fists up, a tiger in Everlast trunks and BenLee shoes. The tough Jewboy who destroyed Irish Danny Regan in one round. The other was Bobby in the uniform of the Rainbow Division—Private Robert Rimkoff, U.S.A., AEF.

The boxer dragged a khaki-colored metal box from under the bed. "That's my footlocker. Tell me watcha wanna see. My medals? The Joiman helmet? The bayonet?"

Bobby lifted the lid. Jake kneeled. He'd heard Bobby bragging about the stuff he'd smuggled home in a duffel bag.

Jake saw what he wanted.

That afternoon the rented Mack headed north for Canada. Buster started the driving. Vinnie slept in back on the quilted padding with which all of F & C Cereal's trucks were equipped. Jake rode up front with the black man.

In Kingston they switched. Jake took over the wheel, Buster slept in back, Vinnie moved up front. They took turns. Only once Buster expressed his fears. "Them Schonkeit people stop us again, I hope leastwise they don't hit my head."

"This time, maybe they'll be nice."

Buster looked sideways at the big man. He knew about him. He'd heard the stories. Clay pigeon. Shooting gallery. So full of lead, wise guys said, he'd sink if he took a swim at Coney Island.

"What you got in that box in the back?" Buster asked.

Jake had placed a wooden cheese box, the kind in which the schoolkids grew flowers, under the quilting.

"Lunch."

"How come it ain't here where you can eat it?"

"I ain't hungry."

Lamotte, the Canadian mechanic-turned-supplier, loaded the truck and accepted a cash payment from Jake. No receipts were given. Checks were never used. The business was always cash and a handshake. The Mack took less than the usual hundred and eighty cases. Jake told the loaders to leave a space big enough for him to sit.

"Here, Frenchy," Jake said. "I'll pay for the full hundred and eighty cases, twenny bucks a case, right?" He peeled off three thousand and six hundred dollars. "Ten cases you'll hold for the next shipment, okay?" Lamotte counted the bills in his office. Jake had learned that the goodwill of suppliers was always worth a few dollars. "Anything we can bring you from the States, Lamotte?"

"No, but I think of something, I ask." The supplier smiled. He liked this big *type*. The kid's father. Jake Chain, *formidable*. Tall, husky, with long arms and hands, *sacrebleu*, like a lumberjack. And the flat face, from *le box* perhaps.

"You know the new road?" Lamotte asked Buster. "Go

west far as you can on the logging road. *Compris?* The guards let you through for a hundred bucks."

Buster knew. He'd be damned if he'd take the direct route to Plattsburgh. They'd stop for no lunches. They'd eat sandwiches and pray.

The loaded truck, with Jake squatting behind a flapping tarp atop cases of scotch, headed south. The French Canadian shook his head. Too bad he hadn't had the guts to tell him that Schonkeit's gangsters were patrolling every road on the New York side. Two days ago some *salaud* driving a load of gin had his head blown off. He'd tried to run a log barricade. *C'est la vie,* Lamotte thought.

Jake told Buster to stop a few hundred yards before the border. The Customs station was a popular one with the bootleggers. The guards were friendly; they were determined that their children would have better lives. Each man took home close to a thousand dollars a week in "donations." The most popular mode of payment was to drop a matchbook with a fifty-dollar bill folded into it.

"Listen," Jake had told them before they drove off, "if we get stopped—I don't mean by agents or Feds—I'll give a signal. I'll yell 'Union.' "

"Union?" Vinnie asked. "What does that mean?"

"It don't mean anything," Jake said. "It's a signal. When I yell 'Union,' fall down and cover yourself. Roll under the truck or get behind a tree."

"You know what you're doing, Jake?" Vinnie was slim and nervous. He was regarded as dim-witted by the other brothers.

"I ain't sure I like this," Buster said. "You gonna pull some of that Crazy Jake stuff you pull when you with the union? Mr. Chain, your son tell us never shoot, never fight back."

"That's my son. I'm me. Remember, when I holler 'Union,' fall down."

Buster shook his ebony head. *Crazy Jake.* Why did he get mixed up with this man? A man with no fear in him was worse than a coward. His head began to ache again. Frowning, Vinnie climbed into the passenger seat and waited for Jake's signal to move off.

Jake settled into a niche amid the crates of booze. On his lap he held the cream-cheese box. Suddenly he rememberd Mutteh sniffling because they could not afford to buy seeds.

Marigolds. Zinnias. Lily-of-the-valley. Bernie Feigenbaum had three cream-cheese boxes sprouting flowers. Mutt had wept when Jake told him he didn't have the money for seeds.

The guards were their usual accommodating selves. Jake sat behind the tarp, holding the cheese box. He heard Buster and Vinnie talking, first to the Canadians, and then to the American inspectors. Mutt had given his crew standing orders—a hundred bucks a man if necessary.

The matchbox must have been dropped, Jake thought. He could hear the Mack's tired motor rumbling, Buster shifting gears. They were back in New York State.

The old thrill was warming Jake's blood. He could not explain it. He feared death. He feared mutilation. But the anticipation of violence, of someone threatening him, the prospect of striking back, never failed to fill him with a wild joy. Was it because he had had so little as a boy, as a young man? That his fists and his strength and his lack of fear made up for bad food, miserable rooms, harsh work, being despised and unwanted?

He was glad Mutt was smarter. Finished high school—almost. Clever kid. The boy had inherited one trait from Jake that would be invaluable—*courage*. He had observed Mutt since he was a squirt—never flinching, never running away. It helped. It helped even more if you were smart.

Lulled by the bouncing of the Mack, Jake rested against the wall of booze. It was not quite clear in his mind what he would do if the hijackers drove off with the truck with him in it. He might be spotted. Maybe it would be better if he were fully hidden.

He decided to rearrange a few cases. Working slowly, maneuvering his huge frame, he built a wall five cases high and crouched behind it. They wouldn't see him. The imminent violence was damned near as good as sex, Jake thought. Maybe because sex was so bad in his life. A fat whore, a cold wife, a woman he loved and could never have. Getting shot at, shooting back, using his fists, made up for it. Almost.

He must have been dozing. The voices awakened him in his prison of scotch.

"Pull it over, Rastus."

"Both of yez, hands over your heads. Up, dago. Drop the shotgun. Denny, pick it up. Watcha got in there?"

Neither Buster nor Vinnie was responding. They knew enough to be silent. They had been fingered. Schonkeit's hijackers usually knew who was carrying what. Sometimes the Customs guards worked with them.

The truck made loud crunching noises as Buster pulled it off the asphalt to the dirt shoulder. It kept moving, heading into the pine forest, Jake could hear a second motor. A vehicle was following them. He moved a crate and parted the tarpaulin. A huge White truck rumbled no more than fifteen feet to their rear. Dimly he could see a driver and a second man. A third man was riding up front of the Chain truck, either jammed into the cab with Buster and Vinnie or on the running board. Jake could hear a strange voice.

"Over there, nigger. By the stone fence. Stop when I tell you."

"Yassuh, boss."

"You, you wop, sit still or I'll give you a shot in the head. Want an earful of hot lead?"

"I ain't doin' nothin'," Vinnie said.

Heart pounding, Jake wondered when to make his move. If he did it now, with the trucks moving, he might miss. If he waited until they began to unload, the hijackers would be in a better position to hit back. With two men locked inside the cab of the White, they were sitting ducks.

Carefully, he moved two more crates and edged closer to the tailgate. He loosened his right arm, flexed the muscles, braced himself against the cases. He opened the cheese box. Inside a nest of absorbent cotton were two gray-green hand grenades from Bobby Rimkoff's war souvenirs. Bobby had explained how they worked. Yank the small pin, hold it like a baseball, lob it with the whole arm. "Don't snap ya wrist like a baseball or ya'll sprain your wrist and it won't go far. Use the whole arm. Get height on it. With *your* arm you could throw it into Joisey."

"Here, nigger. Stop! Dumb coon."

Through the crack in the tarp, the sun glinting in his eyes and impeding his vision, Jake saw the pursuing truck stop. Buster's Mack rolled a few feet, then jolted to a halt.

Hit them now, Jake thought. While they were in the cab, unarmed, unsuspecting. Then he'd worry about the *mamzer* up front. He hoped he'd get a chance to get his hands on him before he hurt Buster and Vinnie.

"*Union!*" Jake shouted. He parted the tarp. "*Union!*" he shouted again. "*Union!*"

Jake pulled the pin from the pineapple, drew his arm back,

and, with all his strength, lobbed Rimkoff's souvenir in a perfect arc. It crashed against the windshield of the pursuing truck.

The explosion, no more than five yards from the rear of his own truck, shattered bottles around Jake and soaked him with expensive hooch. Goldsturm would never forgive him.

The hijackers' truck blossomed into a fireball, roaring, exploding, as the engine blew apart and the gasoline ignited. Blinded and bloodied, the men staggered from the doors and rolled in the dirt. One stopped rolling. A chunk of glass a foot long was stuck in his throat. His neck spurted a crimson fountain.

Jake leaped over the tailgate. He had the second grenade in his pocket. In his right hand he held his .38. Running low to the ground, he came around the side of the Mack, saw the man on the running board, leveled the .38, and shot him twice in the legs. It was almost funny, the dumb bastard, a fuzzzy-haired thickset man in a red plaid lumberjacket, frozen, wondering who in the hell was yelling *Union*, staring at his exploding truck.

The man dragged himself on his hands and elbows, looking for his shattered eyeglasses. His gun, an army regulation .45, was in the dirt, a few feet away. But without his specs he couldn't see it. Jake picked up the gun, then crunched the eyeglasses with his shoe.

"Ya big bum," the man said.

Jake smashed the butt of the .38 against his ear. He stopped crawling.

"You guys okay? Buster? Vinnie?" He leaped to the running board. Both men were crouched below window level, arms clamped over their heads like a pair of war prisoners. "He hit you? You guys get hurt?"

"I'm okay, boss," Buster said. "I think Vinnie got part of his head blowed off. It landed on me."

Jake pulled Vinnie's arms back. The side of his head was a mass of blood, bits of bone, brain. Jake felt sick; he was bad luck for the Ferrante brothers.

"He dead, Mr. Chain?"

"Looks like it. Anyway, the guy who did it won't be able to brag about it."

Jake fired a shot into the neck of the man on the ground. Might as well, he felt. He'd be no good to Schonkeit anymore with busted legs. No good to anyone. If they wanted a hijacking war, Crazy Jake would be happy to oblige them.

"I can't drive with Vinnie up here. I got me a nervous stomach."

"Gimme a hand, Buster. We'll stick him under the quilts."

Buster got out. He was shivering. Darkness was enshrouding the looming pines. He wanted to be home with his woman and his sons and his pint of gin. Friends had warned him about that wild man Jake Chain. A prudent, churchgoing black, Buster Twine wondered why the young Mr. Chain, so nice and sensible, would let his crazy father do this.

They tucked Vinnie's corpse under the quilting and stacked cases around it. Buster, gagging, cleaned the front seat with a rag. The White truck behind them exploded again. The fire soared higher, threatened the stands of pine trees. Jake ran to the two men on the ground. He lifted the one with the shard of glass on his throat and threw him into the blazing wreck.

As he went for the other, he heard a siren. No way of knowing if it was for them. The roads were full of troopers and Prohibition agents. He looked at the darkening sky. The smoke from the blazing truck was boiling and churning wildly into the sky above the treetops. A forest ranger's station would surely spot it and send someone out to investigate.

"Let's beat it, Buster. You drive." He took a last look at the other man. The burned, peeling face looked familiar. Who?

They backed up the Mack, made a wide circle past the wreckage of the burning truck. Buster covered his mouth and nose and coughed. "Don't like that smell. A man burnin' in there."

"Buster, that kind of *paskudnyak* don't mind getting burned. He was born for that. Come on, step on it. When you hit the main road, don't stop."

Outside Glens Falls the Mack broke down. Jake had to pay a hundred dollars to a mechanic who was getting ready to close down. On the bumpy back roads, a ricocheting stone had cracked the gasoline pump. Jake telephoned Mutt from a pay station. There'd been a "little trouble." But they were all right. They had the load.

"You alone, Mutt?" Outside he could see Buster and the mechanic bending into the engine. The man was working with a huge wrench, struggling to dislodge the broken gas pump.

"Yeah."

"Vinnie's dead. They took his head off. Don't say nothing to the family till I'm back."

Mutt lowered his voice. He glanced at Theresa. She was

checking the seams in her stockings, getting ready to leave. *Another brother shot to hell.* First Frankie. Now Vinnie. Mutt wondered how Sal would react. Maybe he would get sick of supplying corpses for the Chains. "Okay, pop. I'll wait for you here."

"We won't make it till the morning. The guy has to send out for a new pump."

"I'll be here."

Jesus, Mutt thought, *Vinnie dead. I send the old man on his first run to the border and I lose a good man.* But what else was Jake to do? Schonkeit was determined to eat them up, the way he was eating up other bootleggers on the Canada run. He could not blame his father. But he should have guessed that sending Jake north was bound to end in violence and death. He wondered what the old man had done to *them.*

Mutt sweet-talked Hilda into staying after Theresa had left. He sent out for corned-beef sandwiches and cream soda. They discussed their wedding plans. Then Mutt made leisurely love to her on the leather couch.

In the darkness, locked between her naked thighs, he felt confident, buoyed. His father's call had shaken him, filled him with sudden dread. *Vinnie dead.* And God knew what his father *hadn't* told him. Talking to Jake, he had gulped, paled, turned his head away so the girls could not see his face, the tremor in his lips. Now, deep in Hilda's warmth, he sensed a rightness, a fulfillment. It was no longer a joining, a conquest, a release. It was as if her plump body told him that life was full of rewards. It gratified him that she would be his for a long time, always there to embrace and enfold him, to comfort him when he was frightened.

"I love you, baby," Mutt whispered. "I always will. I need you. Maybe I'll do some rotten things. But I'll try not to."

"I love you too, Morty. Oh, my God, so good, so good. We're not supposed to love it so much."

"Who says so?"

When he came, he cried for joy.

In the half-light of dawn, Sal looked at Vinnie's bloodied corpse. Dumb Vinnie. The jerk of the family. Frankie and Sal had been the smart ones. But Sal did not weep. He made the sign of the cross, glanced for a last time at Vinnie's shattered, blood-matted head, and telephoned Locatelli, the funeral director.

Then he called his father, the old barber. They were not to leave the house, he said, papa or his black-layered wife. Sal would come home to talk to them. And the brothers—Baggie, Dom, Luigi, Petey—were all to be present. And Theresa and Iolande.

Locatelli came with his hearse. He and Buster loaded Vinnie into a canvas bag.

"I want an open coffin," Sal said. "Fix his face. And the biggest cross and the biggest rosary you can buy for his hands."

Troubled, Mutt got up from his rolltop desk in the office. Jake was sitting on the couch, legs crossed, cap pushed back on his head. He was weary. Too much for him. He was sorry about Vinnie.

"Mr. Locatelli," Mutt said, "the biggest floral display you can get, from the Chains. A big heart. A big cross. Send me the bills for the whole funeral. They can have any kinda coffin they want. The most expensive. And a nice stone, with angels."

As he spoke, Mutt made mental notes: Benny would have to fix the cops, the coroner, everyone. Better no one knew how Vinnie cashed in. A fake death certificate—heart failure.

Locatelli departed with Vinnie's earthly remains. Sal remained in the doorway of the office. Once he wiped at his eyes. Nothing more. *Cry, damn you, cry,* Mutt wanted to say.

Sal nodded at Jake. "You. You done it to him."

"Me? I killed him? You're crazy. Ask Buster." The black man, exhausted, was outside unloading the rescued shipment.

"Ya *got* him killed. They call you crazy, you're crazy all right. But someone else gets it alla time. What'd you do? Pick a fight?"

Patiently Jake explained what had happened. The other truck, the three men, the grenade. It was tough for Vinnie. But they'd taught Schonkeit's mob a lesson. Three of them dead. A truck blown to hell. Nobody would start with F & C again, Jake said. When you were in a tough business, you took risks. He wished he could bring Vinnie back, Jake said.

Sal sighed and folded his arms. He looked as if he had no spine. He began to bite the nails of his left hand, refused to meet Jake's eyes or Mutt's sorrowing face.

A *creep*, Hilda had called him. *Creepy Sal.* The kid selling hokey-pokey ices from a two-wheeled cart. With a red, green, and white umbrella. The soiled gray apron for change, the torn sneakers, a cap two sizes too large. Darting eyes. *Little punk,* Hilda sneered. Never looked anyone in the eye in his life.

"I started the business," Sal said. "Me and the taxi." The eyes flew to the corner of the office, settled on the electric fan, flitted to the calendar with Clara Bow's face.

"So?" Mutt rested his head on one palm.

"Maybe you guys should realize that."

"Hold it," Mutt said. "We went to Canada partners the second time. And we split the dough. I helped pay for the trucks."

"It ain't *you.*" His reptilian head bobbed toward Jake. "Him. Your old man. He'll get us all killed."

"My old man stays."

"Who says so?"

"I do. You're upset because Vinnie cashed in. We're sorry. It was an accident. Look what my father did. They won't futz around with our trucks again."

"Mutt is right, sonny boy," Jake said slowly. "I can't spend my life riding with trucks. When there are Schonkeits in the world, there's only one way to handle them. Don't be so cute. You once blew a Canuck's head off."

"You wasn't supposed to know." Sal's head sagged beneath his shoulders. These goddamn Chains. They came in. They took over. "Just the two of us from now on," he said hoarsely. "Me and Mutt. When I get enough, I'll buy Mutt out. Just me. No Chains."

Father and son looked at one another. They understood. Jake eased his body forward. He let his hands dangle between his legs. He was a little shaken. And he felt genuinely sorry for Vinnie. With Frankie, he owed nobody apologies. Frankie caught a stray chunk of lead. With Vinnie it was different. If Jake had surrendered to the hijackers, showed a yellow streak, maybe Vinnie would be alive. But that was not Jake's way.

"Salvatore, listen to your uncle Jake—"

"You ain't no uncle. You're trouble. Luigi warned me. Baggie warned me."

"Listen, *walyo.* I like you. I like your family. But you won't get rid of the Chains."

"No?"

"Mutt built the business with you. I'm in it now because I can help. We'll make you a millionaire if you stay calm. Know why?"

Sal did not answer.

"I'll tell you why, *walyo.* You know that girl who sits in

the office with your sister, the girl Mutteleh is going to marry, Miss Hilda Otzenberger?"

"Pop, leave Hilda out of this."

Jake ignored his son. "Salvatore, her father is Mr. Benny Otzenberger, and he's the key to every fix we have. Every cop, every Fed, every judge, every D.A. You can't run an operation like we have without fixing. The store has to be open. Mr. Otzenberger is our fixer. Right? If you decide we're out, Mr. Otzenberger will fix for us, but for people like you there'll be shit."

"You guys always got an angle."

"It's not an angle, Sal," Mutt said placatingly. "It's good for all of us."

Sal picked his nose thoughtfully. "Your old man goes on payroll. No split."

"Sorry, Sal," Mutt said. "We cut everything three ways. A third to you, a third to me, and a third to my father."

Mutt was surprised: His voice did not shake and his hands were steady. He leaned back in the swivel chair and picked up the ringing phone. An early morning order, even before the girls were in. A rich guy in Lawrence, Long Island, throwing a wedding party. He'd heard from Mr. Dullahan, the politico, that F & C handled a high-class line of imported booze.

All politeness, Mutt took the order. Jake put an arm around Sal. They walked out of the office. As they did, Theresa entered from the exterior steel door. She'd heard: Vinnie was dead. She had disobeyed her father and come to work. Her screams and howls slammed and reverberated around the cutting plant. A few seconds later she fainted. Jake and Sal carried her into the office and placed her on the couch.

She revived after Professor Goldsturm arrived, learned of the tragedy, and forced her to drink some of his "French Cognac." Her howls became weird strangling noises. She began to give Jake a headache. He gestured to Sal to follow him to the street.

"I'm sorry about this, Sal. But don't try to screw us. Stay with the Chains."

"What choice I got."

"None, *walyo*. I like you. I like your family. They'll forgive me."

Chapter 31

"So. Pregnant at age what? I lose track. Or maybe it isn't polite to ask." Dr. Abraham Heilig smiled at his sister. "You look the same. The same way you looked when you were a *pisherkeh* on the picket line. *Oi,* that voice."

"You know how old I am, Abe. I'm thirty-six."

"A little late for a kid, but it should be all right."

"You're sure it's in there?"

"The tests don't lie, Eva. I'm sorry papa isn't alive. Proof of the power of sour milk! His daughter conceives in her mid-thirties. You should have had kids sooner. It's easier. What am I giving you advice for? You never took it anyway."

"It won't be any burden for me. I'll never nurse a child. I'll never change a diaper. I'm rich, Abe."

"Don't sound so bitter. It should happen to all of us."

Eva laughed. He looked very much at home in his green-shaded, oak-paneled consulting room. An up-and-coming surgeon, he had a red brick house and office on President Street, a few doors down from Glauberman the lawyer. The houses were completely detached on plots of manicured grass. Through the rear window, Eva could see a garden, with maples and oaks flaunting autumnal colors.

"Sol sent me this," Abe said. "Our eminent brother was in Albany for a committee meeting and this turned up in the local newspaper."

Eva put on her rimless eyeglasses. She had taken to wearing them more frequently. My God, Dr. Heilig thought, the way she's used those green eyes. Even with glasses, they were something. Reading, writing, *hypnotizing* people with them. But she seemed tired. He wondered if the pregnancy was a good idea. Evidently she and Halstead had agreed that their lives needed more than causes. *A child.* Abe, a keen psychologist, thought to himself: *Perhaps a child to save the marriage.* She rarely volunteered a word about Garrison or about their friends. Eva, once so open and frank, had become secretive where her personal life was concerned.

Eva read the short newspaper story:

TWO DEAD IN MYSTERY EXPLOSION
NEAR PLATTSBURGH, THIRD INJURED

Two men were found dead, one in and one near the burning remains of a truck in a clearing off U.S. Route 9, ten miles south of Plattsburgh, state police reported today. A third man was found alongside the wreckage, seriously burned.

State Trooper Sgt. William Hernley said that the surviving man has been identified as Philip (Futka) Frummer, a New York City bootlegger, age 33. The dead men are as yet unidentified.

The truck is believed to be one used on bootlegging runs from Canada, since it contained quilted pads used for transporting liquor. The wounded man and one of the deceased were trapped in an explosion that destroyed the truck and set it on fire. The other unidentified victim was shot three times. His body was thirty feet from the truck.

Police said they have no suspects. Shootings and ambushes have become commonplace in the frontier area because of "wars" between rival gangs.

"So?" Eva asked. "Why show it to me?"

"Sol had the same idea I did. It might involve our esteemed cousin."

"Jake?"

"Don't look surprised. Evitchka. Ordinarily I'd say so what? Gangsters killing each other, good riddance. But it so happens, on the day after this was reported in Albany, they buried one of Jake's partners. One of the Ferrante brothers, Vincent. Could be Jake's trying the Canadian air."

"It proves nothing."

"Just thought you'd like to see it. You always were a sort of heroine to that rogue. I must say, he isn't stupid. When Solly and I gave him lessons, he learned fast. He's still learning. Maybe *giving* lessons now."

"I don't see any connection. . . ."

Dr. Abe didn't press the point. He didn't care that much about Jake Chain one way or the other. But surely Eva knew that Jake's son was up to his *pupik* in bootleg booze. He had heard from patients about Mutt's booming business. One of the fastest-growing industries in Brooklyn. His "calling cards" turned up everywhere—price lists, special offers, catering.

"To heck with the Chains and the Ferrantes," Dr. Heilig said. "Someday Crazy Jake'll catch the right bullet. The one with his name on it."

"Don't say that."

"Why did he stop *shtarking?*"

Eva winked and pointed at her chest. "Your big sister. I had a talk with Jake."

"*Hoohah!* You can think that if you want to! The word I get is that Mutt convinced him there was more money in booze and that it was safer."

They chatted about the old neighborhood. All three Heilig children had outgrown it. Eva, in her elevated position as the wife of a socialite, Abe in his medical practice on President Street, lawyer Sol with an office on Court Street and a house on Carroll Street in Crown Heights. Sol was in line for an appointment as a deputy attorney general, a special post to investigate rackets. Sol would never be rich, but he'd be happy, they agreed.

Dr. Heilig stroked his brown moustache and stared for a moment at his bookcases and the framed photographs of Dr. William Osler and Dr. William Welch on his wall. He mentioned to Eva that someday, *someday,* Sol might find himself trying to send Jake and Mutt Chain to jail. Or maybe even the electric chair.

"Abe, please. That's ridiculous."

"I'm kidding. But face it, Eva, there's something destructive about the Chains, *père et fils.* I won't say that they are genetically criminal, or even that they're basically antisocial. But they can't resist anything crooked."

"That doesn't make them much different from our big corporations. Or our esteemed President Harding and the criminals around him. I'm not so sure the Chains are out of step with society. Labor violence was inevitable. Bootlegging? I can't get exercised over it. The Volstead Act was the real crime. All those holier-than-thou Methodists and Baptists forcing their fanaticism on the people. So now we have gang wars and murders and people dying of wood-alcohol poisoning."

"Don't tell me. I see them. Blind, lame, ruined from drinking anything in a bottle." Abe sighed. "Anyway, Doc Abelman tells me that Mutt sells only nontoxic beverages. Their poison might give you a bad headache and the runs, but it doesn't kill."

Eva laughed. "Oh, goodness! How does Abelman know?"

"He's still the Chain family physician. He patched Jake up after the famous banana attack. Sam tells me Sarah is doing quite well. Gets around the house without the cane, wears spiffy clothes. She gets her hair done twice a week and plays poker."

Eva shuddered. *Limited aims, limited ambitions.* Her heart went out to Sarah Klebanow Chain, that maimed woman. But dammit, why couldn't she take courses at the Hebrew Educational Society? Or be something other than a drone? She repressed a bit of guilt: Sarah might have been more of a woman if Jake had not abandoned her to nurture a hopeless love for Eva.

"Enough on the Chains," Abe said. "How are you, sister?"

"Fine. See for yourself."

"I see a new short haircut, very attractive, maybe from a Fifth Avenue salon. I see an expensive blue velvet dress with a skirt maybe a little short for your age, but you have the legs to justify it. I see black crocodile shoes with a matching bag. Clear skin, beautiful eyes, the ivory chin. That's all on the outside. Inside?"

"Pregnant. Full of life."

"I mean the things that don't show in a laboratory test. How are you and Garry getting along?"

"Why do you ask? You know we're compatible."

Abe sighed. "We don't see you that often. Leah is a little put off. So's Solly and his wife."

"I'm busy. I'm not a snob. You know that. Maybe that's one of my problems."

"Problems?"

"We just don't socialize. With anyone."

"Snotty little remarks about his Jewess?"

"We try not to let it bother us. Garry's above all that. People think twice before insulting a Halstead to his face. I suspect he has his moments of—"

"Regret?"

"Not at all. He's as kind and good to me as ever. There's no other woman."

She could not bring herself to tell Abe that her passion had never equaled Halstead's. Jewish women, so the rumor went, were supposed to be mother lodes of passion. Levantine Liliths bursting with erotic desires, like the ripe persimmons of the Holy Land. *What nonsense!* But she could never tell Abe or anyone—*he is too hot and I am listless.*

"Are you happy, Eva?"

"What is happiness?"

"Come on, *ketzeleh*, this is your brother Abe."

"Of course I am. Look at all I have. My career. A rich husband. A reputation. I'm thrilled when the garment workers cheer me, when I get a scrawled letter from some girl in the shops."

"But with Garry, everything's all right?"

"Do you think we'd be having a child if it were not the case?"

Abe bit on the templepiece of his spectacles. "I was wondering. After ten years and no kids? Maybe the pregnancy was a way to patch things up. Don't be ashamed. Others have done it. It often works. Motherhood, fatherhood. It makes a difference. Leah and I had a few tough moments before Sidney was born. What a blessing that little *shmendrick* was! I come home from the hospital, tired, angry, maybe I lost a patient, maybe I screwed up a case—for your ears only, Eva—and I see that *mozzik* with his yellow hair and his green eyes and the way he grins at me, and I know the world is a better place. You'll see, Eva. Wait till you have your own."

Eva wondered. Leah Hemkau Heilig was a doctor's daughter, a "Mrs. Yifnif." Furs, jewels, vacations at Schroon Lake. A Crown Heights family, claiming to be German although Eva suspected they had twisted geography a little.

"I'm glad you and Leah are happy."

"You say it as if *you're* not."

"I'm happy in my work. Garry and I are busy, independent people. Maybe we subordinate our emotions to our work, but that's the way we want it."

She's lying, Dr. Heilig thought.

Shikey Frummer entered the Polo Pony Club on East Fifty-fifth Street and worked his way through tobacco fumes, past tables filled with early evening drinkers sipping their cut scotch, rye, and gin at a dollar a shot. A patent-leather-hair dude with a waxed moustache, he found his way to Melvin Schonkeit's private table at the rear. As usual, the Paymaster, comfortable in his own speakeasy, one of twenty-two he owned, was drinking milk.

"So?" Schonkeit asked.

"It was Chain."

"Which one?"

"Crazy Jake. Futka wrote it on a piece of paper. He can't talk. His mouth and tongue are burned up. Maybe he ain't gonna live, Mr. Schonkeit."

Melvin Schonkeit ignored Shikey Frummer's tear-rimmed dark eyes. There was little sentiment in the Paymaster. And Shikey expected no expression of sympathy. With Schonkeit, it was *tuchas af'm tisch*—ass on the table, *get down to facts*. His brother Futka lay dying of third-degree burns and internal hemorrhaging, and from their employer not a word of sympathy.

"Let's see," Schonkeit said.

Shikey, slicking back his gleaming hair, handed the Paymaster the bit of paper. In a quivering faint hand was written the single word: CRAZY.

"Crazy? That proves it?"

Shikey nodded. "It's Jake Chain. We didn't know he was working with his kid. When I think what that bastard done. Two guys dead. Them I don't care about. But my brother maybe ain't gonna live."

Schonkeit signaled for another glass of milk. He did not offer Frummer anything. The man had failed him. A patron at the next table was advised by the Paymaster to extinguish his cigar or get out of the Polo Pony Club. The rule at the speak was that no one within *two tables* of Mr. Schonkeit smoked. He himself never touched tobacco. He wore high starched white collars, bankers' maroon ties, somber dark blue suits. Clear-eyed, smooth of skin, soft-spoken, he might have been a successful obstetrician or surgical dentist. Schonkeit detested violence and physical effort.

"You're to blame," Schonkeit said. He smiled with his mouth. The rest of his face was impassive.

"Me, Mr. Schonkeit?"

"You and your stupid brother. You should have known that Chain was riding the convoys."

"After we tried to kill him with the banana cart, who'd think he'd have the guts to start again? Me and Futka said how many times we got to shoot this bum to kill him?"

"Did your brother say anything else?"

Shikey wept. His waxed moustache wilted. Schonkeit turned his head away in disgust. Bullies, cowards, fools. No wonder he had amassed an empire so quickly. It required brains, confidence, vision, an ability to gauge weaknesses, to dominate animals like the Frummers.

"Well?" Schonkeit said.

"Mr. Schonkeit, he can't talk. Big black blisters all over like he was roasted. But it was Chain. God knows how he blew up the truck. Anyway, we killed that dago Ferrante. That'll learn him."

"You're a bigger fool than I thought. Frummer, we buy and sell and kill people like that for a case of bad scotch. We lose a truck and three men, and they lose a Ferrante."

"Mr. Schonkeit, gimme another chance. I'll put the Meal Ticket on it. He owes Chain. He'll shoot the bastard in the back some night. He'll stick him so full of holes with an ice pick he'll be a Swiss cheese. He'll blow him up with TNT."

"No. You're all stupid. You're stupid and maybe yellow."

"That ain't fair, Mr. Sch—"

"Shut up, Frummer. Beat it."

Dabbing at his eyes, Shikey left. Suddenly he hated the high rollers, the society people and the newspapermen, who patronized Schonkeit's elegant speak. The Polo Pony Club was the prize of his collection. And what did Shikey have? A dying brother, and not much of a future. He'd kill Jake Chain someday. And as he thought of it, fear twisted his guts. He knew he wasn't man enough to do it.

When Frummer had left, Schonkeit telephoned Leo Glauberman and told him about the bungled hijacking, the unexpected appearance of Crazy Jake Chain and the dire consequences. Both men found the incident grimly amusing.

"Melvin," Glauberman said, "take my advice and let the Chains alone. Brooklyn isn't your bailiwick. I'm glad he's out of the labor business. We have enough problems with Reds these days."

"Leo, he's a bigger problem. And I have the feeling his son will be an even bigger one someday. I agree, let's stop trying to—ah—eliminate him. But maybe we can put him out of business politically. Why be violent when you can do things other ways?"

"You mean get to his rabbi? Knock off his connections?" Glauberman chuckled. "Fat chance, Melvin. The Chains and Benny Otzenberger are on the same team. The Chain kid is going to marry Benny's daughter."

"Otzenberger is a small-time ward heeler."

"Not quite, Melvin," Glauberman said firmly. "Not *quite.*" He felt impelled to defend Brownsville and Benny. The attorney had used Otzenberger, been used by him, fought him at times. But he knew that the fat man had power. He paid off.

"Melvin, Otzenberger has Dullahan's ear. There isn't a cop or a judge or a prosecutor that can't be bought out of Dullahan's office. So don't tell me we can short-circuit Mort Chain and his father."

The two agreed: For the time being, the Chains would enjoy special privileges on the Canada run. It amused Schonkeit. It tickled his sense of the romantic. A coward who never carried a gun and ran from fights when he was a little rich kid in blue velvet knickers, a sissy who went to dancing school and had a German nanny, he admired the coarse strength of a Jake Chain. He'd seen the man once. Slavic-faced, with a mop of dark blond hair, something of the Viking about him.

Chapter 32

By Thanksgiving, Jake was working full-time with Mutt. Sal reluctantly accepted him. The money was pouring in in such staggering quantities that it barely mattered whether it was split two ways or three. No papers of partnership were drawn up. All transactions were in cash, including salaries to the girls (a third had been hired), drivers, warehousemen, and Professor Goldsturm. Buster, for loyal service on the Canada run, was given a raise.

The old Kolodny plant was becoming cramped. They had to use one of the truck bays for the storage of raw alcohol. Mutt did not like leaving the trucks on the street at night. He began to look for a bigger place, something secure, isolated, with more office space and maybe a reception room for clients.

Sal, a loner who lived with his parents, while all the surviving brothers were married and raising new broods of Ferrantes, remained their "outside" man. He organized trips to Canada, dispatched trucks, provided protection, bribed "dry" agents, handled the purchases of alcohol, real booze, flavoring agents, barrels, bottles, and labels. Mutt wondered if he was a secret fairy or if he couldn't get it up. Girls made him stammer.

Crazy Jake proved a decided asset to F & C Cereals and its

affiliate, Pacific Breeze Hair Tonic. His presence alone would have justified his third of the profits. The word spread quickly in the underworld. *Crazy Jake Chain was in bootlegging.* The muscleman they couldn't kill was back in business. Politicians and rich sports who did business with F & C, and heard that Jake Chain was a partner, expressed a desire to meet him and shake his hand. The newspapers made a quasi-celebrity of him: the colorful scoundrel who once boasted to a reporter about his price list for *shtarking*—a hundred bucks to wreck a small factory, up to six hundred for a big place. He was always good for a story.

Mr. Jacob Chain [a reporter for the *World* wrote] has turned his talents to greener pastures. Interviewed at his pleasant home in Brownsville, with his attractive wife, Sarah, listening, he explained he is an executive of a cereal company and a hair-tonic firm. Bootlegging? Ridiculous, Mr. Chain said. He would not indulge in anything that circumvented the law. He expressed sympathy with the temperance movement and efforts to enforce the Volstead Act.

At thirty-seven, Mr. Chain is powerful and muscular, a forbidding presence with a flattened nose, high cheekbones, and calm blue eyes that tell the visitor very little indeed. He is almost handsome.

"One thing I don't like," Jacob Chain said, "is this Crazy Jake business. I'm not crazy. I never was. I had little education. I was an orphan. I didn't learn to read or write until I was twenty-five. Does that make me crazy? I wish you people would cut it out. It doesn't look nice for my wife and my son to see that in the papers."

In their living room—Sarah had just bought a new white mohair couch—Jake read the article to her. She smiled. She had come to look more favorably on Jake's career. They had a lot of money in the bank. Morty would soon be married to a lovely girl. Socially, it would be a step up. Benny Otzenberger was moving to a three-story brownstone on Montgomery Street. Brownsville was getting a little dingy—more Italians, more Polacks, even a *shwarzer* family here and there.

She looked at Jake, sipping his tea, reading the paper slowly, missing nothing. She had never imagined he was so smart, so interested in reading. Sadly, she felt unequal to him. She had remained mired in her ignorance. Yet she was a pretty woman. Face, hair, figure had all improved as she aged. Away from the rattling sewing machines, concerned now with her elegant apartment, her husband and son, she looked very much the prosperous housewife.

"Jake . . . maybe we could go together again?"

"Where? The movies?" He regretted the words as soon as he uttered them. He knew what she meant. His heart yearning for Eva Heilig all these years. Sarah knew. A lot of people knew. He had used his wife's deformity as a cheap excuse, gone to hoo-ers.

"I got a new nightgown. You'll like it. Lace, pink silk. A present to myself before Chanukah. Do you want me to wear it?"

He walked from the table to the couch, sat down alongside her, and lifted her bent legs. One had all but healed. The lower bones on the left leg remained thin and shortened. The surgeons had done all they could.

"Sarah, *ketzeleh*, I love you. I do. It's hard for me to be romantic, like Valentino. I'm a *bulvan*. I don't know fancy words."

"Then you could kiss me sometimes. Hold me. Do what we used to do."

He kissed her cheek, her forehead, her lips. She shoved her tongue between his teeth. "Please, Jake. Be a man with me."

"I can't."

He wondered: How can guilt grow in a man like weeds until it chokes out everything else? It was like a child being bad. Mutteh had been like that. If he lied or stole from the candy store and was punished, it only made him lie again and steal again. As if to prove to Jake and Sarah that he was right and they were wrong. So now did he nourish his own guilt; repelled by his wife, he refused to change.

"What did I do to hurt you?" She wept. "I am young. I have a body. You were so good to me after the accident, in the hospital. You give me everything now. Nobody has what I have—furs, jewels, nice clothes. So give me something else."

"I can't."

"You have another woman."

"You are my only woman. You worked when we were poor. You worked harder than I did. You suffered. You were a good mother. Who else could I love?"

"Then come to the bed with me. I'll wear the new nightgown. We'll be like young people. I need you, Jake."

He smiled. "You have me."

"Only like a boarder. A greenhorn off the boat who lives here. I feed, I make his bed, I wait till he gets a job and moves. You are no greenhorn." She cried, burying her face in his shoulder. "You are my husband."

He stroked her back, ran his hand down her thigh, sniffed the expensive perfume. Women envied her and whispered about her. *Yentas* gossiped about snooty Sarah Chain who couldn't read or write. What else from a gangster's wife? A disgrace for Haven Place!

He carried her to the bedroom, kissed her face and her naked arms. But he could not love her.

Later, alone in the living room, listening to the radio—a runner had been killed off Montauk, Henry Ford was fighting the Interstate Commerce Commission, the League of Nations wanted to cut European armies in half—he picked up the newspaper again. Boy, that Dempsey. *There* was a man!

On an inner page he saw a small item: MRS. HALSTEAD DENOUNCES PROHIBITION, CALLS IT CRIME. Again Eva. She managed to make the papers about once every two weeks. Last time what was it? Handing out birth-control pamphlets? Chuckling, he shook his head. They couldn't stop her. Now she was forming something called the Woman's League to Repeal.

"I do not drink myself, and I deplore the ravages of alcohol," she was quoted as saying. "But this monstrous legislation is making us a nation of criminals. The government is party to this fraud, an act passed by bigots and hypocrites. Let the people have access to pure, unpoisoned liquor, and the gangsters will wither away. In the Congress of the United States, in the halls of the Senate, the reek of illegal liquor is pervasive. Legalize!"

And put me out of business, Jake thought. Funny, he could never be in harmony with her. Or understand her. The Heilig children were a different race. The surgeon Abe, a man of talent and wealth, Sol, the lawyer, who had been named to investigate the rackets. And Eva, so bright, so full of ideas. How could he be of the same blood?

The radio crackled and whistled. He switched stations. Another newscast filtered through. Again, the dead rum runner. The report was more detailed. Off Montauk and the south shore of Long Island, the announcer said, vast fleets were assembling, selling booze in unimaginable quantities. It was like an armada. Rowboats to huge oceangoing craft. Buyers and sellers did business past the three-mile limit under the noses of the coast guard.

Jake had never been on anything more dangerous than the Staten Island ferry. Of boats he knew nothing. But about whiskey he was learning a great deal. He would have to do some investigating. As a partner, some contribution was expected from him. If Canada was getting crowded, there was apparently lots of space in the ocean.

The next day, Jake asked Professor Goldsturm for a bottle of their best scotch. *"Uncut,"* Jake emphasized. "Not that horse piss you bottle for our customers."

"Of course, of course, Mr. Chain," Goldsturm said. He emerged from toxic vapors with a sealed bottle of Glenlivet. The professor turned it in the harsh light. Jake inspected the revenue label. No fakery, no counterfeit stamps. As of last week Mutt had ordered the chemist to start cutting the booze by a *fourth*—one-quarter real liquor, the remainder water and questionable alcohol.

Jake told Mutt he'd be gone for the day. Personal errands. Mutt nodded. Things had calmed down up north, thanks to Jake's appearance. Schonkeit's mob was laying off since the grenade incident. Futka Frummer had died three days ago in a Plattsburgh hospital. That made three Jake had dispatched. His reputation was becoming legend up north, just as it had been magnified in Brownsville. Big operators along the border were honored to learn that Crazy Jake was in their ranks. It was as if an exclusive golf club had landed a Vanderbilt or a Whitney.

Jake put the bottle of scotch in a paper bag and drove through gray November streets to Sheepshead Bay. He knew the waterfront area slightly, having taken Sarah and Mutt there on the trolley years ago. It was picturesque, pleasant— the bracing sea air, the pungent odor of fish and clams, the restaurants, boats slapping gently against the wooden piers in the autumnal wind.

He drove by Lundy's restaurant. Maybe he'd have dinner there. Maybe invite some person who could help the business. He had discovered that his bold, big appearance, or even the mere mention of his name, often evoked a friendly reaction. He marveled at how his reputation had grown since the years of the strikes. It was one thing to be a stupid wagoneer, and another to be celebrated as a "labor consultant." And now he was a businessman.

He parked on Emmons Avenue. With the bottle in the pocket of his blue cheviot topcoat, he strolled along the waterfront. Flapping wooden signs advertised fishing boats. It was off-season. Most of the berths were filled with idle craft. The boats looked wide, sluggish, and sturdy. They were designed to hold up to a hundred fishermen packed against the iron railing that circled the deck. There was usually a small cabin for gear, and a high bridge for the skipper.

At the end of the sea walk he noticed some smaller, sleeker boats. These were built differently, with broad aft decks to accommodate a few fishermen, and equipped with swivel seats. The cabin and wheel were toward the pointed bow. A sign read: PRIVATE CHARTER ONLY.

For rich guys, Jake thought. The boats looked fast. Not as big as the open boats, but classier. A few salty types in blue denims wandered by. On an empty lot, kids tossed a wool sock filled with sand—a homemade football. In front of one of the charter boats a grizzled one-eyed man was cleaning whiting, tossing slimy innards to screaming gulls.

Jake came up and watched him slice and gut with a thin razor-sharp knife.

"Nice day," Jake said.

"Nice for gulls. They ain't nothin' a seagull does but eat and shit. It'll eat anything. I seen guys throw their baited hooks out offen the side of a boat and a seagull will grab the bait, hook and all. Customer catches a seagull 'stead of a bluefish. Of course, all a bluefish does is eat and shit also."

"Why should they be different from us?"

"You're right and you're wrong, mister. They got more brains than us. See my bad eye? From drinking wood alky. Some bum give me a bottle of the stuff. Claimed it was pure corn liquor. Sent me into Kings County for a week, and when I came out—well, look at that right eye. Blinder 'n a dead porgy."

Jake looked at the gray film over the old man's eye. Nobody could accuse the Chains of selling stuff that bad. Nobody had ever reported anything more than nausea, vomiting, a headache, a three-day hangover, or the enamel flaking off their teeth.

The half-blind man asked Jake if he was from Sheepshead Bay. Want a charter? Like to go after deepwater cod? Too bad bluefishing was over. His boat, right in back of him, the *Deepwater Angel*, was one of the best. Mr. Dullahan hisself and his friend Judge Younghusband chartered it once a month in the summer. And drink? The booze didn't stop all day.

"Fast?" Jake asked.

"She does fifteen knots. For fishing you don't need to do much more."

The one-eyed man sliced a whiting from gullet to tail, yanked out the guts with one hand, and tossed them into the air. Two gulls swooped down and battled for the entrails. The bigger one triumphed, batted its wings, flew off. The other squawked and buzzed the fish cutter's head as if complaining.

"You work on this boat?" asked Jake. "What's your name?"

"I'm cap'n's mate. I'm Chick Muncie. Ask anyone around Sheepshead Bay about Chick Muncie. I drove dogs in Alaska. Drove steers on the Chisholm Trail. Château-Thierry and St. Mihiel. First Marine Division. Gunnery sergeant."

"Very nice. What's the captain's name?"

"Tommy Tuttle. Don't go aboard 'nlessen you're invited. Guests ain't welcome."

"Just a friendly call. I'm interested in a charter for a few days. Some important people."

"Cap'n don't want visitors today."

"I like the way you handle that shiv," Jake said. He gave the old man a dollar bill. "Maybe someday you could teach me how to slice fish."

Chick Muncie winked his good eye and jerked a thumb over his shoulder. "Go ahead. You look big enough to git your way."

Jake descended two steps to the wooden planking, hopped from the pier to the gunwale of the rocking craft. He stepped down and looked at the wide rear deck. Plenty of space to store cases. And another storage area belowdecks.

He poked his head inside the cabin and saw a broad-beamed backside in salt-streaked blue coveralls bending into the engine of the *Deepwater Angel*. In the darkness he could discern a huge wrench. He heard a few muffled curses.

"Excuse me," Jake said. "Mr. Tuttle?"

"No business today."

The voice was high, with a lilting quality. It dawned on him. It was a woman's voice.

"Maybe I can help."

The figure in blue coveralls and boots turned around. "The pump is stuck. No charters for a week."

"I'll make a date for a week from now."

The woman stood up. She was tall, with broad shoulders.

The coveralls could not hide a full bust and rounded hips that stretched the worn denim. She had an unlined throat, and a long, strong neck. Her face, although windburned, was exceptionally pretty. Jake looked her over approvingly— widely spaced dark brown eyes, eyebrows that rose from the bridge of the nose at a sharp angle, a high forehead. Her nose was a bit short, the nostrils large. Her chin was square and cleanly molded, and her chestnut hair was bound with a red bandanna.

"*You're* the captain?"

"I'm not the messboy. What are you staring at?"

"You'll excuse me. I ain't seen many boat captains of any kind in my life, and you're the first *lady* captain I seen."

She laughed and threw her head back. Jake stared at the throat—a deep hollow, skin whiter than the weather-darkened face. "You're not a fisherman, mister. You don't know Sheepshead Bay. Captain Tommy Tuttle is part of the scenery. Come back in a few days."

She turned her back and knelt. Jake saw the long curve of her buttocks, thigh, leg—a powerful woman, yet graceful. In a fancy dress, in silk stockings and jewelry, she'd be a knockout.

"The pump is barely moving. I think it caught a fifty-caliber slug. Those coast-guard kids will shoot at anything, even an honest charter boat." She grunted as she yanked at a stubborn valve.

"Gimme a try at it," Jake said. "I done a little hard work in my day."

"You? All duded up in that fancy suit and topcoat?"

"It's a disguise."

He took off his coat, making sure not to injure the bottle of Glenlivet, removed his suit jacket, and rolled up his sleeves. The lady skipper watched. She noted the oaken forearms and the enormous hands.

"About car engines I know a little," Jake said. "Just show me what has to be moved."

She spread a canvas at the edge of the oil-blackened boards and pointed to a lead elbow coupled to a threaded housing. Jake could see that bolts had been removed. But the connection and the coupling appeared to be out of true. She had doused the recalcitrant joint with oil, but the wrench could not budge it.

"Bilge water's driving me nuts," Tommy said. "This scow has more leaks than a senator's luggage after a trip to Bermuda. Go on, Dempsey, give it a whirl. Don't dirty your fancy pants."

"I been dirty before, captain."

Jake knelt, spit on his hands, and got a grip on the long wrench. He locked the head around the coupling and began to apply leverage. Muscles and veins bulged his forearms. The wrench slipped and he almost fell into the hold. His face turned scarlet. He had to admire the woman for even trying. The thing was cemented, immovable.

"What's the matter, Dempsey?"

"It's the rocking. Every time I get a grip on it, your boat moves."

"Oh, boy, some sailor. Three more tries and then out. Chickie and I will manage it."

Once more Jake locked the wrench on the coupling. He braced his body and used his back, his shoulders, and the power of his hands. Instead of trying to yank the rusted metal apart, he moved it slowly and firmly, the way he had lifted wagons when he was a kid. Never a fast, sudden move.

The coupling squeaked and rotated slightly on the worn threads. Jake gritted his teeth, applied pressure, grinned as the threads turned.

"By golly, you did it," Captain Tuttle said. "Watch out you don't get a faceful of bilge water."

Warned too late, Jake did not have a chance to escape a jet of brackish water that spurted out of the opened valve.

Laughing, the skipper dragged him back and let the water splash around until the pump emptied itself. She got down on her knees alongside him. "Too bad, big guy. That ten-dollar shirt and the silk tie look ruined. But you volunteered."

"I don't mind. I learned something. Anytime you need a pipe opened, ask Jake Chain."

"Hi there, Jake Chain. Tommy Tuttle. My real name is Henrietta Mae, can you imagine? My daddy was Mac Tuttle. He ran boats out of here and horses at Sheepshead Bay track. Tommy stuck to me 'cause I was a tomboy."

"What do I do now?" Jake asked. "I'm all *shmutzed* up so I might as well finish the job."

"Stick your hand down the pipe and see if anything's blocking it."

Jake reached into the rusted metal pipe. He probed and brought out a misshapen chunk of lead.

"What did I tell you?" She laughed. "A coast-guard souvenir. I ought to sue them. Shooting at a woman. And me with nothing but fishermen on board."

Rotating the lump of lead in his hand, Jake guessed it wasn't the first time she'd been shot at. There was a kind of knowing look that bootleggers developed—friendly, wary, a bit satisfied with themselves. Captain Tuttle had it.

"So what now?" Jake asked. "Do I get paid for all this labor? Watch it, I'm an old union official."

"Unions, huh? You don't look like a bricklayer to me."

"I was a consultant. I'm not kidding. What do I get as a reward?"

"Finish the job. What'd you say your name was?"

"Jacob Chain."

"Jew? No offense. I like anyone who plays it straight. Some of my best cust— Well, I mean, lots of my fishing clients are Jews. Doctors, lawyers, judges. A bluefish or a striper doesn't ask who catches him."

She handed Jake a shiny brass fitting. "Go on, Mr. Chain, use your muscles and get this new coupling on. I get sick of having to do heavy work myself. Old Muncie out there hasn't got the strength to bait an outrigger since wood alky almost killed him."

Jake removed the worn metal and replaced it with the new one. He whirled and pushed the giant wrench as if it were a toy. Then he wiped his hands on a rag, dusted rust from his shirt, tie, and vest, and climbed up to the cabin.

"Nice work, Jacob."

"Jake is better."

"Jake is no fake. Good job."

"My pleasure, captain."

"You look like a sport, so I won't offer you any money. But we'll sample some of my private stock."

She opened a mahogany cabinet in the cozy living quarters—two berths, gas ring, cabinets, a door to a toilet—and took out a square bottle with a label that read "Edinburgh Mist." Jake smiled. Some of Schonkeit's horse piss.

Tommy poured two half-tumblers and shoved one toward Jake across a table that was attached to the bulkhead with copper hinges. "Sit down, big man," she said. "Anyone who handles a wrench like that can be my friend."

A restrained drinker—he had firsthand knowledge of what went into what was marketed—Jake sniffed the liquid. Then he let a few drops fall on his index finger. He rubbed thumb and finger together until the "scotch" vaporized. He held his hand to his nose.

"What's that all about?" Tommy asked.

"Testing. Smell it, lady."

The skipper sniffed Jake's hand. "So?"

"Creosote and fusel oil. You know about boats, Captain Tuttle, but about whiskey, nothing. Try some of mine."

"Where'd you learn that trick?"

Jake ripped the seal from his bottle of Glenlivet and asked her for two clean glasses. She washed out the two with Schonkeit's liquor in them. Jake studied her strong figure. A different kind of woman. Inside the work clothes, a body without marks, no sagging. From all that work. Good muscles. Take the red handkerchief off her head, fix her up with a permanent, rouge, eye shadow. Pearls, a fancy black dress, silk stockings. She'd be as pretty as a movie star.

"I'm in the business, captain."

"I should have figured. Bootlegger."

"So who isn't?"

Jake raised his glass of scotch. "On the job I don't usually drink, but this is a celebration. I never fixed a pump for a lady captain before. *L'chayim.*"

"Sorry, big guy. I'm not up on my Yiddish."

"It means *life,* and it's Hebrew."

"I'll go along with it." Tommy Tuttle drained the half-glass. She moved not a muscle. Jake looked at the strong line of her throat. Something clean and alive.

"What we are now drinking isn't what my company usually sells. Too good even for rich people."

"I know. You cut it."

"Right. But any decent bootlegger should have a supply of real stuff."

"And that's why you're here. Supplies low?"

Jake nodded. They lifted glasses again. This time he only filled a quarter of the tumbler. No use getting stinko on the job. He could take or leave liquor. He never could understand what it did for people, why they fought, risked getting killed, and indeed got killed for it. They hid it in baby carriages, inner tubes, oil cans. They bought it in drugstores, paint shops, barbershops, from undertakers. Men had been caught crossing from Canada with their trousers lined with rubber hoses full of scotch. Women wore brassieres and corsets with rubber compartments next to their titties and tushies. *Goyim,* he decided, were insane. Liquor was their life. They gave up families, mistresses, homes, careers—their very lives—for it. Who was he to deny them their fun?

Captain Tuttle took Jake abovedecks. She leaned over the

side and showed him a row of holes in the boat's lapstraked flank. They were bigger than any bullet holes Jake had seen.

"Coast guard," Tommy said. "That slug you took out of the pump is the last one. I need at least a week for repairs. I'm not sure I want to play ring-around-the-rosy again with them. It's a sharks' convention on Rum Row."

"I got long teeth," Jake said. "I been around. How many cases can you handle?"

"Couple of hundred."

A drop in the F & C's bucket. But if he started with the woman, he'd learn the seagoing trade, hire other boats. Better yet, with the way the money was rolling in, they could buy their own boats. Run a fleet. The ocean trade was bigger and safer than truck convoys.

"We do a big volume. What do you charge?"

"Two hundred a day for the boat. Chickie gets fifty bucks a week. You got to make good for damages, fuel, and maintenance."

It was a bargain. On two hundred cases, they could gross over ninety thousand dollars after cutting. Each bottle of real scotch or gin now yielded four bottles of Goldsturm's scorching brews.

"Tell me, Miss Tommy," Jake said. "Why don't you go into business yourself? Buy, sell, handle goods. Whaddya want to be a taxi service for? All you need is cash, connections, and guys to wrestle cases for you."

She straightened up. The sea wind whipped strands of chestnut hair peeking from the bandanna. "I couldn't get customers. The big shots didn't like a woman horning in. Bad enough getting shot at by the Coasties. I got winged by some hoodlums in a private gunboat. No, thanks. I'm a sailor. A professional captain like my daddy, not a hooch peddler. I only ran whiskey when I had bills to pay."

"But you've done it."

"A woman's got to eat. I got a daughter to feed, clothe, and send to school."

Jake smiled at her. Her motherhood pleased him. The mannishness, the coveralls, the rubber boots, hid a woman, someone who could cook, worry about a kid, sew a dress.

"Husband?" he asked.

"Ran off to Florida. He works the Keys, smuggling rum from the West Indies. I know more about boats than he ever did. My father taught me."

"Where's he?"

"Lost at sea. He had a fast fifty-footer. Fancier boat than this. Took out a party of Wall Street lawyers during the war. Nineteen sixteen. They must have hit a loose mine. The rescue parties never even found a life preserver. Just some boards. Six lawyers and Captain Mac Tuttle, gone."

Jake suggested he take her to lunch. The eighty-six-proof scotch had left him giddy, his stomach yawning for food. Lundy's? he asked. She said she'd have to change; it was a spiffy place. Why not just go to a clam bar? Jake was insistent.

He waited on the wooden pier with Chickie, who was hosing down the deck and flanks of the *Deepwater Angel*.

"Heard you talking to the skipper," the mate said. "You're in the business."

"A little bit."

"It gets scary out there. See them holes? Should have heard the noise they made when they hit. Dang near sunk us if it wasn't for Captain Tommy's nerve. She beached us off Captree. By the time the Coasties got to us we'd dumped the booze in the Atlantic or throwed it into rowboats."

"Rowboats?"

"These people are so thirsty they'll cross the ocean in a dinghy for a sniff of scotch. Quite a sight when Billy McCoy and the rest of the boats come in from the islands. Like a dang armada. All them skiffs and speedboats and cruisers coming out to load up."

"Who decides who gets the stuff?"

"Oh, contacts. Some load off to their own boats. Some got regular customers. Some hold an auction. I seen a fella fall out of a thirty-foot cruiser. Man in black suit and a derby. The skipper of the rum schooner spent two hours right under the coast guard's nose trying to fish him out of the water."

"Why was he so valuable?"

"The son of a bitch had fifty thousand dollars cash in his pockets. Can't let a buyer drown."

Tommy emerged in a blue pea coat and a light blue skirt, dark stockings, and black pumps. She'd put lipstick on, combed her long chestnut hair, and tied a royal blue band around it. Jake felt his blood jump. A different kind of woman. No whining Sarah. No preaching Eva. No fat Minnie.

They ate steamers and lobsters at the rear of the restaurant. The waiter discreetly furnished them with teacups—Captain Tommy was an old friend—from which they drank "French" wine. Jake asked to look at the bottle and laughed.

It was some of Goldsturm's Château Magloire, distilled from a bit of kosher sweet Concord, grain alcohol, and bitters.

Jake's plainspoken manner appealed to her. After a few glasses of Château Magloire, Tommy became talkative.

She lived alone aboard the *Deepwater Angel*. Her daughter, a lively two-year-old named Lisa, boarded with her father's married sister in Coney Island. Tommy felt guilty. She told Jake she wanted to devote more time to the child, but the boat kept her busy—hustling charters, running booze, repairing it.

"You're not as tough as you make out," Jake said. "I like that. You're a woman. You got a right to be scared when they start shooting."

"You're not scared?"

Jake had to smile. She didn't know him. She hadn't heard the stories. "Miss Tommy, I been shot at a whole lot. You read the papers? Ever read about a guy called Crazy Jake?"

She laughed. "Yes, I make the connection. I know who you are now. You bust heads on picket lines."

"Used to. No more."

"Oh, sure. Look at those hands. I saw the way you handled the wrench."

"But I keep the palms soft for ladies." He touched the back of her tanned hand. "You are a beautiful woman. Your husband had to be a *shmendrick* to go running off to Florida."

"He was afraid of me. I had more courage than he did. Can you imagine a yellowbelly who'd hide belowdecks when he saw a coast-guard boat? Or one of the go-through boats?"

"What's a go-through?"

"Hijacker. Fast boats with machine guns and boarding hooks. They go after little guys like me. They wait until you're loaded, ram you and board you. They're worse than the Coasties. They'll kill you for a case of gin."

Jake absorbed the information. It sounded risky, but there were huge hauls of booze to be made off Long Island and Jersey. The important thing was to connect with a big operator, offer more money, get a "first" on his shipment. Even better, he thought, would be to own your own ocean-going ships, your own craft for unloading, and a fleet of trucks for the trip to New York.

Over Lundy's blueberry pie and vanilla ice cream, Jake gave her two of his cards—the F & C Cereal card and the one advertising Pacific Breeze Hair Tonic. There were phone numbers on each.

"I don't need corn flakes or hair goo, Jake."

"Let me know when your boat is ready to sail again," Jake said. "I'll pay."

"You'll pay before I go out, Dempsey. I haven't got the money to get the hull patched."

Jake pulled the roll from his pocket. "What do you need?"

"She has to go into dry dock. Four or five days' work. Fix the pump. Four hundred should do it."

"Here's five hundred. As soon as she can sail, call me. You can tell me the best time and place for buying."

"Outside the three-mile limit on a foggy day. You always carry that much cash?"

Jake paid the check, tipped liberally, and complimented the headwaiter. He held the chair back gallantly for Tommy.

"Listen, Dempsey," she said, with a mocking gleam in her eyes, "there's a horse hitched down the street. Want to see if that roll you carry will choke him?"

"It's a cash business, captain."

They parted on a windy corner on Emmons Avenue. A steel-gray sky lowered over the docks and the rocking boats. A clumsy open boat was churning the waters, nosing toward its berth. It was laden with frigid cod fishermen.

"A week maybe?" Jake asked.

"I'll call when I need corn flakes or hair tonic. You people really are a sketch. Thanks for lunch, and thanks for working the wrench."

He watched her stately figure walk off. No weakness in her. A little shy about men. A crazy life—raised on boats, no mother, her father drowning. A different kind of woman.

It was early evening when Jake got back to the plant. As soon as he had parked his car he heard screaming from within. He saw no police cars parked on the cobbled street. The double-size garage door was locked, so he entered with his key through the smaller steel door. As he crossed the threshold, he identified the shrieks as issuing from the mouth of his future daughter-in-law, Hilda.

Cautious as always, Jake waited in the brick-lined hallway that led to the office with its frosted-glass walls.

Hilda screamed again. "Mutt, Mutt! Watch the *knife!*"

Jake could hear muffled curses and angry voices. One was Mutt's, full of menace and warning. The other was a guttural snarl. Who?

He walked into the plant and glanced at the office. Hilda was wailing, pressing her hands to her face. Theresa had gone for the day, as had the third secretary, Mrs. O'Neal. Mutt was standing behind a copper mixing vat, holding a broken bottle in his hand. Opposite it, Sal Ferrante was pointing a six-inch blade at Mutt.

"Fuckin' crook, fuckin' kike," Sal was muttering. "I'll cut ya heart out."

Puzzled and wary, Jake kept a cool head. He always counted the house, figured the odds. None of the other Ferrantes was present. Buster was probably out driving a truck. Only the professor, his bulging bald pate gleaming under the overhead lights, was in the barnlike room, jigging up and down, appealing to the partners to calm down.

A good situation, Jake thought. No Baggie, no Dom, no Luigi. Even Theresa was gone. The odds were with the Chains. Jake was unarmed. He made it a point not to carry weapons. Why give the cops an excuse? He could remember when Dopey Benny Fein, an untouchable mobster, got in big trouble in 1915 for a Sullivan Law violation.

The dispute could be handled. But he would need room to swing, arms unencumbered. He took off his topcoat and jacket and placed them on a stack of wooden crates. Then he walked stealthily into the factory.

Goldsturm saw him first. *"Mr. Chain!* Please, Mr. Chain, stop them! It's my fault! I take the blame!"

Hilda also saw Jake. "Sal says he'll kill him! Jake, do something!"

"Sure." Jake laughed. "Call a cop."

"Screw you, too," Sal said. He backed away so he could see both Jake and Mutt. Hilda danced in terror. Her breasts wobbled.

"Sal, *walyo*," Jake said gently. "What's all this?"

"I told him to shove his home-cooked alky up his nose," Mutt said. "It's ruining the booze. We had a dozen cases sent back. The professor says we can't use it anymore. Right, Goldsturm?"

"I'm sorry I started," Goldsturm wailed. "Mr. Chain, it's true. What Mr. Ferrante brings in is *poison*. Bedbugs, mouse crap. We can't use it. Better we should buy more denatured alcohol and purify."

"No," Sal said. "My whole family's inna business. All my friends. I ain't puttin' them outta work."

Poor Sal, Jake thought. On a hot afternoon Pacific Street smelled like a garbage dump. Stinking fumes hovered over the pavement, made eyes tear, noses twitch. In each three-story building, alky cookers bubbled. The cottage industry gave income to a horde of Ferrantes, their relatives and friends.

"But, *walyo*," Jake said sweetly, "nobody wants to take the bread from your family's mouth. It's just we can't kill our customers."

"It's awful, Mr. Chain," Goldsturm sputtered. "A disgrace. We found a sparrow in a bottle of Tennessee Morning."

"Dead, I hope," Jake said.

"Our best line," Mutt said. "Sal, put the knife down. Pop, stand back. I don't need you. I'll fight him."

Jake pondered his move. No cops, of course. Cops were people you bought, bribed, and owned. You never involved them in family disputes. But Mutt was not afraid. He was lean as a whip, leather-strong, fast on his feet. Lacking his father's size, he had inherited his strength. At Jefferson High he had won medals for the two-hundred-yard dash. Jake could remember cheering at the PSAL games when Mortimer Chain won the four-hundred-yard relay with a mighty sprint on the anchor leg. *Bright sunlight, a cool day at Boys High Field* . . .

"Okay, I'm out of it," Jake said. "Both of you drop the stuff in your hands. The knife, the bottle. You wanna fight, fight with fists."

"No!" Hilda shrieked. "No! Mr. Chain—stop them! Stop them!"

"Giddadahere," Sal said, turning to Jake. "I ain't a-scared a you."

"Sal, boychick. My little buddy who used to sell ices," Jake said. "Who wants you to be afraid?"

"Yez are after me. Your kid made me take you in. So you get two-thirds of the business and I get shit. I started it! Mutt learned it from me. Then he brings you in. Who needed you? Now it's two against one."

Jake sat on a barrel and crossed his legs. No point in using his fists on Sal. He could get the knife and beat the daylights out of him in seconds.

"You got my brothers killed," Sal said. He sounded as if he were ready to weep. "Frankie. Vinnie. You use us up like we was snot rags."

"I loved your brothers. I love you like a son. That is why you got to listen to Uncle Jake. Was I ever rotten to you? Did I ever say Salvatore Ferrante was a bum who took pennies from kids for selling lemon ice?"

Mutt winked at Hilda. She was shuddering. She had always feared Sal. Ever since the day he'd blown off the farmer's head. Mean as a snake, the eyes never looking at you.

Mutt was smiling. The old man was going to soft-soap Sal, work a con on him. He had seen his father do this before. Years ago when he was a "labor consultant" with Glauberman. Mr. Jacob Chain, playing with a gold watch on a chain, discussing a contract with a union official.

"Sal, listen to Jake. I know your poor mother is sick. I know that has upset you. Put down the knife and I'll tell you what we will do."

"No."

Mutt tried to stifle the smile. *Oi, the con game the old man was pulling*. Like the pea under the shells.

"Sal, you can keep all the rotten alky that stinks like dead fish, that your *goombahs* are making. We can't use it."

"Screw you, Chain."

"Sal, you got to listen to me. Your mother liked me. Didn't I pay for the masses in Holy Family? A whole year of candles? Be nice."

Jake thought: *If he is not nice, if he turns me down, I may have to crack his head*. But that would be a desperate move. The Ferrante muscle, manpower, and contacts were useful. A man and his son were not enough. They needed an organization. Maybe they had been unfair to Sal.

"You keep your alcohol," Jake went on. "But we'll furnish, below cost, bottles, corks, revenue stamps, and the mixers. Professor Goldsturm will be happy to hire you a cutter to make the booze. His advice will be available. Only two things we won't do?"

"Whazzat?"

Sal was hooked, wiggling, Mutt saw.

"Your *own* labels. Your brands can't compete with ours. No Aberdeen Dew, no Juniper Tree, no Tennessee Morning. It's easy. Our printer will design them. So your line won't be competitive with ours."

"What's the other thing?"

"Stay away from our customers. Sure, you're still with us. But you got a second line. You can charge less. Sell to the Polish Falcons and the Ukrainian Social Club and the Sons of Erin. They're also thirsty. For F & C, you're a partner. We keep the Brooklyn Democratic Club, the speakeasies, the restaurants, the society people. You have your own business on the side. None of the alky your family makes goes to waste, right? And who else in the home bottling business gets free bottles, corks, mixers, and flavors?"

"It's a good deal, Sal," Mutt said. "You could clean up."

Sal blinked. He looked chastised. All breathed a sigh of relief. The baloney slicer went into Sal's belt. "You mean it? I get bottles and stamps and all the crap that goes into the whiskey?"

"Please," Goldsturm said. "My additives, Mr. Ferrante, are not crap. They can do nothing but improve your vile alcohol."

"My word," Jake said. "Mutt's word. Partners, aren't we? Just don't compete for customers. Make an inexpensive line. The Polacks and the micks and *shwarzers* will be happy to pay. Use extract of Jamaica ginger. Old antifreeze. The iron in it is good for the blood."

Within a week, Sal was running a cutting plant in the cellar of his father's barbershop. If the product was inferior to F & C's, it was nonetheless in demand, even though the president of the Polish Falcons went into semi-paralysis after a wedding at which Ferrante's Society Club Special Rye was served and much praised by Polish *Feinschmeckers*.

Chapter 33

Each day Jake waited for a call from Tommy Tuttle. Normally a patient man—he had learned that if you waited long enough you got what you wanted—he found himself eager to see the tall woman again.

She was something refreshing to him. The women he had known (except for Eva, the unattainable) were soft, beaten, lesser beings in a man's world. The women of Brownsville—Italian, Jewish, Irish—seemed to him depressed, frustrated, and empty. He pitied his wife, was disgusted by Minnie, and found Hilda, his daughter-in-law-to-be, selfish and conceited. The Ferrante women were not much better than slaves to tyrannical brothers.

Tommy's independence and courage astonished him. Her strength intensified the sexual thrill he anticipated. She liked him. He knew it. She knew who he was. Crazy Jake. The tough guy. A man carrying a grand in cash around.

There was no telephone aboard the *Deepwater Angel*. He did not know how to reach her. But he did not ride out to Sheepshead Bay again. He preferred to wait, to delay their meeting. Then an odd thing happened. With the woman on his mind continually—*Am I in love?* Jake wondered—he approached Sarah one night, came to her bed, and made love to her. She could not believe her good fortune.

"It was like when we were young," she said. "So good."

"Because I love you, *ketzeleh*."

A shadow of guilt hovered over his affection. Considerate of Sarah's frail body, he understood the act was a lie. He was making love to Tommy. In his mind were pictures as vivid as photographs—how he would join his body to the strong woman. What difference? he decided, as he and Sarah rested in the dark, arms around each other's body. What difference? Sarah did not know. The moments of passion had made her joyful.

"Jake, I am happy. I'm glad you came to me."

On a mild breezy day in early December, Tommy Tuttle phoned Jake at the warehouse. She was ready to sail. The *Deepwater Angel* was repaired—the holes sealed, the pump replaced, the engine reconditioned.

"You go out in winter?" Jake asked. "I don't know what kind of a sailor I am."

"What happened to the tough guy, Dempsey?"

He laughed. "I'll be there. How much money should I bring?"

"How much do you have?"

She had gotten a tip from a speakeasy owner in Coney Island. The *Grecian Venus*, under command of the legendary Captain Bob O'Hara, was due off Freeport the following morning. O'Hara always notified a few choice customers. The speak owner liked Tommy and let her in on a good thing.

Jake scrawled some notes. He was to meet Tommy at the dock in Sheepshead Bay at five the next morning. She would have Chickie and another man on board to help with the loading. She was to be paid cash in advance. As for trucks, that was his business. She told him to have the trucks wait for her boat at Rayburn's Boatyard in Clamshell Inlet east of Freeport. Tommy said she did not like to take her boat into heavy surf or land on a beach. It was asking for trouble. Mr. Rayburn was reliable. He kept numerous coast-guard employees and Prohibition agents on his payroll. If all went well, they would be able to unload cargo by six or seven that night.

"Food?" Jake asked. "Guns?"

"I'll supply the food. No guns, Dempsey. My rule is, when in trouble, run, ditch the cargo. Pay off if you have to. The Coasties have fifty-caliber machine guns and three-inch cannons."

Jake told Mutt and Sal about his plans. He'd need three trucks. Since two were out making pickups on Lake Champlain—they'd located a hotel owner who let them use his resort as a drop—they would have to rent vehicles. Buster Twine would drive the lead truck. Baggie and Stroonz Rizzo would follow.

Sal was suspicious of the seaborne operation. But he had become more subdued now that he was becoming Brownsville's chief purveyor of "nigger gin." Sullenly he consented to the new venture. When Sal left the office, Mutt asked his father if he knew what he was getting into.

"I won't know until I try. It sounds good. This lady captain knows the angles."

"A *lady* captain?"

Jake tried to be offhand. "You should see her. Tugboat Annie. Tough as nails."

"Enough drivers?" Mutt asked. "Cash?"

"Sure. Buster's got the most brains so I'll give him instructions. The *walyos* can take orders from him. I'm taking ten grand in cash. I want to see what it'll buy."

Mutt's eyebrows arched. "*Ten grand?* Did you tell Sal? Remember, he's a partner."

"You tell him."

The following morning was colder and windier. Jake got seasick a half-hour into the Atlantic. He heaved his breakfast and requested a warm mackinaw from Tommy. She laughed at him. Some tough guy. A landlubber, a baby at sea. He'd better get a pair of sea legs if he wanted to work Rum Row, she taunted.

The *Deepwater Angel* chugged noisily and left a wide churning wake, but it made good time in the choppy seas. Tommy had brought along a flat-bottomed barge. It was tied to the fishing boat with a hawser. It slowed them down, but it would be useful in case Jake planned a big purchase. She had known buyers to weep in frustration at their lack of planning.

Rum boats would come in with ten or fifteen thousand cases, and buyers would have to settle for a small purchase for lack of storage space.

Chickie and Anton, a chubby Slavic-looking youth, labored about the deck, while the skipper, puffing a Fatima, handled the wheel.

"I feel useless," Jake said. "Can I help?"

"Just flash your roll when we pull alongside the *Venus*. O'Hara has sharp eyes. He can count your money from twenty feet away. What'd you bring?"

"Ten grand."

"That should get you five hundred cases, or a thousand burlocks. He'll think you're a piker. Guys come out with pokes of fifty and sixty thousand."

She explained why O'Hara had been so successful. He had a contact with the coast guard, a warrant officer who earned $153 a month. O'Hara paid him ten times that amount to look the other way. He also furnished the officer with payoffs for his crew. Unhappily, the warrant officer was not always on duty. If some other boat took up the chase or fired a shot or tried to board, O'Hara had to play it cute. Usually he presented a fake bill of lading from Bermuda or Nassau. *No need to inspect cargo, officer, we're carrying palm oil.*

Tommy, guiding the boat along the south shore and munching a liverwurst sandwich, regaled Jake with stories of Rum Row. He abstained from lunch. There was a working day ahead and his stomach was trying to crawl into his mouth.

"Getting tougher for small operators like us," she said. "Heck, I've seen customers row out four times in one afternoon to load up. Wait'll you see Rum Row. Speedboats, skiffs, fishing boats. But the big guys are closing us out. They send their buyers to the West Indies and purchase a cargo in advance. They charter schooners and meet them with speedboats off Montauk or Coney Island. Sometimes they unload under the Statue of Liberty."

Jake absorbed more information. Bootleggers were ordering rum runners built to specifications. Fast craft that could reach fifty knots, ten knots faster than a coast-guard vessel. One smuggler was experimenting with armor plate.

"People get killed doing this?" Jake asked.

"You bet they do. I've seen rum runners shot dead in New York harbor. If not by the Coasties, by some crook trying to hijack."

"I didn't bring my guns. You told me not to."

"If there's trouble, we run and dump cargo, clear?"

Jake inhaled the salt spray, the sea air. Not a bad life. Better than hanging out in the stinky plant. Goldsturm's mixtures were permeating bricks, timbers, flooring. The place smelled like the inside of an old beer barrel. Theresa, Hilda, and Mrs. O'Neal complained about the stench.

Jake stood next to Tommy at the wheel. She was perched on a high stool, eyes on the compass, guiding the boat through a choppy sea.

"You like this life?"

"What else do I know? This and my little girl are everything. I don't date much. They all think I'm one of the boys. Good old Tommy. Even the name. Sometimes I wish I were a Lydia or a Cynthia."

"You're a beautiful woman. Even in dungarees and a heavy blue sweater."

"Step down, Dempsey. The fee is the same. Two hundred for me, fifty for each of the boys."

Young Anton clambered to the bow and sighted through a pair of binoculars. "I think I see dem, cap'n. O'Hara's ship and a whole lot of others."

"Word gets around," Tommy said. "Are they loading?"

"I can't tell."

She turned the wheel to the right and headed toward open sea. "Hold on, Dempsey, it might get rough. You look gray."

"I'm okay. I'm getting excited. Listen, how does he decide who gets what?"

"Some deals are made before he leaves. We're small-timers, so we get leavings. But Bobby likes me. He gives my clients a break."

"He's a boyfriend?"

"No, he's not. He's happily married with a wife in Florida and seven kids. He just likes me. That's all."

Soon they were able to see the fleet of boats. Around the tall silhouette of the *Grecian Venus*, a score of smaller boats—cruisers, charters, outboards—circled like suckling pigs around a brood sow.

Anton hopped down from the foredeck. He gave the binoculars to Tommy. "Somethin's wrong, skipper. Nobody's unloadin'."

She left the wheel to him and ordered him to turn the boat to port. She took the binoculars.

"No wonder. Coast-guard cutter's got the *Venus* stopped. The Feds are off to starboard. If O'Hara wanted to give him a run, he could. But that would leave an awful lot of sorry customers. I guess his warrant officer isn't working."

Jake shivered and drew the plaid lumberjacket over his throat. He had overcome his queasiness. He was almost enjoying the roll and pitch of the boat, feeling himself part of the crew. But it bothered him that he was apparently on a useless errand.

"I'd guess he's outside the three-mile limit," Tommy said. "But they still won't let him unload. In fact, friends, they got the three-incher pointing at him. Look. Where the sun hits it."

Jake took the spyglasses. He could see the white government boat. A spark of gleaming metal indicated the cannon.

As they watched, some small boats started toward shore.

"Yellowbellies," Tommy said. "Well, the more leave, the better for us."

A cabin cruiser and a charter boat was turning in the choppy seas and sailing to harbor.

"What's he gonna do?" asked Jake.

"I don't know. Maybe put out to sea for another day. Then hit the island further east—Montauk, East Hampton. I sure hate to see us lose out."

"You mean I got to pay even if we strike out?"

"That's life, Dempsey. You ought to carry insurance." She winked. "Some days it doesn't pay to start up the engines."

"It's just I hate to quit. We got trucks waiting in Freeport."

The coast-guard cutter hove into full view. The craft sailed from behind the dark hull of the rum runner. Clean and white, it made O'Hara's booze ship look dingy and disreputable. Tommy said that O'Hara deliberately kept it so to fool pursuers. His engines could outrun anything the government owned. But this time he must have been surprised.

"Damn," she said. "Looks like the ball game's over."

Jake scratched the scar on his chin. Cold, damp weather. The old wounds seemed to bother him on days like this. The scars in his legs and his groin began to twitch.

"Tommy, I'm no sailor, and I never bought booze on the ocean. But I think I got an idea."

The *Deepwater Angel* lurched and righted herself. The towed barge bumped the stern, butting the rubber tires with a sucking noise. A fast cabin cruiser passed them, sending out a boiling wake that made Tommy's boat rock, rise, and settle again. A man in a captain's hat and a handsome navy blue coat was standing on the aft deck. He bellowed through a megaphone: "No use, Tommy. The Coasties won't go. O'Hara's got twenty thousand bottles of booze on board. I think they're going to board to search. It's an outrage."

Tommy thanked him through her megaphone.

"Who's he?" Jake asked.

"Van Dyke. Rich guy from Old Westbury. Polo player. He likes to buy his booze off the boat so he's sure it isn't cut."

The speedboat flew past them, churning the steel-gray waters. Gulls wheeled and squawked in its snowy wake.

Jake asked: "You got extra gasoline on board? Engine oil?"

"Sure."

"We used to do this when I was *shtarking*. To get the cops off our back when we wanted to throw a bomb or hit the scabs."

"You're ahead of me, Dempsey."

"Soak the barge with gasoline and oil to make it smoke. I know from fires. When it starts to burn, we shove it off. I'll give you five to two the coast-guard ship comes after it."

"You're crazy," she said.

"Crazy Jake."

"If we wreck the barge," Tommy said, "we'll have only half as much space for the whiskey."

Jake said, "I always take what I can get when I can get it. Tomorrow, your friend O'Hara could be arrested and the government could grab the booze."

She turned to Chickie. "Get out a gasoline can and five quarts of engine oil."

"Miss Tommy, we could all go up in smoke," the mate said. "Blown to hell."

"You'll go first, Chickie. All that alcohol in you. Turn the barge loose when it starts to burn."

"Not me, Miss Tommy. Let that big guy try it. He ain't no sailor. If we lose him, so what?"

Jake suggested they pull several hundred yards closer to shore to give the coast guard a longer run. Tommy agreed. But she didn't want the flaming wreck to run aground. It would be too easy to put out the fire. Drifting in the choppy seas, it would be harder to control.

Chickie came from belowdecks with a ten-gallon jerrican of white gasoline and two five-quart cans of motor oil. He was breathing heavily. *Scared*, Jake saw. He'd do the job himself. He'd show them how Crazy Jake got things done.

Tommy raised O'Hara on the radio. She spoke to him in code words. For all she knew, the coast guard had boarded him already. He acknowledged her as "Angel," and she called him "Venus." Had he any news of her aunt in Miami Beach? O'Hara said she was sick again. Lung trouble. She sent Tommy her love. But the doctors wouldn't let her go north.

Tommy guessed he was being detained. Maybe searched. Jake Chain's daring plan sounded better and better.

"I ain't gettin' on that barge," Chickie said. "Blow me clear to hell. One spark from the engine. A backfire and *wham*."

Jake leaped onto the barge, trying to land lightly. The boards moaned beneath him. He could see how splintered and stained the barge was. The most he'd pay for its loss, he decided, was three hundred bucks. "Chickie, toss me the cans."

Anton, the younger man, took over from the frightened mate. He threw the jerrican to Jake, then the oil cans.

"We far enough from him?" Jake called to the skipper.

"Let me swing around once more, so when we cut loose she'll drift west. If we're lucky we can load up while they're still chasing it."

Jake sprinkled gasoline and oil on the wooden deck and sides of the barge.

"How ya gonna light it?" Chickie called.

"With a match, how else?"

From the wheel, Tommy watched him. Quite a man. Nerve, brains. Like her father, Captain Mac. Same size, same coloring, same blunt hard face. And with a streak of the gambler in him.

"Not while you're in it, Mr. Chain," Anton said. "C'mon back on board. I'll untie the hawser."

Jake shook the cans vigorously. *Every last drop.* He felt like Goldsturm emptying detoxified methyl alcohol into a vat. Anton gave him a hand and pulled him over the stern of the *Deepwater Angel.*

"Gimme a hunk of cardboard," Jake said. "Like an old box, something that'll burn slow."

Chickie found the cardboard container that had held the oil cans. Jake stuffed it with newspapers and sprinkled them with gasoline."

"Untie the rope, kid," he ordered Anton. He called to Tommy: "Skipper, when I holler *go*, give her all her power."

They worked like a trained team. Anton undid the painter. He held the loose end until the last minute. Jake threw a book of lit matches into the newspaper-crammed carton and heaved it onto the barge.

"Full steam, Tommy," Jake shouted.

The *Deepwater Angel*, free of the sluggish barge, spurted away. *And just in time*, Jake thought. He felt his eyebrows singe, his skin prickle with the burst of flame. The gasoline roared. The oil sent up clouds of boiling black smoke. The old wooden craft listed away from them, staining the clear wintry air with choking bursts of smoke.

Jake came into the wheelhouse. "Can you raise a coast-guard station? Or the harbor cops?"

"I can try."

"Tell them you saw a floating wreck. Big boat burning. People in the water. Give a different name for this boat. Say you're going to try to pick people up but you need help."

She cocked her head and smiled. The arching eyebrows that had attracted him, rising from the bridge of her nose, arched even higher. "You not only have muscles, Chain, you know how to lie."

"Nobody's getting hurt."

After a few attempts on the crackling radio, Tommy was able to contact the Freeport harbor police. She did as Jake suggested, identifying herself as the *Ocean Beauty II* out of Captree. A sergeant replied he'd get to the coast guard at once. There was a cutter just off the three-mile limit.

"If I were you," Jake said, "I'd head for your friend O'Hara."

Within a half-hour they pulled alongside the *Grecian Venus*. O'Hara and his crew were tossing oddly shaped crates to a speedboat riding alongside the rum runner.

The cutter was nowhere in sight.

"What happened to the Feds?" Tommy shouted.

O'Hara laughed. "Fire at sea. They took off like war was declared."

Tommy shouted up to him: "That was our barge, skipper. You owe us seven hundred bucks, O'Hara. My customer had the bright idea."

"Same Tommy," O'Hara called back. "Stand by. I'll load you next. Who's your client?"

"Mr. Jacob Chain."

O'Hara looked through a spyglass, sizing Jake up. New face to him. The name meant nothing, but the man's size was impressive. And if it had been his idea to fake out the Coasties with a "fire at sea," he had to be a helluva man.

O'Hara ordered a Jacob's ladder lowered. He shouted at a

returning customer to get out of the way so Captain Tuttle's boat could be loaded first. There was some picturesque cursing from a gray-bearded skipper in a wide-beamed open boat.

"Prior deal, Anderton," Captain O'Hara called. "She had a date."

Tommy nudged Jake's side. "Anderton hated my father's guts. He's an old crook, smuggler, go-through man. The bum has an arsenal belowdecks."

Jake looked at the name on the bow of the bearded captain's boat. *Ocean Beauty II*. The name Tommy had given the harbor cops! *By God, that was a woman for him.* If a stink was raised about the fire, the Feds would come looking for Anderton.

"He wants *you*, Dempsey," Tommy said. She shoved him toward the rope ladder.

"Come aboard, Mr. Chain," O'Hara said.

A bit uneasy, Jake dug his heel into the lowest rung, then hauled himself up and aboard the rum boat. The deck was piled six- and seven-high with wedge-shaped packages swathed in burlap.

"No wooden crates?" Jake asked O'Hara.

The two men sized each other up. Both were big and wide-shouldered, with calm unemotional faces. There was a sense of recognition in their flat stares.

"My invention," O'Hara said. He was windburned, with a shock of white hair, intelligent brown eyes.

Jake picked up one of the cloth cases. "Feels like six quarts."

"You guessed it. Pack 'em three, two, and one. Each bottle gets a straw jacket. Then the colored girls in Nassau sew them into a double burlap wrapping. They use a third less space than wooden crates with twelve bottles. Every dollar counts, Cohen."

"Chain."

"Excuse me. I ever meet you?"

"No. I run an operation in Brooklyn. Me and my son. Take a few cards."

O'Hara smiled. *A cereal company. Hair tonic.* He had met bootleggers who claimed to represent pharmaceutical houses, paint and shellac factories, industrial machinery manufacturers, antifreeze producers, insecticide makers.

"I'll buy all you can get into Captain Tommy's boat."

O'Hara nodded. "Seeing as she's a friend, and how you got the Feds off my neck, it's a deal."

Prices were going up. Two burlocks—twelve bottles, the equivalent of a full case—went for fifty dollars. Two years ago, Jake remembered Mutt telling him, they were able to buy whiskey in Montreal for *ten dollars a case*.

The *Deepwater Angel*, with the aft deck crammed, every inch of the wheelhouse filled, more burlocks stacked on the foredeck, a few jammed into the hold around the engine and the pump, would take a disappointing two hundred and eighty burlocks. The loss of the barge hurt.

Tommy complained. They'd have to limp back to shore with the gunwales dangerously deep in the water. They were looking for trouble if the seas turned rougher.

Jake counted off seven thousand dollars in hundreds from the ten grand he had locked in his money belt. O'Hara's black crew paid no attention. They had seen rolls of forty, fifty, and a hundred thousand aboard the *Grecian Venus*. And their skipper never carried a gun. His fists, his reputation, and his honor were protection enough.

The deal concluded, Jake, Anton, Chickie, and two black Bahamians began securing the wedge-shaped packets with rope and tarpaulins. The seas were heavier now. The *Deepwater Angel* bumped fretfully against the steel ship. Captain Tuttle held her steady, gave orders, supervised the stowing of cargo.

Coatless, in his candy-striped shirt, sleeves rolled up, Jake outworked every man in the crew. He lifted, tossed, stacked. And did not once breathe hard. Captain O'Hara watched him, thinking, *That is one big tough Jew.*

They were exhausted and freezing when, under the cover of night, the *Deepwater Angel* sailed through narrow channels, past rickety waterfront homes to Rayburn's Boatyard. Tommy had ordered the two-man crew to sit on the tarpaulins. If they were stopped, they would stall for time.

But all was quiet in the marshy channels east of Freeport. They scudded past a long jetty with a red light winking on its outermost pilings, then turned into a smaller channel.

"Good haul, Dempsey?" Tommy asked.

"Yeah. But I wanted to spend ten grand. Too bad we lost the barge."

"You owe me five hundred."

"Take three. Piece of junk, good only for what we used it for."

She smiled. Dimples dented her long cheeks. A *woman,*

Jake realized again. The rough blue work clothes would have to go. There were curves, and smooth skin, and warmth under the seaman's disguise. "Make it four hundred," she said.

Jake peeled off the bills. Then he gave her an extra fifty. "Buy something for your little girl."

"I like that. I also like the way you got dirty stowing burlocks. You made O'Hara's deckhands look like weaklings."

Jake touched her hand. "I done my share of hard work. I never been ashamed of it, either."

She thought: *Like my old man.*

An anxious Buster was waiting in the parking lot of Rayburn's Boatyard. The trucks had been there since late afternoon. Colin Rayburn, the owner of the boatyard, anchorage, and "drop" for rum boats, had picked up the radio signal reporting a burning derelict. Harbor police and coast-guard vessels had responded. Rayburn, a chunky egg-bald man, chewing on a cold cigar, was concerned. The signal had come from the *Ocean Beauty II*, Ulf Anderton's boat. And Anderton was first boat out that morning to contact O'Hara.

"Don't worry about it, Colin," Tommy said. "It's under control. The coast guard came through. Any word on survivors?"

"Petty officer thinks it was a fake. By the time they'd finished looking for them, O'Hara had unloaded and sailed. Bobby's on his way back to Nassau by now."

Jake ordered Buster to start unloading. To Jake's amusement, three local policemen, in uniform and armed, were enlisted to help stack burlocks in the F & C trucks. They worked hard, stacking expertly, as if they had done it many times.

"Ten bucks a man," Tommy informed Jake. "Fifty for Rayburn."

"A bargain."

Within an hour the trucks were loaded. Jake said he would ride in front with Buster and pay off. Route 25 was known as "whiskey highway." There would be six or seven payoff points before crossing the New York City line. Since the cutting plant was in Brooklyn, they could avoid the biggest payoff, the Queensboro Bridge.

Jake shook hands with Tommy. "I think I was a pretty good customer. If you contact O'Hara, tell him I'll buy his whole cargo next time."

"Two hundred thousand dollars' worth? C'mon, Chain, that's not your league. You're no Schonkeit."

He watched her walk off to her scruffy fishing boat, and he felt sorry for her. No job for a woman. And the daughter she missed so much. The dead father she had loved. In his chest were odd flutterings. Like nothing he had felt since his young manhood and his love for Eva.

The truck convoy was shot at just after leaving Oceanside. But it was a halfhearted attempt. A few bullets whistled over the hood of the first truck. Buster and Jake ducked below the windshield, ran a red light, signaled to the rear trucks to follow as fast as they could move with the heavy loads. They bounced along the highway. On a stretch of uninhabited sandy land, a motorcycle cop, siren screaming, halted them.

"Exceeding the speed limit," the helmeted officer said. "Driving on the wrong side of the double yellow line. Let's see your driver's license, Bojangles. Let's see the registration for the trucks."

It was ten after midnight, the end of a long, wearying day. Jake had no intention of losing his booty now. The two hundred and eighty burlocks held *one thousand, six hundred and eighty* bottles of genuine scotch, brandy, and gin. These could be cut four-to-one, resulting in damn near *seven thousand bottles* of phony brands, which could then be sold at eight or ten dollars a bottle.

Gross earnings on the haul from Captain O'Hara could come to more than *sixty thousand dollars*. Not bad for an outlay of seven grand, plus a thousand bucks in miscellaneous expenses. To have all this ruined by a dumb motorcycle cop? Never, Jake thought.

"Officer," Jake said politely. "I am with the F & C Cereal company. I'm bringing in a load of grain. Someone shot at us outside of Oceanside. I feel you should look for those criminals."

A flat smile transformed the cop's face. He knew, he *knew*. The word was out. O'Hara had been offshore near Freeport. Some local hoodlums were trying to scare the drivers.

Jake gave him a card. "There it is, sir. A respectable Brooklyn firm. I think it is outrageous the way we get shot at, stopped and questioned. If we violated traffic laws, then I'm ready to pay fines. Could you arrange it for us, on account of this shipment is a day late already?"

"What's your name, wise guy?"

"Dr. Jacob Chain. Consulting chemist for our company."

Trucks roared by on Route 25, some bound for Montauk, some returning to the city. The great booze parade. The cop studied Jake's innocent, wide face.

"You might be interested in our subsidiary company, officer," Jake said. He gave him a Pacific Breeze Hair Tonic card. Under it were a pair of hundred-dollar bills. It was exorbitant. A holdup. But Jake was edgy. No use in looking for bargains. Buster's eyes opened wide.

"I'll let you off this time, doctor. But watch it. Traffic laws were meant to be obeyed."

"Absolutely. Next time we'll be more careful. Buster, I think we can go on. Thank you, officer."

Jake's trucks rolled off the dirt shoulder, hit the asphalt, and sped toward the city line. He kept performing primitive arithmetic in his mind. Someday not far off, he would buy an entire cargo from Captain O'Hara. He had a little trouble calculating how much bootleg hooch, how much *real* money could be made from a two-hundred-thousand-dollar purchase of the real stuff. The amount was so huge it eluded him.

Goldsturm was ecstatic. Mutt and Sal were impressed. The whiskey from the sea assured that they would have more than enough for the holiday season. Almost six hundred additional cases of fake booze. Goldsturm was so overjoyed he decided to try a new line of gin, something with a piquant dash of sulfuric acid. He called it Tavern Table Gin and awarded it medals from the St. Louis Exposition and the Brighton Pier Centennial. Buster tasted it and said his tongue curled up like a window shade.

"No more small sales," Mutt told his father and Sal in the office. "We're getting too big. From now on, no retails, no cards in hotel rooms, no individual deliveries. Only speaks, stores, and distributors. Minimum purchase is twelve cases. We give a ten-percent discount on anything over twenty-four cases."

Jake nodded. Sal flickered his eyelids. Mutt imagined it meant yes. More and more Sal was finding himself an "outside" man—supervising deliveries, picking up alcohol, checking inventory. He seemed to have changed, to have grown more moody ever since the Chains refused to buy his *goombahs'* home-stewed poison. Luckily he was getting a rep in Brownsville and East New York—The King of Nigger Gin. Fussed over and pampered by his mother, he stayed at home, set his thick black hair in a net, and listened to a Zenith through elephant-hide earphones.

"I think we can start charging a flat ten bucks a bottle, one hundred and twenty a case," Mutt said. "Schonkeit's getting eleven and twelve, and I'd love to undersell the Paymaster."

Chapter 34

"He's carrying twenty-four hundred cases, Dempsey. Damn near five thousand burlocks. Interested?"

Was Jack McGraw a manager? Could Bobby Jones play golf?

In the F & C office, Jake listened on the phone to Tommy's breathless account of O'Hara's imminent arrival. In two days the *Grecian Venus* would be returning to Freeport. And because O'Hara had been a seagoing mate of Old Mac Tuttle's, he was giving Jake Chain "firsts."

Her fluty voice aroused him. What was better than money, adventure, and a handsome woman? Aboard her chugging fishing boat she had seemed mannish, curt, a bit tough. On the phone her voice suggested silk gowns and soft bedroom lights.

"He'll let me buy it all?"

"That's what the man said. And O'Hara's word is good. He phoned before leaving Nassau. He's damn near loaded. Scotch, brandy, and gin. A big shipment came in from England."

She told him to bring cash. Twenty-four-hundred-odd "cases" would come to *one hundred and twenty thousand dollars*. If he only wanted part of the shipment, O'Hara might not play. There were no secrets on Rum Row. Schonkeit or some other big operators would pounce on the cargo if Jake had the shorts. Word would get out.

She outlined the plan. She would hire extra boats for the ship-to-shore run. Again they would unload at Rayburn's Boatyard. But this time they would need at least fourteen trucks.

"And we're doing it *at night*," she said. "Captain Bob's got some deal worked out to discourage the go-through guys. Our fleet will leave Sheepshead Bay at midnight. You should be out here by eleven."

"Let's make it nine o'clock. I'll buy you dinner at Lundy's."

"Sounds good. Go to the bank and get a second mortgage. Sell the farm. This'll make you and your son rich. You can buy your wife a mink coat."

Lusting for her, he kept business foremost in his mind. Jake had learned to prepare, to anticipate. He took a ruled pad from Hilda's desk and did some calculations. Thirty thousand bottles of whiskey could be cut to one hundred and twenty thousand quarts of Goldsturm's mixtures. Sold at ten dollars a quart, the gross receipts would be in excess of a *million dollars*. They had to get bottles, crates, storage space, as soon as possible.

Mutt and Sal were in the garage arguing. Mutt wanted to buy a grocery jobber's warehouse across the street and use it for storage. They had no room to move around in, Mutt complained. So much stuff was being turned out that Goldsturm needed four new vats and an automatic pumping system for filling bottles. Crated booze would have to be stored elsewhere.

Cautious as ever, Sal objected. "Whadda we wanna spend all that dough for? Who needs a new building?"

Wait, Jake thought, *wait till he hears what I got in mind.*

"Boys," he asked politely, "we can spare maybe a hundred and twenty thousand in cash?"

"The new building, pop?" Mutt asked. "Hell, we can buy that old dump for ten grand. A few thousand more to fix the bricks, put in steel doors, bar the windows."

"Not for the building, Mutt. Sal, listen to your uncle Jake. I got a tip that is gonna make us rich like we never believed. A hundred and twenty thousand for real booze. Another five grand for boats, bribes, trucks, and helpers. I got new friends."

Tommy was waiting for him in the lobby of Lundy's. She was wearing stockings and low-heeled black shoes, a black suit, a pink blouse.

"You look better this way. I can see the lines. When you're dressed like a boat captain, it's like a good racehorse under a heavy blanket."

"Thanks a lot, Dempsey."

Her hips and thighs were full and long, melding gently into a pair of well-formed legs. Her full breasts, high and firm, poked at the silk stuff. There was a double strand of pearls around her strong throat. Her wind-darkened face, a bit lined and worn, while lovely and elegantly proportioned, seemed apart from the femininity of naked throat, high breasts, well-fleshed limbs.

"All set?" he asked. "Boats and crews?"

"If you have the money."

Jake lifted a black valise. "The money belt wouldn't handle it. I had a hell of a time convincing my partners that we should take it out of the bank."

"I bet. You belt them around?"

"No. One's my son, I told you. And the other one likes money as much as we do. He agreed. In fact, he and my boy, Morty, are going to Rayburn's."

A whiff of her perfume made him giddy. He was guiding her toward the restaurant. Suddenly he felt he would swoon if he did not make love to her.

"Table for two, sir?" the headwaiter asked.

Jake edged her away from the entrance to the dining hall. "I'm not hungry. Tommy, I'm in love with you. We'll go to the Half Moon Hotel. We got time until the boats leave."

"No. Don't ask me to, Jake."

"Please. I think—I think—I'm not good with words. I can't say it. I love you."

"Then don't ask me."

"It's not just a business deal anymore."

He was moving her toward the coat check. He told the waiter they'd changed their minds.

"What will we use for luggage? They won't let us in." She looked ashamed.

"This," Jake said. He held up the black leather valise. He had a hundred and fifty thousand dollars in it.

"Maybe you'll be sorry."

"Never with you."

They made leisurely, restrained love. Jake saw at once that she was hesitant. He was considerate and undemanding. Yet the sight of her long curved body, free of wrinkles, full of strength and grace, gave him a joy he had never experienced. Her refusal to abandon herself, the suppressed noises she made in climax, made her all the more desirable.

A wintry moon sent shafts of light into the darkened bedroom. Tommy sighed and rose from the bed. With a feathery touch, he ran his hand down her spine.

"You tickle. Soft hand for a big man."

"I'm in love with you, lady captain."

"It's late, Jake. We'd better get to the boats. I'm not a lady anymore. Just an old salt. You know they call me 'one of the boys' in the bait-and-tackle shops. Maybe it's why I'm not a good lover."

"You're the best woman I ever—"

"Oh, I bet. You mobsters get show girls and models, right?"

"Not Jake Chain. My wife, God help her, is a cripple."

"Maybe I am also."

"You? You're *perfect*, Tommy. There's no woman like you anywhere."

She put on her underwear and slip, nestled close to him, and began to cry. He tried to undress her, but she did not want to be loved again. "One of the boys," she said, sniffling. "A drunken husband who used to beat me, and a father who was too good to me. Captain Mac. Maybe I'm still looking for him."

"You found him, kiddo. I'll be any kind of man you want. Papa, boyfriend, husband. I'll be a customer for your boat. I'll protect you, I'll buy you fancy silk things, furs, pearls. Maybe I said the wrong thing, huh?"

"No, Jake. You made me happy."

But she did not look happy. Her long face was solemn as he stroked her hair and kissed her forehead.

"Alligator skin," she whispered.

"You make fun of yourself too much."

She began to talk. Tommy wasn't her real name. It was Henrietta Mae, but she had been a notorious tomboy as a kid in Sheepshead Bay. She could remember her grandfather walking horses at the racetrack. As a girl of ten she would go help him, insist on "walking off" some overage plug that her grandpa, Big Joe Tuttle, owned. Neither horses nor the tough gangs frightened her. *She was a Tuttle*. When the track folded, her grandfather seemed to die a little every day. The few dollars he had left went to Mac, who bought a boat and traded his way up to the *Deepwater Angel* and a steady business in charter fishing. Business was good, especially in late summer and early fall when the blues were running.

Her mother "died of the booze," Tommy said. Alone a great deal, uneducated, a handsome Irishwoman, she felt that Cap'n Mac loved his rusty tub more than he did his wife. She was a secret drinker. She gave Tommy little love.

"And your husband?"

"I hated him. I thought he'd be like daddy. He wasn't. Stupid, vain man. It's no good being stupid, Jake. I'm sorry. I know you have no education. But people who don't know anything go to hell faster. I quit after two years of high school. I've always been sorry. My daddy read a lot. He and grampa *understood*. People have minds also, they knew. I feel cheated."

"Don't be ashamed, Tommy. I learned to read and write when I was twenty-five."

"I'm sick of being a—a—fake man. Boots, sou'westers, heavy sweaters. They think I'm a roundheels or a lesbian."

"I could tell them different. Listen, you want to go to school? I'll pay. You want to sell the boat and open a business?"

She rested her head on his massive chest. "No more baiting hooks with skimmers? Skin my last bluefish? It would take a carload of cold cream, Jake, to get the calluses off my hands. And my face is a mess—an old sea horse."

"It's a beautiful face. Get rid of the boat. I'll buy it. I'll hire some guy to run booze. That ain't for a lady like you. A lousy two hundred bucks a trip? While I make a fortune? You can go to Brooklyn College. You can do anything you want."

Such words, spoken with such tenderness and sincerity, he had never used to Sarah. He felt guilty.

"Nuts," she said. "Old Dempsey." She tousled his hair, got out of bed, and finished dressing. "I hate this. I have to change again on the boat. I dressed for you. Now I have to go back to dungarees and slickers and a watch cap like a merchant seaman."

"Henrietta Mae, I love you."

"Stow it, Jake. You better get dressed too. You might as well check out and save another night's rent. No encore tomorrow, understand?"

"But maybe the day after tomorrow?"

He could not remember such pleasure. Merely watching her dress—maneuvering her long body into the sheer blouse, the skirt, the jacket, the high-heeled shoes—aroused him. The magic, the strangeness of women's clothing tantalized him, all the hooks and snaps and elastics. As she was brushing her hair, he seized her from behind and ran his lips over her neck and cheeks. He took her one last time on the bed, fully clothed.

Chapter 35

The waters were reassuringly calm. A mile off Sheepshead Bay, the *Deepwater Angel* rendezvoused with three other boats of Tommy's flotilla. Two, like hers, were open fishing boats. The third was an old seagoing tug. None of them had much speed. They would be sitting ducks for the coast guard or a hijacking craft.

"Prices went up for a night haul," she said. "They get three hundred each. I gave them half of it. You can pay the rest when we unload at Rayburn's place."

"A bargain," Jake said. They wore heavy-weather garb—navy blue watch caps, knit sweaters, boots. Jake was enjoying the life. It got him out of the warehouse.

Distantly, through fog and spray, Jake could see searchlights flashing. It seemed to be a code—three fast flashes with intervals of about a second between them.

"Trouble?" he asked.

"Heck, no. That's O'Hara's friend."

"You mean the coast guard is leading us out to him?"

"What else are they paid for? For a mobster, you can be a boy scout sometimes. You know that Dwyer, the biggest rum runner of all, uses coast-guard boats to unload his schooners? He's got New York City cops loading his whiskey into trucks. Everybody plays."

Several hours later, as the swells increased and the fog dissipated, they were able to discern the silhouette of the *Grecian Venus*. The government cutter hove to a quarter of a mile away. She had stopped flashing her blinkers.

"It's safe to pull up," Tommy said. "There's one skipper can put in for an early retirement. By next Christmas he'll be a rich man."

O'Hara's schooner looked dingier and rustier than the last time Jake had seen it. Moreover (unless his eyes deceived him), he noticed a row of huge bullet holes in her starboard side.

Lanterns glowed aboard the schooner. They could see O'Hara and a black deckhand lowering a Jacob's ladder.

"He wants you, Jake," Tommy said. "Don't forget the satchel."

Chickie and Anton gave him a shove upward. The two boats nudged each other's side tentatively. He dug his work shoes into the rope and climbed aboard with one hand, holding the valise in the other.

"Good evening, Chain," the skipper said.

"Good evening to you, captain. You done me a real favor. I'd invite you to my son's wedding, but I know you stay out of New York."

"A kind thought, Chain. I like a family man. Got seven kids of my own."

"I hope you got more cases of booze."

O'Hara showed him a manifest. The heading read:

O'HARA & BEECHAM, LTD.
IMPORTERS
PRINCE STREET, NASSAU

"Read it and weep, Chain. I've got twenty-eight hundred cases, thirty-three thousand six hundred quarts. Half are sewn into burlocks. The rest are crated. We didn't have time to sew them all. The island's overloaded with liquor. Every distiller in the United Kingdom is shipping. I can't even rent warehouse space."

"Gimme a price."

"Since you're Tommy's friend, it's the same as last time. Fifty dollars a case."

"I make that a hundred and forty grand."

"Nice round figure. Plus five thousand for the United States Coast Guard who escorted you here and is standing off my port bow."

"Tommy said you'd split the payoff for the Feds."

"Did she?" O'Hara leaned over the rail and hailed Captain Tuttle. "You giving your friend ideas? What's this half-and-half on the Coasties?"

"Be a sport, Bobby," she called back.

O'Hara laughed. "Okay. Two and a half grand. Why argue over trifles?" He shouted to his crew. "Start unloading, boys. Two of you get on board Captain Tuttle's boat and stack."

Jake decided not to work that night. He opened the valise. He and O'Hara sat on a hatch cover. The purchase and the money for the coastguard boat left him with seven thousand five hundred dollars. The drivers and loaders and bribes would eat into that. But what did it matter? He'd landed a fortune in clean booze. It would teach his kid a few things. And wise Sal up. They would be small-timers no more.

After O'Hara had counted the green bills and stowed them in an iron safe belowdecks, he came back with a submachine gun and two .45 automatics in his arms.

"I thought you never carried hardware," Jake said.

"We got word that the go-throughs are around. They're mostly dumb micks and wops, and, excuse me, Chain, a few sheenies. They can't take a good run at sea. Start heaving their guts as soon as there's a wake. But they might give you trouble on the way in."

"So?" Jake said.

"You paid up fast and you're Tommy's friend. Take these with my compliments."

Jake thanked the skipper. He tucked a .45 in his belt and handed the submachine gun and the other .45 over the side to Anton.

"No dice," Tommy said. "Give them back. If we get hijacked, Jake, it's your neck, not mine. I have no interest in your booze. Remember? I get three hundred dollars a boat and expenses."

"Obey the lady," O'Hara called. Burlocks and crates flew past his head. Jake had never seen a crew work so fast. They unloaded a fourth of the cargo in minutes, tossing wooden boxes and burlap packages, securing them with rope.

Jake gave the machine gun and one automatic back to O'Hara. The second automatic he kept in his belt.

By four in the morning all the boats were loaded and groaning under the weight of more than thirty-three thousand quarts of rye, scotch, gin, and brandy. It was by no means a record haul, O'Hara told Jake. Some of the big operators had come ashore with loads worth seven and eight hundred thousand dollars.

"I'm getting there," Jake said.

"Good luck, Chain. I'll call Tommy when I'm ready again."

Jake descended the rope ladder. Tommy took the wheel. O'Hara was a considerate purveyor. He had arranged for the coast-guard boat to escort them beyond the three-mile limit.

"We can't make any speed," Tommy said nervously. "We're loaded like pregnant whales. Just pray that when Uncle Sam says goodbye, there won't be any pirates around."

"It would be a shame," Jake said innocently. "And not a gun on board." He put his hand on the .45. He'd never used one, but he knew the trick. Aim low, *very* low. The damn thing kicked like a mule.

The boats labored through the now choppy seas. Toward the shoreline the December fog thickened. Each boat kept running lights on. Tommy had ordered the captains to keep a short interval between boats. Once they got into the main channel, they could relax. It was unusual for go-through boats to try to intercept there.

They saw the red jetty lights of Freeport, waves breaking on the long rock pilings. The cutter turned east.

As Tommy guided the *Deepwater Angel* between rocking buoys, she let out a gasp. "Trouble," she said.

"Where?" Jake asked.

She cut their speed. The overloaded boat came to a shuddering halt a hundred yards short of the channel entrance.

"Look left. He's coming our way."

A long, sleek speedboat, white as death, was cutting the water, focusing twin searchlight beams on the *Deepwater Angel*. Jake was momentarily blinded. The damn fool piloting the white boat was headed straight for them. It had a long curved bow. He could see men standing on the foredeck, others on a narrow rail-enclosed contraption.

"Flying bridge," Tommy said. "They spear swordfish from it. Only I think someone else is getting speared. Dammit, we were almost home free."

A burly man in a wool cap and pea jacket was standing on the narrow metal bridge. He was pointing a submachine gun at the wheelhouse of the *Deepwater Angel*.

"Remember what I said," Tommy said. "To hell with the cargo. I want to live. I'm a mother."

"I'm a father. It don't mean we quit. Not with me out a hundred and fifty grand."

"Heave to," the armed man called. "Stop the tub or I'll blow your brains out."

Jake grabbed her arm. "You're gonna give in?"

"You never saw anyone so yellow."

Chickie began to shiver. He looked dolefully at Anton. "Jesus, I wish we could just go fishin', like the old days."

The white boat had no name on its bow, no identifying numbers. Tommy had told Jake about them. Fast boats, built for the rum trade. They could run rings around a government boat. They'd steal every case they could stow, force the boats to follow them to a beach, and steal the rest.

"Ask the guy in charge to come aboard," Jake said. "Tell 'em they can have anything they want. You got no guns on board. But you need help to off-load. I'll hide behind the oil drums."

"Scared, Dempsey?"

"Just trying to figure something out. Listen to me. I know these *mamzerim*. I talk their language. Do anything you want, tell him you'll kiss him, but get the top guy on board."

The white boat came alongside the *Deepwater Angel*. Tommy told Anton to signal the other boats to stand by. Their skippers understood. They would never stand a chance making a run for it. They'd be overtaken in minutes.

"You've got us," Tommy shouted down to the speedboat. "Just don't start shooting. We don't carry guns."

"But booze, huh? From O'Hara? Move, bitch."

"I don't know any O'Hara," she said. "And please speak with respect to a lady."

Crouched behind oil drums, Jake thought he recognized a voice. A whiney high-pitched voice.

"Tell the whore to start throwin' the stuff over the side, don't go on board. . . ."

"Whaddya think, I'm scared?"

"Ya goin', boss, take a piece. Manny, give the boss a rod."

"Against a skirt I don't need a rod. Hey, she's good-lookin'. . . ."

Jake could hear Tommy ordering Anton to throw a ladder over the side.

There was a clatter of heavy heels, waves lapping, the noise of the boats bumping. Then thudding, as a man landed on deck. Then the sounds of two more men.

He peeked from behind the drums.

Shikey Frummer.

No question about it. Short, dapper in a fur-collared greatcoat and a black beaver hat pulled over his ears. The lanterns pinpointed lights on his waxed moustache. The little thug removed his hat and bowed. "A pleasure. Lady, what's your name? Whaddya got on board? It don't look like bicarbonate of soda."

Tommy lied. It was cheap booze, she said. Stuff from a floating "cutting plant." The other boats were empty. He'd waste his time unloading a lot of fake liquor.

"Good try, lady, but you're a liar," Shikey said. He smashed the butt of his gun against a burlock, reached in with a gloved hand and took out a shard. "Cut, my Yiddish ass. Look at that. Old Cumberland, eighty-six-proof. Start unloading. Anyone gets smart, this broad here'll have an extra hole to go with the ones she's got already."

"Anton. Chickie. Do what the man says."

Tommy's crew began tossing crates over the side. Two of Shikey's crew clambered aboard to help. Shikey did not pull his gun. He had two toughs with him who did no work but kept shotguns trained on the loaders. The bulky man on the flying bridge aimed the Thompson at the wheelhouse.

All my life I took chances, Jake thought. Then, stupidly, he said to himself: *Sarah will never forgive me if I miss Morty's wedding.* The old lust for violence was bursting inside him. Like sex, like the way some men craved the booze.

"I never seen a dame running a rum boat," Shikey said. He guffawed. "Jesus, look at the size of that broad. Tony, ya'd get lost in there, right?"

Tony, one of the men armed with a shotgun, said nothing. Women were not to be insulted. Even rum runners.

"What's ya name, beautiful?" Shikey asked.

."Captain Tuttle. Take what you want and go. I don't want any trouble."

Shikey patted his moustache and peered around the wheelhouse. He could see the other boats turning. "Hey, you wanna get your head blown off, captain? Tell those guys to stay where they are. They move, you're dead. Dummy, give 'em a blast."

The man on the flying bridge leveled the Thompson at the first boat. Bullets peppered the side of the turning boat, caused tiny waterspouts. The boat stopped.

"Through the horn," Shikey said to Tommy.

Tommy picked up the megaphone. "Stand to, Ole. Tell the others. No one will get burt."

"Atta girl," Shikey said. He pinched Tommy's behind. "I seen it *all* now. A lady bootlegger. Ya must be workin' with somebody. Anyone I know?"

"Some man sent me the money. It's not my booze, you know that. I get three hundred dollars a boat, that's all."

"What else do you get, baby?"

Tommy walked toward the drums. Jake waited. She was working with him. Shikey had no weapon in his hands, but he probably was carrying one. Jake edged to the side of the drum nearest the open deck. Ten feet away, Anton and Chickie were tossing burlocks into the speedboat. Jake suspected they'd be there for hours. The armed men would keep them riding outside the channel. The white speedboat would need a dozen trips to off-load.

"Three hundred a boat?" Shikey asked. He followed her across the slippery deck. "Whaddya get without the boat? I mean, like if I wanna *shtup* you?"

A few hours ago Jake had been in bed with her. He had decided that he loved her and would marry her. To hear Frummer insulting his woman was more than he could tolerate. He yanked the .45 from his belt. It was a chance. They all might be blown to hell. But the old brute confidence, the stolid belief in the Chain luck, asserted itself.

Stealthily Jake came out of the darkness like a footpad. In one swift move he grabbed Shikey, coiled his left arm around the furry neck, and pressed the barrel of the automatic to his victim's right temple.

"Tommy!" Jake shouted as Shikey floundered. "Put the lantern on us so they can see!"

The brief struggle drew the attention of the men with shotguns. The man on the flying bridge had temporarily left his post. He was shouting orders at one of the boats.

"I got Frummer!" Jake shouted. "I got a forty-five next to his head! You want a dead man here? You want I should blow his brains out?"

"What the fuck's going on?" Tony asked. "Shikey? You there?"

"He's here, wop," Jake said. "Look at him."

Tony halted. He saw his boss locked in Jake Chain's iron embrace. Shikey's eyes bugged. His cheeks worked like pink bellows. The moustache seemed ready to crackle and fall apart.

"Kfff—kffff—kfff—Ch—Ch—Chain—"

"Take a good look, gentlemen," Jake said. "Look at where the gun is. Maybe you'll get me, but you'll have a lot of explaining to do to Mr. Schonkeit if I kill this *mamzer*."

"Shikey, whah?" Tony cried. "Who? Whah?"

"Eh, who's 'at guy?" a man shouted. He aimed the machine gun at Tommy.

Jake released his grip slightly. "Tell that son of a bitch to throw the violin in the water! Fast! You wanna choke to death?"

"D—dr—drop it," Frummer called.

The submachine gun splashed into the water.

"Now the guys with shotguns. Give them to the old guy and the kid. Anton, Chickie, get 'em."

"I want one," Tommy said. "Chickie, give it here."

Jake braced his back against the door of the wheelhouse.

He dug a knee into Shikey's kidneys. The barrel of the black automatic never moved from the right temple.

"Listen to me. This is Crazy Jake Chain. You heard of me? This is my booze. These are my boats. First, you'll load back every bottle you stole. You don't move fast, this guy's brains'll be all over the place. Schonkeit'll cut your balls off."

Tommy leveled the shotgun at Tony. "You, start loading. *Move!*"

"Shike?" the hoodlum asked. "Is it okay?"

Before Frummer could nod his head, Tommy double-pumped the shotgun and fired a blast past Tony's head.

"Jesus, lady. I heard you. Jesus!"

"Move, assholes," Jake said. "Excuse the language, Miss Tommy. It's all these people understand."

Wheezing, pissing his pants, Shikey Frummer tried to squeeze words out. That bastard Chain! A gorilla! He was barely letting him breathe. There was no killing him, no stopping him.

"Listen, Jake," Shikey gasped. "Go easy. I'll choke. I'll die. I'm dead, they'll kill you."

"Your brother's dead and nobody killed me."

"Yeah, I figured. It was you blew him up."

"And you're next, if those ginzos don't work faster. Tony, move your ass. Tommy, next time take the bum's head off. Nobody'll miss him."

"Ch—Chain, gimme a break," Shikey cried.

"Never. Not to people who insult women. Me you can insult. But a lady you should never insult, Shikey. That's why I'm angry."

"Yeah, and a hundred thousand bucks' worth of booze."

"Booze I can always get. Apologize to the captain. Say, 'Miss Tommy, I am sorry I made dirty remarks to you.' Say it!"

Reduced to a lump of boneless flesh, Shikey mumbled his apologies.

In fifteen minutes the burlocks and crates had been reloaded. Jake now had to take a chance. He guessed there were still guns aboard the hijackers' speedboat. But they had three weapons of their own now. And Rayburn had surely paid off the local police to assist O'Hara's customers.

"Okay," Jake said. "All of you, back on your boat."

"Lemme go," Shikey whimpered. "Ten grand for you, Chain. Lemme go. I ain't kilt no one. I ain't even carrying a rod."

"Shut up. Who's the captain there? Show your face, sailor, or you'll have a passenger with no head."

A light went on on the bridge and a stout man appeared. "What do you want, Chain? Don't make trouble for me. I was just hired for a job."

"Get out of here fast. Don't follow us into the inlets. Just beat it."

"Understood."

Tommy added a few instructions. She thought she recognized the skipper. A man from Bayshore, a ferryboat skipper who'd graduated to whiskey speedboats.

"What about my client?" the captain called.

"He comes with me. You pull anything, you get out any hardware you haven't used, he gets it in the *kugel*. He won't be the first I had to stiff."

The crew of the white boat needed no further orders. They returned to the deck, cursing. Jake heard Tony refer to him as "a Jew ape, so crazy he's kilt ten guys already."

Tommy reversed engine and let the white boat pass. Then she led her convoy past the red jetty lights, through the bobby buoys, and into the waterway to Rayburn's.

Mutt, Sal, and the brothers were waiting nervously. They had heard the bursts from the machine gun. Rayburn had heard that Schonkeit was determined to clean up along the south shore.

Jake tied Shikey's hands behind his back and prodded him off the boat to Rayburn's dock.

"Who's the cake-eater, pop?" Mutt asked. "Man, look at that fancy moustache. Fur-collar coat, shine on his kicks."

"An old friend. Shikey—what is your real name?—say hello to Mortimer Chain, my son and partner."

"My name is Saul. Chain, gimme a break. I'm just a guy on the make like you. I take orders."

"I don't. I give them."

The Ferrante brothers stared at the man. They wanted to burn him alive. Or perhaps weight him with cement and leave him to the crabs. Wasn't he the guy who got Vinnie killed in Plattsburgh?

Jake was glad Tommy did not hear any of this. She remained aboard the *Deepwater Angel,* giving instructions to the off-loaders. Rayburn had outdone himself. Half the local police department, two deputy sheriffs, three volunteer firemen, and a Prohibition agent were hired for the night's work. Each would get fifty dollars and a bottle.

"Nah," Jake said. "Why make more trouble? I want this

bum to go to Schonkeit and tell him to leave the Chains alone. They tell me the Paymaster respects people with guts. Right, Shikey?"

"Burn the bastard," Baggie said.

Sal stroked his melting nose. "I'll do it. First ya stuff his mouth so he can't holler. Then you tie him up to a post or a tree. One can of gasoline. Burn like a Fourth of July sparkler. Right, Dom?"

The brothers nodded in solemn agreement. This man had murdered Vinnie. He had to be destroyed.

"I like cement better," Dom said thickly. "Two blocks tied to his feet. Cut his belly open so he sinks, and the crabs have a feast."

Vaguely frightened, Mutt listened, aware of the awful power his father had. As dreadful as the Ferrantes were, his father dominated them. Jake was smiling, enjoying Frummer's terror. They had shoved him, trussed, onto a stack of lobster traps. Behind them, the loading of the trucks proceeded. Buster Twine supervised.

Jake said, "We'll let Frummer walk home. With his hands tied and his mouth stuffed, he might make it by 1925."

"Chain, I'll make a deal with you."

"Shut up. You used filthy language in front of a lady."

"Lady?" Mutt asked. "What lady?"

"The captain. The woman on the deck."

Mutt squinted in the gloom. He saw a tall woman in a bulky sweater, moving among the men. A new one on him.

"I'm sorry, Chain. I apologize. Don't let these dagos kill me, please. I'll make it up with Schonkeit. You'll have your own territory."

Baggie hit him on the nose. Blood squirted, covered his mouth.

Rayburn ran to them. "Chain, no rough stuff around here. Nobody gets stomped in my boatyard. Take the guy into the woods. How dumb can these guys be? There's fifteen cops working around here."

"You're right, Mr. Rayburn," Jake said. "Dom, Baggie, lay off."

He settled the issue. Shikey would be left bound and gagged on the sandy shoulder of Sunrise Highway. It was five in the morning. At daylight, his fur-collared figure would be noticed by a motorist and he would be returned to the Paymaster.

The trucks were loaded and ready to move. Jake paid everyone off. He had enough money left to cover the police in the towns and the big payoff at the city line. The Brooklyn cops had doubled the price for passage. He'd handle them himself. They knew Jake Chain. Sergeant Pope had spread the word about the big guy with the free hand.

"Be with you in a second, kid," Jake said to Mutt.

He jumped aboard the *Deepwater Angel* and entered the wheelhouse. He took Tommy gently in his arms, kissed her, explored her mouth with his tongue, kissed her neck and throat and cheeks and ears, and said he would call her in two days.

"You're all right, Jake. But for God's sake, no more nights like this."

"On the boat or in bed?"

"You know what I mean. I value my life. I have a child. Go on. I can see your son trying to peek in. I hate breaking up marriages."

"Maybe mine needs breaking. So long, sweetheart."

Mutt could barely see into the dim cabin. What was going on? Was his father holding the big dame?

The haul from O'Hara's schooner made rich men out of the partners. They would now be able to buy a new cutting plant, own their own boats, and make deals with the biggest suppliers.

The new booze was contracted for and sold as fast as Goldsturm could mix it. The thirty-three thousand, six hundred quarts of unadulterated liquor translated into *one hundred and thirty-five thousand* bootleg quarts, labeled, corked, stamped, and crated. As an added insult, they decided to *undersell* Schonkeit by a dollar, charging nine dollars a bottle.

Gross profits from the shipload came to a little over one million dollars.

The money was a problem. They soon had fifteen bank accounts under a variety of names. Sal kept his share separate, a great deal of it stored in sealed tin cans buried in his father's tomato garden. Mutt and Jake shared some accounts, owned some independently. Others were opened in Sarah's name, in Hilda's, and under the names of Sarah's aged parents, the Klebanows.

The empire was expanding, a power that defied the lazy law, murderous rivals, and the bluenoses who feared legal alcohol.

Chapter 36

"Every time Brunstein looks at you, he looks like he's going to faint," Dr. Abe Heilig said. He glanced across the crowded beflowered tables at the Buffalo Manor. Mortimer Chain had married Hilda. The wedding feast had begun.

Eva smiled, shifted her weight. She was five months pregnant. The loose blue chiffon gown camouflaged her abdomen. She had come to the wedding without Halstead. No explanations were given. Seated with her family at the table near the dais, she tried to make herself heard over Willy Klugman's Brownsville Society Six. They were playing minor-key melodies from the old country. A drunken Heshy Otzenberger was trying to do the *kazotzky* and kept falling on his ass.

"Ike always looks as if he's going to faint," Eva said. "Poor man. I'm glad he's married."

Abe sighed. Brownsville was getting on. It was 1923. A good year loomed. *Brunstein married?* Progress of sorts. Brokenhearted by Eva (who wasn't?), he had married a radical firebrand, Yetta Maltz.

"I like the way the crowd is divided up," Abe said. "What a mixture. Only with the Otzenbergers and Chains could you find such a mob. One-fourth are carrying guns, one-fourth copies of *Das Kapital*, and the rest are respectable, hardworking people who don't know from such *chuchmas*."

"Abe, you're being a snob," his wife said. "Isn't he, Dr. Abelman?"

"He's telling the truth," Abelman said. "For a hoo-hah wedding, there are lots of *gonovim* around."

The union of bootlegging and politics, long honored in the city and the nation, had been personified an hour earlier in the marriage of Mortimer J. Chain and Hilda Otzenberger.

That they were two young people in love, none doubted, least of all the Heiligs. As distant relatives of the groom, they knew the misery of his early life, the dreadful poverty of his parents' early years. And now *triumph!* Wealth, power, a career—and the ripe daughter of Brownsville's political boss.

"Take a look, Sam," Abe Heilig said. "A whole table of

Hibernians. Old Dullahan himself, O'Toole, Mulqueen, Roark. All drunk."

"Not so drunk, Abe." Abelman winked. "They hold it. It's a game with them. I was in Polachek's office in back. Jake's got a bar set up. His best booze. Those Irishmen are drinking it like it's seltzer, and look at them. Not a bleary eye. They live for it."

Eva shook her blond curls. "Dr. Abelman, you and my brother are a pair. Racial stereotypes! All Irishmen drink, all blacks are dumb, all Jews smart—"

"I never said that," Dr. Abelman said. "I just meant that some of Benny's friends are here because they like Jake's whiskey. It's their reason for living. It keeps them going. Dullahan's got to be eighty. I can remember the crook handing out cigars from the back of a Cadillac on election day. The bum once voted my father's name four times. Ten years after my old man died."

Sol Heilig rubbed thumb and forefinger together, said, "Benny knows where the power is. Someday it'll catch up with him. Maybe it'll even catch up with the Chains."

"Don't hold your breath till it happens," Abe said.

Sol's wife, Rose, a thin woman who affected a pince-nez and was studying for a Ph.D. in education, kicked her husband under the table.

"Ouch." Sol said. "Rose doesn't like me to make cracks about our cousin."

"She's right, Sol," Eva said. "Bootlegging is the government's fault. If they repealed Prohibition, the hoodlums would wither and die. People wouldn't get murdered, or die from poison liquor. Am I right, Dr. Abelman?"

"Like always, Eva."

"Anyway, the Dullahans and the rest of those bosses are through," Sol said. "They'll go the way of the dinosaur."

"Don't bet on it," Abe said. "While you and your kid investigators are interviewing witnesses, Dullahan will be a hundred and three years old and still running Brooklyn."

"Not true," Eva said. "I'm with Sol. We'll change the system."

"To what?" asked Abe. "To what *you* want? Or what Brunstein wants? Everyone's happy, kiddo. Jobs, food, booze, the stock market, Babe Ruth. This is *America Gonif*, Evitchka. I'm glad papa forced sour milk on us, so our bodies can handle it all."

Matla Heilig, the matriarch, blinked her eyes and dragged on a Sweet Caporal. She was sixty and worked seventy hours a week in her stationery store. She wore a black bombazine dress, two heavy necklaces of antique gold, and had her white hair done up in a pile of buns. The mention of her late husband's name awakened her.

"What? What about sour milk?"

Her three children roared. Memories of the house on Haven Place! The pitchers of sour milk, the old man's ledgers with his equations! Socialism must triumph! The square root of wealth divided by the square of man-hours, extrapolated as x to show productivity, and plotted on a graph to show profits . . .

Ike Brunstein's mind could not digest it. How explain the Chains? Were they part of the fabric of American life, like the flamboyant Jewish gangs of Odessa from whence his own parents had come? (Ike always felt a bit superior about his Ukrainian origins, amid the Litvaks and Galitzianers of Brownsville.)

No matter. The Chains were a force, part of the scheme of things. If not labor *shtarking* (how well Brunstein knew the value of a strong arm or a lead pipe), then bootlegging and God knows what else. He could say this for Jake and his son: The dynasty had begun with a noble heart, and was merely supplying a service now. Maybe there were worse things in the world. What he could not answer in his own mind was whether the Chains impeded or accelerated the triumph of the proletariat. *Neither,* he decided. When the workers' paradise dawned, people like Jake and Mutt would be crushed.

Other matters muddied Brunstein's mind. His own failures. He was in Glauberman's clutches. Hiring gangsters to win him contracts. Forced to sell out, compromise, pay off. A fine model to the Third International! He was glad Glauberman was not present to lord it over him. Something mysterious hovered about the Jewish Teddy Roosevelt's breakup with Jake Chain; it had come suddenly and angrily. Glauberman was now Melvin Schonkeit's man in Brooklyn. A man to be feared.

If I had Jake's courage, Brunstein thought bitterly, *I could tell the comrades—the party functionaries and theorists—what really makes America go, what the people want, what they respond to.* Not red flags and *Das Kapital.* Otzenberger, Chain, Dullahan—they understood Alexander Hamilton's great beast.

Ike watched Mort Chain, plug-hatted, in white tie and tails, getting a faceful of wedding cake. Morty returned the favor, ramming a chunk into Hilda's mouth. Flash powder popped smokily. The bride sputtered, hammered at him with soft fists. Mounds of white satin, her breasts shook in mock anger. Morty embraced her. Cake-to-cake, they kissed feverishly. He all but ran his hands over her rear end. She was lush and lavish, a woman suggesting harems. Her head would never be shaved and she would wear no *sheytl*. Hilda and Mortimer, Ike Brunstein realized gloomily, would inherit the earth. And maybe they deserved it.

And Jake Chain would get his share. Brunstein saw him— rugged, handsome, wearing his white tie and tails and shiny black topper like a society swell on his way to J. P. Morgan's.

Eva, too, was staring at Jake as he rose to toast the bridal couple. Ruddy-faced, his body straight and powerful, his gestures those of an athlete, he spoke haltingly but with authority. He knew he possessed power. Unlettered, crude, probably a killer, surely a mobster, violator of too many laws to even think about, he commanded respect.

"To my new daughter, beautiful Hilda, and my only son, my dear boy Mortimer, long life, happiness, lots of children, *l'chayim!*" Jake Chain said.

Applause. Cheers. Morty kissed Hilda again. He would not let go.

"By the way, what are we drinking?" Sol Heilig asked his brother.

"Real Concord," the doctor replied. "The rabbi gave it his blessing. It isn't cut with wood alcohol or prune juice. Jake saved a dozen cases for the wedding."

Rabbi Piltz, seated at a table with Shimen Klebanow and other elders of the synagogue, was rising to leave. He had done his work. The holy words had been uttered beneath the canopy. The glass broken. Vows made. Rings exchanged. No need to observe these goings-on. Austere, craggy-faced, a scholar of repute, he told his *shammes* to get his hat and coat.

Jake approached. "Rabbi, we haven't paid for your services."

"Mr. Otzenberger took care."

"Please, could I talk to you? In Polachek's office, if you don't mind? It'll be an honor."

Jake and Rabbi Piltz walked past the dancers, the wedding table, the remains of the giant cake ("shoulda had a bottle of gin on top," Dr. Abelman commented), and into a storage room, where the bar had been set up. A bartender dispensed the best Chain line—uncut scotch, rye, brandy, and gin. Clear-eyed, Dullahan and O'Toole and Roark were drinking purposefully and slowly, savoring the velvety goodness.

Each man bowed as the rabbi walked past. "Your Honor," Dullahan said, "a grand service."

"So it was. Grand." Roark winked at O'Toole.

And O'Toole: "An honor to all of us, rabbi."

Rabbi Piltz nodded but did not smile. Better these Irishers than the Lithuanian anti-Semites who had stoned synagogues and beaten Jews in the old country. In a sense he was grateful to men like Otzenberger, and possibly even Chain. They were Jews, they were Americans, and they understood the system. They spoke the tongue of the angry *goy*. God in his infinite wisdom sometimes put bad people on earth to perform (unwittingly perhaps) certain good deeds.

A Roman Catholic who drank whiskey with you and attended the wedding of your children (Rabbi Piltz reflected as he followed Jake into Polachek's office) was less likely to burn down your synagogue or beat your children.

In the office, Jake sat behind Polachek's desk. *Wrong*, he thought. It is the rabbi who should be there. Not me. He is the teacher, I am the pupil.

"A nice ceremony, rabbi," Jake said. "I am sorry I am not a better Jew. I never learned Hebrew. You know how I lived."

"And how do you live now?"

"I make a living."

"Mr. Chain, I hear stories. I know about you. The Jewish community is a good one. In Brownsville we are building. Doctors, men of law, rabbis. Our children go to college. Merchants open stores. Life is rewarding. People worship God. Our faith must be part of our life. You are part of this, Mr. Chain?"

"Of the life, yes. I have no secrets. That I have no faith, I apologize. All right, I'm not a good Jew. I don't go to shul. I am not proud of it. I never learned anything. I had no parents. I learned to use these instead of my brains." Jake held up his blocklike fists.

"Joshua was a soldier. So was David. But they were good Jews."

"Maybe it was easier to be good then."

"The Jewish soldiers of our forefathers fought and died for their faith and for the Almighty. For whom do you fight, Mr. Chain?"

"For myself. I admit it."

The rabbi shook his head. "Solomon tells us to avoid those who 'lie in wait for blood,' to 'walk not with them,' and 'make not haste to shed blood.'"

"I'm sorry, rabbi. I told you I was a stupid man."

"Not so stupid that you do not understand, Mr. Chain. Solomon also says, 'So are the ways of every one that is greedy for gain, which taketh away the life of the owners thereof.'"

He spoke in Hebrew. Jake was lost; he admitted it. Rabbi Piltz translated what he had said into Yiddish.

"You make me ashamed of myself," Jake said. "I know what I am and what I'm doing. I don't hurt innocent people. The people I hurt are worse than I am. Thieves and murderers. Chain only hits back. He doesn't hit first."

"But you are part of this world of violence and blood and death, Mr. Chain. Maybe it is wrong for me to lecture you. But I performed your son's marriage and his bar mitzvah and I feel I must say this."

"I can't change, rabbi. What I do is part of the world."

"No, Mr. Chain. I knew about people getting their heads broken, thrown down stairs, factories burned, goods destroyed. Now perhaps you are doing worse things."

Jake did not smile. He reminded Rabbi Piltz how he had gotten into the labor movement. Had not the rabbi heard of the day he had rescued old Jews at Amsterdam Creek?

"Today what you do is different. But I am not a policeman. I am not the law of America." He got up. "Mr. Chain, I am pained to say this. You bring shame to the Jewish community."

"I'm sorry I'm not a doctor or a lawyer. But each of us makes his way the way he can. Mine was with my fists."

"Wrong. Especially for a Jew."

Jake escorted Piltz to the door, then stopped him. "I know Mr. Otzenberger paid for your services. But I want to help also. For the shul, rabbi."

He took a huge roll from his pocket, peeled off a thousand dollars in hundreds, and handed them to Rabbi Piltz. "Nobody has to know. For the school. The building fund. And there'll be more."

The rabbi shook his head. "Mr. Chain, tell me something."

"Yes?"

"This money you give me. It came maybe from the wine you stole from the government with my stationery? Forged papers, forged copies of my signature? Men who should know better, pretending to be rabbis? To you, it is clever. To me, it is a desecration. I have said nothing because I know you will bribe your way out of it, the way you bribed the *goyim* in the warehouse."

"I made sure you got your wine also."

"I do not want your thousand dollars. I will pray that you can be a different man. If not you, your son maybe or his children. Goodbye, Mr. Chain."

"With all respect, rabbi, I hope you are right. I'll give the money to the Brownsville Hebrew Orphan Asylum in the name of your synagogue. All right?"

"The deed is a good one. The man who does it might be a good one someday. Good night, Mr. Chain."

Rabbi Piltz left, and Jake made his way through the dancers to the Heilig table and asked Eva to dance. Just then, one of Polachek's waiters approached.

"Mr. Chain, excuse it, but there's a cop to see you."

"Cop?"

"Give him his ten bucks and tell him to beat it," Dr. Abelman said.

"A sergeant," the waiter said.

Everyone laughed.

"Make it twenty-five," Dr. Heilig said. "Jake, I hear prices have gone up. Some nerve, those chumps, coming around for a *shmear* during Morty's wedding!"

Jake excused himself. "Next dance is mine, Eva," he said. "And maybe a few after that." He followed the waiter.

A whiff of Eva's perfume lingered in his nostrils. The maddening desire for her would never leave him. It was useless, he realized. People regarded him as a clod, a killer with no feelings. He would go back to Tommy, his lady captain. Maybe he could love her and be good to her. And forget Eva.

Sergeant Pope was standing outside the checkroom. He looked pale and sweaty.

"Jake, bad news. Your place is burning."

"The plant?"

"Went up like a bonfire. A four-alarmer. The firemen been trying for fifteen minutes, but all that alcohol burns like gasoline. You can hear the bottles popping four blocks away."

Morty followed Jake into the lobby. Hilda, waltzing with her father, was oblivious to the crisis. She blew a kiss to her top-hatted husband.

"What happened, pop?" Morty asked.

"Fire. Our place."

"Bad?"

Sergeant Pope nodded sadly. Oh, the income he would lose! The drop in earnings that would affect the morale of his men! The Chains had been good providers. "Total loss, the chief thinks. They can't control it. Jake, you guys must have bought up half the alky in New York."

"Let's go," Jake said. He took Pope by the elbow and started for the glass double doors, past the banks of carnations and geraniums, the displays of daisies, dahlias, and roses. No expense had been spared to make the Chain-Otzenberger nuptials the event of the Brownsville social season.

"I'm going with you," Morty said. "It's my place too."

"It's also your wedding, Mutteh. You got to stay."

"Like hell I do."

Father and son got their coats from the checkroom girl and followed the sergeant. Sal Ferrante, in a tuxedo two sizes too large, slithered after them. He had a sixth sense. He knew something bad had happened.

Hilda, gliding around the waxed floor with her father, holding the hem of her satin gown high, saw Morty leaving. She hobbled on spiked heels toward the doors. "Morty! What are you doing? What kind of way is this to treat your wife?"

"Be back soon, honey. Wait for me."

Hilda collapsed into her father's arms bawling. Benny understood them better than she did. You married a Chain, you asked for it. Who knew what those bandits were up to at eleven o'clock at night, in their cutaways, boiled white shirts, and stovepipe hats, running off with a sergeant?

"Papa, papa," Hilda wailed. "Make him come back."

"He'll come, he'll come, *ketzeleh*. It's his wedding night, right?"

Angry and vengeful, the three partners of F & C Cereal and Pacific Breeze Hair Tonic looked on as roaring flames devoured the cutting factory.

The scene had its idiotic overtones: Jake and Mutt in black toppers, soup and fish, snowy starched shirts and white satin vests stained with cinders. Sal slunk around, his eyes unwilling to focus on the gusting flames and choking smoke that spewed from the blackened warehouse.

A half-dozen engines pumped water on the long brick building. Kolodny's old place, expanded, fortified, the garage added. Loading platforms, office, mixing room, storage rooms, all were engulfed in roaring cones of fire. The stench was overwhelming. The roof was a sea of boiling black smoke.

"It's Goldsturm's flavoring," Jake said unemotionally, sniffing the air. "He was using too much fusel oil."

"Son of a bitch," Mutt said. He wiped tears from his smudged face. "You think Schonkeit did it, pop?"

"Who else?"

"We'll cut his balls off," Sal whispered.

"Shikey Frummer," Jake said. "He gets it first."

Revenge, however, was hardly the answer now. Times were changing. They were in the big time. Like a corporation. Only they were not insured. Who would insure an illegal business?

"On my wedding night, the bastards," Mutt said. "Wasn't anybody on duty?"

"I forget," Jake said. "The wedding and all. Sal, someone was working here?"

"I don't remember. Maybe Buster."

The firemen had brought the flames belching from the doors under a semblance of control. But the smoke was undiminished, bubbling dark clouds of alcohol-fed fumes, pouring out to the street, fouling the air. Behind the brick walls they could hear bottles popping like cherry bombs.

Three firemen were prying at the oven-hot steel door with crowbars. A hose kept dousing and cooling it so they could approach it. The water sizzled and formed clouds of steam. Finally the red-hot hinges gave way. Under showers of water, the rubber-coated firemen pulled the door apart.

Two bodies were lying athwart the entrance. They seemed to have died—suffocated or scorched to death—trying to claw their way to freedom. Although the faces were blackened and peeling, Mort, Jake, and Sal saw at once who they were. Buster Twine. Professor Goldsturm.

Firemen dragged the corpses into the street. Chunks of flesh peeled from Buster's mighty black arms. Goldsturm's chickenlike body appeared to have shriveled to half his size. Crazily, the pince-nez was still on his nose. Cracked, but in place.

"Burned to death?" Jake asked. He felt a surge of emotion. The two had been loyal workers. Good men. Buster preached in the Holy United Army of God church. Goldsturm was sending a son to CCNY.

Pope and an intern from Brownsville Jewish Hospital leaned over the bodies. "Oh, boy," the doctor said. "Somebody slit their throats first."

The sergeant and the intern flipped the bodies of the chemist and the black man on their backs. Their heads lolled, unhinged. From ear to ear, each man's neck had been slashed, one long deep cut, severing arteries, ending life in a rush of blood. The blood had congealed in the furnace heat of the fire. Their faces and throats seemed smeared with raspberry jam.

"Run them hoses through the front door," the fireman said. "Bust everything standing."

Great arching jets of water splashed on the tar roof, on the ember-hot brick flanks of the building. Five firemen in rubber coats, helmets, and boots went through the broken door. Axes smashed against walls, doors, partitions.

"Bastards," Mutt said. "Buster was a good guy. And there wasn't a better mixer than Goldsturm. Pop, we oughta get those guys. Tonight."

Jake knelt next to the corpses. *You played rough, you lost sometimes.* Schonkeit, of course. Probably Shikey. But there were no witnesses. The two who had seen the arsonists were dead.

There was a chunk of scorched material in Buster Twine's right hand. Jake touched it. *Fur.* The fur collar on Shikey's fancy coat? The coat he wore the night he tried to hijack the *Deepwater Angel?*

"At least the new place didn't burn," Jake said. He looked across the cobbled street to the building they had bought for storage. Jake did some quick calculating—maybe three hundred, four hundred thousand dollars' worth of booze in there. Enough to get them started again.

Mutt was crying. Jake put an arm around him. The kid was nineteen. The Boy Wonder of Bootleggers. But a boychick, a child. And on his wedding night. Schonkeit's present.

Sal was on his knees, vomiting noisily into the murky river flowing along the curb. He had taken a look at Buster's head, at Golsturm's slashed throat.

Jake thought: They had done a job. Killed the witnesses. A little torture, maybe. Maybe they had tried to tie them up and let them burn in the fire. Buster had probably fought back. A decent man. Jake would have to do something for his wife and his four kids. Goldsturm was widowed. They'd make sure his son finished college.

A fireman came out with a scorched case of Aberdeen Dew. "Here's one we saved." He laughed. "But there ain't much left in there. Jake, can you drink this without going blind?"

"Our top of the line," Jake said. "But look for some Glenderrie. It's the real stuff."

"We're ruined, pop, and you're kidding around?" Mutt sniffled.

"Not ruined, Mutteh. Stop with the tears. You're a Chain. You're not a dumb guinea like our partner. Look at him puking."

Sal was leaning against the red fender of a fire truck, heaving his cookies. Wedding cake, roast chicken, stuffing, the works. Polachek's kosher dinner was working its way up.

"What do we do, pop?" Mutt asked.

"What else? Go back to the wedding. I don't want your mother and Hilda to holler on us. Pope, you'll give us a lift?"

"Sure, Jake."

Jake turned to the fire chief. He was a popeyed man named Gallagher. Jake had kept him on payroll for over a year, contributed lavishly to firemen's charities, Christmas fund drives. They all knew Jake. A tough hebe who kept his promises.

"Chief Gallagher," Jake said. "Whatever's left inside and is fit to drink—"

His voice was smothered. There was a massive explosion. Flames roared through the roof. Goldsturm's vats, Jake figured. The big copper mixing kettles, detonating in the blast that drove them across the street, sent a dozen firemen flying out of the opened doors behind a sheet of flame.

"—whatever's left is for you and the cops."

"Pop!" Mutt shouted. "It's all we got left!"

"Eh," Sal gagged, wiping his bleached face. "Eh, I got a say in it."

"Calm down, kids," Jake said. "It's a present for your men, chief. For Pope and all of his boys. You fellas decide how you divvy it up. Chief, for yourself, make sure you take only Mount Vernon rye and Glenderrie."

They walked toward Pope's prowl car. Coated with cinders, their formal garb wet with spray, the partners were silent a moment. Pope held the door open for Jake. He knew class when he saw it.

"Pop," Mutt moaned. "There's over a hundred thousand bucks' worth of booze left in there."

Pope gunned the engine. They splashed through the flooded street. A crowd had gathered. People knew what went on behind the brick walls of the F & C Cereal company. The curbs ran not only with water but the bootleg alky. Two stumblebum drunks were on their knees, sniffing the runoff, licking at it.

"Nah, it's almost finished," Jake said. He nudged Sergeant Pope in the ribs. He winked at Mutt and Sal. No point in being gloomy. Not on his son's wedding night. There was always the extra warehouse, where they had put away a supply. And there was Tommy and her fleet, and other friends he had made. And most of all, his undiminished strength and courage and cunning.

"It's generous of you, Jake," the cop said. "The guys will appreciate it."

"Appreciate, *fongool*," muttered Sal. "Givin' away my share. Who said you could?"

"It's goodwill for the future, Salvatore," Jake said. He tipped his plug hat to Pope. "Ask the sergeant. His pals would have taken it anyway, right? Between you and the firemen and the snoopers, there'd be nothing left. Right, Pope?"

"Right, Jake."

"So let's go back to the party. I ain't danced with my daughter-in-law yet."

Jake Chain was planning ahead. Shikey and his friends could expect a few surprises. And Schonkeit the Paymaster would someday learn about Crazy Jake, a man who enjoyed a fight.

1960
Myron Malkin's Notebook

We're sitting on a screened porch of a luxurious log-cabin lodge, Mr. Mortimer J. Chain, fifty-six (a tough and stringy fifty-six), and me, boy reporter.

The porch is on the second story of the ritzy rustic bungalow. *Bungalow?* It's like Wotan's palace—bearskins, stone fireplaces, beamed ceilings, redwood furniture. M. J. Chain's retreat in the Adirondacks. The place where his son, Martin, hides him for most of the summer. There's a twenty-room mansion in Palm Beach, I'm told, where they stow Mortimer the rest of the year. To keep him away from nosy people like me.

Below us an intercamp baseball game is in progress. Camp Spruce Grove, once owned by the Chain family, battling the visitors, Camp Holy Spirit, a Catholic charity camp further south on Lake Champlain. Distantly I see the cool blue of the mountain lake.

"What's the score?" Mortimer J. Chain asks me.

"Your kids are ahead. Bottom of the fifth. Spruce Grove five, Visitors zip."

He laughs. "I figured we'd have an undefeated season. The rich people from Great Neck pay six hundred bucks a summer to send us their *pishers* from Horace Mann and Poly Prep. But I always give a few free athletic scholarhips to tough kids from Brooklyn. That pitcher we got? Blum? He's an all-city ballplayer from Tilden. His old man drives a truck. The catcher, the big kid? Brooklyn Tech. Joe Tuttle. I knew his family."

Mortimer Chain taps my knee. "Malkin, in kids' baseball, all you need is a pitcher and a catcher. You could put dummies in the other positions and win. Another winning season for Camp Spruce Grove. Four years in a row we'll be the Adirondack League champions."

He tells me he has no financial interest in the boys' camp anymore. Sold it after the war to an old NYU football star, Ed DiBiasi, who gives speeches on Americanism and sportsmanship every Sunday. But the Chain family kept the lodge overlooking the ball field, and a private beach on the lake.

"I never knew you were in the camp business," I say. "Uncle Doc never mentioned it."

"*Camp?* Who cared about a *camp?* I needed a place to drop booze from Canada. The camp was for fun."

I'm stupid. Lake Champlain. *Canada.* A gorgeous way to smuggle whiskey into the country. Mortimer J. Chain sits, lean, dark, hard-faced, long-nosed, in his wicker chair, hands clenched around his knees. He has black hair, parted in the middle, sun-browned skin. Kafka as criminal. He's smiling at my stupidity.

"I got a lot of laughs out of this place. Would you believe, Malkin, the counselors carried guns at night? That's right. When the campers were asleep, after the bugler played taps, we'd let the boats from Canada tie in at the swimming dock. You saw our waterfront? A nice cover."

I nod. A beautiful, immaculate waterfront on the pine-bordered lake—floats, docks, a huge canoe rack. And a hard dirt road.

"The trucks would be waiting. The speedboats would come

in after ten o'clock. The counselors got five bucks each for helping with the loading. Before dawn the trucks were on their way to Brooklyn. That was after I took over from my father. He had good ideas, but I think I was smarter. I think I ran in almost as much hooch here at Camp Spruce Grove as he did on Long Island. And never a word from the Feds or the state troopers. To them, it was a boys' camp. Counselors from Cornell and Syracuse."

"How'd you get the idea?"

He shrugs. There is a lot of lean power in his shoulders and his arms. He's wearing a white LaCoste shirt, white duck pants. No fat on him. No signs of wear. Except for the huge dark glasses. At the edges of the smoked lenses, white scar tissue on his cheeks.

"My older kid, Martin, went to this camp. You talk to Martin?"

Yes, I tell him. No cooperation from the emperor of the Chain dynasty. But a pleasant meeting. (A lie on my part; Martin sent me packing.)

"I took one look at that lake, that coastline, the way the lake runs to Canada, and I said, Pop, we need a *camp*. DiBiasi was the perfect front man. A great running back for NYU. He beat Fordham single-handed twice. Anyway, that's how it started. Around 1928. Anyone score?"

"No. Your pitcher, Blum, struck out the side. Those kids from Holy Spirit can't touch him."

Morty Chain chuckles and shakes his head. "I hate to do it to them. Father Gurney is a good friend. But what the hell, winning is all that counts. I wish I could see a ball game again. We had a box on first base at Ebbets Field for years. I knew Max Carey and Dazzy Vance personally. Martin and his wife, they know from horses, not the Brooklyn Dodgers."

John Tuttle, the rawboned catcher for Camp Spruce Grove, belts a home run far into a stand of pine trees. Two men on base. The home team leads eight–nothing. Kids are screaming. Holy Spirit is taking its lumps.

Mortimer Chain hears the cheering and gets up. I tell him what's happened. His "scholarship" campers are annihilating the opposition. The former "Mutt" Chain sits on the log rail around the porch. In his excitement he whips off the smoked glasses.

He's blind. Photostats of the New York papers' reporting the attack on him are in my briefcase. God, he's been blind damn near ten years.

His eyes are two filmy gray orbs, disfigured, the eyes of a cold statue. But the face is alert, intelligent, hard.

"Your catcher is touching home plate," I say.

"Atta boy!" M. J. Chain shouts. "Give 'em good! I get a kick out of a winning ball team. I could have been a ballplayer myself but I started working when I was eighteen."

He's reminiscing. The taxi ride to Montreal with one of the Ferrantes. The details elude me. They're not in the literature on bootlegging, but there are old newspaper accounts about his start. One thing about the Chains: They laid low, gave no interviews, had a wondrous talent for evading the law. No strong-arm stuff unless necessary.

The Tuttle kid is big, rangy, and blond. The other ballplayers, rich Jewish kids from Fieldston and other fancy schools, swarm around him, lift him to their shoulders.

The name rings a bell with me. Wasn't there a Captain Tuttle? I'll have to check my files. Something about a rum-running boat skippered by a *woman,* a friend of the Chains'?

Mortimer puts on the dark glasses. "You saw my eyes, Malkin? What's left of them?"

"I'm sorry. I remember when it happened. My uncle Doc took you to a specialist on Park Avenue."

"Your uncle was right. We lived on Ocean Parkway then, but Abelman was a doctor I trusted. It was no use. They did a job on me." His voice is flat and calm. He's accepted his curse. The way he has accepted Martin's domination of the empire. "What good am I blind? I never read much even when I had eyes, so who could bother with Braille? Thank God for the radio. And I'm alive, right?"

"Right, Mr. Chain."

It's pleasant on the screened porch. Giant oaks and soaring pines cast late afternoon shadows. Cries rise from the ball field. I hear the sound of ball cracking on bat. A wonderfully nostalgic noise. Yet I can't help marveling at the lunacy of it. Mortimer Chain bought a boys' camp in 1928 so he could run booze from Canada!

"Didn't the parents complain?" I ask the sightless man. "All those rich people sending their kids to a camp that was a front for smuggling?"

Most of them didn't know. Those snooty Central Park West *Yiddlich!* German Jews. They drank my booze. They liked the camp. They were honored to shake hands with the immortal Ed DiBiasi."

His wife is dead. Three years now. Hilda Otzenberger Chain, dead at fifty-five of a heart attack. She'd been a diabetic, overweight. I gather she was a tough one, with more than a little of her father's cunning and gall. It must have destroyed her when Morty was blinded. Schonkeit's mob had waited a long time to get him. (I've heard a story that a *woman* blinded him.) But in the end the Chains won. They survived. They made it to the top.

He asks me again: *What do I want?* A book? A magazine article? Never, he says. Plenty of stuff in the newspapers about the Chains. Why don't I talk to Lillian Halstead, who tried to prosecute them? Or talk to Eva Heilig, her mother? I tell him I have spoken to Eva. She's old. She wants no part of the story. It's history. Jake is dead. Morty is blind. Martin is a young tycoon, a prince of money and power, running his corporations from a tower on Park Avenue.

"Martin married one of our campers. My daughter-in-law Dorothy. A real German Jewish aristocrat." Pride in his high voice.

"DeeDee? The former Dorothy Grau?"

"Her parents were so ritzy they looked down on Sephardim. Old money from Nashville, Malkin. Can you imagine a German Jew from Nashville and my cocker of a Marty marries her? Her parents hollered, until they figured out I was richer than the whole Grau family together. By then we were in legitimate distilling, proprietary drugs, war surplus. You know something, Malkin? I once controlled every pound of calcium carbonate in the country. I never saw a barrel of it. I never stored it anywhere. But I owned it. I could sell it for my own price."

"Calcium carbonate?"

"That's right. And four or five other basic chemicals. Prussic acid. Sodium oxalate. I had five congressmen on my payroll and two federal judges. A director of the War Surplus Commission took orders from me. I set the *vontz* up for life."

"And he set you up in chemicals?"

"Up to my ass. I showed Marty a few things. We cleared over twenty million on chemicals. I figured it was time to get out. Real estate looked better." His pointed ears seem to twitch. I see Kafka again. Kafka as hoodlum, with his sharp nose, low-growing inky hair, blade of a nose, taut mouth. Cocking an ear, he listens to my ballpoint pen scratching on a copybook.

"Taking notes, kid?"

"If you don't mind."

"Do me a favor and don't write about us. Martin's got a few little problems with the SEC. Who needs this?" He cranes his corded neck and muscular throat, listens to the cheers of the campers. Uncle Ed DiBiasi is leading a sportsmanlike cheer for the losing visitors.

Two, four, six, eight,
Who do we appreciate?
Holy Spirit, Holy Spirit, Holy Spirit!

"We win big?" he asks.

"Eleven—nothing. That big kid, the catcher, hit a double with the bases loaded."

"Joey. Great kid. Don't tell anyone, Malkin, but he's eighteen. The age limit in this league is sixteen."

"But that's cheating."

"So? A few years? All the camps do it. If Father Gurney had a good eighteen-year-old pitcher, he'd use him. Who checks birth certificates?"

I watch a downcast Holy Spirit team pile into a yellow bus. They have natty maroon uniforms. I comment on them. Morty Chain tells me he bought them for the charity camp. He remembers when he was poor—as he puts it, "on the balls of my ass."

I explain my notion. A history of the Chain empire from Crazy Jake, the *shtarker,* to Martin, the young captain of industry, breeder of prize-winning horses.

"No. Sorry you had to shlep all the way to Lake Champlain to get a turndown. What do you want from me anyway? I'm out of the rackets for years. So I was a bootlegger. So what? Yeah, I made a fortune. I made even more after 1934, I made even more during the war, and my son is still making it. You know why?"

"No, Mr. Chain."

"We don't quit. We don't take crap from anyone. Most of all, we're never afraid. *Never.* It's in the Chain blood from Crazy Jake down."

He wants to know about Cousin Eva. Is she happy in Long Beach? Does she need anything? She was always loyal to the Chains, even when she hated what they did. It goes back a long way, he says. Back to sweatshop days in Brownsville. . . . Did she talk about her brothers? Who could guess the Heiligs were related to the no-good Chains! Mortimer J. Chain chuckles. Dr. Abe, a surgeon. Sol, who ran for Congress twice, a special prosecutor, an aide to a governor.

A woman appears in the high-beamed living room. She's about thirty, very pale, and with soft yellow hair and a bovine face.

"My nurse," Morty says. "Miss Hanratty."

Some nurse. Hilda is dead, a victim of overeating and a bad heart. Of course he needs a companion. No eyes. But everything else is in working order. Young Martin keeps him out of harm's way, away from boardrooms, exclusive clubs, the corporate offices, comforted by a nurse-mistress.

"Go talk to my other kids," Morty says. "I'm as proud of them as I am of Martin. They didn't want the business. Okay by me. Davey's on a kibbutz in Israel. He makes jokes about our money, but I financed their hydroelectric project."

"And Iris? Your daughter?"

"A famous Hollywood writer. You saw her last movie?"

I confess that I haven't. A crappy love story. It's apparent to me that his two youngest children have opted to break away from the empire. Martin carries on.

A file of younger campers, in swim trunks, slapping at each other with towels and herded by a weedy counselor wearing a T-shirt that reads DARTMOUTH A.A., parades under the porch.

Hi, Uncle Morty!

We won, Uncle Morty!

The nurse helps Mortimer Chain to his feet. "Hi, kids," he shouts back. The elder statesman of Camp Spruce Grove. Unbelievable. He now spends summers here like an old sage. Later Miss Hanratty tells me that he is widely loved in the area, endowing local hospitals and fire departments.

I shake hands with Mr. Chain. A grip like a clamp. Crazy Jake's strength. But he looks like his mother. I've seen photos of the late Sarah Chain—dark, pretty, with birdlike features. On his face the sharpness suggests a fox.

"Forget the whole thing, Myron," he says warmly. "So I was a bootlegger. The Chains provided a service. People needed us. Today, look what we do. Nothing but good. Maybe my two ringers beat Camp Holy Spirit this afternoon, but I buy Father Gurney uniforms, bats, balls. I painted his mess hall. The Chains go first-class and don't forget it. Give my regards to Mrs. Abelman. I never had a doctor as good as your uncle."

Miss Hanratty escorts me down the wooden stairs and into a clearing in a grove of pines, where a taxicab waits to take me to the Trailways Bus Company depot.

"He was glad to see you," she says. "He talks a lot about the old days in Brooklyn. People think he's so hard and tough, but he isn't."

There's more than professional care going on here, I speculate. I imagine Mort remains something of a sexual athlete.

High-rumped and thick-thighed, Miss Hanratty is more than your everyday R.N.

"Thank you, Miss Hanratty. If he changes his mind about discussing the family, will you let me know?"

"He won't. Goodbye, Mr. Malkin."

The cab drives along a dirt road, past the neat green-and-white bungalows, the empty ball field, a mess hall glittering white in the afternoon sun, past a vista of Lake Champlain, where, years ago, the Chains smuggled oceans of booze.

PART III

1931

Chapter 37

Mort parked his white Pierce-Arrow, locked the doors, and squinted through thin January sunlight and banks of gray-black snow at the breadline.

It was twice as long as last week. A muddy river of shabbily dressed men. Ragged caps, lumpy coats, beat-up shoes. They hunched in the chill morning air, blew on callused hands, waited for the sluggish file to move into the Salvation Army soup kitchen that had been set up in an abandoned laundry.

Suckers, Morty thought. Bowl of soup, a margarine sandwich. That would be their day. When things went bad, you went out and scratched and screamed, made noises, made the guys in charge uncomfortable. And you trusted no one.

He and Jake had agreed years ago. Not a penny of their bootleg profits was to go into the stock market. Jake didn't understand it. He didn't believe in it. Mort, a shrewd twenty-two at the time, turned down brokers and salesmen with a smile and a handshake. He sold them his best booze even as he rejected their offers to make him even richer than he was. "Screw General Motors," Mort would tell them. "I don't trust any of them. I trust what I can see."

The breadline snaked past the empty lot where the old F & C warehouse had once stood. All that remained were piles of scorched bricks. Schonkeit's revenge. They had salvaged nothing. But Mutt's foresight in buying the auxiliary building had saved them. It was now three times as large; an adjacent "tax-payer" joined to it via sliding doors. It was no longer F & C Cereals. The phony grain company, along with its hair-tonic affiliate, had been liquidated. A discreet shingle outside the metal door read:

BROOKLYN GENERAL SUPPLY COMPANY

Mort paused and looked at the shuffling file of hungry men. He shook his head. They were blocking the garage. Deliveries would be a problem. Worse, they would be pestered all day by men wanting jobs. It was no secret what went on inside the blind walls of Brooklyn General Supply. Even as Mort crossed the street, dapper in black cashmere coat and dove-gray hat, he could see Baggie Ferrante talking with three men. Italian words dropped into the conversation now and then. They were *goombahs*, begging for a day's labor. Italians, like Jews, detested handouts, the "relief." They wanted work.

"We ain't got nothin'," Baggie was saying. "*Niente, amici.* Full up. Every guy in Brownsville wants we should hire him. It's full up." His one-inch brow furrowed in commiseration.

Two trucks were turning the corner. The morning shipment from Freeport, from Jake's operation. On oiled hinges the steel doors opened. A whiff from Harris Weltfish's vats wafted out to the cold street. A few unemployed men sniffed the illegal air. The cops grinned. Steady income. Sergeant Pope had retired with sixty grand in his poke before Christmas of 1930. The Chains had made him a rich man.

Morty followed the trucks into the garage and nodded at Luigi and Stroonz as they locked the doors. The new cutting plant was twice the size of the place that Shikey Frummer had burned to the ground. The office, enclosed in frosted glass, was separate from the mixing and bottling area and the storage bins. It was a handsome office, well lit, spacious, furnished with heavy oak pieces. There was a wide oak desk for Mort and a smaller one for Sal. On the stuccoed rose walls were reproductions of "The End of the Trail" and "The Last Post." There were also framed photographs of Mort Chain with Mayor James J. Walker, Francis Fagan Dullahan, Benjamin Otzenberger, and other noted political figures. There were autographed photos of ballplayers, boxers, and entertainers.

Mort was well liked in all areas—politics, sports, show business. Handsome, dark, soft-spoken, a man of his word, a supplier of decent whiskey, always on time, he was ever willing to give a hard-pressed speak owner (now that the Great Depression was beginning to hurt) an extra week or two to pay. M. J. Chain had developed a reputation as the "Gentleman Bootlegger." Often he was called upon to supply beverages for society weddings on Long Island or in Westchester. He got to know polo players, men who played court tennis, traveled first class to Europe, bred horses, sailed yachts, and screwed each other's wives. They all liked the sharp-featured young Jew. He had excellent manners, never raised his voice, and, for all his polite demeanor, carried with him a whiff of sulfur, of a murky underworld of mutilation and murder.

Theresa Ferrante helped Mort off with his cashmere coat, took the dove-gray Borsalino with the slanted brim, lingered long enough at his desk for him to finger her breasts. She shuddered. "Stop. Not in the office, Mort."

"Why do you think there's frosted glass on the partitions? To keep your brothers from peeking in."

"They suspect us, Mort."

"They're too dumb."

She was forty. He was twenty-seven. Unmarried, enslaved for years by her slightly daft mother, she had accepted a spinster's life. Yet she was a darkly attractive woman, slender, long-legged, with small assertive breasts and enough of a rise and swell in hip and buttocks to make men stare.

Mort had been making love to her in a room in the St. George Hotel for five years. She was a compliant and passionate mistress. Miraculously, her grim brothers had not the faintest idea that she was bedding down twice a week with their boss. Mort Chain would always have a remarkable talent of telling little, hiding things, giving nothing away. In that respect he was his father's superior. Blunt and iron-headed, the old man had used fists and courage to make his way. Mortimer was a different breed of cat—cautious, a planner, a man with a capacity to see ahead, to organize, to outguess.

"Anything important from yesterday?" Mort asked. He sat behind his desk. In the office, he rarely took off his pinstriped blue jacket. Beneath it, he wore a sedate matching vest, a gold watch chain. His white collars were starched by a Chinese laundryman, and he favored dark blue or maroon ties. He rarely smoked or drank and he worked out four times a week at the Brooklyn Jewish Center, playing furious handball.

"Your father called. They're giving the new boat a trial run."

Theresa lingered. She looked twenty-five, not forty. Morty was intrigued with her. The age difference excited him. He could not explain why. And she was slender, mysterious. She always smelled of musty perfumes and wore a gold cross on her dusky throat.

"The big one? The seventy-five-footer?"

"Who knows? He said the new boat."

Mort nodded. Jake spent most of his time at the waterfront

warehouse and dock. Five years ago they had bought Rayburn's Boatyard and converted it into a vast efficient operation for the delivery of seaborne booze. Radio operators worked with their fleet. Local cops helped guard it. Tommy Tuttle no longer went to sea but supervised a dozen boats under the Chain flag.

"Theresa," Mort said softly. "Five o'clock today. The St. George."

"No. I told you, my brothers are suspicious."

"Tell them it's school. You're taking bookkeeping at Brooklyn College, right?"

"I've been taking that course four years, Morty. They know I'm lying."

"Five o'clock." She placed his mail on his desk. He ran a strong hand under her skirt, stroked her naked thigh.

"Stop." She sighed. "Stop. I can't say no to you."

When she left, he stared a bit guiltily (or as guiltily as a Chain could) at the photographs on his desk. There was a new one of his wife, Hilda. She was getting fat. But a beautiful soft woman, with chubby red lips, a snub nose, staring dark brown eyes. She wore her hair bobbed and spit-curled. Diamond earrings dangled from pink ears. A five-thousand-dollar brooch decorated her proud bosom. Yet she did not look joyful. The red brick mansion on Ocean Parkway, surrounded by clipped privet hedges and a brick wall, the summer home on Lake Champlain, the vacations in Florida—none of these erased her moroseness.

The truth was, Mort reflected, Hilda was a spoiled, lazy, conceited woman. She did not golf. She rarely read. She ate too much. She refused to do any charity work. He wondered how she got through a day. There were three in help at the Chain house to look after the three children, to cook, clean, sew, wash, and drive.

But Mort was not a man to moon over a somewhat soured marriage. Theresa, thirteen years his senior, a moaning bed partner, supplied what Hilda no longer could. Dutifully, he made love to his wife, lavished gifts on her, and tried to keep her reasonably happy. Benny looked after the Chain interests, and Mort knew a happy daughter would keep Benny on his side. The Irishmen who ran Brooklyn politics—the judges and commissioners, Jimmy Walker's buddies—listened to Benny and did him favors. The next year, 1932, would be a Democratic year, Benny said. Hoover was a dead duck. The micks would want every Jewish vote they could get in Brooklyn. Thus Mort Chain and his hoodlum father remained favored men among the bootlegging fraternity. These high political connections, Mort understood, had often saved them from Schonkeit's wrath.

He checked his mail—bank statements, orders from customers, a complaint about the quality of the booze. One of the chief Prohibition agents in New York had "an interesting proposition" for Mr. Chain. Why not set the snooper up in a speakeasy of his own? He would take the heat off the Chain organization, and operate as a *customer* instead of a prosecutor. At a reduced price for booze, of course. He would expect to be supplied at half the going rate. It was not a bad idea, Mort thought, not bad at all. Corrupt them at their own request and keep them on the string.

Bored, Morty yawned. He looked forward to his five-o'clock rendezvous with Theresa. Forty years old and she often came nine and ten times in an hour. By contrast, Hilda had become lazy in bed, sluggish. She gave lavish bridge parties, entertained a growing crowd of "girls"—wealthy young matrons, wives of physicians and lawyers and "allrightniks."

Gloomy thoughts about Hilda were sweetened by the photographs of his children on his desk. In gold frames they smiled at him. The oldest boy, Martin, was seven. He was a Klebanow. Like his grandmother Sarah Chain and her deceased father, he was sharp-featured and slender, with intense deep brown eyes. There was a feverish energy in him. But the younger children were throwbacks to Jake, their paternal grandfather. They were large-boned and fair-skinned, with clear blue eyes and thatches of yellow hair. The younger boy, David, was five. He grinned good-naturedly at Papa Morty and the world. His chunky legs were astride a kiddy car. The baby, Iris, a year old, was fat and fair and resembled Davey.

Mort spoiled them all. He tried to make up for Hilda's finicky attitude, her disdain for the grubbier aspects of motherhood. She was affectionate but standoffish. Since the Chains were rich and help was cheap, there had always been a nurse or a maid to change diapers, wipe up after accidents, clean pools of vomit. On the maid's day off, Mort changed diapers. Often he fed and burped Iris. Hilda sniffed when he grew angry at her inadequacy.

"I can't help it," Hilda cried. "I'm sensitive. I'm afraid of *drek*. But I love them. I do."

"You're lazy."

"I want to go back to work. Why can't I work at the place? You could use me. I helped you get it started."

"Stay home and be a mother and a housewife like everyone else."

And, he wanted to add, don't come to the warehouse, because you'll get in the way of my happy hours with Theresa.

Chapter 38

"Sixty miles an hour," Tommy Tuttle said breathlessly to Jake, "and not even breathing hard."

"And with a thousand cases." He laughed.

The newest boat of the Chain fleet ripped through the Atlantic, cutting a creamy wake, roiling the choppy waters. They were well inside the three-mile limit, after a wave-lashed night unloading from a boat from the St. Pierre and Miquelon islands. As usual Jake paid in cash. He was a "priority" customer along Rum Row.

The new boat was seventy-five feet long, streamlined, powered by three Liberty engines. They had taken her out for laughs and she had run rings around a coast-guard cutter. Jake had two more like it on order. Soon the fleet would number twelve boats, all built with ample deck and hold areas for stacking burlocks and cases.

Long Island boatbuilders vied for the Chain business. The Depression had hit them hard. But rumrunners were flourishing. The demand was for even bigger and faster boats. Tommy had designed the new boat herself. A craft, she said, unfit for anything but carrying booze on short runs.

Anton was at the wheel. He was the best of Tommy's skippers, cool, bright, as skillful at navigating the channels around the coastal villages as he was at evading a Coastie or pulling alongside a rum boat. Now he was guiding the craft into the safe harbor of what was still called Rayburn's Boatyard, but which was, in fact, the Chain maritime branch.

Jake had long ago conquered an early disposition to seasickness. Tommy had taught him to be a sailor, helpful on deck, knowledgeable about lines, rigging, engines. She was in her late thirties now, a statuesque woman with the same open gaze, the broad pretty face, the thick chestnut hair. The woman who had attracted Jake nine years ago in Sheepshead Bay.

The new boat nudged the dock gently. A light snow was falling, dusting the pilings, the pier, the cream-colored stucco house Jake had had built over the foundation of Rayburn's place. It was a thick-walled Tudor mansion with fifteen rooms, a double basement, and living and working quarters. In the third-floor attic, Jake had installed a shortwave radio transmitter, with which he communicated with his own boats and, via code, with the rumrunners. A retired navy petty officer, a gray-haired man named French, ran the radio and kept track of seagoing trade.

Alongside the house was a three-car garage for storage purposes. It was rarely used. Jake had deliveries down to a tight schedule. As soon as a boat arrived, the work gangs, recruited from local police, firemen, and other civil servants, got to work stacking the whiskey into waiting trucks. No time was lost in trucking the cargo to Brooklyn.

Years past, Jake had taken care of every cop along the route. New policemen were broken in by old-timers. The last truck was the payoff vehicle. One of Jake's loaders was always there with a leather briefcase to *shmear* the bagman.

In the swirl of January snow, Jake and Tommy paused a moment to watch the crates being manhandled from the boat to the trucks. Jake had set up a portable conveyor—oiled rollers bolted between steel rods—to speed the process. Tommy shivered, squeezed his hand, and walked to the Tudor house. The only part of the business that interested her was the work at sea. They might just as well have been carrying sacks of turnips.

A northern wind whipped across the inland canals, piling snow against the high fencing around the Chain piers, around the edges of the great house. Jake could see a light in the attic. French, the radio operator, was on duty. He was widowed and lonely and never left his transmitter when a boat was out. A reliable man.

Patsy Camilli, a Ferrante relative, came by for the payoff money. Jake took him into the ground-floor office. From a Mosler safe he took out a black leather briefcase. It contained a thousand dollars in cash, more than enough to fix every cop along the way, and extra money for emergencies.

"The usual road," Jake said. "I'll call the plant and tell them you're on your way."

Patsy nodded. He seemed brighter than the other Ferrantes. He had attended Boys High School for two years.

"Give me an accounting," Jake said. "Pay the drivers and the guards the usual, and you get fifty, Patsy."

"Thanks, boss."

Jake took a .45 from his belt and gave it to the young man. "Only in an emergency, Patsy. And never on a cop. Them you *buy*."

Jake waited until the trucks were almost loaded. Grizzled old Rayburn, on the Chain payroll as a caretaker, opened the fence. He batted his arms, dusted snow from his beard.

Snow bit at Jake's face. He was pleased with the night's work. The haul was worth more than a million dollars after cutting, mixing, bottling, and sales. And they handled shipments like this two, three times a week. The Depression might not have existed as far as the Chains were concerned. As poor as people were, they were always thirsty. The rich especially seemed thirstier than ever. They joked about booze, sought it out, compared brands, and looked upon their bootleggers as romantic heroes. The government's agents were the real criminals.

Jake returned to the house, after checking the trucks, wondering if perhaps he owed Sarah more than the two-story yellow brick house on Haven Place. It was by no means a bad house. Jake had bought it from Rimkoff three years ago and they now used both floors. But by comparison to his home in Freeport, it was a dump. Sarah never came to Freeport. The rule was firm.

It bothered him. He had a second wife, a second home. By all that made sense, he should divorce Sarah, marry Tommy, and cut his ties to Haven Place. But it was unheard of. One did not desert a crippled woman who had stood by you when you were a bum driving a wagon. A woman who had worked long hours, lived in a basement, raised a son. So the existing situation seemed to him the easiest: two wives, two lives, two homes . . . and two sons.

He dusted the snow from his boots on the veranda, removed them, and set them in the rack outside the door. Everything about the Freeport house was solid and durable. Oak, plaster, and cement had gone into it. "Strong enough to stop bullets," Jake told the contractor and winked. "Maybe strong enough to stop a cannon."

The builder understood; he appreciated his client.

In a bright yellow kitchen, Tommy, who had changed to an aqua velvet robe, was making an omelet with American cheese and green peppers. She was a talented "fry cook," able to turn out superb dishes using only a skillet and the stovetop. From years of going to sea, she told Jake. She could make do with a bare minimum of utensils and ingredients.

He kissed her cheek and hugged her. One hand stroked the firm buttocks beneath the robe.

"As your mother would have said, Jake, eat first." She pushed him away.

"I never knew my mother. Maybe I don't want to remember her or my old man."

"I bet he's sorry for what he did to you."

Jake wondered. He had no idea what had happened to Yussel Chain, the ne'er-do-well farmer from Lithuania. Maybe they could have been a happy father and son. Worked together. The way he and Morty got along. Two against the world. They had handled Sal Ferrante, made peace with Schonkeit, kept the cops and the judges happy, and now had an empire worth fifteen million dollars and growing.

They sat at the kitchen table, enjoying the tangy omelet, sipping hot English tea, munching on buttered muffins. It had been bitter cold at sea. Returning, they had been covered with icy spray.

Tommy laughed. She wanted to take the speedboat out and race the *Ile de France* or the *Normandie* just to see how fast she could push it.

"Kid stuff," Jake said. "Don't take it out unless it's for money."

"Oh, my smart Jewish lover."

"It's not the Jew in me, kid, it's the businessman. Never forget it, Tommy: There's more *goyim* bootlegging than there are Jews. Dwyer, Duffy, Higgins, Madden, all that crowd."

"They're Irish. They aren't *my* people."

"Close enough. I tell you something else I'm proud of. Morty and me haven't killed anyone in eight years."

Tommy shuddered. She did not want to hear about killing anymore. A tolerant woman, betrayed by a drunken husband, she had looked for security, someone to give her strength. The tall booted woman in the sou'wester, her hair tied in a blue kerchief, suggested a seagoing Amazon, a distaff pirate. But the image was a fake. As Jake had learned in their eight-year liaison, she was unsure of herself and lonely until they began their life together.

"Don't tell me any more," Tommy said. She stroked his hand.

"I won't. I was never that kind of guy when I was a kid. I didn't start fights. It started with the union business. But I only hit back when I was hit."

Jake wondered: *Am I going soft?* Forty-six, and ashamed of his violent past. He thought of Moishe Nigger drowning in chicken blood. Of what he had done to Futka Frummer and his mob in the woods. And others he had *klopped,* leaned on. Most of them deserved it. But he had little stomach for violence now. He loved Tommy Tuttle. Someday he would figure out a way to get rid of Sarah. Guilt, a strange dependence, an old loyalty born in poverty, sent him back to the house on Haven Place.

A seven-year-old boy, rubbing his eyes, wearing a green wool bathrobe, walked into the kitchen. He was barefoot.

"Ma, I couldn't sleep. The trucks woke me up."

Outside they could hear the last of the convoy gunning its engine, leaving.

"Come here, precious," Tommy said.

The boy was towheaded. He had Jake's Slavic face and the rangy long-limbed body of both parents. His name was Mackenzie Tuttle, after his grandfather. To Jake and Tommy he was Little Mac. Jake was his father. Jake sometimes referred to him as "the Half Moon Kid"—the product of their affair in the Sheepshead Bay hotel. After Tommy became pregnant, Jake was more careful. They adored the blond handsome youngster but they wanted no more children. Her daughter, Lisa, was in a boarding school in Connecticut.

A story had been concocted for Little Mac's benefit. His father had died in Florida. The big man who gave him presents and came to his birthday parties and took him fishing was "Uncle Jake." Relationships were left vague. Little Mac was a happy child. He attended public school in Freeport, and was fast becoming a water rat, wise in the ways of the channels, streams, and beaches in the area, a powerful swimmer, a cunning fisherman. Summers, he went crabbing and clam-digging. His skin turned brown-gold.

"Uncle Jake, you gonna get me a two-wheeler?"

"Sure, Little Mac. Wait till the weather's better. The snow is no good to ride in."

Little Mac stretched. *My God,* Jake thought. *My son.* My little *shagitz.* He had lied to Morty about the boy, said he was Tommy's, son of a vanished boyfriend. Morty saw through Jake's clumsy subterfuges. He knew at once that the blond kid was his half brother. *The same age as his son Martin!* Mac, meet Martin, your nephew. How do you like being an uncle at age seven, Mac Chain? Mort wanted to ask. No matter. He did not hold the *mamzer* against Jake. He knew that his parents had no life in bed. Let the old man have his *shiksa* mistress, with the wide hips and the legs like a two-miler.

Jake asked the boy to come to him. He lifted him to his lap and stroked the yellow hair. A small version of Jacob Chain. Broad face, blunt nose, fair skin, big feet, strong hands. More of him in the kid than in Morty, or Morty's eldest, Martin. It was funny the way things worked out. He wondered what kind of life Little Mac would have. Jake resolved he would take care of him the same way he would take care of his three grandchildren.

"Kiss Uncle Jake."

"Nope. That's for sissies."

A true *goy*, Jake thought. No caressing and fussing for him.

"Go ahead, Little Mac," Tommy said. "Kiss Uncle Jake."

"He ain't my father."

"He's almost a father," she said. "And he loves you."

"Maybe the two-wheeler could come tomorrow or the next day," Jake said. "So there's snow, so what? When the streets are clean, you can ride. Right, mama?"

"If he's careful."

The boy bounced off Jake's lap and clapped his hands. "Oh, boy! Uncle Jake, I want an Ivar-Johnson! With a Troxell saddle!"

"You'll come with me to the store, Little Mac. Only one thing I got to ask you. You'll give the bike a name?"

"Sure. All the kids do. Racing Queen. Speedy."

"This bike I want you to call Half Moon."

Covering her mouth, Tommy laughed. Her crude lover was a romantic at heart.

"Half Moon? That's a dopey name."

"A favor for Uncle Jake."

"What's a half moon?"

"Something beautiful," Jake said. "Someday you'll know."

Tommy took her son's hand. She reminded him to kiss Uncle Jake, then led him to his upstairs bedroom. It was twice as large as Mutt's old room on Haven Place. But Jake felt no guilt. Mort lived lavishly now. He owed his first son nothing; he owed his wife nothing.

French, the radio operator, knocked on the kitchen door and walked in. "All under control, Jake. Patsy called in from Queens. They'll be at the plant in fifteen minutes. The cops took a little over five hundred this time."

"A bargain," Jake said. "I guess it's the Depression. They'll settle for less."

He yawned, stretched, looked forward to losing himself in

Tommy's warm body, unwinding, restoring his manhood. In winter, on wet days, the old wounds ached and gnawed at him. His jaw became taut. The white scar seemed to expand, as if the jaw had been glued together ineptly. He rubbed it. He wished he were through with violence, shooting, killing, all the rotten stuff he had endured and inflicted. Maybe he was. They were secure, vastly wealthy, respected. Morty deserved a great deal of the credit. Smooth, secretive, a step ahead of everyone, he had built the business. With guile and planning, he had kept the most vicious killers, the Italians and the Irish gangs, away from Chain trucks and boats and warehouses.

We are good combination, Jake decided. A father who could not be killed. The man with iron fists. And a son who used his brains and his nerve and let nobody get the jump on him.

Chapter 39

Eva stopped at the apple vendor's crate alongside the newsstand in front of Bryant Park. She bought six apples for thirty cents, more than she could possibly eat. A gesture, she thought as she paid the vendor, a pointless one.

"Thanks, lady," the unshaven man said. His gray coat was held together at the waist with a rope, and there were streaks of dirt on his neck.

"It's shameful," Eva said. In her mid-forties, she had not lost her urge to lecture, improve the unfortunate, spread understanding. "The way you're forced to do this. Can't you find work?"

"You kidding, lady? I'm a machinist. They closed down my place in Joisey. The boss took the gas pipe. Every cent he made on the business was in the stock market. Hunnert and forty of us out of work."

"It's a crime."

"Don't tell me. *Apples, hey, apples, fi' cents!*"

Eva shook her head in anger. Nineteen twenty-nine had come. The prophets of Marxism were proven right. The built-in contradictions. The inevitable collapse. Nobody was in charge. Nobody cared. What next for the country? She cursed herself for not having answers. She saw nothing hopeful in the future. President Hoover and his dull-headed advisers (several of whom were friends of her father-in-law) kept assuring the people that prosperity was just around the corner.

The truth was, the labor movement depressed her. Between the Communists, the gangsters, and the stricken bosses—many of them ruined—the movement was in disarray. Her heart still went out to the underpaid, exploited, weary people at the machines. How they remained so honorable and hardworking, how they raised children who struggled to go to CCNY, to improve their lives, continued to astonish and delight her. Garrison agreed. It was what had fascinated him about Jews. The life force in these ghetto people amazed him. And there were good, honest, overworked union officials—bedeviled, underpaid, hounded by criminals.

Perhaps, Eva thought ruefully, I was never anything more than a symbol of Garrison's admiration for working Jews. Less of a wife, hardly a mistress, a late-in-life mother, but always a symbol. Not the soundest basis for a good marriage.

Sol, in a brown tweed topcoat and a vested green suit (as befitted a newly appointed state official), was motioning her toward a bench. He had picked one in the sunlight. A few bums in various states of alcoholic decomposition surrounded the bench.

A chunky man with frizzy brown hair and a wry smile on his gentle face, Sol Heilig fooled people. Beneath the paunchy exterior there was a core of steel. A scholarship boy at NYU Law School, he possessed a keen mind. A "reform" Republican, a freak in Brooklyn, he had decided to devote his life to public service. Let the Leo Glaubermans make the big bucks. Let others struggle to worm their way into fancy New York firms. Sol liked politics. He enjoyed being an underdog. Old friends in Brownsville had never understood why he had become a Republican. The party of the rich, the bosses, the oppressors, the party of Harding, Coolidge, and Hoover?

Sol would wink and laugh his noiseless laugh. "Democrats and Socialists we got by the barrel in Brooklyn," he would say. "Some Jews should be Republicans. Besides, how else do I get to be county chairman, get on committees, get my name in the paper?"

Benny Otzenberger, Democrat to the marrow of his mammoth bones, scorned Solomon Heilig for this defection. A Socialist he could understand, even a Communist. Like that shmuck Brunstein, who had to beg Melvin Schonkeit to save his *tuchas*. But Eva Heilig's brother?

Sol kissed Eva's cheek and hugged her. A ragged bum tipped his frazzled fedora and rolled off the bench to make room for her.

"Oh, I'm sorry," Eva said. "We could move . . ."

" 'S all right, lady."

The man walked away, his feet slithering, his legs dancing to a diseased rhythm in his muddled head.

"Jake leg," Sol said. "From bad alcohol."

"Named for our esteemed cousin?"

"Hardly. Although it might be appropriate. They get it from drinking alcohol distilled from Jamaica ginger."

"How do you know so much about whiskey, my abstemious brother?"

"We prosecutors get to know these things. Eva, I'm becoming an authority on loan sharks, goons, bootleggers, *shtarkers,* and other assorted villains. It's fascinating. Things Marx and Engels never dreamed about."

"Coming from Brownsville must be an asset."

"And how. I'm regarded as the office tough guy."

"You, Solly? You're a cream puff, a charlotte russe."

"Don't be so sure, Evitchka. I was a great punchball player in my day. I could hit two sewers. I didn't like to fight, and mama said I had weak ankles, but I was a champ at Chinese handball."

Sol's wife and the kids were fine—healthy, vigorous, showing all of the Heilig enterprise and cheerfulness, plunging into schoolwork and neighborhood activities. His older boy had won six merit badges with the Boy Scouts and was on his way to becoming a Life Scout.

"A whiff of fascism just passed my nose, Sol."

"Eva, for God's sake. That stale radicalism of yours."

"Not so stale. Look at Europe. Mussolini, Hitler. Every country has some kind of reactionary demagogue. And here, Coughlin and all kinds of right-wingers surfacing. Your Republicans are better?"

"We are. So are the Boy Scouts. And so are the Democrats. I don't sell the system short."

He opened a *New York Times* he had under his arm. Governor Franklin Roosevelt was cracking down on the rackets. He'd asked his special commissioner, Mr. Seabury, for minutes of the hearings on rackets. A district attorney was about to be removed for inefficiency. The man had complained to Seabury that "racketeers are virtually immune from punishment." The D.A., an elderly man, had protested that he was helpless against gangsters who infested the business structure of the city.

"Don't tell *me*," Eva said. "My old enemies in the needle trades."

"Not just there. Trucking, building trades, food. From both ends. And not only in the unions. The bosses also. In fact, these rats *are* the bosses today. They were sneaked in, they did their dirty work, and they took over."

Eva was solemn: memories of Jake as her first enlistee.

Sol explained that the belief was the Franklin D. Roosevelt would make a run for the presidency. He had to come in clean in his own state, a crusader who had knocked the political-underworld alliance out. Mayor Walker was sure to get hit. Most of the crooked politicians were in Roosevelt's own party and most of them were in New York City. But the governor was shrewd and tough. The wheelchair and the aristocratic manner hid a man of vision and strength. He'd picked the Republican Seabury, thorough and intelligent, to investigate rackets. The D.A.'s were scared stiff of the new prober, a circumstance that delighted Sol.

"I'm a small fish in a big pond," Sol said happily. "But, boy, will I enjoy nailing some of these rats."

"Sheriff Sol Heilig to the rescue," she giggled. "Two-gun Heilig."

"Luckily I got a famous surgeon for a brother. I get shot up, the way our cousin Jake used to, Abe can stitch me up. Anyway, these bums don't go after people like me. They kill their own kind. Every time Jake got shot at, it was some other gangster. Police, D.A.'s they leave alone."

With new respect, Eva studied his round, good-natured face and remembered him as a boy, with his eyes riveted on a textbook, furiously making notes on a yellow pad, making *extracts* of his notes, getting the pith and substance of his courses. His mind could summon up a word or a phrase— *separation of powers*—and a whole paragraph would flow from his pen, accurate, precise, worthy of a teacher's "A" and a "well written." He'd graduated Phi Beta Kappa from CCNY and at the top of his class from law school. Withal, he wore his intelligence lightly. People liked Sol Heilig. Even the hoodlums he interrogated found they enjoyed talking to this rumpled pudgy man from Brownsville.

Sol told Eva that Schonkeit had emerged as the First Lord of Crime. It had begun in the mid-twenties, when union leaders had come to him for help. The Paymaster, a respected figure, soon became a mediator between employers and workingmen. For these services (and for fixing police and judges) he was paid vast sums, by *both* sides. Fees as high as half a million dollars to settle a strike were not unusual.

"Ike?" Eva asked.

"He's been to him. Ike's in trouble up to his neck. He paid Schonkeit to back the Communists and now he's sorry. Ike is not an immoral man, Eva. He's got a good heart. But when he saw that the Red flag wasn't going anywhere, he hired guns. Schonkeit couldn't care less about politics. Money interests him. What's soured Ike is that, at the last furriers' strike, Schonkeit worked for the bosses. His goons, Frummer and Wesselberg, were beating up strikers."

"He is a fascist," Eva said. Rage splotched her cheeks.

A panhandler shuffled by. Eva gave him an apple and a quarter. He tipped his hat.

Sol shook his head sorrowfully. A city, a nation of beggars. "Melvin Schonkeit is no fascist. He's a moneyman. They all come to him—real estateniks, gamblers, garment-industry people, bookmakers." Sol frowned. "It's crazy. He's a middle-class boy from a good family. He has the golden touch. Know how he got it?"

"With guns."

"Wrong. By betting on sure things. Schonkeit is a gambler. But only when the odds are big and he knows he has to win. He started past-posting when he was a teen-ager."

"Past—?"

"Getting the results of races from a tipster at the track. Then placing a bet *after* he knew the winner. They've never found out how he did it. He's fixed fights, ball games. He's run fifty stock swindles. He pulled out of the market with ten million dollars from his bucket shops a week before the crash. He's a wizard."

"A disgrace."

Eva sighed and crossed her silk-clad legs. Two bums stared and staggered away. Bryant Park. Memories of gracious old New York. And the library, full of books that could save the world. But the world hardly seemed ready for salvation. The foundations were shaking. Nothing was simple anymore. Old answers were immaterial. Melvin Schonkeit seemed to run half of New York.

"He's taken over several firms in the garment industry. You see, they depend on trucks. He controls trucking through his gangsters. All he has to do is pull a drivers' strike, and goodbye to the fall line. Frummer and Wesselberg took over factories in the garment district. They forced them to close, then moved in. Ike was in a rage. The father and son who owned one factory committed suicide. Now the workers are forced to accept a wage cut and have to kick back a buck and a half a week to Schonkeit."

"This is outrageous." *Wesselberg*—who tried to rape her.

"Eva, being married to Garry and making hoo-hoo speeches on birth control and interviewing Mr. Gandhi aren't the same as getting your hands dirty in the labor movement. Anyway, we're going to nail Frummer and Wesselberg. Ike is getting ready to cooperate with us. He knows enough to send Schonkeit to jail. And maybe send Shikey and Herman to the electric chair."

"Good God. Will Ike be protected?"

"Of course."

Eva blinked in the morning sunlight. A rush of pity for Ike overwhelmed her. Poor adoring Ike with his mooning eyes and ratty moustache. Chained now to Yetta, a firebrand writer for the *New Masses* and *The Daily Worker*. He was in double jeopardy. The Communists would disown and denounce Ike for revealing that the party had hired gangsters. The hoodlums would seek vengeance.

"Ike wants to do this?"

"I convinced him on the basis of old Brownsville loyalties. He asked me a funny thing. He said, 'Sol, I've known you for a long time, and I know you know how I admire your sister Eva.' I said I knew. So he asked me did I think you would approve of his talking and would I ask you."

"You never did."

"So what? I told him you approved. You do, don't you? The labor movement is changing. There are good men gaining power. Real leaders, men concerned with hours, wages, conditions, education, medical help. People like Potofsky, Dubinsky, Hillman. They want the movement cleaned up. Ike can help us get rid of parasites like Frummer."

"You used my name without my permission?"

Sol tucked the *Times* into his bulging briefcase. "The magic words. Eva Heilig Halstead. He's in love with you, the shnook. I mentioned your name and he looked like a bloodhound with a bad stomach. Sorry, but that's how a special investigator gets things done."

"I don't admire you for duping Ike that way."

"He'll recover."

Sol got up. They munched on apples and walked toward the subway station at Sixth Avenue. "Listen, Eva. There's racketeering in twenty-six industries in New York. The poor guys on the machines, at the cutting tables, with paintbrushes in their hands, they're getting a screwing. It's got to stop. The bosses get away with it because Schonkeit is the connection between gangsters and politicians. Roosevelt can't allow that if he wants to be president. We're helping workingmen get rid of murderers like Frummer. Ike's doing the right thing."

"But his safety—"

"Forget it, will you, Eva?"

He asked her about Garrison, about her seven-year-old daughter, Lillian. Eva seemed tentative in her responses. Garrison was traveling a great deal. He was in California at the moment, reporting on Upton Sinclair's EPIC movement, doing articles for the *Nation*. Lillian (whom Sol could not have seen more than a dozen times) was attending the Little Red Schoolhouse. She was a bright, moody child, already competing with her mother by writing compositions.

"Got a picture of her?"

"I'm afraid not, Sol."

He said nothing. Eva seemed cold and detached. Something compassionate and warm was lacking in her. All her heart, her emotion, had gone into political movements, social reform. The marriage had to be a bit sour. He invited her to a Passover seder the following week. Garrison always enjoyed those he had attended. He remained a sincere philo-Semite. Little Lillian, Sol recalled, had loved the singing and the rituals. Matla would be there. And Abe and his family.

"I'm not much on religion, Sol. I never have been."

"So what? We're your family, kiddo. The Heiligs of Haven Place. It's a short ride to Brooklyn."

She shook her head. Sunlight gleamed on the edges of the tight curls. How beautiful, Sol thought. Brainy, courageous. Maybe she'd been loved too much. All that worship—from the laboring girls, from Jake, from Ike, from her rich husband.

"I'm going out of town next week. Speech in Chicago for the birth-control movement."

"As usual."

They stopped at the subway entrance. Sol looked at an afternoon headline. The king of Spain was out on his royal *tuchas*. They were declaring a republic. Progress, progress. "You and Garry are away a lot. Who looks after Lillian?"

"Sol, we're rich. There's always three in help. Lillian likes it better that way. At least that's what she tells mommy."

When he had descended the IND steps, leaving her to hail a cab—she was off to a meeting at the League for Industrial Democracy—he worried about her.

Curious, Sol thought. She had not asked about Jake and Mort Chain, their underworld relatives. But what was there to ask? Sol had seen the file on the Chains. It was three inches thick. Under the protection of Otzenberger and Dullahan, they had prospered beyond anyone's imagination. Phone taps, stolen records, interrogation of disaffected hoodlums who had worked for the "Brooklyn General Supply Company" indicated that the Chain bootleg empire was now worth in excess of twenty-five million dollars.

Hoo boy, thought Sol as he put his nickel in the slot, will they be in for a surprise when Prohibition ends! They could retire on their millions, of course. But it was no secret that Roosevelt would run. And Roosevelt would win. And that would be the end of the Volstead Act and fortunes made from illegal booze. He shed no tears for the Chains.

A week later Ike Brunstein began to talk. Once his lips opened, the flood of words drowned Sol's office. Two stenographers were needed to get the story down. Ike had made his mind up. For once in his life he would do something courageous.

For a week Brunstein sat in a guarded hotel room, while Solomon Heilig got him to spill his guts.

Shikey Frummer, under Schonkeit's patronage, had formed a "truckmen's association," Ike revealed. Delivery prices for the garment industry were hiked. Frummer got the biggest share. His *shtarkers* divided another huge chunk, leaving the drivers with less than they had earned before.

For Shikey, the sleek brother of Futka, this was a mere start. Along with Herman Wesselberg, the elephantine Meal Ticket, he founded "partnerships" with terrified manufacturers. They began to ship unfinished garments out of New York for completion in nonunion shops. Honest union officials of the Amalgamated Clothing Workers and the International Garment Workers Union battled Shikey and the Meal Ticket. These honorable men demanded better wages, hours, and conditions for their people, and no more out-of-city work. In defiance, Shikey increased the scab work. A protesting shop steward had his throat slit.

Cutters, most of them aged Jews who were wary of a fight with the gangsters (Ike told Sol), tried to keep tabs on garments being trucked out of New York for "finishing." It was useless. Garments kept leaving New York to be completed by low-salaried workers in New Jersey and Connecticut.

Acting on Brunstein's information, an attempt to strike back at the gangsters was launched. Sol demanded—and, surprisingly, got—the cooperation of the police commissioner. FDR's cleanup was having good effects. For once Schonkeit's power was frustrated. Public officials feared the Seabury Commission. They saw that Roosevelt meant business and that his appointees could not be bought off. A corrupt local run by stooges of Frummer and Wesselberg was raided and the books impounded. It took no mathematical genius to see that the crooked officials, besides indulging in illegal trucking, had misappropriated eight-five thousand dollars of the unemployment relief fund.

The morning after the raid, younger union officials, elected by the workers, took over the local. For the moment Frummer and Wesselberg were stopped. They were forbidden to use their trucks to remove unfinished garments. The new leaders had won a temporary victory on the basis of Ike's testimony.

Ike, under police guard twenty-four hours a day, whether in the investigator's office or at home at Flatbush with pouting Yetta, or in the secret hotel room, sang and sang and sang. Frummer and Wesselberg raged. *That punk! That dirty yellowbelly of a Red!*

Three weeks after Ike began to talk, subpoenas were served on Saul "Shikey" Frummer and Herman "Meal Ticket" Wesselberg, together with six union officials they had illegally installed.

The investigator who took the depositions from the new union officials, and the outraged cutters, furriers, pressers, and deliverymen in the needle trades, was Solomon Heilig. The source of his information—the former Socialist, former Communist, full-time idealist Isaac Brunstein—was now locked into a suite of rooms in the Whitman Manor Apartments in Dyker Heights, Brooklyn. Ike had a view of the Narrows, of April's greening trees, and two city detectives who lived with him around the clock while he sang.

"A bird in a gilded cage," Ike said humorlessly to his guardians.

Out on bail and in defiance of a court order, Frummer and Wesselberg came to see Schonkeit at the Polo Pony Club.

"We got to lean on that canary Brunstein," the Saratoga Avenue Meal Ticket said. "We shut his mouth, we'll be okay."

Shikey sipped celery tonic. "Heilig got no case without him."

Schonkeit counseled caution—at the right time he would fix a judge. His subordinates looked glum and frightened. It wasn't working too good anymore. The industry wasn't totally in their control now that Roosevelt demanded action. The crippled *shmuck!* He wanted to be president. Seabury would not stop until they caught a few big fish.

"I don't like being a pike or a carp, Mr. Schonkeit," Wesselberg said. "I been loyal to you. Me and Shikey. What are you gonna do to help us?"

"When you need help, you'll get it," the Paymaster said. He sipped milk.

"We got to kill Brunstein," Shikey whispered. "Before he kills us."

"No," the Paymaster said. "You do, you'll be sorry."

"How about that *putz* Heilig?" the Meal Ticket asked. "He started this."

"Herman, you never kill a cop or a D.A. or an investigator. You kill them only if they take and then double-cross you."

They didn't like it. Shikey and his friends feared indictment. Heilig was getting tons of information from old union stiffs—the frightened, pasty-faced shlemiels who worked in the lofts. Brunstein, opening his yap, had given them courage. There were rumors that the Wallowitz case was being reopened. Shikey shuddered.

"I'll get Leo Glauberman to defend you," Schonkeit said airily. Through the smoky haze, he signaled a waiter by tapping a diamond solitaire against his glass. He wanted another tumbler of Borden's Grade-A. It was good for his ulcer.

Shikey's manicured hands brushed his sleek ebony hair. "Mr. Schonkeit, from what I hear, Glauberman is next. Heilig ain't stopping with us. If Leo sings, what happens? Maybe even you—"

"Please, Shikey," Schonkeit said. "You're giving me a

headache. Glauberman will plead lawyer-client privilege. When the time comes, we'll handle Brunstein, Heilig, all of them. Anyone can be bought."

Chapter 40

Morty, refreshed after his hour in the St. George Hotel with Theresa, came home to a late supper. He always approached the three-story sprawling house slowly, his eyes alert for movement, signals. If there was trouble, Hilda and the servants knew, the tall exterior lamp, standing amid the privet and hawthorn, was to be lit. Real trouble: the carriage lamps on either side of the massive front door were to be turned on.

It was dusk. Only the interior lights, behind pale yellow chiffon curtains, illuminated the high mullioned windows. He always stopped the Pierce-Arrow outside the garage, unlocked the door, and turned on the interior light before parking it. His father had taught him caution. Ever since the ambush at Haven Place, when Jake had absorbed twelve bullets, the old man had told him: *Go slow, look, see what's behind you.*

The garage was immaculate. Harry Twine, Buster's twenty-two-year-old son, employed as a man-of-all-work at the Chain household, opened the door from the garage to the house. "Evening, Mr. Mortimer." He was carbon black, tall and broad-shouldered. Harry served as a butler, in white coat and white gloves. He could also rake, seed, and fertilize the lawns and backyard garden. And he was a whiz at repairs, from carpentry to wiring. His younger brother, Eddie, was a foreman at the Chain warehouse. Jake and Mort were supporting six members of Buster's family. If a man got his throat sliced for them and was burned to a charred chunk by monsters like Frummer, then his family deserved a break.

"Hi, Harry. Quiet?"

"Your-in-laws here."

Mort groaned to himself. *Benny and Jessie.* All he needed.

After a strained dinner—Hilda full of complaints, Mort engaged in reading box scores to Martin—they retired to the living room. Hilda and her mother sat near the arched stone window and listened to Rudy Vallee on the floor-model Zenith. Soupy music issued from its mahogany hull. Mort and his father-in-law settled into easy chairs apart from the women.

"You better look ahead, son," Benny said. He lit a dark brown Partagas. "When Roosevelt lets everyone buy real booze, the game is over. You and Jake should start looking for another business. But not unions. That'll be even worse. They'll be honest."

Mort nodded. He'd see to it that the next generation of Chains would never suffer the stain of the preceding two. No strong-arm stuff, no guns, no bribing of cops. It would all be legit. And far more lucrative than selling rotten whiskey.

"I think I'll give Hilda a birthday present," Mort said suddenly.

Hilda's ears perked. She looked across the parlor. *"Huh? What kind of present? That sunburst brooch I wanted from Tiffany's?"*

"No, sweetie. A trip to England. Maybe France also."

"Ooooh, Morty!"

"You'll need a whole new wardrobe, *tsatske*. The works. The Chains go first-class."

She heaved herself out of the overstuffed chair, jiggled toward her husband, embraced him, and covered him with soggy kisses. He liked it. She was beautiful, *zaftig*, smartly dressed, aromatic of expensive perfumes. He patted her bountiful butt. "When, *when*, Morty?"

"Soon, Hilda. Just you and me. No kids."

"Like another honeymoon! You hear that, ma? Papa?"

"My son-in-law, God bless him."

Mort, locking lips with his wife, thought ahead. *Contacts, contacts.* And lots of cash. Money would have to be transferred to English and French banks. A lot more money than they would need for a deluxe trip. And for more important reasons.

"Mussolini can't be all bad," Garrison Halstead said, "if he's cracking down on the Vatican."

Eva looked quickly around the candlelit dining-room table. The only Catholics present, she quickly decided, were Mr. and Mrs. O'Loughlin, Long Island aristocrats. They did not take umbrage—at least they did not manifest any—at Garry's blunt remark.

"Remarkable fellow," Garrison went on, as a white-gloved

butler passed the cheese tray. "Mussolini suspended Catholic Action, closed down the Knights of Columbus, and has thrown guards around the Vatican."

"Well, he did start as a Socialist," Eva said uneasily.

"What makes you think that's admirable?" asked Mrs. O'Loughlin.

Eva, radiant in a bare-shouldered pearl-gray gown, a necklace of lapis lazuli and onyx on her alabaster neck, said nothing. *Let goyim fight goyim,* Dr. Abelman used to say.

"Oh, they'll work it out," Mr. O'Loughlin said. "After all, the church and the fascists have the same goal—stopping communism in its tracks."

Someone laughed. The host, Mr. Van Dorn, tried to change the subject. He was a Yale classmate of Garrison's, a polo player and banker. (He spent very little time at the bank.) His wife, Dorinda, was six feet tall, with an elongated tanned face and muscular arms. Eva suspected Garry had had an affair with her before their marriage. Perhaps they still enjoyed an occasional "return engagement." Garry and Dorinda Van Dorn seemed to share small secrets, arch glances. They laughed at the same jokes. Eva was uneasy.

"Mind you, I'm not exactly a friend of Mussolini's—"

"Garry," Eva said tautly. "He jailed *five* intellectuals this week. Professors, economists, bankers, lawyers. Hardly Reds. Everyone at this table should be concerned about him. He is a menace. And Hitler is worse. I wonder why people never take these monsters at their word."

"Hear, hear," Dwight Enos said. He was a fat, unraveled, perpetually boozed "world traveler." Secretly he envied Halstead his career as a "journalist," lusted for his exotic "Jew wife." *And how is the fair Deborah, the temptress of West Tenth Street?* Enos would ask. He had a drunk's shrewd eye. Eva's white shoulders, her blazing green eyes, the bobbed yellow hair were too much for one man to contend with. Enos had known Halstead in college. A rake, a lecher. He could not have changed. *Oh, the mythical Jewish woman!* Enos had read about the heroine of the picket lines. And he divined that she and Halstead were in trouble. Their daughter was said to be the problem. Too smart for her own good. Jews, Enos decided, suffered from a surfeit of brains.

"All I'm saying is that Mussolini, like him or not, seems to have some kind of plan, some vision of the future," Halstead said.

"His plan is murder, torture, lies, and exploitation," Eva said.

The women listened with bovine expressions. None of them trusted Eva Halstead. It was a good thing that she was (a) beautiful; (b) famous; and (c) married to a Halstead. Otherwise this slum-bred woman would never be allowed to sit at a table on East Sixty-first Street.

"Now, Eva, no soapbox," O'Loughlin said, winking. Corpulent and walleyed, he was a Knight of Columbus, a Knight of Malta, a Knight of Saint Gregory, a rather genial man. He entertained warm feelings for the fair-skinned girl Halstead had married. In fact, grudgingly he admired her. Dullahan was an old friend of his, and Francis Fagan had more than once paid tribute to her as a tough cookie. Moreover, Dullahan informed O'Loughlin, Eva Heilig came from tough stock. Know the Chains, O'Loughlin? the boss asked. The bootleggers? *Her family.* Crazy Jake and his tough kid. The Irishmen winked. Nothing generated respect as did violence, power, wealth, and illegal hooch.

"I've graduated from soapboxes," Eva said. "Those lunatics in Europe are heading for a war."

"Maybe a good idea," Van Dorn said. "Get rid of the Bolsheviks. I'd support that war."

"Would you fight in it?" Eva asked.

"Too old, Eva, my dear. Too old for war, sex, or politics."

Later, Garrison backed Dorinda Van Dorn into a corner of the living room. They sipped brandy and appeared to be laughing a bit too loudly.

Eva sat, a lone missionary amid the Zulus, with a sozzled Dwight Enos. He had turned a shade of pale violet, but he made more sense than the others. Writers missed an essential about the very rich. They were dull, dull, *dull*. Not necessarily bad people, but of a dullness that parched the throat and glazed the eyes.

"Eva, I agree with you," Enos said. He had once entertained radical notions. Daringly he had ridden into Mexico to observe the peasant revolution, been shot at, written an article for *Scribner's*.

"About what?"

"Europe. A mess. Fascisti all over the place. We asked for it. It's obvious our class—not yours—ruined everything. No one in charge. No one making rules—or if there were rules, no one obeyed them. Good for you for popping off."

Cigar smoke, the aroma of brandy, filled the room. Eva felt vaguely nauseated. She had been to too many such parties. The guests had learned to check their anti-Semitism with their coats when she was present. But a lifetime of such inane blabber appalled her. Garrison did it because he had no choice. He could not offend his father's friends, the class in which he had been raised.

"Roosevelt is a Red," O'Loughlin was saying. "If the Democrats nominate him and he's elected, he'll wreck the country. Pauperize the people. Giveaways, socialistic notions. Someone should assassinate that crippled madman. Besides, the Depression's over."

Eva was tempted to respond. Dwight Enos was stroking her hand. A well-meaning idiot. Tempted by a soapbox Venus. Oh, the utter *shmuckiness* (as Sol would have said) of these people.

She saw Garrison in his odd tippy-toed way walk into the Van Dorns' library, one hand on Dorinda Van Dorn's naked shoulder blades.

At Eva's insistence they now slept in separate rooms. Sex had never been a success with them. Less and less Garrison came to her at night. She did not mind. She was trying to give more of herself to their daughter, Lillian, a difficult and distant child. It was likely that Halstead, jealous of the girl—he had claimed he wanted a child, but paid little attention to her—was having affairs. Mrs. Van Dorn, surely. Like getting into bed with a racehorse, Eva thought. Good breeding, po-ten legs, an elongated face.

My fault, she thought. I was never responsive enough. Something in my repressed Jewish background. All those taboos that I scorned, all those *don'ts* that I claimed to have mocked, have left their mark. Stir a crowd, get an audience to its feet, confront a politician, present a challenge to the mayor, talk back to a policeman . . . all these she had done. There was no shortage of passion in her. The *Eagle* called her "Fighting Eva," the workingman's Joan of Arc.

But her emotional life had suffered. She and Halstead led discrete lives. His magazine assignments (which rarely paid the cost of the trip) often sent him to Europe, around the country. He wrote for radical or eccentric periodicals. The Halstead fortune, untarnished by the stock-market crash, supported his travels and their comfortable style of living.

"I don't need all this," Eva told him one day, over their morning grapefruit. "I came out of poverty, and I can manage with a great deal less."

"I know you can," he said kindly. "But I need *you*. You are important to me."

"Your conscience? Your sweatshop protége?"

When you are pumping away at Dorinda Van Dorn's body? she wanted to ask. When you are meeting your Yale friends' wives for an afternoon of semiclad sex? And do they gossip about your Brownsville Salome?

Eva was too strong to let these matters deter her. She lectured continually. Radicalism was on the rise. As a sometime Socialist she stood her ground—no bolshevism, no fascism. A middle-way. The country would be saved by a peculiarly American red-white-and-blue radicalism. In small stages, reforms would be enacted.

She rearranged the pillows on the four-poster. After almost twenty years of marriage, she felt an intruder in the ancestral bed. *Does my Hebraic flesh recoil from these boards and springs and comforters fashioned by the purest of Americans?* she wondered. Maybe if she and Garrison had made love in hotel rooms she would have responded more ardently. Whenever their bodies were conjoined (less and less the past few years), she sensed that platoons of fierce Halsteads glowered down on them, venerable Puritans, nonplussed, if not horrified, by the Jezebel opening her legs to the thrusts of their fine-boned heir.

"*That,* Eva Heilig," she said in a loud whisper, "is a plate of yesterday's *tsimmes.*"

She could hear Garrison in the bathroom. His bedroom was across from hers. He gargled, spit, worked at his morning ablutions with military snap. Her husband was one of the most orderly of men. He wrote flat declarative sentences, searched Webster's unabridged for the precise word, edited galleys with a needle-pointed pencil.

Lillian had left her homework for her mother to check. A gesture, Eva knew, one that made her sad. She should have been more attentive to the child, a precocious third-grader. Lillian wrote brilliant original compositions. She was far ahead of her class in everything. Garrison and his parents hated the school. They wanted her enrolled at Emma Willard or the Madeira School. Halsteads did not attend these free-form progressive schools. And of course, Mount Holyoke, which four generations of Halstead women had attended, was inevitable.

Eva looked at the photo of Lillian on her night table. Not a pretty child, possessing Garrison's extended jaw, his narrow face, the high color that hinted at hypertension. Eva's fair hair and green eyes were evident, to be sure, but the effect was diminished on the elongated face. A lonely child, Eva realized. She had come to them late, and they were both a bit selfish, too much involved with causes.

I *will* pay more attention to her, Eva thought. I owe it to her.

The child seemed to enjoy her visits to Brooklyn, an afternoon of romping along Eastern Parkway with Abe's children, or playing with Sol's garden at his modest East Flatbush house. Grandma Heilig, the cigarette-puffing old lady in the high-buttoned black dress, amused her. (And Grandma Heilig always loaded her with pencils, pens, paper, pads, scissors, glue, colored paper—a rich haul from the stationery store.)

After breakfast, when Halstead had left for an appointment with his stockbroker and Lillian had gone off to school, Eva took a call from Ike Brunstein.

"Can't tell you where I am, Eva," he said huskily. "You've been reading about me, I suppose."

"Yes. Is Sol being rough on you?" She was overcome with pity for Ike.

"He is the essence of kindness."

"Can I help?"

"Isaac Brunstein is past help. I dined with the devil and he had a long spoon. Eva, as I'm talking to you, Sergeant Cooney and Sergeant DeVitale are standing on either side of me listening to every word."

"Yetta is all right? Can I bring her anything? Is the Trades Council looking after her?"

"Hah! Trades Council! I'm a pariah, Eva, a diseased dog. You would think people would be grateful that I'm telling everything. There'll be fifty indictments by the time I'm through. Gangsters, crooks, union chiselers. But Brunstein will be branded a traitor. The Communists hate me. The Socialists hate me. The regulars hate me. And the *shtarkers*—" His voice became a convulsed sob.

Oh, dear, Eva thought. *The old days*. When she, Ike, and old Flugelman had talked Jake Chain into protecting their girls. How had it come to this? It was no one's fault. It was inevitable in *America Gonif*. You played tough. You struck back. You won respect. Ike had gotten caught in the middle.

"Why did you call me, Ike?"

"I don't know," he sobbed. "It was so wonderful years ago. Our plans. We were sure of ourselves. Now look at me. I'm a prisoner. Talking, talking, talking."

She lowered her voice. It would be foolish of her to mention the Chains. Surely, one of Sol's young lawyers was monitoring Ike's calls. "Have you talked about . . . the early days? . . . I mean . . . you know. The man who saved the people at *tashlik?*"

He caught on. The battle at the creek. "No. I haven't. Your brother knows everything. He'll get around to it. Eva, I'm sorry I bothered you."

Distraught, she worried about him. Maybe she should have married Ike. She could have put starch in his spine, made him a leader, not a weakling playing at revolution. But then she would not have had a townhouse in New York, an estate in Sag Harbor, a grand career.

A few days later, two husky men in police uniforms entered the Whitman Manor Apartments. It was four in the afternoon, the time at which the detectives guarding Brunstein changed shifts. Detectives Flannery and Cane had been delayed at the station house by a malfunctioning squad car. Someone had poured granulated sugar into the tank. While the detectives tried vainly to get the engine to turn over, the two uniformed men rode the elevator to the penthouse.

Sol, having concluded his interviewing in the morning, had left for a meeting with his boss, one of Seabury's aides. The men on duty, Cooney and DeVitale, liked to leave early and were glad to see the uniformed men. They asked why their usual relief men were not on hand. "Car busted at the precinct," one of the men said. "I'm Carretta and this is Wahlstrom. We'll watch Mr. Brunstein until they show. How'd the Dodgers do?"

Cooney glanced at Ike. Their ward was stretched on the couch shoeless, smoking his fortieth cigarette of the day. The former radical, the man who confessed he had hired criminals to win local elections, looked like an Egyptian mummy. Yellow-brown skin, shrunken cheeks, lips like leather shoelaces, ears like dried apricots. The graying moustache drooped below his chin. *Poor dumb bastard,* Cooney thought. *And hebes were supposed to be smart.*

"Why uniformed men?" Ike asked.

"Until the detectives get here," Wahlstrom said. "Don't worry, Mr. Brunstein. The captain said we should order dinner for you. Care for me to call the deli? Something to drink?"

"It's too early," Ike said. He slumped deeper on the sofa, turned his back, drew his scrawny legs up into a fetal position. "I'm not hungry."

"Never eats," Cooney said on his way out. "The Dodgers got beat again. Braves knocked 'em off, ten to eight. Berger hit two."

"As Berger goes, so go the Braves," Carretta said.

His partner listened to the elevator rising, the clank of the door closing, the rattle of cables as it descended.

Ike never had a chance to shout. The two "policemen" leaped upon him and bludgeoned him into silence with one blow of a blackjack across his temple. They dragged him to the eleventh-story window. It was a clear drop, unimpeded by landings or setbacks.

For a terrified moment Ike regained consciousness. He flailed about and grabbed at a radiator. He tried to scream. The men stuffed a rag soaked with gasoline into his mouth, jammed it deep into his throat. One of them smashed his clutching hand with a lead sap. Tormented eyes pleaded. He wept gouts of tears. All for nothing—Marx, sacrifice, his love of the workingman.

"Fa chrissake, throw him," Wahlstrom said. "Grab an arm."

They each took an arm and leg. They waved Ike's frail body back and forth three times. On the fourth airborne sally, they hurled him out of the window. Ike sailed down eleven flights to an enclosed courtyard. They heard the heavy *splat*. One man grinned and said: "The bum could sing but he couldn't fly."

Swiftly they left by the fire stairs. A stolen car and a driver awaited them on the street. Inside, the men discarded their police uniforms. Beneath, they wore dark business suits. An hour later the driver and the "cops" were on a Greyhound bus for Cleveland, sitting separately, never speaking to each other. In Buffalo a fourth man came aboard and gave each voyager five hundred dollars. None of them would ever know that their employer had been Melvin Schonkeit.

Although a professed atheist and a former Stalinist, Brunstein was buried in the faith of his fathers. Yetta objected. It was sheer hypocrisy, she said. But Ike's aged mother insisted. The workers for whom he had toiled so long, suffered so much, taken beatings, humiliations, insults, turned out en masse. Political differences were temporarily laid aside.

"Isaac Brunstein, whatever his failings, and for these we forgive him," said Rabbi Piltz, "was one of us, of our blood, and of our faith, and had the Almighty permitted him to live longer, and not to have fallen victim to the jackals who stalk our city, would surely have returned to the Jewish faith. Let the King of the Universe accept him now, and let us join in prayer for Isaac Brunstein."

The procession extended for two blocks, behind a stark pine coffin on the bed of a laundry delivery truck. In his later years Ike had done the wet-wash workers much service. He had tried to unseat the gangsters he had helped bring in. Perhaps Wallowitz's memory stirred him.

Yetta rode in the cab of the truck. Behind the "hearse," limousines from Eckowitz's Funeral Parlor bore Ike's relatives. In one car sat Eva Halstead, her brother Sol, his wife Rose, and Dr. and Mrs. Abe Heilig.

"I'll never get over a feeling of guilt," Sol said. "Those dumb cops. The way they let those killers in. If I find out those detectives were in on it . . ."

"Any idea who they were?" Abe asked.

"Not a trace. They import them."

Eva wiped her eyes. Ike was gone. A part of her life. For a moment she regretted having spurned him. Had he ever kissed her? Once, twice, three times? A few pecks. Panting, worshipful Ike. He would have died for her. In a sense, he had died for her younger brother. The Heiligs had been no help to him.

"Yetta?" Eva asked. "Is she taken care of?"

"She won't take a cent from us," Sol said. "She says her political allies will pay the funeral expenses and give her a job."

"The Trotskyites," Eva said hopelessly. "Ah, the way they kill each other off. The Nazis will take over Germany, the fascists will run Europe, and the left will be denouncing each other."

It was an unnaturally cold rainy day in late May. The procession rolled at a measured pace through Brownsville, down Pitkin Avenue, past Leo Glauberman's law office (the mob's attorney watched from his window), past Otzenberger's Democratic Club (Benny was sorry Ike was dead but he felt that the man was a *shmuck*), toward East New York and thence to the cemetery.

The routing of the procession, because of a Consolidated Edison blockade on Liberty Avenue, took the wet-wash hearse and the limousines past the four-story fortress of the Brooklyn General Supply Company, the heart of the Chain empire.

Dr. Abe Heilig shook his head. "The Chains go on and on, and poor Ike is dead."

"Yeah," Sol said. "With a rag stuffed in his mouth. We found traces of his skin on the radiator. They had to pry his hands off."

Eva shuddered. "I don't want to hear any more." She cried again. "Ike was part of our growing up. That he should have to die this way— It's wicked."

"He tried to use rotten people," Sol said. "And they used him. Cruel world, Eva."

Two buildings down from the Chains' whiskey warehouse was a large machine shop with high opened windows and smoky gray walls. The hideous building housed the Unruh Tool and Die Works.

As the truck bearing Ike's coffin passed by, a hail of stones cascaded from the opened windows. Bricks bounced off the wooden lid. One smashed the truck's windshield. The limousines stopped. Behind them, people ran for cover. Chauffeurs were not going to undergo that hail of dornicks and debris.

"Red!"

"Commie!"

Stones and bricks clattered and skipped. The truck proceeded alone. Yetta had been cut on the forehead.

"Your beloved working class," Abe said to Eva. "Behold, the noble proletariat, paying tribute to one of their fallen. Those bricks are being thrown by machinists and mechanics."

"Ignoramuses, galoots," Eva said. "What do they know about Ike?"

The limousines were still halted. *"Move!"* Eva shouted. "Follow the truck!"

"Not me, lady." The driver signaled to the drivers behind him to back up to the corner and take another route.

None of them saw Jake Chain standing in the doorway of Brooklyn General Supply. Two of his workers were with him, Stroonz Rizzo and Baggie. Jake had a gutter awareness of violence.

As Eva and her brothers watched in amazement, Jake and his friends raced to the front entrance of the tool-and-die factory. They hurled a watchman into the street and vanished inside the building.

In minutes the brick-throwing ended. Eva and her brothers, peering from the window of the Cadillac, saw Jake Chain holding a gangly youth by the ankles, dangling him outside a second-story window. Every now and then Jake shook him a little to let him know that he could be dropped. He was educating a brick-thrower.

Wild shouts, sounds of objects being thrown, issued from the factory. Baggie and Rizzo were keeping order. Amid the hubbub, Jake Chain stood his ground, gripping the white ankles of the writhing boy, shouting at the drivers to proceed. All was secure now.

Not another brick was thrown.

"Holy jeez," Eva's chauffeur said. "Get a loada that big guy up there. Now he's holdin' him by *one hand*."

He was indeed. One of Jake's fists gripped the brick-thrower's leg. The other, waving a crowbar, was fending off the youth's co-workers.

"So much for the united front, dear sister," Abe said. "Behold the enlightened worker. Jake has the right idea. All those men inside Unruh's? They believe every word in the Hearst papers. Ike was a Communist. Ike deserved what he got."

Sol laughed. "A Jake Chain they'll always understand."

Eva lit a cigarette. She crossed her legs and pulled down her too-short black silk skirt. She'd bought an elegant Saks dress for the funeral. "Both of you are disgusting cynics. We can't spend the rest of our lives depending on the Jake Chains to effect reform. They're as bad as Schonkeit."

"Not quite, Eva, not quite," Sol said.

An idea was germinating in his mind. Jake had always had a bit of the knight-errant in him. Maybe he could help where Ike had failed. An unlikely reformer, that *bulvan*, that smuggler of booze. But who knew what went on inside that iron skull? And was it worth finding out?

Chapter 41

In June of 1931 Mort and Hilda, with twenty-one pieces of luggage, sailed for England on the *Queen Mary*. Mort carried fifty thousand dollars in a money belt. He also bore letters of introduction to three London banks and letters of credit which would allow him to open accounts in the United Kingdom totaling five million dollars, a fifth of the family fortune.

Mort had developed a cool, low-keyed manner. He had

spent a great deal of time (as a supplier of goods and services) with North Shore society people and wealthy residents of Manhattan mansions. He had learned to wear dark well-tailored suits, white shirts, dark blue ties. His conservative shoes gleamed. His nails were manicured. He wore no jewelry except for a gold watch and a simple gold wedding band. A gifted mimic, he soon picked up the locutions of the rich, lost his Brooklyn cadences. They regarded him as a curiosity—a refined hoodlum, a mannerly gangster, a fellow whose word was his bond, and whose best whiskey was bottled in bond. Darkly handsome, sharp-featured, graceful, he impressed the rich and influential.

Hilda had not kept pace with him. But cruelly corseted in boned elastic, she made a decent appearance. Her clothes—Mort insisted on this—were always sedate and demure and her jewelry was expensive but never showy. When in doubt, he ordered her, keep your mouth shut and smile. She managed to do both quite decently. Her hair was her glory—naturally curly, lustrous, the color of Coca-Cola, and usually piled high over her round face. Fashionably clothed; always in low-heeled shoes (Mort insisted that spikes had a whorish look), she held her own in snooty company. Often, suffocating her Brownsville accent, she used her Brooklyn origins to tell funny stories about her roguish father, a man who knew Governor Roosevelt, senators, corporate presidents.

Of all the documents that Mortimer J. Chain, dapper in black homburg and black chesterfield, carried to London in his Mark Cross attaché case, none was of more value than a letter that his cousin, Eva H. Halstead, had secured for him. It was from her father-in-law, Garrison Halstead, Sr., chairman of the board of two New York banks and a member of the presidential commission to reform the stock exchange.

Eva had always gotten along well with Garry's white-haired father. The old man admired "Hebrews." They worked. They produced. They did not commit crimes. They were good at business. Their sons became excellent physicians. His daughter-in-law's radicalism (like his son's) could be overlooked. Besides, she was quite a beauty. Old Halstead, a bit of a goat, had more than once stroked Eva's knee, pinched her behind.

Knowing the value of an ally, Eva had not discouraged the lusty gentleman. She did not tell Garry. An accomplished flirt, she winked at her father-in-law, a Byzantine temptress teasing a Crusader knight. At dinner parties old Halstead demanded that Eva be seated next to him. At the opera or the theater, the patriarch insisted on sitting next to his son's "Deborah" and occasionally sneaking a mottled hand up her skirt. *Let him*, Eva thought. *Some day he'll be of use*. To her radical friends she said that when the revolution came, they'd spare old Halstead a violent death. He would ride to the gallows with dignity, reading the *Wall Street Journal* and the *Yale Alumni News*.

"Cousin Eva," Mort had asked, in his sincerest manner, "can I get a character reference from your father-in-law? The old cocker?"

"He is no old cocker, Morty, and your character is unknown to him."

"Ah, come on, Eva. I'm Crazy Jake's son. Just a letter. That he knows me, he knows my company, and I'm a terrific guy."

"I'd phrase it more felicitously, Mort. Let me compose it. I'll talk to Mr. Halstead."

All that was needed was an open-mouthed kiss on Daddy Halstead's shriveled lips. Eva did not mind. The Chains continued to intrigue her. She'd had the feeling, ever since Ike's murder, she might be needing Jake. Odd, how she kept returning to him for help. The brutish flat-faced man. She shuddered remembering her last view of him. An angry giant, holding the brick-thrower out of the window.

On his bank letterhead, a name recognizable in any financial office in the world, Halstead, Sr., wrote:

This letter will introduce Mr. Mortimer J. Chain, president of the Brooklyn General Supply Company of New York City.

Mr. Chain and his associates are known to me personally. They are men of the highest caliber, both professionally and in their private lives. This young executive is active in charitable organizations, and conducts his affairs with probity and respectability.

Any services you can give him will be appreciated by the undersigned.

On reading the letter at her father-in-law's Wall Street office, she gave him a second kiss and let him squeeze her left breast. She left him gasping and gaping.

* * *

A month later Morty was seated in the gloomy offices of the Caledonian and Northern Distilleries, Ltd., of the United Kingdom. He produced his references, his letters, his bank accounts, and talked business with a bloodless man named Colin McVey. (*Oi vay*, Morty called him later, when he and Hilda celebrated with champagne in their suite at the Savoy.)

"But you chaps can only do this—ah—illegally," Mr. McVey said. He had a glass eye. It had more life in it than the real eye, Morty thought. Both were snot green in color. His smooth flesh was the color of borsht before the sour cream was added. The Scotsman's nose, round as a tennis ball, was a road map of burst blood vessels. Senior partner of one of the hugest distillers of scotch whiskey in the world, Colin McVey often sampled his product.

"It's going to change," Morty said. "And we're willing to gamble."

"We are not so sure. We are told Mr. Hoover has made a commitment on repeal. The Methodists and Baptists who support him will carry the election. He needs their vote."

Mort let him talk. *Shmuck. Putz. Farfel-head.* The British knew about America the way Americans knew about the monarchy. Mort let him believe that Hoover was a sure thing; that Roosevelt, or whoever the Democrats ran, would be pictured as a "drunken bum." What they had done to poor Al Smith in 1928! Why, then, was Mr. Chain willing to make an investment in whiskey he could not sell, or only sell illegally?

"Mr. McVey," Mort said again, "we're gamblers. I am told you British understand that. You are sporting people. Horses, cards. We're willing to take a chance. We want to be your exclusive representative in the United States. You have read the letters."

"My dear Mr. Chain. You are a bootlegger."

"So? I'm the first one you ever saw?"

"You break the laws of your country with impunity. I am not sure . . ."

Morty was not sure what "impunity" meant, but he was not a man to be discouraged by what Hilda called a "ten-dollar word." He offered McVey a Havana cigar, lit one for himself, crossed knife-creased dark blue trouser legs. "Ask anyone who has done business with us. We don't cheat. We don't haggle. We pay on time. I assure you, Mr. McVey, we never kill anyone. Unless *they* make trouble first."

It took five seconds for the last part of Mort's sales pitch to register. *"Trouble first! Trouble first! Oh, that is jolly good! Jolly good!"*

Mr. McVey laughed so hard his throat clogged with phlegm. He coughed for thirty seconds. When he was composed, Mort handed him an envelope containing fifteen thousand dollars in cash.

"Mr. McVey, count this. It has nothing to do with any business arrangement we might come to. It is for *you.* I am told you are a racing fan and you own horses. What's in that envelope will buy you a prize yearling. The Chains are grateful people. You give us the concession, you'll have a racing stable as good as the king's."

McVey lost no time in counting the money. Before Mort left they agreed to a second meeting, which their solicitors would also attend, to draw up a contract between the Brooklyn General Supply Company and Caledonian and Northern Distilleries, Ltd., for the purchase, importation, and distribution of whiskey and gin.

"I don't get it," Hilda said nervously, as they dined at the Savoy before leaving to see a Noel Coward play. Hilda looked lush and Oriental in a flowing black gown, strands of pearls. "I don't get it. Suppose there's still Prohibition?"

"So what?" Mort asked. "We'll stash the booze in the Bahamas and run it on boats. Pop is buying a big ship like a fishing schooner. We can cut, mix, and bottle on board so we don't lose any time. We win either way."

Mort sipped a dark claret. Not much. The English went nuts over it. Wine was not a big money item. Years ago, after Rabbi Piltz's tirade at Jake, they'd given up the business with fake rabbis. *Wine, shmine.*

The money was in booze. Americans were the thirstiest people in the world. It was not just drinking, getting drunk, but the ceremony, the religion they made about it. Jokes, talk, teasing, as if to take a slug of gin were the greatest sin since the first guy screwed another guy in the ass. Jake, in his primitive way, had understood this love-hate relationship with alcohol. Mort understood it even better. He saw the shining light in their eyes when you mentioned the real stuff, listened to their dumb jokes about "hollow legs" and "human sponges," their college boys bragging, "Boy was I pissed last night," businessmen laughing their heads off over a colleague's ability to "put it away."

"So long as there are Christians who have to have alcohol, even if it's the piss we sell now, or the good whiskey we will get from McVey," Mort told his wife as he toasted her, "the Chains will do all right."

The play bored them, but they enjoyed sex in the hotel suite later. Almost as good as with Theresa, Mort thought with surprise. He would have to make more trips abroad with Hilda. New business contacts would demand it, anyway.

Dispensing large cash bribes in fresh hundred-dollar bills, presenting his letters of recommendation and bank accounts as evidence of his reliability, Mortimer J. Chain won distribution rights from two more distilleries. He signed contracts. He hired a graduate of Oxford, who wore a double-breasted vest and glasses on a black string, to run the London branch of the Brooklyn General Supply Company.

Mort took the wavy-haired blond man to lunch at a private club—Mort's banker was a member and accompanied them—and told funny stories about his father's career as union organizer, enforcer, bootlegger, and now captain of a seagoing rum fleet.

The new employee, Horace Bain-Foxx, found it jolly amusing. So did the banker. Both were intrigued by the sharp-faced, gentle-voiced young man who informed them that he was a graduate of Dartmouth and had already registered his sons (in the English tradition) for that fine college.

"But that's a lie," Hilda said, as they made afternoon love, half-clothed. "You never finished Thomas Jefferson High School."

"They'll believe anything I tell them so long as the money keeps coming."

Chapter 42

Soon after Mort and Hilda left for England, Sol had Wesselberg picked up for questioning. After several hours of interrogation, Sol stepped outside his office and signaled to his assistant, a young lawyer named Bertram Dunphy. Dunphy was an ex-cop, unshakably honest. A married man with five children, he had attended law school at night while walking a beat in Brooklyn Heights. He was fair-skinned, dark-eyed, with the characteristic shock of thick dark brown hair of many Irish. He and Sol worked well together. Dunphy was tough and unsubtle. Sol could be gentle and conciliatory.

"How's your shorthand, Bert?" Sol asked.

"Good enough."

"I don't want the secretaries to hear this. Can you sit by the tube and make notes? Wesselberg is beginning to sweat. Maybe he's ready to pop."

"Good luck. The fat bum. I wish I were on the force again. Fifteen minutes with the slob."

"Be nice, Bert."

Dunphy seated himself at a camouflaged aperture in the plaster wall through which Sol Heilig's interrogation could be heard. Sol winked at him and reentered his office.

What a monster was Herman Wesselberg, thought Sol. Now in his late fifties, the Meal Ticket sagged and drooped. His gut was a great ball of flesh encased in specially tailored gray trousers. His cannonball head was mottled with red-brown warts, and the pouches under his eyes looked like uncooked gray blintzes. His hair grew long and unkempt, in ratty strands that covered his ears and his creased neck. Wesselberg had asked for a hard-backed chair, complaining that once he sank into a stuffed chair he fell asleep.

Sol studied the fat man's hands: delicate, dainty, manicured. How many people had he killed with them? Sol could guess. Ten, twelve, more. He was a merciless, useless son of a bitch, with nothing to redeem him. For a moment, Sol, who tried to make excuses occasionally for Schonkeit, found himself detesting the Paymaster for elevating this monster to be his lieutenant. And Wesselberg was rich now; he and Shikey had made fortunes.

"Why do they call you the Saratoga Avenue Meal Ticket, Herman?" Sol asked genially. He sat behind his desk. One neighborhood kid to the other.

"In Brownsville, when I was a kid. I always was good for a free meal. Y'know, Mr. Heilig? Before I moved to the East Side, I had a good heart. I still got one."

Sol laughed, as if appreciating the man's high estimate of himself. "But what about Wallowitz? You remember a steward in the wet-wash union named Wallowitz?"

"Nope."

Sol read a clipping from the *Times*. It was ten years old. Hyman Wallowitz, 42, a shop steward for the laundry workers, shot to death as he lay recovering from a beating in Brownsville Jewish Hospital . . .

"I never heard a him. What do I know from wet wash?"

"Herman," Sol said, "you're in trouble up to your big *tuchas*. We have witnesses. They were afraid to talk ten years ago. No more. They saw you and Frummer in the hospital that day."

"Which Frummer?"

"Futka."

"He's dead. If he did it, good riddance. I never touched Walkowich, whatever the *putz's* name was."

"Suppose I told you we've subpoenaed records from the office of Leo Glauberman and that there are some interesting letters between Glauberman and Schonkeit." He got up.

Wesselberg placed his soft hands on his paunch, as if trying to keep it from falling to the floor. An old killer, he had undergone his share of interrogations. He did not scare easily. He had always been bailed out by political connections, sharp lawyers. But this *vontz* Heilig was bothering him.

"Name somebody who might have shot Wallowitz," Sol said.

"Jake Chain."

Sol halted halfway across the room. "Good try, Wesselberg, but Jake was clean."

"He's your relative also, right?"

Sol did not smile. "Distant cousin. He's been checked out. He has an alibi. Besides, he liked Wallowitz. Chain was getting religion. That's why he got out of *shtarking* and into booze. He worked you over once, right?"

"Screw Jake Chain. I got no idea what happened to Halavich."

Sol ignored him a moment. What he was really after was the Brunstein case. Wallowitz was a red herring. He began to ask the Meal Ticket about kickbacks from union members, the beating of elected officials, sweetheart contracts that sold out the union to the employers. Sol asked about the control of trucking, something Shikey and Wesselberg had organized into a fine art. Then he got around to Ike.

"Why was Brunstein killed, Herman?"

The fat man did not flinch. "Don't ask me. I hardly ever saw the bum."

"You knew him."

"So did you, Mr. Heilig. Could be lots of reasons. Maybe he welshed on a bet."

Sol sat on his desk. The Cleveland police, on a tip from an informer, had arrested a man named Santo, a killer-for-hire.

Santo wasn't talking, but they had found the stub of a Grey-hound bus ticket to New York in his coat.

"You got friends in Cleveland?" asked Sol.

Outside, Bert Dunphy, taking notes, whistled softly to himself. Heilig was playing his best card early.

"Cleveland? I never been in Pennsylvania."

"Know a man named Santo?"

Wesselberg shifted his butt, lowered his head. *Oi, that bastard Schonkeit. The things he did for him.* It did not trouble Wesselberg or Frummer to kill a stool pigeon like Brunstein. But Heilig was a tough bastard. *Thirty indictments in the works.* Who knew if he and Shikey would be included? As much as Wesselberg detested the Paymaster, he needed him. He needed the smooth, quiet man who paid off judges, assemblymen, aldermen, and political leaders.

"Thinking it over, Herman?"

"I got nothing to think. I never been in Cleveland."

"Schonkeit'll do the same to you someday. But it'll take more than two men to heave you out of a window. They'll need a platoon of marines to throw you."

The Meal Ticket gargled a laugh. "You just lost your case, counselor. Why should I talk to you, if that's what's gonna happen? Brunstein was a Red who shouldna played with tough guys. I run a trucking business. I pay taxes. I'm a well-known person in the garment industry."

Outside, Sol's secretary gave Bert Dunphy a memo. An anonymous caller from Cleveland. Mr. Heilig was advised to use the name Calabrese in his interrogation regarding the Brunstein murder. Dunphy recognized the name at once. A mob boss, an underworld power. Santo's employer.

Dunphy knocked on the door, summoned Sol, whispered to him, and gave him the slip of paper.

In the chair, Wesselberg yawned and scratched his balls. He drank a tumbler of water. *Boy Scout Heilig.* He should know that he almost screwed his sister once. In a hallway in Brownsville. That blonde with the round ass and neat boobies who married the rich *goy.* Oh, he remembered Eva Heilig with the big voice. The rainy day they'd boiled his pal Moishe Nigger. It was that bastard Jake Chain.

"Who is Mr. Calabrese?" Sol asked.

Wesselberg tugged at his collar. "Never heard a him."

"Mr. Calabrese in Cleveland."

"Ya wastin' ya time. Mr. Heilig." But he was turning grayish, the fat on his face like softened tallow, the bags under the eyes darkening. "I been here long enough. Ya can't keep me here all day. Next time I'm coming with Mr. Glauberman."

"Mr. Calabrese and his employee Santo are getting cooperative. They think they know you. How about it, Meal Ticket?"

"I wanna lawyer. I ain't talking no more."

"Okay. You can go."

Driving back to New York, Herman Wesselberg thought it over. He wouldn't talk. Never. Schonkeit would protect him. Anything could be fixed. But that scumbag Heilig! How had he found Calabrese? The man he had met in Cleveland, the man to whom he had given ten grand to finish Brunstein. If those Cleveland wops talked, H. Wesselberg would be in trouble.

"They'll have to build a special electric chair for you, Herman," Melvin Schonkeit said jovially. "Louise dear, would you leave us?"

They were in the Paymaster's penthouse apartment on Central Park West. Schonkeit's wife smiled and departed. Usually the more disgusting of Melvin's associates—like this fat man—were not received at home.

"It ain't funny, Mr. Schonkeit."

"Just deny everything. Our friends in Cleveland are protected."

A phone was off the hook, near enough to Schonkeit so that he could hear a voice. Someone was shouting into it. Wesselberg watched. He knew what was going on. He was amazed that the Paymaster would let him see his dirty work. Schonkeit picked up the phone and nodded. He listened for a fraction of a second, hung up. Then he asked the operator for a number. Into the phone he said softly, "Four."

Oh, the sly bastard, Wesselberg thought. Always on sure things. Somehow he was getting race results from Jamaica. The number-four horse had won. A "beard" had just been given the word and was placing a bet with some sucker of a bookie. The bookie would be paying through the nose when the results came through on the wire.

"This punk Heilig," Wesselberg said. "You got to buy him off, Mr. Schonkeit."

"He can't be bought. You and I are crooks in our hearts. There aren't many Jews like us. We're the exceptions, freaks. We—"

"I ain't no freak, Mr. Schonkeit."

"I was not referring to your weight, Herman. I know about the Heiligs. His brother is a surgeon. His sister, the one who writes and lectures. They're better than we are. A lot better. And they don't frighten. So I'm afraid we will have to let Solomon Heilig proceed and let the chips fall where they may." Schonkeit believed every word he said; he admired achievement, respectability.

"I think, Mr. Schonkeit, you want me to be the fall guy."

"Don't be concerned. If Heilig gets an indictment, it won't stick. I'll see to that."

Wesselberg got to his feet. "Mr. Schonkeit, I don't like the way this is going. I may have to lean on Heilig."

"I forbid it."

"Scare the guy. Maybe threaten his wife or his kids."

Schonkeit got up. His manner was calm, but there were scarlet splotches on his shiny cheeks. "I warn you, Herman. You are not to touch the prosecutor. We have rules. That's why I was put in charge. People like you and Shikey, left to your own devices, would ruin everything. An honest lawman like Solomon Heilig cannot be touched. We'll move around him. We'll handle him in court."

The Paymaster escorted Wesselberg to the private elevator. "Remember, I'll be annoyed if you try any rough stuff on Heilig. Let nature take its course. We'll all survive and prosper."

The meeting enraged Wesselberg. He had lived with violence since he was a fat boy of eleven. A *psychopath*, a doctor had once called him in court. Heilig and Schonkeit were two of a kind—one on the side of the law, one working against it. Brains. Nice clothes. Rich friends. And he was fat, hideous, hated and feared. He would not only get Heilig but arrange to have it pinned on Schonkeit. Let the Paymaster work on that one.

Not long after Wesselberg's audience with Schonkeit, Eva was typing furiously in her cluttered study. She took a morning telephone call from her brother Abe. "Busy, busy, Abe. I can't talk."

"Rest easy, kid," Dr. Heilig said. "Bad news, but not that bad. Solly's been shot."

"Good God. Is he—"

"He's all right. In front of his house. He was getting into his car. Two wounds, one in the arm, one high in the chest.

No vital organs. He's going to be all right. He's conscious, he's fine, he'll make it."

She began to cry, forced herself to stop. The Heiligs handled themselves with courage and self-discipline. "Where is he, Abe?"

"Crown Hill Hospital. I operated on him myself."

"Operated?"

"Just to remove the bullets. One of them shattered his collarbone. We called in an orthopedic surgeon. He says it'll be okay, maybe with a bump on it."

"Rose and the kids?"

"They're all right. Rose had a bad time at first, but she's gutsy. A car pulled alongside when Sol was getting into his and they opened up. He must have been suspicious, because he hit the ground at once. The rest of the shots bounced off his Buick."

"Are you at the hospital now?"

"With Rose and mama. Mama's in bad shape. I didn't want her to come. Grab a cab and get out here."

Crossing the Brooklyn Bridge in a taxi, Eva cried again. They had tried once. They would try again. Sol was too courageous for his own good. She knew about the underworld. For a moment she wondered why the secret rulers had permitted the attack. The unspoken law was never to go after D.A.'s, investigators, or cops. It served no purpose but to arouse public fury. Anger replaced fear. She knew at once where she would go for advice to protect Sol.

Bertram Dunphy, Sol's young assistant, met Eva outside the hospital room. There were three uniformed cops standing guard. Eva could hear her mother weeping in the room. But Sol's voice was comforting and unafraid.

"He could have used the police this morning, Bert," Eva said.

"He refused. He didn't want to scare Rose and the children. The judge just issued an order. He's to have twenty-four-hour guards, at the house, the office, everywhere." Dunphy looked pale, controlling his fury.

"It's outrageous. Do you have any suspects?"

"Just suspects. No evidence. No one saw the car. No one got a license number. Your brother leaves early, even before his children go to school."

In the room Eva gingerly embraced Sol. He was sitting up in bed, left arm and shoulder in an elevated plaster cast. An IV dripped plasma into his right arm.

Abe was talking to the orthopedic surgeon. They were not concerned. He'd be out of commission only a few weeks.

"But the gangsters will come again," Matla Heilig wailed. She was old and feathery. "Once they try, they'll try again. Solly, Solly, why *you*? Why you with this gangster business? Let someone else go after them."

Eva watched Sol's eyes. As ever they were bright and merry. He was putting on a good act. "Eva, explain it to mama. It was an accident. They had me mixed up with someone else."

Rose Heilig entered. She had done her crying already. It served no purpose now. She was an elementary-school principal, an ambitious woman. She and Eva embraced.

"Room's too crowded," Dr. Heilig said. "This isn't a family reunion, it's a hospital room."

Eva found a pay phone. A talk with Jake Chain was in order.

Sarah answered the phone. She had been sitting in the kitchen, fanning herself, watching Jake eat a late breakfast—orange juice, corn flakes with cream, three fried eggs, rye toast, and coffee. It was one of his twice-a-week visits to the house on Haven Place. She overfed him, looked after his laundry, hovered over him. She knew about the woman in Freeport.

"Eva," Sarah said, "you're lucky you caught him. He came in last night. More and more he's at the place on the island. Business, business."

Eva's voice was shaky. Hearing that Jake was in the house, she sounded calmer. "Please, Sarah, could you put him on?"

Just like her, Sarah thought. Nothing to ask about me, my health, the house, Morty, the grandchildren. Only Jake interested her. Bitterly Sarah thought, She's rich and famous and pretty, so what does she want with my husband? Sarah blamed Jake's alienation on Eva. Jake's ideal. His dream. No wonder he had run off to other beds, to that *shiksa* tramp, that lady pirate.

Irene Twine, widow of the murdered Buster, who worked as Sarah's maid (the only maid on Haven Place), came in. She complained about the awful heat, switched on a fan, and began clearing the kitchen table.

The clatter of dishes, the hum of the metal fan, the chattering of his wife and the black woman unnerved Jake. He told Sarah he would take the call in the living room.

"You hang up, Sarah," he said, "after I get on."

"So what's to listen? She only calls when she needs a favor."

Nagger, Jake thought. And yet he pitied her, hating himself for the way he neglected her. He could not help it. He loved Tommy. He loved their bastard son, Little Mac. The sprawling stucco-and-timber house was his real home.

The living room was shaded against the hot morning sun. The thick leaves on the Lombardy poplars Doc Abelman had planted formed checkered patterns on the drawn blinds. Jake sat at his desk and heard Eva's voice. It never failed to make his blood jump.

"Jake, someone shot my brother Sol."

"He's all right?"

She filled him in. A car had paused in front of Sol's house on Eastern Parkway. Someone—the police guessed there were at least two men—had emptied guns at him. Luckily Sol had taken only two bullets. He would live.

"What do you want me to do, Eva?"

"Find out. Tell them not to hurt him. You know all those people."

He was thinking: Always me when there is dirty work. Always Crazy Jake. Loving her, he was resentful. Never a kiss. Never embracing her, never seeing her naked. But full of desire for the small woman. So smart, so brave, so much a part of his life. She did not go running to her rich husband Halstead, or to his millionaire father, or to her brother, the surgeon. But she appealed to Crazy Jake, the bad one, the violent one, the *verdamte blut*.

"Sol must have more Chain blood in him than I thought," Jake said. "He learned how to duck. Not like Brunstein."

"Don't make fun of us, Jake."

"Who is making fun? I'm glad Sol is okay."

She asked him who he thought had tried to kill her brother. Dunphy, Sol's assistant, was certain it was Wesselberg and Frummer or their hired killers. The same monsters who hurled Ike out of a window.

Jake sighed. He saw Sarah standing sullenly in the doorway, seething over the way her husband was being dragged into the Heiligs' affairs. Jake Chain was wealthy, feared, respected, a businessman like any other. Why did Eva Halstead have to bother him? Why didn't she mind her own business, that ritzy one?

A mischievous notion seized Jake. Yes, he would talk to Eva. He would discuss what they could do. But only at the place in Freeport. He'd pick her up at the hospital in an hour. She argued a bit at first. Why all the way out there? She had appointments, lunch with the women's reform movement, a dozen things to do.

"Cancel everything, Eva. You make enough speeches," Jake insisted. He wanted her to see Tommy. To let her know she was not the only woman he could love.

"Freeport, *Freeport*," Sarah mocked. "Getting all your *nafkas* in one place? Is that it? Look at me, Jake. Look at your wife. I am a pretty woman. I am young. Is this my life? Card games and shopping, and a *shwarzer* to do my work?"

No anger generated in him. He pitied her. He longed for her to be happier. "I'm sorry, Sarah. This summer maybe we could take a place in Long Beach. Near the ocean. It'll be nice. I have this customer who runs a hotel a block from the boardwalk."

She slammed the door.

Chapter 43

"I'm ashamed to ask for lemonade here," Eva said. She smiled her most charming smile, smoothed her white linen skirt.

"It's all right, Mrs. Halstead," Tommy said. "I hardly ever drink myself."

"Eva, please. I'm family."

Jake watched the two women warily. His pale eyes were amused and gratified. A little lesson for Eva. A bit of showing off to Tommy. A high-class lady, his cousin. A society lady. A well-known writer. But in a crisis, her brother wounded, she had come to him, the mobster.

"Lemonade is easy," Tommy said. "Jake?"

"Same all around. It's funny how, working with booze all my life, I lost the taste for it."

Tommy laughed and threw her head back. "Jake, really. Who wouldn't lose their taste, considering the poison you sell to people!"

"I dunno," said Jake. "Whoever pays the right price gets the good stuff. You pay less, you get rotgut."

A breeze from the Sound ruffled strands of Eva's curling blond hair. Jake stared at her a moment. Forty-five. Almost his age. And she looked twelve years younger. Unlined skin, clear green eyes.

Tommy noticed the way her man was looking at the visitor. He had told her often about Eva. She went inside the house and left them on the second-floor veranda with its view of the winding canals and the distant white-capped ocean. A Chain boat was chugging slowly into dock. In broad daylight it would unload a cargo of English gin.

"Just like that?" Eva asked.

"Why not? The guys unloading and stacking are the local cops. The Feds, Morty and I took care of long ago. We set them up in their own speakeasy. How can they turn us in if they're customers?"

"Same Jake. Same Morty. Same Chains."

"Yeah, we manage."

Eva could see the woman inside the house preparing lemonade for them. A fine-looking woman. Tall, big-boned, with a strong throat and somewhat coarse skin, but stunning features—a high brow; a fall of chestnut hair, luminous in the afternoon sun; arched eyebrows; sharply defined features. She was a different kind of woman.

"You love her," Eva said.

"Yes. We have a son."

She smiled and took his hand. "I'm glad. A good boy?"

"Sure. Little Mac. After her father. Mackenzie Tuttle. That's a name for a half-Jew?" He laughed. "There he is, by the truck."

Eva got up and leaned over the wooden railing. She saw a muscular blond boy of about seven or eight. He had the same shock of thick blond hair that Jake had had as a boy. He was barefoot, in ragged pants, his skin a golden brown. He carried a bamboo fishing pole with a red-and-white bobber.

"Good God, Jake. He's so—so—*American.* Huckleberry Chain."

"What? Oh, I get it. I never read the book, but I get it."

He told her about Tommy's daughter, who was in the boarding school in Connecticut. Money was no problem. Jake supported two households and what amounted to two wives.

Tommy came out with a tray, pitcher, and three glasses filled with ice. Eva had to smile. Surrounded by oceans of booze, warehouses and boatloads and trucks, they drank lemonade.

It was balmy and sun-warm on the broad veranda. Wicker chairs, chintz pillows, a sense of peace and isolation. No wonder Jake loved it, Eva thought. And the woman had a certain strong quality. No great beauty, but graceful, despite her large body. There was honesty and independence on her sun-lined face.

Eva had to keep reminding herself. Jake Chain was a mobster, a man who made his living outside the law, a violent man. He had killed people. She had lost track of the Chains the past few years. Sol said that father and son had become enormously rich and powerful. So powerful that the secret rulers of the underworld let them go their way. Schonkeit, arbiter, decision maker, was content to let the Chains run their operation untouched.

"It's lovely here," Eva said.

A second Chain boat was moving slowly through the inland canal, cutting a gentle swath in the shallow waters. Eva could see that it was loaded with wooden crates and wedge-shaped burlap packages.

"Ours," Jake said. He was smiling. "We buy whole cargoes. No more *shnurring* around, picking up a load here, a load there."

"The wonders of modern capitalism."

Tommy Tuttle laughed. "Jake told me you were a radical, Mrs. Halstead. We're sort of outside the economy. You know, not part of the system."

"I realize that." She wanted to say, Economic systems come and go, but crime and the Chains go on forever. A Communist friend had told her that in the Soviet Union the black market flourished.

Jake was as rugged and handsome as ever. The flattened face, broad cheekbones, calm blue eyes. The blond hair, a bit graying, was still thick, falling over his forehead. His body had not run to fat. Strong, lithe, broad-shouldered, he looked indestructible.

Below, Sal Ferrante was shouting instructions to the drivers. A convoy assembled on the driveway. So it goes in big business, Eva reflected. Organization was everything. Ike had predicted that the Chains were doomed. They were *lumpenproletariat*, criminals who would die when the perfect society evolved. But the perfect society, to a disillusioned Eva, seemed light-years away. Everything was going downhill. In 1929 all belief had been shattered. What if the Chains inherited the earth?

"Let's go for a boat ride," Jake said. "Come on, Eva. I'll show you how fast we can go. It'll be safe. There won't be a drop of booze on board. You, me, and Tommy. We'll let Anton skipper."

"I'm not dressed for an outing at sea, Jake."

"The boat is like a hotel. Tommy?"

She shook her dark hair. She knew of Jake's lost love. "I'll stay here. You two go."

Anton guided the speedboat through winding canals, past bulkheads and piers,. into the "rip" where the deep blue ocean broke against the stone jetties in foaming bursts. It was a hot July day, but refreshingly cool on the water. Gulls and terns dipped about the flashing boat.

Eva sat on a canvas chair, laughing, tucking her flapping white skirt under her legs. Very good legs, Jake thought. Slender, tiny ankles. She wore smart little flapper's shoes. White and brown straps.

"Cut the speed, Anton," he said. "Let her drift."

"Right, Jake."

Jake took her hand. "So? Always me when there's trouble."

"I'm frightened for Sol. They almost killed him. I want you to help."

"Shoot somebody?" He smiled. "I never do those things. Not anymore."

"But you know those people. You know Schonkeit. Sol's been questioning Wesselberg. He's that garment-industry gangster."

Jake rubbed his knuckles. He thought: *I should have killed him*. Outside Frummer's political club, a long time ago. After what they tried to do to Eva . . .

"I don't want you to get hurt or to hurt anyone," Eva said. "But Mr. Dunphy says that Wesselberg is insane. They think he has syphilis and it's affected his brain. He has a notion he must get rid of Sol."

"So let Schonkeit take care of him."

He wondered how much weight he could swing with Schonkeit. The Paymaster had made his peace with the Chains long ago. They were too tough, too smart. Brooklyn was far enough away so that he could surrender the territory. Jake wondered how much control Schonkeit exercised over Wesselberg and Frummer.

"I'll try. But, Eva, it's a long time since I used my fists on anyone. I don't take chances like I used to. You saw why."

"I did. She's a beautiful woman. And the boy. I'm glad for you."

Aimlessly, he hated Halstead. In her. Joined. His *shagitz* body, pale and knock-kneed. How white she was, unlined, graceful. A small woman, all courage, passion, devotion. But something was wrong with the marriage. He'd heard gossip.

From Rose Heilig, via Matla, Eva's mother. Separate bedrooms. Traveling without each other . . .

Anton turned the speedboat. It rocked gently in its own wake. Distantly they could see two large boats riding at anchor.

"More booze," Jake said. "Everyone's stocking up. We're buying shiploads." He was glad to change the subject. Self-pity was a waste. Her silken legs, exposed by the insistent wind, were driving him wild. That fancy Halstead. Too good for him. She was too good for anyone.

"You'll talk to Schonkeit?"

"Could I ever say no to you?"

She kissed his cheek, ran fingers through his hair. "Jake, I know you'll get them to stop. People listen to you."

Everyone except you, he thought. "I love you," he whispered.

"No. You love Tommy. Remember that."

Eva called him three days later. Rose Heilig had been threatened on the phone by a muffled voice. Rose and Sol's daughter, Celia, had been stopped in the street by a dark man in a black suit and handed a note. It read: YOU AND YOUR WHOLE FAMILY GONNA GET IT. Terrified, Celia had run home. Dunphy took her to police headquarters and had her look at mug shots. Celia could not identify the man.

A reinforced police guard was ordered for Sol's home and family. Two men were assigned to Sol's house on Eastern Parkway—one monitoring phone calls, another watching the door. Sol never traveled anywhere without a detective escort.

Again Wesselberg was called in for questioning. This time he threw a tantrum in Sol's office, cursed him and threatened to "get" everyone connected with it.

"He's off his nut," Bert Dunphy said.

"Or it's an act," Sol said.

Leo Glauberman, the aging Teddy Roosevelt of Pitkin Avenue, showed up to complain that his client was being unjustly persecuted. From now on he would not cooperate.

"How about Shikey Frummer?" Sol asked. "You represent him also?"

"I do."

"He's next. If you want, you can sit in on the meetings. Glauberman, maybe *you* want to answer some questions. About Wallowitz. About Brunstein."

Glauberman did not rise to the bait.

"Warn Wesselberg to lay off Mr. Heilig," Bert Dunphy said. "He should know better."

The following day, Rose Heilig took her children and moved for the summer to a boardinghouse in Liberty, New York. Again, two police officers were assigned to the family. She complained to Sol that she felt that she was in jail. She wept a great deal, begged Sol to resign from the investigator's office. The hoodlums got her phone number in the Catskills. Threatening calls continued.

Just back from Europe, Mort heard about Eva's appeal to his father, the attacks on Sol and his family. On learning of Jake's intention to meet with Schonkeit, he was upset.

"It's not our business, pop," he said. In a vested blue suit, newly barbered, getting his nails manicured, Morty sat in his private office in the Brooklyn General Supply Company. He had relegated Sal Ferrante and his brothers to an outside "workroom." They shared space with file cabinets, desks, telephones, three secretaries. Sal was spending less time at the place. He was learning the ropes in narcotics, investing time and money with an old mobster named Mafalda.

"For Eva," Jake said. "Schonkeit I can talk to. Wesselberg is a lunatic. Nobody knocks off cops and D.A.'s. I should have killed him ten years ago, when I—"

"It's okay, pop. I won't try to stop you. Just be careful."

"I owe the Heiligs." His father appeared to Mort strangely innocent and trusting. "They taught me to read. I respect people like the Heiligs. It's like Rabbi Piltz told me when you and Hilda got married. There's all kinds of Jews. I ain't the best kind and I know it."

"You're good enough."

"Eva, Sol, the doctor—they're the kind of people the rabbi meant. I done rotten things."

"So have I. But if we stopped to worry about it, we'd go out of business."

London was calling Mr. Mortimer Chain. Urgent. Something about the wording of a contract. Morty winked at his father, as if to say, *Don't worry, pop, we're going legit soon.*

"You're smarter than I am," Jake said. "You got class, brains. You look ahead. Maybe I can retire in a year. We won't need the place in Freeport if repeal comes in. We can unload right on the New York docks, right?"

"Right, pop. Give my best to Schonkeit. You want to carry something?"

"I ain't carried a gun in years. Except on the boat, and only when Tommy is along. Nobody'll start in with a Chain. It's like starting in with a Rockefeller."

Mort laughed, talked into the phone. Funny, Jake thought, he's got a different voice, a different accent when he talks legitimate business. Almost like an Englishman, or one of those Long Island society people.

"Ah, Mr. McVey," Morty was saying. "How are you, sir? Yes, the contracts look fine. . . ."

Jesus, Jake thought, Thomas Jefferson High School! And fighting in the gutter twenty years ago with Bernie Feigenbaum! For a moment he recalled the day Sarah was crippled when the K & R factory collapsed. Driving the wagon to the tenement, having to tell Mutteh that his mother had been injured. And Eva. A vision in her shirtwaist and skirt, her hair undone, more beautiful than he could ever remember her, walking toward him with a bowl of soup.

Schonkeit was convinced that Wesselberg was going insane. The fat man's physician had warned him. The Meal Ticket had paresis. Latent syphilis. Wesselberg had become violent in the doctor's office, threatened a nurse, smashed equipment. He was obsessed with Solomon Heilig.

The Paymaster decided Wesselberg would have to be killed. Moreover, something besides the demise of the Meal Ticket loomed. Some brilliant scheme that could wound the Chain dynasty. The Paymaster had long ago made a shaky peace with them. But he had been getting disturbing reports from England. That young entrepreneur, Mort Chain, had been signing contracts in the British Isles, grabbing liquor-distributing rights. When Prohibition ended, the Chains would be ready.

Schonkeit was jealous of this kind of foresight. Melvin Schonkeit should have been doing it *first.* Who knew how far the Chains could rise? And while they were not bred-in-the-bone killers, not bloody bastards like Frummer, they would be an impediment. Too big to control. A future source friction, of rivalry for the big dollar.

And so he looked forward to seeing Jake Chain. They met at Schonkeit's private table in the rear of the Home Stretch Club on East Fifty-sixth Street off Park Avenue. It was another of Schonkeit's own speakeasies, an elegant one, frequented by the kind of people to whom Mort sold his most expensive brands.

"Jake, you look good. You never get old."

"I stay in shape."

Schonkeit signaled a waiter. Jake wanted a glass of ginger ale.

"Wesselberg has to smarten up," Jake said.

"You understand, Jake, I can't control him anymore."

"Why not? He's yours. You set him and Frummer up in business. Trucking, extortion, kickbacks. This was your way of getting union contracts, Melvin?"

Schonkeit detested his given name. Jake enjoyed calling him by it. The Paymaster did not smile. He smoothed back his gleaming black hair. Patent-leather Kid, they once called him. Jake knew he disdained violence, ran from fights, never packed heat. He was a thinker, a brain, a schemer.

How much was real and how much was crap? Jake wondered. You get a reputation, and it grows and grows, and people believe it. He admitted that it was also true of the Chains. They were unbeatable, the other mobs and the police had begun to think. Too tough, too smart. It wasn't true. And he wondered for a moment why he had let Eva sweet-talk him into this errand.

"The guy has got to lay off Sol Heilig and his family," Jake said. "It's bad for everyone. He hurts anyone in Heilig's family, Melvin, it's the end for you also. They know you financed Wesselberg. You use him. You're the one should be stopping him, not me."

Schonkeit smiled. "Why don't we both try? He's here."

"I figured. The Paymaster knew when I called what I wanted."

"No rough stuff. I'll take you to him and you can talk. But keep your hands to yourself. He's under orders to do the same. He's afraid of you. You beat him up once, didn't you?"

"I should have killed him."

Schonkeit got up. "Wrong. If I did anything for the mobs, I taught them not to be violent, and especially to lay off cops. We can do anything we want with a fix. Come on."

Jake followed the Paymaster's dapper figure through the speakeasy. Society people ogled him. A famous reporter waved to him. He was a celebrity. He never missed a World Series, a championship fight, a theater opening. But there were rumors he was losing his grip. If the Democratic bosses went under, if Seabury nailed some crooks, Schonkeit would not possess the same power.

He led Jake down steep stairs and into a room where a poker game was in progress. Five men, unknown to Jake, were deeply engaged in reading their hands. They did not even nod at the two passersby. Down a corridor to a metal door the Paymaster led Jake. He knocked twice and the door opened.

"Go ahead, Jake. It's all right."

Jake stepped into a storage room. High shelves full of booze. The room had a cement floor and high cement walls. It smelled musty, winy, the way Goldsturm's old mixing vats used to smell after a busy day. There was a drain in the floor, a gutter running around the walls. For broken bottles.

Wesselberg was the only one in the room. There were two chairs and a small desk.

"Hello, Chain."

"Hiya, Meal Ticket."

"If it's all right with you, Jake," the Paymaster said softly, "Hymie would like to frisk you. You do the same to him. Then I'll beat it."

"Okay."

Jake held his arms up. If they tried anything, he was confident that he could move fast enough. Strangle Wesselberg and throw the fear of God into the coward Schonkeit.

Wesselberg felt Jake's pockets and trousers, nodded his head. When it was Jake's turn, he felt disgust and revulsion as he fingered the gross body of the old killer. No, he did not have a gun. So far so good.

"Both of you listen to me," Schonkeit said. "I want an agreement. I made peace with the Chains a long time ago, Herman. And you owe me plenty. So work something out. I'm going back upstairs."

Schonkeit motioned to them to sit. Nobody would listen in. Two businessmen, two men who had been around and could talk to one another. He left.

Bulging his elephant-gray suit, unshaven, Wesselberg gave off a stink like a swamp.

"So. You want I should lay off Sol Heilig."

"That's it, Meal Ticket."

"It ain't me. I didn't shoot at him. But I'd be happy if the slugs took his head off."

"Meal Ticket, you and Shikey are bringing in hit men from out of town. Dagos. You don't pull a trigger, but you got people who do. Schonkeit feels the way I do. It's lousy."

Wesselberg's face contorted with rage. The fat cheeks inflated, the eyes retreated in fleshy pouches. "He's trying to burn me. I never done what he said I done."

"So why are you worried? You come to trial, you'll beat it."

"Schonkeit says I got to take the fall. I'm the stand-up guy."

"Get any fatter, you won't be able to stand up."

"You Polack bum. You been on my back a long time. I remember when I seen you shoveling crap in Kolodny's stable."

"That's right. Remember what I did to Bunchik and Mendel with a shovel?" Jake leaned forward and cracked his knuckles under Wesselberg's nose. "I won't need a shovel. Big as you are, I could tear you apart. There's so much fat on you it might take a little longer to choke you, but, believe me, it'll be a pleasure."

Wesselberg said nothing. He gulped, mopped his brow.

Jake crossed his legs and smiled. "Get smart, Meal Ticket. Leave Sol Heilig alone. You'll have *tsuris*."

Wesselberg folded his hands on the table. "What do you know? I got a legitimate business. I'm well known in the garment industry. People respect me."

"Not for long. Labor rackets are finished. There's new guys in the needle trades. They'll get rid of you and Frummer. They'll cooperate."

"Not for long."

"Do me a favor. Lay off Sol Heilig."

"Screw you, Chain. You tell Heilig to lay off *me*. I'll get him the way I got his sister——"

Jake lunged from his chair. He yanked Wesselberg's flabby arms apart and went for his throat. The man was enormous, a dead weight of three hundred pounds. Lard, garbage. His odor infuriated Jake. He cracked the Meal Ticket across the face, tried to yank him from the chair. Wesselberg did not fight back; he bent his gray, long-haired head, ducking blows, whimpered, fell to the floor. Jake yanked him to his feet and hit him once in the gut.

"Bastard!" the Meal Ticket wailed. "I screwed your broad."

Jake punched him again, his fist swallowed by the gluttonous gut.

"Hit, hit, Polack. I'll kill Heilig. I'll kill his wife, all of them."

Jake stopped hitting him. What good would it do? He had *shtarked*, hit, beaten, gotten hit, for a long time. Violence was not for him any longer. Morty was smarter. Do it with contracts, papers, lawyers. What was he trying to do, beating this useless son of a bitch? There had to be another way. Let the cops protect Sol and his family. That was their job. He had his own life to live. Tommy, Little Mac, the boats . . .

The metal door opened. Both men were heaving and gasping. Wesselberg was wiping blood from his face. He looked at the doorway, goggling.

Sal Ferrante walked in. He looked sheepish and apologetic, as if he had interfered in something important. He stood in the doorway, hunched, his head drooping, his melting brown eyes full of self-pity.

"Sal?" Jake asked. "Morty sent you? I don't need help."

"No fair," Wesselberg growled. He blotted blood from his nose. "No fair. Beat it, wop."

"Mr. Schonkeit said I could help."

The suspicion formed too late in Jake's mind. He was vaulting across the cement-floored room. But Sal was twenty feet away. Too late. Jake could duck, hit the floor. But the chances were bad.

He was figuring the odds, reaching for the nearest chair as a weapon, when Sal opened fire with a .45 automatic.

Jake, who had taken twelve bullets and lived, took one this time and died.

Sal's first shot struck him in the forehead, made his face a crimson mask. Jake staggered forward. The body responded blindly. But there was no brain left. He clutched at the racks of bottles, dragged a few with him to the floor.

They clattered, broke, spilled liquor. Odors of fake scotch and adulterated bourbon clotted Jake's nose. He went slowly to his knees. His hands tried to wipe the blood from his eyes.

Sal shot him again at close range. The side of Jake's head blew away. Bits of brain and bone splattered the racks.

"Dead, ya bastid," Sal said.

Wesselberg wiped his face and stumbled away. He gagged and vomited into a grate-covered drain. "Leave it to the Paymaster. Using Chain's guinea."

His back was turned to Sal. Sal fired four times into Wesselberg's padded, hunched-over body. As the fat man, clutching at bottles, collapsed, Sal walked up to him and fired a final shot into the base of his brain.

When the five poker players entered the room, Ferrante was leaning against the racks, weeping discreetly.

One of the men shook him. "The gun, asshole. Gimme the gun."

Sal gave him the .45. He turned his head away as the men carried the bodies out of the storeroom and into the corridor.

One of the men came back and threw a wet sponge and a towel at Sal. "Clean up, jerk-off. We tol' you to keep it clean."

Three men dragged Jake's body along the floor, lifted it over the threshold, and bore it down a flight of stairs. The others followed with the Meal Ticket. The corpses went into separate cars to separate destinations.

Chapter 44

"He isn't at home," Sarah said shakily to her son. "Is he at Freeport?"

"No, ma. Don't worry. Pop is probably calling on a customer."

Morty stayed late in the office. Slow day, hot July weather. He turned on the Zenith behind his desk. Post and Gatty were due to end their record flight. Around the world in eight days! A record heat wave was under way. The estate of Baron Astor had just won a sixteen-million-dollar tax case. That's the way it goes, Mort thought. You had it, you kept it.

He wondered about Jake. He'd probably finished his meeting with Schonkeit and was on his way out to Freeport. Tommy had not seen him all day.

Mort had Schonkeit's private number. He called it. A secretary said that Mr. Schonkeit had left town. But she would leave a message that Mr. Chain had called.

It was now past six. Mort had forgone his evening session with Theresa. Too hot, too clammy. He had sent her home early. He called Long Beach, where Hilda and the kids were spending the summer in a palatial house a block from the beach. The kids were fine, she told him. Spent the whole day at the Lafayette Pool. But they missed him. Would he promise, for sure, little Marty asked, that he would come out for the weekend? And bring him a great big beach ball?"

"Promise, Marty. Kiss mama for me. Be nice to Davey and Iris. Learn to swim."

He began to worry about the old man. Crazy Jake. The wild man. Believing in his own power to survive, to wade into guns.

Over the years, Mort realized, his father had changed.

Tommy had been the difference. Calmed him down, made him less prone to violence, rid him of that wild fearlessness. But Jake would do anything for Eva. Anything. Sol was in danger, and Jake had ridden into combat again. Like an old western movie Mort had seen: Jesse James taking his guns out of a trunk to avenge someone.

Hell, life was not a cowboy movie. Schonkeit would surely have more sense than to lean on a Chain. But Wesselberg, that maniac . . .

To ease his mind, he called in Harris Weltfish and they talked about future plans—their line of legitimate brand names, how they would run their own distilleries for blending whiskey. It was bound to come about. If not after Hoover lost, soon enough. The country could not tolerate any more gang killings, deaths from poison whiskey, corruption. Wealthy people, politicians, university presidents, even ministers were against Prohibition. It would go. And the Chains would be ready.

Dr. Weltfish agreed. The key would be "blending." A less expensive process, turning out a cheaper line with a gentler taste, a light color, something easy on the mouth and digestive system. After years of throat-scorching poisons, vile and sickening concoctions, the public would appreciate soothing "blends." Weltfish wanted money for experiments. He wanted to hire distillers from England or Scotland.

Mort agreed and dismissed the young man. He liked him. A Ph.D. in Chemistry from City College was nothing to sneeze at. Mort respected learning, dedication, intelligence, loyalty. Sometimes he regretted he had not finished high school. Or taken courses at night. Still, a man could read, improve himself, learn about the world. Maybe this fall he and Hilda would not only visit England and France (he was arranging contracts to import French Cognac) but go to Germany, Austria, Switzerland. The world didn't end in Brooklyn. Of one thing he was certain: His children would go to the best colleges.

At six-forty-five he called Tommy again. No word from Jake. She was concerned also. He was usually in Freeport by midafternoon. He would take a swim, stretch his powerful body in the sun, look over the purchases.

A little past seven, as Mort was wondering whether a call to the police would be in order, his phone rang.

It was Sergeant McHenry, the new bagman.

"Mr. Chain, I got bad news. You better come out here before we move the car."

"Car?"

"Your father's dead. We found him in the trunk of a stolen Buick. In an empty lot down from the hardware store."

"You're sure? You're positive, McHenry?"

"Mr. Chain, I knew your father real good. I'm sorry as hell. You want us to take him to the morgue or you want to come out here? I could send a car for you."

"I'll drive myself."

It was a few minutes to the sooty garbage-strewn street. Police ropes had been set up. An ambulance was on hand with its flasher blinking.

A mob of beanie-hatted kids were standing behind the restraining ropes. One kid had a wooden gun made of the end of an orange crate and a rubber band and was miming shots into the opened trunk of the old car.

"The guy is dead."

"Hey, he got no face. Ya seen it, Mikey, no face?"

"Jeez, what a mess."

Heat, dust, stink. Mort braced himself as he walked through a gathering crowd of the curious. Mothers in cotton dresses yanked their children away. *Don't look, don't look, it's a disgrace.*

The words bounced against Morty's ear. His Brownsville. He was part of the streets, the gutter. He and his father.

"A dead guy. Someone got shot."

"Morris! Come upstairs! Geddada there!"

Sergeant McHenry shoved people away. He yelled at the police to make room. Two interns were removing a stretcher from the back of a Brownsville Jewish Hospital ambulance.

"It ain't pretty, Mr. Chain," the sergeant said. Mort was *Mr.* Chain. Jake was always Jake to the cops.

"How long . . . when was it . . . ?"

"They left the trunk slightly open. Wanted to make sure it was found. Some kids opened it. About fifteen minutes ago. He ain't been dead long."

Dusk settled over the steamy street. Hot, hot, as only asphalt and cement could be in July. Mort swallowed. He tried to calm himself. Not just a dead father. An empire was under threat. To kill a Chain was no small matter. Whoever did it had connections. For years the Chains had avoided violence. Mort had taught his father a better way—pay off, make it profitable for everyone, give service, organize.

He stared at his father's ruined head. Half of it blown away. A hole in the forehead, small, neat. A dark red gouge. But the side of his head . . .

"At close range, we figure," McHenry said. "If I know Jake, he wasn't ready for it. Someone pulled a fast one on him."

"Pop was getting careless, I guess." His voice was hoarse, distant. "Oh, my God. Oh, pop . . ."

They wrapped the corpse in a rubber sheet. It wasn't long enough. Jake's polished brown-and-white shoes, expensive summer kicks, protruded from the stretcher.

Mort made his mind up. Closed coffin. Short service. And he would get the murderers.

Sarah collapsed. She had to go back to the wheelchair. She rarely left it after Jake's murder. At the cemetery she wailed uncontrollably. Mort and Hilda stood behind her and tried to comfort her.

In the funeral home on Pitkin Avenue, Rabbi Piltz had been brief and casual, a little too much so for Mort's comfort. But the son did not take issue with the rabbi's stingy words. You lived hard, you died hard. The rabbi had no use for people like Jake Chain, or even Morty, he had made clear on many occasions.

It was a surprisingly small turnout. The Ferrantes came, Sal unable to look anyone in the eye. Baggie, Dom, and Theresa, she in appropriate black.

The Otzenbergers were there, and Eva and her daughter. Halstead was not present. Nor was Sol, who was still recuperating. Old Yussel Kuflik showed up, and Kalotkin the roofer and a wheezing Flugelman.

The last prayers were said. Stones were tossed on the burnished walnut coffin. Mort had selected a giant stone to be unveiled in a year's time. Sorrow was eating at him internally, but his vulpine face showed nothing. *Control. Confidence.* Courage in the face of disaster, he told himself. Somewhere, people were celebrating Jake Chain's death at age forty-six. A hard man, a troublemaker who couldn't be stopped, finally dead.

In the limousine on the way back to Haven Place, where they would sit in mourning for five days, Hilda took his hand. "Cry, Morty, cry."

"I cry inside."

"I really liked your father. I really did. He was a great guy. Who would want to do such a thing?"

Sarah's mouth was hard. "He lived bad, he died bad. Oh, my Jake."

Love had gone out of the marriage years ago, Mort understood. He was sorry for his mother, but he sensed a bitter sound of fulfillment in her mourning. Jake had provided well, comforted her, helped her to walk again. But there had been no love. Mort flinched inwardly. Was his own marriage going the same way? Were the Chains incapable of love?

"Some guy, your old man," Benny was saying. "Strong? I never seen a guy like him. Afraid of nothing. Right, Eva?"

"Right, Benny." Eva had sat down with Sarah in the parlor on Haven Place after they arrived and was holding her palsied hand. In the backyard, her daughter, Lillian, a shy, solemn girl, was climbing a sour-cherry tree. Marty Chain, seven, was trying to look up her skirt.

"What a man," Benny said. "No more like him. Afraid of nothing."

Dr. Abelman and his wife dropped by to pay their condolences. "A damn shame," Doc said. "I liked Jake. He was the only man on Haven Place could lick me at arm wrestling. You all right, Sarah?"

"Yes, yes, I'll manage, doctor. I'm going to live with my son."

Hilda looked horrified. She opened her red mouth. Her eyes popped slightly. News to her.

Abelman asked Mort how his children were. He had delivered all of them—Martin, Davey, Iris. Hilda and Mort bragged about them. They apologized for not calling Dr. Abelman more often, but it was a long trip from Ocean Parkway to Brownsville. He would understand. . . .

Abelman looked into the backyard. Weeds and stunted trees. Only the cherry tree, in which a leggy girl was climbing, was worth anything. His own yard was magnificent—peonies, roses, pepper bushes, magnolia. But the Chains were not people of the soil; they were people of violence.

Eva took Mort aside in the yard. They sat on a slatted bench and watched their children playing. Lillian had come down from the tree. Martin was showing her his marbles. He took out a "realie" and a "purie" and two "immies" and marked off a square in the packed dirt. "Ya ever play marbles?" he asked.

"No."

"I'll learn ya."

"Teach you, *teach* you." Mort shouted to his son. "Go on, Lillian, it's fun."

Eva laughed. "Very good, Mort. Lillian is a bit protected.

It would do her good to learn some of the games we played. Hide-and-seek. Boxball. Potsy."

Mort smiled. No wonder his father had loved his cousin. What a face. What a woman! But today she was subdued, something gone out of her.

Lillian hiked her skirt, knelt, knuckled an "immie," and tried to hit one of the stationary marbles. Martin shook his head and showed her how.

" 'My mother, your mother live across the way,' " Eva said. " 'Every night they have a fight, this is what they say.' I forget the rest. Mort, do you remember it?"

"No. I never had much time for games. I wanted to work with pop as long as I can remember."

Through the opened rear window they could hear Dr. Heilig and Dr. Abelman discussing Jake's death.

The coroner says the first one killed him. . . .

Second to make sure, took his head apart. . . .

Funny, Sam, I had the feeling no one could ever kill Jake. . . .

"Eva, you asked pop to help you, didn't you?" Mort asked. "About Sol?"

She nodded and put a handkerchief to her mouth.

"You wanted him to see Schonkeit."

"I—I—was sure Jake could help. Mort, I'm sorry. I don't know what he did, who he talked to. He said maybe he could stop them. Everyone said that fat man, Wesselberg, was part of Schonkeit's mob, I thought . . . Oh, my God, if I had anything to do with Jake's death . . ."

"Jake could take care of himself. Schonkeit didn't want any more killing. But the Meal Ticket . . ."

She looked at him. Tears filmed her eyes. Hard to believe Jake was dead. That powerful presence. Protector of the pickets. His primitive mind was never quite sure what it was all about—hours, wages, working conditions. Only that if you got hit, you hit back. She had induced him, with her smile, her face, the charms that made him dizzy and desirous, to go back into violence. And now he was dead.

"I can't apologize to you enough, Mort. You, Sarah, your children. Jake wasn't even fifty years old."

"It's all right, Eva. They won't get away with it."

Their children ran to them. Lillian liked her cousin Martin. He was so smart! He was giving her a "realie" and a "purie." He had taught her how to shoot marbles.

Mort stared a moment at Eva's daughter. Long, thin, pale, like her father. Not pretty, the way Eva was. Too much jaw and a narrow head. Suddenly he felt competitive. The need to match Eva's child with his own. She had found an easy way, marrying a rich *goy*. Nothing had been easy for the Chains. Everything had been dangerous. But for his children, it would be pie and ice cream all the way.

Hilda was summoning him from the window. Mr. Dunphy, Sol's assistant, was on the phone. Mort entered the house and took the call, pausing to kiss his weeping mother, accepting condolences from Dr. Heilig.

Dunphy had interesting information. On the same day that Jake had gone to meet Schonkeit, Wesselberg had vanished. Nobody knew where he had been that afternoon. His girlfriend said he had been checking his trucks in the morning, had lunch at his office, and then had gone to an afternoon meeting. Nobody knew where. It was not unusual for the Meal Ticket to make the rounds, intimidating customers, picking up bribes.

"What do you think, Mr. Dunphy?" Mort asked. "You think it's connected with what happened to my father?"

"I don't know, Mr. Chain. It could be. You said you think your father saw Schonkeit that afternoon?"

"He said he was."

"We'll have to have a chat with Schonkeit. And Wesselberg."

As Dunphy spoke, Herman Wesselberg was lying in six feet of lime in a grove of swamp maples and pin oaks ten miles from Route 17, the Catskills highway. The nearest habitation was a farm seven miles away. The grave had been well covered, and the Saratoga Avenue Meal Ticket was doomed to remain buried there forever, mourned by few.

Chapter 45

"You can stay here," Mort said to Tommy Tuttle. "You and the children. My father would have wanted it that way."

They sat on the upper veranda of the stucco house. It was a quiet afternoon. The Chain fleet rode quietly at the moorings. Bobbing gently, water slopping their sleek sides, they rested like domesticated dolphins.

"I loved him," she said. "I'm sorry. It's not the right thing to say to you. Your mother must hate me. And hate my children."

Mort looked over the railing and saw his half brother, Mackenzie (*Mackenzie?* What kind of a name for a Chain?), fishing for snapper blues from the pier. The boy was rugged, towheaded. Mort felt no kinship with him, but no enmity. A stranger. He was glad his father had known the good-looking woman, had the kid. They were nothing to Mort, less than nothing. But in deference to his father, he owed her favors.

"There's no will," Mort said.

"I guess that leaves me broke. I'm not worried. I managed for a long time on my own."

Mort knew about the lady captain running open boats out of Sheepshead Bay. Some reporter had called her "Madame Pirate," printed a lurid account of how she carried guns in her skirt, cursed like a petty officer. All lies. Tommy had dignity and style.

"We'll take care of you," Mort said. "And your children. You can stay in the house as long as you want. Pick out any of the boats. It's yours. Take two for yourself."

She shaded her eyes. She did not want to discuss property or money. She had loved the big man. "Stop," she said. Weeping, she turned her head. "Don't talk about those things. He's dead. He was the best man I ever knew. He wasn't afraid of anything. And he was kind. If he'd been educated or treated decently when he was little . . ."

"I know. But you'll be looked after. The company will keep you on as manager. In a few years we'll close this down, but you can have the boats, I'll see to it your kids go to school."

Tommy wiped her eyes and got up. Below, Sal Ferrante, in white-on-white shirt and brown silk trousers, appeared from the warehouse. He watched Little Mac fishing. Sal spit into the water, squinted up at the veranda, but did not wave to Tommy or Mort. He slithered into the garage. He liked dark, damp places. Mort thought. Always in the shadows. He belonged in warehouses, underground garages, storage rooms. A goddamn lizard or a spider.

"Why was he killed?" she asked Mort.

"I'm not sure. Maybe he was killed by mistake. I can't figure it out." He would tell her no more. She was not of the Chain blood. His plans for revenge were of no concern to her.

There was in Mort Chain a gutter instinct, street wisdom, cunning. Like his father, he could often anticipate connivance, treachery. He had not liked the way Sal had stared at them silently. Usually Sal came to him. He whined, complained, moaned. Another odd circumstance: Since Jake's death, Sal, a perpetual *kvetcher*, had not come pleading for a bigger chunk of the profits. *The little bastard*, Mort thought. You'd think he'd be breaking my chops, demanding part of Jake's profits. But not a word. The same shuffling creep, the same cockroach eyes. Why?

"The day my father said he was going to New York," Mort said. "Remember? The day they found the body?"

"What? Six days ago?"

"Yeah. Thursday. Was Sal around here?"

"Let me see. He's usually here afternoons, four or five days a week. Thursday . . . I don't think so. Wait. I'm sure he wasn't. Baggie came in with Anton. He was upset because Sal wasn't here to check the cargo. Baggie thought the skipper had shortchanged them. In fact he tried to call Sal in Brooklyn."

Mort dropped the subject. It was a tough one to figure. Schonkeit didn't usually resort to violence. And why be suspicious of Sal? Ferrante had gotten rich with the Chains. Stubborn as he was, he understood that he was a cheap hoodlum, a *cafon'*, without the Chain brains and muscle. Mort and Jake had built the business, come up with the big-money ideas. When they went legit, Mort decided, he'd buy Sal out. Maybe he'd keep Theresa on the payroll.

He was leaving Tommy, kissing her dutifully on the cheek, assuring her again she'd be taken care of, when an overseas call came through for him. London wanted Mr. Chain.

Mort took it in the radio operator's shack. Slow day, French, the old navy man, said, greeting Mort. No calls from the big boats.

It was McVey, the British executive. He was a bit upset. A New York attorney with important bank references had come to see him. Poking about, telling McVey of the unfortunate death of Mortimer Chain's father—"Awfully sorry, Mr. Chain, terrible tragedy"—and that McVey's firm might be making a dreadful mistake getting involved with people like the Chains. Odd thing was, this very lawyer showed up in Edinburgh two days later and gave the same story to the North Border Distillers, Ltd., another of the firms Mr. Chain had a contract with.

"It sounds as if he wants me out and his people in," Mort said. "What was his name?"

"A Mr. Bunthorne. Rather elegant young man. Wall Street firm."

"Who did he say he represented?"

"It was in confidence, Mr. Chain. Ah, well, you and I are partners, so to speak." (Mort had a secret deal with McVey and the other British distillers he had lined up. They were getting huge kickbacks, more money than they earned in three years' salary from their pinchpenny firms.) "He said he represented a Mr. Melvin Schonkeit."

Mort thanked the Englishman. It didn't take the Paymaster long to move. Whether he had anything to do with Jake's death or not, he sure as hell was going to use it. *Only sure things* was Schonkeit's creed. Mort felt confined, threatened. He had to move fast. He remembered the name: Bunthorne.

In early September, after Jake had been buried, and Wesselberg listed among missing persons, Mort relaxed in the Ocean Parkway mansion, eating a lonely dinner and listening to the radio.

. . . a canvas by supporters of Governor Franklin D. Roosevelt revealed that he will have enough delegate support for nomination on the first ballot, an Albany citizens group announced today. Governor Roosevelt's friends say he can muster eight hundred and six first-ballot votes, more than enough to secure the Democratic nomination for the presidency. . . .

Goodbye bootlegging. Mort made notes on a lined pad as he ate his chicken salad and sipped ice tea. Harry Twine, the Chains' man-of-all-work, served him. The black youth sat opposite Mort, waiting his employer's word. Hilda would never have permitted the help to sit at the table. But Hilda was in Long Beach with the children, the nursemaid, and the cook, cool in a ten-room house. Buster's son stayed in Brooklyn to help Mort.

"That Roosevelt, he good?" Harry asked.

"Yeah, I guess so. Don't interrupt, Harry."

Mort continued making notes. They had more capital, more cash, than they needed. What they would need was plant space, a delivery system, and, above all, unlimited supplies of neutral grain spirits. They would have to start distilling alcohol in advance of the inevitable repeal of the Volstead Act. There were millions of gallons of pure alcohol remaining in government warehouses. The Chains had tapped much of it. But not nearly enough.

Mort decided that was his next order of business. Sharp operators like Remus, in the Middle West, had made a fortune working scams with government alky. Mort needed the same kind of access until such time as Harris Weltfish could start manufacturing pure grain alcohol on a mass scale. It would no longer be possible to make a living selling rotgut, detoxified alky, fake scotch, phony gin.

"Mist' Chain," Harry said as he served Mort a dish of chocolate ice cream, "can I get an advance on my salary?"

"Why? You lose a big one to the bookie?"

Harry cleaned the table as the radio concluded the newscast. FDR was asking for twenty million dollars to help the unemployed; Hoover was warning that this would lead to communism; the French and the United States were lending the English four hundred million dollars to keep them from going broke.

"No, sir. I'm busted 'cause I *won* my bet."

Mort nailed Harry with a steely eye. He had always liked the kid, loved old Buster. Burned to a chunk of charcoal in the old place. He and Jake had promised Mrs. Twine the boys would always have jobs.

"You *won* on a horse and you're broke?"

"Rocco tapped out. He tell his customers someone hit him for a hundred grand on a horse and he is broke. All of us small bettors got to wait to get paid."

Rocco Lentini was the local bookmaker. He worked out of a speakeasy in Coney Island, one of Mort's customers. Mort knew the bookie, even though he and Jake had never played the horses.

"Someone took Rocco?" Mort asked. "I can't believe it."

"Yeah. He suspicious. Some hard guys make him pay off. So he broke. He think someone past-posting him."

Something stirred in Mort's mind. Something he had heard from Baggie about a racket, a way of screwing bookmakers. Getting race results *before* the bookies got them.

Mort had Harry call Rocco. Yeah, he'd be at the Golden Surf Social Club late. For the time being he was paying off with markers. He was sure Mr. Chain would understand. Harry Twine, that nice coon, would get paid as soon as Rocco got healthy.

An hour later, Mort sat in a damp cellar of the wire room, chatting with Rocco. The bookie was a neckless ex-pug who had fought under the name of Mickey Haggerty. Pinkie ring, a squashed left ear, a few gold teeth. At one time he had been a very hard guy. Two murder raps and countless arrests. But he had gone as straight as he could.

"I catch the punk he'll be floating in the river," Rocco said hoarsely. "There ain't nothing worster in the world than a creep cheats a bookie with a sure bet."

"Tell me what you think is happening."

"Some guy is getting results faster'n we do. He's smart as a snake, because he uses a different beard every time. And he never hits a bookie more than oncet a week. How can we tell when he's gonna hit?"

"How bad was the last one?"

Rocco studied a stack of betting slips. Behind him, his brother, Jimmy Guts, posted results from Santa Anita. A few bettors groaned. Losers again. Mort wondered where all the money came from. Guys selling apples, guys out of work, breadlines, relief, but the wire rooms had no shortage of suckers.

"The prick hit me for near a hundred grand, Mr. Chain. We got a twenty-to-one limit, and he bets five grand on Rosemary Kay at Jamaica. An allowance race. Horse pays eighteen-to-one. Guy's name was O'Toole, a fat mick. Says he's from Gerritsen Beach. If we don't pay, he's got a brother in City Hall. So I pay. I can't shit in my own kitchen."

"Rocco, how do you think they do it?"

"Beats me. A semaphore maybe, like in the navy. From the roof. Or a telegraph hidden somewhere on the track. Phones are out—they're illegal at the track. The Pinkertons patrol the tracks pretty good."

"Any suspicions?"

Rocco scratched his neck. "Every book I know thinks Schonkeit has something to do with it. I can't believe it. With all his dough, picking on bookies? The Paymaster set up half the bookies. It can't be him."

"Suppose I found out."

Rocco's eyes turned the color of raw calf's liver. The lids drooped and his voice was a growl. "Big as he is, he'll end up part of the Belt Parkway."

The following day, Mort visited one of the Pinkerton supervisors at Jamaica racetrack. He gave the man two thousand dollars in cash and promised to deliver a case of scotch to his home in Valley Stream that night. In return, the Pink was to "sweep" the track with a special squad, looking for hidden phones, a signaling system, or a Morse telegraph that might be sneaking out race results.

Two days later the Pinkerton assured Mort Chain (a

pleasure to do business with one of the Chains, and sorry about your father, sir) that the track was clean. His men could find nothing.

Sol Heilig, recovered from his wounds, was back on the job, a bit stiff in the arm and shoulder but ready to pursue his probe of the rackets. Jake's death had added a new element; but Sol and Dunphy were still mainly concerned with the Brunstein murder. They were convinced that Wesselberg and Frummer were behind it. But the fat man had evaporated without a trace. Shikey remained untouchable, secure in his offices in the garment district.

Sol regretted Jake's murder. He knew all about Crazy Jake's past. But he had a Brownsville loyalty to the tough man. After all, he and his brother Abe had taught Jake to read and write. Not a truly bad man, Sol reflected. There were a lot worse. He told Mort he would keep him informed if he learned anything.

One morning he telephoned Mort at the new Brooklyn Supply plant in Long Island City. Mort operated out of a fancy suite of rooms. Dr. Weltfish occupied an adjoining office when he wasn't in the laboratory.

"There's no question, Mort," Sol said. "Your father was with Schonkeit the day he was shot. He says Jake came to talk business. He denies anything to do with Jake's death. They talked, and then Jake said he had to see Wesselberg."

"Where?"

"Schonkeit says he has no idea."

Mort mulled the notion. Logic there. The Meal Ticket could have killed his father, then skipped town. He would lie low until the heat was off.

"We're also working on some old hoodlum who gambles in Schonkeit's game. The guy says he saw your father."

"What's the bum's name?"

"Joe Kuflik."

Mort paused. "He's an old *gonif* who used to work for my father. There's something fishy, Sol."

Chapter 46

"That got to be it, boss," Harry Twine said. "I been round and round the neighborhood. Lookin' for a place with a clear shot at the finish line. Three stories high. Big window."

Mort and the young black man were in the cab of a Brooklyn General Supply truck on a tree-lined street in Queens. Behind them and to their right was the Jamaica racetrack. In the back of the truck was Harry's brother Eddie, a huge muscular man. He worked as foreman for Mort.

"You sure?" Mort asked.

"I cased every house, every street. I climbed on roofs and over fences. Good thing you got me this phone-company suit and the tools."

Lithe and leathery, Harry was dressed in the olive-green uniform of a phone-company repairman. A leather belt laden with tools dangled from his lean waist. He also carried a .22 pistol. Mort had a .38 in his inner coat pocket. It was mid-September. A hot, hazed, nose-choking day, heavy with pollen and grit.

"On the third floor?" Mort asked.

"I figure. Hey, look."

A glint of sunlight bounced off something in the window. A glassy brilliant object was poking between the blue curtains.

"Okay," Mort said. "What can we lose? Park the truck opposite the place. You go first. You mind?"

"For Jake, I do damn near anything."

"Me and Eddie will be behind you. You get any lip, pull the gun."

The three men paused at the house. "Third floor, back stairs," Harry said. "Front door for the ground floor only. Landlord lives there."

They followed Harry up the narrow wooden stairs at the rear. No one seemed to be at home in the other two apartments. In fact, it almost seemed to Mort that they were deserted. Dust, old newspapers, silence.

Harry knocked at the third-floor door.

"A moment, sir, just a moment." The voice was frail and dignified. Mort motioned Eddie to stand behind him.

"Phone company," Harry Twine said.

"Ah, the inevitable phone company. AT and T, avaunt."

The door was opened by a slender, hollow-faced man of about sixty. He wore an eye patch and was smoking a cigarette in an ivory holder. His nose was invalid-thin and his Adam's apple bobbed. Long pepper-and-salt hair was parted in the middle. His tongue flicked at a hairline moustache as he studied Eddie's innocent black face.

"Ah, an Ethiopian. I sent for no phone company."

"There been a complaint," Harry said. "Got it here." He consulted a pink pad and read off the address.

"Cops," Mort said. He moved Harry aside. Eddie, towering, followed him into the room. Mort shoved his gun into the man's kidney. "Turn around. Frisk him, Eddie."

The man was unarmed.

"I daresay," he said. "I daresay, this is irregular."

"Here it is, boss," Harry said.

A pair of enormous binoculars were mounted on a tripod at the windows. Harry looked into them. "*Sheee-it.* Got him a clean look at the finish line. Ain't you smart?"

"A hobby, gentlemen," the man said. "My name is Colonel Elwood Craig, former owner of a large stable in Landona, Maryland. Undone by the events of 1929. This is my only mode of relaxation."

Mort shoved him into a sagging easy chair adjacent to the window. In front of it was a bridge table with four telephones, several pads, pencils, and a stack of *Morning Telegraphs* and *Daily Racing Forms.*

"Schonkeit want action today?" Mort asked.

"I don't believe I know the name."

Mort crashed the .38 against his jaw. Trembling, Colonel Craig wiped blood from his lip. "Dear me. I cannot abide pain. You're wrong, sir. What was the name?"

Mort pulled up a folding chair and sat down, leveling the gun at the man's head. Eddie and Harry wandered around the apartment. Unmade bed, kitchen sink filled with dirty dishes, an old white cat lapping milk from a cracked plate. There were large photos of Man o' War and Regret pinned to the wall. Old racing and horse-breeding journals littered the shabby furniture and the unswept floor.

"Tell us how it works, Craig. I'll blow your head off if you don't. But first I'll let these two guys work you over so you'll hurt like you never hurt in your life."

"He mean it," Harry said. "Eddie, look at this."

Eddie squinted through the binoculars. "Man, he got him the whole homestretch and the finish line. A race finishin' right now. Can see the number on the horse. Number five win."

Mort pointed the revolver at Colonel Craig's nose. "Schonkeit waiting?"

"Ah, no. No, sir. He usually gives me instructions between one and two o'clock. He can't be tied to a phone, so he usually restricts himself to the sixth and seventh races."

"You expect a call?"

"Yes." His filmy eyes pleaded for mercy. "I shouldn't be revealing this. I'm paid rather well, and betraying Mr. Schonkeit . . ."

Eddie and Harry were taking turns looking through the binoculars, shifting the focus.

"Mr. Chain," Harry said, "you ain't gonna believe this. I can see the tote board. Payoffs and all. This a maiden race. Pay five-to-two. Eddie, how come we ain't this smart?"

Mort picked up a telephone and dialed Rocco Lentini in Brooklyn. He told the bookmaker to drive out to the house near the Jamaica track. It might be a good idea, Mort suggested, to bring some other bookie who'd been caught with a big late bet recently.

It took a few more slaps, cuffs, and kicks to open Craig's mouth. It was pretty much as Mort figured. Schonkeit was using an army of beards. Not just in New York, but in Buffalo, Detroit, Cleveland, as far west as St. Louis. He'd get a confirmed winner from the "colonel," and while the bookies were accepting bets before the results came in, the beards would be given a number, bet the horse heavily, collect, and lie low for a few weeks.

"What does he pay you, colonel?" Mort asked.

"A hundred dollars a week."

"Cheap bum."

Rocco arrived an hour later with a bookie named Calloway, a choleric Irishman from Hell's Kitchen. He had tufted orange eyebrows and raging yellow eyes. Mort knew about him. Newsstand Calloway, an eccentric who wore Salvation Army suits, slept on a cot in back of his bookie establishment, and was worth four million dollars. He rarely spoke, but did a great deal of spitting on Colonel Craig's cracked linoleum floor.

They waited in the hot musty room. Eddie Twine went out for sandwiches and beer. It became chokingly warm; too many sweaty bodies lolling about on Craig's ramshackle furniture. Mort sent Eddie out again, this time to buy an electric fan and a cake of ice.

At three in the afternoon, Schonkeit called. Mort warned Craig not to give anything away.

"Yes, sir," Craig whispered. "The sixth race. Allowances for three-year-olds and up."

Rocco rubbed his chin. His bagging eyes were full of hate and sorrow. Any man who would cheat his bookmaker would eat shit, would make a whore of his sister. Schonkeit may have been the Paymaster, King Fixer, but from now on he was a target as far as Rocco Lentini was concerned. Newsstand Calloway agreed.

Post time for the race approached. Mort shoved Craig into the folding chair. The colonel held his head and whimpered.

"You be ready to phone him. Understand, colonel?"

"I do, Mr. Chain."

"You pull a smart one, the colored boys will tear your arms off. They'll pull your eyes out so you can't spot horses."

"Be my pleasure," Eddie Twine said.

"Race started," Mort said. He sat in Craig's chair and watched the race through the magnifying lenses. It was a mile and one-sixteenth. The finish line was in direct line of sight with the Zeiss-Ikon lenses. The number-two horse, Sandycove Boy, won by a length. Not a bad price either. Seven-to-two.

Mort turned to the colonel. "You getting him?"

Craig nodded. He was gray. The operator was buzzing Mr. Schonkeit.

"Tell him number six won," Mort said.

"I can't . . . I can't, really, Mr. Chain."

"Tell him number six or you're a dead colonel." He put the barrel into Craig's ear.

In a hoarse voice Craig said, "Number six." He hung up.

Rocco picked up a phone. "Let's see if the prick picks on me or you this time, Newsstand."

Calloway went to another phone. In a few minutes they had determined that neither of their establishments had been hit with a bet on the six horse in the sixth race. Rocco called a half-dozen more bookies. He hit pay dirt in Queens. Somebody named Lifton had placed a bet for five thousand dollars on the six horse, Andiron Dug, with a Maspeth betting parlor. Lifton had looked like he'd swallowed a live bluefish when the results came in with Sandycove Boy the winner. The Queens bookie told Rocco that Lifton had almost fainted, then raced to a phone when he learned the result.

Rocco grinned and slammed the phone down. "Thanks, Mr. Chain. You're okay. This clinches it. We'll learn Schonkeit a lesson."

Mort nodded. "Give him five minutes to eat his heart out. If he's placing bets around the country, he might have how much bet, Craig?"

"Forty thousand dollars, sir."

"It's forty thousand he can flush down the toilet, not to mention what he won't win." Mort looked at Rocco and Newsstand Calloway. "You guys are gonna have to do something. What's he taken you for over the last few years? Two hundred? Four? Five? The bookies' association is going to have to teach him a lesson."

They waited another five minutes. Mort ordered Craig to call Schonkeit again. The Paymaster was in his duplex penthouse on Central Park West.

Mort seized the phone. "Schonkeit? Mort Chain. I'm here with your spotter, Colonel Craig. We just screwed you on that race. The number-two horse won."

"Chain? What . . . ?" It was a rare moment of panic for the gambler.

"You heard it. A couple of bookies are with me and they watched the procedure. Rocco Lentini and Newsstand Calloway. There is going to be a meeting of the Greater New York Bookmakers Association tonight. A decision will be reached on how to handle people who indulge in past-posting."

Rocco ripped the phone from Mort's hand. "This is Lentini, Schonkeit. Tell your beard O'Toole he'd better run and hide. I'll blow his head off when I find him."

Mort offered the phone to Calloway. Newsstand waved his hand. No need to waste words. The code had been broken.

"Chain, what do you want?" Schonkeit asked. "This is a mistake. I don't know anyone named Craig. I wouldn't dream of past-posting. Something can be worked out. Tell me what you want."

"Who killed my father?"

"Wesselberg."

"Not good enough, Schonkeit. How? Where? He was with you that day. You better have some more ideas or I won't be able to influence Mr. Lentini."

Negotiations with Schonkeit for the repayment of the four hundred thousand dollars he had bilked from bookies went on for several weeks. Where money was concerned, the Paymaster stood firm: a misunderstanding; Chain had framed him. Craig had vanished. Schonkeit tried to divide the delegation of bookies that called on him—Rocco and Newsstand against the others. He threatened, cajoled, promised to pay off in installments. And he refused to tell Mort Chain anything about the death of Crazy Jake.

The first installment was ten thousand dollars in treasury notes, paid to Rocco Lentini. On attempting to deposit them, Lentini discovered that they were stolen. The bookie spent an uncomfortable day with federal agents.

Schonkeit tried to pay off a lesser bookie from Queens. The money, five thousand in hundreds, was counterfeit. Later, people wondered why he had panicked. They did not understand Schonkeit; cheating someone was more important than cash value.

On Saturday, October 17, 1931, Schonkeit was returning to his apartment on Central Park West in his chauffeured limousine. He had just attended the NYU-Rutgers football game at Yankee Stadium and had won ten thousand dollars betting on NYU, a 27–7 victor.

As he leaned into the window of his car to give the driver instructions, a man in a tan overcoat and a brown cap walked out of the lobby of the building and shot the Paymaster four times in the head and neck. He was dead before he hit the pavement.

The bookmakers' association professed no knowledge of the killing, arguing that, with Schonkeit dead, they now stood no chance whatever of regaining their stolen dollars.

The death of Schonkeit got Mort no closer to solving the riddle of his father's murder. But he was patient. He could wait.

His son Marty, an intelligent seven-year-old, had been enrolled in September in the Polytechnical Preparatory Country Day School (Poly Prep), the fanciest private school in Brooklyn. Davey was in kindergarten. Iris was at home.

Hilda became active in charitable affairs. Mort spent long hours at his new offices with Dr. Weltfish, laying the groundwork for repeal. They were working to beat the clock—a year away, they figured—and get into heavy production of legal whiskey.

Schonkeit's death had left a vacuum in the underworld, and into the void stepped meaner, more brutal men. They were largely Sicilians, once used by Schonkeit as enforcers, but now taking over as executives of the crime empire the Paymaster had put together.

An intelligent and imaginative man of twenty-seven, Mort Chain knew that he could not function in their world, and that in time they would seek him out. It was therefore obligatory that as soon as the Volstead Act was repealed, the Chains shed their underworld connections.

Cerrone, Razzini, Nudo, Notaro—they were names Mort had seen in the papers. Hoarse, dark-eyed men he had met in the past, as customers, suppliers, or as people who had to be paid off. Now they were rising like scum to the surface of a dank pool. Schonkeit may have been a liar and a cheater, but he had, Mort reflected (as he sat with Dr. Weltfish in his office), a kind of shiny class. The new criminal lords would have to be by-passed. Early on they would have to be impressed with the independence and legitimacy of the Chain operation.

Weltfish advised Mort to form a new corporation—a pharmaceutical house legitimately engaged in manufacturing cough medicines, tonics, and the like. Thus they could make new claims for government grain alcohol. Once they impressed the right combination of public functionaries, they would arrange it so that the moment repeal came, Chain interests would purchase entire warehouses and distilleries.

"We need them, Mr. Chain," Weltfish said. He was arrow-thin, with a beaked nose, black eyebrows that met over the bridge of his nose, a pointed chin, piercing black eyes. At City College he had been a champion high hurdler.

Mort and Dr. Weltfish worked long hours planning the takeover of warehouses. The bribes would be staggering. Government employees already paid off would have to be paid off again. Higher-ups and supervisors would have to be reached. Bonded warehouses could then supply them with pure alcohol until such time as Weltfish's distilleries went into operation. As importers of English gin and scotch, they would have a head start in the marketplace. But the big money, Weltfish explained, would be in "blended" whiskey.

"I'm sorry the old man didn't live to see this," Mort said sadly. "He would have appreciated it."

"Quite a guy, your dad," Weltfish said. The chemist did not go beyond that. Like Mort, he had a vision of the future. In it, there would be no place for a thug like Jake.

Mort buzzed Theresa and asked for the name of the firm that employed Bunthorne, the Wall Street lawyer, who had been cruising around England representing Schonkeit and trying to steal the Chains' distillers.

Theresa called back in a few minutes. "Horace Bunthorne is with Weed, Belanger, Ballison, Dean, and Bunthorne. They're at Ten Wall Street."

"Call him, Theresa."

They would need not only supplies, government contacts, customers, and a pharmaceutical company, they also would need the best legal counsel available. Mort studied the books, reviewed their profits and anticipated income, and realized they could afford the best. *Horace Bunthorne*. The name alone, Mort decided, would make him worth his fee.

He thumbed through the *Times*. Al Capone had gotten eleven years for income-tax evasion. Two misdemeanors and three felonies. The Chains would strive for respectability, operate within the law, say farewell to *shtarking*, violence, thuggery.

Except, of course, in the matter of his murdered father. He would pursue the truth until he learned it, and he would exact vengeance in the Chain tradition.

Chapter 47

The week before Christmas, Mort and Hilda shopped on Pitkin Avenue, their old neighborhood, buying Chanukah-Christmas presents for their three children. Prices were much lower in Brownsville, Hilda argued. She was an Otzenberger at heart, part of the old tradition. Her father, Benny, was getting old and lazy, anchored to the padded swivel chair in his office. But he still carried clout. Five times he had been summoned upstate for meetings with Democratic leaders, once by Louise Howe, Roosevelt's right-hand man. Would Brooklyn back FDR? they asked Benny. Was Carl Hubbell a pitcher? he responded.

Mort and Hilda, lugging games, dolls, a kiddy-car for Iris, a paint set for Davey, boxing gloves for Marty, came out of the toy store. Harry Twine jumped from the driver's seat of the Pierce-Arrow to help them carry the presents. He had been reading the morning edition of the *Daily News*. "Legs"

Diamond was dead. The clay pigeon had taken a fatal slug in an Albany hotel.

Mort shrugged when Harry showed him the headline. One more dumb hoodlum dead. The Chains were putting all that behind them. Soon the new company, backed by the Chain fortune, would lead them into corporate America.

"Beat it, bum," Harry Twine said. He was pushing a ragged panhandler, a shuffling vagrant. The man was trying to get to Mort.

"Mr. Chain, please, you got a buck for me? A little Chanukah gelt?" the man asked.

"Morty, get in the car," Hilda said. "Bums I don't need. Harry, get rid of him. Give him a dime."

"You and Rockefeller." Mort laughed.

"Mr. Chain, please?" He was a mass of rags, scraps of patched clothing. An unraveling woolen cap was pulled over his ears.

"How come you know my name?"

"I'm Joe Kuflik. I used to *shtark* for your father, God bless him. I'm sorry he died. They called me Yussel the Bear. I won't sell apples or go on relief. You got a job for an old man? Anything. Because I got something you should know."

"No promises. What do you know?"

"Could I have a dollar?"

Mort peeled off a ten and gave it to him. The hand that reached for it was like a hairy paw.

"Morty, come on!" Hilda called from the car. Harry tucked the raccoon blanket around her legs, stacked the packages in the trunk.

"When your father was killed, Mr. Chain . . ."

Mort grabbed the man's frayed lapels. "What about it?"

"I was working for Shikey Frummer. Shikey sent a bunch of us to the speakeasy where your father came. Later I carried out Wesselberg's body. Someone else got rid of it."

"What about my father?"

"Some—somebody—got both of them. I don't know how it happened. A fight—who knows? Downstairs, like a second basement. So they buried the Meal Ticket. Some other guys took away your father."

"Who killed him?"

"Please don't tell no one, Mr. Chain. That skinny guy who works for you. He was hanging around. I had to take a leak. I went outside and I seen him in the hall."

"Who? *Who?*"

"The kid who sold hokey-pokey. The one with the crazy eyes."

"Sal."

"I swear I seen him there. Maybe he came to protect your old man."

Mort gave him another ten dollars.

"Thanks, Mr. Chain. A Happy Chanukah to you and the missus. A good year, also."

"Same to you, Kuflik. Buy yourself a warm coat."

In the car, Hilda nestled close to him, locked arms, kissed his neck. "What was that all about?"

"An old friend of pop's."

"Such a long talk?"

"He wanted a job."

Careful, careful, Mort thought. Sal would have to be dealt with. With the Chain enterprises ready to turn respectable, there would be no need for Sal Ferrante anyway.

He might, he thought, keep Theresa on payroll for a while, then retire her when her age began to tell and she no longer satisfied him.

1960
Myron Malkin's Notebook

It's a plain office and he's a plain man, Sol Heilig. Mid-sixties. Stocky, rumpled, gray hair needing cutting. He's got tired gentle eyes, a snub nose, and a slightly ornate way of speaking. I can picture him in a courtroom. Polite, patient. *If it please the court, Your Honor, my client, Mr. Chain, has not been given an opportunity* . . .

"So you're out of politics, Mr. Heilig?" I ask.

"More or less. I don't like the way the Republicans are going. My heart was with the Fusion movement. Good government, no party labels. After LaGuardia died, I lost interest."

"How does the election look to you?"

"Kennedy. Close, but Kennedy. The fact that he's an Irish Catholic won't hurt him. It'll elect him. The Democrats are losing their grip on the blue-collars. The workers would run to Nixon in a second, but Kennedy will be one of theirs, so they'll vote for him. The only better candidate would be an Irish Catholic southerner."

"You're for Nixon?" I ask, amazed.

"I may sit this one out. I've always been my own man. I wish Norman Thomas was around."

"You're a Republican-Fusion-Socialist, Mr. Heilig?"

"Why not? I like General MacArthur. Myron, read about what he did in Japan after the war. The man was a liberal reformer. But the right-wing idiots who worshiped MacArthur didn't understand him. Politics is more complicated and subtle than you think."

A good man. Still at 60 Court Street, Brooklyn, the lawyers' building. He handles civil rights, criminal cases, class actions.

He's never gotten rich, like his brother, the noted surgeon, Abraham M. Heilig. He reminds me of my late uncle, Dr. Sam Abelman. A moral, honest man. But he isn't cramped by Uncle Doc's perpetual outrage. There's gentleness in Sol Heilig, a remarkable tolerance for human frailty.

A book on the Chains? He laughs. He anticipates my problems. Mort and Martin will never cooperate. When the time comes, they'll hire a historian and tell the story the way they want it told.

"And leave out all the rich stuff. You know a great deal of it, Mr. Heilig."

"Yeees," he drags the word out and stretches. His air-conditioning isn't working too well. There are cracks in the yellow plaster on the walls. Framed photos of Darrow, Debs, LaGuardia. A photograph of Eva Halstead taken sometime in the twenties. Out of doors, her hair flying, standing on a ladder, addressing a rally in Union Square. About what? Sacco and Vanzetti? She's beautiful in the darkened picture. I stare at it.

"You saw my sister?"

"Yes. She's fine. Too peppy for that old folks' home."

He shakes his head. "What a woman. She influenced Abe and me, let me tell you. Made us stay in college while she worked. I guess not many people remember her. Nineteen ten, nineteen twelve, the big strikes. People are more likely to recall the famous wedding. Jewish radical girl, rich Protestant fella."

"I have the clippings. It made big news."

"All us *shnorrers* from Brownsville, elbow-to-elbow with WASP society. Garrison wasn't a bad guy. But the marriage had to break up. It didn't matter that they were from different backgrounds. They were independent souls, big egos. Garry always felt she upstaged him, and I guess she did."

"And their daughter?"

"Lillian? Takes after me, ha-ha. She went into government work. Youngest deputy attorney general in the state. One of the first women to head the special prosecutor's office. She's in Washington now."

Sol Heilig shrugs. His successors came close to nailing Mort. I want to ask about the Ferrante murder, the blinding of Mort.

I tell him about the sightless man sitting on the screened porch overlooking a baseball field. And how he's rigged the game by recruiting over-age high-school stars for Camp Spruce Grove and how he loves a winning team. *That's Mort,* Sol agrees. And does he know the story of the counselors hefting guns during Prohibition, while the Chains smuggled whiskey across Lake Champlain?

He knows, he knows. What about Martin? Have I seen him?

I tell Sol that Martin was polite, firm, emphatic, and unemotional. Too busy with his horses, his estates, his corporations. In fact, there was almost a threat from him when I said I wanted to do a book on the Chain family.

"Marty's all right. Got a lot on his mind. Hell, he isn't even forty and he's the head of America's rising conglomerate. Liquor, pharmaceuticals, real estate, vending machines. Martin's so smart he scares me. Not that I see him much. I hear the other boy, Davey, the one in Israel, is a sweetheart. Big, tough, blond kid. Looks like Jake."

"Do you handle any legal work for the Chains?"

"Me? You kidding, Myron?" He laughs noiselessly. No, he's just a Brooklyn lawyer, shlepping along. Do I know the name Horace Bunthorne? he asks. Of Weed, Belanger, Ballison, Dean, and Bunthorne? One of those unpublicized multimillion-dollar Wall Street outfits. Not a Jew in the place, Sol says. But their biggest client is Chain Enterprises. A funny story, he says. Bunthorne, a young hotshot lawyer in the thirties, representing Melvin Schonkeit, went to Europe to try to steal Mort Chain's distilleries.

"Mort not only kept the distilleries but he hired Horace Bunthorne."

His mention of the legendary Schonkeit prompts me to ask him about the Paymaster's death in 1931. Unsolved. Wasn't Sol Heilig a rackets investigator then? Did they look into Schonkeit's murder?

"The story was that he outsmarted himself. Cheating bookies. They tried to get their money back, he refused, and pretty soon he was dead. Right in front of his apartment house on Central Park West. Nobody cried except his wife."

"But—the Chains—were they . . . ?"

"Nobody ever proved anything. Mort and Jake were never in gambling. I might be a prejudiced witness, being related to them. But we never could figure out a connection. There were rumors. Jake was probably murdered by one of Schonkeit's thugs. And it might seem logical that Mort would want to avenge his father. But it wasn't Mort's style to hire gunsels. We also felt Schonkeit was too sharp to be involved in Jake's death. But he did use those monsters, the Meal Ticket and Shikey."

"You sent a Frummer to the electric chair. Which one?"

"Shikey."

"That's right. In 1936, for the murder of a union official named Isaac Brunstein."

"Poor Ike."

"Eva said he was in love with her years ago."

"Who wasn't? I've become an anti-capital punishment man but I didn't mind nailing Shikey. He was no good. A heartless bastard. A disgrace to the unions. Bert Dunphy and I found the Italians in Cleveland who pitched Ike out of the window. Shikey and Wesselberg had put out the contract."

"And out of that kind of—of—horror, the Chain empire grew?"

"Hold it, Myron. The Chains were bootleggers. Culture heroes. Morty was invited to society parties in Great Neck. Mr. Chain, the importer. Jake had a wild streak in him, but his rule was to hit you only if you hit him first. Mort was never a real mean guy. He didn't carry a gun, can you believe it? And Martin? He's so respectable he makes me dizzy. If I see his photograph at one more worthy charity event, raising money for orphans, medical research, scholarships, and the Clean Up New York Campaign, I'll puke. Morty and Jake were more fun."

I remark that it's odd how many loose ends there are in the Chain saga. Nobody knows who killed Schonkeit. Nobody knows who killed Jake. And what about a thug named Salvatore Ferrante? Found floating in a Catskill lake with a dozen bullets in him? Was that ever solved?

"I'm afraid not, Myron. These people have a tendency to knock each other off. Sal was a spooky little creep. Big family. They were kind of expendable. The Chains used them up. Couple of them got killed in the early days. There was this good-looking sister who never married. Terrific body, long hair, skin like porcelain. She was an old friend of my sister Eva's. A sewing-machine heroine."

"And a friend of Mort's."

"Could be." He shrugs. "She was beautiful for a long time. Dropped out of sight during the war, sometime after Mort was blinded."

Another mystery. Two assailants. One a woman. Hurling acid into Mort's face as he came out of Loew's Flatbush in 1935. They couldn't save his eyes. One was destroyed, the other slowly deteriorated. The man and the woman escaped. Hilda went a little batty after that, Sol says. I make a quick connection: Sal Ferrante's corpse showed up for roll call around that time.

He's hiding something. Playing dumb. Weren't the Chains suspects in the Ferrante murder? I ask.

"But why kill Ferrante? Guys like that you can buy. And nobody ever beat the Chains at that. They bought half a congressional committee in 1946 when they wanted war-surplus chemicals."

"What's your guess?"

Sol says, "When people like Sal, or even a Schonkeit, get killed, it's not easy finding a suspect. Not that there's a shortage. The opposite. Too many people. In Brunstein's case, we narrowed it down pretty fast and were able to pin it on Frummer."

"It's funny, Mr. Heilig . . ."

"What is?"

"You and your family. And the Chains. Not the blood relationships, but the way you both came out of Brownsville. And it's like you and your brother and sister are one side of the coin, and the Chains are the other."

"I'm flattered. Look at me, a lawyer with two suits. I had to take loans to get my sons through college."

"It's not the money that counts. You've done a hell of a lot of admirable things. You still do. Your sister helped build the trade-union movement for women. And your brother—"

"Professor of surgery at Mount Sinai. Inventor of the Heilig procedure in thoracic surgery. We're what you might call achievers. Martin Chain can buy and sell all of us in one afternoon."

"But look how he got it. You can't kid me. There may have been a lot of bootleg whiskey in their rise, but there had to be a lot of blood also."

"Some. Some."

He won't be of much more help than the Chains themselves, than his sister Eva. It's not exactly a conspiracy of silence. It's a kind of grudging admiration for those skirters of the law, survivors, hard guys. A willingness to overlook their faults?

"What do you think of them? Make believe I'm not a reporter, just Dr. Abelman's nephew. What made them tick? What made them go?"

Sol Heilig brushes back his mussed gray hair. His eyes are misted with memories of Haven Place. "I don't know. Jake was a good egg. Not very bright. Good instincts. Morty was different. Smarter, meaner. My God, eighteen years old and he was running booze in a taxi. Ran the whole bootleg business when he was twenty. And Martin? Mort with a Dartmouth education, Harvard Business School, horses, a fancy wife."

"But they all must have had something in common, Mr. Heilig."

"Guts. Sheer guts. One thing about the Chains, kid. They were never afraid of anything or anybody."

PART IV

1950

Chapter 48

On the flagstone patio of the Roaring Brook Country Club (of which he was past president and founder), Mortimer J. Chain, with his one good eye—the left—watched the women's foursome, dragging a bit, walk off the eighteenth green and trudge up the vivid green incline.

Hilda had been dieting. She looked marvelous, although the iron girdle she wore, a tough contraption covering waist, butt, thighs, and the tops of her knees, gave her the appearance of a woman made of poured cement. But her lush hair gleamed black. Red lights winked in the wavelets. When she took off her white visor and shook her head, men stared. A big, well-formed behind and a smooth white face is much admired, Mort thought. Forty-eight. Two years older than he was and turning heads.

"Morty?" she called. "The gals and I are going to play a rubber of bridge before lunch."

He nodded. A happy family Sunday at Roaring Brook. The average annual income of members at this glossy new club, Mort estimated, was a quarter of a million dollars. There were (he had access to records) not less than twenty-six millionaires, and twelve men with net worths in excess of ten million.

Mortimer J. Chain, one-eyed, handsome, tanned, polite, helpful, was the richest member of Roaring Brook. He could not estimate his worth. Nor could the Internal Revenue Service. But he guessed that Chain Industries, Inc., the parent corporation, had to be worth over three hundred million dollars in inventories, plant, sales, cash, investments.

The club was elegant but not showy. Mort, planning it with a dozen other millionaires, had consulted the Chain lawyer, Horace Bunthorne, and asked for a tour of *his* club, the restricted, all-Christian Heather Cliff Country Club in Greenwich, Connecticut. Mort wanted to see how they did it.

As a result, the food at Roaring Brook was far better, the liquor was as good (the Chains' top lines), and both clubs manifested the same subdued elegance. Platoons of gardeners, maintenance men, and private police worked ceaselessly to keep Roaring Brook the showplace of the North Shore of Long Island. When problems arose, the helpful "Mr. Morty" was always available to solve them. He was a man, the members learned, who could talk to police, garbage collectors, town officials, golf pros, and his fellow oligarchs with equal ease. A few knew his background and understood why.

The women's bridge game included Mort's daughter-in-law, DeeDee Grau Chain, married to his son Martin; Martin's sister, Iris, recently graduated from Smith; and Horace Bunthorne's crosshatched, ash-blond, assless wife, Tucky. Mort hoped that Tucky Bunthorne, a reckless drunk, would stay sober long enough to finish the bridge game. She'd forgo lunch, of course. Christians, Mort knew (and was grateful), *drank* at country clubs. Eating was considered a sin against their religion. Roaring Brook, on the other hand, set a buffet table of such lavishness that the desserts alone were said to have caused more coronaries among the clientele than the crash of 1929.

"That's a nice bridge game," Martin said. "Mom's the best, by far. She can beat the other three with one hand. They ought to play three against one."

He and his father were seated, after a relaxed eighteen holes, at a mosaic table. They sat in the sun, away from the green-and-white-striped awning (Mort had ordered it from the English firm that made the Wimbledon awnings), soaking up warmth and heat.

Father and son could have been brothers. Both were dark, thin men with foxlike faces. Handsome, with thick hair rising in a black mane, growing somewhat low on the broad forehead. Long straight noses, rather harsh mouths, small ears flat to the narrow heads. The black patch on Mort's right eye, anchored with two bits of Scotch tape (a trick he'd learned from an advertising salesman who'd lost an eye in the Battle of the Bulge), seemed a device for telling the two apart. They wore white LaCoste shirts, identical Patek watches. Speaking, they made identical small emphatic gestures.

There was one outstanding difference, of course. Horace Bunthorne had noticed this as soon as he became aware of young Martin, then a student at Poly Prep (before transferring to Choate). Mort retained the cadences and dentalized *T*'s of Brownsville. The hint of gutter would never fully leave the patriarch of Chain Industries. Martin, while not speaking Eastern Seaboard Lockjaw (Bunthorne, an Iowa man, noticed these things), had adopted constricted vowels, a slurring of consonants. Poly Prep, Choate, Dartmouth (where he'd played varsity lacrosse), and Harvard Business School. All of these overlays, the observant Bunthorne understood, had minimized the Brooklynese in Martin Chain and created a strange-sounding, Christian-appearing young man, mysterious and candid at the same time. Martin, now twenty-six, would be more than a worthy successor to his father, Bunthorne felt.

"Mrs. Bunthorne's off," Martin said quietly. "Second martini, dad."

"Don't worry, Marty. She has her keeper with her."

A table away, in the cool shade, a large young black woman in a white uniform sat reading the *Daily News*. She looked powerful, slightly angry, and unimpressed by the surroundings. She sipped a Pepsi.

"I only hope she grabs Tucky Bunthorne before she hits the flagstone," Marty said. "All those fine bones. *Cr-ack*."

Mort rubbed his nose and sipped his club soda. "Margaret's got fast moves. Reflexes. Harry trained her. Bunthorne says she's the best nurse Tucky's ever had. And between us, she ain't afraid to belt Tucky on her chops when she needs it."

Margaret Twine was Harry's oldest daughter. The Chains took care of those who were loyal. Harry and Eddie Twine and their children would always have jobs in the empire. Fidelity and honesty were rewarded. Betrayers were destroyed. Of the multitudinous Ferrantes, none remained in the distilling corporation or its subsidiaries.

Although none knew the details (the secret had been buried with the death of old Kuflik), the police had long suspected that someone acting for Mort Chain had sent a perforated Sal Ferrante to the bottom of a pond in the Catskills. And the acid attack on Mort's eyes, years later, had been the obligatory act of vengeance from Sal's family.

Behind the Chains, hidden by a green canvas windscreen anchored to a Cyclone fence, Mort and Martin could hear the popping sounds of a tennis ball struck by good players. David, Mort's younger son, bursting with energy, was playing the club pro, Paco Guerrero. Paco had been a Davis Cup player for Venezuela. He could beat Davey any day of the week, but Davey would never stop trying. His tennis was rusty, but his strength and his desire were limitless.

"If only he had that kind of interest in the business." Mort sighed. He caught a glimpse of Davey's flashing figure. Tan, white, a shock of yellow hair. Jake's hair. Davey reached up, smashed, laughed as the ball sailed yards out.

"He's happy, pop," Martin said. "Let him alone."

"Happy. Yeah, I guess so."

Through the green screen, Mort watched the outlines of his son's leaping body. Yes, he was Jake. The strength, the long limbs, the huge hands and feet, the need to use the big body. This, as much as ideals, Mort sensed, was what had sent Davey to Israel in 1948. Mort remembered Hilda's ear-shattering hysterics, her buckets of tears, her threats to kill herself. Marty was away at Harvard, Iris at Smith. Davey was deserting them. Why not stay, now that he was out of the marine corps, and help pop in the business? My God, it was a miracle he had lived through the marines! Pop needed someone from the family at the corporate headquarters on Park Avenue. Mr. Bunthorne was fine, and so was Dr. Harris Weltfish, and the lawyer Sol Heilig had sent to Mort, Bertram Dunphy. But a Chain needed a Chain to work alongside him—Hilda sobbed her misery—especially now that his father was blind, *blind, do you hear, Davey?*

"In one eye, mom," Davey had said. "Pop's one eye is better than three on most people."

More shrieks. Sobbing in the bathroom. Fainting in the bedroom.

"You want to go kid, *go*," Mort had said.

Former Marine Lieutenant Al Seligman, Davey's platoon commander on Okinawa and Iwo, embraced Davey and hugged Mort. They'd leave that night and join a Palmach unit, special attack forces, at a camp outside Haifa.

"Mr. Chain," Al Seligman had said, "I hate to do this. It's not fair. I've been a guest here three days, brainwashing your son, and I've made your wife hysterical. But those people need everything. Medicine, guns, signal equipment. I took a son. Can I take something else?"

Mort took the chunky young man and Davey into his study. "What did you have in mind?"

"Money."

Mort gave Seligman a business card. "Come to my office with Davey tomorrow at noon. You'll get a check for a hundred thousand dollars. Tell me how to make it out, the best way to convert the funds."

"No problem. We've got banks all over Europe. The guns come from everywhere."

"Seligman, one more thing. Bring Davey back alive and there's another hundred thousand. Win the war against those *mamzerim* and there's another hundred thousand. Maybe more."

Davey shook his thick blond hair. Embarrassed. Humiliated. "Holy smoke, pop. If you think this means I'm going to be Al's stooge, a cook, or a clerk, you're nuts. They need soldiers. I'm qualified with twelve weapons. Al, don't listen to him."

Seligman winked at Mort. "No favors for you, Dave. You weren't that kind of marine, and you won't be that kind of *Palmachnik.*"

Mort understood. He'd suddenly cried, risen from his desk, and embraced his younger son. The wild one, the lousy student, the college dropout, the taker of chances, the fighter.

Jake, Jake again. Hit me, I'll hit you back.

Davey and Seligman left three days later, with the international money transfer to be deposited in the Athens branch of a London bank. A month later they were smuggling M-1 rifles onto deserted beaches. In late May their unit helped capture Safat and liberate the northern Galilee.

Now what for Davey? Mort wondered. He decided not to worry. The kid would always have something to do. But the business, no. That was Martin's. Martin had brains, tact, education. He enjoyed handling money, lunching with bankers and investors, buying French wine, selecting fine horses.

The waiter brought club soda for father and son. They rarely drank. Mort knew too much about booze. Martin, a bit of a health nut, found it did nothing but parch his throat. He never understood why people who craved alcohol said they were "thirsty." Or writers about Prohibition who spoke of the "thirst" of the people.

"Thanks, Juan," Mort said. He handed him five dollars.

"Thank you, sir. Note from the gentleman at that table."

Mort's left eye looked across the sun-splashed patio, the bright green plantings of ilex, yews, and privet, the burnished flagstone, the tables at which animated, handsomely dressed golfers drank and ate. He located the sender of the note. It was old Leo Glauberman, waving feebly, pointing to a dark thickish man seated with him.

Glauberman! Good God, he went back to Jake's era— 1910, 1912. The "labor consultant," the Teddy Roosevelt of Brownsville. He had to be in his eighties. But fixing, *hond-*

ling, arranging. He'd outlived his old rival for power, Benny Otzenberger, and was an enormously rich man, sleek and fat on profits from labor rackets, fees for defending hoodlums. After the death of Schonkeit, the Sicilians had moved in. Glauberman had survived among those snakes, advising, consulting, trying to make them appear respectable.

"Old bastard," Mort said. "My father hated his guts. I think he tried to finger Jake once."

With cold shaded eyes, Martin glanced at Glauberman's beaming face. The hair was roached, white, stiff. The skin was the color of an oiled bicycle saddle. "What does he want, pop?"

"The guy with him wants to shake my hand."

Mort showed the card to his son. Four tables away, Mort could hear Hilda saying to Mrs. Bunthorne, "Tucky, never play trump on my honor."

"Sorry, Hilda."

"Mother, stop being so *technical,*" Iris said. She was bored by bridge. But her father had asked that she be nice to Mrs. Bunthorne.

Martin read:

Dear Morty,
My friend and client Mr. Ruggiero Pisano wants to say hello and shake your hand. He's a sweet guy. I'll stay here and sip my tea. I'm old and I don't move too good.
Leo

"Important?" Martin asked.

"As important as horse shit in the street."

"Why does Glauberman do this?" Marty asked. "He knows you hate him." He twisted his Dartmouth ring, winced inwardly. The scum that surfaced from time to time! Memories of his grandfather's bloody past. He yearned for the day when no one would remind him.

"Leo's soft in the head. But who knows when people will be useful?"

"You know this ape?"

"No. But I can guess."

Mr. Pisano, potbellied, in crimson shirt and rose Daks, exuding Habit Rouge and patting his artfully barbered hair, silver-gray on coal-black, approached the Chains' table. He wore, Martin noticed, black alligator shoes that sold for a hundred and fifty dollars.

Thwack. *Thwack*.

Mort heard the sounds of Davey's racket, of Paco's hard strokes. He envied them. Someone said Davey could have been tournament caliber if he hadn't screwed around so much with contact sports. He'd broken a knee, sprained a shoulder, sustained a concussion. Enlisted in the marines in time for two of the bloodiest invasions of the war. Then Israel, and getting wounded again, and enduring God knows what with Al Seligman.

The cleanness of Davey's life and character filled Mort with a murky hatred for the likes of Ruggiero Pisano. He could not explain it. It was as if he would like to kill Pisano, throttle him then and there, to preserve Davey, to let Davey live forever.

"A pleasure, Mr. Chain," Pisano croaked. "I think we met after the war. When you was in the chemical business."

"I still am."

"Oh, I din't know. I think we done some hauling for ya."

Mort made no move to introduce Martin. His children did not have to be exposed to such vermin. Marty, more tolerant, extended a tanned hand. "Mr. Pisano, I'm Martin Chain, Mr. Chain's son."

"Pleasure, pleasure. Hey, ya look like your father. I wish I could buy a drink, but it's your club. Mr. Glauberman, he won't let me pay for nothin', and, gennulmen, I'm the kind of guy who picks up tabs." He stopped talking as the Chains regarded him with stony eyes. "What am I sayin'? Since when do the Chains need anybody should buy a drink for them?"

"That's right," Martin said.

Mort had gone rigid, silent. Martin, a more polished man, feared these moments. The old Chain capacity to hate. To draw back. To calculate. Yet Pisano seemed harmless enough. A hoodlum looking to meet "high-class" people.

Martin glanced away from the uninvited guest's swarthy face. He'd seen many such faces working for his father— drivers, warehousemen, sweepers. But there was more in Mr. Pisano's morose features. A sense of command.

Martin could see Davey toweling off, shaking hands with Paco, who was a head shorter. They were laughing, teasing. Jock talk. "That's all she wrote," Davey said. "You beat me like a gong, *amigo*."

Across the patio, his mother, his sister, his wife, and the blond woman with a face like a road map of drunken disasters were bidding.

Three hearts.

Pass.

Three spades?

Four diamonds.

Oh, is it my turn? Sorry. Three hearts. I guess.

"Tucky," Hilda said with great patience, "you bid three hearts *last* time. Iris just bid four diamonds. It's got to be four hearts, if you want to stay in hearts."

DeeDee turned her head and blew a kiss to Martin. He winked at her. German-Jewish by way of Central Park West. And he was Russian-Jewish by way of the Brownsville gutter. And they'd ended up on Fifth Avenue. A fun couple. A couple everyone wanted at their parties. *Bullshit,* Martin thought. DeeDee's beautiful and I'm rich.

"My idea is this, Mr. Chain," Pisano was gargling. "I got services to offer. Maybe cost you less than what you're paying. Cartage. Pickups on chemical waste. A contract for the distillery workers, the clerks, to your advantage. I got connections."

"What else do you have?" Mort asked.

Bulky white sweater thrown over his shoulders, Davey walked up the stone steps. He sat on the brickwork balustrade some distance from his father and brother, and listened. Around his neck was a gold chain. The Hebrew letter *Ch'ai* on a gold amulet.

"Like I said, Mr. Chain, connections. You would never have a day's labor trouble—"

The sons watched attentively. Davey was puzzled. Martin (who spent much of each day with his father and knew him well) was smiling. Mort interrupted Pisano. "Hold it, Pisano. Hold it."

"Whatever you say, Mr. Chain."

"Two years ago I had labor troubles. Some bastards tried to organize my drivers. We already had a contract. We pay more than scale. We got better pensions. Some tough guys come to see me. Mr. Chain, we'll give you a better contract so you can fuck the drivers—"

The word "fuck" hung in the hot clear air like a fart, and DeeDee's alert pearly ears caught it. She glanced archly at her husband, as if to say: *Oh, your elegant family.*

"—and I said, if you dagos think you're gonna get my drivers to strike or organize them in a union they don't want, think again. I'm a Chain. My old man was Jake Chain, and he was the toughest bastard ever walked the streets of Brownsville. So I—"

"Please, Mr. Chain," Pisano said. "I'm only trying to help. Mr. Glauberman said—"

"I said to this *walyone,* you throw a picket line around my distillery, I'll be the first one to drive a truck through. And there'll be a shotgun on the seat next to me and a forty-five in my lap. The first picket, whether he's a coon, a wop, a hebe, or a mick, who tries to stop a Chain truck gets a head full of lead. *Capisce,* Pisano?"

"Yeah, sure, Mr. Chain." His jaw dropped. The silver-on-black head looked debrained. "But look—take cartage, for example—"

"No cartage. No hauling. Go home and kiss your godfather's hand. You don't scare a Chain. Pisano, the worst thing you could have going for you is that Glauberman recommended you. Beat it. I'm having lunch."

Chastised, Pisano walked back to Glauberman.

"Easy, pop," Martin said. He locked his hands, watched the hood closely. Pisano looked as if he'd been pistol-whipped.

An innocent, Davey was astonished by his father's vehemence. He pulled the sweater around his shoulders. In the shade of the awning he was chilled. So little contact had he had with his father, and his father's way of life, that the savage encounter had shaken him.

"Pop," Davey said, "you really let him have it. You turned him down and you insulted him."

"That's what he understands. To a bank president I talk different." Mort patted the black patch. He made sure the Scotch tape was anchored. People used to whisper that he could see out of the right eye, that there was an invisible pinhole in the patch through which he clearly saw his rivals, associates, government officials. More than they wanted him to see. Mort's *camera oscura,* Horace Bunthorne called the patch.

Martin was shaking his head in appreciation of his father's performance. He got up. The bridge game was over. There'd be seven for lunch. Tucky Bunthorne would join them, eat nothing, swill martinis. Margaret Twine would be seated out of view, watching for the first signs of collapse.

Davey lifted his rackets and followed his father and brother toward the bridge table. "Pop, who was the guy tried to muscle you a few years ago? The one you mentioned to him?"

"It was *him.* Ruggiero Pisano. The dumb bastard called

himself Rocky O'Brien then. They always want to be Irishmen."

Mort kissed Hilda's cheek. Even with Tucky as a partner, she'd thrashed her daughter and daughter-in-law.

"Mom's too good," Iris said. "She should play with a handicap, like in golf."

They were given a prize table overlooking the golf course. Halfway through the meal, Tucky Bunthorne began sliding toward the floor. Margaret Twine, gliding on rubber-soled white space shoes, was there to prop her up and walk her to the car. She would drive her home and put her to bed.

"I wish Horace were here," Hilda said. "Why he lets his wife run around getting boozed like that . . ."

"He's doing his own weekend boozing on his boat," Mort said coldly. "It keeps them alive. That's why I hired him. In my *ganze leben* I never saw a man drink so much, stay so clearheaded, and get so much work done. Right, Martin?"

"He's a damned good executive. Great lawyer, too."

As they ate—tangy seafood, satiny avacados, crisp salads, hot rolls, iced drinks—Martin studied his wife. She was disdainful of Roaring Brook. It was a "new money" place, DeeDee complained. A bit excessive. Martin would have to learn the advantages of the worn look, casual understatement.

Mortimer J. Chain, her father-in-law, did nothing that was not distressingly in excess. He had supervised the kitchen, found the best lobster pound, ordered vegetables directly from Chinese growers on Long Island.

This Central Park West snootiness had not deterred DeeDee's father from permitting his ivory-skinned daughter to marry the grandson of a gangster. The truth was that the rarefied Graus were broke. Mr. Grau had lost it all in 1929 and was supported largely by his second wife, an aristocrat with a small inheritance.

"Money is not everything," DeeDee's stepmother, Grace Korn Grau, told father and daughter when DeeDee announced she would marry Marty Chain.

"Yeah," Mr. Grau said moodily. "Confederate money. Czarist rubles. What the Chains have is real money. We should not complain, Grace dearest. DeeDee can take off their rough edges."

The in-laws had nothing to do with one another. Both Martin and DeeDee liked it that way. DeeDee was talking about taking a master's degree in business. The Chain empire intrigued her. She wondered if she could work somewhere in it. Martin had no objection. Hilda and Mort thought it a dreadful idea. DeeDee was much too refined, too exquisite, for the rough-and-tumble of the Chain businesses.

Sulking, DeeDee secretly met with Mr. Bunthorne, Mort's operating officer and chief counsel. Horace Bunthorne thought it was a sensational idea. So DeeDee registered for business courses at NYU, dropped them in a week, and was now trying her hand at ceramics.

Squeezing her knee under the table, Martin decided she could do anything, be anything, so long as she remained his wife, let him possess her long body, share the fineness, the good breeding, the indefinable superiority that coursed in her veins. Through the magic of sexual union she would make him a better person. It was no small thing to be a Grau. They were Jews who had come to the United States in 1849, and at times seemed to Martin more Christian than the mid-western likes of Horace Bunthorne and his sodden Tucky.

"My children are all together for a change," Hilda sighed. "I'm so happy today. Just as well that drunken lady went home. Our dear family, seated at one table. If only my father, your father, Morty, were here to see us. Look at Davey, how big, handsome! And Marty, handsome also. And what a head for business! And DeeDee, our new daughter. And—"

Iris held up a hand. "Stop. *Stop*, mother. I don't want to hear about your dollink daughter Iris. The black sheep. Or ewe, or something."

"Never mind, Iris. It's very few people got a daughter who graduated from Smith's."

"Smith, Mother. No apostrophe *s*."

"So I'm proud of you," Hilda said. "No matter how much you knock it. Tell me, Martin and DeeDee, you have heads on your shoulders. Why do young people knock everything? All Iris does is poke fun at her achievements."

"She's kidding, mother," DeeDee said. "Aren't you, Iris?"

"Like hell I am."

Iris planned a future as a screenwriter. She had not told her parents. They would not have understood. Writers? What were they? But she had confided in Davey, with whom she had been close since childhood. She was physically similar to Davey. Both were throwbacks to Jake. Broad-shouldered, heavy-breasted, she had long strong limbs, a superb throat, fair skin that freckled easily, and thick brown-gold hair. She was not a beauty—a wide Slavic nose, narrow slanted eyes— but she carried herself well and her flippant manner attracted men.

"Language, Iris," Hilda said.

Iris marveled at her mother's gentility. Out of a steamy slum, daughter of one of New York's more flamboyant political fixers, Benjamin Otzenberger. Hilda never read a book, merely glanced at newspaper headlines, owned a head full of bridge games, Mah-Jongg, beauty parlor appointments, benefits. And yet so genteel, so grand. Iris preferred her father's coarseness. Martin? A bit too slick. Eldest son, beneficiary of primogeniture, plunging into the family millions, the super-corporation that had exploded after the war.

Davey was her favorite. A little empty-headed, wonderfully naïve. He would not have lasted a day making the rounds of bars peddling Chain brands, bribing owners, buying drinks for the boys—the usual apprenticeship for a Chain executive. Davey was a man you could never nail to a desk and a swivel chair, with an adding machine, a date calendar, *In* and *Out* baskets. Indeed, Iris thought as she looked at Davey's unsubtle face, he was a man you could hardly force to wear a tie and a suit. She had seen pictures of him as a marine corporal in battle fatigues, as a *Palmachnik* dynamiter in desert tans and jump boots. Dusty, sweaty, full of courage.

"I'm so proud of my children," Hilda sobbed.

Mort cautioned Iris, who was tossing her hair angrily, not to interrupt. Let Hilda have her *nachas*, her pleasure. It was rare that all of them were together. Mort, too, was glad that Mrs. Bunthorne had gotten herself sodden and been carted home to Greenwich. Let six-foot-eight Horace, with his praying-mantis face and arms, have his Sunday ruined. When he got back from his "drinking boat," they'd battle all night.

"Marty, my oldest, the executive. DeeDee, God bless her, from Wellesley's. Iris, a graduate of Smith's."

"It's plain Wellesley, mom," Iris said sharply. "It's Smith, not Smith's."

"Let me enjoy," Hilda said. She sniffled into a handkerchief. In her mind she was recalling the day she'd taken the taxi ride to Montreal with Morty and the repulsive Salvatore. And how Sal had blown the Canadian's head off. The mad chase across the border. Hilda sobbing and puking all the way to Plattsburgh. It was as if her relationship to Mort had been sealed in blood.

"And Davey, who'll finish college now that he fought two wars, my hero," Hilda went on.

Davey smiled tolerantly. Not a conniving or ambitious bone in him, Iris knew. The best of the three. No plans, no commitments, not even a steady girl.

"I'll finish college in Israel, mom," he said.

"Come on," his father taunted. "You told me your Hebrew stinks. If all the guys in your outfit weren't mostly Americans, you'd be dead by now. You couldn't holler 'duck' in Hebrew."

"I'll learn."

"No!" Hilda said. "Enough being a hero! You'll stay here! You'll go to college. You'll work for your father!"

"Do what you want, Davey," Iris said.

"He will without you telling him," Martin said. "He always has."

Mort sipped iced tea, accepted obeisances from club members who wanted to exchange stock-market talk or political chatter.

Christ, Iris thought, they do everything but get on their knees and kiss the old man's ring. She loved her father, but she was rendered uncomfortable by his power. It was not just the massive wealth, the millions that poured in endlessly, but a kind of mystical power that he possessed. She knew the old stories. The origins of the fortune in blood, violence, and crookedness. She did not fear it. But she could not fathom it, nor did she wish to be part of it.

Paco, the tennis pro, came by. He was doll-size and muscular, with forearms of a man twice his size. Browner than a Polynesian, he spoke softly to Davey. "I got no lessons, *amigo*. You wanna try to beat me again?"

"Why not? If I get three games from you it's a moral victory."

Davey was on his feet. A big man with an agile body. "Sorry, folks. Paco's not happy unless he gets in three hours with me."

When they had left, Mort laughed. "He thinks the pro lets him play for free. Wait, it'll be on my monthly bill. Tennis lessons at twenty bucks an hour."

"You can afford it," Iris said. "You can afford a pro, a court, and your own tennis team. Daddy, what can't you afford?"

"Iris, stop at *once*," Hilda said. "Don't ruin what has been a lovely day."

Mort pinched his daughter's tanned cheek. A big blond woman, twenty years old, a bit unformed. "*Ketzeleh*, you're right. I can afford anything. As a matter of fact you got an appointment with United Artists on Wednesday. They heard my daughter was interested in writing for the movies and they loved the idea."

Hilda beamed.

Martin nudged DeeDee under the table, as if to say: What we want, we get.

Iris overcame her humiliation. She gritted her teeth.

Chapter 49

"I thought you might have chosen Luchow's out of sentiment," Eva said. "Good God, wasn't that a long time ago . . . ?"

"Our first date," said Halstead. "No, my dear, the memories are hazy and a bit painful. Our very first date was at Gage and Tollner's. Luchow's was later. The German barbarousness didn't faze you in the least. Not even the enormous schnitzel. But then nothing ever did."

They were in the Sixty-Eight restaurant on lower Fifth Avenue, not far from the brownstone Eva had been awarded in their divorce settlement. Halstead had not remarried. He lived with a woman thirty years younger, an abstract artist of ancient Boston lineage. a gaunt woman with a face like white granite. They shared an apartment in the West Village. He and Eva had been divorced in 1941. Prior to that, they had not slept together for many years. The breaking point (insanely, Eva recalled) was Halstead's refusal to accept lend-lease.

Garrison Halstead, once a devotee of Eugene Debs and Norman Thomas, a man of moderation, a believer in democratic reform, had nestled closer and closer to the Stalinists. Ultimately he had become, to Eva's distress, an avowed Communist. True to her Social Democratic principles, she backed Roosevelt on aid to Britain and France. She had seen what had happened in prewar Germany—Communists letting the Nazis take over, rubbing their hands, convinced they'd pick up the pieces. *After Hitler, us.* Outsmarted, beaten into submission by the SS, they ended up in the same concentration camps with the Socialists they'd attacked as "Social Fascists."

It's strange, Eva thought, how two of the men who loved me drank of the Red cup. Ike Brunstein, who ended up sailing out of a window. And now Halstead, a millionaire's son, one of the walking wounded, a brand from the burning. When the anti-Red probes had started in Congress after the war—the House Un-American Activities Committee, McCarthy, others—Halstead had proved a voluble, cooperative, blabbing witness. He named everyone he could think of, including his ex-wife, the writer and lecturer, Eva Heilig. His communism, overnight, became anticommunism. His wife's socialism, for the benefit of congressional probers, became communism.

"I'm glad you're not angry with me," Halstead said now.

"But I am. I think you're dreadful. How do you sleep at night?"

"Not too well. But I did the right thing. The Hiss case bears me out. Guilty. A traitor."

"As usual, you haven't got it right. Hiss was convicted on two counts of perjury. Not treason."

Halstead stroked his iron-gray hair and lifted his prognathous jaw. "Precise as always, Eva. Good God, you're the most beautiful sixty-four-year-old woman in New York City. Snowy hair, not a lock out of place. I like it piled high like that. And the carnelian earrings I bought you in India. Oxford-gray suit, elegant legs, smart pumps. You look ravishing. How do you manage?"

"Garry, you are a bore."

They ordered mussels, veal piccata, tossed green salads, a pale dry Chablis. Indifferent to food, Eva had always let him order. She listened to his slightly cracked voice and marveled at his staying power. Liberal, radical, Socialist, Communist, anti-Communist, reactionary. When would he agitate for a corporate state with pink-cheeked prep-school storm troopers?

. . . The chairman, and the rest of the committee, Mr. Halstead, is most appreciative of your cooperation. Mr. Halstead, it puzzled many of us that a man of your background and education could involve himself with such subversive and un-American elements, that you should give them funds and advance their causes, and the committee wants to thank you for so frankly revealing . . .

"I'm sorry I named you, Eva," Halstead said, as he extracted a hot *moule* from its silvery-black shell. "Why did I do it? You were never a party member. You fought us. You denounced us in little magazines."

"Revenge."

"Oh, no. Don't think that."

"Of course. I was better known than you for many years. I think that I had twice as many articles published as you."

"That's not so. I was traveling a great deal."

"Fellow-traveling?"

"I guess I didn't hurt you too much, did I? I mean, your income, and so on?"

Like most of his class, he was conveniently deaf, dumb, and blind when it suited him. The committees hadn't called her. They had the files. She had anticommunist credentials. And besides, she was not a name that would make a headline. A forgotten white-haired woman who had once had something to do with the labor movement. They craved big names. Actors, writers, professors, state department officials. Eva Heilig was not a headline-making name. She wasn't worth a subpoena.

"I like to think," Halstead said, "that I didn't hurt anyone. They already had all the names I gave them. Except yours, of course. I called up some of our old radical friends and asked their permission to give their names. They didn't care. I even offered a *quid pro quo:* You can give my name if you let me give yours."

"Garrison, you continue to astonish me. That conviction that you can do anything you want, anything in the world. The Chains have more honor than your kind."

He blinked behind rimless eyeglasses. More and more, Eva thought, her ex-husband looked like FDR. He prided himself on the resemblance, although he had never had much use for Roosevelt. During Roosevelt's first two terms he regarded him as a fascist. Now that Halstead had made a sharp right turn, he looked back upon Roosevelt as a crypto-Red, a conniver with the international communist movement. Eleanor was even worse, more treacherous.

These political meanderings, these excesses, Eva understood, were games for Garry, the way his Yale classmates became absorbed in squash, yachting, or horses. Yet she could not eradicate the memory of the man who had stood bail for her many years ago. And the good years in the house on West Tenth Street.

"Are you all right financially?" he asked her.

"I manage. I've rented the two upstairs floors of the house."

His cheeks splotched scarlet, an old Halstead habit. The house had been all that Eva had asked for. And some minimal payments until she got a job. She had been fifty-five at the time, with a daughter in college. (Halstead agreed to pay for Lillian's education.) But she wanted no money from him. Her pride, self-wounding, was as lofty as it was when she battled policemen and strikebreakers. No money, just a place to live. She'd managed all these years writing for the *New Republic*, the *New Leader*, union publications, birth-control magazines, tenants' groups. But her income was meager. She was not in much demand anymore as a lecturer. For a period during the war she had sold books in Brentano's. Miserable pay, but nice surroundings. The manager had remembered her. He confessed to having heard her lecture at the Community Church during the Depression.

"I'm sorry," Halstead said. "I'll have my lawyers look over the alimony agreement. I'm a cad, Eva. I should have insisted . . . tenants, good God." Giving up the townhouse had embittered him.

"Your ancestors would be horrified. A marvelous young Japanese sculptor has the top floor and we've put in huge skylights—"

"Oh, God. All that plaster and marble dust."

"Worse. He's a welder. We've had two fire alarms since Sunichi moved in." She laughed. "And below him, two homosexuals, polite, sweet, middle-aged men who are gourmet cooks."

"Poets? Set designers? What?"

"One's a stockbroker and the other is a claims adjuster. And they both went to the University of Alabama."

"You have this tolerant view of the world and its people. Why doesn't it include me? Would you feel triumphant if I told you I miss you terribly? That I love you? I've never been happy since we broke up. And why in God's name *did* we break up?"

"Garrison, this is a lunatic conversation for two old people suffering from arthritis and hypertension. We should be comparing medications, not trying to revive a dead love."

He seized her hand and kissed it. "I mean it. Why don't we . . . ? Damn, what did I do wrong to get you so angry? *You* asked for the divorce. I know there was no other man."

"I wasn't passionate enough for you. Admit it. You strayed. So what? My slum-bred body didn't respond. Nothing as proper as a working girl. Maybe I nursed guilt over getting so much wealth, such fame, such power, for no other reason than my face. Your intoxication with an exotic Jewess. Hildah the prophetess, whom some biblical scholars contend was a sacred prostitute. Sorry I didn't fill the bill."

"Wrong. I enjoyed our—our—sex."

"No you didn't. You probably are very good in bed even now, very satisfying to handsome ladies and artistic girls. How is the incumbent?"

"Not as beautiful as you."

Halstead poured Chablis for Eva. "You overestimate my powers. I saw a lot of women. Not one of them diminished my respect for you. I remember that day in court. Your battered face and torn shirtwaist. And those weeping girls. Brunstein flapping his arms like a wounded crow."

"You were gallant. I appreciated it."

"Then . . . let's try again. We'll get the homosexuals to move out so I can have my study back."

"No, Garry. Never. Do you remember the last screaming fight we had? The night after you debated a Columbia professor on American aid to the Allies? There you stood. The voice of the pigheaded self-destroying left. The voice of the idiots in the Communist party. 'This is an imperialist war,' you brayed. 'Aid to England and France is aid to encourage inperialist expansion.' As if Hitler were the same thing. As if the Jews were being arrested and killed in England the way they were in Germany. How stupid could you have been? How much Stalinist nonsense could you swallow and still respect yourself?"

"The Russians were buying time. After all, the western Allies had been their enemies as much as the Nazis."

"You still believe that?"

"To an extent. You know how I've changed. I'm unshakably anticommunist. What I'm saying is the Russians and Germans were two sides of the same coin. We should have let them destroy each other. Rid the world of both."

"Stop *funfering*, Mr. H. How a man could equate England and France with the Nazis! And my relatives were soon to be gassed and burned in the Vilna ghetto. I could have strangled you. And how you changed once Hitler invaded Russia? Oh, what a different tune you sang!"

"You shame me with these recollections. That's why I've changed again. I now believe—"

Eva clapped her tiny hands and guffawed. The waiter turned his head. "Coffee, folks?"

"Yes, black," Eva said. "Strong. And brandy. We're celebrating Operation Barbarossa."

Crazy lady, he thought.

"Eva, less exuberance," Halstead said.

" 'This is no longer an imperialist war!' " she cried. "Remember that one? After June 1941? What a thrilling line! *This is no longer an imperialist war!* So long as the English and the French and the Low Countries—and the Jews—were dying and suffering, but the Soviet Union had a pact, you were neutral. But when the panzers moved east, the party gave you a new speech, right, Garry? That's when I decided we'd gone far enough. Your trouble was you followed too many banners and too many women."

"You're the only woman that's ever mattered to me. Eva, I do wish you'd call a moratorium on these hurtful reminiscences. Nothing is gained by them. Give me credit at least for a certain broadness of mind. A willingness to change."

"It was party-line poison you were spouting. And look at you now. Running off to committees, blabbing your old friends' names, editing a magazine that considers Eleanor Roosevelt as bad as Stalin, denouncing the New Deal as a plot to socialize America, telling your readers that Joe McCarthy is a great patriot and the savior of the republic. Disgusting."

"I believe deeply in everything that's printed in *Manifest Destiny.*"

At the mention of the monthly magazine that Halstead financed and edited, a rallying ground for ex-Stalinists, disaffected Trotskyites, right-wing Brahmins, fringe fascists, and witty anti-Semites, Eva pounded the table. "Believe that garbage if you will, Garry. Maybe it's where you belonged all the time. Why is it that former party members are the worst of the lot? Is it because you hate yourself so much?"

"Unfair, my dear—"

"Unfair, my foot. I hope you take pride in that snotty fascist rag you publish. Death to the Rosenbergs. Hang Hiss. Democrats and liberals are worse than Communists because there are so many of them. *Preventive war!* Drop atom bombs on Russia and China before they catch up! Cut spending, cut taxes, no welfare! Do you really believe you have a constituency with such wicked nonsense? As Dr. Abelman would have said, you and your new colleagues are a bunch of galoots."

"We will soon have a much larger following than you can imagine. Your musty liberal convictions will fall of their own weight soon enough."

"I love you ex-Communists. Anyone who favors child-labor laws is suspect. *You* were deceived by Stalin, so anybody who *wasn't* is a traitor. Go on, throw out the humanist baby with the communist bath water. That's what you'd like to do. Maybe put a few of us in concentration camps while you are at it."

"That is unkind."

"You sicken me. Tell me how you're going to get this vast constituency."

"Quite simply. Spies and traitors being exposed by Senator McCarthy and others will convince people of the Red plot. A *liberal* plot, I might add. There is no difference. Beyond that, we have a much stronger card to play."

"The Jews?"

"Oh, goodness, no. They're by-and-large business and professional types. If they had any sense they'd support us. People like your multi-millionaire relatives the Chains should be casting their lot with us."

"The Chains are too smart for you, and too tough. They have no politics. They understand what makes the country go. Much better than you do. But enlighten me. What is your secret plan to take over Washington?"

Halstead set a fresh cigarette in his ivory holder, lit up, cocked his head. *Damn,* Eva thought, *he still thinks he's Roosevelt.* Some curious aberration was at work in his mind. Admiring FDR years ago (one of his own class who rebelled), he now hated him, but could not shake the identification. Self-hatred, Eva concluded. Detesting and defaming Roosevelt, Eleanor, the New Deal, liberals, was a way of despising himself. And he probably hates me, she thought, for never having gone as far left as he had, for refusing to dance to Stalin's tunes, for refusing to defend the Soviets no matter what bloody excesses they committed. That was the secret. He, like other former Communists, could not exorcise their own demons without convincing themselves that reformers, humanists, liberals, and socialists *were worse than they ever were.*

"Negroes will be our salvation. And the nation's."

Eva cocked her head. "Negroes?"

"They will soon be demanding rights, as they call them, upsetting the natural order, trying to replace whites in the social and economic order. They will become violent and angry, commit crimes, destroy cities. Liberals will encourage them. We old-fashioned patriots will seize on this ravaging of America to create a new social conservatism. The criminality and brutality of coloreds will be the anvil on which we smash the spine of the left-liberal conspiracy."

He exhaled a thick cloud of smoke, rested back in his seat, and waited for her explosion. A bit of the old Heilig temper seemed in order. The angry voice of the picket captain. It was what had drawn him to her: that undiluted courage, pristine anger, moral outrage.

"I am so repelled by you, Garry, that I can't even respond. You'll use Negroes the way Hitler used Jews. Is that it?"

"Not at all. The Jews were innocent. They did not mug or steal or rape or ruin neighborhoods. I've said many times I sympathized with their plight. You and I signed petitions for them and tried to increase the immigration quotas. But Negroes are a different matter. I have no grudge against them, but their fate is inevitable. They'll give us the excuse to form an honorable, virtuous, moral society."

"You are insane. I'm leaving."

He followed her to the door, pausing to sign the check, scrambling after her on birdlike legs. Furious, Eva walked south on Fifth Avenue. Halstead caught up with her. He took her arm. She yanked it away.

"Don't be wroth with me, Eva. A lot of what I say is intellectual doodling. But I see the future. I see an opportunity to move this country away from gnosticism, creeping socialism, all the liberal-left dogma that have failed, that have betrayed—"

She cracked him across the face with her tiny hand. "Get away from me. I don't want to see you. I despise you."

"Pity," Halstead said, rubbing his inflamed cheek. "I was going to offer you a monthly column in *Manifest Destiny*. That was the reason for the lunch. Let you give us the view from the left for balance. I'll overlook what happened. Are you interested?"

"Go to hell."

He watched her walk off, a slender and vigorous woman, looking fifteen years younger than her age. He realized he had failed to ask about their daughter, Lillian. Lillian was quite close to Eva. Halstead rarely saw her.

Chapter 50

Lillian Halstead, twenty-seven, graduate of Columbia Law School, was one of the few women in the office of the New York State attorney general. She was a tall, solemn young woman, with her father's gangly limbs and rather awkward physical appearance. But she had clear green eyes like her mother, fair skin, and curling tawny hair. She might have been beautiful were it not for the prolonged Halstead chin and her disregard for hairdressers, cosmetics, artifice of any kind. "Plain" was the word used to describe her—an honest face, an interesting face. The young lawyers who worked with her decided she was a rather sexless woman. Talked little about herself. Very private. No coasting on the Halstead name. She had gotten the job on merit after outstanding volunteer work in the office of the Brooklyn district attorney during summer vacations. From both parents she had inherited a talent for expressing herself effectively—verbally and in her written briefs.

In the New York office of the attorney general, Miss Halstead, a rather odd sort to her co-workers, studied a long report on illegal practices in the liquor industry. Her superior wanted a review.

Distillers were complaining about the unfair practices of Chain Industries and Chain Distillers. It was an old file. To Lillian's surprise, no action had ever been taken to investigate the charges. Revealingly, several distillers of much greater size, and vaster income than the Chains, were the complainants.

Lillian crossed her legs, let a low-heeled shoe dangle on one foot, and smiled. Mr. O'Neal, her boss, would be shocked out of his shoes if he knew that Mortimer J. Chain and his son Martin Chain, accused in the file of bribery, kickbacks, and payoffs, were her distant cousins.

She knew little about the Chains. Her mother had sometimes spoken of them. Jacob Chain, a violent hoodlum, dead some nineteen or twenty years, was the progenitor of the line. Quite a man, Eva used to tell her. A third cousin on her mother's side, related to old Grandma Matla, herself long dead. A man who had been shot at with depressing regularity and survived, until a fatal ambush.

The son, chief target of the accusers, was Mortimer J. Chain, a reclusive man of uncountable wealth. She vaguely remembered visiting his home once with her mother—climbing a tree with his son Martin. A newspaper clipping in the file showed Mr. M. J. Chain, darkly handsome, nattily dressed, a piratical black patch over his right eye. He was coming down the steps of the Federal Courthouse with his attorney, Mr. Horace Bunthorne, and other lawyers. The appellate court of the second district had reversed a lower court's findings against the Chains for unfair labor practices. She looked at the date—1948. Only two years ago.

Strange, Lillian thought. Her mother had always depicted Jake Chain, for all his crudeness and violence as a friend to workingmen. What a difference, Lillian thought, a generation makes.

Mortimer Chain was quoted in the article. "We feel vindicated. This was not a labor-employer matter," he told reporters, "it was a fight between two unions, one that we recognize, and one run by a bunch of gangsters who want to take over. Our wage scale and our pension benefits are the best in the distilling industry and we don't need hoodlum-run outfits in our corporation."

That took courage, Lillian knew. Gangster-dominated unions did not take kindly to such accusations. There seemed to be a fearless, outspoken strain in the Chains. Old Jake (she could recall her mother telling her) had been a hero to beaten pickets. The essence of courage. A huge and enormously strong man. Lillian mused: Can courage, boldness, and daring be inherited? She wished she knew more about the son she dimly remembered as a boy, Martin. His name appeared only once in the file, as executive vice-president of the corporation.

One of her predecessors had summed up the complaints:

Although the Chain organization is not among the top half-dozen distillers and importers of alcoholic beverages, it is the most aggressive in selling and distributing its products.

Much of this has to do with imaginative advertising and the exploitation of trends in the liquor business, which is subject to fads and fashions. Moreover, they seem to have established an effective, if somewhat involved, method of maintaining inventories of neutral grain spirits and the straight whiskeys needed for the best-selling blends.

None of the above practices are *per se* illegal. Complaints from competitors stem rather from the Chain corporation's illegal payments to retailers, bars, and restaurants to push their lines. There are three complaints on record to the effect that the Chain salesmen resorted to veiled, and not-so-veiled, threats when meeting resistance from retailers. These, of course, are accusations by their competitors and must be carefully weighed. Van Alst and Rimmelberger, the giants in the liquor trade, are not themselves angels of mercy.

The bulging file amused Lillian. A perceptive woman, with her mother's tolerant view of people, she almost had to laugh at the complaints. They had the ring of the whinings of bullies, the mean boys in the schoolyard, who had been shown up by a tough upstart kid.

There were letters and affidavits from haughty law firms, from the rival distiller Van Alst, making accusations. One irate corporate president accused the Chains of theft, of "stealing" neutral grain spirits from a government warehouse to launch their business in the thirties. The businessman charged that the Chains were still, in 1950, not above such chicanery—paying off government storekeeper-gaugers and bribing suppliers as well as retailers. In short, bringing their bootlegging habits into a gentlemen's industry.

One line caught her eye. It seemed to her to sum up the argument, or indeed the lack of any. She scanned the paragraph.

Distillers admit they fail to understand why some brands catch on and some do not. They concede that, in terms of the market, each corporation enters the field with more or less identical products, all priced within a given range. Labels differ, content is the same. Success or failure is the result of a mystical affair called "brand loyalty," a capricious matter. The Chains have apparently been very apt at developing this "brand loyalty." A great deal of money and energy is devoted to advertising, promotion, public relations, contacts with retailers, packaging, display, and distribution.

420

Good for the Chains, she thought. A disreputable, crude, ambitious, hard-handed branch of the family. Richer than any Heilig, light-years removed from her respectable uncles, Sol the idealistic lawyer and Dr. Abe. Mortimer Chain, she had heard, had never finished high school. Martin? She was not sure. He looked shrewd and knowing in his photographs.

Lillian decided to make a few calls, to see if any new evidence was available on the alleged improprieties of the Chain liquor interests, and then write a report for her superior. She was about to close the file, having jotted down names and phone numbers of informants, when she noticed a few yellowing clippings. The first was from the *Times* of July 1931.

JACOB CHAIN, MOB FIGURE, SLAIN
BODY FOUND IN BROOKLYN

Jacob Chain, 46, a bootlegger and labor racketeer, was found shot to death in the trunk of a stolen automobile in the Brownsville section of Brooklyn yesterday.

Chain, known to police and the underworld as "Crazy Jake," had been shot twice in the head. Police said the murder had taken place that day. The body had been driven to Sutter Avenue, four blocks from Mr. Chain's place of business, Brooklyn General Supply.

Chief of Detectives William Kane said there were no suspects, or any motive, as of yesterday evening. Chain had a long record of arrests for assault in connection with labor disputes. At one time he ruled a mob that specialized in wrecking factories and beating up nonunion laborers. He was, a source said, no longer involved in union activities.

Chain and his son, Mortimer, 27, were said to be Brooklyn's major bootleggers, operating behind the facade of a chemical supply business, a cereal company, and a hair-tonic factory.

Lillian Halstead was her mother's daughter. She could smile at life's absurdities, the ironies of the world. *Hair tonic! Cereals! Chemicals!* She laughed, then read on.

There have been several attempts on Mr. Chain's life in the past twenty years. In 1911 he survived twelve bullets, and about ten years later he survived a second barrage from underworld rivals, earning him a reputation as Brownsville's foremost "clay pigeon."

This time, police theorized, Mr. Chain was shot and killed by people he knew, and whom he had no reason to fear. . . .

Lillian paused, listened to the hum of the electric fan in her cubicle. She heard the voices of her fellow prosecutors outside the frosted glass partition.

"Something about Korea on the radio . . ."
"What? A communist invasion? Jesus, and I'm in the reserve. . . ."
"It can't be for real. . . . Who needs another war so soon?"

The Chain past preoccupied her. The invasion, or whatever it was—probably a border incident; the radio newscasts had a way of magnifying these things—could wait.

She wondered about Jake Chain, ignominiously murdered; a young man. Her mother had often spoken of him with grudging affection. Yes, he was a terrible man in many ways. But at heart a gentle hulk, simple, with decent instincts. "I got him into his business, Lil," Eva would say. "Maybe it was a mistake, but I can tell you, we would not have won those strikes without him. And he wasn't crazy, not at all. . . ."

A second clipping reported the discovery of a hoodlum's corpse in a lake in the Catskills.

BODY SURFACES IN CATSKILL LAKE
BELIEVED TO BE MOBSTER FERRANTE

Local police today discovered the bullet-riddled, decomposed body of a man believed to be Salvatore Ferrante, a Brooklyn gangster, who vanished three years ago.

James Collins, a farmer, discovered the body floating on Carrington Lake yesterday afternoon, while looking for lost cows. The body had apparently been weighted down with cinder blocks, but the wires attaching them to the corpse's limbs had rusted and come loose. Tentative identification was made from dental work and fingerprints.

Ferrante, member of a Brownsville family of mobsters, union strong-arm men, and bootleggers, vanished in February of 1932 without a trace. A coroner's report was awaited to determine the cause of death.

Lillian decided she would have to talk to Dugan, the man who drew up the file. Why the clippings? She knew the name Ferrante. Her mother had spoken of a family of thugs who had worked for Jake and Mort. The connection had been broken in 1934 after the repeal of Prohibition. She looked at the date on the clipping: *1935*. For three years, Salvatore Ferrante had rested amid the sunfish and perch of Carrington Lake.

The third clipping was about an attack on Mortimer J. Chain by unknown persons. It was from the *Daily News*.

ALKY EXEC VICTIM OF ACID ATTACK
M. J. CHAIN BLINDED OUTSIDE THEATER

Lillian saw the date: 1935. The report stated that Mortimer J. Chain and his wife, Hilda, of Ocean Parkway, Brooklyn, were coming out of Loew's Flatbush theater at 10:00 P.M. when an unidentified woman threw sulfuric acid in his face. The woman, clad in a dark coat and black hat, escaped in a car. Some observers said she was accompanied by a man. In the confusion that followed the attack, no one got a clear look at her or noted the car's license number. Preliminary medical examinations, the *News* said, indicated that Mr. Chain, president of Chain Industries would lose the sight in his right eye, but that the left, though suffering damage, would heal.

She called the office of George X. Dugan, the man who had collected the file some years ago and was now in private practice.

"Lil," Dugan said, "that Chain thing is a bat's nest. Why the boss wants to reopen it—"

"I'm curious about the clippings. Jacob Chain's murder, the Ferrante case. Why are they in there?"

"Ferrante was a two-bit bootlegger who worked with the Chains."

"Who were the suspects?"

"Half of Brooklyn."

"And who were the suspects in the Chain murder?"

"The other half."

Lillian laughed. "Thanks, George. I won't even ask you about the acid attack on Mortimer Chain."

"Another spin-off from their bootlegging, we figured."

"Nothing like private enterprise, right, George?"

"Who am I to argue? Excuse me, Lil. I got to turn the radio on. All hell's breaking loose in Korea. Truman's sending in troops."

Chapter 51

The weekly executive meeting took place in Mort's board-room on the twentieth floor of their Park Avenue head-quarters. Around the table sat his high command. Son Martin, executive vice-president. Horace Bunthorne, vice-president, chief operating officer, and counsel. Bertram Dunphy, vice-president for the Imports Division and assistant counsel. Dr. Harris Weltfish, vice-president for quality control and production. Mr. Mackenzie Tuttle, storekeeper-gauger at the major Chain distillery in Wisdom, New Jersey. There were three others, all respectable, bright, aggressive men, all under forty, all skilled in the savagely competitive liquor business.

"This damn Korea thing," Bunthorne was saying. "We have no idea how long it'll last. If it runs on, we may have a problem with inventories. The Big Four may not want to sell to us."

"Horace, I'll be counting on you to convince them it's in their own interest," Mort said softly.

Bunthorne's goggling eyes wandered to the buildings on Park Avenue. "Mort, I'll try like the devil. But they're trying to crowd us now for using leverage with retailers."

"Look who's talking," Martin said. "Monopolists, price fixers."

"They want it all, Van Alst and Rimmelberger." Bunthorne stroked his purplish cheek. "Of course, our inventories are high, aren't they, Harris?"

Dr. Weltfish, with his stone-gray hair parted in the middle, a curved pipe drooping from his ragged moustache, hid in a fog of smoke. Rum and maple? Martin wondered. Walnut? Weltfish's pipe always made him think of the dormitories at Dartmouth.

"Horace, I'd say we have a three-year lead. A long war could hurt us. The problem will be straight whiskey, the four-year-old stuff. Neutral spirits may also be a problem until our own distilleries make us self-sufficient."

Mort listened and made notes. They had pioneered blended whiskeys in the late thirties. They had set the pace for other distillers. And he had to admit that lanky noodle Bunthorne had showed him the way. Whiskey was Horace Bunthorne's only religion, his reason for living, his guiding light.

Listening to the discussion—big Mackenzie Tuttle, Mort's half brother, was talking about neutral spirits available in government warehouses—Mort smiled, and recalled his first meeting with Bunthorne.

Nineteen years ago. Bunthorne had returned from his fruitless errand for Schonkeit—fruitless because Mort had already bought off the British distillers. Still, Mort had to hand it to the Paymaster for picking so refined and well-spoken a front man. Bunthorne was invited to lunch with Mr. M. J. Chain at the Chambord.

The two men had studied each other warily. Mort, in his late twenties, dapper in a vested blue suit, starched white collar, his foxlike face and thick ebony hair suggesting something of the gypsy to the Iowa-bred Bunthorne. The youthful lawyer, in turn, intrigued Mort with his dead-center, on-the-nose, middle-of-the-road *goyishness*. At once Mort realized this was the kind of man he wanted to help him run the business after repeal. An absolute American Baptist who could drink forever and never fall down.

"What are you earning now?" Mort asked. "You're with one of those old-time Wall Street outfits, right? Harvard and Yale fellas?"

"I'm a very junior member, Mr. Chain. I went to the University of Iowa and its law school."

Even better, Mort thought. "That isn't what I asked. What do they pay you?"

"Thirty thousand a year."

"I'll give you sixty."

"But, Mr. Chain . . ." The six-foot-eight-inch man, with his beet-red cheeks, a capillary-bursting boozer at age thirty-one, an all-day, nonstop drinker with impeccable taste and a rich farmboy's voice, opened his eyes wide. Horace had huge staring eyes. The pupils were the color of burned sugar. Already the whites were yellowing, the sure sign of an orthodox alcoholic. What impressed Mort was that Bunthorne never behaved drunkenly, never slurred a word, never staggered, never became noisy, or goosed women, or threw up, or showed physical damage. He golfed, sailed, and played bad tennis, worked fourteen hours a day, looked lovingly after his sozzled wife and was active in community affairs in his hometown of Greenwich.

"I know very little about the liquor business, Mr. Chain," the lawyer said cautiously.

"Like hell you don't. You ran around England trying to steal my suppliers. You ran errands for Schonkeit. You're worth sixty grand. Whaddya say, Mr. Bunthorne?"

"Let me be candid, sir. You ask me to leave one of New York's most prestigious law firms to be counsel for a bootlegger? I know a little of your history, Mr. Chain."

"Those guys you work for on Wall Street? They're bigger crooks than any Chain ever was. In a couple of years we'll go legitimate. I want you to be with us. If you took a job for Schonkeit, you can't be that fancy. All money is the same color. Besides, we haven't killed anyone in years, and the few we killed deserved it. Deal?"

Bunthorne opened his mouth, as if the mantis were ready to eat a horsefly. He laughed soggily and shook Mort's hand. "Deal, Mr. Chain."

"Mort."

"Mort. My goodness, I've never called any of our senior partners by their first names. And I've been with the firm four years."

They would be a great combination. Bunthorne knew secrets about the vast American heart, the people who hated New York and distrusted Jews but wanted their liquor served well and abundantly, in nice bottles and at a decent price. Horace possessed that wondrous faith in booze that had made rich men of bootleggers, that half-jesting, worshipful, dear-to-the-heart love of drunkenness, of wobbly feet and dulled minds, that characterized a basically puritanical people. As they drank, they joked, teased, lost their inhibitions. To drink was to be a patriot above reproach.

"Every time I look at that *langhe luksh*," Mort later told Hilda and the children, as they sat around the dinner table in the Ocean Parkway mansion, "I see all of America out there, making their cockamamie jokes about whiskey, hollow legs, human sponges, all that kidding around. Men falling down, women puking on expensive dresses, college boys boasting how potted they were, the marines Davey was with making hooch out of raw alcohol and grapefruit juice, the little *shiksas* in Iris's class at Smith sneaking bourbon from daddy's bottle—I see all of them combined in this one skinny man who never eats, but who gets healthy and smart and nicer, the drunker he gets. God gave me Horace Bunthorne."

"Daddy, you have to be teasing," Iris said. "Jews also drink."

"I have no idea what your father is talking about," Hilda said.

"I do," Martin said. "But it's more complicated than that. Pop likes to kid about Bunthorne, but he's a hell of a lawyer."

Davey listened a bit opaquely, never quite sure what his father meant, faintly jealous of Martin's quickness, of Iris's sharp tongue. He was more comfortable in battle fatigues. He knew he could never work for Chain Distilleries. What could he possibly do around sharpies like his father, his brother, Bunthorne, Weltfish, Bert Dunphy? Even the thick-bodied quiet man, Mackenzie Tuttle, the storekeeper-gauger, who (officially at least) was a United States government employee, was smarter than he was. Funny kind of guy, Tuttle. With that flat face and soft blue eyes, and the slow movements of a man laden with more weight and strength than he knew what to do with. Davey liked him.

"God bless Bunthorne," Mort said. He patted his black patch. "He gave me a peek into people's minds. Legitimate booze was different from bootlegging. I needed him."

As the men around the conference table talked about advertising campaigns, better distribution, competition from cheap brands, marketing experiments with gin and vodka, the need to covertly establish their own banks to meet enormous prepaid taxes for the removal of bonded whiskey, Mort let his mind wander back again to those early years, the bursting thirties, when he had expanded, gambled, battled competition, paid off the right people, and gotten into liquor production in a big way.

He could recall Bunthorne gently agitating the bourbon in his glass, sipping it, rolling it over his tongue, and rendering his verdict to Mort. It was the spring of 1934, Mort recalled, a few months after repeal. The Chains had started slowly. Their one small distillery was lagging. They could not produce enough neutral grain spirits. The law required that straight whiskey had to be aged in charred oak barrels, which were hard to come by. The big boys—Canadians, English, Van Alst—came in with a head start. Undaunted, Mort had set the Chain company up as mere "rectifiers," purchasers and mixers of whiskeys, putting their own labels on blended brands created from a combination of products.

"Too strong, too hot for the mouth," Bunthorne was saying. "And it costs too much." He was sipping straight bourbon whiskey, distilled from corn and aged in charred oak barrels for a minimum of four years to give it the designation "bottled in bond." There was lots of it, along with bonded straight rye and straight wheat whiskey, being distilled. To Bunthorne it was a waste of time and money. A small market, high costs, a four-year wait.

"Blends, *blends*," Bunthorne told Mort, whose indifference to hard liquor applied to expensive whiskey as much as it had to rotgut.

They were on the verge of concluding the purchase of a large distilling plant in upstate New York. They would soon be ready to threaten the "big four" of the whiskey business. They would be operating from a solid base, their own supply of neutral grain spirits, which formed forty-nine percent of a typical Chain blend. Mac Tuttle, nominally a government man, was explaining how he would see to it that a sympathetic "storekeeper-gauger"—the man who supervised whiskey production—was appointed.

The job was an odd one, little known to the general public. Although distilleries had been privately owned and operated since 1934, "control" was under the eagle eye of the "storekeeper-gauger," a man required to possess absolute integrity and knowledge of the business. (Gone were the good old corrupt days, Mort mused, when they bought and sold shmucks like O'Connor and Curtis, the jerks who were supposed to control alcohol warehouses. Mort smiled as he recalled Jake's squad of fake "rabbis" who regularly procured government-sequestered wine from venal government men with forged letters from Rabbi Piltz.)

Mackenzie Tuttle held the keys to the distilling rooms, the cisterns, the grain bins, all functioning parts of the distillery. Not a single employee, not Mort Chain or Martin or Bunthorne or Dr. Weltfish, could go from one part of the plant to another until the federal employee gave his permission and unlocked the area. In theory, the distilling process was carried out under Tuttle's bland blue eye. Tuttle and two assistants examined grains, extracts, and sampled all spirits. Even the affixing of the green federal revenue stamp was part of Tuttle's job.

Through an intricate process of influence, visits to key congressmen, a sympathetic assistant secretary of the Treasury, M. J. Chain had arranged for Mac Tuttle to get the job at the Chains' main distillery. No one knew that Tuttle was Mort's half brother. Indeed, Mort suspected, possibly Mackenzie himself did not know. They never discussed the matter. From time to time Mort visited the statuesque gray-haired woman who lived alone in the stucco house in Freeport and ran a fleet of charter boats. *Mrs. Tuttle.* Old Jake's mistress, the woman who'd made him happy and given him another son.

Sometimes Mackenzie would look at Mort with his flat eyes as if summoning up the courage to ask something. *Are you . . . ? Are we . . . ?* But the words never came. Just as well, Mort thought. I've taken care of my own blood. Jake probably loved the boy as much as he loved Mort. And Tuttle was a good man, intelligent, reliable, extremely knowing about the business.

I do better with my associates than my father did, Mort thought. Jake had been stuck with the Ferrantes most of his life, and one of them, that bastard Sal, had surely been involved in his death. Kuflik, the old *shtarker,* had said as much that snowy night on Pitkin Avenue. Schonkeit had used Sal to get rid of the insane Wesselberg and Jake in one cunning stroke. . . .

"*. . . the nerve of those people using prune juice and sherry in their blends,*" Bunthorne was saying. He was talking about a leading competitor. "*Love to tell the newspapers about it, catch them red-handed. . . .*"

Mort Chain had had his revenge. It had been sweet. Honey to the lips. The way he'd trapped Schonkeit, framed him with his own dirty game, gotten the bookmakers to take care of him. It had taken a couple of months to arrange Sal Ferrante's disappearance. The job saddened him a little. After all, Sal with his farting taxi had gotten Mort started back in 1922. But the violent and treacherous streak in the youngest Ferrante was bound to do him in. Mort had wept a little the night he got word that Sal was dead, resting at the bottom of a pond in the Catskills.

Mort thought of the turbulent thirties, the rise of the Chain corporation from rectifiers—people who merely mixed and bottled a "blend into major distillers, innovators in the field, satisfiers of the great American thirst.

Bunthorne backed by Weltfish's skills, put them into blends with vigor and imagination. *Mildness, a uniform taste, something easy on the palate and throat, but with the same gently fuzzing and forgetful effect.* Render the limbs loose, the tongue active, the sex glands aroused, let the world glow rosily. Bunthorne had pointed out that while straight whiskeys required at least two years of aging and bottled-in-bond liquor straight needed four years—an expensive lengthy process—blends could be sold damned near *green.*

To the astonishment of the corporate giants, the Chains' milder product, beautifully bottled, smartly labeled, advertised as smooth, mellow, and satisfying, a drink that left the imbiber clearheaded and bright-eyed, caught on. Straight rye and straight bourbon became regional tastes. Especially among the young, the cry was for "whiskey"—and whiskey meant a lighter, younger product.

When grain alcohol was in short supply during the war, the big boys had vast inventories of it and did not suffer badly. Production of whiskey and grain spirits was shut off for a time. Industrial alcohol took precedence. Daringly Bunthorne and Weltfish flew to Cuba and started buying up vast quantities of sugarcane for alcohol. They also bought up entire crops of potatoes, excess cereal grains, and fruit orchards, to provide them with the clear liquid, distilled at 190 proof, which formed the basis of their popular brands. Chain's Old Oak Tree was soon proving a runaway favorite at officers' clubs, night spots, defense plants.

Some experts complained that Weltfish's cane-based alcohol gave the Chain products a rummy aftertaste, not what they expected in an honest blend. The defect was soon corrected by a neutralizing agent. The public continued to like Chain brands.

Sullen and greedy, the big four, led by the octopus Van Alst, watched angrily. Who the hell was M. J. Chain and his nervy gang of newcomers? *Sugarcane? Potatoes?* The word was spread to bar owners, restaurants, hotels, and retailers: Chain whiskey was rotten whiskey. It was made from anything that would ferment, including garbage. What else could people expect from people who had gotten their start as bootleggers?

But the Chains fought back. Scrambling for grain alcohol, buying up small distilleries, working overtime to make sure they would never be at the mercy of the big operators, they survived. The richest of all the whiskey families, the Van Alsts, had accumulated huge stores of grain alcohol. Quietly, under Bunthorne's shrewd guidance, Mort set up a "cover company," presumably in the cough-medicine business. Hundreds of thousands of gallons were bought from Van

Alst, until he found out and out and threatened to sue. But it developed that he himself was vulnerable to the law on a variety of counts. Bunthorne arranged a truce, and the Chains soon got a share of grain alcohol to tide them over.

Glancing around the boardroom now, Mort felt proud of his organization, pleased with his choices. Bunthorne, Dunphy. Weltfish, Tuttle, and now young Martin, a graduate of Harvard Business School and smarter than the old man. Immediately Martin had understood the value of their subsidiaries—Chain Chemicals, founded on brokering postwar surpluses; Chain Pharmaceuticals, a flourishing line of proprietary drugs; and now the Patriots and Citizens Bank and Trust Company, a means of easing tax payments.

"Any other business?" Mort asked.

"The foundation, pop," Martin said.

"That's a whole other meeting, Martin. Talk to Horace and Bert about it."

For some months Martin had been advising his father to establish the Chain Foundation, a tax-free charitable institution, directing resources toward medical research and education. It not only made sense from a financial standpoint but it was sound public relations. It would also take away the lingering stigma, the snide references in the press, the whispers at conventions, the buzzing about the origins of the Chains, the trail of violence and blood, shadowy memories of a murdered father.

"One other thing," Martin said. "When I made the last European trip, pop? With the trade group?"

"Yes?"

Martin had been active in a campaign to get Jewish survivors of the Holocaust out of Eastern Europe and into Israel. His intelligence, his access to funds, his Washington contacts were invaluable. The trip to Europe had been one of several he had made in the company of affluent businessmen, bankers, and educators. The distinguished group had rejected him at first. But Martin, with his Ivy League charm, his discreet manner, his ability to listen and then add constructive ideas, won them over. DeeDee had been a great asset, too. She was, after all, a Grau.

"Quite a trip, as I recall," Bunthorne said. "Maybe we can tie some rescue and rehab work into the foundation."

"I didn't mean that," Martin said. "I did some shopping in Poland. Look at this."

He put a bottle on the table. Colorless liquid, clumsily corked and without a label.

"Vodka, gentlemen," Martin said. "One hundred proof, distilled in Krakow, Poland. No taste, no smell, no congeners, less headaches, no whiskey breath. Mixes with anything."

"Hell, it isn't even booze," one of the men said.

"Martin, we know about vodka," Harris Weltfish said politely. "A fraction of the market. Our blends are for the masses. Who wants a whiskey you can't see, smell, or taste? No one buys vodka."

"Horace, do me a favor," Martin said. "Take this home and try it out. With orange juice, tomato juice, any way you want. With quinine water, vermouth, with Rose's lime juice. You and Tucky have a ball."

"I have never been known to refuse a free bottle of the disturbance." Bunthorne said solemnly.

"It's got to succeed," Martin said. "With college kids. With women. Less headaches, less hangovers, less puking, no bad breath. And you can flavor it any way you want. Mix it with vitamin-rich juices."

Mort adjourned the meeting. He was pleased with Martin's enterprise. But a colorless booze that looked like water? . . .

His musings were interrupted by his secretary. Mrs. Chain was on the phone and was having hysterics. "Again?" Mort asked. He took the phone. David had just tried to reenlist in the marines, Hilda sobbed. He had been rejected because of wounds he'd gotten in Israel, but he was calling a senator to use his influence. The boy was crazy. Only his father could stop him. *Korea! Who needed Korea?*

Martin followed his father to his office. "Something wrong at home, pop?"

"Your brother wants to fight a war again."

The older son volunteered to ride out to Brooklyn with Mort and talk Davey out of it. Mort dissuaded him. Davey'd been rejected already, and Mort would see that the rejection stuck, if it involved calling the secretary of defense. No military unit would ever accept former sergeant David Chain.

Martin was relieved. DeeDee was jumping that weekend in a horse show in Armonk, and they had invited guests over for a Friday night "bird and bottle."

Chapter 52

When Mort got home, he found the house on Ocean Parkway cluttered with trunks, valises, and packing cases. In two days Hilda would be moving to Lake Champlain for two months at the lodge at Camp Spruce Grove. Mort owned a minor interest in the prosperous summer camp, but was little concerned with it apart from ensuring a winning baseball team by giving "scholarships" to New York City high-school stars. Spruce Grove had a twenty-seven-game winning streak. Looking at the luggage, Mort had a wistful reminder of Davey, as a counselor, making an incredible running catch in center field against an army team from Plattsburgh. The tall, suntanned figure racing into the woods to turn a home run into the final out . . .

"Thank God you're here," Hilda wept. "He's driving me crazy. I listen to the radio. Americans are getting killed, and your son wants to reenlist. Already they told him his leg is no good. He called two congressmen."

In a Dior robe, Hilda rested on a white velvet sofa. A year ago Iris had demanded that the house be redone by a fashionable decorator. Mort hated the new furniture, the cockeyed paintings and screwy statues. Mostly blacks, whites, and grays. It looked like an old movie. No color, no life. But Iris loved it. The house had been featured in the *New York Times Magazine* section. *Bauhaus in Brooklyn,* whatever the hell that meant, Mort thought gloomily.

"Is this true, Dave?" he asked.

"It's true."

Iris tossed her golden mane. They were so much alike, the younger Chain children. Jake's big body, strong limbs, fair skin, blond-brown hair. Even the hands. Long, thick, corded with veins and muscle. Mort always thought of his father when he saw them.

"Let Davey do what he wants, pop. The world doesn't begin or end with neutral grain spirits." Iris winked at her brother.

"No, but that's what pays the bills," Mort said. He sighed,

sat down, summoned Harry Twine to bring him a glass of seltzer.

"I don't want to be paid off," Davey said. "I never have. I'm no hero. I just want to go."

Hilda hefted her weary body into a sitting position. The gold-and-black dressing gown dazzled against the white sofa. Her thighs stretched the gossamer fabric of the seven-hundred-dollar robe. Mort looked at her hips approvingly. Still round and unmarked. Forty-eight years old and men stared at her soft, seamless face, the staring dark eyes, the crimson mouth. He loved her. They had been through a great deal. He did not like to see her hurt.

"You fought two wars, David," she sobbed. "You were lucky the first time. I know how you were wounded in Israel, how you almost lost your leg and lied to us. You and your father tried to keep it from me. But your friend Al Seligman—who needs that *nudnik?*—he let the cat out of the bag. Now you have a knee with a brace, and thank God you won't have to go to Korea or anywhere else. . . ."

"Your mother's right," Mort said wearily. Jesus, how did kids contrive to make their parents so miserable? He'd never been a burden to Jake. He'd begun smuggling booze when he was eighteen, taken the old man into the business. They'd been partners and friends.

Davey ducked his head, sat hunched over on the famous Otzenberger ottoman that was shaped like a hideous frog. Iris and her decorator detested it. Mort insisted it stay. When they entertained, Iris hid it in a closet.

Mort smiled. "Dave, take that job I offered you. You'll run the chemical division—"

Iris got up, frowned, paced the wall-to-wall steel-gray carpet. "Daddy, forget it. Davey can do anything he wants."

"Iris, sweetheart," Mort said, "this isn't your argument. It's Davey, mama, and me. Dave, the chemical end is a piece of cake. We don't have a single warehouse, a truck, no manufacturing. It's all done on the phone. We broker government surpluses. We find the customers and take the commission—"

"We've heard it, daddy," Iris snapped. "Whatever the traffic will bear."

"Don't make fun of it. It sent you to Smith. It paid for your Jaguar. It set Martin up to be a millionaire with a horse farm in Armonk and a society wife. And I won't apologize to anyone. I support every charity around. When the cardinal wants help, he comes to me. The UJA got a problem, it's

Mort Chain they call on. The NAACP, the Protestant charities. They don't care that your grandfather was a *shtarker*. He was more of an American than a lot of people who went to Smith and Harvard."

"What in God's name does that have to do with the subject under discussion?" Iris asked.

"A lot, a lot," Mort said.

He felt his younger children slipping away. What the hell, they'd never go hungry. The Chain fortune would make it easy for them. Good kids, both of them. But what did they understand about his struggles, the death threats, the shootings, the bombs, snakes like Schonkeit and Wesselberg and Sal Ferrante? How little they knew—even Martin—about the battles, the bloodshed, the dangers.

"All right, forget this Korea business," Mort said firmly. "You did your share. Iwo Jima, Okinawa. Navy Cross, Bronze Star. We're proud of you. So why do you have to go back?"

"To show them Jews aren't afraid."

"Oh, God, Davey," Hilda cried. "Some reason! We don't owe anyone any apologies. After what they did to us in Europe?"

"That's exactly why," Davey said.

"Don't try to change his mind," Iris said. "Davey, remember when we spent summers in Long Beach? And those redheaded kids would come out of Mass on Sunday and shout 'Go back to Hitler' at us?"

"I never forgot," Davey said. "I fought five of those kids one day under the boardwalk. Iris was there. Tell them, Iris."

"He won every fight. My brudda." She jabbed at her nose, tossed a right at Davey's towhead. "I stopped his bloody nose. We never told you. So there."

"Listen, mom, pop," he said earnestly.

No guile in him, nothing hidden, Mort saw. He loved David for his openness. No, he could never run the chemical division, or sell Chain brands.

"The Korea business is probably a punk idea," Davey said. "My leg might give out, I know that. I'm leaving anyway. Seligman called me last week from Tel Aviv."

"Oh, another fine offer!" Hilda cried. "Who needs him, that lunatic with machine guns and grenades? He almost got you killed! He left you with a broken knee! You had to fight the whole Syrian army!"

"I've made my mind up," Davey said. "I'm going back. Maybe for good."

"No!" his mother shouted. "No! Since when are you a Zionist? You had trouble reading for your bar mitzvah!"

"Hilda, sweetheart, please," Mort took her hand.

"Terrible, what I have to live with," she said. "All the blood I had to look at in my time. Never mind, you kids don't know the half of it. Better you shouldn't. Never knowing if your father would be all right."

"Oh, mom," Iris said. "What are we, morons? We know about grampa. And the old days. The boats. The gangsters. Who cares anymore? We're so respectable it's disgusting. Martin belongs to fancy horse clubs. Pop is best friends with the cardinal. The president of NYU calls him on the phone. Money talks."

"That's why I want my children *here!*" Hilda nestled under Mort's protective arm. "I grew up with all that rottenness, people getting beaten up, and worse. Now, at least let me enjoy my children in peace."

"Davey, what do you want?" Iris asked.

"You're no help!" Hilda cried. "Mort, talk to him. I want him here, in the business, not getting shot at by Arabs. I read how they torture Jewish boys, cut off their hands. I read—"

"Dave, give it some thought," Mort said. He sounded exhausted.

"I have, pop. Seligman says they need trained soldiers to work with the kids on the border *kibbutzim*. They call these places *Nahals*. It's a farming community, but they have to stand guard, do military jobs. Most of them are kids who've never fired a gun. So they need instructors. I'd travel from one place to another and give lessons."

"Some lessons," Hilda said. "To blow people up. To shoot people. To get your head blown off. Let your crazy friend Seligman do it. For this lunacy you have to volunteer? Davey, think of us!"

Harry Twine knocked and entered. He asked if the children would be staying for dinner. He and his wife would be happy to make fried chicken for four. No problem.

"I'm in," Davey said.

"I'm not," Iris said sharply.

"You're finished with college, you have no job, no steady fella, and we never see you," Hilda said. "Once maybe you could have a meal with us and tell us a little about yourself?"

"Why? So you can jump all over me the way you're jumping on Davey now?"

Mort waved a hand, pleading with her to abandon the argument. A tough, shrewd man, he was gentle, considerate, and accommodating with his children. Especially Iris. His golden-haired baby. A woman now. A bit heavy-bodied and slightly mannish but a beauty nevertheless. She'd have the finest wedding ever. The Plaza, the works. He'd connive for her to fall in love with the proper man. Maybe an inheritor of vast wealth, who could merge businesses with the Chains.

Iris got up and started for the stairs.

"So where are you going?" Hilda asked petulantly.

"New York, if you must know."

"It's a big city. Where exactly?"

Iris turned dramatically on the curving marble staircase. Was there another stairway like it in Brooklyn? Mort wondered. Sometimes he longed for the narrow house on Haven Place. Doc Abelman still lived on Haven Place. Eva's mother, Matla Heilig, had died in such a house a few years ago. It it weren't for the invasion of wild *shwarzers*, it was a pretty decent place. But of course corporate giants did not live in Brownsville. Damned few, as a matter of fact, lived anywhere in Brooklyn.

"I might as well give you a double dose," Iris said imperiously. "Steady, mama. Hold her, pop. I'm leaving town also. I'm meeting with a producer tonight, a very important producer. Mr. Ernest Parvus. He's interested in a script idea I have. He says they'll pay me four hundred dollars a week at the studio to develop the screenplay. We'll make the final arrangements tonight and then I'm leaving in two or three days."

"What? What is this?" Hilda shrieked. "Mort, stop them! We're losing our children, God help us. This one off to the desert to shoot guns. That one off to be a movie writer. I know what women do to get jobs there. Even Martin we hardly ever see. He likes his horses better than he likes us."

Iris ran up the stairs.

Eager to avoid further recrimination, Davey went after her. They would talk, arrange strategies, examine their satisfaction in throwing off the Chain stranglehold. They loved their parents. But they had made their minds up long ago. The empire was not for them. Let Martin, the sharp one, the favorite, the dynamo, inherit it.

"What did I do so terrible to them?" Hilda cried. "Why? Why? Are they ashamed of us?"

Mort stroked her uncreased neck. White, white, his true love. He regretted his hours of passion with Theresa Ferrante. Unquestionably the woman who had blinded him, sought her revenge for the death of her brother Salvatore. Mort kissed Hilda's cheek, wiped the salty tears.

"Think of it this way, *ketzeleh*," Mort said. "You always wanted to travel. Now we have excuses. To California to see Iris. To Israel to see Davey. I'm thinking of buying up wine in a big way. Maybe whole vineyards. Weltfish says it's a coming thing. I'm looking forward to the trips already."

"I'm not happy."

Mort patted her shoulder and kissed her. She smelled of Joy. Hilda Chain went first-class. So did Iris and Martin. All except Davey, who would never need the Chain money. The kid would make his own way, training Jews to fire guns, string barbed wire, handle explosives. It was what he wanted, and Mort would not stop him.

David knocked softly on Iris's door. She told him to come in. The room looked like Beverly Hills, not Brooklyn—nubby fabrics, raw silks, Japanese grass cloths. Everything in beige, brown, and cream. The colors made Davey think of the desert.

"We rocked them a little," he said.

She turned her back, hooking stockings to her girdle. A big woman, she had to work on her figure. They had joked about her at Smith: the Hebrew Amazon, the Brooklyn Bomber. It didn't bother her. A poor student, she had been popular, generous, unashamed of her Brooklyn accent (somewhat diminished by her years away at school) and her reputation as a "hot neck."

"They'll get over it, Dave. We have to shake this Chain crap sooner or later or it'll smother us. Martin can bottle gin the rest of his life."

"They love us, Iris. But I don't want it. I liked the easy money and the cars and the expensive clothes. Summer camps. Ski vacations. But I don't belong here. In this house or on Park Avenue or in the corporation. I'm dumb to begin with. I never understood the Dow-Jones."

"If *you* don't, what about me?" She dabbed at her face with cleansing cream. Her skin tended to dry in the warm months. She saw faint wrinkles from too much golf, tennis, and riding. Mature, yet youthfully strong, Parvus had said. If Parvus tried to lay her, Iris thought, he was in for a shock. She had Jake's strength. She had inflicted bodily pain on more than one amorous swain.

"You think you can write movies?" he asked. "That would

be a switch for a Chain. Oh, I forgot about Cousin Eva. She was a writer. A pretty famous one, once."

"Keep a secret, Davey?" She constricted her mouth and applied vermilion lipstick.

"Who would I tell? I'm no snitcher."

"Parvus wants to marry me. Imagine. A Hollywood producer. He says we'd made a great husband-and-wife team. He hates his wife and kids."

An uncomplicated young man, Davey Chain rubbed his chin. He could not think of anything appropriate to say. "How old is he?"

"Forty-six."

"Holy smoke. The same age as pop. Are you serious? I mean, would you . . . ?"

Iris brushed her hair with fierce strokes. "Hell no. But he'd leave his wife and kids and the fifteen-room house in Beverly Hills in a second if I said I'd marry him."

"Did you—I mean . . ."

"No. Would you believe I'm a virgin?"

"If you say so, sis."

She strode toward the door in a hurry to escape the Chain house. "We can do anything we want, Dave. Or we don't have to do a damn thing. Don't forget it."

After dinner, in the soft dusk of a late June day, Mort sat with his son in the large garden. Phlox, forsythia, iris bloomed about them. Hilda had retired to an air-conditioned bedroom. Too much emotion all day. She claimed her heart was missing beats. Father and son listened to the radio. Truman was sending the works into Korea—army, navy, air force. MacArthur was on his way. The stock market had rallied after a big drop.

Mort talked about business. Chemicals, drugs, liquor. The war would give a tremendous boost to Chain products. He was sorry, of course, that the fighting had broken out. It all sounded like a stupid mistake, a screw-up, something that could have been avoided. But now that it was here, the Chains would try to make the best of it.

"A tricky business, Dave," Mort said. The radio droned on. Harry Twine moved amid lilacs and azaleas, cutting flowers for the house. His workday never seemed to end, but he didn't mind. He and his brother Eddie had an iron loyalty to Mort. They remembered their father's murder. Both men knew that the Chains had evened the score with the people who had slit old Buster's throat.

"What is, pop?" Dave thought his father was talking about Korea.

"Whether we should buy more straight whiskey. The price is too damned high. We'll take a loss on every bottle."

Davey looked blank. "Pop, I don't understand the business. That's Marty's department."

Mort laughed. "I know, kid. It bores the hell out of you. Too bad. You'd have made a hell of a salesman. A vice-president in no time."

Davey barely heard him. His mind was on the sun-bright desert country of prefab homes, tractors, apricot and orange trees, suntanned young people. He would leave as soon as he settled his affairs. A girl named Aviva whose parents had been murdered in Treblinka was on his mind.

"You're not listening. So why am I talking business? What do you care whether I buy or sell or whether the booze is four years old or a day old?"

"Sorry, pop. I never was good at paying attention."

Mort said huskily, "But you were one hell of a linebacker. Your coach at Poly Prep used to say he never saw a kid hit so hard or take so much punishment. Maybe you should have played in college."

Dave leaned forward on the green plastic chair. He locked his huge hands between his knees. "I let you down, I guess. Every way. No interest in the business. Never even stayed with football. Lousy marks. Getting myself wounded. Making mom cry all the time."

The sorrow clotted in Mort Chain's throat, and he realized how painfully he loved the hulking youth. His son, his blood. Martin was like a brother, a crisp colleague around a polished conference table, Iris was his baby, precious and spoiled. But the innocence and the generosity in Davey made him want to weep. He got up from the chaise and put his arm around Davey's shoulders.

"Listen, kid, I love you. Don't be embarrassed. I don't care if Harry hears. Harry knows. And *my* father loved *me*, poor Jake. Davey, do what you want. Go to Israel. Don't worry about mama or me or what anyone thinks. And, Davey, you're not dumb." He was crying. "You're the best of the lot. You're what—what—my old man could have been if things had been different."

*   *   *

Some days later, Mr. Ernest Parvus called on Mortimer Chain. He proved to be a diet-slender tanned man with a creased face, a moustache thinner and nattier than the late Shikey Frummer's (which made him suspect to Mort at once), and a button of a nose. He wore a honey-colored Italian silk suit, and his eyeglass frames were shiny black and a half-inch wide.

"My daughter has writing talent?" Mort asked.

"Unquestionably, Mr. Chain."

"You're not just giving her a fast shuffle because she's rich and pretty?"

"Ernest Parvus is in business to make films. There are lots of rich pretty women around. I respect Iris. Our relationship is nothing more than professional."

It developed that Parvus was not, as Iris had said, with a studio, but was an "independent," who put together "packages" and then tried to get financing and induce a "major" to make the film. Mort knew nothing about motion pictures. He much preferred a baseball game or a prizefighter to any movie, since the outcome was unknown; whereas in any film or play or TV show, *somebody* knew how it was going to end.

It did not take Mr. Parvus long to plead his case. Mort was a leap ahead of him. The slender man in the silk suit, with the airy manner and death's-head smile, wanted *money*.

"I'm not in the movie business," Mort said. "I don't know what my daughter told you, but we don't go into those fancy things. Not that we aren't gamblers. What my son Martin would call innovators. Nice word, huh, Mr. Parvus?"

"The Chains have a way with words. I'd like to meet your sons. Iris has spoken a great deal about them. The young business tycoon and the war hero."

"The war hero is in Israel. He's got a notion Jews should stop apologizing and should hit back when somebody hits them."

"I admire that. I'm something of a fighter myself."

Mort suppressed a sneer. Some fighter, this Hollywood *shmeichler*. But he was reasonably cordial. He'd discuss the matter with his son Martin. But Martin was at a meeting of the distillers' association.

"Fascinating," Parvus said. "You're almost like a—a—separate nation. I mean, you and your competitors."

"Yeah." Nation, my ass, Mort thought. "Mr. Parvus, what kind of money do you have in mind?"

"A million, a million and a half. We call it *front* money. To get the project started. Some of it would go to pay your daughter's weekly stipend and the agreed-upon price for the screenplay."

A hustler, Mort thought, a scam artist. The moustache was the giveaway. If he was such a big wheel in Hollywood, why was he working a con on a twenty-year-old girl who had never written anything but poems for her college magazine? But he wanted his baby to be happy. And he was certain she could handle this dapper *vontz* if he ever made a pass at her.

"I need more information," Mort said. "A financial statement. Points, risks, guarantees, tax angles. I can't make the decision myself. It'll go to our board. They're cold-eyed business people, Mr. Parvus."

Parvus understood. He bragged a moment about his own business expertise.

"By the way," Mort said, as the nifty man got up, "what is this movie about?"

"I thought Iris told you. It's a period piece. Nineteen ten, nineteen twelve. About a wonderful woman, a relative of yours, Mrs. Halstead. A marvelous story."

So that was Iris's big idea. A movie about Eva?

"Mr. Parvus, I don't know anything about movies, but that sounds to me like a lousy idea. People want to laugh, to forget their troubles in the movies."

"I agree. But from what Iris says, Mrs. Halstead led a dramatic and romantic life—"

"She was a radical in the labor movement. Sweatshops, strikes, boycotts. So she married a rich man and it was a sensation in the newspapers. But this isn't my idea of a movie."

"Iris says her grandfather was close to Eva Heilig. He must have been a colorful fellow, your late father, from what she says."

"What does she say?"

"Heart of gold. But a very tough man."

And anything else, Mort thought, is none of your damn business. Iris was getting on his nerves, as only a beloved, indulged daughter could.

"One other thing, Parvus," Mort said. "No fooling around with my daughter. By you or anyone else."

"I wouldn't dream—"

"The Chains have long memories and a long reach. I'm sure you've heard talk about us. Don't hurt her. Don't make trouble for her. I can't stop her from this nonsense, but I'll see to it that our people in Los Angeles keep an eye on her. And on you."

Ernest Parvus swallowed, and thanked Mr. Chain for his

time. He left with a queasy stomach. He'd heard stories of the Chain mob, the labor racketeers and bootleggers. He would have to be extremely careful with their daughter. She was a princess whose touch could kill. Luckily, Parvus was impotent, and married to a stern older woman who watched him constantly.

Chapter 53

"Daddy's flipped," Lillian said to her mother. "Can he take this garbage he prints seriously?"

Lillian Halstead was having lunch with Eva in the kitchen of the townhouse on West Tenth Street. Once a month the unwed daughter came to visit. She knew that her mother was lonely, had few friends, rarely traveled. A faded red rose of the twenties and thirties, Eva called herself. The New Deal had preempted a great deal of socialism's programs. Norman Thomas said so. Minimum wages, plant safety, child-labor laws, social security, labor negotiations. Who needed the old organizers and pamphleteers of yesteryear? Disdaining Garrison Halstead's money, Eva lived on the rentals from the upper floors, wrote a bit, lectured at the New School, thought about writing her memoirs.

Lillian made herself a tongue-and-cheese sandwich (cooking had never been Eva's strong suit) and looked at the blue-and-gold cover of her father's magazine, *Manifest Destiny*. The articles advertised on the cover astonished her.

"Why Not Nuclear Bombs on Korea?"
"There Are More Alger Hisses!"
"FDR: Hero or Traitor?"
"The Plot to Communize Harvard"

"What's gotten into him?" Lillian asked.

"He's following new banners. Lillian, your father always lusted after strange gods. And maybe strange women. I never could figure out why he wanted me."

"Exotica. The Oriental beauty."

"Me? I looked more Polish or Russian when I was a girl.

Dr. Abelman used to say the Heiligs and the Chains had cossacks in the family tree. More coffee?"

"Thanks, mother. I really enjoy these visits. Do you have everything you need?"

Her needs were minimal, Eva said.

Lillian marveled at the strong sound of her voice. She looked well, had kept her figure slim, her white hair bouffant, always dressed in a simple black or gray suit. They had never been too close during Lillian's childhood and adolescence. Both parents had careers and spent long hours at meetings, parties, fund raising. They traveled a great deal, left Lillian with governesses. They had battled for sharecroppers, Tom Mooney, Sacco and Vanzetti, the Scottsboro boys, Angelo Herndon, the Jews in Germany, migrant workers, anarchists in Spain.

Such dedication took its toll on personal relationships. After the Little Red School House, Lillian had attended boarding schools, college, law school—a shy plain girl, incapable of flirtation, jealous of her mother's beauty. Even now, in her sixties, Eva had grace and flair. Lillian was uneasily aware that her new tweed suit did not flatter her angular figure. Her mother's old tailored jacket and pleated skirt were damned near seductive.

"I manage, Lil. The rentals are good. I get some interest on bonds Garrison gave me."

"I'll never understand why you refused alimony. With all his money? Why such pride?"

—"Oh, we old Socialists. When all else fails us, we retain our pride. Most of us, anyway. Do you know—I hate to sound like this rag your father publishes—that there are editors who won't print my articles because I never was a Red? Because I was wise to them from the time they corrupted Ike? Those noble Stalinists! They used gangsters the way everyone else did. And they ruined good unions, sold out to Hitler, and looked the other way when the Jews were persecuted in the Soviet Union."

She mentioned two left-wing editors. Powers, major names in the literary world. And oddly, they were "reformed" Communists. But they had no interest in the memoirs of Eva Heilig. Only the *chosen,* those who had been through the fiery furnace, yes, even Communists-turned-reactionary, were welcome.

"It's like McCarthy said to the witness who protested he was anti-Communist," Lillian said. " 'I don't care *what* kind of Communist you are.' Your editor friends *do* care."

Eva sipped her black coffee. "It's senseless, this political *Sturm und Drang*. One thing Marx was right about, maybe the only thing. Economics is at the root of everything. Just about everything, anyway. The Korean business will end when someone decides it's bad for business."

"It won't end with nuclear bombs? The way father seems to want it?"

Eva flicked the pages of Halstead's magazine. "Be tolerant, Lil. I predict that, within a year, your father converts to Roman Catholicism. It's the logical end for him—socialism, communism, right-wing reaction, the mother church. I hope he'll be happy."

"So do I. I don't have any mean thoughts about him. He was sort of—well, a presence. The long face, the pince-nez, that upper-crust accent. I liked him even if I never loved him."

"And me? The mama who was never home?"

"I love you, mother. Really. Everyone does."

"Lillian, stop. Who remembers the Golden Voice of the pickets? The last time anyone wrote about me was that book from the WPA Writers' Project. I was embarrassed. They got everything wrong."

Lillian took her mother's hand. It felt like a bird's wing.

"Old Social Democrats never die," Eva said. "They just write for Hearst."

Her daughter laughed. "That's funny! Who said that?"

"Dr. Abelman. I went to see him last week. We have all sorts of fancy doctors around here. Beth Israel, University Hospital. But I like him. He and his wife, that lovely woman, they're still in Brownsville."

"And you're all right?"

Eva cocked her head, as if to say, More or less. "You notice how I limp? Dr. Abelman took X rays. I'm going to see an orthopedist next week. There's some kind of bone deterioration in my left knee. Nothing serious. Part of getting old."

She talked mistily about Brownsville. It was half black now. The old-time Jewish families had by and large departed, except for the Abelmans, Kalotkin the roofer, a few others. Sarah Chain was long dead, surviving Jake by less than five years. Rabbi Piltz, in his eighties, carried on a lonely struggle in the moldering synagogue, aided by a young rabbi from Poland, a scholar who had been mugged twice by blacks.

"It's sad," Eva said. "I'll never go back. I went to where the old K and R factory was, the one that collapsed. You know the story. . . ."

"My mother the heroine. The strikes, the battles. Mama, you're part of history."

"A relic. There's a school there now. Mostly black and Puerto Rican kids. Half the windows were broken. It made me want to cry."

Lillian moved the chair closer and put an arm around the white-haired woman. "Mama, I do love you. And I admire you. We sometimes get union cases at the office, and I want to say to people—my mother, a little woman with a big voice, made this law possible. She's the reason you get raises, pensions, and benefits."

"Stop, Lil. I didn't do that much. You exaggerate."

They talked about Eva's brothers. Uncle Sol, with his law practice in Brooklyn, working as a public defender, devoting spare time to Israel, the resettlement of concentration-camp survivors, improving black slums, organizing good-government groups, battling for tenants' rights. Sol would never be rich. At one time he could have had a lucrative job with Mort Chain. But he had sent Bert Dunphy instead to make his fortune as a Chain lawyer. Candidly, Sol told Mort he would never feel comfortable arguing cases involving shipments of grain alcohol, truth-in-advertising, brand labeling.

And Abe? A rich man, an eminent surgeon. Performing specialized thoracic surgery, conducting experiments for a new kind of operation, teaching, lecturing, traveling, revising medical-school curricula. Like Sol, he and his wife were *involved*. Fund raising was one of Abe's specialties. Find a good cause and Abe and his wife were on the letterhead. Right now they were concerned with training black doctors and nurses, integrating hospital staffs, and supplying better medical services to Harlem, Bedford-Stuyvesant, and the South Bronx.

"The Heilig syndrome," Lillian said. "I guess I have a little of it also."

"I'm glad you do."

Lillian mentioned the request from the major distillers for an investigation of the Chains. The state liquor authority had asked her office to look through their files. It was no secret that Mortimer J. Chain and his late father had been among the East's most successful bootleggers.

Eva snorted. "Hmph. They should talk about illegal operations? My cousins were small-timers compared to them. Van Alst, the others."

"Not so small, mother. Give the Chains another ten years, they'll be in the *Fortune* Five Hundred."

"What's that? It sounds like a track meet or an auto race."

Laughing, Lillian explained the magazine's ratings of corporations. The Chain empire was growing, diversifying. Besides chemicals and drugs, they were now into nutrient additives for cattle and poultry, soft drinks. Mortimer Chain was rumored to be investing in motion pictures and television.

"I don't doubt it," Eva said. "Where there's money to be made, Mortimer will be there. God, I remember him with snot dribbling out of his nose, no shoes, dirt on his face. Fighting with Bernie Feigenbaum. They lived in a cellar. Jake and Sarah and the boy. No wonder he was always such a shrimp."

"Your shrimp is now a captain of industry. His son Martin may end up a general."

Hesitantly, Lillian got around to the clippings about the murder of Jake Chain, the discovery of Sal Ferrante's body some years later, and the blinding of Mort. Did her mother recall anything? Did she know Sal Ferrante?

"Of course. I didn't know him well, but his sister Theresa was one of my picket captains. Let's see, later she went to work for the Chains. She went to secretarial school. An interesting girl."

By the twenties, Eva said, she had lost track of the Chains. She rarely saw them. She recalled attending Mort's wedding to Hilda, the politician's daughter. But Sal Ferrante? He had been around for years, she remembered, he and his brothers. They seemed to get picked off by attrition, used up like spare parts. A connection between Jake's death, Sal's death, and the attack on Mort? Eva had no idea. She had become respectable, a rich man's wife, a writer and lecturer. Part of another world. Odd, she told Lillian, how the people in this world—the rich, the brainy, the elite—had so little knowledge of that other world. She conceded that the Chains were hardly subjects for veneration. But they existed. They served a purpose. Yet they remained imperfectly understood, ignored. And it seemed to Eva that, in some perverse way, they were closer to something in the national ethos, in the structure of society, than all the hoo-hoo intellectuals and snobs she had known.

Lillian said if that was so, it was terrifying.

Eva agreed. The question was, she said, why had the Chains risen to eminence? Why were they tolerated and encouraged? Was there something in the nation's soul that hungered for this stew of violence?

"One thing I've learned, Lil," Eva said, cleaning the table

and walking to the sink with a distinct limp. "In this great country, the right things get done for the wrong reasons."

Lillian wasn't sure what her mother meant. But she had an inkling. She told her mother she had spoken to the Brooklyn district attorney. He had looked up the old file on Jake's murder and the killing of Sal Ferrante. Nothing. Closed cases. No one had any information.

"What do you intend to do?" asked Eva.

She wasn't certain. Some old loyalty stirred in her. The Brownsville strain was getting the best of the Halstead genes. Jake Chain and his son were names to her, poorly limned memories. But she had heard the old tales from her mother. Would it not be worth a few inquiries? There was no statute of limitations on murder.

It all seemed far away to Eva. Lost in the mists of two wars, a depression, union battles, Red scares, bootlegging, the Roaring Twenties. She had been a part of it. So had Jake and his precocious son. For a moment she wanted to warn her daughter: *Let it rest, ignore it. They're dead, and they lived the kind of lives that courted death.* There was blood on Jake's hands.

As Lillian was leaving, Eva said. "There was a woman Jake lived with for a long time. A Mrs. Tuttle."

"What do you know about her?"

"She helped Jake and Mort run the ships that transported the liquor. She's still alive. In Freeport. She even had a son with Jake. There was once a write-up about her in the paper a long time ago. A lot of nonsense about a pirate queen who carried guns. None of it true. I met her once. She was quite nice."

"And I thought you were his only love."

"Who ever told you that, Lil?"

"Father. He said Jake worshiped you."

"Your father was inclined to exaggerate, dear. It's only since he's become a right-wing publisher and a professional informer that he's become an out-and-out liar."

Mother and daughter embraced affectionately. They kissed, wondered why they did not see each other more often. They made a date to meet again for dinner.

"Don't worry about me, dear. I'm a tough old hen, on one leg or two. I promised you I'd never be a Jewish mother to my half-Jewish daughter. But aren't there any eligible men around the office? Someone who won't be frightened by all that money your father will settle on you someday? Think of it! *An heiress!* And a magazine into the bargain!"

"Mama, I won't spurn father's money, but the magazine he can will to the Liberty League, if it's still in business. I'll let you know if someone proposes."

When she had left, it occurred to Eva that she had been less than honest. Perhaps intentionally forgetful, perhaps hypocritical. She had not mentioned to Lillian that it was Eva Halstead who had come to Jake with a last appeal. In my old age, Eva thought, perhaps I have the right to protect myself.

Chapter 54

"How did you find me?" Tommy Tuttle asked.

"Not hard. Our office can find people." Lillian smiled, and was relieved that her smile was accepted by the woman.

Mrs. Tuttle had iron-gray hair, swept back off a serene forehead and gathered in a bun at the nape of a strong neck. She wore a blue denim shirt, revealing a suntanned throat. Her body, seated in a wicker chair, looked fatless and well formed. She wore a darker blue denim skirt, no stockings, leather sandals.

Beyond the old stucco house, over the dock and the pilings, was a large green-and-white sign:

TUTTLE'S BOATYARD
CHARTER AND OPEN BOATS
MARINE REPAIRS AND SUPPLIES

A breeze from the Sound undid a strand of gray hair. The older woman tucked it in. She had an unwavering gaze. Lillian understood how Jake could have loved her. There was a palpable strength and honesty in the face. An outdoor woman, an independent one, someone who earned her own way.

"I met your mother once," Tommy said. "But I never knew there was a daughter."

"And here I am."

"What do you want to know? You say you're a lawyer?"

Lillian explained her job—the inquiries about Chain business practices. Then she mentioned the old newspaper articles. Jake's murder, Sal's. Mort blinded.

The woman shook her head slowly. "I don't know anything. Jake kept his business to himself. I was part of the Chain organization. Just the boats. Nothing else. I've become a local character in my old age. They know I used to be a lady bootlegger. It helps to have a reputation, even a bad one. The truth is, Jake and Mort did all the buying and selling."

"He loved you," Lillian said.

The gray-haired woman did not respond. She looked out to the white-capped steel-blue Sound. A Tuttle boat, a charter flying sassy pennants, with long whiplike outriggers shivering in the wind, was easing into a berth.

Tommy squinted at it. "Two blue shark," she said. "They'll be angry they didn't catch stripers. I can't guarantee the catch. It's a little different from rum-running. In the old days we knew exactly what we'd bring in, down to the last bottle."

A self-contained, honest woman, Lillian could see. No wonder Jake had been attracted to her. A look of the sea about her. The skin was lined, healthy, wind-reddened.

"I don't know what I can tell you," she said. "I have a son who works for the Chains. Actually for the government, but he supervises one of their distilleries. He's married and has a son."

Why does she tell me this? Lillian wondered. Perhaps because she knows I have Chain blood in me. The woman talked easily. No, she did not see Mortimer or Martin. They were very rich, very important men. They wanted to blot out the old lawless days.

"About this man Salvatore Ferrante . . ."

"I never trusted him. The other brothers weren't too bad, and Jake was loyal to them. Sal was the worst. He'd killed several men. They say Jake went to see Schonkeit. I remember some terrible man named Frummer whom Jake almost tore apart when they tried to hijack our first boat. Jake was afraid of nothing."

"I got curious when I saw these newspaper articles. All those unsolved deaths. Some connection, perhaps."

"May I give you some advice?"

"Of course."

"Don't keep asking questions. Of me or anyone else." She got up. "It won't bring Jake back. But if you insist on trying to find out, at this late date, you might ask your mother."

"My mother?"

Tommy sat on the heavy wooden balustrade and exchanged a few words with Anton. He was making the painters fast, securing the boat bearing the blue sharks. She turned back to Lillian.

"Miss Halstead, Jake was more honest with me than with anyone in the world. He told me that Eva Heilig was the one person in the world he couldn't refuse. He'd worshiped her when he was young. She was an ideal to him."

"I'm aware of my mother's past."

"Ask the people who lived there. Her brothers, the old doctor on Haven Place, the girls who worked in the factory with your mother. They all knew that Jacob Chain worshiped his cousin."

Lillian zipped up her briefcase. What was she searching for? What answers did she want? Perhaps some explanation of the relation between the Chains' violent world and her mother's altruism?

"Your mother sent Jake to see Schonkeit. To ask him to stop some men from trying to kill your uncle. I'm convinced it led to Jake's death."

Horrified, Lillian covered her lips with a hand. "Oh, I am sorry, Mrs. Tuttle. I never heard anything about that."

"Mort might be able to tell you about it. He didn't want to cooperate with the police. The Chains did things their own way."

She thanked Tommy Tuttle, lifted her briefcase, and descended the stairs. Gulls and terns wheeled over the inland waters, snatching at garbage, chasing baitfish.

A boy of about seven or eight, waving a large crayon drawing, walked down the gravel path leading from the blacktop road into the boatyard. He had Jake's flat face. He was towheaded and strong-limbed.

"Hey, grandma," he called. "Last day of school. I made a pitcha for you of the big boat."

"That's nice. Come up for your milk."

Lillian turned on the steps. "Your—"

"Grandson," Tommy said.

Jake Chain's grandson, Lillian thought.

Chapter 55

"Your father looks like an old pirate up there on the porch," DeeDee said. "Captain Kidd on the foredeck. All he needs is a spyglass."

"Lay off, DeeDee," Martin said irritably.

"But he does. He *is* a pirate. God, why doesn't he get a glass eye instead of that hideous patch?"

"I said lay off." He pinched her thigh: firm, muscular, well nourished.

Martin and his wife were returning to the lodge after a morning of golf. The Chains had built the nearby country club and sold it at a profit. Martin parked the Olds convertible under a soaring hemlock adjacent to the lodge, his father's "headquarters" at Camp Spruce Grove. Beyond stretched the immaculate green campus, the white-and-green bungalows, the ball field and grandstand.

"Good God," DeeDee said. "I thought I'd seen my last sleep-away camp when I was fifteen. Schoolgirl crushes and masturbating. So I marry a man whose father insists we spend a week here to help root for a baseball team."

"There are worse eccentricities, DeeDee. I'll do anything you want for the rest of the summer. East Hampton? Europe?"

"No you won't," she said. "I heard you talking to Mort. The Chain empire is in some kind of gloves-off fight."

Dazzled by her ineffably beautiful face—high forehead, long assertive nose, wide red mouth, intense brown eyes, arched eyebrows—Martin hugged her as they walked toward the lodge. "Don't pout, Dee. You had fun this morning, didn't you? We can drive to the summer theater tonight. We'll have dinner away from the family. We can screw in the back seat of the car. You always liked that."

"Vulgar."

"That's why you fell in love with me. A Brooklyn gutter rat with a veneer of Dartmouth and Harvard. You know I won you in a crap game?"

She laughed and put an arm around his waist. Martin was handsome and lean, a pantherish man. A cleaned-up Mort, with black hair growing low into a widow's peak, lush side-burns, piercing dark eyes. All the features were sharply hewn, alert.

"I don't believe anything a Chain says."

"It's true. I used to run the big crap game at Harvard Business. There was that rich little shit you used to date—"

"Martin, for God's sake—"

"An Oppenheim, or a Loeb, or a Lehman. Fine old money. I cleaned him for seven hundred dollars one night, and then I said I'd roll him once, high point, for you. First time a Wellesley girl was the stake. The punk rolled an eight. I fingered the dice the way Harry Twine taught me when I was a kid. Then I rolled a nine. A five and a four. He almost fainted."

From the porch, Mort waved at them. He had a letter in his hand. Hilda was sitting nearby crocheting. A reporter from the *Wall Street Journal* had once remarked that Mortimer J. Chain and his wife remained "plain Brooklyn folks," for all their power and wealth, and had to be admired for their simple pleasures.

"You lie, Martin Chain," DeeDee said. She kissed his ear. Their sex was vibrant, quivering. It sometimes seemed to pass electric shocks, waves, between their young bodies.

"I rolled the dice and I shouted something I'd learned from a South Philadelphia guinea in army ordnance: *'What killed Jesse James? A forty-five!'* "

"Oh, God."

"Up came a four and a five. I said to Oppenheim, or whatever his name was, never shoot craps with a Brownsville poolroom bum."

"Another lie. You were raised in a twenty-room house on Ocean Parkway."

"The doctor who delivered me was from Brownsville. I told your fella, from now on *I* date DeeDee Grau, not you. You just lost her. If I catch you with her, I'll break your arm. A week later, you and I were in a motel in Boston finding out how much we loved each other."

"You're a horrid man. Like all of your family. Nothing stops you. Anyway, you're handsome, and a pretty good golfer."

Martin took her hand and squeezed it as they walked on to the lodge. "You left out rich, cocky, mean, and a great lover, husband, and father. Hi, pop. Mom, still on that afghan? In midsummer?"

"It keeps me from getting bored. I could use a nice bridge game. Mah-Jongg I'd never find up here."

It was odd, DeeDee reflected: Nobody except Mort enjoyed these vacations at a noisy boys' camp, yet to please the one-eyed *capo di casa,* they migrated north.

"Letter from Davey," Mort said. "Some kid. They put him in charge of ten of those settlements. He's got a girl, a small house, four soldiers, and some old machine guns and rifles that don't work. Martin, we have to help Davey."

Gunrunners, DeeDee Chain thought. Smugglers, evaders of the law, undercover men.

Martin agreed with his father. Davey, the simple idealist, the blond kid with the innocent face and the heavyweight boxer's body—Jake's body—would be helped. Through normal channels the Chains had contributed lavishly and often anonymously to Israel. Guns were a special matter.

"Get in touch with that guy in Italy," Mort said. He held the flimsy airmail letter in his lap, as if reluctant to let go of the remainder of his younger son. "What was his name?"

"Levin."

Martin made a note in a memo book and tucked it into his back pocket. The mysterious Levin, who had once looked into the purchase of European vineyards for the Chains. Levin floated in and out of Rome, smuggling camp survivors, orphans, the lost and scarred and bereaved, into Palestine. Later he purchased and transported arms, darting in and out of France, Sweden, Cyprus.

"Make sure Davey gets whatever he needs, Davey *personally,*" Mort said.

"Mort, really," DeeDee said. "You can't have everything your way."

"Will you please call me pop, or daddy, or whatever German Jews call their fathers?"

"Mort!" Hilda snapped. "Your manners!"

"It's all right, Hilda," DeeDee said. "Daddy, pop, papa, we understand one another." Delicate as a ballerina, she walked up to her father-in-law and kissed his cheek. Mort patted her backside. Ah, the flesh of good inbreeding, fresh air, country homes, the right food.

"What else does Davey say?" Martin asked.

"That he's happy," Mort said. "Here, read it."

Martin sat on the log railing and read. It was rest hour at the camp. The vast lawn, the neat houses, the towering pines and spruce were silent, save for a lulling hum of summer insects. A squadron of angry jays chased two invader crows.

Not much in Davey's letter. A few misspellings (why

couldn't he learn? Martin wondered), words crossed out, fumbling attempts at expressing his love for his family, his decision to make a new life without the benefits of being a rich man's son. He and Aviva were thinking of getting married. It was dry, hot, and dusty in the border settlements. But they loved it. Davey was not only training the settlers in the arts of self-defense but running a sports program.

Martin gave the letter back to his father. Hilda began to sniffle and excused herself. She wanted all her children together, the way it was when they were little. Iris? She rarely phoned. She had been gone a month, rooming in a garden apartment in Westwood with a Smith classmate. Mort and Hilda were relieved. They didn't want her living with "producer" Ernest Parvus.

As for the great project, the movie based on the career of Eva Heilig, it had gone nowhere. Mort had made a decision. He would support Iris, give her a chance to try her hand at writing. But the dude with the moustache, who reminded him of Shikey Frummer, would get not one penny of Chain money. Iris sulked and accepted the judgment. Like all Chains, she took rebuffs in stride and proceeded to the next business at hand. But she appeared to have cut the ties to Hilda and Mort.

Whistles blew on the green campus. Ed DiBiasi, director and head counselor, was comg out of his cabin. NYU baseball cap, T-shirt, lanyard with whistle around his size-seventeen neck, clipboard.

Mort stood up and overlooked his former domain. He could hear DeeDee and Martin ordering soft drinks from Harry Twine, kidding about the golf game. He watched Uncle Ed DiBiasi gathering his staff, bellowing through a megaphone to get the campers out for afternoon activities.

Sophomores, softball . . . juniors, volleyball . . . seniors, boating and canoeing . . .

Slowly, in a manner that terrified him, Mort was seeing Ed DiBiasi and the group of T-shirted boys and men in blurred, shaky outlines. Ed's thick body was losing its hard edges. The arms and legs were going soft and melting into the green background. The boys looked wobbly, formless. As if seen underwater.

Damage to the corneas, Mr. Chain. One eye is gone, but the other appears to be all right. Of course, we'll have to watch it, and you'll need periodic checkups. . . .

Jesus Christ, Mort thought, *I'm going blind.*

He dug his hands into the log railing and braced his feet.

The figures shifted in focus. Blurred, muddled, watery. He waited, hearing his daughter-in-law and his wife discussing lunch with Harry. A door slammed behind him. A phone rang. *Goddammit,* he thought, *Chains do not accept punishment.* For a moment the old Chain urge to avenge, to refuse to be hurt, caused the blood to rush to his head, to roar in his ears.

In a minute or so his vision seemed to clear. Ed DiBiasi was waving at him, making some joke about the nature counselor's snakes. Mort saw the brawny figure more clearly and waved back.

A curious sense of rightness steadied him. He breathed deeply and stared into the cloudless summer sky, the soaring stands of evergreens, not hearing Hilda's plaintive voice. There seemed to Mort a rude justice in all that had happened. He remembered Theresa's wild sexual encounters with him, her demonic cries. Forty, she had been nurturing erotic fires inside her belly for a long time. In bed, her black hair tumbled over his chest, her mouth devoured his lips. She had bit him, dug nails and heels into his young back. And had surely hated him for years, even before Sal vanished.

Score's even. Mort thought grimly. Jake dead, Sal dead, Theresa in a mental institution on Long Island. And I'll be blind soon, rid of the violence, but ravaged by memories. Once he had overheard Iris and a girlfriend talking in that funny way those rich girls had. It was about love, sex, dying. Sex, one of them was saying, was like death. It killed you a little. Especially if it was wild enough. Mort was not quite sure what they meant. Now he thought he was beginning to understand. A flashing memory of Theresa, dark, lithe, her black curly mound confronting him like a magical symbol. Oh, once more, once more. . . .

Bunthorne was on the phone. Pop, something urgent, Martin called from inside the house. The lawyer was taking the private seaplane up that evening.

"They're after us," Horace Bunthorne said when he arrived.

His flight had been delayed by a thunderstorm. Now, with summer thunder and lightning crashing in the Adirondack woodlands around the lodge, the lawyer sat, nursing a straight vodka, with Mort and Martin in the den.

Hilda and DeeDee had gone to the movies in Crown Point. Bunthorne had brought his wife along. Tucky had promptly drunk herself into a snoring stupor. It did not seem to bother Bunthorne.

"Who, *who*, Horace?" Mort asked angrily.

In the dimly lit pine den, with logs flickering in the stone fireplace, Harry Twine refilled glasses, emptied ashtrays. Mort, Martin, and Bunthorne talked in low voices. On the campgrounds outside, a bugler blew a woeful taps.

Fortified by Chain vodka, Bunthorne relaxed. He admired the tapered bottle with its white-and-gold label. It was giving the Big Four fits. White Prince. No one knew exactly who the white prince was. The assumption was that it was a drink of nobility. The whiteness conveyed purity. The prince himself appeared in gold chain mail, bearing a lance with black pennant, resembling Tyrone Power. Actually the beverage was one hundred percent neutral grain spirits, distilled from "choice American grains," in case any purchaser got the notion he was supporting Red Russian communism by drinking it.

"Go, Horace," Mort said. "Your tank is full."

"Right you are, Mort. It's been a hell of a day. Van Alst and Rimmelberger have made a deal. They're going to put us out of business."

John Van Alst's Global Distillers and A. M. Rimmelberger's American Beverage Corporation were the giants of the field. They permitted lesser liquor companies to exist at their sufferance. Now, Van Alst and Rimmelberger wanted it all. Mort had met the two men. Van Alst was old Long Island money, deeply rooted in a bootlegging operation that made the Chains look like a "ma and pa" store. He was gray, cold, retiring, and hated Jews. Rimmelberger, of Alsatian-Jewish ancestry, was another variety of business glutton. He was showy, loud, a backer of Broadway shows, and, in his seventieth year, an escort of young actresses. He and Van Alst detested each other.

"So, Van Alst and Rimmelberger have got together finally?" Mort asked.

Bunthorne gargled vodka. "It started with their own problems with each *other*. A Mexican standoff. They figured one way to settle their differences was to put *us* out of business."

"What's the fight about? Why do they want to put the shiv in *us*?" Mort asked.

Bunthorne explained. Rimmelberger had accumulated th largest stock of whiskey and neutral spirits in the countr Van Alst, more conservative, had concentrated on well-pr moted brand names and higher-priced blends, for which required considerable outside buying. Van Alst was faced with a dilemma. He could pay Rimmelberger's high price for whiskey and make less profit on his brand names, or he could switch to cheaper brands and make less money.

As for Rimmelberger, his position was the reverse. He could make an immediate profit by selling to Van Alst, and suffer reduced sales of his own cheaper products, or he could sit on his stores and use them to blend more costly brands in competition with Van Alst.

"If Van Alst sustains his name-brand sales," Bunthorne said, "Rimmelberger gets most of the profit. It's *his* straight whiskey that's being sold. If Rimmelberger starts emphasizing brand sales, he makes less money in the retail end. Van Alst can stay ahead of him just by waiting. But they don't like that idea."

"Sounds like a draw," Martin said. "Which way will they jump, Horace?"

"On us," Bunthorne said.

"Why us?" Martin asked.

Bunthorne covered his face. "I hate to say this, Mort, but they think we're vulnerable. Old stuff. About Mr. Chain, Senior, the founding father."

Mort betrayed no emotion. It could touch him. The whole Schonkeit-Ferrante-Wesselberg mess. Blood and more blood. Christ, why couldn't people stay in their graves?

"To hell with that," Mort said. "Ancient history. What's their plan?"

The lawyer had spies inside the rival distilleries. What he did not learn from them, he learned from Mackenzie Tuttle.

"Rimmelberger will take over light whiskeys, white stuff, vodka and gin. Van Alst will grab all the straight whiskey we own."

"How can they do that?" Martin asked. "We don't issue stock. We're a privately held corporation."

"With the help of Uncle Sam," Bunthorne said. "They're going to have the Feds and the state people crack down on us. We'll be nailed for violations that the big guys have been pulling for years. They'll accuse us of unfair advertising, harassment of their salesmen, and goodness knows what else. Dunphy got word from the Brooklyn district attorney that people have been asking questions about your grandfather's death. And other murders connected with it."

Mort was immobile. A dark brooding figure. The eye patch seemed to have grown, in the half-light, covering half his shadowy face. "What else, Horace?"

"They'll refuse to sell us neutral spirits. They'll force the third, fourth, and fifth distillers to go along with them. A boycott of the Chains. In a few months we'll be desperate to sell at bargain prices. That's the plot."

Mort rubbed his hands. "Sounds like the old days. We could use Crazy Jake."

"Now, now, Mort," Bunthorne said. "That doesn't work anymore. But I'm not finished. They've hired that thug Pisano. He's going to hit us with a wildcat strike."

Scribbling on a pad, Martin reviewed what Bunthorne had told them. First, the leaders in the field were going to unearth what they believed to be old scandals involving the Chains. Second, they would complain to government agencies of illegal practices. Third, they would refuse to sell the Chains whiskey for blending—a standard practice among distillers. Fourth, they would pay Pisano to hit the Chains with a strike.

"Great," Martin said. "How do we start?"

"Counterpunch," Mort said. "If they're cutting off our supplies, it's restraint of trade. We can win that one, Horace, can't we?"

"I would think so."

Mort nodded. "The illegal practices, so-called. Worse comes to worst we sign a consent decree. We promise to be nice boys. The labor crap I'll handle myself. One thing I learned long ago is how to deal with filth like Pisano."

"And the old stuff?" Bunthorne asked warily. "The unexplained deaths, your father's problems?"

"Nobody ever learned anything," Mort said.

Among his many virtues, Bunthorne knew when to be silent. As a young lawyer he had worked briefly for Schonkeit. Although he had no precise knowledge of what had set off the chain—apt word!—of murders, he had his suspicions.

Mort got up. The Olds was pulling into the parking space behind the lodge. His wife and daughter-in-law were home from the movies. "It won't be the first time people have tried to knock off the Chains. Marty, we'll go back to the city tomorrow and go to work."

In bed with her husband later, Hilda asked for, and got, vigorous love. His virility was that of a man of thirty. She was soft and pliant. He was like metal. They made love like teen-agers.

Afterward, caressing his thick hair, kissing his chest, Hilda said: "I can't sleep. Tucky is snoring."

In the guest room, Bunthorne and wife, pickled in booze, slept as if under anesthesia.

Mort did not answer. Awake, his good eye stared at the beamed ceiling. Were the brown logs melting into the white plaster? The way DiBiasi and his counselors had turned mushy on the campus under the summer sun?

"You're worried about something," she said.

"Me? Never. A few business adjustments."

"I never saw you upset like this," Hilda said. "Hold me, I'm cold."

So am I, Mort thought. And scared. A terrifying recollection of Jake's ravaged head, sticky with blood and brains, the huge figure doubled up, crammed into the trunk of a car, made him shudder. He turned to Hilda. Old love, old partner.

"I ever tell you I really liked your father?" Mort asked. He stroked her smooth back, the ample rise of rump, thigh, unblemished, seamless.

"Why shouldn't you have liked him?" She grasped his member with soft hands, kissed his throat. "He bailed you and your father out often enough."

"And I love his daughter."

"Even if I'm two years older. I'll kill you if you ever tell anyone. I've been lying about my age since Martin was born."

He allowed himself to be drawn into her again. Cursing to himself, he regretted, in dull middle-class fashion, his affairs with chorus girls, high-priced hookers (not too often, and not with much pleasure), and especially his tempestuous sex with Theresa. Cracking her body like a whip. And blinding him.

DeeDee, lithe and lean, her white ass tantalizingly rounded, walked around their bedroom, shivering as she got into her nightclothes.

"Jesus, you'd think your old man could afford a fireplace in here. A gas heater. My boobies are like a pair of refrigerated muffins."

"Get in the sack, I'll warm them."

Martin, sitting up in bed, reading the *Wall Street Journal*, watched her trotting around the rustic room. Their baby daughter was in Armonk with a Scottish nanny. Sarah Babette Chain, they'd named the child. Sarah for Martin's dead grandmother, memorialized by the family as a heroine of the K & R disaster. Babette was a Grau name. For generations, going back to the late eighteenth century in Frankfurt, Germany, Graus had named daughters Babette. A dumb name, Martin thought, but if it indicated class, he'd accept it.

In a polka-dotted flannel nightgown, bright with pink ribbons at the collar, DeeDee got into bed and cuddled next to her husband.

"Why does a bride have fur on the bottom of her nightgown?" she asked Martin.

"Give up." He'd gone back to checking big-board listings. Chemical companies, distillers, drugs.

"To keep her neck warm, stupid."

"You learn that in college? Or at Dalton?"

"My first date told it to me. I was fourteen. It took me a week to figure it out. His name was Arnold Hoffenberg and he is an abstract painter today. I hated him. He had yellow teeth."

DeeDee always seemed to know artists, writers, theatrical people. *Interesting people.* It frosted Martin's ass. What was wrong with selling liquor and making a fortune at it? She sneered: *business.* What did intrigue her, she told him, as they wrestled for position, rearranged each other's nightclothes, made the lubricious connection, was his family's bloody past.

She enjoyed taunting her well-married former classmates with tales of terror in her husband's background. Poly Prep, Choate, Dartmouth, Harvard Business, none of this cut any ice with her Wellesley friends and their husbands. Nor, indeed, did Martin's eminence as a young executive. But the old stories of battles royal, gunfire and stabbings (DeeDee invented a great deal), were always good for laughs.

"You're not yourself tonight," she said. "Is it the mountain air?"

"Business problems."

"Ah, that's better. Now you're with me."

She made love the way she played tennis or golf, Martin concluded. It could have been a lot worse. In fact, he rather enjoyed the atmosphere of teamwork and competition. It was as if, in an adjoining bed, another young executive and his wife were humping away, keeping score with the Chains. We'd win two out of three, Martin thought.

"I'm glad, Dee."

"But—*ah, ah, good*—what's it all about? Why did the praying mantis fly up here on gossamer wings?"

"Not for you to worry about, angel."

Chapter 56

Lillian Halstead sifted through the stack of information she had accumulated on the Chain case. State and federal liquor authorities were pestering her again for the data. Everything her office could put together via interviews, searches of old newspapers, reviews of business deals, sales figures, mergers, acquisitions, court proceedings.

It did not take Lillian long to realize that an orchestrated assault against the Chains was under way. Queries came from local, state, and federal authorities. Could a request be made for records, tax returns? Had anyone interviewed salesmen for Chain products? What about that war-surplus business? Which congressmen had been friends of Mortimer and Martin Chain? Did they not often entertain government officials at expensive restaurants, furnish them with theater tickets, vacations, and perhaps women?

How much was true and how much was the work of partisans of Van Alst and Rimmelberger she could not tell. But she could see a convergence of tactics aimed at destroying the Chains.

An old loyalty stirred in her. Perhaps memories of stories her mother had told her about Crazy Jake. Eva had hinted at other acts of generosity and courage on the part of the hard-fisted founder of the dynasty. Her knight, she had joked, her champion in a checked cap and a celluloid collar.

What her mother had *not* told her was even more disturbing. The Tuttle woman had spoken of an errand Eva had asked Jake to perform. An appeal, a visit to the potent Schonkeit.

One day a batch of material, what Lillian assumed to be old investigations and court proceedings, was left on her desk. She lit a cigarette, sipped her morning coffee, got out her pad and pencil, and started to read.

The first papers were copies of an interrogation of a bookmaker named Rocco Lentini, seventy-six, retired, living in Central Islip, Long Island. The more she read, the more unnerved she became.

Q.: Mr. Lentini, did you know Melvin Schonkeit?

A.: Sure, I knew him.

Q.: In what capacity?

A.: The way I knew most people. He made bets with me.

Q.: Big ones?

A.: Big enough. The bum took me for plenty. He was past-posting. He cheated plenty of bookies.

Q.: So you weren't sorry when he was killed?

A.: You kidding? If ever a guy deserved to get his head blowed off, it was Schonkeit.

Q.: Can you tell us anything about his murder?

A.: No.

K.: You ever hear any rumors about why he was killed?

A.: There got to be a hundred reasons when a bastard like Schonkeit gets knocked off.

Q.: Do you know Mr. Mortimer Chain?

A.: Who?

Q.: Mort Chain.

A.: Oh, the bootlegger.

Q.: Did he have any dealings with Schonkeit?

A.: What are you asking *me* for? I'm a bookie. Ask Chain.

Q.: Did you know his father, Jake Chain?

A.: Yeah, yeah. I heard of him. He was a bootlegger also. Very tough guy.

Q.: Did you have business dealings with the Chains?

A.: Nah. They weren't horseplayers. They sold booze. Then they went legit.

Q.: You know that Jacob Chain was murdered? A few months before Schonkeit was killed?

A.: Yeah. Well, he was a stand-up guy. His kid, Morty, he was tough also, but he never used his fists. Brains. He had every cop in Brooklyn on the payroll.

The interrogation meandered on. Rocco Lentini was a closemouthed fellow, typical of his breed. He revealed nothing. But the questioner, an assistant D.A., was clearly trying to connect the Chain and Schonkeit murders.

Lillian lit another cigarette—dreadful habit, her mother said—and reread the bookie's responses. Old stuff. Nothing that could be acted on. Then she noticed, for the first time, the date of the interview. *August 15, 1950.*

* * *

Martin and Bunthorne were going over a list of Rimmelberger's major stockholders. The Chain heir, at age twenty-six, was proving as cunning as his father. Perhaps more so."

"What fascinates you about Bernard J. O'Toole?" asked Bunthorne. At ten in the morning, he was sipping an apple juice and vodka.

"He's the son of an old speakeasy owner my family used to supply. Made a fortune in contracting. Political clout also."

"And he is now the second biggest stockholder in the Rimmelberger corporation."

"If we can get his ear, maybe talk to a few more big stockholders, we may be able to educate them," Martin said.

"I think I see where you're going."

"They might like the idea of quick profits. Who knows how long this Korean business will drag on?"

Bunthorne shut his eyes. "See if I read you. You work the Chain charm on Mr. Bernard O'Toole, others. You convince them that Mr. Rimmelberger should sell off an ocean of his whiskey to Mr. Van Alst. Huge profits are realized at once. Rimmelberger stock rises. O'Toole can then reap great rewards by selling out or banking the dividends."

"Right," Martin says. "It takes the heat off us. Van Alst may decide it's advisable. Avoid tangling with us, avoid getting other distillers sore at him. Horace, we can shout conspiracy in restraint of trade. We put pressure on Rimmelberger through his stockholders to sell to Van Alst. Van Alst keeps bottling brand names in volume. We let them fight over brown whiskey. We keep shifting into whites."

"My palate tells me you may be right."

"How do we reach O'Toole?" Martin asked. "How do we convince him to rally his fellow stockholders and prevail upon Mr. R to sell?"

Bunthorne cleared his throat as the buzzer on Mort's desk sounded. "Oh, a hundred thousand dollars might get him started," the company lawyer said. "With the promise of another hundred if he can deliver for us. I hear he enjoys a glass. I could have a few with him."

Martin nodded his approval. It was worth a try. He was even more certain that this back-door approach was obligatory when he heard Dr. Harris Weltfish's shaking voice on the phone.

"Martin, we've got troubles. A wildcat strike. They've burned a delivery truck and thrown up picket lines. There were fights all morning. We've got the police out, but the men are walking off the job."

"Who called the strike?"

"Pisano's goons. The police captain told me that half the guys picketing have records a mile long. Martin, it's bad. They slashed tires and broke windshields, including mine."

"Why didn't the cops stop them?"

Harris stuttered. "Th-they got here too late. Nobody'll identify the men who did it."

"I'll be right out."

Weltfish felt his confidence surge. There was something about the Chains that made you feel better when things went sour. Perhaps it was their absolute faith in themselves; the hard way they looked at the world, refused to quit, showed no fear.

He told Martin that Mackenzie Tuttle, the government man at the New Jersey plant, was on the phone with Washington. Mac knew people who could help. If the strike and the violence did not stop, they would seek injunctions.

Martin called for his car. Without chauffeur, he told his secretary. He'd drive it himself. Meanwhile Bunthorne was to get in touch with union leaders with whom they had contracts. The Chains had always paid generously, both in contractual agreements and in gifts to union officials.

On Martin's way out of the office, his father met him in the anteroom. Mort looked grayish under the tanned skin. He was wearing a thick lens over his good eye. It distorted the pupil.

"Trouble in Jersey, pop," Martin said. "You all right?"

"Yeah, yeah. The doctor put drops in. Nerve fatigue. I got to rest it a few days. What kind of trouble?"

Martin told him about the wildcat strike by their drivers. Weltfish had sounded worried. Bert Dunphy was bargaining with Ruggiero Pisano and his hoodlums. Martin did not tell Mort that a truck had been wrecked, fires set, that the plant was in danger of shutting down.

"So where are you going?" Mort asked.

"To settle it. Pisano is part of the competition's scheme."

"I'm going along."

Martin tried to stop him as they waited for the private elevator. The receptionist and the uniformed guard watched as father and son argued.

"You have a bad eye, pop. Dr. Shapiro said to rest it. Do me a favor. Go home. Relax. Since when does a hood like Pisano worry the Chains?"

"And since when does a Chain back down? Move, kid. I'm going with you."

They could see the ruined hulk of the van, lying on its side, scorched and twisted. A large area of the macadam entrance to the distillery was littered with smashed bottles, pools of whiskey, cardboard cases. Three trucks, loaded and ready to leave, were halted inside the parking area behind the Cyclone fence with its barbed-wire crown. Fifty feet away on the grassy shoulder of the state road, a Chain tank truck, loaded with neutral grain spirits, waited. The windshield was cracked. No driver was in evidence.

"Go through the gate," Mort said to his son.

"Maybe we should park here and walk in," Martin said. "Those animals may throw a brick. If we walk, at least the cops can protect us."

About thirty men in work clothes had formed a picket line at the gates to the distillery. The Chains saw Ruggiero Pisano at once. A golf-playing strong-arm man. He carried no sign, but wore a white cap with the name and number of his local on it.

"I only see about nine or ten of our men on the line," Martin said. "There's a couple of hundred inside the plant, still on the job."

Strike Chain!

New contract! New contract!

Twenty more a week!

The pickets charged and waved their signs but kept their distance from the fence. Ten local cops and a dozen state police in dark blue breeches and jackboots lolled about, resting against prowl cars.

"Can't you clear them out?" Mort asked one of the troopers on the highway.

"Oh, hi, Mr. Chain. We're waiting on a court order. Mr. Pisano claims he's got a permit."

"You see it?"

"Yessir."

Four men in work clothes, newer employees, came out of the gate and joined the pickets. Behind the gate, Eddie Twine, wearing his union button, in peaked cap and green coveralls, watched with solemn black eyes. If there was going to be action, he wanted part of it.

In one of the casement windows Dr. Weltfish and Bert Dunphy looked out gloomily at the scene.

"This plant is *struck!*" Pisano was shouting. He was standing on the bed of a red pickup truck. His voice was a croak, as if he had been hit too often in the throat.

"Cheap bum," Mort said. "In the old days, we'd give a bum like that a cement overcoat."

"It's not the old days, pop," Martin said.

Mort, seeing dimly, figures vague and blurred, lights flashing where they should not flash, corners of his field of vision turning muddy, told his son to drive through the gate.

"We'll escort you," the trooper said. Two motorcycle cops preceded the blue Cadillac.

The big car was halfway through the gates when the pickets surged around it, trying to strong-arm their way through the police cordon.

"That's them!"

"Get the Chains!"

"Tear his fucking eye patch off!"

"Crooks! Bloodsuckers!"

"Bastards! Robbers!"

From the truck bed, Pisano egged his goons on. "Police brutality! Lay off my guys! We got a right to a living wage!"

A rock bounced off the roof of the car. Another struck a side window, shattering it. Bits of glass stung Martin's neck, cut Mort's cheek.

Unwilling to run over their tormentors, Martin inched the big car forward. He could see Weltfish and Dunphy pleading with two men, obviously asking them not to leave the plant. Hell, he thought as a third rock bounced off the truck, it doesn't matter. If they won't take trucks out with deliveries, or bring in spirits for blending, we'll have to close anyway.

"Stop the car," Mort said.

"Why?"

"I'm getting out. No dago bastard is going to get the best of us. I told him at the golf club I'd be the first one to drive a truck through if he pulled a strike, and I never back off a threat."

Martin did not try to stop him. A trooper shoved a burly man in a windbreaker away and leaned in the window. "I wouldn't if I were you, Mr. Chain."

"You aren't me. Let me out."

Once his father was out, feet planted on the tar parking lot, Martin inched the car forward again. stopped, and also got out. Strangely, the shouting pickets, quick to throw rocks at the car, now retreated a few steps.

Mort stood his ground. A slender dark man in a tan suit.

The black patch suggested a pirate clothed by J. Press. Martin looked at him. It was in the blood, in the nervous system, this appetite for combat.

"Pisano," Mort said. "You want to talk? Come up to my office. I don't talk with a gun to my head."

Shuffling his feet, the union boss did not descend from his perch on the red pickup.

"Come on, Pisano. You a man or a coward? I won't hurt you. You want to be a man, you'll sit down with me in my office and we'll talk. The way my father used to talk to union guys. Want an election? NLRB? A mediator? Or you want a funeral with lots of flowers?"

Eddie Twine and two other black employees, muscle-heavy men, came out of the area behind the opened gates. They watched with understanding eyes. One thing they knew about Mr. Mort Chain and young Mr. Martin Chain—they had more black people on payroll than any factory in the county. Your color never counted with them. Your work did. Your loyalty.

"Wise guy, huh, Chain?" Pisano yelled. "Think you can sweet-talk me? We're gonna unionize your goddamn plant all over. Close you down. You see that delivery truck?" Pisano pointed to the tank truck on the grassy roadside outside the gate, like an abandoned space ship. "That's the last one gets as far as any distillery of yours. Try *sucking* the alky out of it."

Mort pounded a fist into his palm. "You won't come in like a gent and talk? What kind of *walyo* are you, Pisano?"

The state trooper whispered in Mort's ear: "Let us handle it, Mr. Chain. They aren't distillery workers. They're Pisano's hoods."

Mort smiled at the officer. "Captain, you think the Chains don't know about wrongos? I guess you're too young to remember Prohibition. We've been on that side of the fence."

From the line of pickets two more rocks were thrown by the hooting, cursing men. One glanced off Mort's arm. The other sailed toward the gate and hit Eddie Twine in the chest.

Mort understood Pisano's strategy. He could not possibly strike the plant. He would never get enough men to walk off. Dunphy had taken care of the shop steward and the business agent. But if they could put a crimp in deliveries, they'd be serving the purposes of the men who wanted to destroy the Chains—Van Alst and Rimmelberger.

"All right, Pisano. Have it your way. You see that tank truck? I am going into the truck and I'm driving it through the gate. Me, Mortimer Chain. I promised you I'd do it. Every time you stop a truck, I'll be here to drive it through. Anyone tries to stop me gets his head ventilated. Understand, *paisan?*"

"Scab!" Pisano shouted. "Try it!"

Martin pulled the Cadillac to one side and swung it into a parking area. He wanted the entrance to the distillery clear. More rocks were hurled. Three state troopers unhooked their clubs and started to shove Pisano's people away. The mob churned, struggled, cursed. Two of Pisano's gang unfurled an American flag.

Martin got out of the Cadillac and surveyed the scene. He seemed an unlikely participant in the confrontation—a handsome, whippy-looking man in a khaki-colored Ivy League suit, white button-down shirt, green and white Dartmouth tie. His cordovan loafers gleamed.

Eddie Twine and friends came toward him. "You need us, Martin?"

"No. Maybe later, Ed."

Martin walked across the tarry pavement and looked at his father, as if assuring him that he, son and heir, was a true Chain. Something worried Martin. His father looked hesitant. It was the eye, Martin knew; it had been a long time since Mort had indulged in rough stuff.

"Pop, I'll drive it," Martin said.

To Martin's surprise, his father did not dissuade him. "Okay, kid. It's part of our life, right?"

Pisano shouted, "Anyone goes near that truck gets a pair of broken chops. Augie, Angie, Mike, stop them."

Four men ran from the picket line to the truck. The terrified driver, who had been sitting on the shoulder of the highway, got up and ran. As Pisano's men neared the cab, Eddie Twine and his friends converged on them.

"Nigger assholes," one snarled.

"You get near that truck," Eddie said, "you be suckin' nigger assholes. Devoe, Morland, git on either side of me."

Pisano's men stopped short. Sneaks, experts at the low blow, the shot in the back, they did not like the look of these huge coons. The Chains always had a few big dinges hanging around. Besides, Augie, Angie, and the others were hired help. Their contract did not require them to get beaten or arrested.

Father to son, Martin thought as he walked to the truck. *We have to prove it in every generation.* He recalled his grandfather, the stories of his battles. And his father, daring when he had to be. *Now me,* Martin thought. His heart pounded as if wanting to tear itself loose and burst through the sternum. *Thank God I'm in shape,* he thought. He was tireless, leathery, a boxer in college and the army.

"You know how to drive that big mother, Martin?" Eddie asked.

"You kidding? I drove semis in army ordnance. I'll double-clutch her all the way to the loading dock."

Pisano's apes picked up stones. They tossed a few, then retreated as Eddie lumbered toward them.

An incongruous driver, Martin thought. *In my narrow lapels and green argyle socks. I smell of Habit Rouge, my hair was styled by Dmitri of Fifth Avenue, and I'm wearing a one-thousand-dollar Philippe Patek watch.*

He gunned the motor. Double-clutching the giant tractor, Martin eased it off the slope and swung it wide.

"You got no union card!" one of the men shouted. "You ain't allowed to drive!"

"Scab bastard!"

A brick sailed at the windshield. The glass blasted itself into a crystalline fretwork but did not shatter. Martin eased himself toward the door and looked out the side window. He completed his turn at five miles an hour and moved through the open gates.

"Get the guy who threw the brick!" Mort shouted at the troopers.

Pisano's mob had moved off, willing to concede a temporary victory to the Chains. They'd get their ten bucks for the day and go home. Pisano would call his contact later for new orders.

Mort saw the truck dimly, the long gray metallic body, the giant double tires, as it passed through the chain-link gate and rolled toward the loading platform.

The pavement shimmered in the sunlight, the beige flanks of the four-story distillery wavered and shook. Light was vanishing, clouds hemming in the enormous building, the storage areas, the parking lot.

Outside the gate, Eddie and his friends had been attacked by Pisano's thugs. The state troopers and the local cops were trying to separate them. There were curses and shouts.

Get the big nigger!

Cut his balls off!

'Ey, Angie, look out, he got a knife!

The police separated the brawling men, thwacked heads

and backs with their clubs. Eddie floored Pisano with a left hook; swung at two clawing men.

Mort tottered, covered his eye. Bert Dunphy came running out of the building to take his arm.

"You okay, Mort?"

"My eye. Everything's turning gray. Cloudy, Bert?"

"No, Mort. It's sunny."

Outside, Pisano's men were hurling rocks and bricks again. Eddie, his head a bloody mass, was trying to choke Angie. The hoodlum spit, slavered, struggled. Eddie's friends Devoe and Morland were retreating to the gate, warding off blows and bricks. Two state policemen pulled Eddie away and dragged him into the factory area. His shirt was a mass of dark blood. He did not mind. He would give blood for the Chains.

A rusted four-inch bolt, thrown as if from a crossbow, whistled through the closing gates and struck Mort's forehead. Blood spurted and flooded his eyes. Dunphy caught him.

"Son of a bitch," Mort said. "You see the guy who threw it?"

"No, Mort. It's a mob scene. You hurt?"

"Nah, nah. But I can't see. Wipe the blood away, Bert."

A local policeman came running to Mort's side. "Want an ambulance, Mr. Chain? A doctor?"

Dunphy took his handkerchief and stemmed the flow of blood from a long gash over Mort's right eye. "Better?"

"A little."

The blood was gone from his eye. But everything looked darker than it should. He saw Dunphy's face turning slate, the sharp edges going furry. He barely discerned Martin—a blackish smudge—getting out of the tractor and talking to someone. Weltfish? Tuttle?

Christ, he thought, it's all cloudy, everything covered with a curtain of soot.

"Send for a doctor," Dunphy said to the policeman.

Chapter 57

Mr. Bernard J. O'Toole had mauve dewlaps, a burnished pink pate, a nose like a crimson mushroom cap, and popping gray eyes. He was chunky and solid, and although well into his fifties, he looked mean and tough. In fact, he informed Horace Bunthorne as they sat down for lunch at the University Club, he had just played two hours of strenuous four-wall handball.

Earlier, in the bar, Mr. O'Toole, tightly suited in navy blue, a stiff white shirt collar constricting his neck so that a purplish coloration infused jowls, jaw, and cheeks, had gulped three scotches. He had ordered Rimmelberger's top name brand, Highland Drum, and downed the amber booze without taint of water or ice.

"Loyalty to the firm, Mr. O'Toole?" Bunthorne asked.

"I believe in brand names and brand sales. Mr. R does too. Except for that bastard Van Alst, we'd own the market."

Bunthorne measured his man. Rich, very rich. Son of a speakeasy owner. The son, like Mort Chain, had risen higher. Bootlegger, nightclub owner, patron of the turf. Mr. O'Toole had kept his nose clean, muted the rough stuff, gone legit about the time the Chains had; then found it expedient, profitable, and conducive to his leisure to sell his considerable interests to the voracious Rimmelberger.

At once Bunthorne realized the key to Bernie O'Toole's character. He would have to match him drink for drink. If necessary Bunthorne would have to outdrink him. Perhaps drink him into unconsciousness. There was, Bunthorne knew in his midwestern heart, a variety of rich and powerful person who is awed, and can be ultimately won over, by someone who can demonstrate a superior thirst.

At the preliminary session in the bar, Bunthorne had downed three White Prince vodkas, unblemished except for freshly ground black pepper. The condiment intrigued O'Toole and he asked about it.

"The Russians like it that way. Claim it gives a bead."

"A *bead*. I haven't heard that since Prohibition. When we

poured fusel oil or sulfuric acid into the piss for the suckers. I didn't know you worked for the Chains then, Bunthorne."

"I didn't. But you pick up a lot of interesting folklore around Mort."

"How is the one-eyed wonder?"

Bunthorne gauged O'Toole. A bit of Irish sentiment in him, probably. Sheds a tear when he hears sad songs about Galway and Cork. Heavy infusions of alcohol would undoubtedly increase his sympathy quotient.

"I thought you might have heard," the lawyer said. "He's lost the sight in his other eye. He was injured when Pisano tried to strike the Jersey plant. It was always a chancy business, ever since he lost the right eye. Mort's blind, I'm afraid. Sees a little light and shadows, but the doctors say it's hopeless. They've decided against an operation."

O'Toole drained his scotch. He shook his head. "Jesus, Mary, and Joseph, I'm sorry to hear that. I never was a close friend of the Chains, but I knew Mort when he ran trucks up to Canada. Well, anyway, they didn't turn yellow at a few dagos. There never was any ki-yi in the Chains."

Stroking his pink scalp, Bernie O'Toole, over bluepoints and double lamb chops and three more scotches (Bunthorne matched him, White Prince to Highland Drum), reminisced about the rough old days. He and his father, the departed speak owner who had made the first ride north with Ferrante, had always respected the Chains.

"Y'see, Mr. Bunthorne," the Irishman said candidly, "hebes are usually soft. White hands, yellow in a fight, full of schemes. The old guys with long whiskers and faces the color of dry dog shit, the young ones with them little round hats, burying their noses in books to be doctors or lawyers. Like those Heilig kids." Not that Bernie O'Toole didn't admire learning. It was just that mockies went at it too avidly and closed other people out. They were a race who would rather study than drink. It was unnatural.

"Their privilege, sir," Bunthorne said. "America is wide open for everyone. I was a dirt farmer's son."

"That ain't what I mean. The Chains were smart even if they never went to college. But, besides brains, they weren't afraid. My father told me about the old man, Jake. Lift a wagon by the rear axle. Unload an ice truck faster than a gang of spades. And fight? Eat bullets? You had to admire a son of a bitch like Crazy Jake."

"I'm sorry I never knew the man. He died before I joined the firm."

"Died? Schonkeit had him killed."

"A shame."

"Yeah. He never learned to duck, Crazy Jake. I am sorry about Mort losing his vision. In the old days we never got in each other's way. Territorial rights, respect for each other. In fact my later interests were largely in improving the breed."

"An American success story," Bunthorne said. He ordered another round. His quarry's face was turning scarlet, inflating, cheeks puffing out like a blowfish's belly, the tracery of burst blood vessels on the nose fiery hot. Scotch seemed to issue in droplets from O'Toole's fuchsia forehead, as if bypassing the digestive system and oozing from gullet to skin.

As for Horace Bunthorne, who had consumed as much one-hundred-proof vodka as O'Toole had imbibed ninety-proof scotch, he showed no sign of wear. He was clear-eyed and clear-skinned. His loud midwestern voice was warmer and more sincere than ever.

Skillfully the lawyer soft-soaped Bernard O'Toole. Terrible, all that bloodshed. Did Mr. O'Toole know that the Chains were reputed to have had something to do with the departure of Melvin Schonkeit? And was that not a blow for liberty, for honest horse breeders, turf enthusiasts, bookmakers?

O'Toole agreed. It was a boon to mankind, an act of kindness that the Paymaster had been removed.

Disdaining dessert or coffee—it left less room for alcohol—the men retired to a quiet corner of the bar. Bunthorne calculated that O'Toole had drunk the equivalent of a fifth of scotch.

The Irishman comprehended he was in a battle of heroic proportions. Finn McCool against Brian Borrhu. If there was one other thing Bernie O'Toole respected beyond raw courage, it was a capacity for the disturbance. He looked at Bunthorne's sloped face, the enormous eyes, the imprinted American smile. Sweatless, steady. No wonder Mort Chain and his kid had such confidence in this tall bag of bones.

"Brandy," Bunthorne commanded. "It helps the digestive process."

O'Toole nodded dreamily. He would go to the mat with this sponge, match him shot for shot.

On the third round from the decanter—it was Courvoisier—Bunthorne began his appeal to the second biggest stockholder in A. M. Rimmelberger's American Beverage Corporation. Yes indeed, Mr. O'Toole, Mr. R would do well to start selling his whiskey to Van Alst. Profits, enormous profits beckoned. A rise in American Beverage stock, dividends, benefits for all . . .

O'Toole's eyes turned to jellied yellow lumps. Sweat drenched the rim of his shirt collar. Bunthorne assured him that the Chains' government contacts hinted that there would be no curtailment of whiskey production because of the Korean War.

After the fourth brandy, Mr. O'Toole excused himself and went to the men's room. He returned fifteen minutes later, looking bleached and wet-eyed. Bunthorne greeted him with a poisonous-looking green drink, a grasshopper. Vodka and green crème de menthe.

"Jesus God," the Irishman said. "What's that green piss you're drinking?"

Bunthorne revealed the ingredients. His voice was loud and cheery. It settled the stomach, the lawyer said. It would do wonders for Mr. O'Toole's tormented gut.

The poor fellow had just heaved his cookies. And met his match. But he could not let a WASP skeleton drink him into blind paralysis. "I'll try one," O'Toole said shakily. "You long-legged prick." He drained the goblet, spit ice cubes, and fainted, sliding from the leather club chair to the mahogany parquet floor.

Bunthorne smiled. He had his man.

"Our proposal was accepted," Bunthorne told Mort and Martin briskly. "Mr. O'Toole said he understood the validity of our arguments re the sale of Rimmelberger's whiskey to Van Alst. He agrees that we must not be made the victims of their unseemly greed."

Mort's face was hidden by dark eyeglasses. The black lenses were connected to black plastic sidepieces that rested against his temple and locked out light. He nodded. "You're a genius, Horace. You can talk to these people better than me. They know you have an edge on them."

They were seated on the sun porch of the house in Brooklyn, amid slants of sunlight passing through louvered windows. In the living room, DeeDee and Hilda's voices drifted out. There was some strain evident. Hilda was complaining that DeeDee never came to visit, that she kept their granddaughter, Sally, from her grandma. There was an unspoken accusation: We aren't fancy enough for you.

Martin wished they would shut the door. He loved his mother, but he had come to regard her as a spoiled and selfish woman. Uneducated, uninterested in books, theater, or politics, she had grown increasingly lazy, sullen, and humorless. Men stared at the busty figure, the high crown of gray-streaked black hair, the immaculate white skin and dark red lips. Her eyes burned with what seemed feverish passion, but her mind was constricted. Martin pitied her. But he was learning a valuable lesson. You needed resources beyond money to survive. Education helped. So did an active mind, interests beyond family, money, acquisitions. His brother Davey knew this.

"You'll come for dinner next weekend?" his mother was asking.

Jesus, Martin wanted to scream, *food, family, home, possessions, prices! Open your mind!*

"We can't, Hilda," DeeDee said. "We have horses entered in the Carillon Show." No invitation was extended to Hilda and Mort.

Martin tried to close out their conversation as he listened to his father and Bunthorne.

"Rimmelberger will come around," Bunthorne said. "Dunphy tells me the old guy is having marital problems with his twenty-eight-year-old wife. He's getting monkey-gland injections. Nothing gets a man on edge as much as woman troubles. He may lack the kidney for a knockdown fight."

Removing the dark glasses, Mort blinked. "Good work, Horace."

Martin felt a draining sorrow. His father's sightless eyes were unfocused, recessed.

"See anything, pop?" Martin asked. He held up his manicured tanned hands. "See my hands?"

"Just some light from the window. The rest is dark."

Nursing his fourth vodka, Bunthorne thought sorrowfully: He can't see the hands of his heir. Or the beige twill hacking coat, the polished brown boots. Young Martin Chain, horseman. A shame the father couldn't perceive the glory. Bunthorne never ceased to admire the awesome leap these intense Jews had made. Three generations. Horses to horses. But no taking of anyone's horse shit. Not even from giants like Van Alst.

"When do you see Dr. Shapiro again?" Martin asked.

"Next week. He says that, for now, all I should do is rest. The cornea may heal. If it doesn't, what the hell, I'll get a dog."

Bunthorne and Martin saw his jaw go taut. The teeth

flashed in the old Chain anger. But his voice did not crack. His big hands remained clenched in his lap.

Compassion gnawed at Martin's heart. The old man—*he was only forty-six!*—was doomed. He had talked to the doctors. The cornea was shot, the old trauma worsened by the new injury. Darkness for the rest of his life. We Chains, Martin thought, are hard and mean and smart, but we don't wear too well. Jake blasted into a bloody ruin at age forty-six. His own father blinded at the same age! Martin struggled with the cold fears and gray doubts in his heart, sensed shudderings in his soul. He looked into the sun-bright living room where Hilda was now weeping gently as she held DeeDee's hands.

"I think the cops know the guy who threw the bolt," Bunthorne said. "Some small-time bum." He helped himself to another shot. "Bert and I had a meeting with the local D.A. Pisano was questioned. He isn't the tough cookie he thinks he is. We may be able to hang a few old raps on him unless he talks about who paid him."

"I'd like to see long enough to meet him," Mort said softly. "Blow his head off."

"Easy, pop," Martin said. "It's different today."

"Not much. We do it in boardrooms, courtrooms, government agencies. We kill each other nicely."

Things were looking better for the Chains, Mort agreed. It was not like them to roll over and die, to surrender, to let competitors and hoods walk all over them. Jake knew this when he was upsetting wagons carrying scabs in pickle barrels. Young Martin, full of Dartmouth and Harvard wisdom, understood it also.

There remains, Mort thought, the old bloody business. Ferrante, Schonkeit, Jake, Wesselberg. He'd gotten a call from the old bookie Lentini. Interrogated again. Who knew some surviving Ferrantes, those unlucky bastards they'd used up like spark plugs, might decide to break the code of *omertà?*

DeeDee and Hilda came out on the porch. Hilda had pulled herself together.

Martin got up. "Horace, anything you need to make the Jersey cops more helpful and keep Pisano on ice, you'll get. Just ask. What about the government? All that nonsense about us restraining trade?"

"Not to worry. Once Van Alst and Rimmelberger start trading booze, they'll lay off. You know who tells government agencies what to do. If the big guys can dominate the market without killing us, the government will go away."

"I got something else in mind," Mort said. He patted Hilda's soft hand. The ride to Montreal kept forming images in his mind. Hilda; Lamotte, the garage owner and whiskey supplier; the wild ride back; Sal blowing out the brains of the Canuck who tried to hijack them . . .

"I'll tell Horace, pop. You relax."

Bunthorne, assembling his stalklike limbs, his face the color of a Burpee tomato, got up. He could guess. He knew his employers. One did not threaten them with impunity. Not even a Van Alst.

"We intend to file that countersuit we talked about," Martin said. "You and Bert will talk to some congressmen. There's one guy who owes his election to us, another whose brother is a federal judge, thanks to the Chains. We're going to ask the Feds to turn the thing around. Van Alst and Rimmelberger are about to be investigated for restraint of trade and unfair competition."

"Fighting, fighting, always *fighting*," Hilda said. She rested her head against Mort's dark thick hair. "Retire, Mort. Let Martin run it."

"As soon as I have my innings, Hilda."

DeeDee, in riding habit, her ass a perfect tan peach, her waist constricted and muscular, watched these alien presences. Jews unlike any she had been raised with. Not like the people who sent daughters to Dalton or Emma Willard or Madeira. Nor did you meet such as the Chains at the Winding Ridge Hunt Club.

"I'll drink to that," Bunthorne said.

"Since when do you need an excuse?" DeeDee laughed. In a way she understood Bunthorne better than she did her inlaws. He was shrewd, energetic, manipulative, but he seemed less concentrated, less ready for combat, less the coiled spring. The Chains were another species. Struggle, violence if necessary, was in their genetic code.

"To what?" Hilda asked.

"The Chains going on the offensive," Bunthorne said.

"Take a look at the *Wall Street Journal*, page two," Garrison Halstead said to Eva on the phone.

"I never read it, Garry."

"Your cousins the Chains are about to pull off one of the great corporate coups of the year. Listen." He read the headline: " 'Justice Department to Probe Major Distillers: Chain Organization Brings Suit Against Others.' "

"So?" Eva asked.

"It's unbelievable. I've talked to banking friends and people in government."

He reviewed the astonishing turn of events. Two giant distilleries had been trying to destroy Mortimer and Martin Chain. Suddenly roles were reversed. Someone in Washington had seen the light. Certain powers had decided that the real offenders were not the Chains but the very people trying to wipe them out.

"I'm not surprised," Eva said. "How does it concern me?"

She'd been feeling ill all morning. A hot Indian-summer day. Her legs aching. Short of breath after climbing stairs to collect overdue rent from the artist. She had listened to radio newscasts. The Americans landing at Inchon. MacArthur trying to trap the North Koreans and liberate Seoul. She no longer had strong political interests. Her radicalism was subdued, tolerant.

"I want you to do a piece for *Manifest Destiny* about the Chains," Halstead said. "Eva, you know them. You can recall that gamy stuff you used to tell me about. The old days in Brownsville. Darling, remember when I put up bail for you?"

"I do, Garry. But don't hold me in debt forever. I married you. That was enough."

"But you said you wanted to start writing again. We don't pay much, but we're widely read."

"By the John Birch Society, the Committee Against Taxation, and every right-wing, crypto-fascist group in the country. I would no more have my name in your rag than in the *Daily Worker*. People like me will end up in the same concentration camp with the Reds when your friends come to power."

"Take a little insurance, Eva. Join us. Really, you could do a marvelous article. We believe in free enterprise. Who could be freer than the Chains? I admire them. I really do. You never gave them enough credit."

"More than you think. The answer is no."

"Did you know that Lillian is looking into them? She's had requests for investigations from the state liquor authority and the Treasury Department."

Lillian, Eva thought, you should never tell your father a damned thing. Garrison, in his groping way, would be bound to misuse it. He was the ultimate political dilettante and nincompoop.

"Lillian says it's of no importance," Eva said. "I'd advise you not to print anything in your magazine."

"I would print nothing to hurt the Chains. I wanted a sympathetic piece from you. As believers in the laissez-faire system, I feel that the Chains are paradigms of the system."

Gagging, Eva bid him goodbye. There would be no article from her on any subject. She cautioned him not to call their daughter for information about the Chains.

Before hanging up—Halstead always seemed reluctant to leave off—he asked, like an embarrassed boy, if he could call Martin Chain about a contribution to the magazine. For all of Halstead's wealth, he was losing money keeping *Manifest Destiny* afloat. Would not a beneficiary of the private-enterprise system, a man harassed by government regulation. be happy to give a hundred thousand dollars toward the furtherance of the free market?

"Don't waste your breath, Garry," she said. "Martin Chain is ten times as smart as you. He won't sleep any sounder at night knowing you're in his corner." She hung up.

"I miss Davey." Mort wept that night. "I miss the kid. Why doesn't Iris call? Why do we always have to call her?"

Hilda embraced the blind man in the canopied double bed. "Please, Mort. We can't hold them here. I should be the one crying. Jewish mothers, that's our business. We'll make a trip to California to see—"

"See? Me? Who can I see?"

"You will see again."

The doctors lied to you, or you are lying to me, he thought. Waste no tears, he told himself as he embraced Hilda's pillowy roundness, stroked her back.

Davey kept haunting him. He'd neglected the youngest son, ignored him for the favorites—Martin, the brainy one; Iris, the flashy daughter. Davey had always gone his own way, quiet, uncomplicated, making his own decisions.

What was it he missed with the boy away? A simpleness, a goodness that he knew had always been lacking in himself. He cried again. Never to see Davey's trusting flat-nosed face again, the shock of dark blond hair, the half-smiling eyes, a little cautious, as if ill at ease in the complex world in which his father and brother moved so easily.

"Make love to me, Mort."

"Sure, baby. I'll try."

"You're the only man I ever had sex with, and no one could have been better."

He wanted to say: We are some lovers—wife forty-eight, husband forty-six and blind as an earthworm.

Mort decided to call Davey in the morning. "That Davey," Mort said. "He has the right idea. He doesn't own two pairs of shoes, but he's happy. Maybe we should try it."

"Mort, don't be crazy. We're used to this life. Servants, cars, homes. I admire what Davey is doing. But he'll wake up someday. What sort of existence is that for a boy with his advantages? Marching around the desert, getting shot at by Arabs, training boys and girls to throw grenades?"

Dear wife, Mort thought. Truly, Otzenberger's daughter. But he forgave her. She had shared a great deal with him; he could be tolerant. Sightless now, he would need her more than ever. A practical, humorless, efficient woman, and still—he gagged as the thought surfaced—beautiful.

Chapter 58

"Signals are switched," Bunthorne said on the interoffice phone. "Game plan is changed." Two weeks had passed; the Chain counterattack was under way.

Mort with his therapist Miss Hanratty at his side, took the phone. She gently guided his hand to the receiver.

"What's up, Horace?"

The lawyer had good news. Van Alst and Rimmelberger were asking for a truce. They'd lay off if the Chains would withdraw their counter-complaint to the Justice Department. Bunthorne was letting them sweat. Their lawyers had decided that the game wasn't worth the candle. But they both now realized they had stuck their hands into a snake pit.

"Pisano started to sing," Bunthorne said. "I think that's what got them to come around. That and Mr. Bernard O'Toole's complaints. Bernie felt he owed me one since I outdrank him in a fair fight."

Mort chuckled. Bunthorne related new developments. Another mob of thugs masquerading as pickets had gathered outside the New Jersey distillery. There had been acts of sabotage against Chain trucks. An overturning, tires slashed. Martin had given firm orders. An armed man was to ride with each driver. Eddie Twine and friends, armed with shotguns, manned the trucks. The attacks stopped.

The enemy, Bunthorie said, was in retreat. However, it would be wise to spare them humiliation, to accept a truce. At the appropriate moment, Horace would withdraw the brief filed with the Justice Department.

Good news and a good future, Mort thought. Yet he was restless.

He put in a call to Iris. She was working on another "screen treatment" for Parvus. It was on "spec," she said. "No money until a studio accepted the outline and authorized a script. It sounded like a scam to Mort. A pity she wasn't raised in Brownsville, he told her, so she could spot bucketshop operators.

Iris's voice grew cold. Before she hung up, she asked for an additional ten thousand dollars from her trust. Without a moment's hesitation, Mort agreed. Let her learn. Who could tell? She might turn out to be Brooklyn's gift to Hollywood.

Displeased with his daughter, he felt the need for Davey's voice. The kid who was never good with words, but knew how to tackle, forecheck, block home plate. The operator could not get through to the frontier outpost. Communications were down.

"Miss Hanratty, I can't hang around the house. Tell Dr. Shapiro I want to work in the office. I feel like a baby. Tell Mrs. Chain I want to talk to her."

"She's shopping, Mr. Chain."

He suspected his nurse was pretty. She used pungent perfume, rustled her starched uniform, brushed soft hair against his face when she waited on him or led him from one part of the house to the other.

When she brought his lunch tray, he stroked her behind, thrust his hand under the skirt, let it linger over her full thigh.

"Please, Mr. Chain. That isn't part of the training."

"Why not? I bet you're beautiful."

"I'm plain and rather fat."

"You smell delicious. Your hair is like silk."

She removed his hand. "Really, Mr. Chain. This won't do."

No, it wouldn't, he decided. One mistress had taken out an eye and left him with a damaged cornea. It would be pointless, humiliating. A blind man stumbling around the house, clawing at his nurse.

"Nothing serious, Miss Hanratty. Just let me touch you now and then."

"Just a touch, that's all. I wasn't hired for that."

Once more he slipped a hand under her skirt, probed, stroked, listened to her sigh. As efficiently as if she were about to give him an intravenous, she disengaged his fingers. "Time's up, Mr. Chain. I'll get your coffee."

A hell of a thing, he thought. Grab-ass with a middle-aged nurse. No point in wasting tears or feeling sorry for himself. The Chains took chances, ran risks, hit, got hit, adapted. Someday, when Hilda was away for a long spell, Miss Hanratty would oblige him. He wasn't dead yet. Not by a long shot. Sightless, he would crush self-pity, go to work, oversee the expanding business, donate to charities, maintain his friendships. He would reward those who were friends to the Chains, and punish enemies.

Miss Hanratty bent over him to take away the luncheon tray and he nuzzled her starched breasts. "Thirty-six B?" he asked.

"C."

"You seem to be a nice person, Miss Hanratty. I think I'll learn braille in no time."

Lillian Halstead enjoyed the drive through the rolling hills, past the white-fenced pastures of northern Westchester County. Her father had cousins in the area—Cross River, Lewisboro. They were members of a world he had forsworn when he chose to be a radical. Perhaps, now that he had moved to the right, extolling Chiang Kai-shek, finding virtue in Calvin Coolidge, raging at the Securities and Exchange Commission in his magazine, Garrison Halstead would return to these places.

Odd, she thought, as the car radio spun out the day's dread events, how Martin Chain, two generations removed from Brownsville, now owned the most lavish estate in the area. He and his wife bred prizewinning hunters, ran the local horse shows, dominated politics. She, who could have moved easily into that world, had rejected it without a second thought.

Bert Dunphy, her uncle Sol's old lieutenant, laughed when he telephoned Lillian to invite her to the Winding Ridge Horse Show.

"Martin is the local laird up here, Lil," Dunphy said. "Didn't take him long. The old guard learned he was brighter than any of them and that he had the touch."

"The Chains are noted for that, Bert."

"Underneath that Harvard veneer, there's a very hard and very smart guy. Martin can talk to the fire department and the sheriff and get things done. The Episcopalians love him. They adore DeeDee. How many of their wives own three Monets and four Renoirs? And once visited Picasso in his studio?"

"They sound formidable."

"Just folks."

"But why am I invited to the annual show?" Lillian asked. "I don't ride."

"Martin thought it was a good idea. You're family."

"Could it be because I'm reviewing the file on the Chains? Bert, don't gasp. You know it. I've been collecting interviews, court records, police papers. Does the name Rocco Lentini mean anything? An awful lot of people were getting themselves killed in those days."

"Don't tell me, Lillian. It was the way things were. Thank God they only killed each other."

So she agreed to the trip to Armonk. Now she was glorying in the fall foliage, the air, the chance to have a look at the world of Martin Chain and wife. There was grand irony to all of it, Lillian realized. The setting could have been her natural habitat, had she so chosen. Instead, Crazy Jake's grandson had saddled up and become an Honorary Gentile.

She had been her mother's daughter. Concepts of work and justice had been bred into her. Eva had been a less than attentive mother. But the gawky, long-faced girl, boarded in private schools, left to herself, had learned to respect her mother's life and ideals. She read old newspaper clippings, the yellowing magazine articles. In a course in labor history at Mount Holyoke she had come across a reference to Eva in a book on the early days of the labor movement.

Among the most eloquent and colorful of the needle-trade organizers was a young girl, Eva Heilig, a sewing-machine operator, self-educated, the daughter of immigrant Jews. In her twenties, Miss Heilig single-handedly called a strike of workers in the bathrobe industry. It became a landmark, one of the unions' first victories. Articulate, forceful, and courageous, she was a legend among working girls. Because of her stirring powers of oratory, Eva Heilig was known as "The Golden Voice." . . .

Quite an act to follow, Lillian thought. She turned at a rustic sign reading WINDING RIDGE HORSE SHOW and drove down a dirt road lined with red oaks. The upper branches had been pleached to form a shimmery green and yellow bower.

She parked on a golf-green lawn, directed to a space by a golden-haired boy wearing a T-shirt reading GROTON. The car door was opened for her by a matching golden-haired girl in jeans.

People in riding habits and sports clothes were eating tailgate lunches around folding tables. Aromas of potent martinis and char-broiled steaks endowed the nippy air with an appropriately aristocratic edge. Faces were ruddy and healthy. Bodies were lean and strong. Lillian noticed that the guests spoke in unnecessarily loud and uninhibited tones. They laughed a great deal. They made bold jokes, shouting across tailgates. Is it, she wondered, because the foundations are shaking underneath them? Will they have to be saved by a Martin Chain?

"Grandstand's that way, ma'am," the Groton T-shirt said to Lillian.

Bert Dunphy spotted her as she entered the grandstand area. In front of the green wooden seats, on the sunlit lawn, riders and horses, to polite applause, were taking the jumps. Judges wearing ribboned badges sat at a long table.

"Lillian. Welcome to horse country. Don't laugh when you see your cousin. Squire Chain himself."

"Hi, Bert. Nobody laughs at the Chains. Not for long, anyway."

The lawyer complimented her on her outfit—tan suede and tweed, with low-heeled brown suede shoes, a matching bag slung over her shoulder. "Miss Abercrombie and Fitch," Dunphy said. "You've got more of a right to that rig than half the people here. And you handle it better."

"Flattery, flattery, Dunphy. Sol always said you were an Irish *shmeichler.*"

"Oh, I've become very Protestant since I started working for Mort and Marty Chain. Nothing like a pair of Jews to teach you how to act like an Episcopalian. What's a *shmeichler?*"

Laughing, Lillian shook her hair and took his hand. "It means you're a soft-soaper, Bert. A flatterer."

Mr. Martin Chain, seated in the president's box, was watching intensely as DeeDee, high in the saddle on Field of Rye, spurred the roan gelding gently, eased him into a canter, and took the first fence effortlessly.

Martin saw Dunphy with a young woman. He gestured to her to join him. "You're Lillian. Come in."

Lillian shifted her shoulder bag and entered the enclosed area. "Hi, Martin. It's sweet of you to ask me up."

"My pleasure. We shouldn't neglect our cousins."

A woman in her eighties, built like a Patton tank, layered in leathers and nubby clothes, her powdery face dotted with freckles, her hair rising in an orange duplicate of Mrs. Katzenjammer's coiffure, glared balefully at Lillian.

Seated next to the huge woman was a starveling man in a riding habit. His scarlet face was crosshatched like a cartoon by Hype Igoe; he sported a guards' moustache and a monocle. On his undersized head was a wicker riding helmet. *He has to be kidding,* Lillian thought. Human beings do not dress like that. The skinny man kept slapping a riding crop against the sides of his blood-red Kauffman boots.

She studied Martin. He was handsome as sin, dark and lean, with his foxy face and low-growing tarry hair. A scent of Habit Rouge rose from his corded throat. Pale gray jodhpurs and black boots emphasized his muscular figure. No fat, no sloth.

Martin kissed her cheek. "What a nice reunion."

"I think so, Martin."

She looked at the gold badge pinned to his Brooks Brothers shirt, windward of the lambkin. It read: CHAIRMAN, WINDING RIDGE HORSE SHOW. "I'm impressed," she said.

"Hold it, Lil. DeeDee's ready for the jump-off."

All necks were craned—the dowager, the man in the wicker basket helmet, Martin, Bert.

Grimly authoritative on the horse's broad back, DeeDee turned the gelding, picked up speed, and cleared the wooden fence with room to spare.

Lillian had ridden for a few years and found it tiresome.

"Nice jump, Dee," Martin called. He motioned Lillian to sit next to him. "Oh, excuse me," he said. "This is Miss Halstead, my cousin. Mrs. Redfern, our vice-president. This is Colonel Dodge Buchanan, master of the Abingdon Hunt."

They shook hands. The old woman did so warily, the man with a lecherous vigor. Lillian wanted to say, *And I am the grand duchess of Luxembourg*. She felt proud of her alienated father for having deserted such as Mrs. Redfern and Colonel Buchanan for Eva Heilig.

DeeDee finished her round of jumps to much applause.

There were murmurs that she was a certain winner. Her "seat" was superb and her control of the mount perfection.

Mrs. Redfern leaned forward and tapped Lillian firmly on the shoulder. "Did I hear Mr. Chain say your name was *Halstead?*"

"Yes, that's right." Lillian smiled. Her long face was tolerant and patient.

"Your husband is a Halstead?"

"I am. I have no husband."

The woman kept staring at Lillian. "I knew the Halsteads quite well. Which branch are you? Are you—*the* Halsteads? The Garrison Halsteads?"

Lillian marveled (as Martin called everyone's attention to the dressage) at the utter lack of grace and manners among these people. No wonder they kept losing elections to FDR, to Harry Truman. They could not be polite.

"I'm Garrison Halstead's daughter."

"Oh, I see. I knew his father. Your grandfather. He had a superb collection of hand-wound clocks."

"I guess he did."

"Yes," Mrs. Redfern went on. "Your father was an odd sort. As a matter of fact I may have attended his wedding in Sag Harbor. If I remember correctly, the bride was a Jewish girl, quite a beauty—"

"She was my mother."

Colonel Buchanan was squinting through his monocle at Lillian as if she were some species of undersea life. "Halstead. *Halstead.* They were quite a family. Knew the daughter. Became some kind of Florence Nightingale. Died."

"My Aunt Mildred."

Martin asked her if she wanted a drink. He had a Thermos filled with martinis. Chain's best. White Prince vodka and Treviso vermouth. He didn't touch it himself, but his guests took a nip now and then.

"No, thanks, Martin. Have to keep a clear head. It's the Heilig in me."

"We'll have a bite later on the terrace," Martin said.

"I can't wait to meet your wife. I'm envious of the way she handles horses. It's wonderful the way life reverses roles. If my father hadn't married your cousin, *I'd* be out there. Tall in the saddle, winning medals."

"You're where you should be," Martin said. He took her hand. He told her he remembered climbing a cherry tree with her after his grandfather's funeral. And hadn't they crossed backyard fences on Haven Place that day and visited Dr.

Abelman, who had given them peonies from his garden? "I can still smell them. You smelled wonderful, too."

Lillian said, "I remember the street. The house where my grandmother lived. And Dr. Abelman's. And your grandfather's house. Yellow brick, two stories. And poplars on the street."

"I like *this*," Dunphy said. "We're at the world's snootiest horse show and my friends are talking *Brooklyn*. I'm a Williamsburg boy myself. Boys High School. Ask me about Indian Yablock."

DeeDee, alarmingly beautiful with her alabaster face, high brow, and proud nose, dark hair tied in a jigging bun, commanded the gelding through a series of mincing steps.

"Your wife is beautiful," Lillian said. "You deserve her."

"Thanks, Lil. Eva okay? Your father?"

Eva managed. Independent, living with memories, collecting marginal rents in an old townhouse. Her father? She found it hard to talk to him. He would spend the rest of his life proving that Roosevelt was a traitor and that Communists in the State Department lost China.

"And you?" Martin asked. He took her hand.

"Investigating the Chains."

"We know."

"Is that why I was asked here? No dice, Martin. Not for a free lunch and a few lecherous winks from the master of the Abba-Dabba Hunt."

They were silent for a while. Bumpy gray clouds appeared suddenly; a fall chill hovered over the sunny arena and the grandstand. Decorous, restrained applause was swallowed in the rising autumn winds.

"Why are you staring at me?" Martin asked.

"You're a wonder."

"You're like Eva. You talk in circles when it suits you. Come on, Lil. I'm Crazy Jake's grandson. Level with me."

"I'm marveling at the leap across the Grand Canyon. From horse and wagon to this. The ultimate glory."

"Don't knock it, Lil."

Martin waved to DeeDee. He indicated he'd meet her in the clubhouse. She doffed her helmet and glanced at Lillian.

"It's easy, Lil," Martin said. "Money makes the difference. The blood has run thin in a lot of these people. They need a Chain to get them cranked up. I bought a hundred more acres for the club. I rebuilt the grandstand. I get us better coverage in the *Times*. I do it all."

"I'll bet you've figured out a way for the club to make a profit on manure."

"That's next. A little bit of Brooklyn goes a long way."

Dunphy excused himself. He had to leave early. A long drive back to Jersey. The lawyer liked living within fifteen minutes of the distillery. He shook Lillian's hand and kissed her cheek. "My best to Sol, to Abe, all the Heiligs. God bless them. They hang in. And most of all your mother. Tell her that Bert asked about her. I'm a sentimental harp, I guess."

Martin got up and greeted several couples. People with the assured, secure glow of winners. He escorted Lillian past groups of noisy people with scrubbed tanned faces, women with high cheekbones and lank blond hair held in place with a gold clip, snowy-mantled men with patrician features and flesh tones suggesting cold borsht, children of such physical perfection that Lillian wanted to cry for them.

Very much the monarch of the club, Martin pointed out a senator, a man who advised the governor, an undersecretary of the treasury, three corporate presidents, the board chairman of a bank, the board chairman of a coal company, a heart surgeon, an owner of racetracks in Maryland, and a deputy director of the CIA.

Martin turned down (Lillian noted) five invitations to have drinks.

"Bend the elbow, Marty?"

"Have an El Belto with the old man."

"Try some of your own poison, Mart?"

"They love you," Lillian said. "It is love, isn't it?"

"More or less."

Martin guided her toward a table on the flagstone terrace. It was unbearably beautiful. A lake, lush willows, lawns of preternatural greenness, rustic buildings. Beyond, horses grazed in a corral behind the obligatory white fencing. They nuzzled, broke into spirited gallops.

"They love the way I got them on their feet," he said. "That's the secret of their love."

"How many Jews are members?" asked Lillian.

"Three couples. I decide. We can't let too many in at once, but I'm working on it. Nobody says no to me. Anyway, Jews aren't interested in joining until I improve the food. The kitchen stinks. The people at pop's club would revolt. There's DeeDee."

Sweating delicately, DeeDee Chain was removing her helmet, setting it carefully on a mosaic table. She looked flushed and radiant.

The women conversed cautiously. DeeDee, who knew of Lillian's odd parentage, was less her acerb self. With fools and *arrivistes* she could be knifingly sarcastic, uttering insults with a bland innocence that set Martin's teeth on edge. With Lillian, she was on her best behavior.

"So you're up in Albany saving us from stock manipulators or whatever your office does?"

"The New York office, DeeDee."

"How wonderful. Martin tells me how smart you are. I admire you. I wish I had a career."

"Dee, you know how you hate to let the servants run the apartment and the house."

The apartment. The house. Cocking her head, smiling as if to let them know she understood them too well, Lillian thought of the apartment. A fifteen-room duplex on Fifth Avenue. The house was a twenty-room 1775 clapboard set on a hundred acres of undulant meadows and forests.

Amused, Lillian wondered about DeeDee's desire for a career. The woman was as finely crafted and assembled as a Fabergé, or one of those mechanical marvels that Da Vinci designed for royal festivals. The serene pale face was more than beautiful; it was harmonious. Modulated voice, precise gestures. Yet there seemed to be a great deal of passion in DeeDee Grau Chain. No fragile shepherdess she, who at a sparrow's death, would dissolve in tears.

DeeDee excused herself. She wanted to change. It was getting cool; she felt sweaty, a bit weary.

"You have a lovely, lovely wife," Lillian said.

"Thanks, Lil. I adore her."

"The baby?"

"Sally's a dream. Looks like—you won't believe this— Davey and Iris. Not the dark look, Mort's face or my face. She's a big blond girl who laughs all the time. We're going to have three kids. Or keep trying till we have a son."

"To keep the dynasty going."

"Why not? The Chains built it. It should stay in the family. We hope to go public in a year or so. Interested in a ground-floor investment? At an insider's price?"

"Martin, that could be interpreted as attempting to bribe a public servant."

"I'm kidding. I know better. Maybe your mother would like some Chain stock. She deserves a break."

"Mother manages."

Martin studied his cousin's long earnest face. Something strong and able and decent there. Probably hadn't married because she couldn't find a man to measure up to her. Moreover, she might have had personal problems—the weakling father, the heroic mother. Is Lillian ever sure who she is? he wondered. Or where she belongs? It was easier when you were a Chain. You understood money, power, politics, and force.

"I could open an account for her," Martin said. "She wouldn't have to know about it until it was done. We could say it's for research, tie it into the foundation."

"Foundation?"

"The Chain Foundation."

Martin clicked his fingers for a waiter. He ordered Heinekens, draped a tan cashmere sweater over his broad shoulders. Colonel Buchanan came by. He looked elated.

"Great news," the man in the wicker helmet said. "A couple of Puerto Ricans tried to assassinate Truman."

"That was on Wednesday," Lillian said. "Not again?"

The colonel winked at her. "It's a joke, Miss Halstead. Two more just tried. They went to Washington to shoot the shit."

Martin did not smile. Nor did Lillian. The colonel sashayed off in his jodhpurs.

"My apologies," Martin said. "He's drunk."

"Tell me something, Martin. Why did it mean so much to you not only to get into this mob of horse lovers but to run the place?"

"To prove that a Chain can do it."

She shook her head. "The old sidewalk toughness. I'd have thought you'd outgrown it."

"Maybe my kids will. Me, never. With pop out of commission, it's my ball game."

With pride, Martin talked about Davey, training kibbutz youngsters to fire weapons, to track in the desert, to string barbed wire and lay mines. Iris's movie was temporarily held up. But her first television play, a half-hour murder story, would be aired in a month. Mort had promised to find a sponsor.

"I'm glad," Lillian said. "Mother will be happy to hear about them. She always felt a close tie to the Chains. She was fond of your grandfather."

"A lot of people liked Crazy Jake." Martin sipped his beer. "Tough old bastard. He took a lot of killing."

"The Chains are a hardy breed," Lillian said. "I suppose I should say 'more power to them.' But, as you know, I'm on the opposite side of the street these days. Martin, I know why you asked me here. You have the virtue of frankness. You want to know about the investigation into the Chain corporation."

"Only whatever you want to tell me."

She hesitated. It would be breaking every tenet of law enforcement. But it was sometimes done. Enforcers had friends. And their friends got special treatment. She thought she could never act in that way, giving away information, playing favorites. But Martin's dark face was profoundly appealing. It was a face that was part of her past.

"Much of the investigation has come to a halt. Your competitors are pulling back. I don't know the details."

With a tolerant smile, he summed up events of the last few months. Van Alst and Rimmelberger had agreed to help one another, take their chances on quick profits, and let the Chains fend for themselves.

"So you're in the clear," she said cautiously. "Government, unions, competitors, all rendered impotent."

"You could say so." He rapped his riding crop softly against his boots. The breeze stiffened. People left the terrace for the clubhouse. A piano was playing "This Love of Mine."

A husky black man in a chauffeur's uniform approached. "When will you want the car, Martin?"

"Half-hour, Harry."

The man left. He walked with an athlete's tread. He had sorrowing dark eyes, a mass of graying kinky hair.

"A chauffeur who calls you by your first name?"

"Harry Twine's been with the family since he was a kid, Lil. He and his brother Eddie helped raise us. Before I was born, our old place in Brooklyn was burned to the ground by Schonkeit's mob. Harry's father, Buster, worked for us. They slit his throat before they torched the factory. We lost one hell of a man and a lot of booze."

"I'm glad you put the man first."

"Friends, business, same thing. Harry and Eddie have been with us ever since. He wouldn't think of calling me anything but Martin. He taught me to box, shoot fouls, and roll dice."

"Better than Dartmouth or Harvard, Mr. Twine's training."

"It helped. Everything does."

Lillian wondered: *How much does he know? How much should I tell him?* She decided she would tell him a great deal. Eva had told her about Crazy Jake. Not just the courage on the picket lines. But hints at how he had protected her from monsters. There was also the mission to Schonkeit to save Sol's life.

"Martin, the investigation into the bootleg murders has

been reopened. They've been interviewing witnesses. No one can tie anything together yet, but it might make things embarrassing for you."

He did not seem concerned. The old Chain bravado, the cocky air, the walk down dark streets, unarmed and defiant.

"Lil, all that stuff was investigated years ago. When my father was killed, when they shot the Paymaster, and after they found Ferrante's body."

"I do wish some of your fellow club members could hear this conversation. It's too rich."

"Tell you what, Lil," Martin said, bending over the green table. "I'm not afraid of this investigation. I just wouldn't want it to harm the foundation. Newspapers can hang you even when you're in the clear."

"The foundation . . ."

"Funded at seventy million dollars for medical research. Grants for research in every branch of medical science. Because of my father's blindness, the first grant is going to an eye hospital in Brooklyn. Some young genius is rebuilding corneas and retinas."

She nodded. It was logical. The wealth went to work.

"Get some of the money out where it can do good. We should be furnishing people with something besides hangovers and cirrhosis of the liver."

"Martin, what do you think was the story behind those killings? The police tell me Ferrante was murdered by imported hoodlums."

"Maybe."

"Weren't you curious? Mort must have been. What did he say?"

"Crazy Jake lived a dangerous life."

"I've had the feeling for some time this shouldn't be my job, poking into the Chain past. After all, I'm family."

"A distinguished branch, Lillian," Martin said with evident sincerity. "I don't fear anything. But it might hurt us enough to put a crimp in the foundation. Whiskey we can always sell. Competitors we can handle. Labor thugs? We eat them alive."

"You seem to have it all wrapped up, don't you, Martin?"

"We understand what the country is all about. Buying and selling. Getting to the top. I admit it. We're not an eleemosynary institution."

"Splendid word. Good for all that money Mort spent on your education. You've almost convinced me that those kill-

493

ings twenty years ago are none of my business. Maybe nobody's business."

"I won't stand in your way." Martin stretched—leathery, strong. "There's an important opening in Bunthorne's department. Bert Dunphy brought your name up. Maybe a job in Bunthorne's old Wall Street outfit. They're looking for a woman. Interested?"

Lillian shook her head. "Martin, please. I'm Eva Heilig's daughter. We can't be bought."

"The Chains aren't subtle. We never were."

Showered, glistening, DeeDee, wearing an olive corduroy suit, came out of the clubhouse. She stopped to talk to a couple whom Lillian recognized from the society pages—a financial boy wonder and a wife who endowed museums.

The utter perfection of the moment made Lillian smile and emboldened her. Bluntly she asked Martin: "Who killed your grandfather?"

"Ferrante. On Schonkeit's orders. Jake was trapped."

"I thought as much. And who killed Ferrante?"

"It wasn't who you think. No professional hoods from Cleveland or Detroit."

"Martin, I've made my mind up. I'm dropping the whole thing. Whatever you tell me is in confidence. I won't leave a memo for a successor. My mother owes your grandfather too much."

"I can't tell you. But you can guess."

Martin let his eyes move significantly to the white rail fence around the pasture. His black-suited chauffeur, Harry Twine, was resting there, one foot on the lower rail, thick arms folded on the upper rail. He seemed lost in a reverie.

"Lil, Harry Twine is a deacon of the African Baptist church. I'm sending his sons to Cornell. Harry and his brother Eddie are two of the finest men I've ever known. So I know you won't say a word, right?"

She nodded. "Right." Old loyalties. The Chains demanded it from her. Just as they had from the sons of Buster Twine.

Clanking gold bracelets, DeeDee strode toward them. She appeared to Lillian Halstead to be the distillation (apt word), the essence, the personification of all the power, beauty, style, status, and high standards that a certain heaven demanded. Martin Chain's heaven.

The week before Christmas, on the Monday after President Truman had proclaimed a national emergency, rolled back auto prices, and terminated the railroad strike, a memo was passed to Lillian by a staff investigator.

An old loan shark named Biagio (Baggie) Ferrante had died in Brownsville Jewish Hospital. It was, the memo said, a natural death, from kidney malfunction. This in itself was odd, in that Ferrante's brothers had a propensity for getting themselves fatally shot.

A detective had questioned the mobster at his bedside about the murder of his brother Salvatore. The dying Baggie professed no knowledge of the death. He implicated no one. He gasped that he barely knew the Chain family. It was, the investigator said, the underworld code at work—silence, *omertà*, to the end.

And I, too, will be silent, Lillian thought. She included the memo in her report to her superior. Then she added:

> It would appear that the murders in the early thirties involving the Chain family and other underworld figures have been thoroughly investigated. Nothing in the files implicates Mortimer Chain or any of his associates. It is recommended that the investigation be terminated, since it is our feeling that it will produce nothing new. Moreover the request to reopen the Schonkeit, Ferrante, and Jacob Chain murders seems to be part of an orchestrated campaign by business competitors who could benefit from defaming the Chain heirs.

That evening, over supper at her mother's house, Lillian told Eva what she had done.

"Just as well," Eva said. She wiped a trickle of tears. "As the poet said, let the dead be dead."

1960
Myron Malkin's Notebook

I'm here by mistake, I'm certain. Mr. Martin Chain's secretary, who helped usher me out of his office a few months ago, probably found my name in her Rolodex and sent me a fancy embossed invitation.

As usual the Chains have gone first-class.

Would you believe Nixon *and* Kennedy are seated on the bunting-bright platform with Mr. Mortimer J. Chain, Mr. Martin Chain, wives, colleagues, and medical big shots?

But why not? It's an election year. Senator John F. Kennedy is running like Eulace Peacock in the hundred-yard dash. Our vice president has made no bones about it. He hungers to succeed Ike.

And believe me, the Chains are worth knowing. I did a little digging. They're backing *both* sides generously. They give to anyone they think has a chance. Why not? It's a free country, isn't it?

Mild October morning. I cross my legs, lean back in the folding camp chair, and glance at the front page of the *Times*. Life goes on, more or less. Korea, the AMA is denouncing Eisenhower's health plan. Trouble in Laos. U.N. debate on the Congo . . .

Plus ça change, plus c'est la même chose. Or, as Mr. Dooley once said, he saw great changes in the country every week, but no changes at all every fifty years.

So I'm back in Brooklyn, about ten miles from Brownsville. On a pass, so to speak.

Behind the speaker's platform rise the sixteen stories of the spanking new Chain Medical Center, a forty-million-dollar addition to Central Brooklyn Hospital. Granite, stainless steel, modular design. The last word in medical construction.

A journalist on my left, a kid from the *News*, whispers to me: "Give the coons two years they'll turn it into a slum. They'll be peddling scag in the clinics and mugging nurses in the parking lot."

I say nothing. I hope he's wrong.

I know the neighborhood. East Flatbush. It used to be largely Jewish, with enclaves of Irish and Italians. Now it's becoming *verschwarz'd* as my late uncle Doc would have said. But at least it stands a chance of surviving. Houses are clean and neat. The blacks who buy them are people with jobs—civil servants, blue-collar workers.

The Chain Medical Center will be a research facility for metabolic diseases of children, and a children's hospital. It's a good idea. Someone in that tower on Park Avenue, the money-filled Chain Building, is thinking constructively. Who am I to be critical? When did I ever fork over forty million for a hospital?

A fellow from United Press is sitting on my right. He's dozing. The uniformed band from the Department of Sanitation wakes him up with a stirring rendition of "America the

Beautiful." He's an older reporter, beery, heavy-jowled. "Who the hell are the Chains?" he asks. "You know anything about them?"

"Anonymous wealth."

Handouts enlighten us about the medical center. Ten years in the planning. The personal project of Mr. Mortimer J. Chain and his son Martin Chain. The foundation has funded many worthy projects in the past ten years, the brochure states, but this is the first major institution to bear their name. Up to now they preferred to keep their benefactions quiet.

Safe enough to go public now, I guess.

I scan the platform. Senator Kennedy, ruddy, too handsome, is talking to Mrs. Martin Chain. She is by far the most exquisite person on the platform. Her beauty is like a reproach, a warning. No one should be that gorgeous, that poised. Clear skin, large features, wide brown eyes, arched brows. Her children are just as magnificent. How do some people get so lucky? There is a blond girl of about eleven, in a blue fairy-princess dress and long braids; two dark bright-eyed little boys.

And blind Mort. My uncle remembered him when he lived in a basement hole and was known as Mutt. A wild street brat, good with his fists, sharp as a scalpel. Running booze from Canada in a taxicab when he was eighteen years old. The last time I saw him was at the camp on Lake Champlain. Now he looks hunched, uncertain, shrunken behind his dead eyes, talking to no one. His starched nurse is by his side.

Martin Chain is seated next to the vice president of the United States. They are in earnest conversation. Hell, a vote's a vote. And a fat campaign contribution is even better than a vote. Nixon looks pretty good—young, trim, his suits fitting better. He gestures a great deal.

The speeches aren't much. Both candidates pay tribute to the generous donation the Chain Foundation has made to maintaining the health of Brooklyn citizens. More such bountiful acts from the private sector are needed, the rivals agree.

Others speak. The mayor, the hospital commissioner, and finally Martin Chain himself, as he hands over the deed to the Chain Medical Center to Hizzoner and says a few pleasant words about his own boyhood not far from here, on Ocean Parkway. He recalls the family's roots in Brownsville, how much they owe the great city and its wonderful people. . . .

Corny? Sure. I wonder if his gratitude includes all the

cops, federal agents, coast guardsmen, and politicians who benefited from the Chains' largesse back in the glorious years of bootlegging. In a way, the family has always been philanthropically inclined. And it all goes back to Jacob Chain. I think of the poor union guys and the exploited girls who got better contracts, increases in salary, because a hardhanded mobster named Crazy Jake was courageous and reckless and hungry enough to take on company-paid bullies.

It's not my business to remind anyone. Besides, DeeDee Chain has just crossed her legs and I'm frantically trying to sneak a look. She should wear longer skirts. Who can listen to speeches about the future of our city when what may be the sexiest legs in New York are on display? How do some people (Martin Chain, for example) win so many good things? I almost cried when I learned he was welterweight boxing champion at Dartmouth and that he finished in the top ten percent of his class at Harvard Business School. He's even a pretty good public speaker.

"With the dedication of the Chain Medical Center," Martin is saying, "we of the Chain Foundation launch our first major effort in improving medical care in the city in which our family was raised. . . ."

The UP man mutters, "How about a center for kidney and liver diseases, considering all the poison hooch they've sold?"

"Cynic," I say.

". . . research in thoracic diseases of children under the direction of Dr. Abraham Heilig and his outstanding staff."

Abe Heilig is giving up his career as a surgeon—he's a bit long in the tooth and maybe the OR is too demanding—to administer the Chain Medical Center. He'll be bringing in teams of hot shots, kids from Mount Sinai, Einstein. He's told his associates he wants them to come up with a Nobel in three years. Don't bet they won't.

I notice lawyer Sol Heilig on the platform. Sol looks weary and gray. Last time his name was in the paper was when he represented tenants being chased out of their brownstones by a landlord who employed thugs. He hasn't lost his ideals. He's a Heilig. They hang on. They don't turn sour or mean or greedy.

Martin Chain finished to loud applause. The Department of Sanitation band strikes up "Stars and Stripes Forever." DeeDee Chain uncrosses her legs. Insanely jealous, I watch her every move. Covering her edible mouth, she is chatting with Senator Kennedy.

Oh, 'tis a grand day, as Mulqueen, the old speakeasy owner, would have said.

The crowd rises. People begin to leave. Lots of white-coated doctors, nurses, technicians, and employees of Central Brooklyn. They're moving up a notch now that the Chain Medical Center has attached itself to their crumbling red brick building. But they look happy. Blacks, Puerto Ricans, Jews, Italians—a nice Brooklyn mix. And who can fault the Chains for what they're doing with their money? It beats buying modern art.

The presidential candidates leave hurriedly. Shave-headed men in gray suits usher them out, although the senator from Massachusetts acts as if he'd like a few more words with DeeDee.

Late-afternoon shadows fall. It's cool. I spot Sol Heilig and his wife Rose—they were Uncle Doc's patients until he died—talking to one of the skinniest, weirdest-looking men I've ever seen. A flunky tells me this is Horace Bunthorne, the top Chain lawyer—boozer, brain, fixer.

Sol Heilig, walking gimpily, his suit rumpled, notices me. "Hey, Myron," he says. "Doc Abelman's nephew?"

"The same, counselor. How are you, Mr. Heilig? Mrs. Heilig?"

"Rose, remember this guy? He used to drive his uncle crazy shooting fouls in the backyard while Doc was taking my blood pressure."

We agree that it has been a beautiful day for Brooklyn. And for the Chain family.

"The speeches were a little stiff," Sol says. "Martin's so buttoned-up he could be an archbishop."

"Sol," his wife scolds. "Not nice. Not nice at all."

"Is your sister here?" I ask. "Mrs. Halstead?"

No, he says, Eva's not in good shape. Confined to a wheelchair. It's hard for her to get around. Paget's disease.

"Know something?" Sol asks. His eyes are bright and laughing. "That's what this clambake needed. A speech from Eva. A little of the old radical fire."

"From what I've heard, it would have been a rouser."

He slaps his thigh. "Eva would have turned them on. She'd have had them standing up and cheering. She was good at that."

We walk to the parking lot in back of the new hospital. Sol is reminiscing about his late mother, the old chatelaine of the stationery store, about his ne'er-do-well Socialist father, raising children on sour milk. And Crazy Jake, the Brownsville Hercules.

"Eva would have given them good," Sol Heilig says to me. "She'd have had the interns and nurses calling a strike the first day the hospital opened."

"I'm sorry I never heard her in action. Is her daughter here today? That girl with the attorney general?"

"Lillian. She's in Washington. New job. Federal Trade Commission."

I'm wondering: Did the Chains have anything to do with it? I recall Mort Chain mentioning the senators and congressmen he knew personally. People who had helped him—and vice versa—when he was buying chemicals, building a fortune with a phone, an office, and an account book.

We pause in the lot. Two motorcycle cops shoo us away with wailing sirens.

"Nixon or Kennedy?" I ask Sol. "Which one gets the first escort?"

"Neither," Sol says.

A black limousine is threading its way through knots of guests, police officials, hospital personnel. Martin Chain sits in the limo with wife and children. A huge black man is at the wheel.

"It figures," Sol says. "Chains go first-class."

"Leave it to them." Rose sniffs.

"No, it's the way it should be," her husband says. "There'll be a Chain Medical Center here long after both those guys are out of office."

A nice thought. But I wish old Eva, the white-haired heroine, the captain of the pickets and the orator of the union halls, had been there.

In some way (I'm not sure how) she has a lot to do with the Chain gift. Someday I'll find out. Someday when the dust has settled and people are willing to talk.

ABOUT THE AUTHOR

GERALD GREEN, who was born and raised in Brooklyn, is the author of 21 books of fiction and nonfiction. He wrote the much-acclaimed television series *Holocaust*, which was viewed by a record 240 million people worldwide and, in novelized form, was published in 18 countries. Mr. Green received the Dag Hammarskjöld international peace prize for *Holocaust*.

THE LATEST BOOKS IN THE BANTAM BESTSELLING TRADITION

☐	13545	**SOPHIE'S CHOICE** William Styron	$3.50
☐	14200	**PRINCESS DAISY** Judith Krantz	$3.95
☐	20025	**THE FAR PAVILIONS** M. M. Kaye	$4.50
☐	13752	**SHADOW OF THE MOON** M. M. Kaye	$3.95
☐	14773	**INDEPENDENCE!** Dana Fuller Ross	$2.95
☐	14066	**NEBRASKA!** Dana Fuller Ross	$2.95
☐	14849	**WYOMING!** Dana Fuller Ross	$2.95
☐	14860	**OREGON!** Dana Fuller Ross	$2.95
☐	13980	**TEXAS!** Dana Fuller Ross	$2.75
☐	14982	**WHITE INDIAN** Donald Clayton Porter	$2.95
☐	14968	**THE RENEGADE** Donald Clayton Porter	$2.95
☐	20087	**THE HAWK AND THE DOVE** Leigh Franklin James	$2.95
☐	20179	**A WORLD FULL OF STRANGERS** Cynthia Freeman	$3.50
☐	13641	**PORTRAITS** Cynthia Freeman	$3.50
☐	20071	**DAYS OF WINTER** Cynthia Freeman	$3.50
☐	20070	**FAIRYTALES** Cynthia Freeman	$3.50
☐	14439	**THE EWINGS OF DALLAS** Burt Hirschfeld	$2.75
☐	13992	**CHANTAL** Claire Lorrimer	$2.95

Here are the Books that Explore the Jewish Heritage-Past and Present.

Fiction

☐	14162	**Exodus** Leon Uris	$2.95
☐	14220	**Mila 18** Leon Uris	$2.95
☐	13564	**Holocaust** Gerald Green	$2.50

Non-Fiction

☐	01265	**The Jewish Almanac** Siegel & Rheins, eds.	$9.95
☐	20153	**Children of the Holocaust** Helen Epstein	$3.25
☐	13810	**World of Our Fathers** Irving Howe	$3.95
☐	20129	**The Holocaust Years: Society on Trial** Chartock & Spencer, eds.	$2.50
☐	14420	**The New Bantam-Megiddo Hebrew & English Dictionary** Levenston & Sivan	$2.95
☐	10199	**The Essential Talmud** A. Steinsaltz	$2.95
☐	14331	**Treasury of Jewish Quotations** Leo Rosten	$3.95
☐	11170	**Wake Up, Wake Up, To Do the Work of the Creator** William B. Helmreich	$2.25
☐	13084	**The War Against the Jews** Lucy S. Dawidowicz	$3.50

Bantam Book Catalog

Here's your up-to-the-minute listing of over 1,400 titles by your favorite authors.

This illustrated, large format catalog gives description of each title. For your convenience it is divided into categories in fiction and non fiction—gothics, science fiction, westerns, mys teries, cookbooks, mysticism and occult, biogra phies, history, family living, health, psychology, art.

So don't delay—take advantage of this special opportunity to increase your reading pleasure.

Just send us your name and address and 50¢ (to help defray postage and handling costs).